# Pedagogical Innovations in AI-Supported Intercultural Communications

Turan Paker
https://orcid.org/0000-0002-3941-3975
*Pamukkale University, Turkey*

Gonca Ekşi
*Gazi University, Turkey*

Çağla Atmaca
https://orcid.org/0000-0002-7745-3839
*Pamukkale University, Turkey*

IGI Global
Scientific Publishing
Publishing Tomorrow's Research Today

Vice President of Editorial — Melissa Wagner
Director of Acquisitions — Mikaela Felty
Director of Book Development — Jocelynn Hessler
Production Manager — Mike Brehm
Cover Design — Jose Rosado

Published in the United States of America by
IGI Global Scientific Publishing
701 East Chocolate Avenue
Hershey, PA, 17033, USA
Tel: 717-533-8845 | Fax: 717-533-7115
Website: https://www.igi-global.com E-mail: cust@igi-global.com



Library of Congress Cataloging-in-Publication Data

Names: Paker, Turan, 1963- editor | Ekşi, Gonca, 1974- editor | Atmaca, Çağla, 1990- editor
Title: Pedagogical innovations in AI-supported intercultural communications / [edited by] Turan Paker, Gonca Ekşi, Çağla Atmaca.
Description: Hershey, PA : IGI Global Scientific Publishing, [2026] | Includes bibliographical references and index. | Summary: "The book offers an up-to-date understanding about intercultural communication (ICC) with a specific focus on AI-supported applications, tools, and platforms"-- Provided by publisher.
Identifiers: LCCN 2025052983 (print) | LCCN 2025052984 (ebook) | ISBN 9798337363257 hardcover | ISBN 9798337363264 paperback | ISBN 9798337363271 ebook
Subjects: LCSH: Multicultural education | Intercultural communication | Artificial intelligence--Educational applications
Classification: LCC LC1099 .P435 2026 (print) | LCC LC1099 (ebook)
LC record available at https://lccn.loc.gov/2025052983
LC ebook record available at https://lccn.loc.gov/2025052984

British Cataloguing in Publication Data
A Cataloguing in Publication record for this book is available from the British Library.

# Table of Contents

# Detailed Table of Contents



**Section 1**
**Foundations and Frameworks**



This chapter examines the growing influence of Artificial Intelligence on language education and intercultural communication, especially in English as a Foreign Language settings where learners gain from adaptive feedback, personalized learning, and broader cultural exposure. It explains how Artificial Intelligence can strengthen motivation, autonomy, and skill development while offering enriched environments for intercultural understanding. The chapter also addresses issues related to fairness, privacy, and dependence on automated outputs, highlighting the need for critical Artificial Intelligence literacy. It concludes by outlining key educational and policy implications that support ethical use and preserve human judgment within evolving learning environments.



This conceptual chapter offers a critical examination of how artificial intelligence (AI)-supported tools employed in intercultural communication (ICC)—including language-learning platforms such as Duolingo, conversational agents like ChatGPT, and translation services such as Google Translate—may inadvertently reproduce and intensify bias. Integrating perspectives from AI ethics, applied linguistics, and intercultural communication studies, the chapter identifies four major bias categories: linguistic, cultural, representational, and accessibility. Drawing on recent analyses, it highlights concerns such as the marginalization of low-resource languages (Wired, 2023), user-reported ethical dilemmas in AI-mediated learning environments (Polygon, 2025), and the perpetuation of gendered translations (Ghosh & Caliskan, 2023). To address these issues, the chapter proposes a Bias-Audit Checklist as a

This chapter proposes a practical framework for using AI to advance educational equity and global fluency by integrating Culturally Responsive Pedagogy (CRP) with Intercultural Communication Competence (ICC). The document presents design principles which include inclusivity, contextual relevance, learner-centered personalization, reflective learning and ethics followed by four classroom integration models. The chapter examines some main systemic dangers which include algorithmic bias, teacher readiness gaps and the digital divide and governance/privacy issues while supporting human-centered design processes that bring together educators, students and community members. The study ends with a research plan that focuses on developing culturally sensitive models, tracking their long-term effects, creating successful human–AI partnerships and evaluating policy effectiveness to demonstrate how AI can establish inclusive learning environments based on cultural foundations instead of conventional standardized education systems.



The Rehumanizing Pedagogical Framework (RPF) advanced herein treats empathy, humor, and ethical awareness as assessable learning outcomes in AI-mediated intercultural communication within distance foreign language education. Grounded in intercultural communicative competence theory and human-machine communication research, the framework identifies four design mediators: task design, feedback design, interface affordances, and governance. These mediators preserve the relational core of intercultural learning while positioning AI as a pedagogical resource rather than an unchecked authority. The analysis situates these mediators within debates on agentic AI, cultural bias in large language models, and governance conditions that covary with perceived intercultural benefit. Evaluation triangulates self-reported dispositions, interactional evidence of repair and audience-safe humor, and ethical practice artifacts. The chapter concludes with a tiered research agenda and recommendations for programs seeking to integrate AI without eroding the human dimensions of intercultural dialogue.

As artificial intelligence (AI) becomes more embedded in children's English language education through story-driven apps, questions arise about the cultural and ecological assumptions encoded in algorithmic narratives. This chapter examines how AI-powered platforms, particularly Lingokids, represent cultural diversity, spatial norms, and nature. Although presented as neutral language-learning tools, these narratives operate as coded stories that subtly reproduce specific cultural scripts. Drawing on intercultural communication theory, ecocriticism, and critical media literacy, the study conducts a qualitative visual content analysis of five alphabet-based Lingokids stories. Findings show recurring Western suburban imagery, anthropomorphized characters, sanitized ecological settings, and simplified story structures indicating algorithmic cultural reductionism. The chapter introduces an interdisciplinary framework for evaluating AI-mediated storytelling and recommends culturally inclusive, ecologically responsive narrative practices for educators, designers, and policymakers.



It is crucial to educate prospective language teachers to create awareness towards intercultural competence and arrange activities in their courses so that they can develop their intercultural competence. Thus, they may be interculturally sensitive to better serve their future students' needs. In this chapter, the importance and the role of intercultural communication, how intercultural competence can be enhanced through employing AI-supported activities, and opportunities and challenges in this process have been discussed. For this purpose, to what extent various AI tools such as Chat GPT, Gemini, QuillBot, Canva, Grammarly, and others can be employed has been discussed in line with the syllabus of the intercultural communication course in the English Language teaching Department. All the activities have been based on Byram's (1997) language-pedagogical model, through diaries, focus group discussions, and reflections of the students.

This chapter examines AI chatbots as intercultural companions in literature education, proposing a framework to develop students' Intercultural Communicative Competence (ICC) and empathy. Based on Byram's ICC model and Davis's empathy framework, it describes a four-week intervention using conversational AI for dialogic exploration of culturally diverse texts. The approach stresses critical AI literacy, treating AI outputs as interpretive texts for analysis, not authoritative sources. A baseline survey of English Literature students at Kırklareli University showed moderate-to-high intercultural sensitivity (M=3.86, SD=0.37) and empathy (M=3.59, SD=0.41), with strengths in interaction enjoyment, respect for differences, and cognitive perspective-taking, but moderate active engagement and affective empathy. The chapter extends ICC and empathy models to digital contexts, offers practical guidance for AI-enhanced pedagogy, and confirms students' readiness for AI-mediated learning while preserving humanistic values in humanities education.



Artificial Intelligence offers modern pedagogical innovations by supporting telecollaboration to develop language skills in authentic contexts. This chapter aims to give insights regarding how AI-supported telecollaboration fosters Intercultural Communicative Competence, grounded in a theoretical framework based on recognized ICC models. The chapter addresses the synergy between telecollaboration and AI, discussing how telecollaboration facilitates authentic interaction while AI helps overcome linguistic/cultural barriers, provides personalized feedback, and supports learner autonomy. The chapter also addresses ethical and pedagogical challenges and outlines implications for both learners and teachers, offering specific pedagogical considerations for integrating AI effectively. The chapter emphasizes the importance of an integrated approach to authentic communication experiences, demonstrating how AI-enhanced tools can fundamentally enrich intercultural education.

In today's interconnected world, clear communication across diverse cultures and languages is vital for success in business, education, and diplomacy. However, language gaps and cultural differences often cause misunderstandings and hinder teamwork. AI-powered collaborative platforms now offer real-time translation, cultural adaptation, and personalized messaging using advanced machine learning and natural language processing. These tools interpret tone and idioms, going beyond literal translation to improve clarity and foster respect among participants. In educational and professional settings, AI customizes interactions based on users' language skills and cultural backgrounds, enhancing engagement through interactive features. This chapter delves into the transformative impact of AI on intercultural communication, exploring practical uses, ethical dilemmas & future opportunities. It advocates for a balanced approach where technological advancements are carefully guided by human values - ensuring that AI supports inclusive, respectful, and effective global communication.



This chapter examines how intercultural communicative competence (ICC) can be fostered through AI-integrated visual arts within Collaborative Online International Learning (COIL) in Vietnamese higher education. Despite the growing use of COIL worldwide, empirical research on its application in visual arts education, particularly in Vietnam, remains limited. Drawing on a qualitative, constructivist grounded theory approach, the study analyzes AI-supported collaborative visual art projects as spaces of intercultural meaning-making and dialogue. The findings indicate that AI-generated visual practices can mediate intercultural interaction, support reflective engagement with cultural identities, and enable new forms of collaborative creativity. The chapter contributes a contextualized pedagogical model for integrating AI and COIL into visual arts education to enhance ICC development in transnational learning environments.

Teacher education plays an important role in shaping cultural and technological transformation. As classrooms become more diverse and digital tools influence instruction, teachers need competences that go beyond traditional expectations. Intercultural Communicative Competence (ICC) and Artificial Intelligence (AI) have therefore become key areas of teacher preparation, yet both remain only partly integrated into pre-service and in-service programs. This chapter examines how teacher education can more effectively embed ICC and AI across the continuum of teacher learning. It outlines the historical development of teacher training, highlights cultural and technological priorities, and discusses how globalization, digitalization, and evolving pedagogies require a reframing of teacher competences. It further explores how ICC and AI can support each other and presents practical models for implementation. The chapter ultimately proposes a coherent, future-oriented framework for integrating ICC and AI in ethical, sustainable, and meaningful ways.



This chapter examines how teacher education and professional development can foster intercultural communicative competence (ICC) in AI-mediated, digitally rich classrooms. Drawing on established ICC models, it introduces intercultural digital literacy, which links digital, media, and critical literacies with intercultural competence and highlights teachers as cultural mediators and critical evaluators of online and AI-generated content. The chapter reviews telecollaboration, virtual exchange, and AI-supported tools such as large language models, authoring and presentation platforms, gamified quizzes, automated writing feedback, and translation systems, outlining opportunities for scenario-based learning, reflection, and differentiation, as well as challenges including bias, limited pedagogical guidance, workload, and unequal access. It argues that sustainable professional development must embed intercultural digital literacy in curricula and build supportive, cross-national frameworks so AI promotes inclusive, dialogic, and socially just education.

# Preface

Artificial Intelligence (AI) within the domain of intercultural communication is among the most significant and underexplored developments in contemporary language education. As AI-driven tools become increasingly embedded in pedagogical practice — reshaping how learners encounter, process, and produce language across cultural boundaries — the field is confronted with an urgent demand for critical, empirically grounded frameworks that can guide both research and classroom applications. This volume responds to that need by bringing together scholarly contributions that examine the pedagogical implications of AI integration into intercultural communicative contexts from multiple disciplinary perspectives.

The chapters collected here address a broad spectrum of concerns central to this emerging field. Foundational questions regarding the current state and future directions of AI in language education are examined alongside more applied investigations into teacher education and professional development, the design and evaluation of AI-supported instructional materials, and the fostering of intercultural communicative competence (ICC) across diverse learning environments. Particular attention is given to issues of bias and equity: several contributors critically examine the cultural assumptions encoded in AI-generated content, propose evaluative frameworks for assessing AI tools against intercultural and ethical criteria, and examine the representation of gender and cultural identity in materials produced for English language teaching contexts.

The volume also engages with a range of pedagogical innovations that have emerged within the overlapping terrain of AI and intercultural education, namely AI-mediated telecollaboration, collaborative online international learning (COIL), chatbot-assisted literature instruction, and AI-integrated visual arts pedagogy. Contributions from diverse national and international institutional contexts, and chapters focusing on young learners and early language education, further extend the volume's scope, raising questions about the values and cultural norms embedded in AI-driven platforms designed for children.

## ORGANIZATION OF THE BOOK

Collectively, the volume offers carefully developed perspectives- grounded in real educational practice- that can guide teachers, teacher educators, and researchers in their practices. The volume is composed of four sections, each addressing a distinct topic. Part one pertains to the foundations and frameworks, while Part two focuses on bias, equity, ethical awareness and cultural representation. The third part of this volume is concerned with the development of intercultural communicative competence, and the fourth and final section focuses on teacher education and professional development.

Chapter 1 sets the stage for the volume by mapping the evolving landscape of artificial intelligence in language education and intercultural communication. Kayaoglu presents a balanced account of how AI enhances personalization, learner autonomy, and intercultural exposure, while also raising critical concerns about ethics, privacy, and overreliance on automated systems. The chapter positions AI not merely as a technological tool but as a transformative force that necessitates the development of critical AI literacy and thoughtful policy frameworks to ensure that human judgment remains central in educational practice.

In Chapter 2, Dogutas offers a timely and incisive critique of bias embedded within AI-supported intercultural communication tools. By identifying linguistic, cultural, representational, and accessibility biases, the chapter provides a structured lens through which widely used platforms can be evaluated. Particularly noteworthy is the proposed Bias-Audit Checklist, which equips educators and researchers with a practical framework for interrogating AI systems and fostering more equitable and inclusive digital learning environments.

Chapter 3 deepens the discussion by turning to the often-overlooked affective and cultural dimensions of communication—humor, empathy, and nuance. Vaishnav demonstrates that while AI tools excel in efficiency, they frequently fall short in capturing the relational subtleties essential for meaningful intercultural interaction. Through illustrative case studies, the chapter underscores the importance of hybrid pedagogical models in which human educators play a vital role in enriching AI-generated content with cultural depth and emotional intelligence.

In Chapter 4, Demir and Uygun provide an empirical investigation into gender and cultural representation in AI-generated ELT materials. Their mixed-methods analysis reveals persistent patterns of hierarchical roles, uneven cultural visibility, and gendered discourse practices. This chapter makes a compelling case for integrating critical AI literacy into teacher education to ensure that AI-generated content aligns with inclusive and pedagogically sound practices.

Chapter 5 advances the conversation by proposing a forward-looking framework that integrates culturally responsive pedagogy with intercultural communication competence. Bozkurt, Cesur, and Ashirkhanova outline actionable design principles and classroom models while addressing systemic challenges such as algorithmic bias and the digital divide. Their emphasis on human-centered design and collaborative development highlights the potential of AI to foster equity and global fluency when implemented thoughtfully.

Chapter 6 introduces the Rehumanizing Pedagogical Framework, offering a powerful response to concerns about the depersonalization of AI-mediated learning. Gökce and Sen foreground empathy, humor, and ethical awareness as measurable learning outcomes, demonstrating how carefully designed pedagogical mediators can preserve the human essence of intercultural dialogue. The chapter contributes both a conceptual model and a research agenda for sustaining meaningful human–AI interaction.

In Chapter 7, Avci and Yalman Polatlar turn our attention to younger learners and the narratives embedded within AI-driven educational apps. Their analysis of story-based platforms reveals how seemingly neutral content can reproduce narrow cultural and ecological perspectives. By introducing an interdisciplinary evaluative framework, the chapter challenges educators and designers to rethink storytelling practices in ways that are culturally inclusive and environmentally sensitive.

Chapter 8 focuses on teacher education, emphasizing the importance of cultivating intercultural competence through AI-integrated pedagogical practices. Paker demonstrates how a range of AI tools can be systematically incorporated into ELT curricula, guided by established theoretical models. The chapter highlights the value of reflective and experiential learning processes in preparing future teachers to navigate AI-enhanced classrooms.

Chapter 9 explores the innovative use of AI chatbots as companions in literature education. Lüta and Tunaboylu present a structured intervention that leverages conversational AI to deepen students' intercultural understanding and empathy. By framing AI outputs as interpretive texts rather than authoritative answers, the chapter reinforces the importance of critical engagement and humanistic inquiry in digitally mediated learning.

Chapter 10 examines the intersection of AI and telecollaboration as a means of fostering authentic intercultural communication. Toscu illustrates how AI can enhance virtual exchanges by supporting language development, personalization, and learner autonomy. At the same time, the chapter carefully considers the pedagogical and ethical dimensions of integrating these technologies into meaningful communicative experiences.

Chapter 11 broadens the scope to include professional and collaborative contexts, highlighting the role of AI in facilitating global communication. Mutsuddi discusses how AI-powered platforms enable real-time translation and cultural adaptation, thereby reducing barriers to collaboration. The chapter advocates for a balanced approach that aligns technological innovation with human values to ensure respectful and effective intercultural interaction.

In Chapter 12, Hong presents an original exploration of AI-integrated visual arts within COIL-based higher education. Through a qualitative lens, the chapter demonstrates how collaborative digital art practices can serve as powerful sites for intercultural dialogue and identity exploration. This contribution expands the field by situating AI within creative and transnational learning contexts.

Chapter 13 returns to the critical domain of teacher education, offering a comprehensive framework for integrating AI and intercultural competence across professional development trajectories. Çokçaliskan and Sener trace the evolution of teacher training and argue for a holistic reconfiguration that reflects the demands of globalization and digitalization. Their model underscores the need for sustainable and ethically grounded approaches to teacher preparation.

Chapter 14 complements this perspective by focusing on intercultural digital literacy as a core component of teacher development. Ilter and Asma highlight the multifaceted role of teachers as cultural mediators and critical users of AI technologies. The chapter provides a nuanced discussion of both opportunities and challenges, advocating for systemic and collaborative approaches to professional learning.

Finally, Chapter 15 brings the discussion to the context of young learners, examining how AI can support lesson planning, engagement, and personalization in early language education. Türkmen, Cesur, and Mikhailova emphasize the importance of maintaining a human-centered approach, positioning AI as a co-creative partner rather than a replacement for the teacher. Their insights offer practical guidance while reinforcing the ethical and pedagogical considerations that underpin the entire volume.

## CONCLUSION

The editors wish to express their sincere gratitude to all contributing authors for their scholarly dedication and professional commitment to this project, and to the students and educators whose lived experiences of intercultural communication have informed the work assembled here.

# Section 1
# Foundations and Frameworks

Chapter 1

# Artificial Intelligence in Language Education and Intercultural Communication: Current Realities and Future Directions

**Mustafa Naci Kayaoğlu**
http://orcid.org/0000-0001-8630-4803
*Karadeniz Technical University, Turkey*

## ABSTRACT

*This chapter examines the growing influence of Artificial Intelligence on language education and intercultural communication, especially in English as a Foreign Language settings where learners gain from adaptive feedback, personalized learning, and broader cultural exposure. It explains how Artificial Intelligence can strengthen motivation, autonomy, and skill development while offering enriched environments for intercultural understanding. The chapter also addresses issues related to fairness, privacy, and dependence on automated outputs, highlighting the need for critical Artificial Intelligence literacy. It concludes by outlining key educational and policy implications that support ethical use and preserve human judgment within evolving learning environments.*

DOI: 10.4018/979-8-3373-6325-7.ch001

# INTRODUCTION

There is no doubt that Artificial Intelligence (AI), particularly Generative AI (GAI), has made itself felt as a transformative force in all spheres of life, meaning that it does more than enhance existing tools or processes. Consequently, it fundamentally changes the way we think, work, learn, and communicate. While technological development has always continued, which is not surprising to us, what distinguishes AI is that it represents an unprecedented moment in the history of technological progress; never before has a tool so profoundly reshaped human creativity, cognition, and interaction. More specifically, in education, it is redefining how knowledge is created, shared, and personalized. Within this broader transformation, in language learning and intercultural communication, GAI enables authentic, interactive exchanges, removes linguistic barriers, and fosters understanding between people from diverse backgrounds. Ultimately, its transformative nature lies in its capacity to merge human creativity with machine intelligence, producing new forms of collaboration and expression that were previously unimaginable.

To better understand this shift, from the earliest tools such as printing to digital platforms and online learning environments, technology has always helped people store, share, and communicate information. Yet these tools were essentially passive. They displayed what humans created. In this respect, AI differs from other technologies as it represents not only a qualitative shift but also a quantitative breakthrough in technological evolution, going beyond merely presenting or storing information. Instead, it can produce, interpret, and reshape knowledge in direct response to human input with unprecedented speed, scope, and precision. Importantly, unlike earlier technologies that served as teaching aids, GenAI behaves more like a collaborative partner, capable of generating original ideas, lessons, explanations, and reflections. This is because it can engage in dialogue, adapt its responses to the learner's needs, and simulate a human-like exchange of meaning. While traditional technologies focused on transmitting fixed content, GenAI allows learners and teachers to co-construct new content dynamically. Specifically, it can generate essays, exercises, feedback, and even creative works tailored to individual goals and styles. Beyond content generation, its strength lies in its ability to adapt contextually, to understand open-ended, incomplete, or ambiguous prompts and to offer responses that fit the situation. In contrast to earlier adaptive learning systems that relied on fixed sets of rules and options, GenAI's neural networks learn from huge collections of data, giving it a flexible, context-sensitive intelligence that more closely resembles human reasoning and communication. Crucially, this shift moves education from the delivery of knowledge to the creation of knowledge. Therefore, in this context, AI is considered a game-changing technology that is rapidly influencing a wide range of fields, including English as a Foreign Language (EFL) instruction.

Another defining feature of generative AI is its use of natural language as its interface, which means that people can simply talk or write to it as they would to another person, thereby eliminating the need to learn special commands or software systems. While previous technologies required users to follow technical commands or use menus, GenAI allows us to learn and create simply by talking or writing naturally. Crucially, this conversational access to knowledge lowers barriers, making learning more intuitive and personal.

However, this new interaction also brings deeper implications. For the first time, technology challenges traditional ideas of authorship, originality, and creativity, forcing educators and learners alike to think critically about what it means to create and understand. In a deeper epistemological sense, generative AI does not merely extend human capabilities; it reshapes how we define thinking, learning, and originality. At the same time, this autonomy brings both opportunities and responsibilities. Learners and educators must now develop new literacies, understanding how AI systems work and how to use them ethically and critically. While traditional educational technologies changed how we teach, generative AI changes what it means to teach and learn. Therefore, it marks a transition from the age of instructional tools to an age of intelligent collaborators, where humans and machines jointly participate in the creation of knowledge. The purpose here is not to draw a simple comparison between the past and the present or between traditional tools and AI generators, but rather to recognize the paradigm-shifting development in the epistemology of knowledge and to understand how these tools reshape the way we think—and how they invite us to rethink learning, creativity, and human agency itself. Ultimately, this represents something that has never occurred before in the long development of technology.

Under these emerging conditions, many EFL teachers are understandably uncertain about how to respond to the growing presence of artificial intelligence in education. In reality, neither teachers nor students, and perhaps the education system, are fully prepared to address the pace and implications of this transformation. Yet this is no longer a matter of choice or preference; it is about finding ways to adapt and move forward with it. Otherwise, we can be left out of the game entirely. The issue is not merely one of keeping up with new tools but of redefining professional roles in a system where teaching, learning, and communication are being reshaped by intelligent technologies. While teachers are expected to foster 21st-century skills such as digital literacy, creativity, and adaptability, they are often given limited support or guidance on how to achieve this effectively. As primary decision-makers in the classroom, teachers face the difficult task of balancing innovation with pedagogical integrity, deciding not only how to use AI but whether it genuinely contributes to meaningful learning.

It is also important to recognize that teachers themselves are learners in this process, experimenting with new technologies alongside their students. The accelerating presence of artificial intelligence in education raises a critical question: will teachers become servants of AI tools, or will they learn to place AI in their service? This distinction is more than rhetorical; rather, it speaks to the core of agency, control, and purpose in teaching and learning. When technology dictates decisions, generates materials, and structures thinking, there is a danger that teachers and students alike will gradually surrender their intellectual autonomy. In this scenario, the tool becomes the master, subtly shaping pedagogical goals and epistemic habits according to its algorithmic logic. Over time, such dependence can turn education into a process of consumption rather than creation, where efficiency outweighs reflection and innovation. It may, in fact, be misleading to speak of "integration," since AI tools have already intruded into and infiltrated nearly every aspect of education, leaving little space for deliberate or gradual adoption. Without structured professional development and opportunities for reflection, many educators may feel hesitant or disoriented in this transition. What is needed, therefore, is a collective and well-informed approach, one that empowers teachers with both the technical knowledge and the critical awareness to integrate AI thoughtfully, ensuring that technology serves human learning rather than the other way around. Institutions will inevitably feel compelled to restructure the entire education system to adjust curricula, assessment, and teacher training within the emerging realities of an AI-driven era.

Within this broader transformation, as a review chapter, this contribution does not aim to develop or test a new theoretical model. Instead, it brings together recent research on artificial intelligence in language education and intercultural communication, using well-established concepts as guiding lenses. Ideas such as learner autonomy, teacher agency, and intercultural communicative competence are not treated as fixed variables within a single framework, but as helpful perspectives for organizing, comparing, and reflecting on existing studies. In this manner, the chapter emphasizes major trends, ongoing debates, and emerging directions in the literature, while staying true to its purpose as a synthesis rather than a theory-building study.

## ARTIFICIAL INTELLIGENCE IN LANGUAGE EDUCATION

While AI technologies have been discussed since the mid-twentieth century, it is only in the last decade that we have witnessed an unprecedented acceleration, and perhaps new challenges, in their application to language education. The integration of artificial intelligence (AI) into language education is no longer a distant aspiration but an ongoing reality that shapes the experiences of learners and teachers alike. Tools such as ChatGPT, Gemini, Siri, Google Translate, Grammarly, Duolingo, and others now occupy a central place in the everyday practices of learners. Beyond mere language practice, these technologies have opened new opportunities for intercultural communication (ICC), a domain long regarded as essential to developing global citizens equipped with empathy, cultural awareness, and the ability to navigate diverse communicative settings (Byram, 1997; Deardorff, 2006).

Parallel to this, there has been a marked increase in scholarly attention to the application of artificial intelligence in education. The clearest evidence of this is that prestigious publishing houses have released an overwhelming number of studies on AI in education, exploring various dimensions of AI in teaching and learning. However, despite their enormous volume, most of these studies remain largely descriptive, offering minimal analytical or theoretical depth. While research on the topic is still in its early stages, this growing body of work reflects the global recognition of AI as a driving force in reshaping pedagogical practices, curriculum design, and learner engagement. At the same time, it reveals our collective astonishment, unpreparedness, and sense of surprise in the face of such a rapid and unexpected breakthrough. This shift forces us to rethink the very heart of how languages are learned. For decades, we've relied on various theories of learning to explain how a student goes from silence to fluency. For instance, we often look to Vygotsky's idea of the 'Zone of Proximal Development,' where a student learns best with the help of a 'More Knowledgeable Other' (MKO). Traditionally, that MKO was a human teacher or a more advanced peer who could sense exactly when a student was struggling. But today, Generative AI has introduced a 'Machine MKO' that is available 24/7, offering a level of persistence no human could match. However, the influence of artificial intelligence extends far beyond the foundations laid by Vygotsky. Similarly, if we look at Stephen Krashen's Input Hypothesis, we know that for a language to stay in a student's memory, they must be exposed to content that they can actually understand. This is content known as i plus one (i+1), which is essentially material that sits just one level above the current ability of the learner. In contrast, in a traditional classroom, a teacher tries to find a middle ground for thirty different students. AI, however, can personalize that 'i+1' input for every single student individually, in real-time. It is like having a textbook that rewrites itself as you read it.

Beyond input and scaffolding theories, we have to consider Bandura's Social Learning Theory, which suggests we learn by observing and imitating others. This raises a fascinating question: if a student's primary 'model' for English is a chatbot rather than a human, how does that change their intercultural communicative competence? While AI is efficient, it lacks the lived experience and emotional depth of a human culture-bearer. This creates a new tension in the classroom: we have more 'input' than ever before, but we risk losing the authentic social 'modelling' that makes language feel alive. This is why we need to look at AI not just as a tool for efficiency, but as a new, complex participant in the social act of learning.

Building on these theoretical considerations, over the past three years, a number of recurring themes and emerging applications have become visible in the expanding body of research on AI in education, revealing where scholarly attention has begun to concentrate and how the field is evolving.

## PERSONALIZATION OF LANGUAGE LEARNING

One of the most prominent themes is the personalization of language learning through AI-driven platforms that can adapt tasks, vocabulary input, and feedback to individual learners' proficiency levels and learning preferences. Building on this idea, a growing body of research indicates that artificial intelligence offers significant advantages to education on a broad scale by making both learning and teaching more personalized for students and teachers alike. In this sense, AI has the capacity to offer each learner a tailored educational experience, enabling authentic, immersive engagement more easily than ever before. More specifically, using technologies such as machine learning (ML) and natural language processing (NLP), AI systems can analyze learners' needs, interests, and performance data to design individualized learning paths that respond to their strengths and weaknesses.

Consequently, this data-informed personalization allows learners to progress at their own pace, accommodating diverse learning styles and promoting deeper engagement. At the same time, it provides teachers with actionable insights into student progress, enabling more targeted instruction and feedback. From this perspective, these features show that AI fosters a more responsive, inclusive, and engaging learning environment that redefines how language education is designed and delivered (Arya & Verma, 2024; Bit et al., 2024; Singh et al., 2025; Karroum et al., 2024; Wangdi, 2024).

Yet despite these advances, it is worth asking whether this move toward personalization truly supports learning in a meaningful, pedagogical way or whether it has simply become a matter of personal comfort and convenience. After all, many people have embraced AI tools not because they transform pedagogy, but because of their speed, ease, and efficiency. As tireless digital assistants, they never rest, pause, or demand resources, continuously saving us time and effort.

## LEARNER AUTONOMY AND MOTIVATION

EFL learners and teachers have long suffered from the absence of tools that genuinely support motivation and autonomy. Historically, English language learning in many contexts has relied heavily on textbook-driven instruction, rigid curricula, and exam-oriented outcomes. As a result, these systems often positioned learners as passive recipients rather than active participants in their own learning journeys. In the absence of adaptive technologies, interactive platforms, or authentic communicative environments, both teachers and students struggled to sustain motivation. This challenge becomes even more visible in EFL settings, where opportunities for real-life interaction and autonomous learning are already severely limited. Consequently, learners found it difficult to see the relevance of what they were studying to real-life communication, while teachers, working within limited institutional structures, had few tools to individualize learning or nurture learner agency.

Moreover, the lack of autonomy-supportive tools meant that students' progress depended largely on classroom exposure rather than self-directed engagement beyond it. Because traditional resources could not easily cater to differences in proficiency levels, learning styles, or interests, many learners became disengaged. At the same time, teachers were burdened with repetitive tasks such as grading and content delivery. As a result, time that could have been devoted to creative lesson design or mentoring learners' independent skills was lost.

In this sense, the emergence of AI-driven tools represents not merely a technological advance but a pedagogical opportunity, the one that directly touches two of the most persistent challenges in EFL education: autonomy and motivation. For years, learners have depended heavily on teachers, textbooks, and exams, often lacking opportunities to make meaningful choices or take control of their own learning pace and content. AI tools, however, allow learners to set goals, receive instant and individualized feedback, and explore language through authentic, context-rich experiences. This personalization helps students see tangible progress, which in turn fuels intrinsic motivation. From the teacher's perspective, AI-supported environments can reduce the mechanical aspects of instruction and free time for mentorship, guidance, and creativity. Instead of controlling every stage of learning, which is often not feasible due to the many demands placed on teachers, they can focus on designing conditions that nurture curiosity and independence. AI becomes a facilitator of learner autonomy rather than a substitute for teaching. By enabling students to take initiative, reflect on their progress, and engage with language in self-directed ways, these technologies can reignite motivation and help learners rediscover a sense of ownership and purpose in their educational journey.

## TEACHERS' ROLES, PROFESSIONAL DEVELOPMENT, AND AGENCY

As AI becomes a permanent reality in everyday teaching practices, it brings both promise and pressure for educators. In this context, the question is no longer whether teachers will use AI, but how their professional roles, identities, and sense of agency will adapt in response. This shift underscores the fact that teachers cannot afford to ignore the profound educational implications of AI, calling for renewed attention to their evolving roles, identities, professional development, responsibilities, and agency in technology-mediated environments.

Reflecting on these growing concerns, it is evident that teachers often approach AI with a mixture of curiosity and caution. Many are eager to experiment with new tools, yet they remain apprehensive about issues related to ethics, assessment, accuracy, and institutional expectations. Yet sustained, hands-on engagement with AI can gradually shift this skepticism toward more critical and thoughtful adoption, where teachers use the technology to support reflection, creativity, and richer feedback practices. Likewise, professional learning communities that explore AI collaboratively through inquiry, experimentation, and shared discussion tend to empower educators to design more adaptive, learner-centered lessons. In these spaces, AI becomes less of a threat and more of a catalyst for pedagogical innovation.

Teachers are emerging not only as facilitators of AI literacy but also as co-learners and designers in an evolving pedagogical landscape. In this sense, AI is not only reshaping the technical demands of teaching but also redefining what counts as professional knowledge, requiring teachers to collaborate with intelligent systems rather than simply use static technologies (Tan, Cheng, & Ling, 2025; Hazzan-Bishara et al., 2025).

Despite these developments, most teachers' AI knowledge remains below the desired level, creating an urgent need for targeted, structured professional development that builds both technical understanding and pedagogical competence. In response to this need, professional development programs are evolving from traditional technology-training workshops to more dynamic, inquiry-driven experiences that foster both pedagogical and ethical competence. Supporting this transformation, the TPACK and extended i-TPACK frameworks emphasize that effective AI-focused professional learning should integrate technological, pedagogical, and moral dimensions, enabling teachers to critically evaluate, adapt, and ethically implement AI tools in classroom practice. Although the field is still in its early stages, such initiatives hold significant promise for cultivating teacher agency, reflective practice, and adaptive expertise in AI-enhanced learning (Dogan, Nalbantoglu, Celik, & Agacli Dogan, 2025).

Nevertheless, while it is widely recognized that AI has the potential to enhance teaching effectiveness and learner engagement, many teachers still feel unprepared and uncertain about its pedagogical and ethical implications. For this reason, they need sustained professional development that promotes AI literacy, reflective practice, and contextually relevant applications (Aguilar-Cruz & Salas-Pilco, 2025).

One practical issue to keep in mind is how assessment and classroom realities influence the use of AI in language learning. Although AI-generated feedback can save time and support personalized learning, there are still open questions about how valid, fair, and transparent this feedback is, especially when it is used for grading or other high-stakes decisions. Automated responses may privilege certain linguistic norms, writing styles, or communicative patterns, which raises concerns for diverse learning contexts. In addition, practical classroom factors, such as existing curricula, assessment rules, and institutional policies, often determine how, and even whether, AI tools can be used in meaningful ways. Even when teachers recognize the benefits of AI, they often have to work within constraints like syllabus requirements, standardized testing, or a lack of clear institutional guidance. Acknowledging these limitations reminds us that AI needs to be used within realistic educational settings, not as a one-size-fits-all fix.

## ETHICAL AWARENESS, ACADEMIC INTEGRITY, AND CREATIVITY

Beyond the opportunities and practical benefits, the ethical dilemmas posed by AI generator tools have become increasingly prominent, especially as the growing presence of Artificial Intelligence (AI) in education has generated concerns that extend far beyond questions of technological capability. As AI systems become more deeply integrated into teaching, assessment, and learning management, educators face complex issues related to data privacy, algorithmic bias, intellectual integrity, and learner autonomy. In particular, the use of Generative AI challenges long-held notions of authorship, creativity, and fairness in academic work, raising concerns about plagiarism, overreliance on automated feedback, and the erosion of critical thinking skills. Perhaps the core of the dilemma lies in the fact that it is becoming increasingly difficult to determine where human effort ends, and machine assistance begins.

Compounding this challenge, most AI systems operate in ways that are not fully transparent, meaning that teachers and students cannot always know how outputs are generated or what kinds of assumptions or biases might be embedded in them. Such opacity can undermine trust in educational assessment and decision-making processes. At a deeper level, the widespread use of AI generator tools may reduce learning to a mechanical process, diminishing the value of human creativity, reflection, and ethical responsibility. Thus, while AI introduces new possibilities for personalization and efficiency, it also compels educators to reconsider how integrity, agency, and fairness can be safeguarded in increasingly AI-mediated learning environments.

If reliance on AI-generated content becomes habitual because it is readily available, engaging, and convincingly written, the academic and pedagogical frame could shift dramatically. Academically, such dependence may blur the boundaries between original thought and machine-assisted production, weakening students' ability to construct, critique, and defend their own ideas. In addition, overuse of AI might erode fundamental research and writing skills, leading to superficial understanding rather than deep engagement with knowledge. Pedagogically, teachers may face greater difficulties in fostering critical thinking, creativity, and intellectual honesty. Classrooms risk shifting from spaces of inquiry and dialogue to environments of content consumption, where polished results are valued over meaningful process.

Another ethical concern relates to the cultural and epistemic bias embedded in AI-generated outputs. Since most AI systems are trained on datasets that are predominantly Western and English-language based, they inevitably reproduce the values, perspectives, and assumptions characteristic of Anglo-American cultural and intellectual traditions. Consequently, this imbalance can reinforce a narrow worldview while marginalizing non-Western perspectives, languages, and epistemologies. In educational contexts, such bias may subtly shape how learners think, write, and evaluate knowledge, normalizing Western modes of reasoning and communication as the default standard. Addressing this issue, therefore, requires fostering critical AI literacy, helping educators and students recognize whose voices and values are reflected in AI tools, and encouraging the inclusion of more diverse linguistic and cultural data to ensure that AI development and use remain inclusive, equitable, and contextually relevant.

AI generators like ChatGPT are trained on large text datasets, not on embodied human experience. This means they learn patterns, correlations, and probabilities in language, but not the contextual, emotional, or experiential understanding that humans naturally develop through life. As a result, AI can sound intelligent, logical, or even empathetic, yet still produce answers that lack common sense, real-world feasibility, or situational awareness. For example, an AI might confidently make assumptions that ignore cultural or ethical complexity simply because it does not understand how things work in the real world. In educational settings, this poses risks when learners take AI-generated content at face value—mistaking linguistic fluency for genuine understanding.

AI tools can produce text that resembles human writing because they are trained to recognize and reproduce patterns within massive datasets. However, their so-called "creativity" is essentially derivative. They recombine existing information rather than generate truly original ideas, at least this is what we know for now. Still, the future is uncertain, and no one can predict what the next generations of AI may bring. Unlike humans, AI lacks intentionality, imagination, and the ability to draw on lived experience or emotional insight. Its outputs are based on probabilities, not purpose or understanding. For instance, an AI model can write a convincing poem or essay, but it does so by mimicking the structures and styles found in its training data, not through genuine inspiration or awareness of meaning. In educational contexts, this limitation becomes particularly relevant: when students depend on AI for idea generation or writing, they risk narrowing their own creative capacities and critical thinking. Genuine creativity in learning involves questioning, connecting disparate concepts, and expressing personal perspectives—all qualities that remain uniquely human. Therefore, while AI can assist and inspire, it should be viewed as a supporting tool rather than a substitute for the imaginative and interpretive power that defines authentic human creativity.

Research shows that algorithmic bias in education can perpetuate inequities rather than reduce them. Bird et al. (2024) found that administrative data often predict the performance of African American students less accurately than that of white students, largely due to insufficient data collection on the achievements of learners from diverse backgrounds. Recent discussions on AI in education increasingly highlight that predictive systems can unintentionally reproduce social inequalities. In many cases, algorithms used to forecast student performance have been shown to misclassify or underestimate the potential of certain demographic groups, particularly those from marginalized racial, gender, or socioeconomic backgrounds. When prediction models generate disproportionately high false-negative rates for specific populations, they risk limiting access to academic support and reinforcing existing disparities rather than alleviating them (Alfredo et al., 2024; Gándara, Anahideh, Ison, & Picchiarini, 2024; Idowu et al., 2024; Švábenský et al., 2024).

More importantly, most of what we know about algorithmic bias comes from Western contexts, meaning that the ways these biases manifest in diverse or non-Western educational systems remain largely underexamined. We still lack comprehensive, context-sensitive research that reveals how predictive tools shape opportunities for underrepresented learners across different regions. This gap underscores an urgent need for more inclusive, globally grounded investigations into algorithmic fairness in education.

In this sense, we know for certain that we are never entirely free from the influence of our upbringing, cultural heritage, beliefs, and experiences, all of which shape how we design and interpret technology. The same applies to the development of AI systems, since these technologies are created, trained, and refined by humans who carry their own social and cultural imprints. As a result, AI cannot be considered truly neutral or objective; it inevitably reflects the value systems, assumptions, and priorities of its creators and the societies from which those creators come.

Given these realities, a large number of AI ethics guidelines have been developed by governments, universities, and research institutions. However, they remain largely symbolic and lack mechanisms for enforcement or accountability. The guidelines, in many cases, outline aspirational principles such as fairness, transparency, and responsibility, yet offer little guidance on how these ideals can be operationalized in real-world technological or institutional contexts. This disconnects between principle and practice leads some to question whether AI ethics frameworks function more as moral declarations than as actionable policies capable of influencing development, regulation, or educational practice. The challenge, therefore, lies not only in translating ethical ideals into concrete standards, governance models, and pedagogical practices that can meaningfully shape human–AI interaction, but also in the fact that there is still no universal agreement on what counts as ethically acceptable in educational settings.

While principles such as transparency, fairness, and accountability are widely accepted, their application in classrooms is often debated. For instance, educators differ on whether using AI tools to assist with grading constitutes innovation or academic dishonesty. Similarly, students' use of AI for brainstorming or language assistance blurs the line between legitimate support and academic misconduct. These tensions reveal that ethical decision-making in education is deeply context-dependent, shaped by institutional norms, disciplinary traditions, and cultural expectations. Therefore, rather than seeking a single fixed ethical framework, the focus should perhaps shift toward developing educators' critical judgment and ethical literacy, enabling them to navigate AI's challenges with flexibility, reflection, and a strong sense of professional responsibility.

Another ethical concern involves the loss of intellectual ownership. AI-generated content complicates questions of who truly owns the ideas or creations, whether it is the student who prompts the system, the educator who guides the process, or the developers who design the AI itself. Such ambiguity can make grading, authorship credit, and even academic publication ethics more complex. Questions of bias and fairness also arise when considering the broader implications of AI use. Because AI systems are trained on vast datasets that reflect not only human perspectives but also human prejudices, they can unintentionally reproduce social, cultural, or linguistic biases. Overreliance on these systems may therefore reinforce inequities rather than promote diversity and inclusion within education.

Closely related to these issues is the risk of dependence and de-skilling. When learners rely too heavily on AI for polished or ready-made answers, their capacity for critical thinking, creativity, and independent problem-solving may weaken—raising fundamental questions about whether education's purpose is to foster deep understanding or simply to generate efficient outcomes. Beyond this, such dependency also risks eroding students' sense of authenticity and individuality. The message we so often give to our students, "be yourself," begins to lose its meaning when ideas and expressions come primarily from machines. If students stop trusting their own voice or feel that their worth lies only in producing flawless results, education may shift from being a space of growth to one of performance. To prevent this, teachers must help learners use AI responsibly while still valuing their originality, reflection, and the imperfect but genuine process of thinking for themselves.

Equally important are issues of transparency and accountability. The inner workings of AI models are often hidden, making it difficult for users to trace how information is produced or verified. When students or teachers rely on such tools without critical evaluation, inaccurate or misleading information may find its way into academic work, undermining trust in scholarship. Ethical concerns also emerge in terms of equity and access, as not all learners or institutions possess equal access to advanced AI technologies. This disparity creates a digital divide that privileges some while excluding others, raising questions of justice and fairness in educational opportunity.

## READINESS OF TEACHERS TOWARD AI INTEGRATION

We all agree that Artificial Intelligence (AI) has created new and innovative opportunities for English as a Foreign Language (EFL) teachers to enhance instruction through automation, personalized learning, rapid lesson design, redesigned assessment strategies, and data-informed decision-making. However, realizing these benefits depends largely on teachers' preparedness to adopt and effectively use AI technologies. Understanding teachers' readiness, along with their perceptions and training needs, has therefore become a growing focus in recent research.

Bautista et al. (2024) examined preservice teachers' readiness to use AI tools within the Technological Pedagogical and Content Knowledge (TPACK) framework. Their findings showed strong levels of Technological Knowledge (TK), Technological Pedagogical Knowledge (TPK), Technological Content Knowledge (TCK), and integrated TPACK, alongside emerging ethical readiness. The authors also reported that higher levels of TK, TPK, TCK, and TPACK were positively associated with stronger ethical awareness, underscoring the need for teacher education programs that develop both technical competence and responsible AI use. Similarly, Karataş and Ataç (2025) surveyed 304 pre-service English teachers and found consistent patterns. Participants demonstrated high levels of technological proficiency (TK) and moderate readiness overall, although their understanding of AI-related ethics was comparatively limited. The study also revealed gender- and experience-based differences, with male teachers and those with prior AI exposure scoring higher in AI-TPACK readiness. Importantly, a positive correlation was identified between traditional TPACK and AI-TPACK competence, indicating that strengthening general pedagogical–technology integration enhances readiness for AI-supported instruction.

In a more recent study, Taşkara (2025) investigated 90 in-service EFL teachers' readiness and perceptions toward AI using a sequential explanatory mixed-methods design. Although teachers expressed generally positive attitudes toward AI, several challenges emerged. Their pedagogical and ethical readiness was limited, as many struggled to connect AI tools with specific teaching goals or to address issues such as plagiarism and bias. Infrastructure problems, including poor access to technology and internet connectivity, especially in public schools, further constrained implementation. Teachers also reported anxiety and uncertainty about AI's rapid introduction, fearing overreliance on technology or loss of professional control. The study revealed a lack of institutional and professional support, with few structured training programs or clear policies to guide integration. Additionally, contextual barriers in Türkiye, such as skepticism and limited exposure to AI-based curricula, hindered adoption. Finally, some teachers viewed AI merely as a practical tool rather than a transformative pedagogical aid, highlighting the need for deeper and more meaningful integration.

Broadly speaking, the reviewed studies, though limited, demonstrate a growing awareness of and willingness to integrate AI, particularly in terms of technological competence. At the same time, they show that many teachers still lack confidence in context-specific pedagogical application and ethical literacy.

## AI-ASSISTED LANGUAGE LEARNING AND INTERCULTURAL COMMUNICATION IN EFL

Empirical evidence from recent studies shows that AI-mediated interventions in EFL contexts can lead to measurable gains in writing accuracy, listening comprehension, and learner motivation. In addition, meta-analytic and review evidence also indicates that AI technologies broadly support language-skill development, learner engagement, and adaptive feedback (Apriani et al., 2024; Xiao, 2025; Toscu, 2025). The common pedagogical driver behind these gains is AI's ability to provide immediate, personalized, and adaptive feedback, enabling learners to self-regulate and practice independently. Recent research suggests that when generative AI is paired with pedagogical strategies such as mind-mapping, it can foster creativity, critical thinking, and learner engagement (Chiu & Hwang, 2025; Khoso, Wang & Darazi, 2025).

Building upon the necessity of addressing specific instructional challenges through technology, research consistently shows AI's effectiveness in supporting student agency. For example, several studies demonstrate AI's capacity to enhance learner autonomy by enabling self-directed and low-anxiety practice environments. Students described AI tools (e.g., ChatGPT and conversational chatbots) as "nonjudgmental tutors" that encourage experimentation, reduce communication apprehension, and sustain motivation. AI-supported feedback not only improves writing performance but also generates positive emotional cycles between enjoyment, engagement, and achievement. In line with these findings, a growing body of recent research demonstrate that AI-supported learning environments contribute to heightened motivation and sustained learner engagement, as students perceive learning tasks to be more meaningful, interactive, and supportive. Such personalization fosters a stronger sense of relevance and ownership in the learning process, which in turn enhances motivation and engagement (Altinay et al., 2024; Artemova, 2024; Mohamed et al., 2025; Moybeka et al., 2023; Nabhani et al., 2024).

Compared to other language skills, writing has received considerably more research attention in AI-integration studies. A review of recent publications (2023–2025) demonstrates increasing pedagogical and empirical interest in the use of artificial intelligence (AI) tools, automated writing evaluation (AWE), and large language models (LLMs) to support writing development across English as a Foreign or Second Language (EFL/ESL) and higher education contexts. Most studies, though descriptive, focus on learner perceptions and acceptance of AI-assisted tools, consistently reporting positive attitudes toward their utility, accessibility, and immediacy of feedback (Sarı & Han, 2024; Taşkara, 2025; Sarıcaoğlu & Bilki, 2021; Ding, Zou, & Kohnke, 2025; Marzuki et al., 2023). Learners particularly value AI systems for grammar correction, vocabulary enrichment, and support with organization while technology acceptance is often predicted by perceived usefulness, ease of use, and trust. However, it is important to note that uncritical dependence on AI tools may limit creativity and depth of thought, suggesting the need for teacher mediation and ethical literacy (Amini et al., 2025). Similarly, the reviewed studies note that while AI tools promote linguistic accuracy, they may risk homogenizing writing styles and discouraging authentic expression.

Moving beyond perception-based research, experimental and quasi-experimental studies provide empirical evidence that AWE and LLM-based feedback can enhance writing quality, self-efficacy, and motivation while reducing anxiety (Rahimi et al., 2025; Sarı & Han, 2024; Mahapatra, 2024). Integrating AWE systems such as Criterion, Grammarly, and ChatGPT into classroom practice leads to measurable gains in grammatical accuracy, cohesion, and revision engagement, though improvements tend to remain at surface levels rather than conceptual or argumentative development. In assessment contexts, studies reveal promising correlations between GPT-based scoring and human evaluations but also point to validity and fairness challenges, as automated scoring may underestimate the performance of multilingual learners. Analytical and conceptual contributions further caution that while ChatGPT can generate context-aware feedback, it may propagate errors or biases if not critically interpreted (Ranalli, 2018). Overall, these studies converge on a common conclusion:

AI-assisted writing technologies function best as collaborative partners—enhancing linguistic accuracy, engagement, and learner autonomy—when used with pedagogical guidance, transparency, and ethical awareness rather than as substitutes for human judgment and instruction. Moreover, research on AI integration in language education is not limited to writing or language learning. A growing body of work shows that AI supported tools also influence other language skills, including speaking, listening, reading, and vocabulary development. These studies reveal how conversational agents, intelligent tutoring systems, and multimodal learning environments can support fluency, comprehension, and interactional competence by providing personalized feedback, immediate scaffolding, and authentic communicative scenarios.

When the literature is viewed as a whole, it becomes clear that several interconnected trends are influencing AI-supported language education and intercultural communication. From a pedagogical perspective, there is a clear move toward more personalized learning, greater learner autonomy, and expanded teacher agency, alongside ongoing challenges related to guidance, control, and meaningful classroom use. At the same time, ethical concerns have become increasingly prominent, particularly around academic integrity, bias, transparency, and the preservation of human agency in AI-mediated learning environments. These developments are closely linked to wider policy and institutional trends, where the rapid spread of AI tools often moves faster than curriculum design, assessment frameworks, and regulatory guidance. Looking at these patterns together, it becomes clear that while AI is reshaping pedagogy and communication, future directions need to address pedagogical, ethical, and policy issues as interconnected concerns.

## AI AND INTERCULTURAL COMMUNICATION

The role of Artificial Intelligence (AI) in facilitating intercultural communication, particularly through spoken interaction in English as a Lingua Franca (ELF) context, has become increasingly significant. Intercultural communication lies at the core of Global English use, encompassing the dynamic exchanges between speakers from diverse linguistic and cultural backgrounds who negotiate meaning through English as a shared medium. Although the diversity of English has long been acknowledged, especially within the frameworks of World Englishes and English as an International Language (EIL), the notion of its global ownership has rarely advanced beyond theoretical discussion. Scholars have long emphasized that English no longer belongs solely to native speakers but to all who use it as a lingua franca for intercultural exchange. Yet, in practice, this vision of shared linguistic ownership has remained largely aspirational because authentic, sustained opportunities for real-time intercultural interaction are limited in most educational settings. Until recently, real-time interaction across linguistic and cultural boundaries depended primarily on physical exchanges such as study-abroad programs like ERASMUS or short-term virtual collaborations, which, although valuable, reached only a small number of learners.

The emergence of AI-based communication and learning tools has dramatically altered this situation. By enabling continuous and globally networked interactions, AI technologies allow users from different linguistic and cultural backgrounds to experience and internalize the diversity of English in authentic communicative contexts. Tools such as intelligent chatbots, automated translators, and virtual communication systems now facilitate intercultural dialogue and real-time interaction, helping learners negotiate meaning, adjust to various accents, and appreciate the legitimacy of multiple English varieties (Rose, McKinley, & Galloway, 2021). Generative AI platforms like ChatGPT can further simulate intercultural encounters, enabling learners to practice empathy, pragmatics, and culturally responsive communication. This shift represents more than a technological innovation. It marks a democratization of English use. AI technologies provide learners from diverse linguistic communities with access to cross-cultural communicative experiences that were once limited by geography or institutional privilege. Through ongoing interaction, users can develop intercultural awareness, linguistic flexibility, and mutual respect, moving beyond passive recognition of English diversity to active participation in it.

AI-supported telecollaborative projects and mobile-assisted learning environments further contribute to this process by connecting classrooms across countries and enabling collaborative tasks in shared digital spaces. These contexts allow students to interact with international peers, exchange cultural viewpoints, and develop awareness of linguistic diversity. For example, AI tools integrated into virtual exchange platforms or intelligent communication apps can analyze interactional patterns, offer feedback on politeness strategies, or highlight cross-cultural pragmatics, thereby deepening learners' intercultural communicative competence. The concept of Intercultural Communicative Competence (ICC), proposed by Byram (1997), extends the traditional understanding of language proficiency beyond grammar, vocabulary, and fluency. It emphasizes that effective communication across cultures depends not only on linguistic ability but also on attitudes, knowledge, skills, and critical cultural awareness that enable individuals to interact appropriately and empathetically with speakers from diverse backgrounds. Byram's view aligns with Global Englishes and English as a Lingua Franca (ELF) perspective, which prioritize intelligibility, empathy, and mutual understanding over conformity to native norms. In this framework, language learning becomes a process of developing intercultural awareness and communicative flexibility, where success is measured not by accuracy but by the ability to build relationships, negotiate meaning, and manage difference constructively. When applied to AI-supported language learning,

Byram's ICC framework provides a powerful pedagogical lens. AI tools that simulate intercultural dialogues, model diverse communication styles, and provide reflective feedback can help learners develop the attitudes and skills necessary for effective intercultural engagement. In this sense, AI technologies can transform language learning from a linguistic exercise into a process of intercultural engagement and global citizenship, empowering learners to communicate ethically and effectively in diverse, multilingual settings.

Among several recent studies investigating the role of artificial intelligence in Global Englishes and intercultural communication, Lee, Jeon, and Choe (2025) conducted research that offers valuable insights into AI-mediated speaking practice. Their study demonstrated that AI chatbots can function as conversational partners simulating speakers of diverse English varieties. Through these interactions, participants practiced spoken communication, engaged in negotiation of meaning, and developed greater confidence in English as a Lingua Franca (ELF) exchange. The findings indicated that AI-mediated dialogues enhanced learners' ELF communication confidence and willingness to interact, performing more effectively than traditional presentation-based tasks. Additionally, the use of AI chatbots created an anxiety-free and supportive learning environment, allowing students to experiment with different English varieties without fear of judgment. Integrating chatbots within immersive virtual environments was shown to bridge theory and practice by offering authentic opportunities for spoken interaction that encouraged intercultural empathy, self-confidence, and awareness of English plurality. Learners displayed greater acceptance of both local and global Englishes and a noticeable reduction in native-speaker bias.

## FUTURE DIRECTIONS AND POLICY IMPLICATIONS

We face a critical dilemma in light of the swift transition toward AI-supported language education. On one hand, existing language policies and assessment frameworks still rely on a monolithic conception of linguistic correctness, rigidly enforcing one specific, "perfect" model of English, even though there have been some modest steps toward change. At the same time, a major concern is that generative AI may end up reinforcing the same linguistic norms—replacing a human-driven monolithic model with an AI-driven one because it is trained on highly standardized datasets. In other words, we may be moving from a human-imposed linguistic monolith to an algorithmically imposed one, raising serious questions about how language diversity and learner identity will be treated in the future. In this context, the role of teachers becomes especially significant, as they are the primary agents who will mediate, filter, or challenge the linguistic norms embedded in AI systems.

Although the topic has received considerable attention from academic circles, as evidenced by the increasing number of online seminars and publications, teachers will remain central in shaping how AI tools are integrated into language classrooms. Yet many feel unprepared or anxious in the face of these rapid technological changes. Within this landscape, three distinct attitudes toward AI integration can be observed. The first group includes enthusiastic adopters who embrace AI because it saves time and effort; however, they often use AI-generated output uncritically, without examining its underlying logic, accuracy, or pedagogical appropriateness. In contrast, a second group consists of skeptics who fear that AI-driven feedback or automated assessment may undermine their professional judgment or even replace essential aspects of their instructional role. Their concerns are heightened by doubts about whether AI meaningfully contributes to learning outcomes, particularly in areas such as communicative competence, critical thinking, or intercultural awareness. It is also noteworthy that some teachers who have built their professional identity around traditional methods may feel threatened by rapid technological shifts that seem incompatible with their long-established teaching philosophies. Finally, the third group includes teachers who hesitate to adopt new technologies largely because the integration process demands experimentation, time, and mindset change. Their reluctance stems not from a lack of interest but from deeply rooted practical and philosophical concerns that create substantial barriers to institutional change.

Collectively, these patterns reveal an important challenge for teaching: teachers who rely too heavily on AI may unintentionally weaken the quality of academic work, while those who are skeptical raise valid concerns about losing professional control and the human element that is especially important in foreign language education. Ultimately, these varied responses show that successful AI integration in language education requires not only technical tools but also thoughtful support, clear guidance, and a commitment to preserving the teacher's central role in shaping meaningful learning. However, these expectations cannot be met unless teachers themselves feel adequately prepared for this transition. Many teachers have not received formal training in AI, leading to uncertainty about the tools' function, reliability, and effective instructional use. This lack of preparedness is partly rooted in the fact that schools and universities often fail to provide adequate professional development, leaving teachers to navigate complex technologies on their own.

At the same time, these complex technologies present a massive opportunity and an obligation for policymakers. AI has the capacity to interpret not only text and speech but also gestures, eye movement, posture, emotional tone, and interaction patterns. Yet this very power also makes it clear that AI systems used in language education are not culturally neutral; they reflect the values and datasets they were built from. For this reason, it is important to develop AI tools that recognize cultural differences and support learners' multilingual and multicultural identities. The datasets behind these tools should include a wide range of linguistic inputs—different accents, communication styles, and pragmatic norms—to avoid reinforcing stereotypes or favoring certain varieties of English. When designed carefully, culturally aware AI can help learners develop intercultural competence by exposing them to diverse communication scenarios from around the world. To achieve this, policymakers and developers should work together to ensure that AI tools include principles of intercultural communication.

From this perspective, learners now naturally encounter a wider and more dynamic range of pragmatic norms and World Englishes. This, in turn, necessitates that policy reform move beyond prescriptive rules and embrace frameworks such as English as a Lingua Franca (ELF). The goal is to use AI's power to reward successful communication and flexibility, not just perfect language use. In practical terms, this means policymakers must immediately revise curricula, assessment frameworks, and teacher education programs to officially incorporate these more flexible and pluralistic views of English, ensuring that AI supports genuine global communication rather than constraining it.

Another area of concern in relation to AI language tools involves data security, privacy, and institutional responsibility. Many of these tools collect sensitive information, such as voice recordings or writing patterns, that is protected by strict data-privacy laws. Schools and universities cannot simply rely on commercial companies to handle these issues; instead, they need clear guidelines for choosing AI tools, storing data safely, obtaining consent, and managing potential risks. Institutions require clear, transparent, and ethical rules. These frameworks should promote transparency in how AI tools operate, the sources of their data, and the limits of their output and feedback. Furthermore, AI's role in assessment and writing support raises questions about academic integrity and authorship that require explicit institutional policies. Ensuring responsible use means protecting learner autonomy, emphasizing AI as a supportive rather than substitutive tool, and setting norms that prevent overdependence. Ultimately, ethical AI governance must combine technological understanding with pedagogical sensitivity so that innovation does not undermine core values of education.

There is also a strong need to focus on ongoing, practice-oriented professional development that helps teachers build real AI skills, such as designing effective prompts, evaluating AI feedback critically, and creating multimodal learning tasks. Teachers also need support in seeing AI not as a threat but as a partner that can help them design richer learning experiences by combining human expertise with machine capabilities. To achieve this, teacher education programs should include AI literacy in their curricula so that future educators develop a balanced, critical understanding of what AI can and cannot do. When teachers feel confident and informed, fears of being replaced decrease, and the essential human role in language teaching becomes even clearer.

Furthermore, assessment frameworks must evolve to reflect the realities of AI-mediated communication. High-stakes testing systems grounded in traditional, monolithic conceptions of accuracy and correctness are increasingly misaligned with the dynamic, global nature of English in digital communication. Future assessment strategies should incorporate AI-mediated tasks such as multimodal interaction, dialogic speaking tasks, and collaborative writing supported by AI. Policies must also clarify how AI-generated work is evaluated, how academic integrity is maintained, and how learners' own contributions are distinguished from machine assistance. Aligning assessment with AI-rich learning environments requires collaboration between policymakers, assessment bodies, and educators to ensure that testing remains fair, valid, and reflective of authentic communication practices.

Sustainable and ethical integration of AI in language education also depends on strong collaboration across sectors. Researchers can provide empirical evidence on how AI reshapes language learning processes, while policymakers translate this evidence into regulatory frameworks and curriculum guidelines. Technology developers, in turn, require input from linguists, applied linguists, and intercultural communication experts to design systems that are pedagogically sound, culturally sensitive, and ethically aligned. Coordinated partnerships help avoid fragmented adoption, reduce duplication of effort, and ensure that innovation meaningfully addresses real educational needs. Establishing national or regional advisory boards dedicated to AI in language education can further formalize these collaborative efforts.

Despite the increasing interest in the rapid growth of AI tools, empirical classroom-based research remains limited, as most studies are descriptive in nature. Future studies should adopt longitudinal designs that examine how AI influences learner identity development, motivation, interactional patterns, and intercultural awareness over time. There is also a pressing need for research that investigates algorithmic bias, cultural representation, and the pedagogical validity of AI-generated feedback and output.

Looking ahead, AI will likely become an always-available language companion built directly into digital applications. As a result, we will increasingly communicate through AI systems, not just with them. AI tools will no longer be optional tools but unavoidable components of teaching and learning. They will complete tasks such as generating personalized materials, diagnosing learning gaps, providing multimodal feedback, and supporting learners with diverse needs. Schools and universities will treat AI literacy as a core competency alongside other essential skills.

In the near future, AI systems are expected to play an even greater role in designing weekly learning plans, tracking motivation, detecting learning fatigue, and adjusting strategies by establishing institutionalized norms. They may simulate complex intercultural encounters, role-plays, and negotiations with near-human authenticity. Private tutoring may shift significantly toward AI-assisted systems. It appears that AI will also be capable of detecting frustration, confusion, confidence, or hesitation, enabling more supportive interaction and becoming a socio-emotional mediator, especially in cross-cultural communication where misunderstandings are frequent. Ultimately, AI will shift from a tool that responds to input toward a system that collaborates, predicts, and co-constructs meaning. It will act not only as an assistant but as a collaborative partner that personalizes learning, mediates intercultural communication, and reshapes language policy while operating under strict global regulations.

Viewed critically, the cited studies here do not merely document technological applications; they revolve around three related theoretical foundations that shape the field. First, a strong learner-centered paradigm emerges, grounded in autonomy theory, self-regulated learning, and adaptive scaffolding models, where AI is framed as a facilitator of individualized progression. Second, a teacher-agency perspective informed by TPACK and sociocultural theory frames AI as a mediational tool whose pedagogical value depends on professional judgment and contextual adaptation. Third, research focusing on ethics and governance, drawing from critical pedagogy and fairness discussions, emphasizes issues such as bias, ownership of ideas, authority over knowledge, and who holds agency in human–AI interaction. While many empirical studies prioritize personalization and efficiency, fewer interrogate the epistemological and sociocultural implications of delegating feedback, modelling, and even intercultural representation to algorithmic systems. This imbalance indicates that technological innovation in the field is progressing more rapidly than its theoretical development. A more integrated research agenda would therefore connect pedagogical effectiveness, teacher mediation, and ethical accountability within a coherent theoretical framework rather than treating them as parallel concerns.

In conclusion, AI in language education and intercultural communication presents a paradoxical field of possibility and risk. On one hand, it offers unprecedented opportunities for personalization, autonomy, creativity, and global interaction, supporting learners as they develop linguistic competence, intercultural awareness, and new forms of participation in English as a Lingua Franca context. On the other hand, it brings complex ethical, pedagogical, and political challenges related to authorship, bias, surveillance, linguistic monoliths, and the erosion of human agency. The evidence reviewed in this chapter suggests that the future of AI in language education will not be determined by technology alone, but by how teachers, learners, researchers, policymakers, and developers collectively choose to shape its use. If AI is to function as a genuine collaborator rather than a silent curriculum, teacher agency, ethical literacy, and intercultural competence must remain at the center of decision-making. This requires sustained professional development, critical policy reform, inclusive and culturally aware design, and a stronger empirical research base that takes classroom realities seriously. Ultimately, the task is not simply to integrate AI into existing practices, but to imagine and enact educational futures in which intelligent technologies expand—rather than diminish—human creativity, dignity, and meaningful communication.

## REFERENCES


Aguilar-Cruz, P. J., & Salas-Pilco, S. Z. (2025). Teachers' perceptions of artificial intelligence in Colombia: AI technological access, AI teacher professional development and AI ethical awareness. *Technology, Pedagogy and Education, 34*(2), 219–238. DOI: 10.1080/1475939X.2025.2451865

Alfredo, M., Potts, R., & Fang, Y. (2024). Bias in student performance prediction models: A large-scale study across diverse demographic groups. *Journal of Learning Analytics, 11*(1), 45–68. DOI: 10.18608/jla.2024.7865

Altinay, Z., Altinay, F., Dagli, G., Shadiev, R., & Othman, A. (2024). Factors influencing AI learning motivation and personalisation among pre-service teachers in higher education. *MIER Journal of Educational Studies Trends and Practices, 14*(2), 462–481. DOI: 10.52634/mier/2024/v14/i2/2714

Amini, M., Lee, K. F., Yiqiu, W., & Ravindran, L. (2025). Proposing a framework for ethical use of AI in academic writing based on a conceptual review: Implications for quality education. *Interactive Learning Environments*, 1–25. Advance online publication. DOI: 10.1080/10494820.2025.2523382

Apriani, E., Indriani, N. L., Samad, I. A., & Hakim, M. N. (2024). Impact of AI-powered chatbots on EFL students' writing skills, self-efficacy, and self-regulation. Glocal English and Research Review, 2(1), 1–12. https://journal.myresearch.id/gerr/article/view/8

Artemova, I. (2024). Bridging motivation and AI in education: An activity theory perspective. *Digital Education Review*, (45), 59–69. DOI: 10.1344/der.2024.45.59-67

Arya, R., & Verma, A. (2024). Role of artificial intelligence in education. *International Journal of Advanced Research in Science Communication and Technology, 4*(2), 589–594. DOI: 10.48175/IJARSCT-19461

Bautista, A., Estrada, C., Jaravata, A. M., Mangaser, L. M., Narag, F., Soquila, R., & Asuncion, R. J. (2024). Preservice teachers' readiness towards integrating AI-based tools in education: A TPACK approach. *Educational Process: International Journal, 13*(3), 40–68. DOI: 10.22521/edupij.2024.133.3

Bird, K. A., Castleman, B. L., & Lohner, G. (2024). Are algorithms biased in education? Exploring racial bias in predicting community college student success. *Journal of Policy Analysis and Management, 44*(2), 332–361. DOI: 10.1002/pam.22569

Bit, D., Das, S., & Ghosh, A. (2024). The impact of artificial intelligence in the educational system. *International Journal of Scientific Research in Science and Technology*, *11*(4), 419–427. DOI: 10.32628/IJSRST2411424

Byram, M. (1997). *Teaching and assessing intercultural communicative competence*. Multilingual Matters.

Chiu, M. C., & Hwang, G. J. (2025). Enhancing student creative and critical thinking in generative AI-empowered creation: A mind-mapping approach. *Interactive Learning Environments*, •••, 1–22. DOI: 10.1080/10494820.2025.2511244

Deardorff, D. K. (2006). Identification and assessment of intercultural competence as a student outcome of internationalization. *Journal of Studies in International Education*, *10*(3), 241–266. DOI: 10.1177/1028315306287002

Ding, L., Zou, D., & Kohnke, L. (2025). ChatGPT as an automated writing evaluation tool: How students perceive it and how it affects their writing. *Education and Information Technologies*, *30*(18), 26777–26799. Advance online publication. DOI: 10.1007/s10639-025-13775-3

Dogan, S., Nalbantoglu, U. Y., Celik, I., & Agacli Dogan, N. (2025). Artificial intelligence professional development: A systematic review of TPACK, designs, and effects for teacher learning. *Professional Development in Education*, *51*(3), 519–546. DOI: 10.1080/19415257.2025.2454457

Gándara, D., Anahideh, H., Ison, M. P., & Picchiarini, L. (2024). Inside the black box: Detecting and mitigating algorithmic bias across racialized groups in college student-success prediction. *AERA Open*, *10*, 23328584241258741. Advance online publication. DOI: 10.1177/23328584241258741

Hazzan-Bishara, A., Kol, O., & Levy, S. (2025). The factors affecting teachers' adoption of AI technologies: A unified model of external and internal determinants. *Education and Information Technologies*, *30*(11), 15043–15069. Advance online publication. DOI: 10.1007/s10639-025-13393-z

Idowu, J. A., Xue, Y., & Moya, J. (2024). Investigating algorithmic bias in student progress monitoring. Computers & Education. *Artificial Intelligence*, *7*, 100267. Advance online publication. DOI: 10.1016/j.caeai.2024.100267

Karataş, F., & Aksu Ataç, B. (2025). When TPACK meets artificial intelligence: Analyzing TPACK and AI-TPACK components through structural equation modelling. *Education and Information Technologies*, *30*(7), 8979–9004. DOI: 10.1007/s10639-024-13164-2

Karroum, S. Y. A., Hammoud, J., Zahili, R., & Rahal, R.Sarah Youssef Abou KarroumNour Eldin Mohamed ElshaiekhKhalfan Zahran Al-Hijji. (2024). Exploring the role of artificial intelligence in education: Assessing advantages and disadvantages for learning outcomes and pedagogical practices. *International Journal of Innovative Research in Engineering & Multidisciplinary Physical Sciences*, *12*(4), 1–14. DOI: 10.37082/IJIRMPS.v12.i4.231000

Khoso, A. K., Wang, H., & Darazi, M. A. (2025). Empowering creativity and engagement: The impact of generative artificial intelligence usage on Chinese EFL students' language learning experience. *Computers in Human Behavior Reports*, *18*, 100627. Advance online publication. DOI: 10.1016/j.chbr.2025.100627

Lee, S., Jeon, J., & Choe, H. (2025). Enhancing pre-service teachers' Global Englishes awareness with technology: A focus on AI chatbots in 3D metaverse environments. *TESOL Quarterly*, *59*(1), 49–70. DOI: 10.1002/tesq.3300

Mahapatra, S. (2024). Impact of ChatGPT on ESL students' academic writing skills: A mixed methods intervention study. *Smart Learning Environments*, *11*(1), 9. Advance online publication. DOI: 10.1186/s40561-024-00295-9

Marzuki, M., Widiati, U., Rusdin, D., Darwin, D., & Indrawati, I. (2023). The impact of AI writing tools on the content and organization of students' writing: EFL teachers' perspective. *Cogent Education*, *10*(2), 2236469. Advance online publication. DOI: 10.1080/2331186X.2023.2236469

Mohamed, N. A. A., Al Dhaheri, A. S. A., Al Menhali, S. K. A., & Al Dhaheri, H. S. (2025). The impact of integration of AI in statistics learning on student motivation and learning engagement in the higher education sector. *International Journal of Research in Education and Science*, *15*(1), 431–447.

Moybeka, A. M. S., Syariatin, N., Tineh, S., Bafadal, A., & Sumarsono, D. (2023). Artificial intelligence and English classroom: The implications of AI toward EFL students' motivation. Edumaspul. *Jurnal Pendidikan*, *7*(3), 1630–1638.

Nabhani, F. A., Hamzah, M. B., & Hassna, H. A. (2024). Learning motivation via artificial intelligence: A bibliometric and systematic literature analysis. *International Journal of Academic Research in Business & Social Sciences*, *14*(7), 952–970. DOI: 10.6007/IJARBSS/v14-i7/22107

Rahimi, M., Fathi, J., & Zou, D. (2025). Exploring the impact of automated written corrective feedback on the academic writing skills of EFL learners: An activity theory perspective. *Education and Information Technologies*, *30*(3), 2691–2735. DOI: 10.1007/s10639-024-12896-5

Ranalli, J. (2018). Automated written corrective feedback: How well can students make use of it? *Computer Assisted Language Learning*, *31*(7), 653–674. DOI: 10.1080/09588221.2018.1428994

Rose, H., McKinley, J., & Galloway, N. (2021). Global Englishes and language teaching: A review of pedagogical research. *Language Teaching*, *54*(2), 157–189. DOI: 10.1017/S0261444820000518

Sarı, E., & Han, T. (2024). The impact of automated writing evaluation on English as a foreign language learners' writing self-efficacy, self-regulation, anxiety, and performance. *Journal of Computer Assisted Learning*, *40*(5), 2065–2080. DOI: 10.1111/jcal.13004

Singh, M., Singh, N., Singh, S. K., Udaiyan, R., Rizvi, S. W. H., Kumar, R., & Rai, D. K. (2025). AI and education: Bridging the gap to personalized, efficient, and accessible learning. In M. Ouaissa, M. Ouaissa, H. Lamaazi, M. El Hamlaoui, & K. K. Reddy C. (Eds.), Internet of behavior-based computational intelligence for smart education systems (pp. 131–160). IGI Global. DOI: 10.4018/979-8-3693-8151-9.ch005

Švábenský, V., Veselý, P., Picek, J., Nečas, P., & Vykopal, J. (2024). Fairness of machine learning models in educational data mining: A study of demographic bias in dropout prediction. Computers & Education. *Artificial Intelligence*, *5*, 100245. DOI: 10.1016/j.caeai.2023.100245

Tan, X., Cheng, G., & Ling, M. H. (2025). Artificial intelligence in teaching and teacher professional development: A systematic review. *Computers and Education: Artificial Intelligence*, *8*, 100355. Advance online publication. DOI: 10.1016/j.caeai.2024.100355

Taşkara, Ö. (2025). Perceptions and the readiness level of EFL teachers towards artificial intelligence (AI) [Master's thesis, Karadeniz Technical University]. Karadeniz Technical University Institute of Social Sciences.

Toscu, S. (2025). A systematic review of artificial intelligence technologies in English as a foreign language education. Sakarya University Journal of Education, 15(1), 152–175. https://dergipark.org.tr/en/pub/suje/issue/94132/1623401

Wangdi, P. (2024). Integrating artificial intelligence in education. *International Journal on Research in STEM Education*, *6*(2), 50–60. DOI: 10.33830/ijrse.v6i2.1722

Xiao, Y. (2025). The impact of AI-driven speech recognition on EFL listening comprehension, flow experience, and anxiety: A randomized controlled trial. *Humanities & Social Sciences Communications*, *12*(1), 425. DOI: 10.1057/s41599-025-04672-8

# Chapter 2
# Unmasking Bias: A Framework for Evaluating AI-Supported Intercultural Communication Tools

**Aysun Dogutas**
http://orcid.org/0000-0002-2928-5156
*Pamukkale University, Turkey*

## ABSTRACT

*This conceptual chapter offers a critical examination of how artificial intelligence (AI)-supported tools employed in intercultural communication (ICC)—including language-learning platforms such as Duolingo, conversational agents like ChatGPT, and translation services such as Google Translate—may inadvertently reproduce and intensify bias. Integrating perspectives from AI ethics, applied linguistics, and intercultural communication studies, the chapter identifies four major bias categories: linguistic, cultural, representational, and accessibility. Drawing on recent analyses, it highlights concerns such as the marginalization of low-resource languages (Wired, 2023), user-reported ethical dilemmas in AI-mediated learning environments (Polygon, 2025), and the perpetuation of gendered translations (Ghosh & Caliskan, 2023). To address these issues, the chapter proposes a Bias-Audit Checklist as a practical evaluative framework and concludes with recommendations for fostering culturally inclusive and ethically responsible AI integration in educational contexts.*

## INTRODUCTION

The quick adoption of artificial intelligence (AI) in almost every aspect of human existence, such as communication, education, and cross-cultural interactions,

DOI: 10.4018/979-8-3373-6325-7.ch002

is one of the hallmarks of the twenty-first century. AI is increasingly mediating cross-cultural and cross-linguistic interactions through conversational bots, adaptive learning platforms, and translation apps. AI-supported solutions have the potential to improve global connection, inclusion, and customization in educational settings, especially those focused on fostering intercultural communication competence (ICC). But new technologies also bring up important issues of representation, equity, and bias. AI systems frequently repeat and even magnify language hierarchies, gender imbalances, and cultural stereotypes since they are based on enormous datasets that mirror prevailing society structures (Blodgett et al., 2020; Crawford, 2021). The goal of intercultural education, which is to promote mutual tolerance, understanding, and cultural awareness, is challenged by such problems.

Globalized education has continuously underlined the value of intercultural communication skills. Scholars like Chen and Starosta (1996), Deardorff (2006), and Byram (1997) emphasize that intercultural competence includes attitudes, knowledge, and critical cultural awareness in addition to linguistic skills. As AI is incorporated into educational institutions to support intercultural learning, it is important to consider if these resources actually advance ICC or if they unintentionally reinforce prevailing cultural norms. According to recent studies, artificial intelligence (AI) has the potential to improve communication and information access, but it can also skew cultural meanings by omitting or simplifying things algorithmically (Floridi, 2023; UNESCO, 2021). In addition to UNESCO's global recommendations, scholars and institutions increasingly draw on complementary ethical frameworks—such as the OECD AI Principles, the European Commission's Ethics Guidelines for Trustworthy AI, and university-level AI governance policies—which emphasize transparency, human oversight, cultural plurality, and contextual accountability in educational AI use. Conversational agents like ChatGPT might not be sensitive to cultural nuances in conflict mediation situations (Weidinger et al., 2022), and machine translation systems have been demonstrated to perpetuate gender stereotypes by defaulting to masculine forms in gender-neutral languages (Stanovsky et al., 2019). These results imply that AI-supported intercultural communication (AI-ICC) technologies could be both beneficial and detrimental, promoting exclusionary behaviors on the one hand and facilitating cross-cultural interaction on the other.

Recent advancements in popular educational platforms exemplify these risks and potential. As an example, Duolingo has launched Duolingo Max, which uses OpenAI's GPT-4 to give students AI-powered role-play and explanations (Duolingo, 2023). Concerns are raised about whether the AI-generated situations accurately represent complex cultural realities or overgeneralize cultural practices, even while these characteristics mimic real-world intercultural conversations and give students practice navigating a variety of communicative circumstances. Similar to this, GrammarlyGO, which debuted in 2023, provides AI-powered writing assistance and promises to modify tone and style for various audiences (Grammarly, 2023). Its dependence on generalized models, however, runs the risk of flattening culturally unique rhetorical approaches and possibly elevating Western academic discourse norms over other writing and communication traditions. Although the accuracy of translation platforms such as DeepL Translate has made them popular, even these sophisticated computers have trouble understanding idiomatic terms and culturally ingrained meanings, which are essential for creating real ICC (Castro & Lind, 2022).

The quick uptake of large language models like ChatGPT has arguably been the most revolutionary use of AI in education. Teachers all over the world are experimenting with its usage in the classroom for critical conversations about cultural stereotypes, intercultural role-play, and writing support. ChatGPT has been demonstrated to replicate biases from its training data, such as reinforcing stereotyped conceptions of cultural groups, despite its ability to simulate cross-cultural interactions (Kasneci et al., 2023). These instances demonstrate the dual nature of AI in ICC education: whereas these tools provide never-before-seen access to genuine engagement and feedback, if educators do not critically mediate them, they run the risk of perpetuating limited or biased cultural representations.

Bias in AI is not a recent issue. Algorithms are not neutral; rather, they reflect the presumptions and attitudes ingrained in their design and training data, as demonstrated by decades of computer science research and critical data studies (Noble, 2018; Benjamin, 2019). These biases have a direct impact on learners' views of culture, identity, and belonging, which is especially worrisome in the context of intercultural communication. A tool runs the danger of reductively or distortedly influencing learners' intercultural understanding if it routinely misrepresents cultural expressions or leaves out minority viewpoints. In this way, prejudice in AI-ICC tools is a problem for education and ethics rather than just a technological one. A multifaceted strategy integrating instructional innovation, AI ethics, and multicultural theory is needed to address this problem.

The lack of rigorous frameworks for curriculum designers, educators, and policymakers to assess bias in AI-ICC technologies persists despite increased awareness of these issues. The pedagogical possibilities of digital intercultural exchange or the technical features of algorithmic fairness are the main topics of much of the present discourse. Still, these topics hardly ever come together to offer practical solutions for educational stakeholders. By putting out a paradigm for detecting, evaluating, and reducing bias in AI-supported intercultural communication tools, this chapter aims to close this gap. The methodology, known as the Bias-Audit Checklist, combines ideas from critical pedagogy, AI ethics, and intercultural communication theory to offer useful recommendations for assessing AI-ICC technologies in educational settings.

This chapter makes three contributions. It begins by reviewing the growing body of research on AI bias in cross-cultural communication, including findings from computer science, linguistics, ethics, and education. In order to assist educators and practitioners in critically interacting with AI-ICC tools both inside and outside of the classroom, it also presents a systematic methodology for bias auditing. Third, it talks about how AI bias affects intercultural learning outcomes and emphasizes the moral obligations of developers, educators, and legislators to make sure that technological advancements support equity and cultural inclusivity. By doing so, this chapter offers specific strategies for properly utilizing AI's promise while also adding to the continuing discussions regarding its place in education.

Given the growing use of AI in international cooperation and higher education, the conversation is especially relevant today. Many universities now utilize AI-based tools for cross-cultural learning, translation, and tutoring, particularly within language education, international programs, and digitally mediated intercultural exchange. Empirical studies and institutional surveys indicate that AI-supported platforms—such as machine translation, automated writing feedback, and conversational agents—are increasingly embedded in higher education curricula, especially following the COVID-19 pandemic, which accelerated the normalization of digital and AI-assisted intercultural communication practices (Godwin-Jones, 2023; Kasneci et al., 2023; Zawacki-Richter et al., 2019). The necessity for moral and culturally aware methods increases as these behaviors become more commonplace. Neglecting bias has serious consequences, including the ability to undermine the transformational power of intercultural education, alienate minority students, and perpetuate inequality. On the other hand, identifying and correcting bias can enable teachers to utilize AI as a tool to promote intercultural sensitivity, inclusivity, and critical reflection.

All things considered, the introduction prepares the reader for a thorough examination of bias in AI-assisted cross-cultural communication tools. This chapter seeks to give educators, researchers, and practitioners the information and resources they need to evaluate AI critically and use it responsibly in cross-cultural learning settings by exposing how bias functions inside these technologies. The theoretical underpinnings of intercultural competence and AI ethics will be further discussed in the following sections. Evidence of bias in commonly used AI-ICC tools will be reviewed, the Bias-Audit Checklist will be presented as an evaluative framework, and the consequences for stakeholders in education and beyond will be discussed.

## THEORETICAL BACKGROUND

### Intercultural Communication Competence (ICC)

For many years, language instruction and internationalized curricula have placed a strong emphasis on the multifaceted concept of intercultural communication competence (ICC). Fundamentally, ICC refers to the capacity to communicate appropriately and productively with people from diverse cultural origins. In addition to language skills, this competency calls for empathy, social awareness, and the capacity to negotiate meaning across a variety of worldviews (Chen & Starosta, 1996; Byram, 1997; Deardorff, 2006).

This chronological ordering reflects the historical development of ICC theory, beginning with affective–behavioral models and later expanding into comprehensive intercultural frameworks.

Byram's (1997) model of ICC remains one of the most influential frameworks. He proposed five "savoirs" (knowledge, skills, and attitudes) that collectively enable intercultural communicative competence:

- **Savoir être (attitudes):** openness, curiosity, and readiness to suspend disbelief about other cultures.
- **Savoirs (knowledge):** knowledge of social groups, products, and practices in one's own and other cultures.
- **Savoir comprendre (skills of interpreting and relating):** ability to interpret a document or event from another culture and relate it to one's own.
- **Savoir apprendre/faire (skills of discovery and interaction):** ability to acquire new cultural knowledge and operate under constraints of real-time communication.
- **Savoir s'engager (critical cultural awareness):** the capacity to evaluate critically, based on explicit criteria, perspectives, practices, and products in one's own and others' cultures.

This holistic view underscores that intercultural learning cannot be reduced to vocabulary lists or grammar rules; rather, it is a deeply ethical and reflective process. By focusing on attitudes (respect, openness, and curiosity), knowledge and abilities (listening, watching, and analyzing), and intended goals (internal shifts in frame of reference and exterior behaviors in intercultural contacts), Deardorff (2006) later improved ICC assessment through her pyramid approach. Because it emphasizes both performance and personal transformation as indicators of intercultural competency, this paradigm has been widely embraced by academic institutions and international organizations.

Chen and Starosta (1996) further contributed by emphasizing the affective (empathy, respect, motivation), cognitive (self-awareness, cultural knowledge), and behavioral (interaction skills) dimensions of ICC. Their early emphasis on affect and relationality provides an important counterpoint to later technology-mediated ICC models, particularly in contexts where AI systems struggle to emulate empathy.

## Additional Models of ICC

### Spitzberg and Chagnéon's Model (2009):

Spitzberg and Chagnéon used the metaphor of "communication competence as impression management" to operationalize their conceptualization of ICC, which combines knowledge, skills, and motivation. According to Spitzberg and Chagnéon (2009), their approach emphasizes that competence is co-constructed during interaction and that what is deemed competent varies depending on the communicator and the cultural context. Because AI-mediated intercultural communication technologies, such as chatbots or translation engines, are unable to negotiate perceptions in the same dynamic way that people do, this relational perspective is especially pertinent. They rely on pre-trained answers instead, which can restrict the flexible adaptability that authentic cross-cultural interactions require.

### Ting-Toomey's Face-Negotiation Theory (2005):

According to Ting-Toomey, negotiating one's identity and self-image in social situations, or "facework," is a common component of intercultural communication. The employment of direct or indirect face-preserving techniques is influenced by cultural differences in individualism and collectivism. This poses important queries in AI contexts: Can AI systems understand face-threatening behaviors in different cultural contexts, such as arguments and refusals? An AI tutor may inadvertently undermine rapport and trust if they give a pupil with a collectivist background too direct corrections. Therefore, while creating culturally sensitive AI communication tools, it is essential to incorporate insights from face-negotiation theory.

### Digital Intercultural Competence (Helm & Dooly, 2017):

Scholars have suggested expanding ICC to incorporate digital literacies in light of the rise in telecollaboration and online interactions. In addition to managing cultural differences, students also need to understand the advantages and disadvantages of digital platforms, according to Helm and Dooly (2017). Understanding how algorithms mediate communication, identifying online power dynamics, and critically evaluating the veracity of AI-generated interactions are all components of digital intercultural competency in AI-enhanced contexts.

### Critical Interculturality (Holliday, 2018):

The assumption that culture is homogeneous and confined is criticized by recent intercultural studies research. Holliday (2018) promotes a viewpoint known as "critical interculturality," which acknowledges the part that ideology, power, and inequality play in cross-cultural interactions. According to this perspective, AI-supported ICC tools need to be critically examined for their potential to reproduce prevailing cultural discourses and exclude alternative worldviews in addition to their instructional utility. Linguistic hierarchies that favor certain learners over others are reinforced, for instance, by translation algorithms that make English the default pivot language.

Rethinking ICC frameworks is necessary for the incorporation of AI into intercultural communication education in order to handle the opportunities and difficulties presented by technological mediation. According to recent studies, artificial intelligence (AI) has the potential to improve cross-cultural communication, but it can also lead to miscommunications because of cultural differences (Sarwari et al., 2024). For example, learners may adopt simplified or prejudiced interpretations of different cultures as a result of AI-generated simulations that fail to accurately reflect culturally relevant communication standards such as courtesy or indirectness. Researchers stress that in order to guarantee genuine cross-cultural learning, critical engagement with AI outputs is required (Jenks, 2025).

## Artificial Intelligence and Bias

Although human-centered communication is emphasized by ICC frameworks, AI tools provide fresh queries regarding the technological mediation of cultural meaning. According to a growing corpus of research in AI ethics, algorithms are not neutral; rather, they reflect the datasets and design decisions that inform them (Noble, 2018; Crawford, 2021).

Recent empirical studies further demonstrate how AI systems reproduce social hierarchies through language. For example, Ghosh and Caliskan (2023) show that large language models and translation systems systematically reinforce gender stereotypes by associating professional roles (e.g., "doctor," "engineer") with masculine pronouns while mapping care-related occupations to feminine ones. In intercultural communication contexts, such biases risk normalizing unequal cultural representations and reinforcing occupational stereotypes across linguistic boundaries.

The UNESCO Recommendation on the Ethics of Artificial Intelligence (2021) provides a global framework for addressing these challenges. It outlines principles such as:

- Fairness and non-discrimination
- Transparency and explainability
- Human oversight and accountability
- Inclusivity and cultural diversity

These values, particularly the focus on openness, respect, and critical cultural awareness, are highly compatible with ICC theory. AI ethics necessitates caution against incorporating negative presumptions into algorithms, much as intercultural competency necessitates putting aside preconceived notions about other cultures.

While UNESCO (2021) remains a key global reference, recent policy-oriented frameworks such as the OECD Principles on Artificial Intelligence (2022) and the European Union's Artificial Intelligence Act (2024) similarly emphasize transparency, accountability, and risk mitigation in high-impact sectors such as education. Together, these frameworks underscore that ethical AI governance must be understood as plural and multi-level rather than anchored in a single normative document.

Critical AI researchers also draw attention to the various ways bias appears. Three types of bias are distinguished in natural language processing (NLP) by Blodgett et al. (2020): interactional, allocational, and representational bias. Intercultural communication is affected by all three areas.

Intercultural communication is directly impacted by AI bias, which can take many different forms, including representational, allocational, and interactional (Blodgett et al., 2020). When AI systems misunderstand cultural quirks in human input, interactional bias results. The unequal distribution of AI-mediated learning chances among cultural groups is known as allocational bias. The way that cultural identities are portrayed in AI outputs, which frequently favor dominant cultural viewpoints, is known as representational bias. Furthermore, empirical research indicates that there are difficulties in attaining cultural alignment, as AI tools like chatbots may promote intercultural empathy for some cultural groups but not for others (Villanueva et al., 2025). To lessen these biases, ethical values including justice, openness, and inclusivity must be upheld (UNESCO, 2021).

## Integrating ICC and AI Ethics

The intersection of technological mediation and human connection in today's classrooms is highlighted by the merging of AI ethics and intercultural communication competency (ICC). AI ethics place more emphasis on justice, accountability, and transparency than ICC does on openness, respect, and critical cultural awareness (Byram, 1997; Deardorff, 2006) (UNESCO, 2021). Together, these frameworks serve as a reminder that AI is an active mediator of meaning, identity, and cultural representation rather than a neutral instrument. Intercultural interactions in AI-supported situations frequently transform from being a direct human-to-human interaction to a human–AI–human triangle, in which algorithms influence not only language but also how appropriateness and civility are perceived.

However, conflicts occur when AI systems reinforce prejudice or are unable to recognize cultural nuances. For instance, grammar checkers may mark non-standard forms of English as erroneous, while translation engines sometimes flatten politeness methods in languages like Korean or Japanese, thus perpetuating "native-speakerist" hierarchies (Kubota, 2019). The significance of algorithmic sensitivity—the ability of both designers and users to identify and critically consider the cultural presumptions ingrained in AI systems—is underscored by such risks. For educators, this entails training students to question AI technologies as cultural agents in addition to using them; for developers, it includes including equity and inclusivity into design.

The need to create AI systems that respect and improve intercultural understanding is highlighted by the convergence of ICC and AI ethics. A human–AI–human triangle is frequently formed via AI-mediated communication, in which algorithms affect not only language usage but also opinions about propriety and appropriateness. According to research, AI systems may fail in culturally varied contexts if they are not carefully designed, but they may also foster intercultural empathy in specific situations (Dai & Hua, 2024; Villanueva et al., 2025). Therefore, algorithmic sensitivity—the capacity of users and designers to identify and assess underlying cultural presumptions—is essential. For developers, this means incorporating equality and inclusivity into system design; for educators, it means helping students to challenge AI results as cultural agents.

In the end, connecting ICC with AI ethics provides a mechanism to develop more culturally sensitive technology and users who are more conscious of their surroundings. Teachers and legislators may guarantee that AI tools promote—rather than impede—intercultural communication by coordinating ICC attitudes, knowledge, and abilities with moral precepts like accountability, transparency, and inclusivity. In a telecollaborative project, for example, an AI tool may translate a Japanese student's formal greeting into excessively informal English, confusing peers. Examples like these highlight the importance of both intercultural competency and ethical AI design for effective digital communication.

This convergence highlights that AI-mediated intercultural interaction is not a neutral enhancement of communication but a reconfiguration of how cultural appropriateness, politeness, and legitimacy are evaluated. As a result, ICC education increasingly requires algorithmic sensitivity—the ability to recognize, interrogate, and contextualize the cultural assumptions embedded in AI outputs.

## Bias-Audit Checklist: A Practical Framework for Evaluating AI-Supported Intercultural Communication Tools

To address the lack of practical evaluative instruments identified in current scholarship, this chapter proposes a Bias-Audit Checklist designed specifically for AI-supported intercultural communication (AI-ICC) tools. While existing research has extensively theorized algorithmic bias and intercultural competence, educators and curriculum designers often lack concrete mechanisms for systematically evaluating AI tools used in intercultural learning contexts. The Bias-Audit Checklist responds to this gap by translating insights from ICC theory (Byram, 1997; Deardorff, 2006) and AI ethics (UNESCO, 2021) into an actionable framework.

The checklist is intended to support educators, instructional designers, and institutional decision-makers in critically examining whether AI tools promote intercultural sensitivity or inadvertently reproduce cultural hierarchies and exclusions. Rather than positioning AI as a neutral facilitator, the framework conceptualizes AI systems as active cultural mediators whose outputs shape learners' understandings of language, identity, and social norms.

## The Bias-Audit Checklist (Core Content)

The proposed checklist is organized around four interrelated categories of bias that are especially relevant to intercultural communication education: linguistic bias, cultural bias, representational bias, and accessibility bias.

### Linguistic Bias

Linguistic bias refers to the privileging of certain languages, varieties, or communicative norms over others, often reflecting dominant or "standard" language ideologies.

Key audit questions

- Does the tool favor "standard" or native-speaker norms (e.g., Standard American or British English)?
- Are non-standard varieties, World Englishes, or multilingual practices marked as errors?
- Does the system flatten pragmatic features such as politeness strategies, honorifics, or indirectness?

Example

- In machine translation tools, honorifics in Japanese or Korean (e.g., –san, –nim) are frequently omitted in English output, resulting in unintended loss of formality and respect.
- Grammar-checking tools such as Grammarly may flag culturally acceptable indirect phrasing as "unclear" or "weak," implicitly privileging Western rhetorical norms.

## Cultural Bias

Cultural bias occurs when AI systems simplify, essentialize, or stereotype cultural practices and communication styles.

### Key audit questions

- Does the tool present cultures as fixed, homogeneous, or nationally bounded?
- Are cultural behaviors explained contextually, or reduced to generalized norms?
- Does the system account for power relations, ideology, and situational variation?

Example

- AI role-play scenarios may depict collectivist cultures as uniformly indirect or conflict-avoidant, overlooking intra-cultural diversity and situational pragmatics.
- Chatbots used for intercultural negotiation practice may provide overly direct feedback that conflicts with face-saving norms in high-context cultures.

## Representational Bias

Representational bias concerns how social groups, identities, and roles are portrayed—or omitted—in AI outputs.

### Key audit questions

- Are certain genders, ethnicities, or cultural groups consistently associated with specific roles?
- Are minority or marginalized groups visible and portrayed non-stereotypically?
- Do outputs reinforce existing social hierarchies?

### Example

- Studies show that AI systems associate professional roles with masculine pronouns while linking care-related occupations to feminine ones, reinforcing gendered labor divisions.
- Conversational agents may reproduce cultural stereotypes embedded in training data, presenting certain regions as technologically advanced and others as underdeveloped.

### Accessibility and Equity Bias

Accessibility bias refers to unequal access to AI tools or uneven benefits across user groups.

### Key audit questions

- Is the tool equally functional across languages with smaller digital footprints?
- Does access depend on subscription fees or institutional resources?
- Are learners with limited digital literacy or connectivity disadvantaged?

### Example

- Advanced AI features (e.g., premium translation or feedback tools) may only be available to well-resourced institutions, widening educational inequalities.
- Low-resource languages often receive less accurate AI support, reinforcing global linguistic hierarchies.

## Applying the Checklist in Educational Practice

The Bias-Audit Checklist is designed to be diagnostic rather than punitive. Educators can apply it when selecting AI tools, designing learning activities, or facilitating reflective discussions. For instance:

- A language instructor might audit ChatGPT role-play outputs for gendered or culturally flattened responses.
- A curriculum designer might evaluate whether a translation tool preserves pragmatic meaning in multilingual projects.
- Institutions can use the checklist to guide ethical AI adoption policies aligned with inclusivity and ICC outcomes.

By embedding bias auditing into pedagogical decision-making, educators can transform AI tools from passive technologies into sites of critical intercultural learning.

*Table 1. Bias-audit checklist*

| Bias Category | Focus Area | Key Audit Questions | Illustrative Example in AI-ICC Tools |
|---|---|---|---|
| **Linguistic Bias** | Language norms, varieties, pragmatics | Does the tool privilege "standard" or native-speaker norms? Are non-standard or multilingual forms marked as incorrect? Are politeness strategies and honorifics preserved? | Grammar checkers flag indirect or culturally polite phrasing as "weak"; MT tools omit Japanese/Korean honorifics, flattening formality. |
| **Cultural Bias** | Cultural representation and meaning-making | Are cultures presented as homogeneous or essentialized? Are behaviors contextualized, or reduced to national stereotypes? | AI role-play scenarios depict collectivist cultures as uniformly indirect, ignoring situational and intra-cultural variation. |
| **Representational Bias** | Social identities and roles | Are genders, professions, or cultural groups stereotypically associated? Are minority perspectives visible? | AI systems associate "doctor" with masculine pronouns and care work with feminine ones, reinforcing occupational stereotypes. |
| **Accessibility & Equity Bias** | Access, inclusion, and usability | Is the tool equally accurate across languages? Does access depend on institutional resources or paid versions? | Advanced AI features are available only via premium subscriptions; low-resource languages receive lower-quality outputs. |

## ALIGNMENT OF THE BIAS-AUDIT CHECKLIST WITH INTERCULTURAL COMMUNICATION COMPETENCE (ICC)

The Bias-Audit Checklist is explicitly grounded in Byram's (1997) model of intercultural communication competence, ensuring that ethical evaluation of AI tools supports—not replaces—core intercultural learning goals.

- **Savoir être (Attitudes)** The checklist promotes openness and curiosity by encouraging learners and educators to *question AI outputs rather than accept them uncritically*. Auditing cultural and representational bias supports the suspension of ethnocentric assumptions.
- **Savoirs (Knowledge)** Evaluating linguistic and cultural bias helps learners develop knowledge of how language, power, and ideology operate across cultures and within AI systems.

- **Savoir comprendre (Skills of interpreting and relating)** Analyzing mistranslations, stereotyped outputs, or flattened pragmatics strengthens learners' ability to interpret cultural meaning and relate it to their own communicative norms.
- **Savoir apprendre / faire (Skills of discovery and interaction)** Applying the checklist during AI-mediated interaction fosters active discovery, enabling learners to adapt communication strategies across contexts rather than relying on algorithmic authority.
- **Savoir s'engager (Critical cultural awareness)** The checklist most directly supports critical cultural awareness by foregrounding power relations, inequality, and ethical responsibility in AI-mediated intercultural encounters.

Through this alignment, the Bias-Audit Checklist operationalizes ICC in technologically mediated environments, ensuring that AI use contributes to reflective and ethical intercultural learning rather than superficial exposure.

While the Bias-Audit Checklist offers a structured framework for evaluating AI-supported intercultural communication tools, its relevance is grounded in a growing body of empirical and theoretical research examining how AI is currently used in educational and intercultural contexts. The following Literature Review situates the proposed framework within existing scholarship on AI-supported language learning, machine translation, conversational agents, and telecollaboration. By synthesizing findings on both the pedagogical affordances and ethical risks of these technologies, the review demonstrates how recurring patterns of bias, cultural flattening, and unequal access underscore the necessity of a systematic evaluative approach such as the Bias-Audit Checklist.

## Illustrative Classroom Vignettes

### Vignette 1: Applying the Bias-Audit Checklist in AI-Mediated Telecollaboration

In an undergraduate intercultural communication course, students participating in an online telecollaboration project with peers in Japan used Google Translate to support asynchronous discussions. During one exchange, a Japanese student wrote a response containing the honorific form *kangaete okimasu*, signaling polite hesitation rather than refusal. The machine-translated English output rendered the message as "I will think about it," which several students interpreted as agreement. Guided by the instructor, the class applied the Bias-Audit Checklist, identifying linguistic bias (loss of honorifics), cultural bias (misinterpretation of indirect refusal), and representational bias (defaulting to Anglo-direct norms). Through discussion, students reflected on how AI outputs may flatten pragmatic meaning and how human mediation is necessary to interpret culturally embedded communication. The vignette illustrates how the checklist can support critical reflection rather than uncritical reliance on AI tools in ICC learning.

### Vignette 2: ChatGPT in Intercultural Role-Play Activities

In an undergraduate intercultural communication course, students are asked to use ChatGPT to practice workplace role-plays involving cross-cultural negotiation. One task requires students to simulate a feedback conversation between a manager from a low-context, individualist culture (e.g., the United States) and an employee from a high-context, collectivist culture (e.g., Japan). When prompted, ChatGPT generates a dialogue that frames effective communication primarily through directness, explicit evaluation, and assertive self-expression. Although linguistically fluent, the response minimizes indirectness, face-saving strategies, and relational cues that are central to communication in many East Asian contexts.

Several students initially interpret the AI-generated dialogue as a culturally "neutral" or authoritative model. Only after guided classroom discussion do they begin to recognize that the chatbot's output reflects implicit cultural assumptions embedded in its training data—particularly the privileging of Western managerial discourse norms. Through this reflection, students identify how AI-mediated role-plays may unintentionally normalize culturally specific interaction styles while marginalizing others. The activity ultimately becomes a productive site for critical intercultural learning, demonstrating that ChatGPT can support ICC development only when its outputs are actively interrogated rather than passively accepted.

## LITERATURE REVIEW

In educational settings, artificial intelligence (AI) has quickly emerged as a crucial intercultural communication (ICC) mediator. Recent studies draw attention to the dangers of bias, stereotyping, and cultural flattening inherent in AI-supported applications as well as their potential to foster intercultural understanding. To avoid redundancy, this section synthesizes prior findings by focusing on mechanisms of mediation and bias rather than repeating descriptive accounts of individual platforms.

### AI-Supported Language Learning Tools and ICC

AI is being used in language learning apps more and more to offer cultural information, real-world conversation scenarios, and individualized feedback. For instance, it has been demonstrated that Duolingo's AI-powered features and adaptive systems enhance learners' motivation and exposure to cultural diversity (Loewen, 2023). Similarly, by highlighting audience expectations and discourse conventions, programs like Grammarly and ChatGPT offer instant feedback on language accuracy and style, which may improve learners' international communicative competence (Zou et al., 2023). Rather than reiterating platform descriptions, recent studies increasingly focus on how these tools shape intercultural norms through feedback standardization and implicit value judgments (Kubota, 2019; Fuchs, 2022).

These advantages do have certain restrictions, though. According to research, AI-driven correction systems frequently favor "standard" forms of English, which perpetuates the divide between native and non-native speakers (Kubota, 2019). This calls into question ICC's core tenet of acknowledging linguistic variety. Furthermore, pragmatic subtleties that are crucial for effective cross-cultural communication, like cultural indirectness or politeness techniques, are rarely captured by AI feedback (Fuchs, 2022).

By exposing students to real-world linguistic and cultural situations, AI-powered language learning apps like Duolingo, ChatGPT, and Grammarly offer dynamic cultural scaffolding in addition to language education (Loewen, 2023; Zou et al., 2023). According to recent research, adaptable AI features can adjust cultural information to students' skill levels, increasing interest and fostering intercultural understanding (Sarwari et al., 2024). AI-based prompts, for instance, might mimic culturally sensitive requests or negotiating situations, giving students practice with politeness and pragmatic variety techniques that are frequently lacking in the traditional curriculum.

However, there are still restrictions. According to Kubota (2019), AI-driven systems have a tendency to standardize linguistic output in accordance with mainstream standards, potentially marginalizing minority or non-standard dialects. Furthermore, cultural nuances that are essential for true intercultural competency, such as humor, indirect speech actions, and context-dependent politeness techniques, are frequently difficult for AI to understand (Fuchs, 2022). According to recent studies, to close these gaps and promote reflective learning, educators must use both human mediation and AI tools (Jenks, 2025; Villanueva et al., 2025).

## Translation Tools and Digital Interculturality

In order to overcome linguistic barriers in cross-cultural communication, machine translation (MT) tools like Google Translate and DeepL are frequently utilized. According to studies, these technologies can help with cross-language comprehension and cooperation, especially in educational exchanges (Garcia & Vela, 2022). However, studies also show that cultural distortion and nuance loss are ongoing problems. Khoshsaligheh and Ameri (2022), for example, discovered that MT systems frequently remove honorifics and politeness cues from Asian languages, which might skew intended meanings and harm cross-cultural relationships. For instance, a Japanese sentence such as “ ” (Tanaka-sensei wa honjitsu irasshaimasu ka), which contains both an honorific title ( ) and a respectful verb form ( ), is often rendered in English simply as “Is Tanaka here today?” This translation omits hierarchical respect and politeness, flattening the interpersonal meaning that is central to communication in Japanese professional contexts.

However, academics note that translation systems run the risk of sustaining linguistic disparities. In AI translation, English frequently serves as a “pivot language,” giving precedence to its idioms and conventions over those of minority languages (Blodgett et al., 2020). This issue calls into question whether AI serves to promote egalitarian interculturality or to reinforce global linguistic hierarchy.

Learners can participate in cross-cultural interactions more effectively because of machine translation (MT) programs like Google Translate and DeepL, which make cross-language communication easier (Garcia & Vela, 2022). Recent research demonstrates their value in cooperative learning settings when quick multilingual comprehension is required (Sarwari et al., 2024).

But MT systems also show enduring bias and cultural flattening. For example, especially in East Asian and Indigenous languages, honorifics, politeness techniques, and culturally distinctive idioms are frequently mistranslated (Khoshsaligheh & Ameri, 2022). Similarly, Korean honorific distinctions such as the contrast between “ ” (to eat, neutral) and “ ” (to eat, honorific) are commonly translated into the same English verb form, erasing culturally significant markers of age, status, and social distance. English is commonly used as a pivot language in MT algorithms, which reinforces global linguistic hierarchies and gives preference to Western-centric viewpoints (Blodgett et al., 2020; Villanueva et al., 2025). These limitations suggest that while MT can bridge linguistic gaps, educators must encourage critical engagement, guiding learners to question AI outputs and reflect on the sociocultural assumptions embedded in translations (Dai & Hua, 2024).

In addition to linguistic loss, recent bias-oriented research demonstrates that translation systems may reinforce gendered and occupational stereotypes across languages, particularly when translating between gender-neutral and gender-marked linguistic systems (Ghosh & Caliskan, 2023).

## Conversational Agents, Chatbots, and ICC

Conversational AI-powered tools like ChatGPT, Google Assistant, and Siri are being investigated more and more as cross-cultural communication partners. Role plays, cultural contexts, and conversations with speakers from various backgrounds can all be simulated by chatbots (Jiang et al., 2023). For instance, students can practice courteous requests or cross-cultural negotiation techniques using ChatGPT, which exposes them to different communication styles right away.

However, studies point to serious hazards. Biases, preconceptions, or discriminatory patterns are frequently inherited by conversational bots that have been educated on vast amounts of internet data (Crawford, 2021). Noble's (2018) groundbreaking study on algorithmic bias demonstrates how AI and search engines perpetuate structural injustices, which also affect cross-cultural communication situations. For example, AI chatbots might fail to accurately imitate politeness techniques in collectivist cultures or replicate gender prejudices in professional role-plays.

ChatGPT, Siri, and Google Assistant are examples of conversational AI systems that have become interactive partners in cross-cultural learning (Jiang et al., 2023). These tools provide instant feedback on intercultural pragmatics, civility, and communication style by simulating role-plays, culturally diverse talks, and negotiation scenarios. According to recent studies, AI chatbots can help students become more interculturally adaptive by exposing them to a variety of communication norms (Sarwari et al., 2024).

However, biases in training data are inherited by AI conversational bots. Research shows that chatbots might mimic culturally particular politeness techniques improperly, fail to identify indirect speech acts, or perpetuate stereotypes (Crawford, 2021; Noble, 2018). Role-play simulations, for instance, may contain gender biases or culturally insensitive outputs, which could serve to further perpetuate preconceived notions about other cultures. It is advised that educators actively monitor AI-mediated interactions and include reflective activities that assist students in critically assessing AI input in order to reduce these hazards (Jenks, 2025).

Empirical analyses suggest that these systems may reproduce not only cultural stereotypes but also gendered interactional norms, particularly in professional or institutional role-play scenarios (Ghosh & Caliskan, 2023; Crawford, 2021).

## Telecollaboration, Virtual Exchange, and AI Mediation

Additionally, telecollaborative projects—online collaborations between students from diverse cultural backgrounds—have used AI tools. According to Helm and Dooly (2017), virtual exchange fosters "digital intercultural competence," which calls on students to negotiate both technological and cultural barriers. While adding AI support—like automated translation or AI-powered discussion starters—can increase accessibility, it also raises moral questions. Recent studies warn that an over-reliance on AI mediation could lead to a misleading sense of transparency across languages and a decrease in learners' critical engagement with intercultural differences (Holliday, 2018; Zou et al., 2023).

AI techniques like automated translation, AI conversation prompts, and real-time interaction analysis have become more prevalent in telecollaborative projects, which are virtual interactions between students from different cultural backgrounds (Helm & Dooly, 2017). AI assistance can improve intercultural cooperation, lower language barriers, and promote communication. According to recent research, telecollaboration facilitated by AI fosters digital intercultural competency, which includes the capacity of learners to negotiate meaning in intricate online contexts (Sarwari et al., 2024).

Over-reliance on AI, however, may lead to pedagogical and ethical issues. Learners might not critically evaluate AI-generated outputs, which would lessen their ability to reflect on cultural differences (Holliday, 2018; Zou et al., 2023). Furthermore, AI-mediated interactions run the risk of oversimplifying cultural diversity, especially when algorithms don't take into consideration ideological viewpoints, power dynamics, or contextual politeness. Educators are therefore encouraged to combine AI tools with guided reflection, explicit cultural instruction, and collaborative discussions to enhance both linguistic and intercultural understanding (Dai & Hua, 2024).

## Ethical Concerns in AI-Supported ICC

Recent policy discussions emphasize that ethical responsibility in AI-supported ICC extends beyond technical bias mitigation to include institutional accountability and equitable access, as highlighted in OECD (2022) and EU-level AI governance initiatives.

The ethical ramifications of utilizing AI in cross-cultural communication are highlighted in an expanding corpus of work. AI is not neutral; rather, it reflects the values and prejudices of its designers, as emphasized by Crawford (2021) and UNESCO (2021). This implies that AI technologies may unintentionally reinforce preconceptions, silence particular cultural viewpoints, or widen the digital gap in educational settings. These risks are categorized by Blodgett et al. (2020) as interactional (distorted communicative practices), representational (mischaracterizing groups), and allocational (unequal access or resources).

These problems highlight the necessity of algorithmic sensitivity for ICC education—the understanding that using AI for intercultural communication necessitates both ethical technological design and human critical evaluation. AI might impede rather than improve intercultural competency in the absence of this dual focus.

Fairness, inclusion, and digital equity are among the ethical ramifications of AI in intercultural education that go beyond bias (Crawford, 2021; UNESCO, 2021). Assumptions made by designers are reflected in AI systems, which may silence marginalized voices and strengthen systemic injustices (Blodgett et al., 2020; Noble, 2018). Furthermore, authentic intercultural learning may be hampered by AI outputs that inaccurately depict linguistic hierarchy and cultural behaviors.

New study highlights the significance of algorithmic sensitivity: developers should incorporate inclusive design principles, and educators and learners should critically assess AI outputs for cultural assumptions (Jenks, 2025; Villanueva et al., 2025). This dual emphasis on human critical appraisal and ethical technical design guarantees that AI promotes intercultural competency rather than hinders it. Incorporating transparent AI explanations, equitable access, and culturally diverse datasets are essential strategies for ethical AI-mediated ICC (Dai & Hua, 2024).

Also, recent empirical studies further demonstrate how AI systems reproduce social hierarchies through language. For example, Ghosh and Caliskan (2023) show that large language models and machine translation systems systematically reinforce gender stereotypes by associating professional and high-status roles (e.g., *doctor*, *engineer*, *scientist*) with masculine pronouns, while mapping care-related or domestic occupations (e.g., *nurse*, *teacher*, *assistant*) to feminine ones. In intercultural communication contexts, such patterns are particularly problematic, as they risk normalizing unequal gender representations across linguistic and cultural boundaries. When AI-mediated translations or conversational outputs repeatedly encode these associations, learners may internalize gendered assumptions as culturally "neutral" or universal, thereby reinforcing occupational stereotypes and undermining the equity-oriented goals of intercultural education.

*Table 2. Summary of key studies on AI-supported tools in intercultural communication*

| Study | AI Tool / Platform | ICC Focus | Main Findings | Challenges / Limitations |
|---|---|---|---|---|
| Loewen (2023) | Duolingo (AI-adaptive system) | Language learning & exposure to cultural content | AI personalization enhances motivation and cultural awareness | Limited attention to pragmatic or politeness strategies |
| Kubota (2019) | Grammarly | Writing feedback & intercultural norms | Highlights linguistic correctness and potential cross-cultural expectations | Reinforces "standard" English norms; marginalizes non-standard varieties |
| Garcia & Vela (2022) | Google Translate, DeepL | Machine translation in educational settings | Facilitates comprehension across languages | Cultural nuance often lost; majority-language bias; limited minority language support |
| Khoshsaligheh & Ameri (2022) | Machine translation systems | Politeness & honorifics | MT struggles to accurately render cultural politeness | Misrepresentation of hierarchical and indirect communication |

continued on following page

*Table 2. Continued*

| Study | AI Tool / Platform | ICC Focus | Main Findings | Challenges / Limitations |
|---|---|---|---|---|
| Jiang, Li, & Zhu (2023) | ChatGPT, AI conversational agents | Role-play & intercultural dialogue | Simulated intercultural interactions increase exposure to diverse communicative styles | AI inherits online biases; struggles with subtle cultural norms |
| Helm & Dooly (2017) | Telecollaboration platforms with AI support | Digital intercultural competence | AI prompts and translation support help manage cross-cultural collaboration | Overreliance on AI can reduce critical reflection on intercultural differences |
| Crawford (2021); Noble (2018) | General AI systems | Ethics and bias in AI-mediated communication | AI reflects systemic inequalities; it may reproduce stereotypes | Risk of perpetuating discrimination and linguistic hierarchies |
| Zou, Huang, & Xie (2023) | Generative AI (ChatGPT, Gemini, etc.) | Language learning, feedback, and intercultural practice | Supports interactive, adaptive learning scenarios; scaffolds communication | Bias, misinformation, and culturally flattened outputs remain concerns |

*Table 3. Mapping ICC competencies to AI ethical principles*

| ICC Dimension | Description (ICC Competence) | Relevant AI Ethical Principle | Practical Implications for AI-Supported ICC |
|---|---|---|---|
| Attitudes (Savoir être) | Openness, curiosity, and willingness to suspend judgment | Non-discrimination & inclusivity | AI tools should avoid cultural stereotyping; interfaces should represent diverse cultures and languages fairly |
| Knowledge (Savoirs) | Awareness of cultural norms, practices, and contexts | Transparency & explainability | AI systems should provide explanations for outputs (translations, suggestions) so learners understand cultural assumptions |
| Skills (Savoir comprendre / Savoir apprendre & faire) | Interpreting, relating, and interacting across cultures | Human oversight & accountability | Educators must guide learners to critically evaluate AI feedback and correct misunderstandings or bias in outputs |
| Critical cultural awareness (Savoir s'engager) | Evaluating cultural practices critically, recognizing power dynamics | Fairness & equity | AI design should address linguistic and cultural hierarchies; learners should be trained to reflect critically on AI-mediated interactions |
| Digital intercultural competence | Navigating cultural differences in digital environments | Inclusivity, accessibility, privacy | Tools should support equitable access, respect data privacy, and provide culturally sensitive content across digital platforms |

## Key Insights from the Literature

Several important themes and patterns emerge from the studied literature on AI-supported intercultural communication (ICC). Rather than reiterating platform-specific findings, this section consolidates cross-cutting insights from the literature.

- First, AI-supported tools demonstrate strong potential to scaffold intercultural exposure and communicative experimentation, particularly through personalization, simulation, and low-risk practice environments (Loewen, 2023; Zou et al., 2023).
- Second, across tool types, AI systems consistently reproduce linguistic hierarchies and cultural biases, including native-speakerism, gender stereotyping, and Western-centric norms (Kubota, 2019; Blodgett et al., 2020; Ghosh & Caliskan, 2023).
- Third, ethical concerns emerge as a unifying theme, emphasizing the need for transparency, accountability, and critical digital literacy across AI-supported ICC contexts (Crawford, 2021; UNESCO, 2021; OECD, 2022).
- Fourth, while AI-enhanced telecollaboration can support digital intercultural competence, over-reliance on AI mediation risks reducing learners' critical engagement with cultural difference (Holliday, 2018; Zou et al., 2023).

Taken together, these insights suggest that AI functions not merely as a pedagogical aid but as an active cultural mediator whose influence must be critically examined rather than assumed to be neutral.

# BENEFITS AND CHALLENGES OF AI IN INTERCULTURAL COMMUNICATION

While there are many prospects for artificial intelligence (AI) to improve intercultural communication (ICC) in educational settings, there are also considerable obstacles to its widespread implementation. If educators, developers, and legislators want to use AI-supported tools responsibly, they must have a thorough understanding of all sides.

## Benefits of AI in ICC

### Enhanced Cultural Exposure and Learning

Artificial intelligence (AI) techniques can replicate a variety of cultural contexts, giving students the chance to safely explore cross-cultural situations. For instance, learners are introduced to greetings, holidays, and cultural etiquette in a variety of nations through Duolingo's adaptive modules (Loewen, 2023). Chatbots like ChatGPT may simulate cross-cultural conversations, including formal encounters in Japanese settings, informal interactions in Latin American Spanish, and role-playing business negotiations in Germany (Sarwari et al., 2024). By giving students the opportunity to practice perspective-taking, empathy, and ambiguity tolerance, these experiences enhance the cognitive, affective, and behavioral aspects of ICC (Deardorff, 2006).

Additionally, learners' comprehension of international communication norms is expanded when they are exposed to a variety of English dialects, idioms, and politeness techniques via AI platforms. Immersion AI-based cultural simulations have been shown to improve pupils' intercultural flexibility and lessen ethnocentric viewpoints (Jenks, 2025). Learners participate in reflective practice by interacting with AI-mediated scenarios, which improves their ability to traverse unfamiliar communicative contexts and grasp cultural nuances.

### Personalized and Adaptive Learning

AI-driven language learning programs, like Grammarly and Duolingo, offer tailored learning routes and adaptive feedback based on each learner's strengths and limitations (Loewen, 2023; Zou et al., 2023). Some AI systems provide cultural modules in addition to grammar or vocabulary support, exposing learners to social norms, idioms, and expressions that are appropriate for their culture. For instance, Duolingo provides information on greetings, festivals, and manners in other nations, which might encourage curiosity and tolerance for diverse cultures. Additionally, learners can advance at their own speed via personalized routes, which increases ICC's accessibility for a wide range of learners with different skill levels.

These technologies can help learners' overall ICC development by exposing them to pragmatic nuances, idiomatic expressions, and culturally appropriate scenarios in addition to linguistic corrections. For example, students who have had little exposure to non-Western cultures before could be led through structured classes that focus on culturally particular metaphors, indirect speech patterns, or politeness cues. Additionally, adaptive modules facilitate self-directed learning and engagement with intercultural information by enabling students to concentrate on areas in which they require additional practice (Sarwari et al., 2024).

## Immediate Feedback and Practice Opportunities

Artificial intelligence tools offer real-time feedback on interaction patterns, discourse tactics, and language usage. Learners can practice polite requests, cross-cultural negotiations, or situational role-plays by using chatbots like ChatGPT, which can mimic intercultural conversations (Jiang et al., 2023). Students who receive immediate feedback are better able to recognize pragmatic language distinctions, such as the directness of English demands against the indirectness of Japanese ones, and modify their communication style accordingly. The language and sociocultural components of ICC are strengthened by this experiential learning.

## Facilitation of Telecollaboration and Digital Intercultural Experiences

AI-enhanced telecollaborative systems, such as AI-assisted conversation prompts or translation tools like DeepL, allow students from different linguistic and cultural backgrounds to collaborate in real time (Garcia & Vela, 2022; Helm & Dooly, 2017). Language barriers are lessened, interactions are scaffolded, and learners are given a structured opportunity to reflect on cultural differences, negotiate meaning, and build digital intercultural competency. AI can, for example, recommend culturally appropriate language for group discussions, exposing students to several communication modalities and improving intercultural comprehension.

## Data-Driven Insights for Educators

According to Zou et al. (2023), AI analytics can monitor learner interactions, spot misconceptions, and point out trends in cross-cultural communication. Teachers can utilize this information to assess students' progress in intercultural competency, address recurring problems, and customize interventions. Additionally, combined insights can guide curriculum design, assisting institutions in implementing evidence-based, more successful intercultural teaching.

Real-time monitoring of learner interactions is made possible by AI analytics, which also show misconceptions, patterns, and regions in which students struggle with intercultural nuances (Zou et al., 2023). Teachers can utilize these findings to create lesson plans that are attentive to cultural differences, offer targeted interventions, and adapt instruction.

For instance, teachers can create microlessons or discussion starters that address recurring misconceptions about honorifics in Korean or politeness rules in Japanese if an AI system identifies them. Furthermore, compiled data can guide curriculum modifications, create intercultural activities, and assess the success of AI-supported ICC interventions, among other institutional decisions (Sarwari et al., 2024).

### Support for Collaborative and Telecollaborative Learning

By facilitating communication and lowering language barriers, AI-mediated telecollaboration platforms improve cross-cultural contact. Students from different backgrounds can work together effectively in both synchronous and asynchronous environments thanks to AI-generated feedback, discussion prompts, and automated translation tools (Helm & Dooly, 2017; Garcia & Vela, 2022).

An AI program might, for instance, provide culturally suitable wording for a Japanese student answering an informal remark from a U.S. peer during a virtual exchange project. This facilitates reflection on cultural norms while lowering misunderstandings and promoting understanding between parties. Additionally, by identifying learners who might want extra help or scaffolding, AI analytics can offer insights into participation patterns and encourage equitable involvement across culturally diverse groups.

## Challenges of AI in ICC

### Bias and Cultural Misrepresentation

Predominant cultural norms and preconceptions may be reinforced by AI systems that inherit biases from their training data (Crawford, 2021; Noble, 2018). Rather than functioning as neutral mediators, these systems often reproduce dominant linguistic and cultural standards embedded in large-scale datasets. Machine translation tools, for example, frequently flatten honorifics, indirectness, or relational markers in languages such as Thai, Korean, and Japanese, thereby distorting intended meaning and interactional stance (Khoshsaligheh & Ameri, 2022).

Similarly, learners who use non-standard dialects or World Englishes may be marginalized by AI-driven writing systems that promote "standard" English norms (Kubota, 2019; Villanueva et al., 2025). This representational bias does not merely affect linguistic form but also shapes whose voices are perceived as legitimate in intercultural communication. As a result, students may unwittingly accept AI outputs as culturally authentic while overlooking pragmatic conventions, power relations, and sociocultural nuance. This risk underscores the need for systematic evaluative tools—such as the proposed Bias-Audit Checklist—to identify when AI tools reinforce cultural hierarchies rather than foster intercultural awareness.

### Overreliance and Reduced Critical Reflection

Although AI offers useful scaffolding, a reliance on it that is too great may impair students' capacity for critical reflection on cross-cultural relationships. Helm and Dooly (2017) warn that assuming AI-generated comments or translations are infallible may lead to a shallow comprehension of cultural norms.

For instance, a learner relying on automated translation might interpret a Japanese peer's indirect refusal as a direct "no," missing the relational and face-saving dimensions of the exchange. Such cases illustrate that the challenge is not technological error alone, but the pedagogical framing of AI use. To sustain authentic ICC development, educators must scaffold AI-supported activities with critical questioning, reflective dialogue, and peer discussion, ensuring that students actively interpret, challenge, and contextualize AI outputs rather than passively consuming them.

## Ethical and Privacy Concerns

AI-mediated communication raises significant ethical issues related to data protection, equitable access, and institutional responsibility. According to UNESCO (2021), educational AI systems should prioritize diversity, transparency, and fairness. However, ethical risk also emerges at the level of classroom practice, particularly when students' interactions, role-plays, or peer communications are processed or stored without clear consent or awareness.

Moreover, digital inequalities may be exacerbated if students in low-resource contexts lack consistent access to AI-supported platforms. If training data remains limited or culturally skewed, algorithmic decision-making may further reproduce social and cultural inequities (Crawford, 2021). These concerns highlight the importance of embedding ethical evaluation criteria—such as accessibility, data governance, and representational fairness—into any framework assessing AI-supported ICC tools.

## Limitations in Pragmatic and Affective Communication

Despite recent advances, AI systems continue to struggle with humor, sarcasm, emotional nuance, and culturally specific pragmatic cues (Fuchs, 2022). Chatbots may misinterpret veiled refusals, sarcasm, or culturally embedded metaphors, potentially leading to misunderstanding or unintended offense. These limitations reveal structural gaps between linguistic competence and intercultural competence.

Accordingly, human mediation remains essential in AI-supported ICC activities. Teachers must contextualize AI outputs and guide students through critical interpretation, discussion, and reflection. When combined with human facilitation, AI can serve as a productive trigger for intercultural analysis rather than a substitute for it (Holliday, 2018).

## Implications for Practice

A careful, introspective approach to AI in ICC is necessary to balance its advantages and disadvantages. Teachers ought to:

- Urge students to examine and challenge AI results, looking for any prejudices and cultural presumptions.
- To promote more in-depth cross-cultural learning, scaffold AI use with facilitated conversations, thought-provoking questions, and cooperative exercises.
- By incorporating algorithmic sensitivity into the curriculum, you may help students understand how AI functions as a language and cultural bridge.

These practices directly operationalize the evaluative dimensions later formalized in the Bias-Audit Checklist. It is also the duty of developers and legislators to ensure that AI tools are inclusive, transparent, equitable, and culturally representative. By working together, researchers, educators, and technologists may optimize AI's pedagogical potential while reducing associated risks, fostering a learning environment where digital literacy and intercultural competency develop side by side.

# DISCUSSION

## Connecting Findings to Theory

This chapter's findings demonstrate a complex relationship between intercultural communication competence (ICC) and AI-supported technologies. By offering culturally contextualized language input, interactive practice scenarios, and adaptive feedback, AI applications such as Duolingo, Grammarly, and ChatGPT support the cognitive and procedural dimensions of ICC—namely knowledge (savoirs) and skills (savoir comprendre and savoir apprendre/faire)—in ways consistent with Byram's (1997) model (Loewen, 2023; Zou et al., 2023). Rather than reiterating their general affordances, this discussion highlights how these tools function as partial contributors to ICC, supporting certain dimensions while leaving others underdeveloped.

However, the analysis also shows that without structured pedagogical mediation, AI tools may systematically constrain the affective and critical dimensions of ICC, particularly attitudes (savoir être) and critical cultural awareness (savoir s'engager) (Crawford, 2021; Kubota, 2019; Noble, 2018). Across the reviewed tools, recurring patterns—such as the privileging of English as a pivot language, the flattening of sociopragmatic markers, and the normalization of dominant cultural scripts—signal not isolated errors but structural tendencies embedded in algorithmic design. These tendencies align with critical interculturality perspectives that emphasize power, ideology, and inequality as constitutive elements of intercultural encounters (Holliday, 2018).

Seen through this lens, AI tools should not be evaluated solely in terms of accuracy or efficiency, but in terms of how they shape learners' perceptions of linguistic legitimacy, cultural normalcy, and communicative authority. This theoretical reframing directly informs the need for a systematic evaluative mechanism—such as the Bias-Audit Checklist proposed in this chapter—to assess how AI tools distribute cultural visibility, agency, and interpretive depth across contexts.

## Implications for Practice and Policy

Educators: Teachers play a crucial role in transforming AI from a passive content provider into a site of critical intercultural inquiry. Rather than positioning AI outputs as authoritative, instructors should explicitly frame them as provisional and culturally situated, using reflective prompts and guided discussion to interrogate assumptions embedded in translations or chatbot responses (Fuchs, 2022). Within the proposed Bias-Audit Checklist, educators can operationalize this role by asking whether a given tool encourages critical comparison, foregrounds multiple cultural interpretations, or obscures sociopragmatic nuance.

Curriculum Developers: Inclusive curriculum design requires aligning AI-supported activities with clearly articulated ICC outcomes. Instead of dispersing similar claims across modules, curricula should sequence AI use progressively—from exposure and practice toward critical evaluation. Telecollaboration projects, for instance, may employ AI for scaffolding interaction while simultaneously integrating checklist-guided reflection tasks that prompt students to identify linguistic hierarchies, representational gaps, or accessibility constraints (Garcia & Vela, 2022; Helm & Dooly, 2017).

Policymakers: From a policy perspective, the findings underscore that ethical AI integration in ICC education extends beyond access alone. Legislators must ensure that AI tools meet standards of transparency, inclusivity, and accountability, particularly in multilingual and low-resource contexts (UNESCO, 2021; Dai & Hua, 2024). The Bias-Audit Checklist offers policymakers a practical instrument for monitoring whether AI-mediated educational practices reproduce or mitigate systemic inequalities over time.

Developers: For developers, the discussion highlights the need to move beyond technical optimization toward intercultural responsibility. Design choices related to training data, language coverage, and interactional defaults have direct consequences for how cultures are represented and valued. Addressing representational and interactional bias through diverse datasets, human-in-the-loop design, and collaboration with intercultural experts can enhance both system reliability and educational trust (Blodgett et al., 2020; Crawford, 2021).

### Synthesis and Future Directions

Overall, the discussion clarifies that AI-supported tools neither inherently enhance nor inevitably undermine ICC; rather, their impact depends on how their affordances and limitations are recognized, evaluated, and pedagogically framed. This synthesis moves the chapter beyond descriptive repetition toward its central contribution: positioning the Bias-Audit Checklist as a connective framework linking theory, empirical patterns, and practice.

Future research should therefore examine how checklist-guided evaluations influence classroom practice, explore longitudinal effects of AI-mediated ICC instruction, and investigate cross-cultural variation in learners' responses to AI outputs. Such work would further consolidate the framework's value as both an analytical and pedagogical tool for inclusive, ethically grounded intercultural education.

## CONCLUSION

Artificial Intelligence (AI) has the potential to revolutionize intercultural communication (ICC) education by facilitating more immersive, personalized, and adaptive learning environments. Recent research has demonstrated how AI tools can improve students' intercultural competency. For example, postgraduate students in a multicultural university setting reported better intercultural communication skills when using AI technology, according to a study by Sarwari et al. (2024). In a similar vein, Klimova and Chen (2024) found that AI-powered resources, such as chatbots and virtual reality simulations, greatly improved students' capacity to deal with cultural differences in higher education.

The use of AI in ICC education is not without its difficulties, though. Careful thought must be given to issues pertaining to the digital gap, cultural misrepresentation, and algorithmic bias. The significance of cultural sensitivity in AI-driven machine translation technologies, especially in translation education, is highlighted by research by Amaro and Zhang (2025). In order to prevent misunderstandings, their research highlights the necessity for AI systems to faithfully capture colloquial idioms and cultural quirks.

In order to overcome these challenges, educators, developers, and legislators must work together to produce AI tools that are not just cutting-edge in terms of technology but also morally and culturally correct. This entails making sure AI systems are open, fair, and able to encourage learners to reflect critically. In their discussion of the use of generative AI for professional communication training in cross-cultural settings, Dai et al. (2025), for instance, stress the significance of including a range of cultural representations in instructional and evaluation resources.

Furthermore, in order to continuously evaluate and solve the changing opportunities and difficulties brought about by AI in ICC education, research, and discussion must continue. It is essential to keep up with the latest developments in AI technology to understand their consequences and modify teaching methods appropriately. This involves creating an atmosphere in which artificial intelligence (AI) is employed to improve cross-cultural comprehension rather than to take the place of interpersonal communication.

In conclusion, even if AI has a lot of potential to improve cross-cultural communication, its successful use necessitates a well-rounded strategy that places a high value on moral issues, cultural sensitivity, and cooperation from all parties. By tackling these issues, artificial intelligence (AI) can be a potent ally in equipping students to interact intelligently and successfully in a world that is interculturally diverse and digitally mediated.

## RECOMMENDATIONS AND PRACTICAL GUIDELINES

It is clear from the research, conceptual frameworks, and advantages and disadvantages that using AI tools in intercultural communication (ICC) instruction calls for a thoughtful and well-rounded strategy. To make sure AI acts as a helpful, culturally sensitive partner rather than a neutral middleman, educators, developers, and legislators must collaborate. Teachers should place a high priority on algorithmic sensitivity in the classroom, helping pupils to assess AI outputs critically, examine possible biases, and take into account different cultural viewpoints. To help students understand that these tools are not perfect, this involves encouraging thoughtful discussion about translation errors, practical misunderstandings, or culturally flattened AI-generated solutions.

AI-supported activities that complement recognized ICC competencies—such as attitudes, knowledge, skills, and critical cultural awareness—should be incorporated into curriculum design. Activities could involve telecollaborative projects, AI-facilitated role-plays, or simulation exercises where students critically evaluate the benefits and drawbacks of AI while negotiating meaning across cultural boundaries. Language variety knowledge should be incorporated into curricula to promote inclusivity, and students should be encouraged to consider how AI systems might favor some language variants over others. By including such critical and reflective methods, AI use is guaranteed to improve intercultural competency rather than detract from it.

Ethical standards should be incorporated into the functionality and design of AI systems for teaching. This entails actively reducing prejudice, integrating diverse datasets that represent many cultural viewpoints, and developing transparent systems that describe decision-making procedures. In order to avoid perpetuating current digital and educational disparities, AI platforms must be made to accommodate learners with different technology resources and linguistic backgrounds. To make sure that AI-mediated interactions complement educational objectives and culturally appropriate participation, developers can work in tandem with educators and intercultural communication experts.

By creating rules and laws that enable fair access, protect privacy, and maintain openness in AI-supported education, policymakers play a complementary role. For educators to stay up to date on the latest developments in AI, pedagogy, and ethics, policies should support opportunities for professional development. In order to ensure that educators and students are prepared to handle AI-mediated interactions responsibly, institutions can facilitate this through workshops, seminars, and collaborative communities that incorporate intercultural and technology literacy.

In the end, a comprehensive strategy integrating critical educational practice, ethical AI design, and supportive policy frameworks is needed for the successful integration of AI in ICC. Stakeholders should leverage the potential of AI tools to improve intercultural communication skills while limiting hazards by addressing the ethical and practical challenges of AI, encouraging algorithmic sensitivity, and advocating for reflective and inclusive education. By doing this, educational settings can become places where culture, technology, and critical thinking come together, enabling students to interact intelligently and successfully in a world that is interculturally varied and mediated by digital means.

## REFERENCES


Amaro, V., & Zhang, X. (2025). Intercultural interfaces: Artificial intelligence and its challenges of cultural sensitivity. *Interfaces Interculturais*. Retrieved from https://www.researchgate.net/publication/391574223_Intercultural_Interfaces_Artificial_intelligence_and_its_challenges_of_cultural_sensitivity

Benjamin, R. (2019). Race after technology: Abolitionist tools for the new Jim code. *Polity*.

Blodgett, S. L., Barocas, S., Daumé, H.III, & Wallach, H. (2020). Language (technology) is power: A critical survey of "bias" in NLP. *Proceedings of the 58th Annual Meeting of the Association for Computational Linguistics*, 5454–5476. DOI: 10.18653/v1/2020.acl-main.485

Byram, M. (1997). *Teaching and assessing intercultural communicative competence*. Multilingual Matters.

Castro, P., & Lind, R. (2022). AI translation tools and intercultural communication: Opportunities and limitations. *Journal of Language and Intercultural Communication, 22*(6), 711–729. DOI: 10.1080/14708477.2022.2050983

Chen, G. M., & Starosta, W. J. (1996). Intercultural communication competence: A synthesis. *Annals of the International Communication Association, 19*(1), 353–383. DOI: 10.1080/23808985.1996.11678935

Crawford, K. (2021). *Atlas of AI: Power, politics, and the planetary costs of artificial intelligence*. Yale University Press.

Dai, D. W., Suzuki, S., & Chen, G. (2025). Generative AI for professional communication training in intercultural contexts: Where are we now and where are we heading? *Applied Linguistics Review, 16*(2), 763–774. DOI: 10.1515/applirev-2024-0184

Deardorff, D. K. (2006). Identification and assessment of intercultural competence as a student outcome of internationalization. *Journal of Studies in International Education, 10*(3), 241–266. DOI: 10.1177/1028315306287002

Duolingo. (2023, March 14). *Introducing Duolingo Max, powered by GPT-4*. Duolingo Blog. https://blog.duolingo.com/duolingo-max/

European Commission. (2024). *Proposal for an Artificial Intelligence Act*. Official Journal of the European Union. https://commission.europa.eu/ai-act

Floridi, L. (2023). *The ethics of artificial intelligence: Principles, challenges, and opportunities*. Oxford University Press. DOI: 10.1093/oso/9780198883098.001.0001

Fuchs, C. (2022). Politeness and pragmatics in digital language learning environments. *Language Learning & Technology*, *26*(1), 1–21. DOI: 10.10125/44742

Garcia, I., & Vela, E. (2022). Machine translation in education: Opportunities and challenges. *Computer Assisted Language Learning*, *35*(4), 879–899. DOI: 10.1080/09588221.2020.1853187

Ghosh, A., & Caliskan, A. (2023). Biases in translation systems: Gender and professional stereotypes in algorithmic outputs. *Journal of Artificial Intelligence Research*, *80*, 123–145.

Godwin-Jones, R. (2023). Emerging technologies: AI-mediated communication and language learning. *Language Learning & Technology*, *27*(1), 1–12. DOI: 10.10125/73494

Grammarly. (2023, April 4). *Introducing GrammarlyGO: AI to accelerate your writing process*. Grammarly Blog. https://www.grammarly.com/blog/grammarlygo/

Helm, F., & Dooly, M. (2017). Virtual exchange and intercultural competence: An introduction. *European Journal of Language Policy*, *9*(2), 139–153. DOI: 10.3828/ejlp.2019.9

Holliday, A. (2018). *Understanding intercultural communication: Negotiating a grammar of culture* (2nd ed.). Routledge.

Jenks, C. J. (2025). Communicating the cultural other: Trust and bias in generative AI and large language models. *Applied Linguistics Review*, *16*(2), 1–9. DOI: 10.1515/applirev-2024-0196

Jiang, L., Li, Q., & Zhu, Y. (2023). Conversational AI and language learning: Potentials and pitfalls. *ReCALL*, *35*(2), 181–199. DOI: 10.1017/S0958344022000192

Kasneci, E., Sessler, K., Küchemann, S., Bannert, M., Dementieva, D., Fischer, F., & Kasneci, G. (2023). ChatGPT for good? On opportunities and challenges of large language models for education. *Learning and Individual Differences*, *103*, 102274. DOI: 10.1016/j.lindif.2023.102274

Khoshsaligheh, M., & Ameri, S. (2022). Politeness in translation: Challenges of machine translation in rendering honorifics. *Perspectives*, *30*(1), 77–94. DOI: 10.1080/0907676X.2021.1931134

Klimova, B., & Chen, J. H. (2024). The impact of AI on enhancing students' intercultural communication competence at the university level: A review study. *Language Teaching Research Quarterly*, *43*, 102–120. DOI: 10.32038/ltrq.2024.43.06

Kubota, R. (2019). Confronting epistemological racism, decolonizing scholarly knowledge: Race and gender in applied linguistics. *Applied Linguistics*, *40*(3), 464–481. DOI: 10.1093/applin/amy034

Loewen, S. (2023). AI-driven language learning: Pedagogical promises and ethical challenges. *Language Teaching*, *56*(2), 187–202. DOI: 10.1017/S0261444822000302

Noble, S. U. (2018). *Algorithms of oppression: How search engines reinforce racism.* NYU Press. DOI: 10.18574/nyu/9781479833641.001.0001

Organisation for Economic Co-operation and Development. (2019). *OECD principles on artificial intelligence.* https://www.oecd.org/digital/ai/principles/

Sarwari, A. Q., Javed, M. N., Mohd Adnan, H., & Abdul Wahab, M. N. (2024). Assessment of the impacts of artificial intelligence (AI) on intercultural communication among postgraduate students in a multicultural university environment. *Scientific Reports*, *14*(1), 13849. DOI: 10.1038/s41598-024-63276-5

Spitzberg, B. H., & Chagnéon, G. (2009). Conceptualizing intercultural competence. In Deardorff, D. K. (Ed.), *The SAGE handbook of intercultural competence* (pp. 2–52). SAGE. DOI: 10.4135/9781071872987.n1

Stanovsky, G., Smith, N. A., & Zettlemoyer, L. (2019). Evaluating gender bias in machine translation. *Proceedings of the 57th Annual Meeting of the Association for Computational Linguistics*, 1679–1684. DOI: 10.18653/v1/P19-1164

Ting-Toomey, S. (2005). The matrix of face: An updated face-negotiation theory. In Gudykunst, W. B. (Ed.), *Theorizing about intercultural communication* (pp. 71–92). SAGE.

UNESCO. (2021). *Recommendation on the ethics of artificial intelligence.* United Nations Educational, Scientific, and Cultural Organization.

Villanueva, I., Bobinac, T., Yao, B., Hu, J., & Chen, K. (2025). AI as a deliberative partner fosters intercultural empathy for Americans but fails for Latin American participants. *arXiv*. https://arxiv.org/abs/2504.13887

Weidinger, J., Mellor, J., Rauh, M., Griffin, C., Uesato, J., Huang, P. S., & Gabriel, I. (2022). Ethical and social risks of large language models. *Proceedings of the 2022 ACM Conference on Fairness, Accountability, and Transparency*, 214–229. DOI: 10.1145/3531146.3533088

Zawacki-Richter, O., Marín, V. I., Bond, M., & Gouverneur, F. (2019). Systematic review of research on artificial intelligence applications in higher education – where are the educators? *International Journal of Educational Technology in Higher Education, 16*(1), 39. DOI: 10.1186/s41239-019-0171-0

Zou, D., Huang, Y., & Xie, H. (2023). Generative artificial intelligence for language education: Applications, challenges, and future directions. *Computers and Education: Artificial Intelligence*, *4*, 100119. DOI: 10.1016/j.caeai.2023.100119

Chapter 3
# The Place of Humor, Empathy, and Cultural Nuances in AI-Supported Tools

**Pankaj Bhanudas Vaishnav**
http://orcid.org/0009-0005-3542-2427
*Al Seeb Vocational College, Muscat, Oman*

## ABSTRACT

*This chapter explores the intersection of artificial intelligence (AI) and intercultural pedagogy, focusing on how humor, empathy, and cultural nuance. They are often represented or misrepresented by language technologies. Through case studies of tools such as ChatGPT, Replika, Duolingo, and DeepL, the discussion highlights both the pedagogical opportunities and the risks of cultural flattening, stereotyping, or superficial affective engagement. The chapter argues that while AI excels in efficiency and personalization, it falls short in capturing the relational and contextual aspects of communication essential for intercultural competence. To address these gaps, hybrid human–AI pedagogies are examined, illustrating how teacher mediation can enrich machine outputs with cultural depth, humor, and empathy. Future directions emphasize the ethical challenges of bias and homogenization, as well as opportunities for interdisciplinary collaboration. The conclusion reasserts the indispensable human role in ensuring that AI serves as an aid rather than a substitute in intercultural learning.*

DOI: 10.4018/979-8-3373-6325-7.ch003

## 1. INTRODUCTION

The integration of artificial intelligence (AI) into educational and intercultural communication contexts is often framed as a story of progress: tools that personalize learning, increase efficiency, and enhance accuracy are celebrated as breakthroughs. Reports such as the U.S. Department of Education (2023) underscore measurable benefits, particularly scalability and adaptability, while Walter (2024) positions AI as central to an "AI-rich learning ecology" in higher education. Yet this narrative conceals a persistent blind spot: the affective and cultural dimensions of communication. When AI is treated as a neutral delivery mechanism for content, its limitations in handling humor, empathy, and cultural nuance remain under examined. This omission is not trivial, for it risks producing forms of communication that are efficient but mechanistic, technically fluent but culturally impoverished.

The "empathy gap" identified by Al-Zahrani (2024) illustrates this problem. He argues that AI-driven conversational agents mimic caring language without genuine sensitivity to context. It results in interactions that may appear supportive but fail to respond to learners' emotional or cultural needs. Jamaluddin and Mokhtar (2025) extends this critique, showing in his comparative analysis that while virtual agents can simulate empathy, they cannot replicate the situational awareness and cultural attunement of human interaction. Together, these findings raise a critical question: what does it mean to "teach empathy" when the mediating system lacks the capacity to interpret affect in culturally situated ways? The analytical challenge lies not in cataloguing what AI does well, but in probing how these surface-level simulations might reshape learners' expectations of interpersonal communication. If learners come to associate empathy with formulaic outputs rather than relational responsiveness, intercultural sensitivity may be diluted rather than deepened.

Humor presents an equally revealing case. Much of the technical literature celebrates progress in humor generation. Zhang et al. (2024), for example, demonstrate how large-scale, crowd-sourced preferences enable models to produce witty captions and jokes. However, the critical question is not whether AI can generate "funny" text, but whether such humor functions interculturally. Humor depends on timing, shared reference, and pragmatic subtlety, all of which vary across cultural contexts. Saumure et al. (2025), in their study, show that AI-generated humor often reinforces stereotypes embedded in training data. This is not merely a technical flaw but a cultural and ethical one: humor that misrepresents or caricatures cultural groups can undermine trust, alienate learners, or even perpetuate harm. The analytical task, then, is to interrogate whether the inclusion of AI-generated humor enriches or diminishes intercultural dialogue.

Emotion-aware systems appear, at first glance, to promise a solution. Fangni's (2025) study of such systems in intercultural classroom dialogue suggests they can scaffold more inclusive interactions by recognizing emotional states. Yet the same study highlights that emotional expression is culturally coded; what counts as "enthusiastic" in one context may be read as "aggressive" in another. Here, the problem is epistemic: by operationalizing emotions as data points, AI risks universalizing expressions that are culturally variable. As Al-Zahrani (2024) cautions, technical fixes cannot substitute for cultural literacy. Instead of assuming that emotion recognition can be generalized, educators must ask whether such tools obscure rather than reveal intercultural complexity.

At stake is more than a question of technical accuracy. When humor, empathy, and cultural nuance are poorly modeled, the risk is that learners internalize distorted representations of communication. In intercultural contexts, where misunderstanding is already heightened, these distortions can escalate into conflict. The challenge is therefore not to discard AI, but to subject its affective and cultural claims to rigorous scrutiny. This requires reframing the pedagogical debate: instead of asking how AI can replicate human capacities, we must ask how AI reshapes the very conditions under which affect and culture are communicated.

To address this challenge, the chapter advances three interconnected lines of inquiry. First, it investigates how contemporary AI systems represent, simulate, or distort humor, empathy, and cultural nuance. This involves mapping not only technical affordances but also their cultural consequences. Second, it examines how these dimensions function in practice by analyzing AI tools widely used in education such as ChatGPT, Duolingo, DeepL, and Replika. These tools are not neutral platforms; each encodes specific assumptions about language, interaction, and culture. By critically interrogating their outputs, the chapter highlights how design decisions influence pedagogical practice. Third, it offers strategies for educators to mediate AI use in ways that foreground authentic intercultural communication.

Such an approach is necessary because technology alone cannot deliver intercultural competence. The importance of intercultural competence as a foundational element of effective communication has been widely established, particularly in educational and professional settings where cultural misalignment can impede collaboration and understanding (Vaishnav, 2024). Empathy is relational, humor is contextual, and cultural nuance is interpretive. These qualities resist easy codification, yet they remain indispensable to communication. If AI systems are deployed without paying attention to them, we risk normalizing communication that is efficient but dehumanized. Conversely, if educators treat AI critically as a site for reflection rather than replication, it can become a powerful pedagogical tool. For instance, a chatbot simulation that produces awkward or stereotypical humor can be reframed as a teaching moment, prompting learners to reflect on why cultural context matters in interpreting humor.

The implications are both practical and ethical. Pedagogically, teachers must make choices about how to scaffold AI use so that learners are not misled by simulated empathy or culturally insensitive humor. Epistemically, they must evaluate whether AI-generated content represents culture faithfully or flattens it into homogenized global English. Ethically, they must confront the risk that stereotypes embedded in training data are reintroduced into classroom discourse. These are not peripheral concerns; they go to the heart of what it means to teach and learn across cultures in an AI-mediated environment.

This chapter therefore argues that the pedagogical value of AI in intercultural communication lies not in its capacity to replicate human affect, but in its potential to provoke critical dialogue about what authentic communication requires. By situating humor, empathy, and cultural nuance at the center of analysis, the chapter underscores that technological innovation must be evaluated not only by what it enables but also by what it risks obscuring.

## 2. RESEARCH QUESTIONS AND METHODOLOGICAL APPROACH

The analytical concerns outlined in the introduction give rise to three guiding research questions for this chapter:

1. How do AI-supported communication tools interpret, simulate, or distort humor, empathy, and cultural nuance?
2. What risks and opportunities arise from incorporating these human dimensions into AI-mediated pedagogy?
3. How can educators and curriculum designers critically engage with AI's limitations while leveraging its affordances to foster intercultural competence?

Together, these questions signal a shift from describing what AI tools can do to critically interrogating what they mean for intercultural pedagogy. They assume that affective and cultural dimensions are not peripheral but central to authentic communication, and they highlight the need for examining not only technical performance but also pedagogical and ethical consequences. This orientation aligns with Vaishnav's (2025) recent discussions on AI–human collaborative teaching, which emphasizes the role of educators in mediating technological affordances rather than delegating pedagogical judgment to automated systems.

Methodologically, this chapter adopts a conceptual and analytical approach. Rather than conducting empirical fieldwork or classroom experiments, it synthesizes insights from three disciplinary strands:

- Sociolinguistics which examines how language is socially situated and how humor, empathy, and cultural nuance function in interaction. Concepts such as context-sensitivity, politeness strategies, and code-switching provide tools for analyzing whether AI-generated communication reflects or ignores the contextual features of real-world discourse (Herring, 2025; Holmes, 2013).
- Intercultural pragmatics which emphasizes how meaning is negotiated across cultural boundaries. This framework allows the chapter to interrogate whether AI reproduces pragmatic strategies such as hedging, humor, or empathy in ways that align with or distort intercultural norms (Kecskes, 2014; McConachy & Spencer-Oatey, 2021).
- AI studies and affective computing, which investigate how systems are trained to model affective cues and simulate human-like interaction. Here, critical attention is paid to both the affordances of generative models and their limitations, particularly around stereotype reinforcement and misrecognition of cultural signals (McStay, 2018; Williamson et al., 2023).

By drawing on these frameworks, the chapter situates humor, empathy, and cultural nuance not as isolated functions but as interdisciplinary problems requiring attention to language, culture, and technology simultaneously.

## 2.1 Case-Based Illustrations

To operationalize the theoretical discussion, the chapter incorporates a set of focused, illustrative case-based analyses of widely used AI-supported tools in educational and intercultural communication contexts. These cases are not intended as empirical field studies, but as analytical exemplars selected to represent distinct AI paradigms through which humor, empathy, and cultural nuance are mediated in pedagogical settings. The selection is therefore purposeful rather than exhaustive, guided by three criteria: (a) widespread educational uptake, (b) representation of a particular AI design logic, and (c) relevance to affective and intercultural dimensions of communication. In this sense,

- ChatGPT is selected as an example of generative conversational AI, where large language models (LLMs) simulate dialogue across diverse communicative contexts. Its relevance lies in its frequent deployment for language learning, academic writing, and intercultural interaction, making it a useful site for examining how humor and empathy are generated, misaligned, or culturally flattened in open-ended exchanges. Prior research by Dwivedi et al. (2023) has shown that while such models can produce contextually plausible responses, they may also reproduce culturally insensitive or pragmatically inappropriate content.

- Duolingo represents gamified language pedagogy, in which humor is embedded deliberately within instructional design to sustain motivation and reduce learner anxiety. It is included to explore how scripted humor and playful feedback function pedagogically, and whether such strategies support or oversimplify intercultural nuance. As Loewen et al. (2019) note, Duolingo's light-hearted tone can enhance engagement, yet its standardized prompts may also limit deeper cultural interpretation.
- DeepL is examined as a case of neural machine translation, where cultural nuance is negotiated implicitly through algorithmic choices rather than explicit pedagogical framing. Its selection reflects its widespread use in academic and professional contexts, particularly by multilingual learners. Although translation quality has improved substantially, studies indicate persistent difficulties with idiomatic language, culturally embedded metaphors, and pragmatically marked expressions (Naveen & Trojovský, 2024), making it a relevant case for interrogating cultural loss and semantic flattening.
- Replika is included as an example of affective computing and simulated companionship, where empathy is foregrounded as a core design feature. Unlike instructional platforms, Replika positions emotional engagement as its primary function, offering a contrasting perspective on how empathy is operationalized in AI systems. Research suggests that while such applications can foster perceived emotional support, they also blur boundaries between relational authenticity and programmed responsiveness, raising ethical and pedagogical concerns (Morton Gutiérrez, 2022).

Taken together, these cases are treated as analytical nodes that connect theoretical frameworks to concrete AI-mediated practices. Each case is examined in relation to the chapter's guiding research questions, illustrating how pedagogical opportunities such as engagement, confidence-building, and extended practice coexist with risks including stereotype reinforcement, cultural homogenization, and the normalization of simulated empathy. This comparative approach enables a nuanced examination of how different AI architectures shape intercultural communication in distinct yet intersecting ways.

## 2.2 Bridging Theory and Practice

The methodological choice to combine theoretical synthesis with case-based illustration reflects two commitments. First, it acknowledges that humor, empathy, and cultural nuance are inherently difficult to quantify, which makes traditional experimental designs insufficient to capture their complexity. Second, it recognizes that educators need not only conceptual insights but also practical guidance on how to navigate the affordances and risks of AI-supported tools.

In this sense, the chapter aligns with a "critical pedagogical approach" to AI in education: one that moves beyond celebrating technical novelty to asking how systems are actually experienced in situated practice. By connecting sociolinguistic and pragmatic theories with real-world AI applications, the chapter provides a methodological bridge between abstract critique and classroom implementation.

## 2.3 Scope and Limitations

It is also important to clarify the scope of this methodological approach. The chapter does not offer large-scale empirical testing or statistical evaluation of AI systems. Instead, its strength lies in critical synthesis and illustrative analysis, designed to generate insights that are academically rigorous and pedagogically useful. This focus means the findings will not claim universal generalizability but will instead highlight key tensions and questions that educators and curriculum designers must address. Moreover, the use of case studies such as ChatGPT, Duolingo, DeepL, and Replika is selective. These tools are chosen because they represent distinct approaches to AI-supported communication, generative dialogue, gamified practice, translation, and affective simulation, each of which illuminates different aspects of humor, empathy, and cultural nuance (Dwivedi et al., 2023; Williamson et al., 2023). Other tools certainly exist, but the ones analyzed here provide sufficient range to surface the methodological and pedagogical issues under investigation.

By articulating three guiding research questions and adopting a conceptual, interdisciplinary, and case-based methodology, this chapter positions itself as both analytical and applied. Its aim is not to measure whether AI tools "work" in a narrow sense, but to critically investigate how they shape the affective and cultural dimensions of communication that are central to intercultural competence. Through this approach, the chapter provides a foundation for subsequent sections, which will examine theoretical frameworks, analyze case studies, and propose strategies for integrating AI in ways that foreground humor, empathy, and cultural nuance rather than reducing them to technical afterthoughts.

# 3 THEORETICAL BACKGROUND

Understanding how AI mediates human communication requires grounding in theories of meaning-making that extend beyond grammar and vocabulary. This section examines three key dimensions; humor, empathy, and cultural nuance that shape intercultural interaction and present distinct challenges for computational modeling. Drawing from sociolinguistics, pragmatics, and intercultural communication studies, each subsection situates these dimensions within broader theoretical debates while considering their implications for AI-supported pedagogy.

## 3.1 Humor in Communication

Humor has long been recognized as a central feature of human communication, functioning as a resource for social bonding, conflict mitigation, and the negotiation of power. As Attardo (1994) argues, humor is not merely entertainment but a pragmatic strategy that can facilitate rapport, reduce anxiety, and subtly challenge authority in interaction. In intercultural communication, humor plays a particularly delicate role: it can bridge cultural divides by fostering solidarity, but it can also sharpen differences when jokes depend on culture-specific references or norms of appropriateness. For this reason, humor is often described as "the most culture-bound of communicative practices" (Chiaro, 2017).

Theories of humor have approached the phenomenon from multiple angles, each offering insights into its communicative and intercultural dimensions. Incongruity theory, rooted in the work of Kant and Schopenhauer, views humor as arising when expectations are subverted, producing surprise or cognitive dissonance that is then resolved. Relief theory, associated with Freud (1928), frames humor as a release of psychological tension, often in taboo or socially constrained areas of expression. Superiority theory, originating with Hobbes, interprets laughter as an assertion of dominance, as when individuals laugh at others' misfortunes or social faux pas. While these classical theories illuminate different functions of humor, more recent accounts such as Raskin's, (1979) Semantic Script Theory of Humor (SSTH) and Attardo's (1994, 2002) General Theory of Verbal Humor (GTVH) bring together linguistic, cognitive, and social dimensions. These models emphasize that humor operates at multiple levels: lexical, pragmatic, cultural, and situational. Importantly, they highlight the interpretive work required by both speaker and hearer, underscoring humor's dependence on shared assumptions.

The cultural relativity of humor is particularly significant in intercultural pedagogy. Research by Holmes (2000) demonstrates that what counts as humorous varies widely across societies, shaped by linguistic conventions, politeness norms, and collective histories. For instance, irony, a pervasive form of humor in English-speaking contexts, may be less common or even confusing in cultures where literalness is valued. Similarly, satire that critiques political authority can be highly effective in liberal democracies but dangerous or taboo in more authoritarian settings. These variations underscore why humor often fails to "travel well" across cultures and why its interpretation can be fraught with risk. Chiaro (2017) notes that even within shared languages, regional or subcultural humor can create barriers to understanding. For educators, this means that the use of humor in intercultural classrooms must be carefully managed to avoid exclusion or misunderstanding.

From a pragmatic perspective, humor functions as a conversational strategy embedded within speech acts, implicatures, and politeness routines. Attardo et al. (2003) show that humor can serve as an "illocutionary force modifier," softening criticism or framing disagreement in less face-threatening ways. In intercultural communication, this mitigative role can be especially valuable, helping to reduce the anxieties of second-language learners and to establish common ground. At the same time, humor's pragmatic functions also raise challenges for AI-supported tools. Computational models often rely on surface-level text features or sentiment analysis, making it difficult to detect irony, sarcasm, or metaphorical play. Even LLM, despite their ability to generate jokes, often produce humor that lacks cultural specificity or misjudges appropriateness.

The intersection of humor and AI brings these theoretical and cultural complexities into sharp relief. Binsted et al. (2006) observed in their survey of computational humor research that machine-generated humor tends to perform well with puns and simple incongruities but struggles with context-dependent or culturally nuanced jokes. This limitation raises important pedagogical questions: if AI tools misinterpret humor, do they risk alienating learners or reinforcing stereotypes? Conversely, can humor generated by AI still serve a positive role in lowering affective filters and encouraging language play, even if it lacks cultural depth? Case studies of platforms like Duolingo show that gamified humor such as quirky example sentences is effective in engaging learners, though it sometimes puzzles or frustrates those who lack the cultural frames to interpret it (Shortt et al., 2023).

Critically, humor in AI-mediated pedagogy should not be dismissed as a minor or ornamental feature. As intercultural communication scholars argue, humor is often the "acid test" of linguistic and cultural competence. Being able to understand or produce humor signals a deeper grasp of pragmatics and cultural nuance than literal comprehension alone. For AI-supported learning environments, this means that the ability or inability of systems to recognize, simulate, or scaffold humor becomes a proxy for how well they support authentic intercultural competence.

Humor exemplifies both the promise and the perils of integrating affective and cultural dimensions into AI-supported pedagogy. Theories of humor emphasize its layered complexity, cultural relativity underscores its variability and risk, and pragmatics highlights its interpersonal utility. Together, these insights point to the need for critical evaluation of how AI interprets and generates humor. For educators, the challenge is to mediate these tools thoughtfully: to harness humor's motivational and relational benefits while remaining alert to the cultural and communicative pitfalls that AI cannot yet fully navigate.

## 3.2 Empathy in Communication

Empathy has been described as one of the most essential capacities for sustaining human relationships, especially in intercultural contexts where communicative intent cannot be taken for granted. Psychologists generally distinguish between *cognitive empathy*, the ability to understand another's perspective or mental state and *affective empathy*, the capacity to resonate with another's emotions (Davis, 2018). Both dimensions are integral to effective communication. In intercultural encounters, empathy facilitates sensitivity to different values, communicative norms, and emotional cues, thereby reducing the likelihood of stereotyping or misunderstanding (Bennet, 1998). Without empathy, intercultural exchanges risk becoming transactional, reinforcing distance rather than building trust.

In educational contexts, empathy has been linked to both cognitive development and socio-emotional learning. Research in pedagogy emphasizes that empathetic classrooms foster student motivation, resilience, and collaboration (Cooper, 2010). Language learning in particular benefits from empathy, as learners who feel understood and supported are more willing to take risks in speaking and experimenting with new linguistic forms. For teachers, the capacity to empathize with students' anxieties, such as fear of error or cultural misfit plays a vital role in lowering the affective filter, a concept central to Krashen's (1982) theory of language acquisition. Thus, empathy functions not only as a moral quality but as a pedagogical tool that enhances intercultural competence.

The rise of affective computing has brought empathy into the realm of artificial intelligence. Affective computing, defined by Picard (1997) as the study and development of systems that can recognize, interpret, and simulate human emotions, seeks to approximate this human capacity in machines. Techniques such as sentiment analysis, facial recognition, and voice prosody analysis allow AI systems to infer emotional states and respond in ways that mimic empathy. Chatbots such as Replika attempt to display empathy by producing language patterns that mirror supportive dialogue, offering comforting or validating responses (Fitzpatrick et al., 2017). In educational settings, similar approaches are increasingly integrated into intelligent tutoring systems, where adaptive feedback is framed not only around correctness but around emotional encouragement.

Yet the notion of "artificial empathy" remains deeply contested. On one hand, researchers highlight the potential benefits of empathetic AI for supporting learners. Zanbaka et al. (2007), for example, show that empathetic virtual agents can enhance learners' sense of social presence, leading to greater engagement and persistence. In intercultural communication, such simulations could help learners feel emotionally validated, reducing anxiety and encouraging participation. On the other hand, critics argue that these interactions remain surface-level approximations, lacking the genuine perspective-taking that defines true empathy. The danger lies in confusing *simulation* with *authenticity*: machines may be programmed to sound caring, but they cannot experience emotions, cultural histories, or moral commitments.

This critique has direct implications for pedagogy. If students perceive AI-supported tools as genuinely empathetic, they may attribute human-like qualities to them, raising ethical concerns about dependency and anthropomorphism. Reeves and Nass's (1996) classic "media equation" research demonstrated that people often respond to computers as if they were human; in the context of empathetic AI, this can create an illusion of relationality that masks the absence of true mutual understanding. From a critical perspective, artificial empathy may risk trivializing the complexity of intercultural empathy, reducing it to affective "signals" such as positive sentiment markers, rather than fostering deeper recognition of cultural difference.

Nevertheless, there are pedagogical opportunities in strategically using artificial empathy. If framed transparently, empathetic AI systems can serve as *scaffolds* that encourage learners to articulate emotions, reflect on their communicative challenges, and practice supportive discourse strategies. For instance, empathetic responses generated by AI could model phrases for showing understanding or solidarity in intercultural interactions, thereby expanding learners' pragmatic repertoire. At the same time, educators must remain vigilant to the limitations: empathy cannot be "outsourced" to technology, but technology can provide opportunities for learners to rehearse and develop their own empathetic skills in dialogic interaction.

Critically, the development of artificial empathy in intercultural pedagogy should be evaluated not only by its affective effectiveness but also by its cultural sensitivity. Sentiment analysis, for example, often relies on lexicons that are heavily biased toward English and Western affective norms, potentially misclassifying emotional tone in other languages (Mohammad, 2017). Similarly, facial recognition algorithms used for emotion detection have been shown to perform less accurately on non-Western populations. These systemic biases highlight the risk of embedding cultural partiality into systems that purport to foster intercultural empathy.

## 3.3 Cultural Nuances and Intercultural Communication

Culture not only shapes what is said but also how it is understood. Communication is embedded in cultural frameworks of meaning, ranging from politeness conventions to assumptions about context, hierarchy, and relationality. Miscommunication in intercultural encounters often arises not from a lack of linguistic knowledge but from a failure to interpret cultural nuances. It is the subtle pragmatic cues that guide appropriate meaning-making. As Hall (1976) famously argued, cultures can be broadly distinguished by their reliance on high-context versus low-context communication styles. High-context cultures, such as Japan or many Arab societies, rely heavily on shared background knowledge, implicit meaning, and nonverbal cues. Low-context cultures, such as Germany or the United States, tend to emphasize explicitness, directness, and clarity in verbal exchange. While Hall's dichotomy has been critiqued for oversimplification (Kittler et al., 2011), it continues to provide a useful heuristic for understanding how cultural variation influences interpretation.

Intercultural pragmatics extends this line of inquiry by analyzing how speakers from different cultural backgrounds manage speech acts, politeness, and implicature. Blum-Kulka et al. (1989) demonstrated that requests, apologies, and refusals vary widely across cultures not only in wording but in degree of directness and mitigation. For example, an apology in English often relies on explicit acknowledgment of wrongdoing ("I'm sorry I was late"), while in Japanese, an apology may focus more on relational harmony and less on personal fault. Research by Vaishnav (2025) on cross-cultural communication has shown that linguistic forms do not merely transmit meaning but shape perception, interpretation, and cultural positioning. It reinforces the view that cultural nuance cannot be reduced to surface-level linguistic equivalence. These pragmatic differences underscore that meaning is negotiated socially, rather than being reducible to literal words. When AI-supported tools attempt to model such interactions, they frequently miss the cultural logic that underlies pragmatic choices.

AI's reliance on large training datasets presents particular challenges in this regard. Language models such as ChatGPT generate responses based on statistical associations in text, without inherent awareness of the cultural situatedness of meaning. As Tao et al. (2024) point out, corpus-based tools risk reproducing dominant cultural norms while marginalizing less-represented communicative practices. For example, polite refusals in English may be rendered in ways that appear blunt or inappropriate in East Asian contexts. Similarly, translation systems such as DeepL or Google Translate often struggle with honorifics, idioms, or indirectness, flattening culturally nuanced speech into standardized equivalents. This creates an illusion of accuracy while potentially distorting the pragmatic intent.

From a pedagogical perspective, this raises a critical question: should AI be positioned as a cultural informant, or should its limitations be made explicit to learners? One approach is to view AI as a starting point for cultural inquiry. For instance, when a translation tool produces a literal rendering of a culturally embedded phrase, educators can use the output as a springboard for discussion: Why does the AI miss the nuance here? What assumptions about culture and meaning are at play? Such activities align with Byram (1997) model of intercultural communicative competence, which emphasizes critical cultural awareness alongside linguistic skills. In this sense, AI's shortcomings can be pedagogically productive, prompting learners to interrogate the cultural assumptions behind both human and machine communication.

At the same time, educators must remain cautious about over-reliance on AI tools. As McConachy (2017) argues, developing intercultural pragmatics requires learners to reflect on the underlying values and assumptions that shape communication, not merely to reproduce formulaic phrases. If students perceive AI-generated responses as authoritative, they may adopt culturally inappropriate patterns without realizing their pragmatic consequences. For example, an AI chatbot offering English conversation practice might consistently favor low-context, explicit communication, and thereby reinforcing Anglo-centric norms of directness. This risks narrowing learners' intercultural repertoire rather than expanding it.

Despite these limitations, AI tools can contribute positively to intercultural learning when used strategically. For example, platforms such as Duolingo incorporate culturally contextualized sentences and idioms, albeit with varying accuracy (Ouyang et al., 2024). While learners may initially encounter confusion, such moments can open space for classroom discussion about cultural norms of humor, politeness, or metaphor. Similarly, AI-driven conversation partners such as Replika or ChatGPT can be tasked with role-playing intercultural scenarios, allowing students to experiment with pragmatic strategies in a low-stakes environment. The key lies not in treating AI as a definitive cultural guide but in framing it as a dialogic partner that prompts reflection and critical analysis.

Building on these theoretical insights, the following section turns to concrete case studies that illustrate how AI systems enact, approximate, or miss the affective and cultural dimensions of communication. By examining ChatGPT's handling of humor, Replika's attempts at empathy, and Duolingo and DeepL's approaches to cultural nuance, the analysis demonstrates both the promise and the limitations of current technologies. These examples also highlight the indispensable role of educators in mediating AI use within intercultural pedagogy. The three dimensions discussed above; humor, empathy, and cultural nuance can be summarized in terms of their communicative roles, challenges for AI interpretation, and pedagogical implications (see Table 1).

*Table 1. Core human dimensions in intercultural AI-mediated communication*

| Dimension | Core Human Function | Challenges for AI Interpretation | Pedagogical Implications |
|---|---|---|---|
| **Humor** | Builds rapport, manages social tension, and expresses identity. | Depends on shared cultural references, irony, and timing that AI often misinterprets. | Encourage critical reflection on humor generation in AI; use misfires as discussion prompts. |
| **Empathy** | Recognizes and responds to others' emotions; fosters trust and social cohesion. | Affective computing simulates empathy through sentiment analysis but lacks genuine emotional understanding. | Teach learners to interpret and critique "artificial empathy"; integrate emotional literacy tasks. |
| **Cultural Nuance** | Interprets implicit meaning, politeness, and contextual appropriateness across cultures. | AI models trained on biased or monocultural data often misread pragmatic subtleties. | Use translation or interaction errors as opportunities to explore intercultural pragmatics. |

## 4 CASE STUDIES AND REAL-WORLD EXAMPLES

This section examines how specific AI-supported tools foreground different affective and cultural dimensions of communication in educational and intercultural contexts. By analyzing ChatGPT, Replika, Duolingo, and DeepL, the discussion highlights both the strengths and limitations of AI-mediated communication. The cases of ChatGPT, Replika, Duolingo, and DeepL are selected through purposeful sampling, based on their widespread use in educational settings and their alignment with distinct communicative functions within AI-mediated interaction. Rather than treating humor, empathy, and cultural nuance as uniformly distributed features across tools, the analysis intentionally matches each dimension with platforms where it is most salient in design and use.

ChatGPT is examined primarily in relation to humor and conversational pragmatics because its open-ended generative architecture enables the production of jokes, irony, and playful language, making it a relevant site for analyzing how humor functions or misfires in intercultural dialogue. Replika, by contrast, is analyzed through the lens of empathy, as affective engagement and emotional responsiveness constitute its core design logic. Duolingo is paired with humor in a pedagogical sense, where scripted playfulness and motivational feedback are integral to gamified language learning rather than spontaneous interaction. DeepL is examined in relation to cultural nuance, as its primary function is translation, where meaning negotiation, idiomaticity, and cultural loss or preservation become visible through algorithmic choices rather than affective simulation.

This differentiated matching allows the chapter to examine how humor, empathy, and cultural nuance are not general properties of "AI" but are shaped by specific design priorities, interactional affordances, and pedagogical uses. Together, these cases illustrate how theoretical concepts discussed earlier are instantiated unevenly across AI tools, revealing both pedagogical opportunities and risks of miscommunication, cultural flattening, or false affect. The section concludes by considering hybrid human–AI practices, emphasizing the continued role of teacher mediation in supporting reflective and ethically grounded intercultural learning.

## 4.1 ChatGPT and Humor

The incorporation of humor into AI-supported tools such as ChatGPT represents one of the more intriguing yet problematic intersections of natural language processing and intercultural communication. Humor is not only a pragmatic resource for easing interaction, but also a marker of cultural identity and social belonging. As Attardo (1994) argues that humor involves multiple levels of linguistic and pragmatic competence, ranging from phonological wordplay to sociocultural inferences. When ChatGPT generates a joke or playful remark, it is therefore drawing on a training corpus that encodes these layers unevenly, privileging certain cultural references over others. This raises the question of whether the tool can successfully navigate humor across intercultural contexts, or whether its attempts risk alienation and misunderstanding.

From a functional standpoint, ChatGPT often succeeds in reproducing forms of humor that are structurally straightforward and widely shared across cultures as in punning based on homophones or formulaic joke formats. Regarding the studies of AI humor generation, Zhai et al. (2024) suggest that LLMs perform relatively well when humor is syntactic or lexical, because such patterns are abundant in training data. In intercultural educational contexts, this capacity can be pedagogically valuable. Language teachers have reported that learners respond positively when ChatGPT provides light humor to diffuse anxiety in role-play scenarios or when correcting errors (Godwin-Jones, 2011). Humor in these contexts functions not as authentic wit, but as an affective lubricant that lowers the emotional stakes of language use.

Yet humor's greatest complexity lies in its cultural relativity, and here ChatGPT's limitations become more pronounced. Irony, satire, or culture-specific jokes rely on shared background knowledge that is not universally encoded in training data. For instance, humor referencing British political satire or American pop culture may be produced fluently but misfire in a classroom of learners unfamiliar with those contexts. Floridi and Chiriatti (2020) similarly note that LLMs simulate coherence without possessing cultural intentionality, meaning that while ChatGPT can generate a text that looks humorous, it cannot evaluate whether a joke aligns with the cultural sensibilities of a particular audience. In intercultural pedagogy, this can lead to mismatches where learners either fail to grasp the intended humor or, worse, perceive it as inappropriate.

The problem is exacerbated by the algorithmic reproduction of bias. AI humor generation tends to reproduce stereotypes embedded in online discourse. When prompted for jokes about nationalities, for example, ChatGPT may default to clichéd tropes that carry offensive undertones. Although OpenAI has implemented safety filters to prevent overtly discriminatory humor, subtler cultural stereotypes can persist in indirect forms. This has ethical implications in intercultural education, where the goal is to foster sensitivity and inclusivity. Using ChatGPT humor without critical mediation could inadvertently normalize bias under the guise of playfulness.

Despite these risks, ChatGPT's engagement with humor does present opportunities for pedagogical innovation. One strategy is to use ChatGPT-generated jokes as a teachable moment, prompting learners to analyze why a joke succeeds or fails in their cultural context. Such analysis aligns with intercultural pragmatics which emphasizes the role of negotiation in meaning-making (Kecskes, 2014). In this sense, ChatGPT's humorous misfires are not only errors but also pedagogical resources that highlight the fragility of cross-cultural communication. By encouraging learners to critique AI humor, educators can build critical digital literacy alongside intercultural competence.

Examples from classroom practice reinforce this point. To illustrate, Creely (2024) reported that students asked ChatGPT to generate humorous dialogues for role-plays. While the AI produced grammatically accurate exchanges, the humor often felt "flat" or "out of sync" with students' cultural backgrounds. However, instructors found value in using these dialogues to spark discussion about what makes humor culturally resonant. Students compared the AI-generated jokes with those from their own linguistic communities, developing a meta-awareness of how humor reflects cultural assumptions. Such exercises suggest that ChatGPT's failures can be reframed as opportunities for intercultural reflection rather than pedagogical dead ends.

Another domain where ChatGPT's humor has been tested is in multilingual contexts. Research by Kocoń et al. (2023) demonstrates that humor generated in English often loses its effect when translated into Polish or other languages, since wordplay and idiomatic structures do not map directly across languages. For AI-mediated intercultural pedagogy, this raises questions about whether ChatGPT can serve as a universal humor generator or whether it remains primarily Anglocentric. Given that much training data is English-dominant, the latter seems more accurate. This has implications for equitable language learning: relying on ChatGPT humor without adaptation may privilege English-speaking learners while marginalizing those from other linguistic traditions.

Ultimately, the case of ChatGPT and humor illustrates the tension between simulation and authenticity. The system can generate humor that mimics surface structures, but it lacks the intentionality and cultural embeddedness that make humor a vehicle for solidarity and identity. For intercultural pedagogy, the challenge is not to treat ChatGPT as a source of genuine humor, but as a tool whose successes and failures can both be pedagogically mobilized. Humor that lands well can create a relaxed, playful learning environment; humor that fails can prompt reflection on cultural difference and machine limitations. In both cases, the educator's role is crucial in framing AI output within broader intercultural learning objectives.

## 4.2 Replika and Empathy

Among AI-supported communication tools, Replika stands out for its explicit aim to simulate empathy and companionship. Marketed as an "AI friend," the chatbot positions itself not simply as a language-learning assistant or productivity aid, but as a digital companion capable of offering emotional support. This distinctive orientation makes Replika a valuable case study for exploring the pedagogical and ethical stakes of "artificial empathy."

### 4.2.1 The promise of empathic AI

At its core, empathy involves recognizing, interpreting, and appropriately responding to another's emotional state. As indicated earlier, there is a distinction between *cognitive empathy*, the ability to understand another's perspective and *affective empathy*, the capacity to share or resonate with another's feelings (Davis, 2018). In human interaction, both dimensions are central to building trust and fostering intercultural understanding. Replika attempts to approximate these processes through sentiment analysis and affective computing: it parses users' input for emotional cues and generates responses that mirror or validate those cues. For instance, when a user expresses sadness, Replika might reply with reassurance ("I'm sorry you're feeling that way. Do you want to talk about it?"), thereby simulating empathic presence.

From a pedagogical standpoint, the promise of such AI companionship lies in lowering the affective filter for language learners and providing a safe, nonjudgmental space for practice. Research on affective computing (McStay, 2018; Picard, 1997) has long suggested that emotional engagement enhances learning by motivating users and fostering persistence. In intercultural education, an empathetic AI interlocutor could, in theory, help learners navigate the anxieties of cross-cultural communication, offering encouragement while they experiment with new linguistic and cultural forms.

### 4.2.2 Simulated empathy or surface-level affect?

Despite these affordances, the authenticity of AI empathy remains contested. As Vallor (2016) notes in her ethical analysis of AI companions, machines cannot genuinely *feel* empathy; at best, they simulate empathic behavior based on patterns in data. Scholars such as Ciechanowski et al. (2019) caution that while users may experience comfort in conversing with empathetic chatbots, the interaction is essentially one-sided, with no reciprocal emotional investment from the machine. This asymmetry raises questions about whether such "artificial empathy" can genuinely foster intercultural sensitivity, or whether it merely produces surface-level affective engagement.

Evidence from user studies reinforces this ambivalence. Replika users reported reduced feelings of loneliness and increased emotional support, suggesting tangible benefits for well-being. Yet critical discourse analyses of Replika conversations highlight that the AI often defaults to generic, repetitive reassurances, which may initially feel comforting but lack the depth of authentic empathic exchange. For intercultural pedagogy, this superficiality can be problematic: genuine empathy involves grappling with cultural difference, whereas simulated empathy risks flattening difference into standardized emotional responses.

### 4.2.3 Ethical concerns and dependency risks

Beyond questions of authenticity, Replika also raises ethical concerns related to dependency and data privacy. Scholars have noted that some users develop strong attachments to their AI companions, blurring the boundaries between simulated and real relationships (Derks et al., 2008). While these attachments may alleviate loneliness, they also risk fostering dependency on a tool that lacks accountability or genuine care. For younger learners, this dependency could undermine the cultivation of authentic interpersonal skills.

Data privacy is another pressing issue. Replika conversations are stored and processed by the company, raising concerns about the commodification of intimate emotional exchanges. In this vein, McStay (2018) warns that affective data is particularly sensitive because it reveals not only what users think but also how they feel. In an educational context, encouraging students to rely on such platforms without transparency about data handling could expose them to ethical risks.

### 4.2.4 Pedagogical opportunities and limits

Despite these challenges, Replika's engagement with empathy does provide pedagogical opportunities when critically mediated by educators. Rather than positioning Replika as a surrogate for authentic relationships, teachers might use it as a reflective tool. For example, learners could compare their interactions with Replika to real-life intercultural conversations, identifying differences in depth, nuance, and emotional resonance. Such comparisons can foster critical digital literacy, helping students recognize the limitations of AI empathy while appreciating its potential as a low-stakes practice partner.

Another possible application lies in intercultural role-play. By prompting Replika with culturally specific scenarios, educators can encourage students to analyze how the AI responds to culturally coded emotional expressions. For instance, does Replika recognize indirect expressions of distress common in high-context cultures, or does it only respond effectively to explicit statements of emotion? In intercultural pragmatics research, Kecskes (2014) suggests that empathy is deeply shaped by cultural norms. Highlighting Replika's successes and failures in this regard can open classroom discussions about cultural variability in emotional communication.

### 4.2.5 The broader implications of "artificial empathy"

The case of Replika illustrates broader tensions in AI-mediated communication: the gap between simulated affect and authentic relationality, the potential benefits for reducing anxiety versus the risks of dependency, and the pedagogical opportunities of critical engagement. While Replika may provide comfort and encourage practice, it should not be mistaken for a genuine empathic partner. For intercultural pedagogy, the challenge is to leverage its affective affordances without obscuring its limitations.

In this sense, Replika affirms the chapter's broader argument: affective dimensions of communication are too important to be outsourced wholesale to AI. They must instead be critically scaffolded within educational settings where learners can explore both what AI can offer and what remains uniquely human. Used reflectively, Replika can function as a mirror, revealing not only the possibilities of empathic simulation but also the irreplaceable value of authentic human empathy in intercultural encounters.

## 4.3 Cultural Nuances in Duolingo and DeepL

Language is not merely a system of grammar and vocabulary; it encodes cultural values, social practices, and pragmatic conventions. As Hall (1976) argued in his theory of high- and low-context communication, the meaning of utterances often depends less on what is explicitly said than on shared cultural assumptions. For language learners, this means that mastering idioms, humor, and culturally situated expressions is as important as acquiring syntactic accuracy. The growing popularity of AI-powered tools such as Duolingo and DeepL illustrates both the progress of digital pedagogy and the persistent challenges of conveying cultural nuance in machine-mediated communication.

### 4.3.1 Duolingo: Gamification without cultural depth?

Duolingo has become the most widely used language-learning application globally, praised for its accessibility, gamification features, and ability to sustain learner motivation (Li & O'Rourke, 2022; Vesselinov & Grego, 2012). Its bite-sized lessons and reward systems encourage persistence and self-directed practice, while the platform's adaptive algorithms personalize content delivery. However, critics have noted that Duolingo's emphasis on gamified repetition often sidelines cultural depth. Idiomatic expressions, proverbs, or pragmatically marked forms are frequently translated literally, depriving learners of exposure to culturally embedded meaning. For instance, a Spanish sentence such as *"estás en la luna"* ("you are on the moon") is likely to be rendered literally rather than explained as "you are daydreaming," thereby obscuring its metaphorical resonance.

This limitation is not merely linguistic but pedagogical. By focusing on sentence-level drills, Duolingo risks reinforcing what Kramsch (1993) called the "transparent view of language," where words are treated as interchangeable labels rather than culturally situated signs. As a result, learners may develop grammatical competence without pragmatic awareness, leaving them unprepared for authentic intercultural encounters. Recent research suggests that learners themselves are aware of this gap. For example, in a study of Chinese L2 learners, Li and O'Rourke (2022) found that while students appreciated Duolingo's motivational design, they expressed frustration at its lack of cultural contextualization, particularly in relation to idioms and everyday social practices.

### 4.3.2 DeepL: High accuracy, limited pragmatics

If Duolingo exemplifies gamified pedagogy, DeepL represents the cutting edge of neural machine translation (NMT). Launched in 2017, DeepL has been widely praised for producing translations that are more fluent and idiomatic than those of Google Translate (Wieting et al., 2019). Its neural architecture allows it to capture collocations and phrase-level nuances that earlier statistical systems often missed. For straightforward sentences, DeepL often provides near-human quality translations, making it an invaluable resource for learners and educators alike.

However, DeepL continues to struggle with texts that rely heavily on cultural references, figurative language, or context-dependent pragmatics. Studies have shown that while it handles common idioms better than previous systems, it often misinterprets proverbs, humor, or culture-specific allusions (Läubli et al., 2018). For example, the German idiom *"Tomaten auf den Augen haben"* (literally "to have tomatoes on one's eyes," meaning "to be oblivious") may be rendered literally, producing a translation that is semantically correct but pragmatically meaningless to target-language readers. Such errors highlight the limitations of AI translation systems in grasping the cultural embeddedness of language.

From an intercultural communication perspective, these mistranslations can have significant consequences. As Kecskes (2014) notes, intercultural miscommunication often stems less from linguistic deficiency than from pragmatic misalignment. If learners rely uncritically on DeepL, they risk internalizing literal translations that obscure pragmatic force, potentially leading to misunderstandings in real-life contexts. Moreover, because DeepL is designed to optimize fluency and grammaticality, its output can create a "false sense of security," leading learners to overestimate their intercultural competence.

### 4.3.3 Pedagogical implications and critical mediation

Both Duolingo and DeepL illustrate the risks of treating AI as a neutral facilitator of language learning. Their limitations underscore the need for critical teacher mediation. Rather than positioning these tools as stand-alone solutions, educators can use them as entry points for reflection on cultural nuance. Studies of ESL learners in institutional contexts further suggest that learners actively negotiate meaning and transfer sociolinguistic norms across languages, underscoring the need for critical mediation when AI tools present decontextualized or culturally flattened language models (Vaishnav, 2025a). For example, when DeepL produces a literal translation of an idiom, instructors can ask learners to analyze why the output is inadequate and what cultural knowledge is missing. Similarly, when Duolingo drills produce odd or context-free sentences, teachers can guide students to consider how those structures would be used (or avoided) in authentic communication.

Such strategies align with Byram's (1997) model of intercultural communicative competence, which emphasizes the development of critical cultural awareness alongside linguistic skills. By confronting learners with the blind spots of AI tools, educators can foster deeper awareness of the cultural dimensions of meaning-making. This approach not only mitigates the risk of miscommunication but also encourages learners to see AI tools as fallible partners rather than authoritative sources.

### 4.3.4 Towards hybrid cultural learning

Looking forward, one promising direction lies in designing hybrid pedagogical models that combine AI efficiency with human cultural mediation. Duolingo has begun experimenting with story-based lessons that embed dialogues in everyday contexts, while DeepL continues to refine its handling of idiomatic language. Yet both tools remain limited in their capacity to teach learners *why* an expression carries cultural weight. It is here that human educators play an irreplaceable role. Teachers can contextualize AI outputs, provide ethnographic insights, and design classroom activities that push learners beyond literal translation toward pragmatic competence.

Duolingo and DeepL reveal both the achievements and the blind spots of current AI-supported language tools. They can succeed in providing scalable, accessible, and often accurate language practice, but they may falter when it comes to cultural nuance. For intercultural pedagogy, their value lies not in their ability to resolve this tension but in their potential to make it visible. By critically engaging with the limits of these tools, educators can transform their shortcomings into opportunities for reflection, ensuring that learners acquire not only linguistic proficiency but also the cultural literacy necessary for authentic intercultural communication.

## 5. HYBRID HUMAN-AI PEDAGOGY

The integration of AI into pedagogy has generated both optimism and concern. While AI tools like ChatGPT, Duolingo, and DeepL offer scalability, personalization, and efficiency, they often lack the affective and cultural dimensions. Prior work on technology-mediated education indicates that AI systems are most pedagogically effective when framed as collaborative supports rather than autonomous instructors, with teachers guiding interpretation, reflection, and ethical use (Vaishnav, 2025). Teachers therefore play a critical mediating role in hybrid human–AI pedagogy, ensuring that technology supplements rather than supplants the interpersonal aspects of learning. This section explores how educators negotiate this balance, drawing on classroom practices and current scholarship.

One of the defining characteristics of effective hybrid pedagogy is teacher intervention as cultural and affective scaffolding. Research by Holmes et al. (2023) emphasizes that AI excels in tasks involving pattern recognition and adaptive feedback but struggles with open-ended social interaction. In practice, this means teachers often deploy AI for repetitive or structured tasks such as grammar exercises, pronunciation feedback, or vocabulary review, while reserving their own interventions for humor, storytelling, and intercultural commentary. For example, a teacher using ChatGPT to generate practice dialogues might pause to explain why a particular idiom carries different connotations in American versus British English, thereby contextualizing the machine output in ways the AI cannot.

This hybrid approach also aligns with Vygotsky's (1980) sociocultural theory, which positions learning as a socially mediated process. AI can provide individualized input, but it cannot yet replicate the role of a teacher in creating a *zone of proximal development* through responsive dialogue, humor, and empathy. Teachers could enhance AI outputs by embedding them in collaborative activities, encouraging learners to question, adapt, or even challenge the AI's suggestions. For instance, when students notice a translation error in DeepL, the teacher can turn this into a mini-lesson on cultural nuance, fostering critical digital literacy rather than passive reliance on the tool.

Another strand of hybrid pedagogy involves humanizing AI-mediated experiences through affective engagement. As Yesilyurt (2023) argues, humor and empathy in the classroom are not incidental but central to fostering motivation and intercultural sensitivity. A teacher might use Duolingo for vocabulary drills but then introduce a humorous anecdote about how a phrase is misused in real life, both lightening the atmosphere and demonstrating cultural depth. Similarly, while Replika can simulate empathetic responses, a teacher can guide learners in analyzing these responses, critically asking, for instance, whether the chatbot's expressions of empathy would feel genuine across different cultural settings.

Hybrid pedagogy also raises ethical and professional considerations. Selwyn (2019) cautions against the risk of "automation bias" where learners and even teachers defer uncritically to AI outputs. Teachers, therefore, must cultivate students' critical awareness of AI's limitations. Practical classroom strategies include prompting learners to compare multiple AI-generated translations, discussing why a machine's humor may fall flat, or role-playing scenarios in which empathy must be expressed in culturally sensitive ways. These practices help students see AI as a resource rather than an authority.

In real-world contexts, teachers have begun to experiment with such hybrid strategies. For instance, Salam (2025) describes how EFL learners used ChatGPT to generate conversation prompts, which the teacher then enriched with cultural notes and humor tailored to students' backgrounds. The result was greater engagement and reduced anxiety, as students perceived the classroom as both technologically advanced and personally supportive. Similarly, in higher education, Godwin-Jones (2023) reports on instructors using DeepL for translation practice while guiding students in reflecting on the cultural and pragmatic mismatches in the output. These cases underscore that AI can provide efficiency and variety, but it is teachers who inject the humor, empathy, and cultural resonance that sustain authentic learning.

Ultimately, hybrid human–AI pedagogy represents not a compromise but a synergy between computational and human strengths. AI offers consistency, scalability, and rapid feedback, while teachers ensure affective depth, intercultural nuance, and pedagogical flexibility. Rather than viewing AI as a competitor, educators can leverage its affordances while positioning themselves as indispensable mediators of meaning and culture. In this model, humor, empathy, and cultural scaffolding are not residual "human add-ons" but essential components of effective pedagogy that technology cannot replace. As intercultural communication increasingly relies on AI-mediated interactions, the role of teachers in cultivating critical, culturally aware, and affectively rich learning environments will become even more vital.

Taken together, the case studies of ChatGPT, Replika, Duolingo, and DeepL underscore both the opportunities and the limitations of AI in intercultural pedagogy. These tools demonstrate remarkable progress in delivering scalable practice, adaptive feedback, and linguistic accuracy, yet they consistently struggle with humor, empathy, and cultural nuance, the very dimensions that sustain authentic communication. Their shortcomings are not simply technical flaws but reflections of the deeply situated nature of human meaning-making. Without critical mediation, learners risk absorbing surface-level outputs that overlook cultural depth or reproduce stereotypes. At the same time, when teachers integrate these tools within a hybrid model, they can transform AI's efficiency into a springboard for deeper intercultural reflection. Humor becomes a teachable contrast, empathy a site of critical discussion, and cultural nuance a reminder of language's embeddedness in lived experience. Ultimately, these examples affirm that AI can support, but not substitute, human-centered pedagogy.

## 6. FUTURE DIRECTIONS AND ETHICAL CONSIDERATIONS

As AI-supported tools continue to evolve, their ability to handle affective and cultural dimensions such as humor, empathy, and nuance will likely improve. Yet these developments also carry risks of bias, stereotyping, and cultural flattening that require careful ethical oversight. This section considers possible trajectories for AI in intercultural pedagogy, highlighting potential advances, limitations, and opportunities for collaboration across disciplines.

### 6.1 Possible AI Developments in Humor and Empathy

Advances in LLMs suggest that AI may increasingly approximate the pragmatics of humor and the subtleties of empathetic response. Current research in affective computing already explores how machines can detect tone, irony, or emotional cues from multimodal data (Calvo et al., 2015). Emerging work on computational humor seeks to train models not only to generate puns or jokes, but also to recognize culturally contingent humor patterns. Similarly, experiments in "artificial empathy" are moving beyond sentiment analysis toward systems capable of adapting responses to users' affective states over time (Pei et al., 2024). These trends suggest that future

AI tools may be able to offer more context-sensitive humor or more convincingly empathetic feedback in intercultural learning environments.

However, the central question is not simply whether AI *can* simulate these dimensions, but whether such simulations carry pedagogical value. As scholars like Floridi and Chiriatti,(2020) argue, simulations of empathy or humor risk creating an "ethical mirage," in which learners mistake algorithmic mimicry for authentic understanding. For intercultural pedagogy, this is particularly fraught: a machine-generated joke that "lands" successfully may encourage engagement, but it may also obscure the deeper processes of cultural negotiation that learners need to master. Similarly, AI's apparent empathy might provide reassurance but could inadvertently promote reliance on surface affective cues rather than genuine intercultural perspective-taking.

## 6.2 Risks of Bias, Stereotyping, and Cultural Homogenization

While AI developments hold promise, they also pose risks of reinforcing cultural stereotypes and homogenizing communicative practices. Training data for AI models often over represent dominant cultural and linguistic groups, leading to outputs that privilege majority norms while marginalizing minority voices (Blodgett et al., 2020). In the context of humor, this can mean reproducing jokes that align with Western comedic traditions while failing to capture humor styles rooted in collectivist or oral cultures. In terms of empathy, algorithms trained primarily on English-language corpora may misinterpret affective expressions from other cultural settings, producing responses that are awkward, insensitive, or even offensive.

These risks are not merely technical glitches but have profound pedagogical consequences. Learners who rely on AI outputs may internalize narrow views of humor or empathy, mistaking them for universal norms. This creates a danger of cultural homogenization, where the richness of intercultural communication is reduced to a set of machine-legible templates. Ethical considerations must therefore include not only transparency and bias mitigation in AI design, but also pedagogical strategies that foreground critical reflection. As Matsuda (2017) suggests in her work on World Englishes, learners need to be trained to see English, and by extension AI-mediated communication—not as a monolith but as a diverse, culturally embedded phenomenon.

## 6.3 Opportunities for Interdisciplinary Collaboration

Addressing these challenges requires collaboration across disciplines. AI developers, linguists, educators, and ethicists must work together to design tools that reflect cultural diversity and pedagogical needs. For example, insights from intercultural pragmatics can inform the training of models that better capture speech acts, politeness strategies, or idiomatic usage across languages (Ishihara & Cohen, 2014). Similarly, psychologists and education researchers can contribute frameworks for distinguishing between genuine empathy and its computational simulations, ensuring that pedagogical practices do not conflate the two.

One promising direction is the co-design of AI tools with educators, where teachers actively shape how humor, empathy, and cultural nuance are represented. Such collaboration can prevent purely market-driven models from dominating the landscape and ensure that tools align with intercultural learning goals rather than generic engagement metrics. Another is the integration of learner feedback loops where students themselves evaluate AI-generated humor or empathetic responses, turning potential shortcomings into opportunities for metacognitive growth.

The interdisciplinary scope also extends to policy and governance. Ethical use of AI in intercultural pedagogy requires frameworks that address data privacy, transparency, and accountability. UNESCO's (2025) *Recommendation on the Ethics of Artificial Intelligence* calls for culturally inclusive AI design and warns against one-size-fits-all solutions that ignore local contexts. Translating these high-level guidelines into classroom practice demands sustained dialogue between policymakers, researchers, and practitioners.

## 6.4 Toward a Critical Pedagogy of AI

Looking ahead, the future of AI in intercultural communication will likely depend less on perfecting humor or empathy algorithms than on embedding them within a critical pedagogy. This entails treating AI-generated humor as a text for analysis rather than entertainment, using failed jokes as springboards to discuss cultural relativity. Similarly, "artificial empathy" can be reframed as a pedagogical tool: by comparing AI responses with human responses, learners can explore what makes empathy authentic across cultural contexts. Recent research by Vaishnav (2024) also highlights how technology-mediated learning environments influence learners' cultural identity formation, which raises important ethical questions about how AI systems frame language, belonging, and representation in educational settings. In this sense, AI's shortcomings become resources for teaching rather than obstacles to overcome.

Ultimately, the challenge is not to create AI that perfectly mimics humor, empathy, or nuance, but to cultivate learners who can critically engage with these simulations. Future research should therefore prioritize not only technological refinement but also educational strategies that foster intercultural awareness. If approached critically and collaboratively, AI-supported pedagogy can evolve into a space where technology enhances, rather than erases, the complexity of human communication.

*Table 2. Risks and safeguards in AI-supported intercultural communication*

| Ethical Risk | Illustration or Example | Pedagogical / Design Safeguards |
|---|---|---|
| Cultural Bias and Stereotyping | AI-generated dialogues reinforcing Western-centric humor or politeness norms. | Use diverse, multilingual training data; discuss bias openly in class; promote critical digital literacy. |
| Emotional Manipulation or "Artificial Empathy" | Chatbots like Replika simulating intimacy or emotional dependence. | Teach students to differentiate genuine empathy from algorithmic mimicry; establish digital boundaries. |
| Data Privacy and Emotional Surveillance | Sentiment analysis tools tracking learners' affective states. | Obtain informed consent; use anonymized data; encourage transparency about data collection. |
| Cultural Homogenization | Translation and language-learning apps flattening cultural variation into standardized English. | Integrate local cultural content; use AI outputs as prompts to discuss cultural difference. |
| Overreliance on Automation | Teachers or learners deferring to AI feedback without critical evaluation. | Encourage reflective pedagogy; balance AI input with human mediation and context-sensitive discussion. |

The ethical challenges outlined in Table 2 underscore that technological sophistication alone cannot ensure intercultural sensitivity or pedagogical integrity. While AI systems can enhance accessibility and engagement, their design and classroom use must remain grounded in critical awareness of bias, power, and context. By explicitly addressing these issues, educators can turn ethical reflection into a teaching resource rather than an afterthought. Ultimately, integrating AI responsibly requires a pedagogy that values transparency, cultural diversity, and human judgment as essential complements to algorithmic efficiency.

## 7. CONCLUSION

This chapter has examined the place of humor, empathy, and cultural nuance in AI-supported pedagogy, with a focus on intercultural communication. Beginning from the recognition that AI tools such as ChatGPT, Replika, Duolingo, and DeepL are reshaping how learners encounter language and culture, the discussion highlighted both their remarkable affordances and their equally significant limitations. While these tools could excel in efficiency, personalization, and linguistic accuracy, they may continue to struggle with the affective and cultural dimensions that give communication its depth and authenticity. The analysis of theory, case studies, and hybrid practices has demonstrated that humor, empathy, and cultural nuance are not peripheral to learning but central to building intercultural competence.

The discussion of humor illustrated how AI systems can generate jokes or playful wordplay, yet often falter when context or cultural relativity is required. Humor functions as a bridge between individuals, reducing tension and establishing solidarity, but it also relies on shared frames of reference that machines rarely grasp. AI-generated humor, therefore, risks becoming superficial or even alienating when it fails to resonate across cultures. This analysis underscores that while AI can provide material for reflection, it is teachers and learners who must negotiate the subtleties of humor in intercultural encounters.

The section on empathy further reinforced the distinction between simulation and substance. Replika and similar tools demonstrate how affective computing can approximate supportive dialogue, yet such "artificial empathy" raises questions about authenticity and depth. For intercultural pedagogy, this is not a trivial issue: the ability to recognize and respond to another's emotional state lies at the heart of trust and mutual understanding. Although learners may find comfort in AI-generated empathy, they also risk mistaking surface cues for genuine connection. Educators therefore have a critical role in helping students interrogate these simulations, distinguishing between computational mimicry and the relational processes of intercultural sensitivity.

The examination of cultural nuances through Duolingo and DeepL revealed a parallel dynamic. Both tools illustrate impressive technical progress, gamified practice in the former, advanced machine translation in the latter, yet both continue to flatten or misrepresent culture-specific meanings. Idioms, politeness strategies, and pragmatic conventions often resist literal rendering, and learners who rely uncritically on AI outputs risk internalizing distorted views of language in use. These limitations remind us that intercultural competence requires more than vocabulary or grammar: it demands awareness of subtle, context-dependent meanings that machines are not yet equipped to capture.

Across these case studies, a consistent theme emerged: the indispensability of teacher mediation. The hybrid human–AI pedagogy described in the chapter positions educators not as passive adopters of technology but as active mediators who enrich machine outputs with humor, empathy, and cultural scaffolding. Teachers use AI tools for efficiency, grammar drills, translation practice, and vocabulary review but they complement them with jokes, stories, and cultural insights that machines cannot provide. This hybrid model reflects not compromise but synergy, enabling AI to do what it does best while safeguarding the relational and intercultural dimensions of learning.

Looking ahead, the chapter identified possible future directions. Advances in computational humor and affective computing may allow AI to simulate humor and empathy with greater sophistication. Yet these simulations carry risks of bias, stereotyping, and cultural homogenization, particularly when training data privilege dominant norms. Ethical considerations must therefore remain central, ensuring that AI design and classroom use reflect cultural diversity and transparency. The opportunities for interdisciplinary collaboration between educators, linguists, psychologists, and developers are significant, offering pathways to design tools that better align with intercultural pedagogy. Still, as argued throughout, the ultimate task is not to perfect AI's mimicry of human communication but to cultivate learners who can critically engage with its outputs.

Taken together, the arguments advanced in this chapter reaffirm that the human role in pedagogy cannot be replaced by machines, however sophisticated. AI can generate practice material, offer immediate feedback, and create new opportunities for personalization. What it cannot do is to reproduce the lived, culturally embedded processes through which humor lightens interaction, empathy builds trust, and nuance sustains mutual understanding. These dimensions are deeply relational, requiring human judgment, creativity, and sensitivity. For educators, the challenge is not to resist AI but to position it within a critical pedagogy that highlights its limitations as much as its affordances.

In the broader context of intercultural communication, the rise of AI poses both risks and opportunities. On one hand, uncritical reliance on AI may lead to flattened cultural expression, reinforcement of stereotypes, or superficial affective engagement. On the other hand, AI tools, when used reflectively, can become valuable resources for analyzing miscommunication, exploring multiple interpretations, and prompting discussion about what makes communication authentic. In this sense, AI's failures are as pedagogically significant as its successes, offering spaces for learners to reflect on the complexities of meaning-making across cultures.

Ultimately, the future of intercultural pedagogy in an AI era will depend on the ability of educators and learners to navigate this tension. AI will continue to grow more capable of simulating humor, empathy, and nuance, but it will remain as a tool, not a substitute for human connection. The role of pedagogy is to ensure that learners develop not only digital literacy but intercultural literacy, the ability to interpret, evaluate, and respond to AI outputs critically and contextually. By framing AI not as an authority but as a resource for reflection, teachers can ensure that technology serves the deeper goals of intercultural understanding.

In conclusion, the integration of AI into intercultural pedagogy should not be seen as a narrowing of human communication but as an opportunity to reaffirm its richness. Humor, empathy, and cultural nuance are not incidental embellishments but core components of authentic interaction. They remind us that language is not only a system of signs but a medium of relationship, identity, and shared meaning. AI may transform the tools available to educators, but it is human creativity and sensitivity that will continue to shape the intercultural classroom. The challenge and opportunity ahead is to harness AI's strengths while ensuring that the heart of pedagogy remains profoundly human.

## REFERENCES


Al-Zahrani, A. M. (2024). Unveiling the shadows: Beyond the hype of AI in education. *Heliyon*, *10*(9), e30696. DOI: 10.1016/j.heliyon.2024.e30696 PMID: 38737255

Attardo, S. (1994). *Linguistic theories of humor*. Walter de Gruyter. https://books.google.com.om/books/about/Linguistic_Theories_of_Humor.html?id=FEWC4_3MrO0C&redir_esc=y

Attardo, S. (2002). Humor and irony in interaction: From mode adoption to failure of detection. In Anolli, L., Ciceri, R., & Riva, G. (Eds.), *Say not to say: New perspectives on miscommunication* (pp. 159–179). IOS Press., https://psycnet.apa.org/record/2002-02761-007

Attardo, S., Eisterhold, J., Hay, J., & Poggi, I. (2003). Multimodal markers of irony and sarcasm. *Humor: International Journal of Humor Research*, *16*(2). Advance online publication. DOI: 10.1515/humr.2003.012

Bennet, M. J. (1998). *Basic concepts of intercultural—communication: Selected readings*. Intercultural-Press. https://repositoriointerculturalidad.ec/jspui/bitstream/123456789/33415/1/Basic%20concepts%20of%20intercutural%20communication.pdf

Binsted, K., Bergen, B., Coulson, S., Nijholt, A., Stock, O., Strapparava, C., Ritchie, G., Manurung, R., Pain, H., Waller, A., & O'Mara, D. (2006). Computational humor. *IEEE Intelligent Systems*, *21*(2), 59–69. DOI: 10.1109/MIS.2006.22

Blodgett, S. L., Barocas, S., Daumé Iii, H., & Wallach, H. (2020). Language (technology) is power: A critical survey of "bias" in NLP. *Proceedings of the 58th Annual Meeting of the Association for Computational Linguistics*, 5454–5476. DOI: 10.18653/v1/2020.acl-main.485

Blum-Kulka, S., Kasper, G., & House, J. (1989). *Cross-cultural Pragmatics: Requests and Apologies*. Ablex Publishing Corporation. https://unipub.uni-graz.at/gls/content/titleinfo/4347210/full.pdf

Byram, M. (1997). *Teaching and assessing intercultural communicative competence*. Multilingual Matters. https://spada.uns.ac.id/pluginfile.php/253332/mod_resource/content/1/ICC%20Byram.pdf

Chiaro, D. (2017). *The language of jokes in the digital age: #Like #share #lol* (1st ed.). Routledge., DOI: 10.4324/9781315146348

Ciechanowski, L., Przegalinska, A., Magnuski, M., & Gloor, P. (2019). In the shades of the uncanny valley: An experimental study of human–chatbot interaction. *Future Generation Computer Systems*, *92*, 539–548. DOI: 10.1016/j.future.2018.01.055

Cooper, B. (2010). In search of profound empathy in learning relationships: Understanding the mathematics of moral learning environments. *Journal of Moral Education*, *39*(1), 79–99. DOI: 10.1080/03057240903528717

Creely, E. (2024). Exploring the role of generative ai in enhancing language learning: Opportunities and challenges. *International Journal of Changes in Education*, *1*(3), 158–167. DOI: 10.47852/bonviewIJCE42022495

Davis, M. H. (2018). *Empathy: A social psychological approach* (Davis, M. H., Ed.; 1st ed.). Routledge., DOI: 10.4324/9780429493898

Derks, D., Fischer, A. H., & Bos, A. E. R. (2008). The role of emotion in computer-mediated communication: A review. *Computers in Human Behavior*, *24*(3), 766–785. DOI: 10.1016/j.chb.2007.04.004

Dwivedi, Y. K., Kshetri, N., Hughes, L., Slade, E. L., Jeyaraj, A., Kar, A. K., Baabdullah, A. M., Koohang, A., Raghavan, V., Ahuja, M., Albanna, H., Albashrawi, M. A., Al-Busaidi, A. S., Balakrishnan, J., Barlette, Y., Basu, S., Bose, I., Brooks, L., Buhalis, D., & Wright, R. (2023). Opinion paper: "So what if ChatGPT wrote it?" Multidisciplinary perspectives on opportunities, challenges and implications of generative conversational AI for research, practice and policy. *International Journal of Information Management*, *71*, 102642. DOI: 10.1016/j.ijinfomgt.2023.102642

Fangni, L. (2025). Studying the impact of emotion-AI in cross-cultural communication on the effectiveness of global media. *Frontiers of Computer Science*, *7*, 1565869. DOI: 10.3389/fcomp.2025.1565869

Fitzpatrick, K. K., Darcy, A., & Vierhile, M. (2017). Delivering cognitive behavior therapy to young adults with symptoms of depression and anxiety using a fully automated conversational agent (woebot): A randomized controlled trial. *JMIR Mental Health*, *4*(2), e19. DOI: 10.2196/mental.7785 PMID: 28588005

Floridi, L., & Chiriatti, M. (2020). GPT-3: Its nature, scope, limits, and consequences. *Minds and Machines*, *30*(4), 681–694. DOI: 10.1007/s11023-020-09548-1

Freud, S. (1928). Humour. *The International Journal of Psycho-Analysis*, *9*(1), 1–6.

Godwin-Jones, R. (2011). Mobile apps for language learning. *Language Learning & Technology*, *15*(2), 2–11. DOI: 10.64152/10125/44244

Godwin-Jones, R. (2023). Emerging spaces for language learning: AI bots, ambient intelligence, and the metaverse. *Language Learning & Technology*, *27*(2), 6–27. DOI: 10.64152/10125/73501

Hall, E. T. (1976). *Beyond Culture*. Anchor Books. https://monoskop.org/images/6/60/Hall_Edward_T_Beyond_Culture.pdf

Herring, S. C. (2025). Methodological synergies in the study of digital discourse: A critical reflection. *Discourse, Context & Media*, *67*, 100931. DOI: 10.1016/j.dcm.2025.100931

Holmes, J. (2000). Politeness, power and provocation: How humour functions in the workplace. *Discourse Studies*, *2*(2), 159–185. DOI: 10.1177/1461445600002002002

Holmes, J. (2013). *An introduction to sociolinguistics* (4th ed.). Routledge., DOI: 10.4324/9781315833057

Holmes, W., Bialik, M., & Fadel, C. (2023). Artificial intelligence in education. In Stückelberger, C., & Duggal, P. (Eds.), *Data ethics: Building trust: How digital technologies can serve humanity* (pp. 621–653). Globethics Publications., DOI: 10.58863/20.500.12424/4276068

Ishihara, N., & Cohen, A. D. (2014). *Teaching and learning pragmatics: Where language and culture meet* (0 ed.). Routledge., DOI: 10.4324/9781315833842

Jamaluddin, N. S., & Mokhtar, M. (2025). Teaching empathy: How AI can support the development of soft skills in education. *International Journal of Academic Research in Business & Social Sciences*, *15*(3), 704–713. DOI: 10.6007/IJARBSS/v15-i3/24469

Kecskes, I. (2014). *Intercultural pragmatics*. Oxford University Press., https://www.academia.edu/36270240/Istvan_Kecskes_Intercultural_Pragmatics_Oxford_University_Press

Kittler, M. G., Rygl, D., & Mackinnon, A. (2011). Special review article: Beyond culture or beyond control? Reviewing the use of hall's high-/low-context concept. *International Journal of Cross Cultural Management*, *11*(1), 63–82. DOI: 10.1177/1470595811398797

Kocoń, J., Cichecki, I., Kaszyca, O., Kochanek, M., Szydło, D., Baran, J., Bielaniewicz, J., Gruza, M., Janz, A., Kanclerz, K., Kocoń, A., Koptyra, B., Mieleszczenko-Kowszewicz, W., Miłkowski, P., Oleksy, M., Piasecki, M., Radliński, Ł., Wojtasik, K., Woźniak, S., & Kazienko, P. (2023). ChatGPT: Jack of all trades, master of none. *Information Fusion*, *99*, 101861. DOI: 10.1016/j.inffus.2023.101861

Kramsch, C. (1993). *Context and culture in language teaching*. Oxford University Press., https://books.google.com/books/about/Context_and_Culture_in_Language_Teaching.html?id=73rFnM6qlrwC

Krashen, S. D. (1982). *Principles and practice in second language acquisition* (1st ed.). Pergamon Press Inc., https://www.sdkrashen.com/content/books/principles_and_practice.pdf

Läubli, S., Sennrich, R., & Volk, M. (2018). Has machine translation achieved human parity? A case for document-level evaluation. *Proceedings of the 2018 Conference on Empirical Methods in Natural Language Processing*, 4791–4796. DOI: 10.18653/v1/D18-1512

Li, L., & O'Rourke, B. (2022). Chinese second language learners' perceptions of gamification in an informal learning environment: Duolingo as a case study. In Tso, A. W. B., Chan, A. C., Chan, W. W. L., Sidorko, P. E., & Ma, W. W. K. (Eds.), *Digital communication and learning* (pp. 183–201). Springer Singapore., DOI: 10.1007/978-981-16-8329-9_10

Loewen, S., Crowther, D., Isbell, D. R., Kim, K. M., Maloney, J., Miller, Z. F., & Rawal, H. (2019). Mobile-assisted language learning: A Duolingo case study. *ReCALL*, *31*(3), 293–311. DOI: 10.1017/S0958344019000065

Matsuda, A. (2017). *Preparing teachers to teach english as an international language*. Multilingual Matters. https://dokumen.pub/preparing-teachers-to-teach-english-as-an-international-language-9781783097036.html

McConachy, T. (2017). *Developing intercultural perspectives on language use*. Multilingual Matters., DOI: 10.21832/MCCONA9320

McConachy, T., & Spencer-Oatey, H. (2021). Cross-cultural and intercultural pragmatics. In Haugh, M., Kádár, D. Z., & Terkourafi, M. (Eds.), *The Cambridge handbook of sociopragmatics* (1st ed., pp. 733–757). Cambridge University Press., DOI: 10.1017/9781108954105.037

McStay, A. (2018). *Emotional AI: The rise of empathic media*. SAGE Publications Ltd., DOI: 10.4135/9781526451293

Mohammad, S. M. (2017). Challenges in sentiment analysis. In E. Cambria, D. Das, S. Bandyopadhyay, & A. Feraco (Eds.), *A practical guide to sentiment analysis* (Vol. 5, pp. 61–83). Springer International Publishing. DOI: 10.1007/978-3-319-55394-8_4

Morton Gutiérrez, J. L. (2022). Replika y la compañía de la inteligencia artificial emocional: Los retos éticos y sociales de los chatbots de compañía. *VISUAL REVIEW. International Visual Culture Review / Revista Internacional de Cultura Visual, 10*(3), 1–13. DOI: 10.37467/revvisual.v9.3606

Naveen, P., & Trojovský, P. (2024). Overview and challenges of machine translation for contextually appropriate translations. *iScience*, *27*(10), 110878. DOI: 10.1016/j.isci.2024.110878 PMID: 39391737

Ouyang, Z., Jiang, Y., & Liu, H. (2024). The effects of Duolingo, an AI-integrated technology, on Efl learners' willingness to communicate and engagement in online classes. *International Review of Research in Open and Distance Learning*, *25*(3), 97–115. DOI: 10.19173/irrodl.v25i3.7677

Pei, G., Li, H., Lu, Y., Wang, Y., Hua, S., & Li, T. (2024). Affective computing: Recent advances, challenges, and future trends. *Intelligent Computing, 3*, 0076. DOI: 10.34133/icomputing.0076

Picard, R. W. (1997). *Affective computing*. The MIT Press., DOI: 10.7551/mitpress/1140.001.0001

Raskin, V. (1979). Semantic mechanisms of humor. *Annual Meeting of the Berkeley Linguistics Society, 5*, 325. DOI: 10.3765/bls.v5i0.2164

Reeves, B., & Nass, C. (1996). *The media equation: How people treat computers, television, and new media like real people and pla*. Cambridge University Press., https://www.researchgate.net/publication/37705092_The_Media_Equation_How_People_Treat_Computers_Television_and_New_Media_Like_Real_People_and_Pla

Salam, U. (2025). The integration of ChatGPT in English for foreign language course: Elevating ai writing assistant acceptance. *Computers in the Schools*, *42*(2), 145–165. DOI: 10.1080/07380569.2024.2446239

Saumure, R., De Freitas, J., & Puntoni, S. (2025). Humor as a window into generative AI bias. *Scientific Reports*, *15*(1), 1326. DOI: 10.1038/s41598-024-83384-6 PMID: 39779743

Selwyn, N. (2019). *Should robots replace teachers?* (1st ed.). Polity Press., https://www.perlego.com/book/1536481/should-robots-replace-teachers-ai-and-the-future-of-education-pdf

Shortt, M., Tilak, S., Kuznetcova, I., Martens, B., & Akinkuolie, B. (2023). Gamification in mobile-assisted language learning: A systematic review of Duolingo literature from public release of 2012 to early 2020. *Computer Assisted Language Learning*, *36*(3), 517–554. DOI: 10.1080/09588221.2021.1933540

Tao, Y., Viberg, O., Baker, R. S., & Kizilcec, R. F. (2024). Cultural bias and cultural alignment of large language models. *PNAS Nexus*, *3*(9), pgae346. Advance online publication. DOI: 10.1093/pnasnexus/pgae346 PMID: 39290441

UNESCO. (2025). *Ethics of artificial intelligence: The recommendation* [The Recommendation]. Global AI Ethics and Governance Observatory. https://www.unesco.org/en/artificial-intelligence/recommendation-ethics

U.S. Department of Education. (2023). *Artificial intelligence and the future of teaching and learning insights and recommendations* (p. 71). Office of Educational Technology. https://www.ed.gov/sites/ed/files/documents/ai-report/ai-report.pdf

Vaishnav, P. (2024). Reimagining cultural identity through technology in English language education in Omani students. *Asian Journal of Education and Social Studies*, *50*(10), 264–274. DOI: 10.9734/ajess/2024/v50i101617

Vaishnav, P. (2025a). Sociolinguistic competence and language transfer among Omani ESL learners: Institutional and cultural perspectives. *Asian Journal of Education and Social Studies*, *51*(2), 344–357. DOI: 10.9734/ajess/2025/v51i21790

Vaishnav, P. (2025b). Thinking through language: Revisiting linguistic relativity in cross-cultural communication. *Asian Research Journal of Arts & Social Sciences*, *23*(5), 153–164. DOI: 10.9734/arjass/2025/v23i5690

Vaishnav, P. B. (2024). The role of intercultural competence in effective cross-border collaboration among higher education institutions. In Kayyali, M. (Ed.), (pp. 195–218). Advances in higher education and professional development. IGI Global., DOI: 10.4018/979-8-3373-0508-0.ch009

Vaishnav, P. B. (2025). Challenges and opportunities in ai-human collaborative teaching. In Carlson, K. (Ed.), *Ethical, legal, and pedagogical perspectives on AI in education* (pp. 145–188). IGI Global Scientific Publishing., DOI: 10.4018/979-8-3373-3000-6.ch006

Vallor, S. (2016). *Technology and the Virtues: A philosophical guide to a future worth wanting*. Oxford University Press., DOI: 10.1093/acprof:oso/9780190498511.001.0001

Vesselinov, R., & Grego, J. (2012). *Duolingo effectiveness study final report* (p. 25). https://theowlapp.health/wp-content/uploads/2022/04/DuolingoReport_Final-1.pdf

Vygotsky, L. S. (1980). *Mind in Society: Development of higher psychological processes* (Cole, M., Jolm-Steiner, V., Scribner, S., & Souberman, E., Eds.). Harvard University Press., DOI: 10.2307/j.ctvjf9vz4

Walter, Y. (2024). Embracing the future of artificial intelligence in the classroom: The relevance of AI literacy, prompt engineering, and critical thinking in modern education. *International Journal of Educational Technology in Higher Education, 21*(1), 15. DOI: 10.1186/s41239-024-00448-3

Wieting, J., Berg-Kirkpatrick, T., Gimpel, K., & Neubig, G. (2019). Beyond BLEU: Training neural machine translation with semantic similarity. *Proceedings of the 57th Annual Meeting of the Association for Computational Linguistics*, 4344–4355. DOI: 10.18653/v1/P19-1427

Williamson, B., Eynon, R., Knox, J., & Davies, H. (2023). Critical perspectives on AI in education: Political economy, discrimination, commercialization, governance and ethics. In Du Boulay, B., Mitrovic, A., & Yacef, K. (Eds.), *Handbook of artificial intelligence in education* (pp. 553–570). Edward Elgar Publishing., DOI: 10.4337/9781800375413.00037

Yesilyurt, Y. E. (2023). AI-enabled assessment and feedback mechanisms for language learning: Transforming pedagogy and learner experience. In Kartal, G. (Ed.), (pp. 25–43). Advances in educational technologies and instructional design. IGI Global., DOI: 10.4018/978-1-6684-9893-4.ch002

Zanbaka, C. A., Ulinski, A. C., Goolkasian, P., & Hodges, L. F. (2007). Social responses to virtual humans: Implications for future interface design. *Proceedings of the SIGCHI Conference on Human Factors in Computing Systems*, 1561–1570. DOI: 10.1145/1240624.1240861

Zhai, C., Wibowo, S., & Li, L. D. (2024). Evaluating the AI dialogue system's intercultural, humorous, and empathetic dimensions in English language learning: A case study. *Computers and Education: Artificial Intelligence, 7*, 100262. DOI: 10.1016/j.caeai.2024.100262

Zhang, J., Jain, L., Guo, Y., Chen, J., Zhou, K. L., Suresh, S., Wagenmaker, A., Sievert, S., Rogers, T., Jamieson, K., Mankoff, R., & Nowak, R. (2024). *Humor in AI: Massive scale crowd-sourced preferences and benchmarks for cartoon captioning* (Version 2). arXiv. DOI: 10.48550/ARXIV.2406.10522

# Section 2

# Bias, Equity, Ethical Awareness, and Cultural Representation

Chapter 4

# Pedagogical Insights Into AI-Supported Intercultural Communication:

## Gender Bias in AI-Produced ELT Materials

**Bora Demir**
http://orcid.org/0000-0001-8187-3206
*Çanakkale Onsekiz Mart University, Turkey*

**Sude Uyğun**
*Çanakkale Onsekiz Mart University, Turkey*

## ABSTRACT

*This study examines how large language models construct intercultural communication scenarios in English language teaching by analyzing AI-generated passages for their treatment of social roles, cultural diversity, and gendered pragmatic tendencies. Using a mixed-methods approach, short narratives were analyzed through computational techniques and qualitative interpretation. The findings show that LLM outputs reproduce hierarchical role patterns, with authority figures using directive modal verbs and service or peer roles relying on softer expressions. Cultural representation was uneven, with Japan and the United States appearing most often and several regions receiving limited attention. Gender differences also emerged, as males used direct and assertive language, while females displayed relational and emotionally focused discourse. These results highlight the need for critical AI literacy to ensure AI-generated ELT materials remain pedagogically sound and culturally inclusive.*

DOI: 10.4018/979-8-3373-6325-7.ch004

## INTRODUCTION

The rapid rise of artificial intelligence (AI) in education has started to change English language teaching (ELT) by offering new forms of content creation, more personalized learning, and greater opportunities for interactive communication (Alm & Watanabe, 2023; Bonyadi et al., 2025). Simultaneously, language educators are increasingly prioritizing intercultural communicative competence (ICC)—awareness and skills that are essential to communicating effectively and appropriately across languages and cultures—as a key objective of ELT in a globalized world (Byram, 1997; Klimova & Chen, 2024; Lee, 2025; Ma & Yang, 2025). AI makes possible new forms of intercultural communication using adaptive learning systems, virtual exchanges, and culturally diverse resources (Klimova & Chen, 2024; Xia et al., 2024). But alongside these potentials lie a new danger: gender bias presented in AI-generated ELT resources. Preliminary studies suggest large language models and other AI-based tools may repeat entrenched gender stereotypes in the texts and images they produce (Crawfurd et al., 2024; Fatima et al., 2025; Gross, 2023; Jiang et al., 2025; Kang & Hirschi, 2025; Li et al., 2025; Mattiazzi, 2025; UNESCO, 2024; van Niekerk et al., 2024; Voutyrakou et al., 2025), creating relevant pedagogical and ethical questions for language educators and researchers in applied linguistics. How can we leverage AI to build intercultural may without replicating harmful stereotypes? This literature review examines this question by engaging with foundational and contemporary research across multiple discourse communities. It will first highlight the role of AI in ELT before discussing the importance of intercultural communication in language education. The next step involves examining - through the lens of bias - systematic reviews of studies on gender and representation in standard ELT materials. This is followed by conclusions on bias specifically around gender bias in educational material generated by AI-led content, then implications for teacher and student education, as well as implications for ethics more generally (Jenks, 2025; Liu, 2023; Messner et al., 2025; Schneider & Oliveira, 2025). From this perspective, the overall aim of this study is to examine how culture, gender, and communication norms are represented in AI-generated English language learning texts. To this end, the following research questions were addressed:

1. What types of social, professional and institutional roles are foregrounded in the dataset, and how are these roles distributed across the intercultural scenarios?
2. How do cultural pairings and national contexts influence the emergence of interaction norms, and to what extent does modal verb usage reflect underlying cultural expectations and obligations?

3. How are gendered pragmatic patterns reflected in the dataset, with respect to modal usage, politeness strategies, emotional responses, and directness versus indirectness?

These questions guide both the eloquent analysis and the qualitative narrative analysis. The research questions explore how AI will generate and reorganize not only its linguistic forms but also cultural values and social norms.

## 2. LITERATURE REVIEW

### 2.1. AI in English Language Teaching (ELT)

AI has gone from speculation about the future to a utility of the present, and has fused itself into the eld of ELT (Alm & Watanabe, 2023; Bonyadi et al., 2025; Crompton et al., 2024; Sharadgah & Sa'di, 2022; Sapuan et al., 2025; Xia et al., 2024). While the term "artificial intelligence" can be broadly defined to mean any AI utility, within the field of ELT, AI encompasses various utilities and applications such as intelligent tutoring systems, automated writing evaluators, speech recognition systems, chatbots, and assistants powered by large language models, all of which serve to support language teaching and language learning (Alm & Watanabe, 2023; Bonyadi et al., 2025; Xia et al., 2024). A systematic review recently published by Sapuan et al. (2025) notes that AI's role in ELT has changed in recent years, as AI technology now plays an important role in supporting numerous ELT practices for both teachers and students (Bonyadi et al., 2025; Sapuan et al., 2025; Uygun & Demir, 2026). Researchers have noted several affordances of AI in the realm of language learning: students' writing, speaking, reading comprehension, and self-regulated learning are all reported benefits (Alm & Watanabe, 2023; Bonyadi et al., 2025; Crompton et al., 2024; Sharadgah & Sa'di, 2022; 2025; Xia et al., 2024). AI-based writing assistants may provide instant feedback on either grammatical or stylistic issues, speech recognition applications support learners in improving pronunciation, and adaptive learning systems could modify vocabulary or reading tasks based on the learner's level (Alm & Watanabe, 2023; Bonyadi et al., 2025; Xia et al., 2024). In a review of 64 studies, Sharadgah and Sa'di (2022) found overwhelmingly positive findings related to the use of AI for many aspects of learning English: AI interventions were found to optimize the learners' language skills, enhance processes of translation and assessment, and even increase learner motivation and satisfaction (Sharadgah & Sa'di, 2022). These findings indicate an optimistic future for the use of AI in ELT, as it may provide additional support for students in their language proficiency and efficiency in the classroom (Bonyadi et al., 2025; Crompton et al., 2024; Sapuan et al., 2025).

However, integrated AI in ELT does raise specific challenges and limitations, in addition to its affordances. Crompton et al. (2024) detail several themes of recurring challenges when using AI in English teaching. Technical issues, such as software glitches or systems "breaking down", may disrupt lessons, and any current AI applications cannot respond to learners' needs with the same subtlety or strategy when addressing complex or open-ended learner tasks. Educators also express some apprehension or outright "fear" with AI, such as whether it will take away the role of the teacher or the possibility of AI making mistakes (Alm & Watanabe, 2023; Crompton et al., 2024). One concern mentioned is the standardization of language in some AI applications, which could prioritize certain "correct" norms of English over others (Bonyadi et al., 2025; Crompton et al., 2024). In Crompton et al.'s article in the British Journal of Educational Technology, they write that there are obvious affordances for using AI to practice speaking and writing but that teachers should be aware of those limits and not believe AI is a perfect or mono solution (Crompton et al., 2024).

In fact, several reviews say AI in ELT is still in its infancy, which requires further research and modification (Bonyadi et al., 2025; Sharadgah & Sa'di, 2022; Sapuan et al., 2025). Some things still remain unclear, including how AI accounts for non-verbal aspects of communication (such as body language or tone), how AI-generated teaching materials are enacted in real classroom contexts, and how best to prepare teachers to use AI (Alm & Watanabe, 2023; Sharadgah & Sa'di, 2022). To conclude, AI is rapidly changing the landscape of teaching English promises of effective resources to support higher levels of proficiency, but consideration needs to be taken to not use AI in ways that do detract from the learning experience. Researchers argue for a "principled manner" to use AI, based on guidelines and ethical frameworks (Compagnoni et al., 2025; Crompton et al., 2024; Sapuan et al., 2025). The following sections delve deeper into one of these ethical and pedagogical principles: intercultural communication and equitable representations of gender across learning material.

To synthesize these developments and provide a cohesive structure for the subsequent analysis, this review adopts a Critical AI-ELT Framework. This conceptual model situates the integration of AI within three interconnected domains: Functional Affordance, Intercultural Mediation, and Representational Ethics. The first domain addresses the immediate pedagogical shifts and linguistic benefits of AI utilities as established in current practice. The second domain, Intercultural Mediation, investigates how these tools influence the development of intercultural communicative competence and the enactment of global citizenship. The final domain, Representational Ethics, critically examines the 'hidden curriculum', specifically the systemic biases and gendered narratives inherent in AI-generated content. By organizing the literature through this tripartite lens, the review transitions from a general overview of technical applications to a deeper exploration of how AI mediates the socio-cultural values of language learning. This framework serves as the structural scaffolding for the remainder of the chapter, bridging the gap between classroom-level innovation and the broader ethical imperatives discussed in the concluding sections.

## 2.2. Intercultural Communication in Language Learning

Intercultural communicative competence (ICC) is described as the ability to engage effectively and appropriately with individuals across cultures, using a foreign language (Byram, 1997). Byram's (1997) seminal model explains that ICC is more than mastering a language, and also enacts skills associated with interpreting cultural signals, thinking critically with openness and curiosity toward another perspective, and mediating between cultures (Byram, 1997). To illustrate this, a language learner demonstrating intercultural communicative competence can establish and nurture relationships and communicate through and by factoring their own culture, and their interlocutor's culture, into their communication (Byram, 1997).

In the modern era of a global society, ICC is a recognized educational goal. As global developments increase cross-culture exposure, mastering a language like English is further linked to being knowledgeable of cultural differences, and the potential consequences of worldviews (Byram, 1997; Klimova & Chen, 2024; Lee, 2025; Ma & Yang, 2025; Zehir Topkaya & Demir, 2021). Still, language education has historically neglected interculturalities through the prioritization of linguistic knowledge (i.e. grammar rules, additional vocabulary), relegating culture to superficial discussions (i.e. food/festivals/other cultures) including attempting to incorporate it into communicative competence and educational outcomes (Byram, 1997).This discrepancy has produced learners who may know the language from a formal perspective, but struggle to participate in real-world intercultural exchanges- this is due to misunderstandings with a lack of opportunities to examine multiple perspectives (Byram, 1997; Klimova & Chen, 2024; Lee, 2025). In the domain of ELT, this is a crisis: as English continues to become a lingua franca spoken across geographic and cultural boundaries, language learners need to be prepared to engage a diverse world through English. Throughout history, educators and institutional bodies, including the Council of Europe, have advocated to embed intercultural communication into language modules and curricula. This means authentically representing cultural texts, and preparing learners to become "global citizens" who are able to engage diversity (Byram, 1997; Klimova & Chen, 2024; Zehir Topkaya & Demir, 2010).

Increasingly, researchers have sought to explore ways that AI and technology can support learners in developing intercultural competencies in ELT. When designed intentionally, AI-based systems can offer personalized and interactive cultural experiences that are impossible in a traditional classroom (Alm & Watanabe, 2023; Klimova & Chen, 2024; Lee, 2025; Ma & Yang, 2025; Shadiev et al., 2020; Shadiev, 2021; Xia et al., 2024). For example, intelligent tutoring systems that offer real-time feedback can accommodate the background and needs of learners and even potentially provide culturally-responsive teaching (Shadiev et al., 2020; Xia et al., 2024). Experimental research has directly incorporated virtual reality (VR) and augmented reality (AR) to immerse language learners into simulated cultural environments. For instance, Shadiev et al. (2020) have created cross-cultural communication scenarios, including allowing students to "virtually" have conversations that took place in other cultures, which improved learners' cultural capacity and communicative ability (Shadiev, 2021; Shadiev et al., 2025; Xia et al., 2024). By practicing in situated contexts (such as replicating a marketplace or social interaction in the target culture), learners can improve their language fluency and become aware of cultural norms and behaviors (Ma & Yang, 2025; Shadiev, 2021; Shadiev et al., 2025).

AI chatbots are yet another avenue being explored for intercultural learning; programming conversational agents with characters from various cultures allows students to interact in the target language with "cultural informants" (Alm & Watanabe, 2023; Lee, 2025). Earlier findings suggest that intercultural chatbots and AI-supported environments can build students' confidence and empathy by exposing students to various speech patterns and viewpoints (Klimova & Chen, 2024; Lee, 2025; Ma & Yang, 2025). Visionaries believe that the emergence of AI presents a "transformative opportunity" to consider the intercultural divide which has long plagued more traditional language education (Klimova & Chen, 2024; Lee, 2025; Shadiev et al., 2020; Xia et al., 2024). By matching students with contrived scenarios, supplying timely feedback, and sourcing ample cultural content, AI tools could allow learners to acquire not only linguistic accuracy but also the pragmatic and cultural awareness necessary to use English effectively across cultures (Klimova & Chen, 2024; Ma & Yang, 2025; Xia et al., 2024).

Simultaneously, it is worthwhile to think critically about AI's role in intercultural communication. More specifically, AI models are fraught with specific cultural and social historical contexts, and, as a result, may have implicit cultural biases (Barry & Stephenson, 2025; Jenks, 2025; Liu, 2023; Messner et al., 2025; UNESCO, 2024; van Niekerk et al., 2024). In a system without checks, an AI might establish a biased cultural narrative (for example, it might highlight Western cultural norms if it was developed primarily on Western data (Barry & Stephenson, 2025; Jenks, 2025; Liu, 2023; Messner et al., 2025). In regards to intercultural learning, this means that teachers should carefully vet any cultural content produced by an AI for accuracy and inclusivity. Nevertheless, when deployed intentionally, AI can be a strong advocate in helping to develop students' cultural horizons as it allows for the virtual experience of distant cultures in the classroom and provides students with safe spaces to practice intercultural encounter (Klimova & Chen, 2024; Ma & Yang, 2025). To summarize, the consideration of intercultural communicative competence has developed into a priority in ELT for global needs, while AI potentially offers viable pathways to enrich the efforts toward this end. The following section will take into account the contents of ELT materials themselves - namely, the representation of genders since the content is among the major dimensions in which both cultural values and bias are transmitted to learners.

## 2.3. Gender Representation in ELT Materials

The representation of gender in language learning materials has historically been an area of scholarly concern and discourse. Textbooks and curricula do not simply provide learners with a neutral input of language; rather, they too transmit societal norms, roles, and expectations - often in a veiled manner (Hartman & Judd, 1978; Porreca, 1984). Beginning in the 1970s, researchers initiated documenting the blatant gender bias that existed in ELT textbooks and reading articles in various contexts around the globe. In the early unit of analysis, researchers engaged in content analyses and documented the numbing patterns of inequality with regards to the representation of women and men. In their groundbreaking research, Hartman and Judd (1978) noted that male characters and pronouns largely outnumbered female ones in textbooks for English as a Second Language (ESL), and that woman (when present) tend to be portrayed in the home or in trivial situations (Hartman & Judd, 1978). A follow-up study by Porreca (1984) examined 15 ESL texts widely used by teachers and found that men appeared not only more often but overall in a wider range of powerful or high status occupations, while women appeared only in a more limited range of roles while typically related to home or traditional "feminine" jobs (Porreca, 1984). These findings led Porreca to assert that there was both sexism in the visibility (or invisibility) of women and in both their depictions as characters in the texts (Porreca, 1984).

Similar studies in other countries corroborated these findings; women were often omitted or underrepresented (a type or a symbol type of exclusion), portrayed in subordinate or stereotypical roles, and sometimes appeared in demeaning situations (i.e., as overly emotional or targets of a joke) (Renner, 1997). Different researchers identified different categories of each bias or exclusion (exclusion, subordination/distortion, or degrading), and pointed out there was often no mention of these biases in the materials in the research studies, use of information in teacher training or education writing (Hartman & Judd, 1978; Porreca, 1984). All these studies highlighted that language instructional materials often reflected, and contributed to the maintenance of the actual gender inequalities in society at the time (Hartman & Judd, 1978; Porreca, 1984).

With the passing of decades, the research question remains, 'how much has changed in the absence of gender bias in ELT materials?' Overall, recent global studies suggest that although blatant sexism may have been minimized in some cases, the existence gender imbalances in textbooks is still common globally. For example, a notable large-scale study by Crawfurd et al. (2024) undertook a study that utilized an automated text analysis of a sample of 1,255 textbooks, written in English, originating from 34 different countries, which revealed significant and consistent biases (Crawfurd et al., 2024). In the books located across this diverse corpus of sources, women and girls were represented in content: female characters were found to be represented far less often as characters than their male peers overall (Crawfurd et al., 2024). Additionally, the qualitative representation remained stereotyped, as the report states that women were more similarly described as passive and far less likely to be characterized by work, achievement, or otherwise, whereas men were more often connected to the public sphere of business and accomplishment (Crawfurd et al., 2024). Women and girls within the textbooks were disproportionately found to be in domestic settings and working in female-identified areas, which contributed to the notion of women in primarily nurturing or supportive roles (Crawfurd et al., 2024). In contrast, male characters were able to occupy a larger scope of occupations (scientist, doctor, leader, etc.) and were more commonly portrayed as lead characters in stories more than female characters were (Crawfurd et al., 2024).

Notably, the analysis also demonstrated variation on socio-economic and cultural factors: countries with a higher number of gender equity (gender status is defined by the legal rights and/or GDP per capita) tended to have more equal representation than countries with extreme female under-representation and stereotyping, like some parts of South Asia in this study (Crawfurd et al., 2024). These results indicate that bias on the basis of gender in educational material is not a relic of the past, but rather a contemporary problem experienced around the globe. As indicated by the authors, in many educational materials, gender and girls "are depicted less frequently, appear more passive, are less likely to be linked with work and achievement, and more likely to be connected with the home" (Crawfurd et al., 2024, p. 3).

This is important because these portrayals present implicit messages which may influence learners' understanding of gendered behavior for themselves (or as a boundary to their potential) – an example of the "hidden curriculum," whereby instructional materials infuse (to varying degrees) social values with language learning (Hartman & Judd, 1978; Porreca, 1984). In terms of intercultural communication, biased materials might even export one culture's gendered stereotypes to another culture (that is, a textbook which shows all scientists as males will signal to learners in other cultures, perhaps contrary to their own views regarding gender equity) (Crawfurd et al., 2024). So, as we shift our focus to AI-produced materials, the question arises: Do newly-produced ELT materials which rely on AI processes follow the same patterns of bias as before, or might this be a moment for course correction?

## 2.4. Bias Representations in ELT Materials

The representation of gender within language learning materials has long been a topic of scholarly investigation and discourse. Textbooks and learning materials are not inherently neutral language input, but reflect shared societal norms, roles and expectations as to how people and identity groups interacts, often implicitly (Hartman & Judd, 1978; Porreca, 1984). Beginning in the 1970s, researchers began to document the systematic bias based on gender in ELT textbooks and reading passages used around the world. In their a landmark study, Hartman and Judd (1978) show that male pronouns and characters outnumbered females to a staggering degree in ESL textbooks, and when women were included, they were frequently depicted in domestic roles or simplistic, trivial situations. In a comprehensive study of 15 ESL textbooks widely used in the 1980s, Porreca (1984) found that men were included in a quantitatively greater representation and held more powerful, higher status occupations – compared to women being afforded little more than decorum in more narrowly defined, traditional "feminine" roles. These studies, from either context and any reference to the materials being used, led to the conclusion that sexism was displayed in the invisibility (or visibility) based on gender characters, and an overall stereotypical depiction of gender (Hartman & Judd, 1978; Porreca, 1984). Following studies in different contexts showed the same patterns – meaning female characters were routinely omitted or underrepresented (symbolic exclusion), were more likely to show subordination or stereotyped actions, or were occasionally depicted in demeaning ways (Renner, 1997). Researchers categorized various bias into generally understood definitions, and often included representations known as exclusion, subordination/distortion, and degradation. The instruction content mirrored the gender inequalities which existed in daily culture (Hartman & Judd, 1978; Porreca, 1984).

Later research extended the empirical foundation and established that asymmetries of a similar nature persist in national and cultural locations. In the Turkish context, Aydınoğlu (2014) reaches similar conclusion when he undertakes a thorough content analysis of Ministry of Education ELT coursebooks in Türkiye. Aydınoğlu demonstrates male dominance in frequency, number of speech turns, and occupational variety, along with spatial stereotyping in which girls and women are depicted in domestic spaces for more than boys, and boys are depicted engaging in action with many examples outdoors. Other review articles such as Nilayam Mihira et al. (2023) further map forms of perpetual gender inequity in English textbooks in varied contexts, and find similar asymmetry in frequency of male characters, more speech turns, greater diversity of occupations and actions in their agency, whereas female characters are strongly aligned with domesticity, emotion, politeness, and have almost no visibility for non-binary or gender diverse identities. Similar patterns have been established in other regions. In his exploration of reading materials utilized in Kenyan primary schools, Kobia (2009) indicates that boys are associated lexically with the actions of "running," "building," "finding out," and "deciding"; the descriptors for girls are of "helping," "waiting," "smiling," and "cooking." Descriptors of boys illustrate the attributes of intelligence, bravery, and independence, and descriptors of girls illustrate beauty, kindness, and obedient behavior that help naturalize and reinforce gender dualisms between masculine competence and feminine feelings and appearance. Ahmad and Shah (2019) gave a thorough CDA of an elementary English textbook, revealing that boys are routinely in roles that were active, agentive, and presented in public-facing scenarios (staring off into the distance, level being fearless, looking after a friend, with visible confidence) while girls appear significantly less frequently and mostly in passive or supportive roles (waiting for a boy, joining in chores); visual analysis reveals boys outdoors, engaged in active and dynamic activities and girls seated, often standing or relaxed with boys and relation-influenced posture. Similarly, for Iranian pre-university textbooks, Roohani and Zarei (2013) show that over 70% of named characters and visual images are male, that respectable, or more highly valued roles are assigned to males with infractions often signaled by females shown competing for roles in limited, narrow, participatory, and often symbolic forms; and their firstness analysis ("he or she," "man and woman") showed the evidence of systematic male precedence; this provides some evidence of historic role assignments and character representations fronted in very narrow terms, in respect to type and value. Overall, the research suggests that ELT textbooks in various environments continue to present common structural asymmetries in visibility, agency, and role assignment histories over years and in various contexts. Over the past few years, there has been a notion that has examined multimodality and discourse structure more deliberately.

At the level of interactional patterns and discourse structure, critical discourse analyses reveal that gender bias is also encoded in who speaks, initiates and controls talk. Asymmetries of discourse at the level of conversation mechanics are identified by Ahmed and Shah (2019), who say that such structural positioning is socializing students "innocuously" into gendered hierarchies of agency. Research that examined teacher cognition adds another layer of complexity. Kızılaslan (2010), moving from textbooks themselves to the preservice teachers' interpretations of textbooks, analyze senior ELT student teachers in Turkey who are unaware of sexist assumptions in excerpts from textbooks, instead often referring to stereotypical representations as normal cultural facts. The participants also stated discomfort in addressing gender in the classroom, and furthermore avoided talking about gender altogether, indicating that despite the materials being biased for educators, the absence of critical awareness in the teacher education program permits biases to be circulated within the program. Exceeding the limited scope of examining ELT textbooks, research on children's literature (as some examples) and broadly defined educational corpuses, not limited to but including films, video documents, and comics indicates/suggests that representational asymmetries exist across genres, and more exciting is that computational methods can reliably account for them, too. Vana–Gür and Damian (2024) create an NLP-based pipeline for detecting gender bias in children's books using labeled entity recognition, co-occurrence networks, and word embeddings. Their analyses reveal how male characters tend to inhabit the central nodes of character networks—by appearing in more chapters, being quoted more frequently, and occupying important connections in the plot—while female characters seem to cluster on the periphery, connected not to each other but to male protagonists. Similarly, Lucy et al. (2020) analyze American educational materials at scale by using NLP techniques and also find evidence that male and white characters are more privileged in visibility and are frequently represented as diverse professionals or intellectual figures, while women or individuals of color appear in more restricted occupational or familial roles; semantic analyses find femininity clustered around care, beauty, and emotion, while masculinity clusters around leadership, science, and technology. These computational audits extend the idea of a "hidden curriculum" and quantify how educational texts make certain identities more salient in national and curricular narratives and marginalize others.

This work connects naturally to research ongoing into corpus-based models and word embeddings, explaining how these patterns in textbooks or literature find their way into AI systems (Bolukbasi et al., 2016). The authors demonstrate adopting the embedding approach to language for conducting their analysis and argue, based on word embeddings trained on large news corpora, that these embeddings did statistically encode gendered stereotypes as part of their geometries in space, portraying associations such as "man: computer programmer:: woman: homemaker," or "he: doctor:: she: nurse." Caliskan et al. (2017) introduce the Word Embedding Association Test (WEAT), which also demonstrates that embeddings capture the same types of implicit associations identified in social psychology (e.g., name associating male names with career words like doctor, and female names with family words like children), and accounts for other markers of racialized hierarchies. The authors of Garg et al. (2018) train diachronic embeddings on historical newspapers, examining how stereotypical associations change over time; stereotypes may become less explicit, but new associations also emerge (e.g., women are described with appearance or emotional descriptors). The studies suggest that bias is reorganized rather than erased. Fast et al. (2016) also show, in their own user-generated online corpus of fiction, that male characters were consistently associated with action, competence, and plot-driving roles, whereas female characters were associated with love, attractiveness, and relational issues—corpora that increasingly form the training data of contemporary models. Hoyle et al. (2019) expand this comprehension to contextualized transformer-based representations where they also find that models still exhibit a bias towards male pronouns for categories of doctors or engineers and female pronouns for categories of nurses or secretaries. Studies of institutional forms of discourse, such as Sevim et al. (2022) on Turkish legal texts, describe asymmetries where male referents explain and cluster semantically around authority, rationality, and institutional power while female referents cluster around vulnerability, dependence, and affect, and women are much more often encoded as grammatical objects that the action happens to them, as opposed to male pronouns being the subject of the action. Lastly, Du et al. (2025), in studying multilingual (12 languages) news media regarding gender culture, find a relationship that men are disproportionately represented as political leaders, experts, and entrepreneurs whereas women are more often represented as a family figure, for their appearance, or for their interpersonal drama.

More abstracted opinions about these representational ways of knowing are structurally similar to how humans and AI learn. Gárate and Hidalgo (2024) suggest that stereotyping in humans and bias in AI share a frequency-based rationale: co-occurring concepts from the past interact to form expectations and predictions and that both human cognition and model parameters play a role in that representation. Since AI is trained on corpora filled with culturally biased pairings of representations (e.g. associating genders and roles/traits), it learns to reproduce that same associative space that is informed by human pre-conceptions. From this perspective, there will be no effective way to "debias" AI until the input and/or social configuration that created that input is taken into account. For ELT, this means that AI tools used to extract or filter learning material are inextricably linked to longer histories of representation in textbooks, storybooks, legal discourse, news, and online fiction. Just decades later, the work conducted in Crawfurd et al. (2024) and others, empirically verifies that significant gender imbalances remain in book publications. According to an automated analysis of 1,255 English-language textbooks from 34 countries, women and girls are still under-represented and stereotyped: female characters featured less often, were portrayed more often as passive, and were less frequently references to work and/or achievement, while men were linked to public domains and accomplishment, with a broader range of occupational roles and more central roles in narratives. More encouragingly, Crawfurd et al. (2024) note that countries with higher gender equality do show representation that is more balanced, while some regions (e.g. parts of South Asia) do demonstrate particularly egregious under-representation and stereotyping of females. These findings correlate with cross-national studies of textbooks and corpora in the Asia, Middle East, Africa, Europe, and North America (e.g. Ahmad & Shah, 2019; Aydınoğlu, 2014; Nilayam Mihira et al., 2023; Roohani & Zarei, 2013), providing additional support for the conclusion that gender bias in educational materials is not a thing of the past, but rather a persistent global issue.

The educational significance of this research is immense. Such portrayals can subtly shape learners' concepts of gender roles and their own potential—an example of the "hidden curriculum," where educational materials impart social values (along with lessons on language) (Hartman & Judd, 1978; Lucy et al., 2020; Nilayam Mihira et al., 2023). In intercultural communication contexts, biased resources may also transport one culture's gender stereotypes to another. For example, Western textbooks may present scientists almost exclusively as men, countering any work toward gender equity. Even if every culture has its own gender expectations, local resources can incorporate their own patriarchal norms in English as a lingua franca. And as research on embedding and large corpora illustrate, the same biased distributions that exist in ELT materials today and other related genres, similarly exist in language models that are increasingly being used to generate new materials. This leads to the question, when we continue discussion of AI-produced ELT resources later in this chapter, will the AI simply replicate or even exacerbate the long-standing biases documented in textbooks, children's literature, and institutional texts, or can the resources be intentionally designed and curated to help course-correct toward more equitable gender representation?

## 2.5. AI-Generated Content and Gender Bias

AI technology is becoming more common when generating educational texts and exercises, from grammar drills and sentences to reading passages and dialogues. Next-generation generative AI models, especially large language models (LLMs), such as OpenAI's GPT line, can generate human-like text on almost any topic; therefore, they are appealing for busy educators creating lessons. Although these models are trained on significant amounts of human-written data, which may reproduce/remove bias as it affected people, LLMs can also reproduce and exacerbate bias in society and in the training data (Gross, 2023; Jenks, 2025; Kang & Hirschi, 2025; Li et al., 2025; Liu, 2023; Mattiazzi, 2025; Messner et al., 2025; UNESCO, 2024; van Niekerk et al., 2024). Notably, a growing body of literature has begun exploring whether AI-generated content may undermine gender bias, and findings indicate that this could be problematic (Al-Samarraie et al., 2024; Arora & Srivastava, 2024; Bai et al., 2024; Deckker & Sumanasekara, 2025; Due et al., 2024; Fatima et al., 2025; Jiang et al., 2025; Kang & Hirschi, 2025; Li et al., 2025; Mattiazzi, 2025;

Voutyrakou et al., 2025). In aggregate, LLMs have been demonstrated to straightforwardly produce gender stereotypes in the content they create, unless explicitly constrained from producing them (Arora & Srivastava, 2024; Fatima et al., 2025; Gross, 2023; Jiang et al., 2025; Kang & Hirschi, 2025; Li et al., 2025; Liu, 2023; UNESCO, 2024; van Niekerk et al., 2024; Voutyrakou et al., 2025).

One stark case is how AI models conceptualize occupational roles and gender. UNESCO (2024) documented an “alarming evidence of regressive gender stereotypes” in the outputs of generative AI (UNESCO, 2024), where across this suite of widely-used LLMs, women were linked to the domestic sphere and family-related words and men were associated with business and high-status occupational words (Jiang et al., 2025; Kang & Hirschi, 2025; UNESCO, 2024; van Niekerk et al., 2024). In this model's analysis, women were described as working in the domestic sphere four times more than men, often using words such as “home,” “family,” and “children” where a woman was referenced (UNESCO, 2024). Male names resulted in words like “executive,” “salary,” and “career,” which depicted an image of men as breadwinners and high-status occupationalists (UNESCO, 2024). Thus, UNESCO's research included evidence of bias toward women in the content generated across three AI models (OpenAI's GPT-3.5 and GPT-2, and Meta's LLaMA 2), therefore providing evidence of systemic bias in AI models (UNESCO, 2024; van Niekerk et al., 2024). Further, the UNESCO study evidenced a significant disparity in the treatment of women between college-educated and non-college educated boys in imagery - this evidence echoes biases seen in human-written textbooks and corroborates the potential impact AI models have on gender bias if unchecked (Crawfurd et al., 2024; Gross, 2023; Jiang et al., 2025; Kang & Hirschi, 2025; Li et al., 2025). Researchers from the field of academia have also dug even deeper into ways that models such as ChatGPT think about gender in particular contexts in education. One notable context is the depiction of professions such as doctors and nurses - a 2024 study published in JAMA Network Open by Currie et al. (2024), who employed AI models to generate thousands of stories about healthcare professionals (doctors, surgeons, nurses), and used an analysis of the gender assignments of the AI in those stories (Currie et al., 2024). The findings were striking: when the AI was asked to tell a story about a nurse, the models (ChatGPT, Gemini by Google, and LLaMA by Meta) presented a nurse as female 98% of the time (Currie et al., 2024). These AI models presumed nurses were female almost uniformly, tapping into the persistent stereotype of nursing as a female profession (Kang & Hirschi, 2025).

While for doctors and surgeons, the AI did present women in those professional roles, and doctor characters were presented as a woman in about 50% to 84% of the outputs from the AI models (Currie et al., 2024). Nonetheless- initially this historical proportion of female doctors may feel positive in terms of equality- the researchers indicated that such adjustments with AI models might just be an “overcorrection” of gender distributions from the developers (Currie et al., 2024). In addition, a closer look did show that there were some subtle stereotypes, rather than just biases, in how the AI model described the female professionals. For example, the AI assignment of gender changed depending on personality and seniority prompts: for example, if the character was described as being agreeable, nurturing, and/or junior role (such as an intern or inexperienced), the models presented the doctor character as female, presumably exemplifying prior stereotypes in their outputs (Currie et al., 2024). On the other hand, if a prompt suggested a doctor was senior, dominant, or had a negative trait—like "arrogant" or "unempathetic"—AI would mostly depict the doctor as a man (Currie et al., 2024). In sum, this means that AI reinforced stereotypical conceptualizations that women often are expected to be compliant and personify lower ranks, while leadership, power—even negative traits like arrogance—were implicitly gendered male traits (Currie et al., 2024; Kang & Hirschi, 2025). The study authors concluded generative AI tools "appeared to reproduce long-held stereotypes related to the expected behaviors of genders…and the appropriateness of genders for certain roles (e.g., senior doctors and surgeons are male)" (Currie et al., 2024). This subtle/unconscious finding may be more troubling than simply a matter of numerical disproportion, as it illustrates AI handing down prejudices at the level of behaviors and status, rather than just at the surface-level of biases. Other research and anecdotal accounts support these observations. In an analysis of ChatGPT's responses, Gross (2023) found that ChatGPT often behaves "performatively" to gender - re-enactive and amplifying existing gender scripts (Fatima et al., 2025; Gross, 2023; Kang & Hirschi, 2025; Li et al., 2025). For instance, when responding to a prompt like, "What does an economics professor look like?", ChatGPT created a robust description of a typically male character, "a well-kept, salt and pepper beard… dressed in cleanly tailored suits… with a leather briefcase (Gross, 2023, p. 8). In the above instance, the AI unconsciously framed the professor as male with masculine-attributed properties (beard, dress) and representation of authority. This is an example of how generative AI can accidentally be infused with gendered assumptions unless it is specifically told not to do so (Fatima et al., 2025; Gross, 2023; Li et al., 2025; Schneider & Oliveira, 2025).

Researchers who study fairness in AI have also found that LLMs tend to stereotype gender with occupations. For instance, it might default to "he" for a doctor and "she" a nurse, and actually correct the user if they resist their stereotype (e.g., Bai et al., 2024; Deckker & Sumanasekara, 2025; Due et al., 2024; Jiang et al., 2025; Kang & Hirschi, 2025; Voutyrakou et al., 2025). Gender bias is clearly a system-wide phenomenon in AI-generated texts - one which will carry over and be reflected into any ELT materials when generated by the AI unless it is specifically countered first by the software prompt string. If a teacher asks the AI to draft dialogue for an English class, there is the genuine possibility that the dialogue will default to include, for instance, male characters in professional roles and female characters in supporting roles. This is an identical framing to the printing of textbooks that have already been documented for skewing and framing (Crawfurd et al., 2024; Fatima et al., 2025; Gross, 2023; Jiang et al., 2025).

It is important to note that bias can also be observed with the AI content beyond gender. The UNESCO report has also noted trends indicating homophobic and racial stereotypes in the outputs generated by LLMs (UNESCO, 2024; van Niekerk et al., 2024). In addition, studies have shown that popular language models trained on predominantly Western text from the internet exhibit Western cultural bias, often resulting in Eurocentric perspectives when generating stories or open-ended questions (Barry & Stephenson, 2025; Jenks, 2025; Liu, 2023; Messner et al., 2025). For example, an LLM might assume certain naming conventions or holidays as the default, potentially sidelining cultural lenses other than Western (Barry & Stephenson, 2025; Jenks, 2025; Liu, 2023). This is critical in an intercultural communication context – if an AI-generated reading passage in an English class consistently draws from predominantly Western contexts or norms, it may actually undermine the intention of providing learners with exposure to multiple world cultures in English (Klimova & Chen, 2024; Lee, 2025; Ma & Yang, 2025).

In addition, different cultural experiences with gender roles intersect – an AI-generated reading may denote the gender role of "professional woman" differently in the context of materials about one country compared to the role in materials about another country. Each of these illustrations shows why AI bias is not solely a technical anomaly, but rather a pedagogical issue, introducing or perpetuating biased content in classrooms, affecting learners' attitudes, and possibly contributing to social inequalities over time (Barry & Stephenson, 2025; Deckker & Sumanasekara, 2025; Dokic et al., 2025; Jenks, 2025; Liu, 2023; Messner et al., 2025; UNESCO, 2024; van Niekerk et al., 2024).

In sum, the composite nature of the evidence – from international bodies such as UNESCO to peer-reviewed scholarship and concrete examples – indicates that AI-generated educational content can be riddled with gender bias. Women may be under-represented or portrayed in stereotypical ways, and mostly, the biases reflect those that are typically acknowledged in past examinations of material created by human writers (Crawfurd et al, 2024; Fatima et al., 2025; Hartman & Judd, 1978; Porreca, 1984). The difference is that using AI can generate the same type of content at a rapid pace and in far greater quantities than the traditional publishing process. Unfortunately, this could embed these biases into educational content faster than traditional publishing has done over time (Li et al., 2025; UNESCO, 2024; van Niekerk et al., 2024). This awareness raises critical educational questions: what sorts of things can educators do to mitigate biases resulting from AI in the classroom? What kinds of pedagogical structures are possible, when using AI, that can challenge rather than reinforce stereotypes in content? The sections of this chapter that follow examine such pedagogical potential as well the ethical obligations that arise when using AI for fair practices in ELT. To synthesize the strands of research reviewed above and clarify how they inform the chapter's analytical focus, the discussion is organized through the following conceptual framework.

## 2.6. Conceptual Framework: AI–ICC–Gender Representation Loop

This chapter adopts an AI–ICC–Gender Representation Loop to integrate the literature and foreground the relationships among technological mediation, intercultural communication, and representational bias. The model conceptualizes AI as a mediating layer between sociohistorical language corpora and classroom discourse. First, existing textual distributions and cultural patterns shape the knowledge base from which AI generates content. Second, AI mediation structures intercultural communicative scenarios by determining which cultures, roles, and interactional norms are foregrounded. Third, these scenarios yield gendered representational outcomes observable in role allocation, linguistic agency, and pragmatic positioning. Finally, pedagogical mediation, through teacher curation, prompting strategies, and critical AI literacy, operates as a feedback mechanism that can reproduce or mitigate bias in subsequent material design. Framing the literature through this loop provides the conceptual bridge to the chapter's analysis, which examines how AI-generated intercultural narratives instantiate these representational dynamics and what this implies for equitable ELT practice.

## 2.7. Pedagogical Considerations for ELT Professionals

The prevalence of AI-generated materials within ELT places a new responsibility on educators and material developers to become critical curators of educational materials. In the past, practitioners could use a textbook that (hopefully) went through a bias review and editing process, but educators can easily curate lesson materials with the click of a button through an AI system. The pedagogical challenge is balancing the benefits AI provides with regard to personalization, engagement, and efficiency, while also attempting to challenge the bias it holds (Budhai & Heath, 2025; Jenks, 2025; Klimova & Chen, 2024; Lee, 2025; Ma & Yang, 2025). Many researchers, educators, and teams have offered a number of suggestions to. to provide a better balance:

### 2.7.1. Critical Creation of Content

Educators should intervene and think critically about AI generation before using in class. Much like one reviews and modifies a text obtained via the Internet, any exercise generated by the AI or generated dialogue should be treated with a critical approach for biased language or skewed representations (Budhai & Heath, 2025, Fatima et al., 2025; Schneider & Oliveira, 2025). Educators Stephanie Budhai and Marie Heath, along with their research studies in critical AI literacies, understand there needs to be an intersection between the textbook and an AI generated text- this 'critical' questioning and intervention comes in the form of questioning of who is being represented and how (Alm & Watanabe, 2023; Budhai & Heath, 2025; Schneider & Oliveira, 2025). For example, a teacher could decide to alter character names or pronouns to reflect a balance of genders when ChatGPT creates a reading passage about male-business leaders, or they could use it as a chance to talk about why the AI might have provided male leaders. In other words, teachers should act carefully, at the very least, do not take for granted that AI content is neutral, or "ready-to-go" as it represents heteronormative bias (Budhai & Heath, 2025; Fatima et al., 2025).

### 2.7.2. Inclusive Prompting Strategies

An emerging skill for educators is 'prompt engineering' or developing the questions or commands they give to an AI to try and result in less biased outcomes. A teacher creating a dialogue could think about prompting the AI with: "provide a mix of diverse profession representations by gender" or "represent characters in ways that push stereotypes." A diverse prompt may be hit or miss in producing diversity but can help push the AI to provide something that reflects a more equitable representation (Alm & Watanabe, 2023; Crompton et al., 2024; Gross, 2023; Schneider & Oliveira, 2025). Some educators have even had their students help prompts in this way and develop it as a CRT task: students are given an AI text that contains bias and, in teams, they provide prompts to the AI to produce a new version that no longer has a biased viewpoint. This process can help to enhance the text and produce students understanding of bias, and how to counter-argue bias (Budhai & Heath, 2025; Schneider & Oliveira, 2025).

### 2.7.3. Use the Lesson as a Bias Opportunity

As a twist, biased AI output can create teachable moments to analyze bias. If there is a system in place, the teacher can present the AI representation of some subtle gender bias and then ask their students to use critical thinking about what they read. For instance, they may ask something like: "In this computer-generated story, why do you think all the engineers were identified as 'he'? What does that mean in terms of assumptions in society?" These types of activities are related to intercultural communicative competence because they push students to think about societal norms, interrogate assumptions, and consider the perspectives of those who are being represented in a less dominate way (Byram, 1997; Budhai & Heath, 2025; Schneider & Oliveira, 2025). Budhai and Heath (2025) stress that we need to be role models of responsibility in the use of AI based on equity and critical engagement. Students should learn how to interrogate AI in the same manner as discretely questioning information or media representation. This practice of developing their critical digital literacy would be a utility for their futures (Alm & Watanabe, 2023; Budhai & Heath, 2025; Schneider & Oliveira, 2025).

### 2.7.4. Curriculum & Policy Support

At a more system level, we encourage schools and education professionals to develop guidelines for the use of AI in teaching - including bias mitigation methods. Sapuan et al. (2025) call for the establishment of systematic guidelines and ethical frameworks - to support educators on using AI responsibly (Compagnoni et al., 2025; Sapuan et al., 2025). Possible approaches could include professional development opportunities on AI literacies, providing teachers with review checklists of AI generated materials (e.g., "Does the text promote gender stereotyping? Does the text use diverse names or cultural context?"), and establishing an inclusive sharing of AI generated material among educators. Certain institutions may elect to curate and pre-vet particular AI-generated resources for instructors, as a way of regulating both innovation and quality (Bonyadi et al. 2025, Crompton et al. 2024).

### 2.7.5. Using AI to Help Combat Bias

Interestingly, AI can also be part of the solution. Researchers are starting to work on AI tools that help detect, and/or correct bias. For instance, AI text analysis tools may note terms that contain gendered language in a text (as a grammar check may signal error) so that teacher can alter their language (Bai et al., 2024; Due et al. 2024; Deckker & Sumanasekara, 2025). Other projects are creating AI modelling that is fine-tuned on more gender-balanced datasets, or follows rules to use gender neutral language in some contexts (Liu, 2023; Voutyrakou et al., 2025). It is hoped in the long-term, that AI would become more "bias-aware" (Liu et al., 2025). Until then, however, educators will still largely bear the responsibility to be the conscientious editors and facilitators toward bias (Budhai & Heath, 2025; Gross 2023; Schneider & Oliveira, 2025).

Despite the above, from a pedagogical stance, it is worth drawing attention back to classroom discourse, and the question of why addressing gender bias in materials matters in terms of language learning outcomes. Biased content can (in nuanced ways), frame, or orient, credibly for learners' attitudes about the language and cultures being studied (Crawfurd et al., 2024; Fatima et al, 2025; Porreca, 1984). If female students do not see themselves represented successfully, and professionally, in English language content, they may actually start to internalize a lesser confidence or motivation when using the language in those domains (Crawfurd et al., 2024). If male students only see other men represented in leadership positions, they may discount what women contribute, or they will simply struggle when they move into real multicultural contexts in which women are their equal or their superior (Hartman & Judd, 1978; Kang & Hirschi, 2025). The goal of intercultural communication training in language classes is to build respect and understanding across difference; inclusion of biased or stereotypical content would directly work against intercultural training by normalizing one group's dominant or stereotypical characteristics (Byram, 1997; Klimova & Chen, 2024; Lee, 2025; Ma & Yang, 2025) to individual students. Therefore, ensuring representation and inclusion should not be seen as an "extra" credit for language educators but rather an important part of effective intercultural language education. Educators have the responsibility to design and create a classroom environment - and curricular material - that reflects values of equality and diversity in order to develop more open-minded communicators.

In summary, the incorporation of AI brings ELT teachers away from educator and course content-focused work but rather extends it into a domain of being critical mediators of content. AI supported pedagogy will require a constant dialogue - between teacher and AI (generating and adjusting content), between students and the AI (using AI-supported tools to practice, hopefully and pending their critical awareness), and students and the biases that may arise (in which teachers support them in noticing and questioning their identification as bias). While creating additional layers of complexity for teaching, instructional methods that create engagement will also build students' engagement with bias from a real-world context, technology, and representation - all through the lens of language learning (Alm & Watanabe, 2023; Budhai & Heath, 2025; Crompton et al., 2024; Klimova & Chen, 2024; Lee, 2025; Schneider & Oliveira, 2025).

## 2.8. Ethical Concerns and Considerations

The use of artificial intelligence (AI) technologies in language teaching has significant ethical implications, particularly with respect to sensitive topics such as matters of gender views and cultural content, which educational practitioners, developers, and policymakers must evaluate. The core principle is equity and do-no-harm in education: AI tools should not reinforce discrimination or stereotypes, and the task of implementation should be congruent to educational imperatives for inclusive and respect for difference (Compagnoni et al., 2025; Jenks, 2025; UNESCO, 2021, 2024; van Niekerk et al., 2024). Recent literature and policy discussions have flagged several broad ethical topics:

### 2.8.1. Amplification of Bias and Inequality

The leading ethical issue is concern that AI systems can unintentionally amplify societal bias while appearing to be objective; it has been previously stated that "small" biases in AI created outputs can be quite significant in the way that they are perceived by learners; an issue that compounds through repetition (Gross, 2023; Kang & Hirschi, 2025; Li et al., 2025; UNESCO, 2024, van Niekerk et al., 2024). In 2024, UNESCO's Director-General, Audrey Azoulay, cautioned that millions of people are interacting with LLMs every day, with biases only very subtle from materials produced by these technologies, which can "enhance inequalities in the real world" (UNESCO, 2024, van Niekerk et al., 2024). For education, this entails the ethical obligation not to let AI become a delivery system for regressive ideas (e.g., sexist or racist) in the classroom. The unmonitored use of AI technology could result in a regression of bias, observing the educational goal of equitable gender education and inclusive education as part of the "hidden curriculum" (Crawfurd et al., 2024; Deckker & Sumanasekara, 2025; Hartman & Judd, 1978; Jenks, 2025).

From an ethical perspective, stakeholders must consider the following: Are we comfortable with an algorithm making the decision about the default gender of a scientist in a story? If it is largely defaulting to male, what are the implications of this, and who is responsible? This is a gender issue, but this is also relevant to cultural biases (e.g., AI systems favoring Western settings) and other stereotypes (Barry & Stephenson, 2025; Dokic et al., 2025; Jenks, 2025; Liu, 2023; Messner et al., 2025; UNESCO, 2024; van Niekerk et al., 2024). The ethical path asserts that active attempts should be made to audit AI systems for these biases, and enact corrective or curative responses or guidelines (Bai et al., 2024; Deckker & Sumanasekara, 2025; Jenks, 2025; UNESCO, 2021, 2024; van Niekerk et al., 2024).

### 2.8.2. Responsibility and Accountability

The second area of concern relates to the issue of "who is responsible" when AI content is de facto biased or problematic. Is it the accuracy of technology or technology companies that designed the model? Is it the teacher's responsibility for using the model without reading its content? Is it the school system promoting AI to teachers? Ethicists argue accountability is shared: AI developers have a duty to continually monitor and improve their model for fairness (Bai et al., 2024; Kang & Hirschi, 2025, UNESCO, 2021, 2024), and educators have a duty of care by curating and presenting content to learners (Alm & Watanabe, 2023; Budhai & Heath, 2025; Compagnoni et al., 2025). The UNESCO Recommendation on the Ethics of Artificial Intelligence (2021), which is endorsed by numerous member countries, calls for governments to develop explicit regulations and standards for AI, including for education, to promote transparency, human governance of that technology, and avoid discrimination (Compagnoni et al., 2025; UNESCO, 2021). In practice, this could mean that AI-generated learning materials would be required to have gone through a bias review or seal of approval, or it could mean that teacher education included training on ethics with respect to the use of AI. Moreover, it would mean that if an AI tool continues to generate biased outputs, there is a system for reporting that bias and holding the AI producer accountable for fixing the incident (Bai et al., 2024; UNESCO, 2024; van Niekerk et al., 2024).

In education, unlike some public uses of AI, the stakes are higher because young minds are malleable and the school has an ethical obligation to provide a safe and equitable learning environment (Byram, 1997; Klimova & Chen, 2024; UNESCO, 2021).

### 2.8.3. Informed Use and AI Literacy

Ethical use of AI in ELT also intersects with the idea of informed consent and informed understanding. Teachers and learners should understand when materials are AI-generated and be aware of potential limitations (Alm & Watanabe, 2023; Budhai & Heath, 2025; Schneider & Oliveira, 2025). There is ethical reasoning for transparent use: a teacher could explain to students that the text they have been reading is generated by an AI and ask the class whether they think the text gives them a different reading experience, and if they think it reads biased in any way. This practice reveals the mystery of AI and also indicates to students that this was not text produced by a specialist human, but instead a prediction produced by a machine that may not be entirely valid or fair (Gross, 2023; Li et al., 2025). Building literacy around AI - that is, understanding and recognizing the limitations of AI and whether AI will reproduce past biases from previous datasets, etc. exists within the frame of ethical pedagogy. As some educators have pointed out, we are not trying to either teach students to blindly trust or avoid AI altogether, but promote a healthy skepticism and critical engagement (Alm & Watanabe, 2023; Budhai & Heath, 2025; Schneider & Oliveira, 2025). This encourages students not to be misled or affected by AI and its outputs unconsciously, with an understanding that they will continue to interact with AI with their own human judgment and values as a guide (Jenks, 2025; Liu, 2023).

### 2.8.4. Privacy and Intellectual Property

While this was not the main focus of this chapter, it is worth highlighting that ethical pedagogy around AI in education also includes ethical concerns around data privacy and authorship (Compagnoni et al., 2025; UNESCO, 2021). Many AI tools rely on user data (specifically, students' input) to work (e.g., adaptive learning platforms leverage user data to interpret the student experience and student performance data). As such, protecting student privacy as well as obtaining consent to leverage student data is critical (Compagnoni et al., 2025).

In addition, questions about authorship and plagiarism arise when AI is unsupervised and generates work. Educators must be sensitive to the possibility that the materials created by AI do not unintentionally plagiarize other copyright materials (if the AI model simply reproduces the copyright portions of the training materials), which is an ethical and legal concern as cited by Barry and Stephenson (2025). Students who use AI such as ChatGPT, as an example, when engaging with assignments, also impact aspects of academic integrity. Therefore, educators must develop short guidelines stating acceptable versus unethical uses of AI assistance with respect to learning task obligations, on one hand encouraging the use of useful tools, and on the other hand, maintaining learning objectives (see Alm & Watanabe, 2023; Budhai & Heath, 2025; Compagnoni et al., 2025).

### 2.8.5. Respecting Culture

In the area of intercultural communication, ethically using AI means that educators must make sure the content generated by AI respects intercultural differences and does not perpetuate culture stereotypes or bias. One example of this might include ensuring that AI generated examples or names of people in the tasks created showcase a plurality of intercultural diversity in representation than representational division that defaults to one culture (see Barry & Stephenson, 2025; Jenks, 2025; Liu, 2023; Messner et al., 2025). Furthermore, it means the educator observing the output of AI, ensuring that educators do not introduce material that might be considered insensitive and/or inappropriate to a group of people from specific cultures (for example, casually using alcohol in content directed towards cultures or age groups that deem consumption inappropriate or taboo). Culture is also not a culturally sensitive entity in itself and will generate content that at any moment could be considered insensitively culturally appropriate depending what instructions are given at the time. Thus, the educators' ethical role is to be that cultural filter (Byram, 1997; Klimova & Chen,

2024; Ma & Yang, 2025). This is consistent with the larger movement in language teaching for culturally responsive pedagogy, which is now looking at AI materials (Klimova & Chen, 2024; Ma & Yang, 2025; Xia et al., 2024).

With this in mind, what recommendations are being made so that the use of AI in ELT is ethical? International organizations and researchers are beginning to establish frameworks. UNESCO (2021, 2024) is calling on governments to develop and apply regulatory frameworks on AI with respect to human rights and equality, particularly to ensure "responsible use of AI in accordance with safeguarding... against potential biases" (UNESCO, 2021, 2024; van Niekerk et al., 2024). In other words, ethical values should not just be additional at the completion of deploying AI, but a part of the entire life cycle of embedded values of AI use in the education context - starting with the design (including different perspectives in the training data), implementation (provision of guidelines and warnings of bias as users), and ongoing assessment (occasional audits of the AI outputs in educational contexts) (Bai et al., 2024; Deckker & Sumanasekara, 2025; UNESCO, 2021, 2024; van Niekerk et al., 2024).

For educators, Budhai and Heath call for "critical AI education" to teach both educators and students about biases and developed values so they can work against these (Alm & Watanabe, 2023; Budhai & Heath, 2025; Schneider & Oliveira, 2025). Some researchers have suggested extending media literacy curricula to include AI literacy, including recognizing bias and fairness in algorithmic outputs (Budhai & Heath, 2025; Li et al., 2025; Schneider & Oliveira, 2025). Teacher PD programs are similarly beginning to include modules related to AI ethics, acknowledging that teachers need support to use these tools responsibly (Alm & Watanabe, 2023; Compagnoni et al., 2025; Crompton et al., 2024; Sapuan et al., 2025).

Lastly, as we maintain a hopeful yet cautious lens, we need to remember AI is still a tool made up of humans and still can be enhanced by humans. That the open-source LLMs were depicted to be more biased but offered more transparency is forward thinking and shows that the community could come together to investigate ways to mitigate bias (Barry & Stephenson, 2025; Dokic et al., 2025; Jenks, 2025; Liu, 2023; Messner et al., 2025; UNESCO, 2024; van Niekerk, 2024). Techniques like bias fine-tuning and reinforcement learning, even human feedback are already being utilized to mitigate harm from AI (Bai et al., 2024; Gross, 2023). Ethically, looking for AI that does not reinforce stereotypes, but even helps can promote positive models, for example, imagine the possibility of an AI that generates stories that, perhaps, support stereotypes or follow gender norms as an intentional story (for example, an AI story or developed text that depicts a female scientist mentoring a male nurse - a subtle counter-stereotypical interaction). Some researchers are even suggesting AI could "undo" some gendered basis by imagining a scenario in a more equitable way (Gross, 2023; Li et al., 2025; Schneider & Oliveira, 2025; Voutyrakou et al., 2025). This is an emerging idea, but it flips the script if instead of AI as a threat to equity, it could be a tool for others to visualize and normalize equality (i.e., AI-generated dialogue where a female scientist is mentoring a male nurse - a subtle counter-stereotype). In practice, this will take thoughtful coding and working with educators and experts in Diversity, Equity, and Inclusion (Compagnoni et al., 2025; van Niekerk et al., 2024).

In summary, the ethical dimensions of using AI in ELT are complicated yet manageable. Acknowledging bias and harm potential, ensuring accountability and transparency, and educating users, as well as championing equity, can assist stakeholders in making sure that AI-enhanced intercultural communication in language teaching meets expectations and does not magnify existing issues (Byram, 1997; Budhai & Heath, 2025; Compagnoni et al., 2025; Jenks, 2025; UNESCO, 2021, 2024; van Niekerk et al., 2024). The ethical intent is outlined clearly: AI in education needs to be an amplifier of human learning and understanding across cultures and genders instead of constraining that learning. That is entirely aligned with the broad purpose of ELT and intercultural education – extending worldviews, countering stereotypes, and preparing learners to act within a diverse world with open minds (Klimova & Chen, 2024; Lee, 2025; Ma & Yang, 2025).

AI-enhanced tools are about to become a staple of English language teaching and learning, and report unprecedented opportunities for personalization in teaching and increasing cultural distances (Crompton et al., 2024; Klimova & Chen, 2024; Lee, 2025; Ma & Yang, 2025; Sapuan et al., 2025; Xia et al., 2024). This literature review has examined ways those innovations intersect with intercultural communication outcomes and challenges related to gender bias in educational materials. The reported research has been a double-edged sword. AI in ELT can improve pedagogical outcomes on the one hand – it can provide personalized practice, can replicate intercultural encounters, and can enliven the learning experience (Alm & Watanabe, 2023; Crompton et al., 2024; Klimova & Chen, 2024; Lee, 2025; Ma & Yang, 2025; Shadiev et al., 2020; Xia et al., 2024). Yet, on the other hand, AI can inadvertently reproduce and even magnify historical biases, including gender biases that have plagued educational materials for decades (Crawfurd et al., 2024; Fatima et al., 2025; Gross, 2023; Hartman & Judd, 1978; Jiang et al., 2025; Kang & Hirschi, 2025; Li et al., 2025; Porreca, 1984; UNESCO, 2024; van Niekerk et al., 2024). Gender bias is not a faraway speculation in relation to AI-generated ELT materials; it is present in the outputs of current models, and mitigating it is urgent and imperative (Arora & Srivastava, 2024; Deckker & Sumanasekara, 2025; Due et al., 2024; Voutyrakou et al., 2025).

Most importantly, the combined findings of both early and recent research from around the globe show that the human element is critical. Technology alone cannot produce content that is progressive or education-focused; rather, it is the interaction between teachers, developers, and learners with technology that will determine the outcome. Educators are called on to be attuned, apply critical thinking and intercultural understanding when choosing and adapting AI-generated texts (Alm & Watanabe, 2023; Budhai & Heath, 2025; Klimova & Chen, 2024; Lee, 2025; Schneider & Oliveira, 2025). By providing teacher training and strong guidelines, educators are empowered to intervene creatively in their use of AI while working to uphold values of gender equity and cultural representation (Budhai & Heath, 2025; Compagnoni et al., 2025; Crompton et al., 2024; Sapuan et al., 2025). At the same time, the responsibilities are to be taken on by AI developers and policymakers who must build ethical/student factors into the AI educational design and regulations so that bias is documented and mitigated (Barry & Stephenson, 2025; Bai et al., 2024; Deckker & Sumanasekara, 2025; Dokic et al., 2025; Jenks, 2025; Kang & Hirschi, 2025; Li et al., 2025; Liu, 2023; Messner et al., 2025; UNESCO, 2021, 2024; van Niekerk et al., 2024). Fortunately, at least there is an increasing awareness of these responsibilities; interdisciplinary partnerships are forming (for example, computer scientists, linguists, educators and ethicists) to fulfill them (Compagnoni et al., 2025; Schneider & Oliveira, 2025; Xia et al., 2024).

For applied linguistics and language education, this moment is remarkable. We now have various AI systems that can provide rich conversations with students, real-time grammar feedback, and simulated cultural experiences – a fundamentally new type of 'assistant' in the classroom (Alm & Watanabe, 2023; Crompton et al., 2024; Klimova & Chen, 2024; Lee, 2025; Ma & Yang, 2025; Xia et al., 2024). By merging pedagogical knowledge with technological innovation, we can shape this assistant into a positive force for good: envision AI-constructed materials that intentionally position diverse cultures on equal footing, or chatbots that allow historically marginalized groups to participate in discussions (Barry & Stephenson, 2025; Jenks, 2025; Li et al., 2025; Liu, 2023; Mattiazzi, 2025; Messner et al., 2025; Schneider & Oliveira, 2025). The opportunity to recreate learning materials that are more inclusive is possible if we are intentional in correcting the course when algorithms veer toward bias. But fundamentally an AI in ELT is not a simple answer, rather it is a catalyst—an enabler that can either perpetuate old biases or dissipate them, contingent on how we shape it (Budhai & Heath, 2025; Compagnoni et al., 2025; UNESCO, 2024; van Niekerk et al., 2024). As we continue working with AI, more studies need to be done in several areas: how to effectively detect and mitigate bias in AI's educational outputs; how use of AI-generated materials impacts learners' intercultural competence and attitudes over time; and how to develop teacher and student AI literacy (Bai et al., 2024; Barry & Stephenson, 2025; Deckker & Sumanaseka, 2025; Jenks, 2025; Kang & Hirschi, 2025; Klimova & Chen, 2024; Lee, 2025; Li et al., 2025; Liu, 2023; Messner et al., 2025; Schneider & Oliveira, 2025; Xia et al., 2024). For example, longitudinal studies may help us better understand if students using AI-supported language learning recognize bias differently than those studying with traditional materials. Studies comparing different languages and cultures will be important because most research to date has focused on English; bias in AI may manifest differently across languages and cultures (Barry & Stephenson, 2025; Jenks, 2025; Li et al., 2025; Liu, 2023; Messner et al., 2025; van Niekerk et al., 2024). Ultimately, continued conversations on bias between the global ELT community and AI developers may help ensure subsequent generations of AI better reflect and fulfil pedagogical principles of inclusivity and cultural understanding (Compagnoni et al., 2025; Crompton et al., 2024; Jenks, 2025; UNESCO, 2024; Xia et al., 2024).

In conclusion, AI use in English language teaching practice elicits both excitement and frustration. Educators can take advantage of pedagogically-based insights and a growing body of research to play an active role in maximizing AI's support of intercultural communication while working proactively to limit gender bias in AI-produced materials (Byram, 1997; Crawfurd et al., 2024; Fatima et al., 2025; Gross, 2023; Hartman & Judd, 1978; Jenks, 2025; Klimova & Chen, 2024; Lee, 2025; Liu, 2023; Ma & Yang, 2025; Porreca, 1984; UNESCO, 2024; van Niekerk et al., 2024). This is no small task, but it is vital. Language education has always been about much more than grammar - it is about communication, it is about culture, it is about the exchange of ideas and values. With the thoughtful implementation of AI use, we may have a chance to extend that exchange to include more students, and we may have the ability to create a more equitable classroom environment. The hope, in part, is that AI-generated content will encourage intercultural communication, but will also model the intercultural communication- we hope to achieve as AI content may reflect the diverse, gender-fair, world we want to create.

In sum, AI has transitioned from futuristic speculation to a vital utility in English Language Teaching, offering transformative affordances for personalized learning and intercultural engagement. However, this shift highlights persistent systemic issues, notably the historical marginalization and stereotypical representation of gender in educational materials. Contemporary research suggests that generative AI often replicates or exacerbates these biases, frequently associating genders with regressive occupational roles and Western-centric cultural norms. Consequently, the role of the educator must evolve into that of a critical mediator. This necessitates a proactive approach involving inclusive prompting strategies and the use of biased AI outputs as teachable moments to foster critical digital literacy. Ethically, developers and practitioners share accountability for ensuring that technology promotes equity rather than reinforcing discrimination. Ultimately, the integration of AI in language education requires a principled, human-centered framework to navigate the hidden curriculum of automated content. By prioritizing inclusivity and critical awareness, stakeholders can ensure that AI enhances human learning and supports a truly diverse and equitable global classroom.

### 2.8.6. Synthesis of Key Issues and Emerging Priorities

Taken together, the reviewed literature indicates that the shift from static textbook production to AI generated discourse represents not merely a technological change but a transformation in how representational patterns circulate in language education. While traditional materials transmitted bias through editorial choices and publishing norms, AI systems reproduce and redistribute these patterns at greater scale, speed, and variability, making their pedagogical impact more immediate and diffuse. Among the issues reviewed, the most urgent concerns relate to how gendered representations intersect with intercultural learning goals. When AI generated scenarios repeatedly position certain groups in limited roles or normalize particular cultural viewpoints, they may shape learners' expectations about social relations and intercultural interaction. Prioritizing these dynamics highlights the need for critical mediation, as the effectiveness of AI supported language learning depends not only on linguistic accuracy but also on the inclusivity of the social meanings embedded in generated texts.

## 3. METHODOLOGY

### 3.1. Research Design

This study employs a mixed-methods design that integrates computational text analysis with qualitative interpretive techniques, reflecting the growing consensus that hybrid approaches are essential for capturing both surface-level linguistic form and deeper pragmatic meaning (Creswell & Plano Clark, 2018). The dataset consists of short intercultural narratives generated by a large language model, an approach aligned with recent work highlighting the need to examine AI-mediated language for its pedagogical and sociocultural implications (Crompton, et al., 2024). The research design is informed by theories of intercultural pragmatics (Kecskes, 2014) and cultural schema theory (Sharifian, 2017), which emphasize that communication is shaped not only by linguistic choices but also by shared cultural knowledge, expectations, and social roles. Accordingly, the data are analyzed both as textual products and as instances of culturally situated interaction. By combining computational measures with qualitative discourse-pragmatic analysis as an approach consistent with critical applied linguistics perspectives (Pennycook, 2021) and bias studies in NLP (Blodgett et al., 2020), the study aims to uncover potential biases, stereotypical frames, and reductive cultural representations that may arise when generative AI models construct intercultural encounters for educational contexts. The design also incorporates principles of methodological transparency in AI research by explicitly documenting prompt construction, corpus scope, and analytic decision rules. This approach ensures that the interpretive findings are grounded in a traceable process linking model outputs to the analytical framework.

### 3.2. Data Collection

The dataset for this study consists of AI-generated intercultural communication passages, produced using a GPT-based large language model under controlled prompting conditions. The goal was to construct a corpus that reflects a range of intercultural scenarios that include characters from different national and cultural backgrounds, embed authentic interactional features such as politeness markers and modal verbs typically encountered in English language learning materials such as travel, workplace interactions, hospitality, classroom communication, formality, and everyday social encounters, while maintaining an A2–B1 CEFR difficulty level consistent with ELT materials. The following prompt was entered into Chat GPT-5.1 from an anonymous account:

> *"Generate an 80-120-word intercultural communication passage at the CEFR A2–B1 level. The passage should present a simple scenario involving characters from different cultural or national backgrounds and include authentic interactional features such as politeness markers and modal verbs. Situations may relate to travel, workplace communication, hospitality, classroom interaction, formality, or everyday social encounters. Use clear, accessible vocabulary typical of ELT materials and avoid stereotypes, ensuring a neutral and respectful tone. The text should be written as a short narrative paragraph, not a dialogue. Make sure each text contains 1–2 characters with names typical of their culture (e.g., Maria from Italy, Kenji from Japan, Aisha from Egypt, Lucas from Brazil, etc.), uses at least one modal verb (can, must, should, may, etc.), include mild emotional expressions (happy, worried, excited, surprised)"*

To enhance procedural transparency, all passages were generated in a single session using the same base prompt, with no iterative refinement or manual editing prior to analysis. This ensured consistency across outputs and minimized researcher intervention in the generation process. The resulting corpus was treated as a purposive sample designed to capture variation in intercultural contexts rather than to represent model behavior exhaustively.

## 3.3. Dataset Structure

The final dataset contains 50 passages, each representing one intercultural episode. The passages include a minimum of two characters from different cultural or national backgrounds, a brief narrative setting, a communicative problem or contrast, and one or more direct speech segments. The passages in the dataset represent 16 countries. The texts include substantial use of modal verbs, cultural norms, politeness strategies, and hierarchical language. The corpus was exported in the following format, as shown in the example below:

*Table 1. Sample dataset from the output*

| ID | Category | Title | Passage |
|---|---|---|---|
| 1 | At the Restaurant & Café | The Tipping Confusion | Kenji from Japan and Sarah from the USA just finished a nice dinner in New York. Sarah left extra money on the table. Kenji looked confused. "Why are we leaving money?" he asked politely. In Japan, tipping is not common. Sarah smiled. "In the US, we should leave a tip for the waiter... |
| 2 | At the Restaurant & Café | Ordering Coffee | Maria, from Italy, visited a coffee shop in Melbourne with her friend Ben. She just wanted "un caffè," which is a simple espresso. Ben looked at the large menu. "They have flat whites, long blacks, and batch brews. What kind do you want?" Maria was a little surprised... |

## 3.4. Data Analysis

The analysis consisted of three complementary components that combined computational and qualitative methods. The first component involved a rule-based NLP procedure designed to identify linguistic markers related to obligation, advice, cultural norms and social roles. The texts were processed to detect modal verbs, references to countries and cultural groups, and role-related expressions. Character names and role titles were also extracted to determine the gender of the characters and who produced each modal verb. Based on these features, each instance of obligation was grouped into a context type and converted into structured outputs such as frequency tables.

The second component consisted of a contextual interpretation of modal uses across passages. At this stage, each passage was reviewed to determine the strength of the obligation being expressed and the underlying source of that obligation. Instead of focusing only on the literal meaning of modal verbs, the analysis examined whether the rule originated from institutional authority, cultural and social context, speaker's role and their relationship with others. This evaluation enabled the categorization of each modal expression into six context types: hierarchical rule, legal obligation, social obligation, cultural expectation, emotional assertion and social advice. The analysis also incorporated role categories, since the speaker's social position shapes how obligations are expressed in the texts. Roles were identified directly from the passages through explicit labels and through contextual cues that revealed the interactional status of each character. Authority roles included managers, professors, teachers and tutors, service roles consisted of officers, clerks, waiters, staff members and other individuals responsible for customer interactions. Peer-level roles referred to colleagues and friends. Learner roles were assigned to characters positioned as students or cultural newcomers adapting to unfamiliar norms. Finally, cultural local guides are speakers who explained or clarified cultural expectations to others.

A third analytical dimension focused on gender-based pragmatic patterns. Speakers were grouped according to gender representations and their modal choices, apology behaviors, emotional expressions and patterns of directness or indirectness. Quantitative comparisons were conducted to identify whether male, female and gender-undefined speakers differed in how strongly they expressed obligation, how frequently they apologized, and how often they softened their speech.

The analytical procedure followed a staged protocol moving from surface-level linguistic extraction to contextual interpretation and finally to comparative pragmatic analysis. This sequencing allowed computational indicators to guide, but not determine, qualitative interpretation.

## 4. FINDINGS

The findings of the qualitative data will be presented with reference to each research question respectively.

### RQ1: Which social and occupational roles appear in the passages, and how frequently?

The role distribution in the Table 2 shows a clustering of characters into four main functional categories. Authority roles such as managers, teachers, professors, tutors, and officers appear most frequently, with 16 passages. This indicates that hierarchical or rule giving figures are the most commonly represented role type in the dataset.

*Table 2. Frequency of social and occupational roles across passages*

| Role Category | Roles Included | Total Frequency (Passages) |
|---|---|---|
| Authority Roles | Manager, Project Manager, Professor, Teacher, Tutor, Officer | 16 |
| Peer-Level Roles | Colleague, Student | 9 |
| Service Roles | Staff, Waiter, Clerk, Housekeeping, Shopkeeper, Cashier, Taxi Driver | 13 |
| Professional Roles | Engineer | 1 |

Peer level roles, such as colleagues and students, appear in nine passages, which is forming the second largest group and reflecting scenarios where interactions occur between equals. Service roles including staff, waiters, clerks, housekeeping, shopkeepers, cashiers, and taxi drivers are present in 13 passages, showing that institutional and commercial service encounters form a substantial portion of the dataset. Finally, professional roles are minimally represented, with the role of engineer appearing in only one passage, making it the least frequent category overall.

*Table 3. Modal verb distribution by role category*

| Role Category | Roles | Must (n) | Should (n) | Must % | Should % |
|---|---|---|---|---|---|
| Manager-type roles | Manager, Project Manager, Professor, Teacher, Tutor, Engineer | 11 | 7 | 61.1% | 38.9% |
| Authority roles | Officer | 3 | 1 | 75.0% | 25.0% |
| Cultural local guides | Colleague | 4 | 4 | 50.0% | 50.0% |
| Learner roles | Student | 3 | 2 | 60.0% | 40.0% |
| Service Roles | Waiter, Clerk, Staff, Housekeeping, Taxi Driver, Shopkeeper, Cashier | 3 | 4 | 42.9% | 57.1% |
| TOTAL | | 24 | 18 | 57.1% | 42.9% |

The distribution of modal verbs across role categories shows clear functional differences depending on the social position of the speaker. Manager-type roles which include managers, professors, teachers, tutors, project managers and engineers in this table, produce 11 uses of must and seven uses of should. This makes "must" the dominant choice with 61.1 percent. Authority figures such as security officers and customs officers also rely heavily on "must", using it three times compared to one instance of "should". With must representing 75 percent of modal use in this category, we can say that institutional control is strongly foregrounded in Table 3.

Colleague roles show a balanced distribution, using must four times and should four times. This indicates a more reciprocal and socially mediated type of interaction where obligation and advice occur at similar levels. Learner roles, represented by students, lean slightly toward must with three instances against two instances of should, corresponding to 60 percent must. This suggests that learners are often positioned in situations where rules or expectations are communicated to them.

Finally, service roles, including waiters, clerks, staff members, housekeeping, taxi drivers, shopkeepers and cashiers, produce three uses of must and four uses of should. Here, the modal "should" accounts for 57.1 percent which indicates a more advisory or polite tone. Across all defined roles combined, the modal "must" appears 24 times and should appears 18 times, meaning that 57.1 percent of modal use involves must overall.

*Table 4. Apology and emotional expression distribution by role category*

| Role Category | Total Apologies | Emotional Expressions (Count) | Dominant Emotions |
|---|---|---|---|
| Manager-type roles | 1 | 11 | stressed, awkward, confused |
| Authority | 1 | 10 | worried, uncomfortable |
| Cultural local guides | 3 | 22 | excited, confused |
| Learner roles | 14 | 48 | embarrassed, awkward, confused |
| Service Roles | 5 | 18 | uncomfortable, confused |
| Mixed | 1 | 6 | shocked, confused |

The distribution of apologies and emotional expressions differs noticeably across role categories. Manager-type roles show one apology and 11 emotional expressions, with stress, awkwardness and confusion being the dominant reactions. For this category, this pattern suggests that individuals in higher-status positions express discomfort primarily through emotional cues rather than direct apologies. Authority roles, such as security and customs officers, also produce one apology but display 10 emotional expressions, most of which convey worry and discomfort. These emotions often arise in interactions involving procedural checks or institutional enforcement.

Cultural local guides, represented mainly by colleague figures, show three apologies and 22 emotional expressions. Excitement and confusion stand out as dominant affects. This indicates that socially dynamic interactions where misunderstandings and enthusiasm frequently occur together. Learner roles account for the highest number of apologies with 14 instances alongside 48 emotional expressions. The most prominent emotions are embarrassment, awkwardness and confusion. This indicates that learner roles consistently occupy positions of cultural vulnerability where uncertainty and politeness pressures are strongly reflected in their responses.

When it comes to service roles produce five apologies and 18 emotional expressions which are most commonly used for expressing discomfort and confusion. These roles often mediate between institutional expectations and customer behavior. Finally, mixed-role interactions contain one apology and 6 emotional expressions, dominated by shock and confusion. These cases typically involve ambiguous role dynamics.

## RQ2: Cultural & National Diversity Representation

The second research question was about how cultural pairings and national contexts influence the emergence of interaction norms, and to what extent the modal verb usage reflects underlying cultural expectations and obligations. Table 5 shows the frequency distribution of countries and regions referenced in the dataset. Japan has the highest occurrence with 20.2 percent of all passages followed by the USA with 16.1 percent which is an indicator of intercultural scenarios are primarily structured around East Asia/Western interactions. The UK appears in 9.09 percent of the passages while Germany and Italy each account for 8.08 percent.

*Table 5. Country frequency distribution*

| Country | Frequency | % |
|---|---|---|
| Japan | 20 | 20.2% |
| USA | 16 | 16.1% |
| UK | 9 | 9.09% |
| Germany | 8 | 8.08% |
| Italy | 8 | 8.08% |
| Australia | 7 | 7.07% |
| China | 6 | 6.06% |
| Egypt | 5 | 5.05% |
| France | 5 | 5.05% |
| Brazil | 4 | 4.04% |
| Korea | 4 | 4.04% |
| Canada | 2 | 2.02% |
| Saudi Arabia | 2 | 2.02% |
| Russia | 1 | 1.01% |
| Morocco | 1 | 1.01% |

continued on following page

*Table 5. Continued*

| Country | Frequency | % |
|---|---|---|
| Spain | 1 | 1.01% |
| Total | 99 | 100.0% |

European countries such as the UK, Germany and Italy appear noticeably less frequently but still represent a secondary cluster of recurring cultural contexts. Australia appears in 7.07 percent of the dataset and China in 6.06 percent. Egypt and France each represent 5.05 percent of the passages. Brazil and Korea have a frequency of 4.04 percent whereas Canada and Saudi Arabia each account for 2.02 percent. Russia, Morocco, and Spain appear least frequently, each contributing 1.01 percent of the total. Overall, in Table 5, the frequencies point to a dataset where cultural diversity is present but not evenly distributed, with a strong emphasis on Japan/USA exchanges while many other world regions remain underrepresented.

*Table 6. Dominant context types by country*

| Country / Region | Must/Should Total | Dominant Context Types |
|---|---|---|
| **Japan** | 18 | Social Obligation, Hierarchical Rule, Cultural Expectation |
| **USA** | 16 | Cultural Expectation, Hierarchical Rule, Social Obligation |
| **UK** | 6 | Cultural Expectation, Hierarchical Rule, Social Obligation |
| **Germany** | 4 | Hierarchical Rule, Cultural Expectation, Social Advice |
| **Italy** | 8 | Social Obligation, Cultural Expectation |
| **Egypt** | 6 | Social Obligation, Cultural Expectation |
| **China** | 4 | Social Obligation, Hierarchical Rule, Cultural Expectation |
| **Authority Roles** | 4 | Legal Obligation, Cultural Expectation |

In Table 6, the distribution of dominant context types shows that most countries are associated with multiple forms of modal-driven interactions. Japan, with 18 instances, displays a balanced mix of Social Obligation, Hierarchical Rule, and Cultural Expectation, which indicates a wide range of culturally guided behavioral norms. The USA with 16 instances is primarily linked to Cultural Expectation contexts with additional appearances in Hierarchical Rule and Social Obligation situations. The UK and Germany both show a combination of Cultural Expectation and Hierarchical Rule at lower frequencies. Italy and Egypt are predominantly associated with Social Obligation supplemented by Cultural Expectation. China includes all three types; Social Obligation, Hierarchical Rule, and Cultural Expectation, which are distributed evenly. Authority-related roles appear almost entirely in Legal Obligation contexts, with only a single instance of Cultural Expectation.

*Figure 1. Heatmap of country pairings*

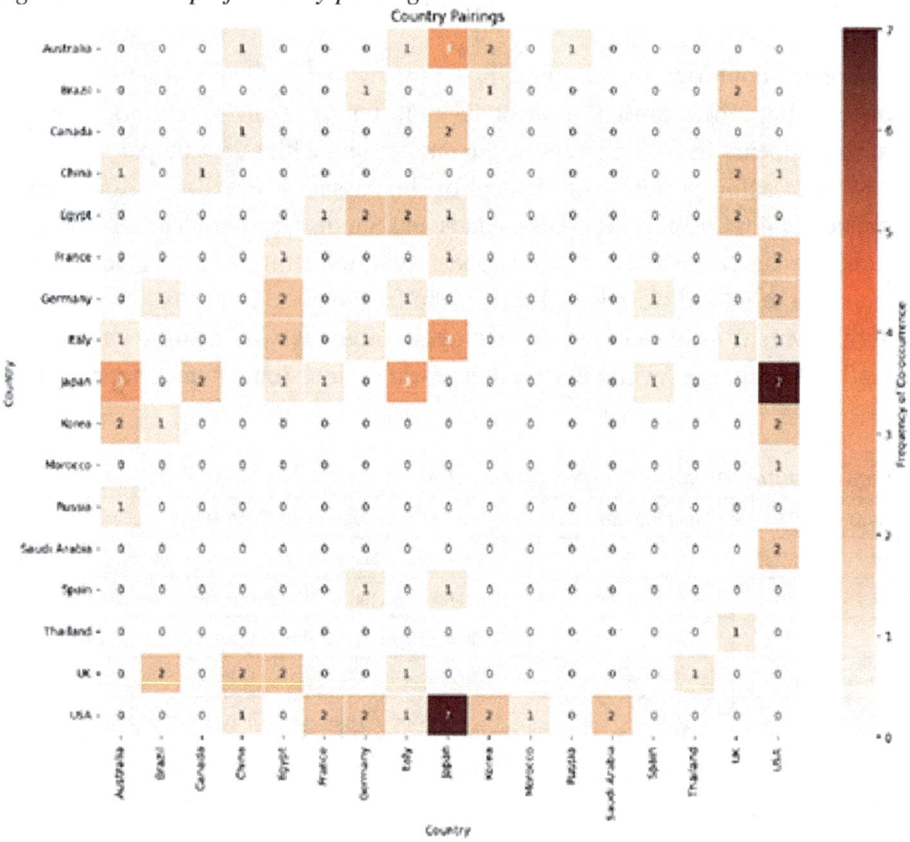


The heatmap visualizes how frequently each country co-occurs with another across the 50 intercultural passages. The distribution shows that certain pairings appear more prominently than others. Firstly, Japan/USA pairings stand out with the highest co-occurrence values. This indicates that a large proportion of scenarios are built around East Asia/Western contrasts. Japan also frequently co-occurs with Australia, Italy, Canada and the UK, which is forming a dense interaction network centered on Japanese cultural norms.

Second, a medium density cluster is visible among European countries such as Italy, the UK, France, and Germany. These pairings show repeated intersections, but at lower frequencies compared to the Japan/USA axis. Their co-occurrences typically involve topics such as punctuality, queuing, and formality.

Third, several low-frequency regional connections appear, including Egypt–Germany, Saudi Arabia/USA, Morocco/USA, Russia/Australia, and Spain/Germany. These pairings occur only once or twice, indicating that Middle Eastern, North African, and smaller European contexts are featured more selectively.

*Figure 2. Distribution of conflict topics within high-frequency country pairings*

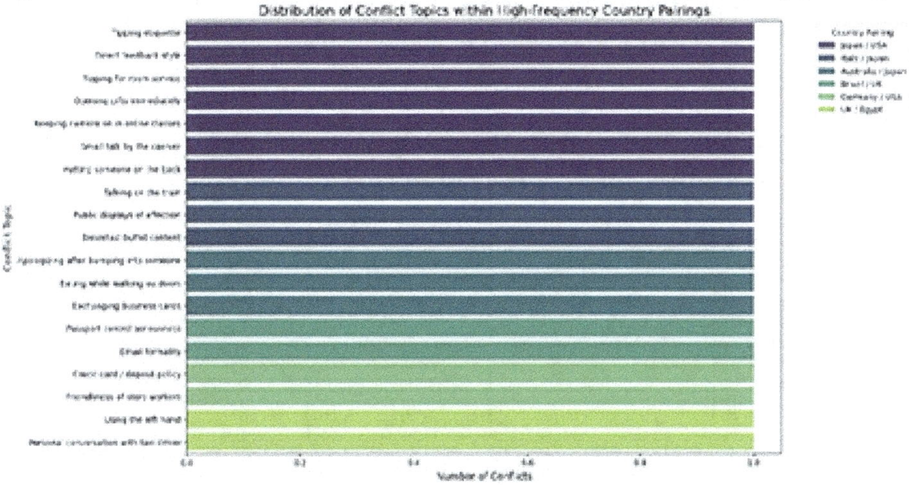


Figure 2 illustrates the specific conflict topics that emerge within the most frequently occurring country pairings in the dataset. Each bar represents a specific intercultural conflict theme, such as tipping etiquette, direct feedback style, opening gifts immediately, keeping the camera on during online classes, small talk by the cashier, or eating while walking outdoors. The chart shows that these topics appear once across the selected high-frequency country pairings, and all items share the same numerical value. The topics cover a wide range of everyday situations, including service interactions, classroom expectations, food-related customs, gestures, transportation behavior, and institutional procedures. The figure lists these conflict types in detail and visually displays how they are distributed across different country pairs included in the analysis.

The figure shows that the Japan/USA pairing includes the widest range of conflict topics, spanning tipping etiquette, direct feedback style, camera-on requirements, opening gifts immediately, cashier small talk, patting on the back, and conversational norms. The Italy/Japan pairing, by contrast, is represented by a smaller set of conflict types focused on public behavior norms such as speaking on the train and public displays of affection. The UK/Egypt pairing contains topics related to bodily etiquette and interpersonal conduct, including the use of the left hand and personal conversation with a taxi driver.

Across all high frequency pairings, the conflict themes span several domains that appear consistently throughout the dataset. Some topics relate to social etiquette practices such as tipping, queuing or apologizing after bumping into someone. Others concern mealtime customs and food-related expectations, including breakfast buffet preferences or norms for eating outdoors. Additional topics involve public-space behavior, institutional rules in travel and hospitality settings such as passport control procedures or credit card policies, as well as academic and workplace expectations including email formality and camera-on requirements.

*Table 7. Distribution of country pairings by conflict category*

| Conflict Category | Types of Modals Used | Country Pairings | Conflict Topic |
|---|---|---|---|
| Hierarchical Rule | Must | Australia / Korea | Using First Names |
| Legal Obligation | Must, Should | Russia / Australia | Customs Declaration Requirement |
| Social Obligation | Mustn't | Italy / Japan | Talking on the Train |
| Cultural Expectation | Shouldn't | Spain / Germany | Appointment Punctuality |
| Emotional Assertation | Must | Germany / Italy | Silence in Conversation |
| Social Advice | Should | Brazil / Germany | Small Talk |

In the Formal Rule category, one of the country pairings identified was Australia and Korea. In this passage, Ben from Australia meets his new manager, Mr. Kim, after relocating to the company's Seoul office. Although Ben has heard that Korean workplaces tend to be very formal, Mr. Kim (Ji-hoon) encourages him to call him "Ji-hoon" for a more friendly style of interaction. However, Mr. Kim firmly reminds Ben that he must continue using formal titles when addressing the company's CEO, stating, "You must still use formal titles for the CEO!".

When it comes to the Legal Obligation category, one of the country pairings here is between Australia and Russia. In this text, Anya arrives in Sydney carrying a jar of honey from her village, which she plans to give as a gift. On the customs form, she marks "No" for food items. When an officer asks whether she is bringing any food, Anya explains that she only has honey as a present. The officer becomes more serious and reminds her that Australia has very strict regulations, stating, "You must declare everything". The officer also warns her that the honey may be prohibited. Anya becomes worried that she has caused trouble, and the officer tells her that next time she should read the forms more carefully.

The story between Japan and Italy is in the Social Obligation category. When it comes to this specific text, Maria, an Italian visitor, is riding a train in Tokyo with her Japanese friend Kenji when her phone rings. She answers it enthusiastically, but soon notices that people around her are staring. Kenji becomes embarrassed and quietly warns her, saying, "Maria, in Japan, you mustn't talk on the phone on the train. It disturbs other people." Maria immediately ends the call and feels ashamed. She realizes that while phone conversations on public transportation are common in Italy, this norm represents a completely different social obligation in Japan.

In the Cultural Expectation category, the story includes Germany and Spain. In this passage, Stefan from Germany is invited to his Spanish friend Javier's home at 8 p.m. When Stefan arrives exactly at 8 p.m., Javier looks surprised and is still cooking. Javier says, "Stefan! You shouldn't have come so early!" Stefan is confused, since the invitation clearly said 8 p.m., but Javier explains that in Spain, "8 p.m." usually means 8:30 or even 9:00, as people tend to be more relaxed about timing. Stefan feels a bit awkward, but he quickly realizes that this is not a personal issue and it reflects a cultural expectation about time and social visits.

In Emotional Assertation category, the example involves Germany and Italy. In the text, Lars from Germany pauses for about ten seconds while explaining an idea to Maria from Italy. Since conversational style in Italy tends to be faster and silence can feel uncomfortable, Maria breaks the pause by changing the topic. Lars is surprised and clarifies that he had not finished speaking and was simply thinking. He explains that in his communication style, it is natural to pause and that silence can be part of formulating a thought. In this interaction, Lars says "We must think before we speak" to emphasize that taking time to think before speaking is important in his context. This indicates a cultural difference in how conversational pacing and silence are understood.

The last category is Social Advice. The story here includes Brazil and Germany. In this narrative, German colleague Lars is waiting for a meeting with his new Brazilian coworker, Lucas. Lucas arrives with a warm smile and immediately begins a friendly conversation. The questions he asks surprise and unsettle Lars, as Lucas casually asks, "Hi Lars! How was your weekend? Are you married? Do you have children?" Coming from a German workplace culture where small talk typically centers only on neutral topics such as the weather, Lars feels caught off guard by these personal questions and answers briefly, saying, "My weekend was fine," while finding the level of intimacy uncomfortable. However, despite his initial discomfort, Lars reflects on the moment and reassesses his own communicative habits, which is captured in the text as: "He realized he should probably be more open."

## RQ3: Gender-Based Pragmatic Patterns

The third research was about how gendered pragmatic patterns are reflected in the dataset, with respect to modal usage, politeness strategies, emotional responses, and directness versus indirectness. Table 8 examines how modal verbs are distributed across genders.

*Table 8. Modals by gender*

| Gender | Must | Should | Total Modal | Must % | Should% |
|---|---|---|---|---|---|
| **Male** | 27 | 15 | 42 | 64.3% | 35.7% |
| **Female** | 11 | 14 | 25 | 44.0% | 56.0% |
| **Unknown** | 6 | 1 | 7 | 85.7% | 14.3% |

Male characters use must a total of 27 times, compared with 15 instances of should. Female characters, by contrast, use must only 11 times, while should appears 14 times in their speech. In proportional terms, male characters account for 64.3 percent of all must occurrences while female characters account for 44.0 percent of the total must usage. The pattern reverses for should. Male characters produce 35.7 percent of all should uses, whereas female characters produce 56.0 percent. For characters whose gender is unspecified, because of how they are introduced through professional labels, the distribution is strongly skewed toward must which has six uses with only one instance of should.

This distribution aligns with prior research indicating that modal verbs differ pragmatically in terms of intensity and social meaning. *Must* expresses strong necessity, authority, or imposition, and can be perceived as forceful in intercultural interaction, while *should* typically serves as a mitigated suggestion, gentle correction, or politeness strategy (Bilobrova et al., 2025). In the present dataset, must is predominantly tied to cultural or institutional obligations, whereas should appears in social advice, softening, and corrective contexts.

*Table 9. Context type by gender*

| Context Type | Male Speakers | Female Speakers | Unknown Speakers |
|---|---|---|---|
| Hierarchical Rule | 13 | 4 | 0 |
| Legal Obligation | 3 | 1 | 5 |
| Cultural Obligation | 12 | 8 | 3 |
| Cultural Expectation | 14 | 11 | 1 |
| Social Advice | 3 | 5 | 0 |
| Emotional Assertion | 2 | 1 | 0 |

The distribution of context types across male, female, and unknown-gender speakers are investigated in the Table 9. Male speakers appear most frequently in Formal Rule contexts with 13 cases, and in Cultural Expectation contexts with 14 cases. They also produce 12 cases of Cultural Obligation. Female speakers on the other hand, while present across all categories, show lower counts in Formal Rule contexts with four cases and in Legal Obligation with one case. Instead, they appear more prominently in Cultural Expectation with 11 cases and Cultural Obligation with eight cases, and they exceed male speakers in Social Advice contexts with five cases compared to three produced by males. Unknown speakers, mostly institutional figures such as officers or clerks are heavily concentrated in Legal Obligation, where they appear in five cases, and show minimal presence in cultural or social categories.

These findings suggest that male speakers are more frequently positioned in directive and rule-giving whereas female speakers show a comparatively greater presence in advisory and socially mediating roles. Additionally, unknown-role speakers, almost exclusively produce legal and institutional must statements.

*Table 10. Apology frequency by gender*

| Gender | Total Apologies | % |
|---|---|---|
| Male | 18 | 52.9% |
| Female | 11 | 32.3% |
| Unknown | 5 | 14.7% |

The distribution of apologies shows a clear gendered pattern. Male speakers produce the highest number of apologies, with a total of 18, which corresponds to 52.9 percent of all apologies in the dataset. Female speakers follow with 11 apologies, making up 32.3 percent. Unknown speakers in the dataset have five apologies, which is corresponding to 14.7 percent. Although female characters appear less frequently in the dataset, male characters are more frequently prompted to produce apologies in moments of cultural conflict while female characters are positioned in roles that involve fewer apologies. The lower rate of apology production in unknown roles is related to these characters being in positions that mostly issue rules or give instructions.

*Table 11. Emotion frequency by gender*

| Emotion Type | Male | Female | Male % | Female % |
|---|---|---|---|---|
| Confused | 22 | 11 | 33.8% | 30.6% |
| Embarrassed | 10 | 7 | 15.4% | 19.4% |
| Worried/Anxious | 9 | 6 | 13.8% | 16.7% |
| Happy/Excited | 14 | 8 | 21.5% | 22.2% |
| Relieved | 10 | 4 | 15.4% | 11.1% |

Table 11 shows how emotional expressions differ between male and female characters. In total, there are 65 emotional instances for male speakers and 36 for female speakers, which indicates that male characters appear in more emotionally annotated passages overall. The most frequent emotion for both groups is *confused*. Male characters produce 22 cases, which corresponds to 33.8 percent of their emotional expressions, while female characters produce 11 cases, corresponding to 30.6 percent. This shows that confusion is the dominant reaction across the dataset, but it is more common among male speakers in absolute numbers.

Female characters show relatively higher proportions of *embarrassed* and *worried or anxious* reactions. Embarrassment appears 10 times in males, making up 15.4 percent of their emotional output, and seven times in females, corresponding to 19.4 percent. Similarly, worry appears nine times in males, representing 13.8 percent, and six times in females, representing 16.7 percent.

Both genders express *happy or excited* emotions, but male characters display this category more frequently, with 14 cases that account for 21.5 percent of their total. Female characters show eight cases, corresponding to 22.2 percent. The emotion *relieved* is also more common in male speakers, who display 10 instances, amounting to 15.4 percent, while female speakers display four instances, amounting to 11.1 percent.

Finally, we can conclude that male characters show more confusion and more relief which suggests that they are more often depicted in situations where uncertainty is followed by a clear resolution. Female characters show more embarrassment and worry indicating that they are more frequently positioned within interactions that demand politeness, sensitivity and social norms. Although female characters appear in fewer passages overall, they produce proportionally more socially oriented emotional reactions.

*Table 12. Directness vs indirectness by gender*

| Gender | Directness | Indirectness | Directness % | Indirectness |
|---|---|---|---|---|
| Male | 61 | 18 | 77.2% | 18 |
| Female | 33 | 22 | 60.0% | 22 |
| Unknown | 28 | 2 | 93.3% | 2 |

In Table 12, an examination of the distribution of directness and indirectness reveals that male characters in the passages use 61 direct expressions, which corresponds to 77.2 percent of their total. They use 18 indirect expressions, which is equal to 22.8 percent. When it comes to female speakers, they produce 33 direct expressions, which corresponds to 60.0 percent and 22 indirect expressions that correlates to 40.0 percent. Unknown speakers show the highest level of directness. They use 28 direct expressions with 93.3 percent and two indirect expressions with

6.7 percent. The table shows that direct forms are dominant in all groups, and indirect forms appear most frequently in the speech of female speakers.

## 5. DISCUSSION AND CONCLUSION

The aim of this research is to study the ways in which large language models design intercultural communication scenarios for ELT resources by looking at how those models represent social roles, how diverse cultural representation is included, and how gendered pragmatic patterns are shown through those resources. Each research question is addressed individually so that readers can better understand the findings of the empirical research in relation to what is currently understood on the topics of intercultural communication and English language teaching.

With the first research question, researchers were able to determine which occupational and social roles were present in the data set and how those roles were used to formulate/modality/apology/emotion. The results revealed a significant imbalance between roles of power (authority) versus those of other types. Manager, professor/teacher, tutor, officer roles make up a substantial majority of the data set. This supports the notion that educational materials continue to replicate the hierarchical nature of institutional authority (Hartman & Judd, 1978; Porreca, 1984). As seen in this study, ELT materials produced by LLMs continue to reflect similar authority-based patterns but will not diversify that experience. The connection between authority roles and their use of modality reinforces the broad view of this perception. Both Manager and Officer roles have a high proportion of "must" usage, indicating directive/top-down modes of verbal behavior, consistent with the language and behavior associated with the institution. Renner (1997) found that ELT publishers commonly depict authority figures as having more powerful voices; and algorithms commonly replicate these hierarchical roles from their training data (Blodgett et al., 2020).

In contrast to the many uses of must by authority figures and expert-level roles where the speaker typically conveys their viewpoint as an expert, the service roles used in this category (i.e., waiters, cashiers, staff) represent the highest number of instances where the word used was should. The majority of these cases are in a more informal or friendly context and are seen as a sign of an advisory position rather than a directive position. The use of should in this context is consistent with findings from intercultural pragmatics studies such as Kecskes (2014), who found that the lower the status or role within a particular culture or social group, the more likely to experience mitigated forms of obligation (e.g., "You should do this"; "It might be a good idea") when interacting with customers to maintain politeness and comply with normative interactional expectations. The balance of must and should, used in peer-to-peer roles and in the roles of local cultural guides, is evidence of the interactional character of the interaction; it shows a more equal, non-hierarchical relationship in these interactions than in peer-to-peer role interaction. Additionally, the balance in the use of must and should is consistent with the cultural schema theory espoused by Sharifian (2017) which states that where there are equals communicating with one another, the communication draws from shared cultural knowledge systems and not from a top-down directive.

The learner role is the most vulnerable emotionally because, in almost all LLM-generated ELT texts, the instances of apology, the emotional manifestations of embarrassment, awkwardness, and uncertainty appear more frequently than any other emotional manifestation. The trends identified above are consistent with other studies of ELT materials such as Ahmed and Shah (2019) and Kızılaslan (2010), who also indicated the emotional burden carried by the character of the learner is disproportionately represented in ELT textbooks compared to other authors and roles in ELT materials. Overall, RQ1 shows that LLM-generated ELT passages do not construct socially neutral interactions; instead, they reproduce hierarchical role structures and pragmatic asymmetries similar to those identified in traditional textbooks.

For the second research question, there was noticeable disproportion of the cultural representations of countries in the dataset. The United States and Japan influenced the cross-cultural encounters of people in these two nations the most. The pairs of countries represent the same pattern found in other studies of ELT texts, which typically have a focus on a small number of "dominant" cultures globally with infrequent coverage of cultures outside the dominant set (Garg et al. 2018, Roohani & Zarei 2013). Moderate representation exists of a number of European countries like Germany, the UK and Italy as well, while very limited representation exists of Africa, South America and the Middle East (e.g., single instances of Brazil, Egypt, Morocco and Saudi Arabia). This perpetuates the previous critiques made by Porreca (1984) and current Analyses of AI Training Data (Caliskan et al., 2022; Schneider & Oliveira, 2025) that show AI models have a bias by conditioning the representation of many cultural contexts in favor of a few.

The dominant types of contexts on which countries are represented (Social Obligation, Cultural Attractions and Hierarchical Obligation) reflect the cultural assumptions underpinning these countries that have been embedded in AI outputs. For example, Japan is associated with strong hierarchical and norm-based obligations, resulting in a perpetuation of stereotypical representations of Japanese society. The concerns reported by Crompton et al. (2024) and also UNESCO (2024), regarding the tendency of AI educational resources to reinforce aspects of cultural essentialism, have been substantiated in this study. The results also reflected that regions like Africa, South America, and the Middle East underrepresented in the data suggests that LLMs reproduce the unbalanced cultural distribution that had been in evidenced in the training data. Other NLP bias studies (Fast et al., 2016; Hoyle et al., 2019) have also indicated that AI models and practices perpetuate existing cultural imbalances, supported by evidence from ELT textbook research studies that show the same phenomenon.

The third research question provided evidence of gender differences in the use of modalities, how they express emotions through their communication and their overall stance when communicating. The way a character uses "must" suggests that a male character has an authoritative and direct style of communication, while a female character's use of "should" implies less authority and a much softer communication style that indicates a relational approach. For decades prior to this study, gendered differences were detected in the content of the educational materials published (Ahmad & Shah, 2019; Hartman & Judd, 1978). Emotional expression patterns also indicate that there is a difference between the genders. Female characters display more emotions associated with shame, anxiety and relational concern than their male counterparts who express the majority of their emotions as being directive and less emotional. Renner (1997) discovered that emotional vulnerability was often used as an indicator of femininity in ELT materials while masculinity was often viewed as being more authoritative and instrumental. Studies conducted by Al-Samarraie et al. (2024) and Caliskan et al. (2022) examining LLM output demonstrated that many gender stereotypes in LLM output are similar to longstanding and contemporary social biases. In the same manner, both Fast et al. (2016) and Lucy et al. (2020) have shown that an AI system generates distinct emotional and pragmatic cues based on the target's gender, reinforcing the current social norms.

Based on the findings of this research question, it seems apparent that gender bias remains in AI-generated ELT content as patterns of gender bias that were previously observed in textbooks created by individuals were also observed in AI-generated ELT materials. Overall, the findings indicate that across all research questions, AI-generated ELT materials contain many of the same representational patterns, cultural stereotypes, and asymmetry between genders found in the historically documented traditional textbooks. The prevalence of hierarchically structured authority roles, disproportionate cultural representations of "East-West" (e.g., Japan-US) interactions, as well as pragmatic differences between male and female characters is an indication that large language models generate more than just linguistically controlled texts; they also embed a hidden curriculum based upon the influences of cultural norms and biases present in the datasets used to train them. Therefore, these results lend support to the assertions made by critical applied linguists (Pennycook, 2021) and intercultural pragmatics researchers (Kecskes, 2014; Sharifian, 2017) that language learning resources, whether developed by humans or AI, serve a fundamental function as objects of social meaning that construct cultural meaning. In order to utilize AI effectively and to minimize the effects of these biases, it is essential that teachers develop critical AI literacy skills which allow them to recognize, challenge, and control the impact of these embedded biases as they continue to incorporate AI within ELT practice.

Although this chapter focuses primarily on gender representation, it is important to recognize that identities are multidimensional. Gendered patterns in AI generated discourse may intersect with other social categories such as race, socioeconomic status, and linguistic background, potentially producing layered forms of representation or marginalization. Acknowledging these intersections helps situate gender bias within a broader landscape of equity concerns and points to the need for future research examining how multiple identities are represented in AI mediated educational materials.

Finally, while large language models provide significant potential for pedagogy, educators need to carefully evaluate output from these models prior to integration into the classroom. The goal of this paper is not to advocate for the exclusion of AI from ELT, but rather to advocate for the inclusion of AI into ELT in an ethical manner and to develop pedagogically sound, culturally inclusive learning environments utilizing AI-enabled ELT.

This chapter has examined how AI generated ELT materials mediate intercultural communication while simultaneously shaping gendered patterns of representation. By bringing together insights from research on AI in language education, intercultural communicative competence, and bias in educational discourse, the chapter highlights both the pedagogical potential and the equity challenges associated with the growing presence of AI in classrooms. In doing so, it contributes to the broader aims of this volume by foregrounding the need for critically informed and ethically grounded approaches to educational innovation. The findings underscore that the integration of AI is not solely a technical development but also a socio-cultural process that requires ongoing reflection on representation, inclusion, and learner experience. Positioning AI as a site of both opportunity and responsibility, the chapter supports the volume's wider goal of advancing equitable and reflective uses of emerging technologies in education.

## 6. LIMITATIONS

Although this research paper demonstrates a systematic breakdown of the roles; the modal verbs; the cultural pairings; and the gendered aspects it reveals; it is essential to recognize certain limitations of this study. First of all, this research paper used a relatively small dataset. The data used consisted of primarily constructed scenarios used as learning tools instead of authentic conversations. Due to this, the role assignments, cultural contrasts, and interaction modalities appearing in the text were written for educational purposes and may reflect what educators want students to understand about intercultural communication as opposed to actual intercultural behavior. Thus, the study was designed to reflect trends represented in the data as opposed to providing generalizations about the broader aspect of intercultural communication around the world. Second, some of the cultural pairings/themes such as East/West appeared to occur at a higher frequency than others. This may lead to an inability to effectively interpret how the data might relate to a worldwide perspective on cultural differences. Results or findings based on countries that only appeared once or twice would not have enough data to provide for adequate comparative analysis. Additionally, the use of simplified and culturally based text may also impact the findings. Finally, the way in which the researcher determined the gender of the speakers was established by names, title, and context, which is an acceptable approach for the course material, but some ambiguity or misunderstanding regarding gender may exist based on these classifications. Classifying all unknown voices (civil service employees, clerks, etc.) as gender-neutral may also impact how modality and emotional expression were analyzed.

## 7. PEDAGOGICAL IMPLICATIONS

The findings of this study highlight the need for ELT practitioners to approach AI-generated materials with critical awareness, ensuring that linguistic input is not only accurate but also socially and culturally responsible. Teachers should actively review AI-produced texts for hidden biases in role hierarchies, cultural representation, and gendered pragmatic patterns, integrating these observations into classroom discussions to promote critical language awareness. Material developers and curriculum designers may also benefit from embedding guidelines for evaluating AI outputs to prevent the unintentional reinforcement of stereotypes. More broadly, incorporating critical AI literacy into teacher education programs can help future educators make informed, ethical decisions when integrating generative AI into language learning contexts.

Beyond immediate classroom practices, exposure to biased AI generated materials may shape learners' perceptions of social roles, cultural norms, and their own communicative identities. Repeated encounters with stereotypical representations can influence learners' expectations about who occupies positions of authority, whose voices are valued, and how different groups are expected to interact. From an intercultural perspective, such patterns may affect not only language development but also learners' openness to diversity, empathy toward others, and confidence in participating in intercultural communication. Considering learner outcomes therefore highlights the importance of critically mediated AI use as part of equitable language education.

## ETHICAL STATEMENT

This study did not involve human participants, personal data, or identifiable human subjects. All materials analyzed were artificially generated by a large language model under controlled prompting conditions. As the dataset consists solely of AI-produced text, no ethical approval was required, and the research adhered to standard guidelines for the responsible use of artificial intelligence in educational research.

## REFERENCES


Ahmad, M., & Shah, S. K. (2019). A critical discourse analysis of gender representations in the content of 5th grade English language textbook. *International and Multidisciplinary Journal of Social Sciences*, *8*(1), 1–24. DOI: 10.17583/rimcis.2019.3989

Al-Samarraie, H., Swinnerton, B. J., Ibrahim Alzahrani, A., Chatterjee, A., & Sarsam, S. M. (2024). Gender perceptions of generative AI in higher education. *Journal of Applied Research in Higher Education*, *17*(5), 1944–1958. Advance online publication. DOI: 10.1108/JARHE-02-2024-0109

Alm, A., & Watanabe, Y. (2023). Integrating ChatGPT in language education: A Freirean perspective. *Iranian Journal of Language Teaching Research*, *11*(3 (Special Issue)), 19–30. DOI: 10.30466/ijltr.2023.121404

Arora, S., & Srivastava, A. (2024). A cross-lingual syntactic investigation of gender bias and stereotyping in GPT-4o: English vs Hindi. *AI and Ethics*, *5*(3), 2497–2514. DOI: 10.1007/s43681-024-00565-9

Aydınoğlu, N. (2014). Gender in English language teaching course books. *Procedia: Social and Behavioral Sciences*, *158*, 233–239. DOI: 10.1016/j.sbspro.2014.12.081

Bai, Y., Zhao, J., Shi, J., Xie, Z., Wu, X., & He, L. (2024). FairMonitor: A dual-framework for detecting stereotypes and biases in large language models. *ArXiv*. https://arxiv.org/abs/2405.03098

Barry, I., & Stephenson, E. (2025). The Gendered, epistemic injustices of generative AI. *Australian Feminist Studies*, *40*(123), 1–21. DOI: 10.1080/08164649.2025.2480927

Bilobrova, Y., Zharko, O., & Batenova, I. (2025). Specifics of modal verbs in intercultural English communication: Implications for communicative competence development. *Scientific Journal of Polonia University*, *70*(3), 16–22. DOI: 10.23856/7002

Blodgett, S. L., Barocas, S., Daumé, H.III, & Wallach, H. (2020). Language (technology) is power: A critical survey of "bias" in NLP. *Proceedings of the 58th Annual Meeting of the Association for Computational Linguistics*, 5454–5476. DOI: 10.18653/v1/2020.acl-main.485

Bolukbasi, T., Chang, K., Zou, J.Y., Saligrama, V., & Kalai, A.T. (2016). Man is to computer programmer as woman is to homemaker? Debiasing word embeddings. *ArXiv, abs/1607.06520*

Bonyadi, A., Kashef, S. H., & Tasouji Azari, M. (2025). The impact of emerging AI platforms on English language teaching and learning: A review of 2022–2025 literature. *Journal of New Advances in English Language Teaching and Applied Linguistics*, *7*(2), 26–43. DOI: 10.22034/jeltal.2025.7.2.2

Budhai, S., & Heath, M. (2025). *Critical AI in K–12 classrooms: Pedagogies, praxis, and possibilities*. Harvard Education Press.

Byram, M. (1997). *Teaching and assessing intercultural communicative competence*. Multilingual Matters.

Caliskan, A., Bryson, J. J., & Narayanan, A. (2017). Semantics derived automatically from language corpora contain human-like biases. *Science*, *356*(6334), 183–186. DOI: 10.1126/science.aal4230

Caliskan, A., Pimparkar, P. A., Charlesworth, T., Wolfe, R., & Banaji, M. R. (2022). Gender bias in word embeddings: A comprehensive analysis of frequency, syntax, and semantics. In *Proceedings of the 2022 AAAI/ACM Conference on AI, Ethics, and Society* (pp. 156–170). Association for Computing Machinery. DOI: 10.1145/3514094.3534162

Compagnoni, I., Oguilve, V., & Wen, W. (2025). Ethical frontiers of AI in language pedagogy: Navigating transparency, accountability, and equity. *International Journal of Linguistics*, *17*(4), 1–18. DOI: 10.5296/ijl.v17i4.22768

Crawfurd, L., Saintis-Miller, C., & Todd, R. (2024). Sexist textbooks: Automated analysis of gender bias in 1,255 books from 34 countries. *PLoS One*, *19*(10), e0310366. DOI: 10.1371/journal.pone.0310366

Creswell, J. W., & Plano Clark, V. L. (2018). *Designing and conducting mixed methods research* (3rd ed.). SAGE.

Crompton, H., Edmett, A., Ichaporia, N., & Burke, D. (2024). AI and English language teaching: Affordances and challenges. *British Journal of Educational Technology*, *55*(6), 2503–2529. DOI: 10.1111/bjet.13460

Currie, G., Currie, J., Anderson, S., & Hewis, J. (2024). Gender bias in generative artificial intelligence text-to-image depiction of medical students. *Health Education Journal, 83*(7), 732–746. DOI: 10.1177/00178969241274621

Deckker, D., & Sumanasekara, S. (2025). Systematic review on AI in gender bias detection and mitigation in education and workplaces. *International Journal of Research in Computing*, *4*(2), 1–11. DOI: 10.64701/ijrc/345/8910

Dokic, K., Pisker, B., & Radisic, B. (2025). Mirroring cultural dominance: Disclosing large language models social values, attitudes and stereotypes. *Societies (Basel, Switzerland), 15*(5), 142. DOI: 10.3390/soc15050142

Du, M., Zhao, Y., & Xie, Q. (2025). Gendered patterns in global news discourse: A computational analysis across 12 languages. *Scientific Reports*, *15*(3303), 1–15. DOI: 10.1038/s41598-025-03303-1

Due, S., Das, S., Andersen, M., L'opez, B. P., Nexo, S. A., & Clemmensen, L. H. (2024). Evaluation of large language models: STEM education and gender stereotypes. *ArXiv, abs/2406.10133*. /arXiv.2406.10133DOI: 10.48550

Fast, E., Vachovsky, T., & Bernstein, M. S. (2016). Shirtless and dangerous: Quantifying linguistic signals of gender bias in an online fiction writing community. In *Proceedings of the International Conference on Web and Social Media* (pp. 209–218).

Fatima, W., Yasmin, M., & Irshad, I. (2025). Exploring gendered language and socio-cognitive impact in AI-generated texts: A critical discourse approach. *Pakistan Languages and Humanities Review.*, *9*(3), 504–524. DOI: 10.47205/plhr.2025(9-III)42

Gárate, M., & Hidalgo, M. (2024). Bias and stereotyping in human and artificial intelligence reasoning: A comparative analysis. *Cognitive Science Review*, *12*(1), 45–67.

Garg, N., Schiebinger, L., Jurafsky, D., & Zou, J. (2018). Word embeddings quantify 100 years of gender and ethnic stereotypes. *Proceedings of the National Academy of Sciences of the United States of America*, *115*(16), E3635–E3644. DOI: 10.1073/pnas.1720347115

Gross, N. (2023). What ChatGPT tells us about gender: A cautionary tale about performativity and gender biases in AI. *Social Sciences (Basel, Switzerland)*, *12*(8), 435. DOI: 10.3390/socsci12080435

Hartman, P. L., & Judd, E. L. (1978). Sexism and TESOL materials. *TESOL Quarterly*, *12*(4), 383–393. DOI: 10.2307/3586137

Hoyle, A., Wolf-Sonkin, L., Wallach, H., Augenstein, I., & Cotterell, R. (2019). Unsupervised discovery of gendered language through contextualized word embeddings. *Proceedings of NAACL-HLT, 2019*, 1708–1718. DOI: 10.18653/v1/N19-1171

Jenks, C. (2025). Communicating the cultural other: Trust and bias in generative AI and large language models. *Applied Linguistics Review*, *16*(2), 787–795. DOI: 10.1515/applirev-2024-0196

Jiang, L., Zhu, G., Sun, J., Cao, J., & Wu, J. (2025). Exploring the occupational biases and stereotypes of Chinese large language models. *Scientific Reports*, *15*(1), 18777. DOI: 10.1038/s41598-025-03893-w

Kang, O., & Hirschi, K. (2025). Bias and stereotyping: Human and artificial intelligence (AI). *Annual Review of Applied Linguistics*, *45*, 69–84. DOI: 10.1017/S026719052500008X

Kecskes, I. (2014). *Intercultural Pragmatics*. Oxford University Press.

Kızılaslan, I. (2010). Student teachers' perceptions of gendered texts in English language. *Procedia: Social and Behavioral Sciences*, *2*(2), 3528–3531. DOI: 10.1016/j.sbspro.2010.03.546

Klimova, B., & Chen, J. H. (2024). The impact of AI on enhancing students' intercultural communication competence at the university level: A review study. *Language Teaching Research Quarterly*, *43*, 102–120. DOI: 10.32038/ltrq.2024.43.06

Kobia, J. M. (2009). Femininity and masculinity in English primary school textbooks in Kenya. *The International Journal of Language. Society and Culture*, *28*, 57–71. https://aaref.com.au/wp-content/uploads/2018/05/28-6.pdf

Lee, Y. M. (2025). Navigating intercultural competence with ChatGPT: Implications and recommendations for foreign language education. *Tydskrif vir Taalonderrig*, *5*(2), 1–8. DOI: 10.54475/jlt.2025.005

Li, M., Enkhtur, A., Yamamoto, B. A., Cheng, F., & Chen, L. (2025). Potential societal biases of ChatGPT in higher education: A scoping review. *Open Praxis*, *17*(1), 79–94. DOI: 10.55982/openpraxis.17.1.750

Liu, C. C., Gurevych, I., & Korhonen, A. (2025). Culturally aware and adapted NLP: A taxonomy and a survey of the state of the art. *Transactions of the Association for Computational Linguistics*, *13*, 652–689. DOI: 10.1162/tacl_a_00760

Liu, Z. (2023). Cultural bias in large language models: A Comprehensive analysis and mitigation strategies. *Journal of Transcultural Communication*, *3*(2), 224–244. DOI: 10.1515/jtc-2023-0019

Lucy, L., Demszky, D., Bromley, P., & Jurafsky, D. (2020). Content analysis of textbooks via natural language processing: Findings on gender, race, and ethnicity in Texas U.S. history textbooks. *AERA Open*, *6*(3), 2332858420940312. Advance online publication. DOI: 10.1177/2332858420940312

Ma, G., & Yang, X. (2025). Fostering intercultural competence through AI-driven tools: A case study of linguistic and cultural adaptability in Chinese EFL education. *Digital Technologies Research and Applications*, *4*(1), 158–169. DOI: 10.54963/dtra.v4i1.1131

Mattiazzi, M. (2025). AI and language: New forms for old discriminations? A case study in Google Translate and Canva. *Feminismo/s, 45*, 118–138. DOI: 10.14198/fem.2025.45.05

Messner, W., Greene, T., & Matalone, J. (2025). From bytes to biases. Investigating the cultural self-perception of large language models. *Journal of Public Policy & Marketing*, *44*(3), 370–391. DOI: 10.1177/07439156251319788

Nilayam Mihira, L. S., Suwastini, N. K. A., Artini, N. N., Jayantini, I. G. A. S. R., & Budiarta, I. W. (2023). Gender inequality represented in English textbooks: A literature review. *Jurnal Ilmu Sosial dan Humaniora, 10*(3), 192–208. DOI: 10.23887/jish-undiksha.v10i3.39209

Pennycook, A. (2021). *Critical applied linguistics: A critical (re-)introduction* (2nd ed.). Routledge. DOI: 10.4324/9781003090571

Porreca, K. L. (1984). Sexism in current ESL textbooks. *TESOL Quarterly*, *18*(4), 705–724. DOI: 10.2307/3586584

Renner, C. (1997). Women are busy, tall, and beautiful: Looking at sexism in EFL materials from: *Annual Meeting of the Teachers of English to Speakers of Other Languages*. Orlando Fl., March 11-15.

Roohani, A., & Zarei, M. (2013). Evaluating gender-bias in the Iranian pre-university English textbooks. *Indonesian Journal of Applied Linguistics*, *3*(1), 115–125. DOI: 10.17509/ijal.v3i1.194

Sapuan, W. N. M., Sulaiman, N. A., & Mohamad, M. (2025). The trends in the integration of AI technologies in English language teaching: Systematic literature review. *Arab World English Journal*, *16*(3), 259–269. DOI: 10.24093/awej/vol16no3.15

Schneider, B., & Oliveira, M. (2025). Developing critical AI language literacy—Prompting experiments on raciolinguistic bias to understand large language models as cultural artefacts. *AI & Society*. Advance online publication. DOI: 10.1007/s00146-025-02727-7

Sevim, N., Şahinuç, F., & Koç, A. (2022). Gender bias in legal corpora and debiasing it. *Natural Language Engineering*, •••, 1–34. DOI: 10.1017/S1351324922000122

Shadiev, R., Wang, X., & Huang, Y.-M. (2020). Promoting intercultural competence in a learning activity supported by virtual reality technology. *International Review of Research in Open and Distance Learning*, *21*(3), 157–174. DOI: 10.19173/irrodl.v21i3.4752

Shadiev, R., Wang, X., & Shen, S. (2025). Effects of immersion and interactive strategies on students' intercultural competence in virtual learning environments. *Education and Information Technologies*, *30*(5), 5883–5919. DOI: 10.1007/s10639-024-13030-1

Shadiev, R., Wang, X., Wu, T.-T., & Huang, Y.-M. (2021). Review of research on technology-supported cross-cultural learning: A sustainable development perspective. *Sustainability (Basel)*, *13*(3), 1402. DOI: 10.3390/su13031402

Sharadgah, T., & Sa'di, R. (2022). A systematic review of research on the use of artificial intelligence in English language teaching and learning (2015–2021): What are the Current Effects? *Journal of Information Technology Education*, *21*, 337–377. DOI: 10.28945/4999

Sharifian, F. (2017). *Cultural linguistics: Cultural conceptualizations and language*. John Benjamins.

UNESCO. (2021). *Recommendation on the ethics of artificial intelligence*. UNESCO. https://unesdoc.unesco.org

UNESCO. (2024). *Challenging systematic prejudices: an investigation into bias against women and girls in large language models*. UNESCO. https://www.unesco.org/en/articles/generative-ai-unesco-study-reveals-alarming-evidence-regressive-gender-stereotypes

Uygun, E., & Demir, B. (2026). Immersive technologies in English language teaching: From theory to practice. In Çelik, F., & Duran, V. (Eds.), *Smart cultural immersion innovations for foreign language teaching* (pp. 335–380). IGI Global., DOI: 10.4018/979-8-3373-3967-2

van Niekerk, D., Pérez-Ortiz, M., Shawe-Taylor, J., Orlič, D., Drobnjak, I., Kay, J., Siegel, N., Evans, K., Moorosi, N., Eliassi-Rad, T., Tanczer, L. M., Holmes, W., Deisenroth, M. P., Straw, I., Fasli, M., Adams, R., Oliver, N., Mladenić, D., & Aneja, U. (2024). *Challenging systematic prejudices: An investigation into bias against women and girls in large language models* (CI/DIT/2024/GP/01). UNESCO / IRCAI. https://mediatalks.uol.com.br/wp-content/uploads/2025/03/388971eng.pdf

Vana-Gür, L., & Damian, C. (2024). *DGBIAS: Detecting gender bias in children's books* [Project report]. TU Wien, FWF 1000-Ideas Programme.

Voutyrakou, D., Katsiampoura, G., & Skordoulis, C. (2025). Fairness in AI: When are AI tools gender-biased? *Advances in Applied Sociology*, *15*(3), 204–235. DOI: 10.4236/aasoci.2025.153011

Xia, Y., Shin, S.-Y., & Kim, J.-C. (2024). Cross-cultural intelligent language learning system (CILS): Leveraging AI to facilitate language learning strategies in cross-cultural communication. *Applied Sciences (Basel, Switzerland)*, *14*(13), 5651. DOI: 10.3390/app14135651

Zehir Topkaya, E., & Demir, B. (2010) The effects of a course about culture and culture teaching: Do pre-service teachers' conceptions change? *X. Uluslararası Dil, Yazın ve Deyişbilim Sempozyumu (The 10th International Language, Literature and Stylistics Symposium)*, 3-5 November 2010, Gazi Üniversitesi, Ankara.

Zehir Topkaya, E., & Demir, B. (Eds.). (2021). *Interculturality and language learning and teaching*. Eğiten Kitap.

# Chapter 5
# AI for Equity and Global Fluency:
## Designing Culturally Responsive and Intercultural Curricula

**Dila Bozkurt**
http://orcid.org/0000-0001-7928-2001
*Çanakkale Onsekiz Mart University, Turkey*

**Kürşat Cesur**
http://orcid.org/0000-0001-5091-9793
*Çanakkale Onsekiz Mart University, Turkey*

**Karlygash Ashirkhanova**
http://orcid.org/0000-0002-6628-5702
*Kh. Dosmukhamedov Atyrau University, Atyrau, Kazakhstan*

## ABSTRACT

*This chapter proposes a practical framework for using AI to advance educational equity and global fluency by integrating Culturally Responsive Pedagogy (CRP) with Intercultural Communication Competence (ICC). The document presents design principles which include inclusivity, contextual relevance, learner-centered personalization, reflective learning and ethics followed by four classroom integration models. The chapter examines some main systemic dangers which include algorithmic bias, teacher readiness gaps and the digital divide and governance/privacy issues while supporting human-centered design processes that bring together educators, students and community members. The study ends with a research plan that focuses on developing culturally sensitive models, tracking their long-term effects, creating*

DOI: 10.4018/979-8-3373-6325-7.ch005

*successful human–AI partnerships and evaluating policy effectiveness to demonstrate how AI can establish inclusive learning environments based on cultural foundations instead of conventional standardized education systems.*

## 1. INTRODUCTION

The modern educational landscape is shaped by global connections and rapid technological change, requiring a shift in teaching methods. The integration of global economies, cultures and societies through globalization has made cross-cultural interaction an essential skill for everyday life. Cultural diversity is necessary as a result of globalization. Students need to learn various cross-cultural communication abilities for achieving effective intercultural communication (Shadiev et al., 2023). Digital platforms have become the central point where economic systems, environmental systems, social systems and political systems merge in modern public spaces (Ebo, 2022). Therefore, the contemporary educational landscape is being fundamentally reshaped by the confluence of two powerful and intersecting forces: pervasive globalization and the extraordinary advance in technology. The current educational system must teach students to become active global citizens through Artificial Intelligence (AI) education because our world has become deeply connected at an international level (Zmire & Chen, 2024).

AI technology is increasingly embedded in educational operations because it operates at the same level as globalization. AI technology is transforming educational institutions through its growing capabilities affecting student learning and teaching methods and school operations (Kamalov et al., 2023). AI technology delivers educational benefits through its ability to customize learning experiences, automate administrative work and facilitate better communication which results in flexible student-centered educational systems (Trivedi, 2023). AI technology enables us to accomplish tasks which were previously out of reach. The educational system benefits from technological advancements which provide efficient methods to help students with different learning requirements and educational needs (Wu, 2024). AI tools promise to customize education, but they end up implementing a single cultural system for all students which results in standardized education across domestic and international borders. AI systems need to be developed with cultural awareness to prevent this problem by incorporating diversity into their design process and ensuring they remain fair and culturally sensitive (Ożegalska-Łukasik & Łukasik, 2023). The educational system needs urgent reforms to develop learning spaces which use human-centered design approaches because of technological progress. The educational sector needs to handle two major obstacles which result from worldwide connectivity and artificial intelligence systems since it must teach both core values and technological skills for a modern digital world (Uche & Uche, 2025).

## 1.1. Digital Global Citizenship in the Age of AI and Confronting Inequities through Digital Conscientization

The present digital environment supports worldwide connections while generating numerous obstacles (United Nations, 2024). The solution to these problems requires an educational system which teaches digital skills while promoting global awareness and incorporates social responsibility, ethical online conduct and civic participation. This framework needs to be centered on global citizenship, which expands traditional citizenship beyond borders to embrace a global community. Students need to develop digital identities and value systems which enable them to participate in online discussions with respect (Harris et al., 2022; Uche & Uche, 2025). The program teaches "digital natives" to become "digital citizens" who follow safe and legal practices while making positive contributions to their communities (Zhong & Zheng, 2023).

AI systems enhance operational efficiency, but they create new security threats. AI systems operate without neutrality because they mirror existing social power structures which they frequently strengthen. They generate content by processing human-produced content which results in the replication of current errors and prejudices (Ansaldo, 2025; Gerlich, 2025). Students need to learn how to evaluate AI outputs based on accuracy, perspective and bias as part of this process. Students who depend on AI without question in their classrooms start to accept false information without any resistance. They function as "containers" which store the biased output generated by AI systems. The digital divide between underrepresented groups and AI datasets results in data poverty because their voices remain absent from these datasets which perpetuates existing racial and socioeconomic inequalities through digital exclusion (Poornesh, 2024). The system delivers reduced performance results and generates discriminatory results (Dolidze, 2025). The digital divide thus becomes a form of systemic injustice. The mission of the educational system, therefore, must be to promote digital conscientization in order to empower students to be agents of critical change.

## 1.2. AI for Inclusive and Culturally Responsive Education

AI offers an array of powerful tools to create a more individualized, effective, and available learning situation. AI can improve the quality of learning and make teachers' jobs easier. It makes individual instructions, based on learners, and enhances students' attitudes and self-confidence relating to instruction (Vieriu & Petrea,

2025). For example, adaptive learning systems can utilize artificial intelligence to continually assess student performance, provide content of changing difficulty and type, allowing each student to progress at his or her rate (Trivedi, 2023). Studies have indicated that students in these individualized learning climates usually state that their self-efficacy is greater and their attitude toward their education is more favorable (Vieriu & Petrea, 2025). This method solves the main problem of educational equity by eliminating standardized teaching methods which result in students being left behind. By replacing uniform models with tailored support, AI promotes fairness. The system enables teachers to concentrate on essential teaching tasks because it performs basic administrative functions automatically (Trivedi, 2023; Göçen et al., 2025). AI functions as an educational tool which helps teachers generate learning spaces that stimulate student inquiry and self-exploration.

AI enables educational development through CRP and ICC because it supports both cultural and cognitive diversity as well as inclusive learning environments (Zmire & Chen, 2024). AI technology supports CRP by enabling students to maintain their personal identities, yet it helps ICC development through its ability to connect people across different languages and cultural backgrounds (Klimova & Chen, 2024). AI tools such as LLM-based CulturAIEd generate customized educational materials through cultural information which helps teachers reduce their work demands (Wang, Xiao, et al., 2025). AI also helps people from different cultures communicate with each other by defeating language and distance obstacles. The translation tools Google Translate and DeepL enable users to work together across different languages through their precise instant translation features (Klimova & Chen, 2024). The tools function as essential instruments for global cooperation which provide additional resources and information to people who communicate in various languages. AI provides computer-assisted language learning through its ability to deliver instant grammar, pronunciation and vocabulary feedback (Macinska & Vinkler, 2025). AI creates training environments with deep cultural elements through its combination with virtual reality (VR) technology. The simulations enable students to practice intercultural communication through simulated real-world situations which improves their ability to manage actual communication events (Zmire & Chen, 2024). AI chatbots generate educational content through character-based dialogues which help students learn how to understand language and social signals. These tools enable students to learn through complete experiences by removing geographical limitations and travel expenses.

Educational applications of AI create ethical problems which stem from the risk of biased algorithms and the need to protect student privacy. AI implementation in educational systems threatens the safety of students because it preserves bias in educational systems while expanding educational disparities and making learning distant and unpersonalized (Vesna et al., 2025; Yu, 2020). AI educational tools must include cultural sensitivity and cross-cultural communication to operate safely. The implementation of AI tools that neglect human-centered approaches leads to greater social disparities. The established guidelines create an ethical foundation for AI systems to function in a responsible and fair manner.

This chapter addresses the given problem directly through a proposal of curriculum design framework strategically useing AI to support educational equity goals and global fluency development. The opening part develops fundamental theoretical underpinnings for AI education which links together CRP and ICC principles. It then synthesizes these theories into a set of actionable principles for curriculum design. Following this, the chapter presents four concrete models for integrating AI into the classroom to support these pedagogical goals. A critical analysis of the significant challenges and institutional considerations, including algorithmic bias, the digital divide, and teacher readiness, is then provided. The chapter ends by presenting a positive outlook on future education that will combine technological progress with ethical values and human-centered learning through AI to achieve worldwide understanding.

## 2. THEORETICAL BACKGROUND

### 2.1. Culturally Responsive Pedagogy

Culturally Relevant Pedagogy (CRP) was established during the mid-1990s when Gloria Ladson-Billings conducted ethnographic research about effective teachers who work with African-American students. The research, conducted between 1988-92 in a predominantly Black, low-income California school, identified eight exemplary teachers through community nomination. The theoretical framework was explicitly grounded in Black feminist and critical pedagogy perspectives. The author used Patricia Hill Collins's Black feminist thought theory to study her own community because she belongs to a marginalized group highlighting real-life experiences and caring methods of teaching (Ladson-Billings, 1995). The three fundamental principles of CRP consist of academic success, cultural competence development which helps students preserve their cultural backgrounds and critical sociopolitical awareness to identify and fight against institutional discrimination. The framework establishes education as an academic process which also serves as a cultural and political system (Ladson-Billings, 2021; Ogodo, 2024).

Ladson-Billings (1995) defined CRP through these three interlocking criteria that effective culturally relevant teaching must fulfill, as the following table presents.

*Table 1. Three components of culturally responsive pedagogy*

| Component | Description | Educational Goal |
|---|---|---|
| Academic Success | Fostering intellectual growth and moral development | Student learning and problem-solving skills |
| Cultural Competence | Supporting students to affirm their culture while becoming fluent in another | Affirming cultural identity and developing cross-cultural fluency |
| Critical Consciousness | The ability to identify, analyze, and solve real-world societal problems | Analyzing and challenging systemic inequalities |

Academic Success requires students to meet challenging standards and high expectations disproving negative assumptions about student abilities because all students excel academically when given challenging and meaningful instruction (Cataldo, 2022; Ladson-Billings, 1995). Teacher education programs develop educational resources that combine artificial intelligence tools to help students who require different learning approaches. The research by Li and Yu (2025) demonstrates that preservice teachers gain knowledge about AI tools (especially generative models) to develop culturally suitable lesson plans adapting to student requirements through a method that combines CRP academic support with AI technology. The global framework for inclusive AI learning by Song et al. (2024) emphasizes equity and wide student inclusion to help teachers create AI learning activities that all students can use. AI tools become effective at delivering personalized educational content when they match the academic success component of CRP to individual student learning styles and needs.

Cultural Competence addresses enabling students to maintain and celebrate their cultural identities while mastering academic content, which involves positioning students' linguistic practices, traditions, and experiential knowledge as pedagogical assets, creating synergy between home culture and school learning rather than treating them as separate or conflicting domains. Ogodo (2024) demonstrates that CRP "empowers students intellectually, socially, emotionally, and politically" through the use of cultural references in their learning process and "cultural competency" serves as the CRP aspect allowing teachers to choose and apply teaching methods that address student requirements and their cultural backgrounds by focusing on their diverse backgrounds as assets rather than limitations. In teacher education, this means preparing teachers to design classroom activities (and now AI-mediated content) that draw on learners' cultures. Taylor and Charran (2025) introduce a "techno-cultural inclusive curriculum design" which unites culturally responsive teaching methods with technological educational tools. The authors present this educational model to help teachers recognize all student identities including multiple marginalized groups through race and gender and disability and other factors to create an inclusive learning environment for all students. Besides, globally, researchers stress the need for

AI curriculum design that accounts for cultural and socioeconomic diversity. The research conducted by Druga et al. (2019) shows that children's interactions with AI technology differ based on their cultural and national backgrounds. The authors suggest educational programs should develop AI learning activities which match these cultural variations. The research findings indicate that AI-based culturally aware educational programs require design approaches supporting worldwide cultural diversity. In short, the cultural-competence component of CRP suggests that the use of AI to create curricula should be grounded in students' cultures, rather than one-size-fits-all content. This also aligns with emerging frameworks for inclusive AI learning as well (Song et al., 2024).

Lastly, Critical Consciousness focuses on developing students' capacity to analyze and challenge social inequities by connecting curriculum to issues of power and justice, which transforms students from passive recipients to co-constructors of knowledge, examining real-world problems affecting their communities and acquiring tools to transform unjust systems (Ladson-Billings, 1995). The AI age requires educational systems to teach students how to analyze technology through activities which include studying AI training data representation and system beneficiaries and how algorithms create social disparities. The educational system needs to develop AI literacy through civic and ethical inquiry because technology must serve both justice and learning purposes yet there are no present examples of AI tools that help students develop critical consciousness.

Recent academic works show that CRP and AI create a strong educational partnership when they are combined in teaching methods. The integration of AI tools and educational content with CRP's three pillars enables education programs to transform AI from a basic tool into a learning enhancement system for students with diverse needs. The training program enables teachers to use AI for academic achievement through culturally relevant approaches while helping them develop cultural competence by using AI-generated content based on student backgrounds and teaching students to analyze AI's social effects. A worldwide education system that uses this approach will create more inclusive learning materials because AI can generate content based on local environments and CRP-based teacher training will help students maintain their cultural identity through these lessons.

## 2.2. Intercultural Communication Competence

Michael Byram established his 1997 ICC model as a basic structure explaining all necessary elements for effective intercultural communication (Hoff, 2020). ICC refers to the ability to communicate effectively and appropriately with people from different cultural backgrounds (Deardorff, 2006). The model includes two main components that contain both factual knowledge about other cultures and the skills and attitudes required to modify behavior when in intercultural situations. The modern world requires ICC as an essential ability because students must learn cultural knowledge and develop intercultural awareness for successful communication across cultures due to increased intercultural contact from technological progress and migration (Deardorff, 2006; Zhang et al., 2025).

Byram's model moves beyond mere linguistic ability, arguing that true competence requires a combination of communicative and intercultural competence (Waliński, 2012). The latter is composed of five interconnected components that describe the necessary knowledge, skills, and attitudes (Hoff, 2020). *Knowledge* concerns the intercultural speaker's understanding of "social groups and their products and practices" in their own and other countries. *Attitudes* are considered the foundational competence and emphasize a disposition of "curiosity and openness" and a readiness to suspend disbelief about other cultures while also questioning one's own. *The skill of interpreting and relating* is the ability to interpret a document or event from another culture, explain it, and relate it to one's own. *The skill of discovery and interaction* involves the ability to acquire new knowledge of a culture and apply that knowledge and those attitudes and skills in real-time communication and interaction. Finally, critical cultural awareness is the ability to critically evaluate, based on explicit criteria, the perspectives, practices, and products in one's own and other cultures. This component has been developed in Byram's later work on intercultural citizenship education, emphasizing democratic values and human rights to defend against intolerance and extremism. Besides, this component also serves as an international parallel to Ladson-Billings' "critical consciousness", providing a clear pathway for synergizing the two models to create a robust pedagogical framework that is both locally grounded and globally applicable.

On the other hand, Deardorff's (2006) pyramid model organizes ICC into successive layers of attitudes, knowledge/skills, and outcomes.

*Figure 1. Deardorff's (2006) pyramid model*

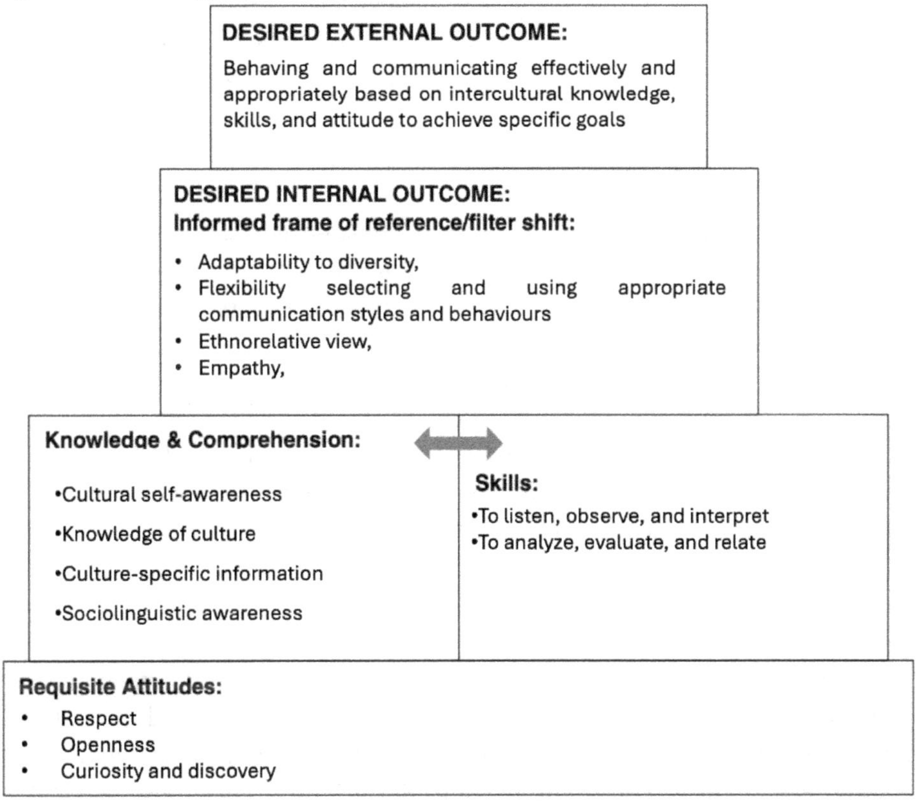


The model operates as a developmental hierarchy. At the base are foundational attitudes: openness, respect for all cultures, and tolerance for ambiguity, which are essential prerequisites for intercultural learning. The next level encompasses knowledge and skills: cultural self-awareness, understanding of diverse cultural contexts including values, histories, linguistic norms, and practical competencies in listening, observing, interpreting, and analyzing cultural information. The internal framework elements create conditions that promote an ethnorelative viewpoint and help individuals modify their communication approaches and develop cultural flexibility and empathy. Intercultural communication finds its optimal result in the apex of this framework: effective and appropriate intercultural communication. The achievement of both suitability and success requires that all pyramid elements develop completely because effectiveness in intercultural contexts depends on the extent of internal growth (Deardorff 2006).

Intercultural competence represents the main purpose of inclusive education services to reach all student populations. AI technology uses adaptable systems to deliver personalized instruction that takes into consideration students' cultural and linguistic profiles. The system creates custom educational materials and assistance devices that enable equal access to learning opportunities for students from any background or ability level (Saborío-Taylor & Rojas-Ramírez 2024).

## 2.3. AI and Pedagogy

The educational environment has undergone a fundamental transformation because of AI implementation in schools. The concept involves moving past technological improvement to transform both teaching methods and educational beliefs according to Ayeni et al. (2024). AI functions as a transformational power generating individualized successful educational spaces yet produces major moral challenges that require careful resolution according to Garzon et al. (2025). The educational environment has started implementing AI technology because educational institutions worldwide conduct experiments to use artificial intelligence for teacher support, curriculum development and the environment of student involvement.

### Personalization and Adaptability

AI delivers its final gift to education through personalized learning adapting educational content to match each student's unique characteristics and learning pace and preferred methods of learning. The collected data allows AI algorithms to create adaptive learning paths generating immediate educational responses that result in superior and varied learning environments (Ayeni et al., 2024). Adaptive learning systems, for example, dynamically adjust the levels of learning difficulty presented in content based on the learner's response, ensuring they are consistently challenged but not overwhelmed. Intelligent Tutoring Systems (ITS) and AI-powered chatbots provide such scaffolding as individually focused information, immediate information and feedback in real time so that the effects of one-to-one tutoring can occur on a larger scale (Vieriu & Petrea, 2025). These systems can identify learning gaps and immediately offer corrective guidance or supplementary materials, allowing students to progress at their own pace and master concepts before moving forward. Because these systems learn from pre-existing datasets which may have societal and historical bias, personalization can unconsciously perpetuate cultural norms, rather than celebrate individuality (Thelma et al., 2024). For example, an AI-based system attempting to personalize a student's content or experience from an underrepresented demographic during its learning phase may not see value beyond standard data and thus, present stereotypical data. The objectives of responsive education become null when these situations occur. The situation needs ongoing human involvement from start to end of the curriculum development process.

## Efficiency

Through its ability to customize instruction AI enables educational productivity because it handles various administrative and standard tasks which used to consume large amounts of teacher work hours (Kasneci et al., 2023; Shi & Aryadoust, 2024). AI systems possess the ability to perform an extensive range of automated tasks. AI enables teachers to produce automatic differentiated learning materials, and the system generates learning activities for students at different skill levels which eliminates the need for teachers to create individual learning content (Cheng, 2025). AI functions as a classroom assistant to handle standard tasks which helps teachers achieve better work-life balance. The method to boost teaching efficiency through AI implementation generates a risk because it might result in complete dependency on AI systems for fundamental educational processes such as curriculum development and assessment while teachers lose their ability to perform essential evaluation work. The practice of educators accepting AI-created lesson plans and feedback without restrictions will create a situation where the "human touch" which efficiency aims to provide will become less evident (Vieriu & Petrea, 2025). AI efficiency achieves its full potential through professional choices which determine whether technology should improve or reduce teaching quality, and these decisions depend on teacher training quality and educational technology adoption practices.

## Ethical Implications

AI systems deployed in education create multiple ethical challenges which need to be solved for responsible and fair implementation. The ethical evaluation of AI in education depends on four essential dimensions which form the basis of current discussions: data privacy and security, algorithmic bias, dehumanization and reduced human interaction, and accountability and transparency. Firstly, the operation of Artificial Intelligence (AI) systems depends on the collection and analysis of sensitive student data which includes learning behaviors and academic results and personal interaction records. The use of these methods creates major privacy risks because unauthorized surveillance and data mishandling threatens student privacy rights and digital freedoms (Deora et al., 2024). Potentially the most important ethical issue is the possibility of algorithmic bias. AI models that are trained on historical data that may reflect social bias may unintentionally perpetuate those biases and perhaps even exacerbate the results of that bias, resulting in inequities (Baker & Hawn, 2022). The educational system displays its bias through grading methods and resource distribution and through the maintenance of false stereotypes which impacts students who belong to marginalized and underrepresented groups (Farheen et al., 2025; Holstein & Doroudi, 2022). Students who depend exclusively on AI programs will give up important direct personal interactions with their teachers and their educational peers. Students face challenges in acquiring vital social-emotional competencies through the "dehumanization of learning" process because it disrupts their development of empathy and collaboration and advanced communication skills which emerge from human interactions. Teachers develop their emotional teaching abilities and psychological depth through the practice of classroom teaching which machines will never achieve (Jia & Zhang, 2021; Selwyn, 2019). Advanced AI algorithms function as "black boxes" which prevents users from tracing the source of problems when they occur. The process of tracking down mistakes and assigning responsibility becomes complex when AI systems generate incorrect recommendations or show biased results thus creating doubt about their reliability (Burrell, 2016; Franzoni, 2023).

## Synergizing CRP and ICC toward a Globally Aware, Inclusive Curriculum

AI faces major ethical challenges because of its inherent biases yet it generates significant possibilities to build an equitable worldwide educational framework. The integration of CRP and ICC as two essential educational frameworks will enable this potential to be achieved. CRP as an educational method requires students' cultural backgrounds to be incorporated into every learning experience by using their life experiences as teaching materials to create culturally relevant education (Samuel et al., 2023). ICC refers to the ability to communicate effectively and appropriately in cross-cultural contexts through knowledge and skills and attitudes that help people handle cultural differences (Cheng, 2025). These frameworks work together toward the common goal of developing learning environments that recognize, value, and engage cultural diversity. The curriculum at this educational center aims to teach students academic skills while developing their cultural understanding and their ability to work with people from different backgrounds (Chen et al., 2025). AI functions as a powerful educational instrument which supports this goal when it is designed and applied with care. AI provides students with cultural educational content and real-time translation capabilities and interactive simulations which help them practice intercultural communication through safe virtual environments (Klimova & Chen, 2024). This approach adopts the Cultural Adaptive Thinking in Education for AI (CATE-AI) framework, demanding that education and tools are engaging globally for equity, but adjusted locally, in order to be mindful of the different needs of all students (Samuel et al., 2023). This framework attempts to move the teaching and learning to an "open and diverse cultural direction", that provides students with the critical literacy and competencies needed for citizenship in an increasingly interconnected and globalizing world (Wu, 2024). Educators are being encouraged to use

AI as a way to enact the principles of CRP and ICC, moving beyond a curricular approach that is individualized to different learning styles to a curricular approach that is culturally responsive to the cultural identities of every learner.

## 3. PRINCIPLES FOR DESIGNING AI-SUPPORTED CULTURALLY RESPONSIVE AND INTERCULTURAL CURRICULUM

AI needs a set of curriculum design principles to achieve its potential of building an educational system that serves all students around the world. The principles function as educational guidelines which direct AI deployment to support fairness and meaningful learning experiences through relevant content (Song et al., 2024). The principles function as a unified system because each individual principle depends on the others to create a chain of mutual reinforcement. Any single principle breach will cause total project failure which will turn an inclusion tool into an exclusion tool. The section presents five fundamental design principles for AI-based curricula which focus on creating culturally sensitive educational materials while teaching students to develop intercultural skills.

### Inclusivity: Ensuring Cultural, Linguistic, and Social Diversity

AI-based syllabi require the first principle to include all students through acknowledgement of their diverse backgrounds which encompass cultural origins and language skills and social circumstances. The principle demands more than symbolic representation because it calls for actual integration of students' cultural backgrounds and personal identities and linguistic heritage into the educational setting to develop a genuine feeling of belonging. An inclusive syllabus, for example, uses accommodating and respectful language, recognizes student cultural backgrounds, and is designed to minimize barriers to participation (Mariyono & Alif Hd, 2025). The implementation of this principle through AI technology depends on three main capabilities which include: (1) providing better access to education for students who face disadvantages when compared to their peers without disadvantages, (2) supporting multiple languages, and (3) delivering content that matches local needs and backgrounds. AI offers various adaptive educational content through its accessibility features which include text-to-speech functionality and automated video captioning and audio transcript generation and image description capabilities (Melo-Lopez et al., 2025). AI tools can support students who speak different languages yet they need to develop algorithms which identify, validate and duplicate students' distinctive dialects and social language patterns for communication instead of enforcing standard English usage to protect their linguistic identity (Albeihi & Rice, 2025).

AI-assisted real-time translation will enhance fair multilingual communication methods for students who come from different cultural backgrounds in their classrooms and during group work activities at school (Fitas, 2025). The educational content of students will become more relevant and culturally appropriate through generative AI technology which produces educational examples and case studies and activities based on local cultural settings (Anis, 2023).

AI-driven inclusivity programs need to undergo thorough risk assessment before they can be implemented. AI models that learn from various content sources tend to repeat discriminatory patterns because their training data contains existing cultural prejudices. AI systems without human supervision produce stereotypical and unverified content which also includes culturally offensive material that affects AI users (Carbajal-Carrera, 2024). The process of making AI content authentic and respectful requires educators and cultural mediators and community members to perform continuous audits of AI-generated material (Anis, 2023). The creation of AI-supported curricula through participatory design practices will become more inclusive because it enables all stakeholders to contribute their perspectives (Lee et al., 2025).

## Contextual Relevance: Adapting Content to Local and Global Realities

The principle of contextual relevance corresponds closely to the idea of inclusiveness. The curriculum needs to undergo a process of "glocalization" because this approach helps students learn through relevant experiences that connect classroom content with their community and worldwide environment. AI technology enables us to achieve new heights in producing content that stays contextually relevant for users. AI systems generate personalized learning materials through their ability to analyze cultural heritage and personal interests (Samuel et al., 2023; Wu, 2024). The main problem with realizing true contextual relevance with artificial intelligence is the largely Western bias of the data used to train most large language models. The application of Western knowledge systems leads to major cultural and factual errors when creating content for non-Western settings (Maisiri & Musonza, 2025). AI development needs diverse multilingual datasets which require local data collection efforts and language acquisition training. The current educational environment requires teachers to function as cultural validators who use their community expertise to evaluate AI-generated content for student accuracy and relevance.

## Interactivity and Personalization: Using AI for Learner-centered Pathways

The basic rule for modern educational methods demands a transition from traditional teacher-led instruction to student-centered active learning approaches (Tapalova & Zhiyenbayeva, 2022). The principle establishes that students must receive additional authority and control over their educational processes. AI enables this transformation through its ability to deliver interactive personalized learning experiences which handle large numbers of students at once. AI supports learner-centered design through its two fundamental components which include personalized learning paths and interactive elements within educational content. AI algorithms generate individualized learning pathways for students by analyzing multiple data points which include quiz scores, learning task effort and discussion forum contributions (Naseer et al, 2024). The educational system delivers automatic support to students who need help through extra resources and challenging tasks for students who have already demonstrated their knowledge of the material. Second, the basis of AI is to generate complex and interactive learning pathways that allow for deep engagement (Wang, Cheung, et al., 2025). AI develops interactive learning materials through educational games, advanced simulations, virtual reality, augmented reality experiences and smart chatbots that provide student assistance. Learning tools transform educational experiences from passive information absorption into interactive discovery, problem-solving activities and creative work.

## Reflective Learning: Embedding Critical Self-awareness and Empathy through Data and Feedback

Educational programs that foster transformative learning require students to achieve content mastery while developing advanced cognitive and affective skills which include reflective practice, critical self-awareness and empathy. In particular, the reflective process can benefit from the unique attributes of AI, which supports emotional experiences, immediate feedback, personalizing of the feedback for each individual, and avoiding human bias. AI can provide meaningful feedback to students without the delay and limitations of their time (Chang et al., 2025).

AI can also be an innovative vehicle for building empathy and cultural self-awareness. AI-facilitated simulations, VR spaces, and role-play chatbots can put students in various, complex social situations which allow them to practice perspective-taking and interact with challenges to intercultural communication in a controlled, safe-to-fail context (Sethi & Jain, 2024). For example, a student could engage in a simulated negotiation with an AI avatar programmed in the communication norms of a different culture in which they would learn to adjust their style and identify their own cultural biases on the spot. This would create a "cultural mirror" through which the AI can make a student's cultural assumptions external by demonstrating how these words may be interpreted through a different worldview and develop critical self-awareness. It is important, however, to acknowledge the limitations with this novel approach. Some studies have noted the lack of genuine empathy in AI-produced feedback and the potential misalignment with subtle cultural and linguistic cues (Vieriu & Petrea, 2025). Therefore, we consider that AI-guided reflection functions as a catalyst to stimulate but not substitute human-led dialogue and deep analysis conducted by educators.

### Ethics and Access: Balancing Innovation with Equity and Responsibility

An AI-based educational framework demands an ethical foundation that focuses on fairness, rapid response and individual student autonomy. Educational systems using innovation maintain proper ethical boundaries. The foundation of all educational systems begins with ethical practices and student access as fundamental elements for personalized and interactive learning. AI testing together with thorough auditing procedures helps to minimize discriminatory patterns and advance inclusive educational practices. The decision-making process of AI systems needs to remain fully visible so that both trustworthiness and stakeholder accountability can be achieved. Organizations should implement well-established data privacy standards which both maintain student secrecy and empower students to control their information. AI technology must improve human educators rather than replace them in its final role. The ultimate authority for student education assessment and support should always belong to human educators (Chu & Ashraf, 2025).

## 4. CURRICULUM INTEGRATION (MODELS, TOOLS, CLASSROOM APPLICATIONS, TEACHER TRAINING)

To bring AI-supported culturally responsive and intercultural curriculum design from theory to practice, identifiable models of integration are necessary. Models provide a scaffold for utilizing certain AI functionalities for specific pedagogical goals. This section evaluates four different models: AI-Augmented Language and Culture Modules, AI-Supported Collaborative Online Intercultural Learning (COIL), Competency-Based Learning Analytics for ICC, and Project-Based Learning with AI Simulations. In addition to considering existing AI tools and classroom applications, the importance of teacher training and institutional support as a basis for implementation will be discussed. The models have an associated pedagogical goal, example tools and technologies, application in the classroom, and primary challenges as described in the following table.

*Table 2. Curriculum integration models*

| Model | Pedagogical Goal | Example Tools & Technologies | Classroom Application | Primary Challenges |
|---|---|---|---|---|
| A: AI-Augmented Language & Culture Modules | Integrate language learning with deep cultural understanding. | Duolingo, Busuu, Rosetta Stone, ChatGPT, Speech Recognition NLP. | Students practice language in AI-generated, culturally specific role-playing scenarios. | AI may lack deep cultural nuance; risk of repetitive or inauthentic interactions. |
| B: AI-Supported COIL | Foster intercultural competence through direct, project-based collaboration between diverse student groups. | NLP-based grouping tools, AI features in Microsoft Teams/ Google Classroom, AI-generated prompts | AI pairs students from different countries for a collaborative project and provides tools to overcome language barriers. | Logistical complexity; requires strong teacher facilitation; potential for surface-level engagement if not structured well. |
| C: Competency-Based Learning Analytics for ICC | Make ICC development a measurable, transparent, and reflective process. | Learning Analytics Dashboards (LADs), AI-powered self-assessment tools based on ICC rubrics. | A dashboard visualizes a student's development of skills like empathy and openness based on their interactions in online forums. | Defining and measuring ICC is complex; risk of reducing competence to simplistic metrics; data privacy concerns. |
| D: Project-Based Learning with AI Simulations | Develop practical skills in intercultural negotiation and conflict resolution in a safe-to-fail environment. | ATLAS platform, VR environments, AI chatbots for role-playing, custom AI avatars | Students interact with AI avatars representing different cultural stakeholders to resolve a simulated business conflict. | High development cost; risk of reinforcing stereotypes if not designed carefully; AI may lack genuine emotional nuance |

## Model A: AI-Augmented Language and Culture Modules

The educational goal of this model requires students to move past vocabulary and grammar memorization toward complete cultural learning which is essential for genuine ICC. Language and culture are inherently intertwined, and active communication requires a sense of the implicit norms, values, and pragmatic rules governing interaction (Whorf, 2012). AI technology enables the development of educational content which unites different learning dimensions into a single integrated system.

The model uses AI technology to perform specific fundamental operations. AI-based platforms such as Duolingo and Busuu and Rosetta Stone provide personalized content through learning paths that adjust to the user's skill level and learning speed. Unfortunately, the cultural context presented appears to be mostly superficial (Munday, 2016). Thus, these systems should provide contextual and cultural alternatives beyond linguistic practice, offering additional culturally relevant content such as articles, videos, and interactive games that provide a glimpse of the cultural consciousness of the language being practiced. Furthermore, generative AI tools such as ChatGPT could also add to interactive turn-taking, generating conversation practice with a virtual interlocutor. They could be a tireless, non-judgmental interlocutor for students to role-play, creating opportunities for students to practice their language in contexts of low-stakes scenarios.

One feasible classroom application might take a hybrid form. Students may do vocabulary and grammar work on an adaptive platform such as Duolingo. The instructor may then create a series of intercultural scenarios for students to practice with ChatGPT. For example, students might be asked to politely decline an invitation from a superior in a high-context culture; it may be difficult to teach such a nuanced interaction through Duolingo alone. A student would engage in a text-based conversation with ChatGPT, and, in the parameters set by the instructor prompt, the ChatGPT would give feedback not only on linguistic accuracy but also on the cultural appropriateness of phrasing, tone, and directness of the student (Kecskes & Dinh, 2025). Such blended practice provides students with an opportunity for structured learning and dynamic, situational practice to support their developmental processes in respective fluency and pragmatic competence.

## Model B: Collaborative Online Intercultural Learning (COIL) Supported by AI for Pairing Students across Borders

The COIL approach connects learners and their instructors across cultures, resulting in students participating in more collaborative and project-based learning experiences, providing opportunities for intercultural competence through authentic, sustained engagement (Rubin, 2017). The conventional method produces operational difficulties which affect both team interaction and communication flow, yet COIL delivers positive results. AI can enhance the COIL format by helping to mitigate some of these issues and augment the learning experience.

The role of AI in this model is primarily as a facilitator. One application is intelligent pairing of students. In this application of COIL, rather than relying on random or instructor-based pair or group formation, AI will serve to analyze student profiles: their learning styles, professed interests, language competence to be able to create groups that are diverse but appropriately balanced - these are groups that may be more likely to collaborate than a random group (Finkelstein & Soffer-Vital, 2025). For example, natural language processing (NLP) could take a student's initial written response to a prompt and smartly put people together with different or opposing viewpoints in order to inspire as many quality conversations as possible (Billings et al., 2024).

AI could assist with communication, using real-time translation tools for the communication platforms, and lower language barriers and support more full participation from all team members (Du & Daniel, 2024). AI can help communication progress further than just translating. In addition to that, it can analyze communication patterns in that group. It could detect potential signs of misunderstanding or disengagement and provide the group or instructor automated prompts to act to intervene and otherwise support collaboration (Wong, 2026). Finally, AI can assist with structuring the collaboration, by generating prompts that are culturally sensitive discussion starters or icebreaking activities to guide students to engage with each other in their initial interactions and navigating their cultural differences constructively (Finkelstein & Soffer-Vital, 2025).

For example, it is imagined that business students in the United States and ones in Japan (in a COIL project) would co-construct a joint marketing plan. The AI could first suggest students based on some complementary, crowd-sourced skills in matching students to strategize classmates from different cultures. Once students are engaged on a platform like Microsoft Teams, an integrated AI for communication may provide translation services, and perhaps add a function for the AI to privately let the instructor intervene when one of the teams was seemingly talking too much or at least had a sustained period of chatter amongst them.

## Model C: Competency-Based Learning Analytics for ICC Progress

One of the principal difficulties encountered when teaching ICC is that its enhancement is generally viewed as intangible and difficult to assess. This model is designed to counter that difficulty by systematically leveraging AI-enhanced learning analytics to make the process of developing intercultural competence more visible, observable, measurable, and reflective for the students and the instructor (Zhang et al., 2025). The anticipated outcome is to provide evidence of progress against defined competencies, alongside data-driven feedback for action.

This is also heavily reliant on LADs. These AI-created data analytics platforms are designed to collect, analyze, and visualize data created from broad-ranging student engagement with tasks such as online discussion forums, group projects, and reflective journaling (Kaliisa & Dolonen, 2023). Current LADs typically report more generalized numerical academic metrics (such as grades and time-on-task) that are not modifiable, while there are LADs that can be used to generate reports of ICC-specific measures (De Vreugd et al., 2024; Susnjak et al., 2022), for example, measures can be linked to scholarly frameworks, such as American Association of Colleges and Universities' (AAC&U) Intercultural Knowledge and Competence VALUE Rubric that identified criteria of cultural self-awareness, empathy and openness (Miller, 2020).

In conjunction with dashboards, this model utilizes AI-powered self-assessment tools. Such technology can facilitate periodic reflection with students on their own intercultural development as it relates to ICC concepts. Rather than employing a conventional assessment questionnaire, an AI tool can develop a dialogue with the student, prompting probing questions based on the student's recent participation and encouraging students to link their experience back to the key concepts from ICC. The platform would provide descriptive analytics (what did the student do), predictive analytics (what is their likely trajectory), and even prescriptive analytics to provide concrete, data-driven advice for improvement (De Araujo et al., 2025; Guan et al., 2025).

Below is an illustration of this process: a student enrolled in an online course engages in weekly discussions about global cases. An LAD analyzes the nature and content of the student's posts and tracks the frequency with which they ask questions of others to learn about their perspectives (curiosity), acknowledge differing opinions in a respectful manner (openness), and employ language that reminds us that they are attempting to understand another's feelings (empathy). In this case, the dashboard communicates whether the student demonstrated curiosity, openness, and empathy in their previous week's participation, possibly even tracking a trend line related to their "empathy" over the preceding months of the semester. Additionally, the student may answer an AI guided self-assessment discussion each week that asks questions to them reflectively such as, "Think about what you discussed in this week's discussion. Did you find there was a moment you disagreed with a classmate from a different cultural background? How did you convey that disagreement?' A weekly self-reflection, in combination with data generated by the system, would push the student to demonstrate a deeper level of criticality, contemplation, and engagement with their own intercultural development process. Based on the student's dashboard data and self-assessment responses, the AI might offer a prescriptive suggestion: "You are doing well at stating your own opinion clearly. Next week, try to explicitly ask a follow-up question about the other person's perspective before sharing your own."

## Model D: Project-Based Learning using AI Simulations

This model focuses on developing practical intercultural skills through simulated learning exercises that train individuals for negotiation and conflict resolution in demanding situations (Sethi & Jain, 2024). The educational rationale is that you develop competence by practicing, and using AI to create simulation-based games provides students with a safe-to-fail environment in which they can experiment, make errors, utilize the immediate feedback, and learn without the ramifications of a real-world event.

The primary technology in this model is the integration of AI-Driven avatars, or Non-Player Characters (NPCs). The developers of Realistic avatars built them to perform as complete digital personalities which show various cultural backgrounds through their unique communication methods and value systems and emotional behaviors. The AI avatars will produce unplanned responses to student input through their verbal and non-verbal reactions. The system enables educational institutions to establish learning environments which deliver customized learning content. AI systems can modify their interaction level during the conversation by increasing conflict or introducing new elements that match student responses to create customized challenging interactions (Fink et al., 2024; Huyen, 2024; Islam & Wang, 2025).

A pivotal aspect of this model is the provision of real-time, data-driven feedback. The AI platform tracks student interaction data which includes their language use and tone, their decision points and strategic approaches. The platform delivers a powerful debrief immediately after the simulation ends to show students their strengths and weaknesses in handling the intercultural interaction (Nadziroh et al., 2025).

## AI Tools that Support Culturally Responsive ICC Teaching

The integrated models mentioned above serve as a base for AI tools which help teachers implement Culturally Rresponsive and ICC teaching at more detailed levels. These tools can be categorized by their primary function. Educators use ChatGPT and Google's Gemini and DeepSeek as *generative AI tools* to develop learning materials which respect cultural diversity. The tools generate diverse educational materials including case studies and role-playing scenarios and examples through particular context-aware prompts which match students from different backgrounds (Stefaniak & Moore, 2024). Mainstream *collaboration platforms* are adding AI technology to their systems to help users work together more effectively across different cultural backgrounds. The AI features of Google Classroom and Microsoft Teams use pattern analysis from student group work to generate teacher alerts about student team interactions. Students can use Flipgrid to submit video responses to questions that they can use to practice role-playing and communication skills while AI assesses their delivery and presentation (Cheng, 2025). Moreover, Virtual Reality (VR) platforms such as ImmerseMe and Mondly VR create *highly immersive environments* where students can "visit" other countries and practice language and culture. The abstract cultural concepts become easier to remember through these experiences (Yan & Lowell, 2025). Finally, *specialized pedagogical assistants* are the tools that focus on creating systems which help teachers implement culturally sensitive educational practices. For instance, the CulturAIEd tool is an LLM-powered system designed to help K-12 teachers adapt existing AI literacy curricula to their students' specific cultural contexts by providing rubric-based feedback and just-in-time coaching (Wang, Xiao, et al., 2025).

## Practical Applications in the Classroom

Theoretical models and tools have become more widely used in actual educational environments through multiple case studies and pilot projects that demonstrate their effectiveness. These applications deliver useful information about AI's learning advantages and practical obstacles when used for intercultural education.

One especially interesting case study was the use of generative AI to design case studies for a postgraduate project management course with a diverse international student cohort (Jayasinghe et al., 2025). Educators used AI to generate case studies contextualized in the specific cultural context of the students. The students gave positive feedback about the culturally relevant materials because they found them interesting and personally meaningful which helped them better grasp the course material. Also, researchers focused on AI-assisted programming education in Taiwan as a specific study that involved multi-ethnic college students (Tsai et al., 2022). Researchers in the study developed an AI system that monitors student academic success alongside their motivation patterns. The study discovered fundamental cultural differences because indigenous learners pursued educational benefits for their clans and Han Chinese students concentrated on personal progress. The teaching approaches of educators evolved to match their students' cultural values. Through AI applications, people can access educational content that reveals the cultural components behind learning motivations.

The increasing implementation of AI in educational institutions reaches the point of practical implementation which demonstrates its potential to revolutionize cross-cultural education. AI systems operate through two main purposes according to the research. The educational content platform generates customized learning materials for international project management classes through AI implementation which provides individualized scenarios to students. The system acts as an adaptable content creation platform to develop culturally appropriate educational resources for students studying international project management. The analytical functions of AI technology help educators identify cultural elements which influence student involvement. Through intelligent cultural-sensitive methods AI demonstrates its ability to develop educational approaches that meet the needs of diverse students and their distinct learning styles together with their motivating factors.

## Teacher Training and Institutional Support

The performance of AI integration systems stands on two fundamental factors which include both the system's technical capabilities and the ability of teachers and educational organizations to handle its operation. Human beings represent the most essential component which will never lose its importance. Thus, strong teacher training and institution-wide support are ideal, and indeed essential, to using AI for valuable and ethical education.

Effective teacher training, or professional development, must go beyond simply training teachers on the basic operation of AI tools (Mikhailova & Cesur, 2025). It must continue to be a contextual, data-informed, and equity-focused process that allows educators to develop a multifaceted set of competencies (Nabi et al., 2025). This process includes AI literacy, or a fundamental understanding of how AI systems work, their limitations, and the ethics of their use (Li & Yu, 2025). It is also particularly vital for professional development to engage in the process of pedagogically integrating AI to help teachers learn the practice of ensuring AI tools relate to their learning goals and use AI tools in educationally appropriate ways (Tammets & Ley, 2023). Professional development must also include learning related to prompt engineering so that teachers can create culturally relevant content in AI prompts, and in response to particular contexts, educate teachers on evaluating bias and accuracy of outputs generated from an AI system (Qian, 2025). Recent study by Temel and Cesur (2024) shows how pedagogically informed use of digital tools, such as gamified Web 2.0 environments, can significantly enhance learner motivation and attainment. This underlines the need for teacher training in purposeful, culturally responsive technology integration.

Institutions need to build a supportive environment for this work to succeed. The first step requires students to access essential technological infrastructure which provides equal access to learning through dependable internet connections and suitable devices (OECD, 2023). Institutions need to establish both their physical infrastructure and their ethical guidelines and privacy standards to guide AI implementation. The organization needs to establish a support system which promotes classroom innovation through AI tools by giving teachers dedicated time and resource access to test new teaching methods and by creating professional learning communities for sharing best practices (Chan, 2023). Research demonstrates that two main factors obstruct the successful use of advanced teaching methods including AI-based COIL because institutions fail to offer support and teachers lack necessary training (Sun, 2025). The most advanced AI systems require substantial funding for human resources and system infrastructure to reach their full educational capabilities.

## 5. CHALLENGES AND CONSIDERATIONS

AI integration into curriculum design shows great promise but its application faces multiple significant obstacles which could eliminate all potential benefits of AI. These challenges are not just technical failures, but are deeply connected to social, ethical and economic structures. Research shows that addressing these problems before they arise will help AI-based education systems prevent from making current social disparities worse (Baker & Hawn, 2022). The four main challenges of algorithmic bias and teacher readiness and digital inequality and ethical management systems form a connected network which amplifies their individual effects. AI tools reveal diversity and bias because they use AI models for training which generates biased data sets due to unequal access to technology resources. When biased tools are in the hands of teachers who have had no training to identify or mitigate bias, they can inadvertently perpetuate harm against the students they are trying to support. Breaking this cycle will require system-based approaches to address each of these challenges simultaneously (Garzon et al., 2025; Poornesh, 2024).

The most pervasive and insidious challenge in deploying AI for culturally responsive education is the problem of algorithmic bias. AI models learn from the data they are trained on, and if that data reflects existing societal prejudices, the AI will learn, reproduce, and often amplify those prejudices (Baker & Hawn, 2022; Idowu, 2024).

Cultural stereotyping is one of the most prevalent types. AI systems, especially those using large language models (LLMs) trained primarily on data from Western, English-speaking cultures, may not be able to fully understand other cultures or global contexts (Usman et al., 2025). Furthermore, generative AI image tools can simply produce images that conform to traditional and biased gender roles in the workplace (Thomson et al., 2026). An even more concerning type of bias is cultural erasure. In pursuit of patterns, AI models can either miss or leave out a fuller representation of marginalized groups who are not included in training data. These biased outputs can negatively affect students by decreasing their sense of belonging, reinforcing negative self-images, and disengaging them from the learning experiences (Lewis, 2025). Solving these problems needs fundamental changes to AI model development methods which must include large representative datasets and thorough auditing procedures to detect and eliminate bias.

AI tool development at a rapid pace continues to produce a major "readiness gap" within educational institutions. Teacher readiness should not be regarded as a technical skill, rather it represents a complex interaction of confidence, AI dispositions, ethical considerations, and a level of institutional support. The present selection of professional development programmes does not adequately prepare teachers for this challenge; they focus on evaluating technical skills for AI usage but overlook the essential element of support. AI systems are frequently implemented as supplemental components that operate independently from the main system. The method of AI surface-level examination enables educational institutions to train students in AI tools yet neglect to teach them the essential AI concepts needed for correct and ethical usage. Acar et al. (2024) demonstrate that learning obstacles stem primarily from educational methods and insufficient teacher training rather than technological blockages. Educational institutions need to address their existing institutional problems because AI system deployment will make current social inequalities worse. Then here, a serious need exists for a new professional development paradigm. The new approach should develop over an extended period while adapting to specific environments to create fair educational methods which go past basic technical skills for AI literacy development (Nabi et al., 2025). The inclusion of literacy training for teachers requires professional development programs which teach basic AI concepts and merge critical teaching methods with ethical and cultural decision-making skills and team-based learning approaches. The educational transformation through AI technology will face limitations because it will only benefit students who belong to privileged social classes.

AI implementation faces major challenges because the "digital divide" threatens to split education into two separate systems which will worsen existing learning gaps through unequal technology availability. The "digital divide" encompasses more than device ownership because it includes multiple problems that affect people's ability to get fast internet service and modern technology and basic digital competencies to operate these systems. The educational system creates particular disadvantages for students from low-income backgrounds and students who reside in rural areas and students who attend schools with insufficient resources (Solomon et al., 2003; Vesna et al., 2025). Artificial intelligence in education will expand existing social and economic and geographic inequalities unless specific measures are taken to address this problem. The solution for digital equity demands multiple organizations to work together through a structured system of collaboration. The development of digital education equity requires government authorities to create suitable policies which will guarantee equal access for all students. The government could reach this goal by providing public funding to build nationwide broadband infrastructure and by supporting AI learning tools for underprivileged students and by creating incentives for developers to produce inexpensive open-source educational AI systems (Vesna et al., 2025). The educational system should go past basic internet access to create an environment which enables all students to successfully use AI-based learning tools.

Local governance systems need to be established for ethical AI use and student data protection. Institutions together with regional and national authorities need to create complete policy frameworks which will enable responsible AI deployment throughout all educational institutions. An operational governance system depends on particular essential components for its successful implementation. Student data protection stands as the primary concern. This must be addressed first. The system needs to establish separate boundaries between collecting data for personalized services and keeping student privacy rights intact. Second, a core ethical implementation principle is adopting "Human-in-the-Loop" design. This design formalizes that AI should complement/distance human judgment (Office of Superintendent of Public Instruction, 2024). AI functions as an educational resource for students and teachers but it lacks the capability to make choices. Third, frameworks should require transparency and accountability. AI systems need to deliver detailed explanations to teachers and students about their operational processes. The systems need to operate under a system which handles all results from their operation while detecting the party responsible for any damage or faults that occur (Chu & Ashraf, 2025). Academic integrity policies should establish specific rules which students need to follow. Students who use generative AI need educational institutions to develop clear rules about acceptable and prohibited uses of this technology.

## 6. IMPLICATIONS FOR THE FUTURE RESEARCH

The development of an equitable and effective future demands a well-defined research plan which will serve as a foundation for its advancement. The academic sector must address multiple critical problems which emerge from the identification of research gaps and challenges presented in this chapter. Research is needed to create AI models which use diverse and multilingual representative datasets. The development of strong methodologies for auditing existing AI systems for cultural bias requires transparent standardized systematic approaches that also include methods for bias reduction or elimination in AI systems (Li & Yu, 2025). At present, the research base includes many short-term studies, and there is a notable absence of rigorous, longitudinal studies relating to the long-term impact of AI on student learning, identity development, and well-being, especially in diverse and intersecting learner populations. The evaluation of academic results needs to be extended by future research through the study of student development regarding their sense of belonging and their critical consciousness and intercultural competence when using culturally responsive AI tools (Tan et al., 2024). Furthermore, it is necessary to move research away from AI's technological capabilities to the pedagogical design that allows it to be effectively utilized. The research needs to explore classroom human-AI collaboration through studies that determine optimal interface designs and workflow processes which maximize the combined capabilities of human educators and artificial intelligence systems (Atchley et al., 2024). Academic research has yet to perform an assessment of the effectiveness of proposed ethical frameworks and policies through empirical studies in various educational settings. Academic research requires an investigation of how particular rules and procedures translate into the implementation of fundamental principles of fairness transparency and accountability within educational institutions and their impact on student achievement. The research will show that ethical guidelines operate as functional tools protecting responsible innovation through measurable and actionable methods (Wieczorek et al., 2025).

AI educational implementation requires more than technological advancements because it needs to follow ethical guidelines and cultural values and educational methods. The creation and implementation of artificial intelligence systems need to follow a humanistic approach which researchers, educators and policymakers must establish. AI will become a positive educational force through deliberate actions which will bring about transformative changes in education instead of expanding existing inequalities. AI enables the advancement of human teaching and learning by creating educational systems which unite intellectual power with ethical values and humanistic principles.

## 7. CONCLUSION AND FUTURE DIRECTIONS

These days education and artificial intelligence have established their initial contact with each other. The future presents two paths which will either cause AI to worsen existing social disparities while strengthening cultural stereotypes and separating students from AI-generated educational content or lead to an "educational renaissance" through AI-human collaboration to assist teachers in building personalized learning experiences that honor cultural backgrounds and promote fairness for every student (Gattupalli & Maloy, 2024). The analysis in this paper contends that there is no inevitability of a technologically deterministic future. The collaborative approach to ethical decision-making enables us to develop a superior future without depending on technology as the solution to past social injustices.

A culturally rooted implementation requires that AI systems harmonize with human values and cultural diversity (Gattupalli & Maloy, 2024). The promise of "AI for all" must not be interpreted solely as equitable technology, but as the right of every learner to engage with educational opportunities that honors, depicts, and enhances their identity, cultural practices (Maisiri & Musonza, 2025) through the use of technology. AI technologies enable learning integration through a social and cultural framework which creates new educational approaches; the primary goal of AI development extends beyond machine optimization because it seeks to create educational tools that produce advanced learning experiences which foster human development.

The development of AI systems which focus on human needs and cultural adaptation requires the implementation of human-centered and culturally responsive development methods. AI systems need to be developed through a fundamental co-design process which requires the participation of all stakeholders including classroom teachers and students as well as cultural experts and community members who represent various backgrounds and life experiences (Xie et al., 2024). AI tools that operate in actual classroom environments with both safety features and usable functionality will be developed through the process of recognizing teachers as educational leaders by combining their professional knowledge and personal classroom experience (Uygun, 2024). The field of educational AI needs to move beyond creating generic AI systems for education through this approach toward developing specialized Educational AI systems which work together with human educators. The upcoming tools will be created with educational methods and fairness and cultural relevance built into their core design because this approach seems to be the most effective route forward.

## REFERENCES


Acar, S. C., Cesur, K., Mikhailova, T., & Akshulakova, B. (2024). A netnographic study on the reasons why people fail to learn English. *Participatory Educational Research, 11*(6), 134–151. DOI: 10.17275/per.24.83.11.6

Albeihi, H. H. M., & Rice, M. F. (2025). Generative AI and language diversity: Implications for teachers and learners. *Arab World English Journal, 16*(1), 43–54. DOI: 10.24093/awej/vol16no1.3

Anis, M. (2023). Leveraging artificial intelligence for inclusive English language teaching: Strategies and implications for learner diversity. *Journal of Multidisciplinary Educational Research, 12*(6), 54–70

Ansaldo, S. (2025). The mirror metaphor and AI: Reflections and realities on education from an emergence perspective. *Globalisation, Societies and Education*, 1–16. DOI: 10.1080/14767724.2025.2543324

Atchley, P., Pannell, H., Wofford, K., Hopkins, M., & Atchley, R. A. (2024). Human and AI collaboration in the higher education environment: Oportunities and concerns. *Cognitive Research: Principles and Implications, 9*(1), 20. DOI: 10.1186/s41235-024-00547-9

Ayeni, O. O., Al Hamad, N. M., Chisom, O. N., Osawaru, B., & Adewusi, O. E. (2024). AI in education: A review of personalized learning and educational technology. *GSC Advanced Research and Reviews, 18*(2), 261–271. DOI: 10.30574/gscarr.2024.18.2.0062

Baker, R. S., & Hawn, A. (2022). Algorithmic bias in education. *International Journal of Artificial Intelligence in Education, 32*(4), 1052–1092. DOI: 10.1007/s40593-021-00285-9

Billings, K., Chang, H. Y., Lim-Breitbart, J. M., & Linn, M. C. (2024). Using artificial intelligence to support peer-to-peer discussions in science classrooms. *Education Sciences, 14*(12), 1411. 1-23 DOI: 10.3390/educsci14121411

Burrell, J. (2016). How the machine 'thinks': Understanding opacity in machine learning algorithms. *Big Data & Society, 3*(1), 2053951715622512. Advance online publication. DOI: 10.1177/2053951715622512

Carbajal-Carrera, B. (2024). AIsplaining: Generative AI explains linguistic identities to me. *Australian Review of Applied Linguistics, 47*(3), 340–365. DOI: 10.1075/aral.24077.car

Cataldo, K. (2022). Culturally relevant pedagogy in the post-COVID-19 era. *Current Issues in Comparative Education, 24*(2), 115–118. DOI: 10.52214/cice.v24i2.9393

Chan, C. K. Y. (2023). A comprehensive AI policy education framework for university teaching and learning. *International Journal of Educational Technology in Higher Education, 20*(1), 38. DOI: 10.1186/s41239-023-00408-3

Chang, C. Y., Lin, H. C., Yin, C., & Yang, K. H. (2025). Generative AI-assisted reflective writing for improving students' higher order thinking. *Journal of Educational Technology & Society, 28*(1), 270–285. DOI: 10.30191/ETS.202501_28(1).TP03

Chen, Y., Macias, H., Granco, G., Hou, Y., & Gomez, F. A. (2025). AI for social good education through a culturally responsive pedagogy. In *Artificial Intelligence for Design and Process Science* (pp. 1-12). Springer Nature, Switzerland. DOI: 10.1007/978-3-031-67886-8_1

Cheng, H. (2025). Research on strategies for cultivating intercultural communication competence in AI-assisted English teaching. *Advances in Educational Technology and Psychology, 9*(1), 101–107. DOI: 10.23977/aetp.2025.090113

Chu, T. S., & Ashraf, M. (2025). Artificial intelligence in curriculum design: A data-driven approach to higher education innovation. *Knowledge (Beverly Hills, Calif.), 5*(3), 14. DOI: 10.3390/knowledge5030014

De Araujo, A., Papadopoulos, P. M., McKenney, S., & de Jong, T. (2025). Investigating the impact of a collaborative conversational agent on dialogue productivity and knowledge acquisition. *International Journal of Artificial Intelligence in Education, 35*(4), 1–27. DOI: 10.1007/s40593-025-00469-7

De Vreugd, L., Van Leeuwen, A., Jansen, R., & Van der Schaaf, M. (2024). Learning analytics dashboard design and evaluation to support student self-regulation of study behaviour. *Journal of Learning Analytics, 11*(3), 249–262. DOI: 10.18608/jla.2024.8529

Deardorff, D. K. (2006). Identification and assessment of intercultural competence as a student outcome of internationalization. *Journal of Studies in International Education, 10*(3), 241–266. DOI: 10.1177/1028315306287002

Deora, Y., Saini, A. K., Yadav, H., & Parewa, R. K. (2024). Ethical implications of AI in education: Data privacy and algorithmic bias. *International Journal of Creative Research Thoughts, 12*(10), 855–866.

Dolidze, T. (2025). The evolving role of artificial intelligence in legal education and research. *Law & World, 11*(33), 92–105. DOI: 10.36475/11.1.7

Druga, S., Vu, S. T., Likhith, E., & Qiu, T. (2019). Inclusive AI literacy for kids around the world. *Proceedings of FabLearn, 2019*, 104–111. DOI: 10.1145/3311890.3311904

Du, J., & Daniel, B. K. (2024). Transforming language education: A systematic review of AI-powered chatbots for English as a foreign language speaking practice. *Computers and Education: Artificial Intelligence*, *6*, 100230. DOI: 10.1016/j.caeai.2024.100230

Ebo, S. (2022). Globalization and social media: Impacts of Facebook on the contemporary order. *International Journal of Research and Innovation in Social Science*, *6*(8), 1–6.

Farheen, S., Cheema, A. A., Ullah, R. S., & Bandeali, M. M. (2025). Equity and bias in AI educational tools: A critical examination of algorithmic decision-making in classrooms. *The Critical Review of Social Sciences Studies*, *3*(3), 67–85. DOI: 10.59075/zqmnpa62

Fink, M. C., Robinson, S. A., & Ertl, B. (2024). AI-based avatars are changing the way we learn and teach: Benefits and challenges. *Frontiers in Education*, *9*, 1416307. DOI: 10.3389/feduc.2024.1416307

Finkelstein, I., & Soffer-Vital, S. (2025). Cultural empathy in AI-supported collaborative learning: Advancing inclusive digital learning in higher education. *Education Sciences*, *15*(10), 1305. DOI: 10.3390/educsci15101305

Fitas, R. (2025). *Inclusive education with AI: Supporting special needs and tackling language barriers*. arXiv:2504.14120.

Franzoni, V. (2023). From black box to glass box: Advancing transparency in artificial intelligence systems for ethical and trustworthy AI. In *International Conference on Computational Science and Its Applications* (pp. 118-130). Springer Nature Switzerland. DOI: 10.1007/978-3-031-37114-1_9

Garzón, J., Patiño, E., & Marulanda, C. (2025). Systematic review of artificial intelligence in education: Trends, Benefits, and challenges. *Multimodal Technologies and Interaction*, *9*(8), 84. DOI: 10.3390/mti9080084

Gattupalli, S., & Maloy, R. W. (2024). *On human-centered AI in education*. University of Massachusetts Amherst. DOI: 10.7275/KXAP-FN13

Gerlich, M. (2025). AI tools in society: Impacts on cognitive offloading and the future of critical thinking. *Societies (Basel, Switzerland)*, *15*(1), 6. DOI: 10.3390/soc15010006

Göçen, A., Akın Bulut, M., & Yurdunkulu, A. (2025, February 10). AI in school management: A new era of leadership. *AIEOU*. https://aieou.web.ox.ac.uk/article/ai-school-management-new-era-leadership

Guan, R., Raković, M., Chen, G., & Gašević, D. (2025). How educational chatbots support self-regulated learning? A systematic review of the literature. *Education and Information Technologies*, *30*(4), 4493–4518. DOI: 10.1007/s10639-024-12881-y

Harris, A., Walton, J., Johns, A., & Caluya, G. (2022). Toward global digital citizenship: "Everyday" practices of young Australians in a connected world. In *Contestations of citizenship, education, and democracy in an era of global change* (pp. 133–155). Routledge.

Hoff, H. E. (2020). The evolution of intercultural communicative competence: Conceptualisations, critiques and consequences for 21st century classroom practice. *Intercultural Communication Education*, *3*(2), 55–74. DOI: 10.29140/ice.v3n2.264

Holstein, K., & Doroudi, S. (2022). Equity and artificial intelligence in education. In *The ethics of artificial intelligence in education* (pp. 151–173). Routledge. DOI: 10.4324/9780429329067-9

Huyen, N. T. (2024). Fostering design thinking mindset for university students with NPCs in the metaverse. *Heliyon*, *10*(15), e34964. Advance online publication. DOI: 10.1016/j.heliyon.2024.e34964

Idowu, J. A. (2024). Debiasing education algorithms. *International Journal of Artificial Intelligence in Education*, *34*(4), 1510–1540. DOI: 10.1007/s40593-023-00389-4

Islam, M. Z., & Wang, G. (2025). Avatars in the educational metaverse. *Visual Computing for Industry, Biomedicine, and Art*, *8*(1), 15. DOI: 10.1186/s42492-025-00196-9

Jayasinghe, S., Arm, K., & Gamage, K. A. (2025). Designing culturally inclusive case studies with generative AI: Strategies and considerations. *Education Sciences*, *15*(6), 645. DOI: 10.3390/educsci15060645

Jia, S., & Zhang, X. (2021). Teaching mode of psychology and pedagogy in colleges and universities based on artificial intelligence technology. *Journal of Physics: Conference Series*, *1852*(3), 032033. DOI: 10.1088/1742-6596/1852/3/032033

Kaliisa, R., & Dolonen, J. A. (2023). CADA: A teacher-facing learning analytics dashboard to foster teachers' awareness of students' participation and discourse patterns in online discussions. *Technology. Knowledge and Learning*, *28*(3), 937–958. DOI: 10.1007/s10758-022-09598-7

Kamalov, F., Santandreu Calonge, D., & Gurrib, I. (2023). New era of artificial intelligence in education: Towards a sustainable multifaceted revolution. *Sustainability (Basel), 15*(16), 12451. Advance online publication. DOI: 10.3390/su151612451

Kasneci, E., Seßler, K., Küchemann, S., Bannert, M., Dementieva, D., Fischer, F., Gasser, U., Groh, G., Günnemann, S., Hüllermeier, E., Krusche, S., Kutyniok, G., Michaeli, T., Nerdel, C., Pfeffer, J., Poquet, O., Sailer, M., Schmidt, A., Seidel, T., & Kasneci, G. (2023). ChatGPT for good? On opportunities and challenges of large language models for education. *Learning and Individual Differences, 103*, 102274. DOI: 10.1016/j.lindif.2023.102274

Kecskés, I., & Dinh, H. (2025). "ChatGPT for intercultural pragmatic learning? Potentially, but not yet"–The question of using AI to develop students' intercultural pragmatic competence. *Intercultural Pragmatics, 22*(2), 369–397. DOI: 10.1515/ip-2025-2008

Klimova, B., & Chen, J. H. (2024). The impact of AI on enhancing students' intercultural communication competence at the university level: A review study. *Language Teaching Research Quarterly, 43*, 102–120. DOI: 10.32038/ltrq.2024.43.06

Ladson-Billings, G. (1995). Toward a theory of culturally relevant pedagogy. *American Educational Research Journal, 32*(3), 465–491. DOI: 10.3102/00028312032003465

Ladson-Billings, G. (2021). *Culturally relevant pedagogy: Asking a different question*. Teachers College Press.

Lee, H., Kim, H., & Yan, W. (2025). Instructional principles for inclusive AI in K-12 education. In *Proceedings of the 19th International Conference of the Learning Sciences-ICLS 2025, pp.* 2007-2012. International Society of the Learning Sciences. DOI: 10.22318/icls2025.109374

Lewis, A. A. (2025). Unpacking cultural bias in AI language learning tools: An analysis of impacts and strategies for inclusion in diverse educational settings. *International Journal of Research and Innovation in Social Science, 9*(1), 1878–1892. DOI: 10.47772/IJRISS.2025.9010151

Li, X., & Yu, S. (2025). Culturally responsive AI module in early childhood teacher education: An action research. *Journal of Early Childhood Teacher Education*, •••, 1–17. DOI: 10.1080/10901027.2025.2552973

Macinska, S., & Vinkler, A. (2025). The role of AI in language learning: Research evidence and strategies for success. *Cambridge Papers in English Language Education*. Cambridge University Press & Assessment. https://www.cambridge.org/sites/default/files/media/documents/The_Role_of_AI_in_Language_Learning_Research_Evidence_and_Strategies.pdf

Maisiri, J., & Musonza, S. (2025, July 20). *The cultural cost of AI in Africa's education systems*. UNESCO. https://www.unesco.org/en/articles/cultural-cost-ai-africas-education-systems

Mariyono, D., & Alif Hd, A. N. (2025). AI's role in transforming learning environments: A review of collaborative approaches and innovations. *Quality Education for All, 2*(1), 265–288. DOI: 10.1108/QEA-08-2024-0071

Melo-López, V. A., Basantes-Andrade, A., Gudiño-Mejía, C. B., & Hernández-Martínez, E. (2025). The impact of artificial intelligence on inclusive education: A systematic review. *Education Sciences, 15*(5), 539. DOI: 10.3390/educsci15050539

Mikhailova, T., & Cesur, K. (2025). Enhancing global awareness and intercultural competence in English language teacher education. In Bafralı, G. (Ed.), *Challenges in teacher education: pedagogy, management, and materials* (pp. 235–266). IGI Global Scientific Publishing., DOI: 10.4018/979-8-3693-7342-2.ch008

Miller, R. L. (2020). Pedagogical techniques for assessing student performance using the AAC&U value rubrics. In *High impact teaching for sport and exercise psychology educators* (pp. 82–91). Routledge. DOI: 10.4324/9780429316210-9

Munday, P. (2016). The case for using DUOLINGO as part of the language classroom experience. *RIED. Revista Iberoamericana de Educación a Distancia, 19*(1), 83–101. DOI: 10.5944/ried.19.1.14581

Nabi, F., Vortia, W., & Shardey, E. (2025). Teacher readiness for AI and digital tools in K-12 classrooms: A review of professional development trends and gaps. *International Journal for Multidisciplinary Research, 7*(5), 55119. Advance online publication. DOI: 10.36948/ijfmr.2025.v07i05.55119

Nadziroh, S., Sunarso, S., & Suyato, S. (2025). Enhancing conflict resolution skills through artificial intelligence-based problem-based learning in civic education at indonesian primary schools. *Educational Process: International Journal, 18*(1), e2025452. DOI: 10.22521/edupij.2025.18.452

Naseer, F., Khan, M. N., Tahir, M., Addas, A., & Aejaz, S. H. (2024). Integrating deep learning techniques for personalized learning pathways in higher education. *Heliyon, 10*(11), e32628. Advance online publication. DOI: 10.1016/j.heliyon.2024.e32628

OECD. (2023). *Digital equity and inclusion in education*. OECD Publishing. https://www.oecd.org/content/dam/oecd/en/publications/reports/2023/08/digital-equity-and-inclusion-in-education_c56b91ad/7cb15030-en.pdf

Office of Superintendent of Public Instruction. (2024, June). *Artificial intelligence (AI) guidance and ethics for educators*. Washington Office of Superintendent of Public Instruction. https://ospi.k12.wa.us/sites/default/files/2024-06/ai-guidance_ethics.pdf

Ogodo, J. A. (2024). Culturally responsive pedagogical knowledge: An integrative teacher knowledge base for diversified STEM classrooms. *Education Sciences*, *14*(2), 124. DOI: 10.3390/educsci14020124

Ożegalska-Łukasik, N., & Łukasik, S. (2023). Culturally responsive artificial intelligence—problems, challenges and solutions. *arXiv:2312.08467*

Poornesh, M. (2024). Through a teacher's lens: Combating bias in AI-powered education for a just future. *The Clearing House: A Journal of Educational Strategies, Issues and Ideas*, *97*(4), 119–124. DOI: 10.1080/00098655.2024.2393153

Qian, Y. (2025). Prompt engineering in education: A systematic review of approaches and educational applications. *Journal of Educational Computing Research*, *63*(7-8), 1782–1818. DOI: 10.1177/07356331251365189

Rubin, J. (2017). Embedding collaborative online international learning (COIL) at higher education institutions. *Internationalisation of Higher Education*, *2*, 27–44.

Saborío-Taylor, S., & Rojas-Ramírez, F. (2024). Universal design for learning and artificial intelligence in the digital era: Fostering inclusion and autonomous learning. *International Journal of Professional Development. Learners and Learning*, *6*(2), 1–8. DOI: 10.30935/ijpdll/14694

Samuel, Y., Brennan-Tonetta, M., Samuel, J., Kashyap, R., Kumar, V., Krishna Kaashyap, S., & Jain, P. (2023). Cultivation of human centered artificial intelligence: Culturally adaptive thinking in education (CATE) for AI. *Frontiers in Artificial Intelligence*, *6*, 1198180. DOI: 10.3389/frai.2023.1198180

Selwyn, N. (2019). *Should robots replace teachers? AI and the future of education*. Polity Press.

Sethi, S. S., & Jain, K. (2024). AI technologies for social emotional learning: Recent research and future directions. *Journal of Research in Innovative Teaching & Learning*, *17*(2), 213–225. DOI: 10.1108/JRIT-03-2024-0073

Shadiev, R., Hwang, W. Y., Altinay, F., & Guralnick, D. (2023). Technology-assisted cultural diversity learning. *Frontiers in Psychology, 14*, 1274292. DOI: 10.3389/fpsyg.2023.1274292

Shi, H., & Aryadoust, V. (2024). A systematic review of AI-based automated written feedback research. *ReCALL, 36*(2), 187–209. DOI: 10.1017/S0958344023000265

Solomon, G., Allen, N. J., & Resta, P. (2003). *Toward digital equity: Bridging the divide in education.* Allyn and Bacon. Michigan University.

Song, Y., Weisberg, L. R., Zhang, S., Tian, X., Boyer, K. E., & Israel, M. (2024). A framework for inclusive AI learning design for diverse learners. *Computers and Education: Artificial Intelligence, 6*, 100212. Advance online publication. DOI: 10.1016/j.caeai.2024.100212

Stefaniak, J. E., & Moore, S. L. (2024). The use of generative AI to support inclusivity and design deliberation for online instruction. *Online Learning : the Official Journal of the Online Learning Consortium, 28*(3), 181–206. DOI: 10.24059/olj.v28i3.4458

Sun, L. (2025). Enhancing intercultural competence of Chinese English majors through AI-enabled Collaborative Online International Learning (COIL) in the digital era. *Education and Information Technologies, 30*(6), 7995–8027. DOI: 10.1007/s10639-024-13143-7

Susnjak, T., Ramaswami, G. S., & Mathrani, A. (2022). Learning analytics dashboard: A tool for providing actionable insights to learners. *International Journal of Educational Technology in Higher Education, 19*(1), 12. DOI: 10.1186/s41239-021-00313-7

Tammets, K., & Ley, T. (2023). Integrating AI tools in teacher professional learning: A conceptual model and illustrative case. *Frontiers in Artificial Intelligence, 6*, 1255089. DOI: 10.3389/frai.2023.1255089

Tan, X., Cheng, G., & Ling, M. H. (2024). Artificial intelligence in teaching and teacher professional development: A systematic review. *Computers and Education: Artificial Intelligence, 100355*. Advance online publication. DOI: 10.1016/j.caeai.2024.100355

Tapalova, O., & Zhiyenbayeva, N. (2022). Artificial intelligence in education: AIEd for personalised learning pathways. *Electronic Journal of e-Learning, 20*(5), 639–653. DOI: 10.34190/ejel.20.5.2597

Taylor, Z., & Charran, C. (2025). Facilitating techno-cultural inclusive curriculum design for teacher educators. In *Developing culturally responsive curriculum in higher education* (pp. 23–40). IGI Global Scientific Publishing. DOI: 10.4018/979-8-3373-2955-0.ch002

Temel, T., & Cesur, K. (2024). The effect of gamification with Web 2.0 tools on EFL learners' motivation and academic achievement in online learning environments. *SAGE Open, 14*(2), 21582440241247928. Advance online publication. DOI: 10.1177/21582440241247928

Thelma, C. C., Sain, Z. H., Shogbesan, Y. O., Phiri, E. V., & Akpan, W. M. (2024). Ethical implications of AI and machine learning in education: A systematic analysis. *International Journal of Instructional Technology, 3*(1), 1–13. DOI: 10.33650/ijit.v3i1.9364

Thomson, E., Chapman, R., Cooper, G., & Cooper, Z. (2026). Exploring bias in artificial intelligence: Stereotypes and gendered narratives in digital imagery of early childhood educators. *Gender and Education, 38(1), 53–72.* DOI: 10.1080/09540253.2025.2546048

Trivedi, N. B. (2023, November). AI in education—A transformative force. In *2023 1st DMIHER International Conference on Artificial Intelligence in Education and Industry 4.0* (Vol. 1, pp. 1–4).

Tsai, C. W., Ma, Y. W., Chang, Y. C., & Lai, Y. H. (2022). Integrating multiculturalism into artificial intelligence-assisted programming lessons: Examining inter-ethnicity differences in learning expectancy, motivation, and effectiveness. *Frontiers in Psychology, 13*, 868698. DOI: 10.3389/fpsyg.2022.868698

Uche, I. B., & Uche, O. A. (2025). "Our work is shaped by culture": Understanding social work practice in Nigeria through the influence of local traditions and norms. *Journal of Evidence-Based Social Work*, •••, 1–23. DOI: 10.1080/26408066.2025.2533381

United Nations. (2024, June). *A conceptual analysis of the overlaps and differences between hate speech, misinformation and disinformation* (Claire Wardle, PhD). United Nations Department of Peace Operations & Office of the Special Adviser on the Prevention of Genocide. https://peacekeeping.un.org/sites/default/files/report_-_a_conceptual_analysis_of_the_overlaps_and_differences_between_hate_speech_misinformation_and_disinformation_june_2024_qrupdate.pdf

Usman, N., Kusumanegara, A., Husnaini, H., Said, Y. R., & Ismayanti, D. (2025). Cultural bias and linguistic representation in AI curriculum design: Implications for society 5.0. In *Advancing society 5.0 through AI-driven curriculum innovation* (pp. 229–258). IGI Global Scientific Publishing. DOI: 10.4018/979-8-3373-1062-6.ch008

Uygun, D. (2024). Teachers' perspectives on artificial intelligence in education. *Advances in Mobile Learning Educational Research*, *4*(1), 931–939. DOI: 10.25082/AMLER.2024.01.005

Vesna, L., Sawale, P. S., Kaul, P., Pal, S., & Murthy, B. S. N. V. R. (2025). Digital divide in AI-powered education: Challenges and solutions for equitable learning. *Journal of Information Systems Engineering & Management*, *10*(21), 1–9.

Vieriu, A. M., & Petrea, G. (2025). The impact of artificial intelligence (AI) on students' academic development. *Education Sciences*, *15*(3), 343. DOI: 10.3390/educsci15030343

Waliński, J. (2012). Enhancing intercultural communicative competence in an online collaborative assessment environment: CEFcult project. *Corpus Data across Languages and Disciplines*, 55-65.

Wang, F., Cheung, A. C., Chai, C. S., & Liu, J. (2025). Development and validation of the perceived interactivity of learner-AI interaction scale. *Education and Information Technologies*, *30*(4), 4607–4638. DOI: 10.1007/s10639-024-12963-x

Wang, J., Xiao, R., Hou, X., Li, H., Tseng, Y. J., Stamper, J., & Koedinger, K. (2025, July). LLMs to support K–12 teachers in culturally relevant pedagogy: An AI literacy example. In *International Conference on Artificial Intelligence in Education* (pp. 152–160). Springer Nature. DOI: 10.1007/978-3-031-99264-3_19

Whorf, B. L. (2012). *Language, thought, and reality: Selected writings of Benjamin Lee Whorf.* MIT press.

Wieczorek, M., Hosseini, M., & Gordijn, B. (2025). Unpacking the ethics of using AI in primary and secondary education: A systematic literature review. *AI and Ethics*, *5*(5), 4693–4711. DOI: 10.1007/s43681-025-00770-0

Wong, J. M. S. (2026). Artificial intelligence-supported group facilitation: Emerging potentials, cautious approaches, and ethical considerations in social work practice. *Social Work with Groups, 49(1), 77-90.* DOI: 10.1080/01609513.2025.2540474

Wu, Y. (2024). Revolutionizing learning and teaching: Crafting personalized, culturally responsive curriculum in the AI Era. *Creative Education*, *15*(8), 1642–1651. DOI: 10.4236/ce.2024.158098

Xie, B., Sarin, P., Wolf, J., Garcia, R. C. C., Delaney, V., Sieh, I., Fuloria, A., Varuvel Dennison, D., Bywater, C., & Lee, V. R. (2024). Co-designing AI education curriculum with cross-disciplinary high school teachers. *Proceedings of the AAAI Conference on Artificial Intelligence*, *38*(21), 23146–23154. DOI: 10.1609/aaai.v38i21.30360

Yan, W., & Lowell, V. L. (2025). The evolution of virtual reality in foreign language education: From text-based MUDs to AI-enhanced immersive environments. *TechTrends*, *69*(4), 853–858. DOI: 10.1007/s11528-025-01086-w

Yu, P. K. (2020). The algorithmic divide and equality in the age of artificial intelligence. *Florida Law Review*, *72*(2), 331–389.

Zhang, Q., Mohammad Ismail, M. I. R., & Zakaria, A. R. B. (2025). Enhancing intercultural competence in technical higher education through AI-driven frameworks. *Scientific Reports*, *15*(1), 22019. DOI: 10.1038/s41598-025-03303-1

Zhong, J., & Zheng, Y. (2023). What it means to be a digital citizen: Using concept mapping and an educational game to explore children's conceptualization of digital citizenship. *Heliyon*, *9*(9), e21264. DOI: 10.1016/j.heliyon.2023.e19291

Zmire, Z., & Chen, X. (2024). AI's role in enhancing cross cultural competence and leadership through online education programs. In *International Conference on New Findings in Humanities and Social Sciences* (Vol. 1, pp. 1–16).

# Chapter 6
# Rehumanizing Intercultural Communication in AI-Supported Distance Language Education Through Empathy, Humor, and Ethical Awareness

**Mehmet Gökce**
http://orcid.org/0000-0003-4690-9693
*Kütahya Health Sciences University, Turkey*

**Mustafa Kemal Şen**
http://orcid.org/0000-0001-8714-0193
*Kütahya Dumlupınar University, Turkey*

## ABSTRACT

*The Rehumanizing Pedagogical Framework (RPF) advanced herein treats empathy, humor, and ethical awareness as assessable learning outcomes in AI-mediated intercultural communication within distance foreign language education. Grounded in intercultural communicative competence theory and human-machine communication research, the framework identifies four design mediators: task design, feedback design, interface affordances, and governance. These mediators preserve*

DOI: 10.4018/979-8-3373-6325-7.ch006

*the relational core of intercultural learning while positioning AI as a pedagogical resource rather than an unchecked authority. The analysis situates these mediators within debates on agentic AI, cultural bias in large language models, and governance conditions that covary with perceived intercultural benefit. Evaluation triangulates self-reported dispositions, interactional evidence of repair and audience-safe humor, and ethical practice artifacts. The chapter concludes with a tiered research agenda and recommendations for programs seeking to integrate AI without eroding the human dimensions of intercultural dialogue.*

## 1. INTRODUCTION

Generative AI has moved fast. In barely two years, it shifted from a peripheral tool to a core layer of online foreign language instruction, reshaping how students draft, translate, and verify intercultural messages before pressing send. Instructors, too, lean on automated scaffolds to plan tasks, triage discussion-board overload, and respond to large cohorts at a pace no individual could sustain (Seo et al., 2021). The promise is real: personalization at scale, on-demand feedback, and multilingual mediation that once required scarce human expertise.

Yet intercultural communication is not merely a language task. The decisive question is whether an AI-mediated interaction lands appropriately and ethically for a particular audience. Without deliberate design choices that keep human judgment visible, AI can flatten cultural nuance, mishandle tone and humor, and obscure who is actually speaking (Ferrara, 2023). These are not edge cases; they are the routine conditions of contemporary distance classrooms.

This chapter proposes a Rehumanizing Pedagogical Framework (RPF) for distance foreign language education. The framework makes three human capacities, namely empathy, humor, and ethical awareness, explicit learning outcomes, operationalized through task and feedback design, interface affordances, and classroom governance. Grounded in intercultural communicative competence (ICC) theory, it positions learners as intercultural mediators who can step outside their own perspectives, engage in dialogue, and repair misunderstandings (Byram, 1997, 2021; Deardorff, 2006). The framework is deliberately pragmatic: it offers designs that distance educators can adopt this term and refine over time.

The urgency of rehumanization arises from converging evidence. During the pandemic, universities worldwide maintained continuity in distance education and discovered that fostering relational design was essential for sustaining meaningful intercultural learning online. A longitudinal account from a culturally diverse bachelor's program shows how students' well-being and participation improved when instructors structured community building as four sequential processes: initial encounter, participation, reciprocity, and the construction of trust and care (Volcic et al., 2024). These findings mirror earlier observations about the challenges of implementing online tuition in distance language courses, where task design and tutor role proved decisive for sustaining interaction quality (Hauck & Hampel, 2005). The practical reality has not changed: time-zone spread, asynchronous multimodality, and uneven access conspire to thin social presence unless it is intentionally designed into the experience.

At the same time, students and staff have normalized AI in their everyday intercultural exchanges. A recent mixed-methods study with postgraduate students from nine countries reports near-universal AI use (93 percent) and a prevailing belief that AI connects cultures and reduces language barriers. Crucially, statistically significant positive correlations emerged between perceived benefits and both attitudes toward AI and the presence of regulation (Sarwari et al., 2024). That last correlation carries pedagogical weight. It suggests that governance is not a bureaucratic afterthought but a condition that covaries with perceived intercultural benefit, and that disclosure rules, attribution norms, and bias checks are themselves learning supports in multicultural cohorts.

A second strand of evidence concerns what AI can and cannot do for ICC. The most promising results arise when AI is embedded in tasks that invite critical comparison between AI outputs and human practices. Telecollaboration designs that position AI as an object of reflection, to be interrogated, revised, and documented, appear to catalyze intercultural awareness, provided teachers scaffold debriefing and model repair (McCallum, 2024). In engineering education, a large survey (n = 990) found that features of AI learning environments positively predicted students' ICC, with learning adaptability partially mediating these effects (Chen & Wei, 2025). The implication is twofold: AI should be framed as a fallible participant whose suggestions are improved rather than merely accepted, and evaluation should include process evidence such as adaptability, repair moves, and reflective notes alongside product-level language measures.

A third strand is conceptual and ethical. The Applied Linguistics Review forum on AI and ICC has argued that our discipline confronts a familiar but amplified problem: we now expect systems to be creative, factual, and norm-consistent at once, aspirations that humans themselves struggle to reconcile (Dai & Hua, 2025). Stereotypes are deeply rooted in human communication and often reflected within the datasets that inform generative technologies. When these biases remain unexamined, AI systems risk reproducing and amplifying them, leading to distorted representations of culture and identity. When guided by an intercultural lens that values diversity and contextual awareness, however, AI can become a meaningful pedagogical ally, one that promotes understanding and dialogue rather than reinforcing bias (Dai et al., 2025). O'Regan and Ferri (2025) sharpen the point from a critical realist depth ontology: AI's semiotic outputs simulate ethical reasoning but cannot ground judgmental rationality. Unless provenance, attribution, and human sign-off become routine, classrooms risk normalizing what amounts to pseudo-empathy, that is, friendly language that masks shallow contextual understanding.

The technological landscape intensifies these questions. Agentic AI refers to systems that plan, reason, and act toward high-level goals through tool calls and multi-step orchestration, with less human micromanagement than traditional prompt-bound generation. While autonomous agents can perform intricate task sequences, the likelihood of cumulative errors rises with complexity, making human oversight and clear auditability indispensable (Hornyak, 2025). For intercultural classrooms, the design question is sharper still: how do we calibrate trust so that learners neither over-defer to algorithmic judgments about tone or politeness, a tendency well documented in research on algorithm appreciation (Logg et al., 2019), nor reject valuable scaffolds out of hand?

Bringing these strands together, rehumanization names a design stance, not a nostalgic retreat from technology. It asks three questions of every AI-mediated interaction. Does the exchange honour the other person's perspective? Does it leave room for play, and for recovery when play misfires? Does it keep authorship and accountability visible? Perspective-taking aligns with the attitudinal and skill dimensions of ICC. Playful engagement fosters rapport and identity negotiation. Accountability maintains trust when authorship is shared between humans and machines (Byram, 1997, 2021; Deardorff, 2006). Because humor can easily falter across cultural boundaries, embedding it in learning tasks as a focus for analysis and revision, rather than leaving it to spontaneous AI generation, preserves a safe space for intercultural exploration (Attardo, 1994; Martin, 2007).

This chapter adopts a deliberately pragmatic orientation. It begins with the observation that benefits attributed to AI in intercultural settings covary with attitudes and regulatory processes (Sarwari et al., 2024). It notes that intercultural progress emerges when tasks and debriefs make interactional processes visible, including stance shifts, mitigation, and repair, and when students document how they prompted, verified, and adapted AI suggestions (McCallum, 2024). It takes seriously the ethical critique that, absent explicit governance, AI can produce polished language that evades accountability (O'Regan & Ferri, 2025). From these premises, the RPF follows: craft tasks that require perspective-taking; design feedback that models empathic repair; instrument interfaces to label provenance and capture prompt journals; and institutionalize governance moves, including disclosure, attribution, and bias checks, so that accountability is built into the course shell rather than appended as a warning.

Methodologically, the chapter proceeds through conceptual synthesis and integrative analysis rather than empirical investigation. It draws on peer-reviewed articles published between 2019 and 2025, retrieved primarily from Scopus and Web of Science using search strings combining intercultural communicative competence, artificial intelligence, distance language education, and generative AI. These sources are supplemented by recent theoretical contributions from the Applied Linguistics Review forum on AI and ICC, large-scale survey findings, and telecollaboration case reports. The approach is consistent with framework-development traditions in applied linguistics and educational design, where the aim is to translate converging evidence into actionable structures that practitioners can adopt, test, and refine (Byram, 2021; Deardorff, 2006).

The analysis adopts a pragmatist epistemological stance, prioritizing designable and assessable constructs over purely theoretical elaboration. Rather than testing hypotheses, the chapter constructs a pedagogical architecture by triangulating three evidence streams: theoretical arguments about ICC and human-machine communication, quantitative patterns from survey-based studies, and qualitative insights from telecollaboration reports. This triangulation is conceptual rather than methodological in the empirical sense; it serves to ensure that the resulting framework is grounded in multiple disciplinary perspectives rather than derived from a single tradition.

As for structure, this chapter is not a technical evaluation of models; it is a pedagogical architecture for distance foreign language education that seeks to preserve the human relational core of intercultural learning in AI-mediated settings. Section 2 consolidates the conceptual foundations; Section 3 reviews current benefits, risks, and gaps; Section 4 details the RPF's design mediators with course-ready examples; Section 5 turns to evaluation and measurement; and Section 6 closes with implications and a research agenda. The aim throughout is to provide distance educators with designs they can adopt this term and refine over time, so that AI becomes a prompt for inquiry and a mirror for culture, never a substitute for judgment.

## 2. THEORETICAL AND CONCEPTUAL FRAME

This section brings together the theoretical foundations for viewing perspective-taking, culturally grounded humor, and ethical accountability as central outcomes of AI-mediated intercultural communication in distance language education. The argument rests on a key premise: intercultural competence goes beyond linguistic accuracy. Byram's influential framework redefined communicative ability through four dimensions, including attitudes of openness and curiosity, knowledge of self and others within sociocultural contexts, skills of interpretation, relation, discovery, and interaction, and critical cultural awareness. Within this model, learners are understood as intercultural speakers who decenter, mediate meaning, and repair understanding across cultural boundaries rather than merely demonstrate grammatical proficiency (Byram, 1997, 2021). Fantini's complementary work reinforced this shift by proposing that ICC comprises awareness, attitudes, skills, and knowledge, with critical awareness serving as the binding element (Fantini, 2009).

Yet convictions about culture do not automatically translate into repeatable design moves. In the Turkish context, a large survey of 503 EFL teachers showed that despite widespread endorsement of culture's importance, actual classroom practices integrating the intercultural dimension were reported only "sometimes," a gap the authors trace to knowledge, resource, and training constraints (Atay et al., 2009). That finding remains instructive: institutional pressure and technological change widen the space between aspiration and implementation. In a related Turkish higher education context, Tuncel and Paker (2018) found that a dedicated intercultural communication course significantly improved students' intercultural sensitivity, reinforcing the argument that structured, intentional design rather than incidental exposure drives measurable growth.

On this view, ICC is enacted in sequences, a point central to Young's (2008) theory of interactional competence and Hall's (2018) work on classroom discourse practices, which locate ability not in individual minds but in the co-constructed practices that participants build turn by turn. A participant initiates, aligns, softens stance, and repairs trouble, often under time pressure and across modalities. Empathy becomes a practice rather than a mood: one marks recognition of intent, proposes a reformulation, and checks understanding. Telecollaboration research consistently finds that learners progress when tasks and debriefs make these interactional processes visible and assessable. When AI enters these sequences, it inevitably nudges stance and selection in tone, register, and the framing of claims, so the question becomes how to design interactions where human judgment remains the locus of repair (McCallum, 2024; Dai et al., 2025).

A second pillar comes from human-machine communication (HMC). Here, AI systems are not treated as inert tools but as perceived interlocutors that shape attention, preference, and deference. Guzman and Lewis (2020) set out a foundational research agenda arguing that communication scholars must treat machines as communicators in their own right, examining how people make sense of, orient to, and relate with technological agents. Their concept of communicative partnership is particularly relevant here: it reframes the AI not as a channel through which humans talk to each other but as a third participant whose contributions shape the interaction's pragmatic texture. The 2025 Applied Linguistics Review forum extends this invitation to ICC: scholars bring thick accounts of stance, facework, and power, while AI researchers contribute insight into how models generalize and when they fail (Dai & Hua, 2025; Hua et al., 2025). This conversation also re-centers an ethical premise. Because generative models simulate sociality and can reproduce stereotyped representations from their training data, they require explicit governance. O'Regan and Ferri's depth-ontology argument is clear: without human judgment in the loop, AI risks producing ethical simulacra, outputs that appear norm-consistent while evacuating accountability (2025).

A third pillar is the sociopedagogical reality of distance education. In remote and hybrid courses, social presence is attenuated by asynchronicity, time-zone dispersion, and the dominance of text-based communication. Moore's (1993) theory of transactional distance offers a foundational lens here: the psychological and communicative space between learner and instructor expands when dialogue is limited and structure is rigid, making deliberate relational design essential. Garrison, Anderson, and Archer's (2000) Community of Inquiry model complements this perspective by identifying social presence, the ability of participants to project their personal characteristics into the community, as one of three interdependent elements (alongside teaching presence and cognitive presence) required for meaningful educational experience. In AI-mediated distance courses, both transactional distance and social presence are at stake: AI can either widen the gap by depersonalizing interaction or narrow it by scaffolding the relational work that sustains intercultural rapport.

Pandemic-era evidence supports the latter possibility, but only under intentional design. Instructors who treated relationality as a staged sequence, progressing from initial encounter through participation to reciprocity and ultimately trust and care, reported better student well-being and participation (Volcic et al., 2024). Those stages map naturally onto an empathy-first pedagogy. Seo et al. (2021) extend this insight to AI-supported contexts, showing that AI can reshape learner-instructor interaction in ways that either enhance or diminish social presence, depending on how the technology is integrated.

These three pillars locate the RPF's triad within a single logic. Perspective-taking and face-saving repair align directly with Byram's attitudinal and skill components (2021). Humor, often mishandled by large language models, is treated not as an ornament but as a cognitively and affectively consequential resource that requires audience design, timing, and a path to recovery when it misfires. Ethical accountability translates HMC cautions into routines: students disclose what the AI contributed, attribute sources, and run small bias checks, calibrating trust rather than granting or denying it reflexively (Dai & Hua, 2025).

Two contemporary developments make this synthesis urgent. The first is the consolidation of agentic AI. As systems shift from single-shot text generation to goal-directed orchestration involving planning, calling tools, and executing multi-step procedures, the risk profile changes. Agents produce longer, more coherent action sequences, but they can also compound subtle errors across steps, especially in pragmatics. If a semi-autonomous agent drafts an email that inadvertently threatens face, who repairs it, who discloses the agent's role, and what is learned from the incident? The answer must be a design that keeps human authorship legible and repair teachable (Hornyak, 2025).

The second is an emerging empirical pattern linking perceived benefits to governance. In a large multicultural sample, students' perceived benefits of AI for intercultural communication correlated positively not only with favourable attitudes but also with the presence of regulation, including rules, transparency, and oversight (Sarwari et al., 2024). When perceived benefits align with governance and transparency practices, these become pedagogically enabling rather than compliance obligations. Studies in professional programmes reinforce the point: learning adaptability mediates the relationship between AI-supported environments and ICC, suggesting that reflective control and metacognitive capacity, not tools alone, drive intercultural development (Chen & Wei, 2025).

The conceptual move from theory to design should not dilute complexity, but it should instrument it. The RPF converts these claims into four mediators that simultaneously act on the interactional, affective, and ethical planes. Task design builds perspective-taking and repair into assignments, for example, by requiring multilingual teams to test an AI's politeness strategies against community-authentic alternatives, to annotate potential face threats, and to co-author revisions with rationales. Feedback design models empathic correction by citing intent, offering an exemplar, and inviting an own-voice reformulation (McCallum, 2024). Interface affordances make provenance visible through badges for AI-generated versus human-verified segments and brief model cards; they cue translanguaging rather than penalize it, consistent with research showing that machine translation can empower learners when paired with critical reflection (Kelly & Hou, 2022). Governance codifies disclosure, attribution, and small bias audits as everyday routines (Dai & Hua, 2025; Hua et al., 2025).

This architecture repositions AI in distance language education. Rather than an oracle or a hazard to be quarantined, AI becomes a prompt for inquiry and a mirror for culture. When an AI suggestion feels off, students are asked to say why in intercultural terms, to repair with attention to audience and relational goals, and to document what the model contributed and what humans endorsed or overrode. The documentation is not bureaucratic; it is the method by which ethical awareness is learned. The connection to teacher development is immediate. The 503-teacher study in Türkiye showed that even when educators value culture, they require specific tools and shared routines to enact it under classroom constraints (Atay et al., 2009). The RPF proposes meeting these constraints by providing templates for task prompts, feedback scripts, and disclosure statements; interfaces that nudge toward provenance and translanguaging; and programme-level policies that normalize frequent, small-scale bias checks. Rehumanization, in other words, is infrastructural.

This synthesis yields a practical architecture for course design. Figure 1 maps how ICC and HMC foundations feed into four interlocking design mediators, which in turn translate the RPF's target outcomes into assessable learning goals.

*Figure 1. Rehumanizing Pedagogical Framework (RPF) for AI-mediated ICC*

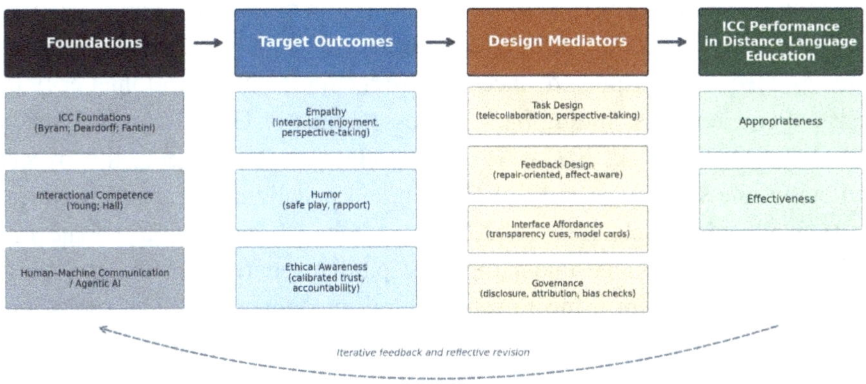


## 3. WHY A REHUMANIZING FRAMEWORK IS NECESSARY

Integrating AI into distance foreign language education offers clear potential for scalability and personalized feedback. In intercultural communication, however, the stakes exceed technical accuracy. Missteps by AI systems, whether pragmatically inappropriate or representationally narrow, constitute relational and ethical failures. The question for educators is no longer whether to use AI but how to govern its use so that human judgment and social presence remain central. This section organizes the core challenges around the RPF's four design mediators, showing why each is necessary.

The first set of challenges concerns what AI brings into the task environment. Models trained on vast and often biased datasets risk reproducing stereotyped cultural representations, a form of representational harm that erodes trust (Dai & Hua, 2025; Ferrara, 2023). These systems can produce what O'Regan and Ferri (2025) call ethical simulacra, outputs that appear well-formed but lack genuine judgmental rationality. At the same time, ICC is fundamentally sequential: it relies on practices like initiating contact, saving face, and repairing misunderstandings. AI systems, however, often exhibit pragmatic brittleness, producing formulaic politeness or tone-deaf responses that alienate interactional partners (McCallum, 2024). Ferrara

(2023) documents how such biases manifest: ChatGPT and similar models may associate certain cultural groups with fixed personality traits or communication styles, generating advice that feels personalized but rests on statistical stereotyping. The RPF's task design mediator responds by requiring learners to interrogate and revise AI outputs rather than accept them.

The second set of challenges involves feedback and relational pedagogy. In cross-cultural settings, misfires in areas such as humor and implicature carry high relational costs, potentially leading learners to disengage or internalize superficial norms as adequate. Despite advances toward mediation and decolonial critique, a persistent risk remains: sliding back into essentialist or Global-North-centric defaults (McConachy et al., 2022). AI-mediated learning can amplify this by subtly privileging one standard variety of English and penalizing nonstandard varieties or translanguaging. Schneider (2022) shows how AI systems participate in the regimentation of language under digital capitalism, narrowing the multilingual repertoires that learners bring to intercultural encounters. In Schneider's terms, digital capitalism flattens the semiotic landscape: the model's training data over-represents prestige varieties, so the "help" it offers quietly nudges learners away from the very code-mixing and register play that marks authentic intercultural exchange. The RPF's feedback design mediator addresses this by modeling empathic correction and framing multilingual flexibility as an asset. At a deeper architectural level, large language models construct implicit world models from their training distributions, such as internal representations of entities, relations, and norms that shape every output (LeCun, 2022). When a model's learned representation of "how communication works" treats one pragmatic tradition as default, its suggestions for cross-cultural interaction carry that bias silently, not as an occasional glitch but as a structural feature of the system's world model.

The third set of challenges relates to transparency and interface design. As AI evolves from text generators into semi-autonomous agents capable of planning and acting toward goals, the potential for compounded error increases. When an agent drafts a culturally sensitive email for a student, questions of responsibility and disclosure surface: who owns the communication, and who is responsible for repairing a misstep? (Hornyak, 2025). The opacity of these systems compounds the problem. As von Eschenbach (2021) argues, the black-box nature of AI undermines the conditions for trust because users cannot inspect the reasoning that produced a given output. The RPF's interface affordances mediator responds by making provenance visible and authorship traceable.

The fourth set of challenges concerns governance. In multicultural educational settings, students themselves associate the value of AI with clear regulation, transparency, and oversight (Sarwari et al., 2024). Governance is not external to learning; it is a variable that conditions trust. In its absence, AI risks simulating ethical reasoning while enabling evasion of responsibility. Von Eschenbach (2021) identifies the black-box problem as a root cause: when users cannot inspect how a system reaches its recommendations, they can neither calibrate their trust nor hold the system accountable. During the pandemic, this opacity became tangible. Instructors in Turkish distance education programs reported that students submitted AI-polished discussion posts that read fluently but contained culturally tone-deaf generalizations about their classmates' backgrounds, and neither the students nor the instructors had tools to trace the source of the distortion (Ergin et al., 2022). Reliance on AI also intensifies existing inequalities: bandwidth, device access, and platform literacy become gatekeepers to participation. The RPF's governance mediator institutionalizes transparency practices, including disclosure, attribution, and bias monitoring, as habitual parts of the course structure.

Taken together, these challenges justify the RPF's central claim. Perspective-taking can be practiced through structured interaction and repair. Culturally grounded humor can be designed with clear recovery paths. Ethical accountability can be embedded in everyday routines of disclosure and verification. Rehumanization is a recognition that the relational and ethical work of intercultural learning can be amplified, but never automated, by technology. The next section operationalizes this stance.

## 4. THE REHUMANIZING PEDAGOGICAL FRAMEWORK (RPF): FROM THEORY TO DESIGN

The argument so far establishes that intercultural competence rests on appropriateness, repair, and ethical responsibility, while the pedagogical value of AI depends on governance and adaptability. The RPF translates these principles into concrete instructional strategies at the course level, ensuring that human judgment and agency remain central.

The framework cultivates its target outcomes through four intertwined design mediators: task design, feedback design, interface affordances, and governance. Each is meant to work with the others; none is sufficient on its own. Because distance learning environments often diminish relational visibility, a core concern of the Community of Inquiry model (Garrison et al., 2000), and because contemporary agentic AI systems are capable of planning, invoking tools, and performing sequential actions, the RPF emphasizes designs that make authorship transparent, enable intercultural repair, and embed routine accountability practices (Hornyak, 2025).

The first mediator, task design, positions AI as a prompt for inquiry rather than a proxy for judgment. In practice, this means crafting assignments in which learners articulate the audience they are addressing, interrogate the cultural scripts embedded in AI suggestions, and collaboratively repair those suggestions in light of community-authentic alternatives. A telecollaboration sequence illustrates the logic: multilingual teams begin with an AI-proposed draft of an invitation or request, then examine how the wording frames social distance, deference, or solidarity. They compare the draft with examples drawn from their own linguistic repertoires and discursive traditions, rewrite the message, and compose a brief rationale naming potential face-threats and the steps taken to mitigate them.

When debriefs are structured to foreground stance-taking and repair, students not only improve the message but learn to justify choices in intercultural terms. Findings from AI-supported telecollaboration reinforce that this object-of-reflection stance can nurture ICC; gains are strongest where debriefs are explicit and iterative (McCallum, 2024; Dai et al., 2025). The same design logic integrates pandemic-era lessons: when courses stage encounter, participation, reciprocity, and trust-and-care as successive phases, affective safety and participation rise, providing conditions in which perspective-taking and humor can be practiced without undue risk (Volcic et al., 2024).

The second mediator, feedback design, makes interpersonal immediacy tangible by modeling empathic correction and treating misunderstandings as teachable moments. In distance education, a significant proportion of "teaching" occurs in written or recorded feedback. The tone, timing, and transparency of these responses become the clearest signals of respect and recognition, a point underscored by research showing that learner-instructor interaction quality in online settings directly shapes engagement (Seo et al., 2021). The RPF borrows the sequential organization of repair from conversation analysis: acknowledge the learner's likely intent, offer a candidate reformulation that anticipates the target audience's expectations, and invite a self-authored revision that holds the learner's voice while adjusting stance. AI can assist in the first pass by flagging hedging, directness, or register shifts. The system's suggestion, however, remains a provocation to be verified, exemplified, or overridden by the instructor. This safeguard matters because AI-generated advice can sound warm without being culturally attuned (McCallum, 2024; O'Regan & Ferri, 2025). When humor is in play, feedback routines include a brief audience-design check ("for whom would this read as affiliative rather than belittling?") and, where needed, a recovery line that restores rapport.

The third mediator, interface affordances, recognizes that platforms are not neutral conduits; they script visibility and power. If learners are to calibrate trust in AI, they must see where AI is present, trace how it contributed, and signal where human verification occurred. In concrete terms, this means labeling AI-generated segments, attaching brief provenance statements, and maintaining prompt journals that record how queries were framed and outputs were checked. It also means enabling translanguaging by tolerating code-switching and providing ways to compare dialectal variants, an approach that treats multilingual flexibility as an asset (Kelly &

Hou, 2022; Schneider, 2022). Trustworthy AI in intercultural settings must keep human control visible, respect privacy, and avoid masking the representational choices embedded in model training (Jenks, 2025).

The fourth mediator, governance, turns ethics into ordinary classroom behaviour. Short disclosure statements, attribution that credits sources and collaborators, and periodic bias audits are not compliance overhead; they are conditions that make trust plausible in multicultural cohorts (Sarwari et al., 2024). Cross-cultural AI-literacy workshops can accelerate readiness; initial evaluations suggest they reduce uncertainty and align expectations across diverse groups (Korte et al., 2024). In courses where agentic tools are available, governance also includes human sign-off on high-stakes communications and least-data-necessary approaches to privacy.

What makes the RPF more than a set of good intentions is its insistence on evidence and repeatability. Task design yields annotated rewrites and short rationales. Feedback design produces side-by-side versions with justification for choices. Interfaces generate prompt journals and provenance badges. Governance creates disclosure forms and bias-audit snapshots. These artifacts provide both formative feedback to learners and summative evidence to instructors. They align with the empirical pattern that gains in ICC under AI-rich designs are partially mediated by learning adaptability (Chen & Wei, 2025). This emphasis on operationalizable mediators, measurable outcomes, and iterative refinement positions the RPF within the emerging discipline of learning engineering, which applies systematic, evidence-based methods to the design and continuous improvement of learning experiences (Goodell & Kolodner, 2022). Learning engineering's core commitment—that instructional designs should be testable, data-informed, and improvable across cycles—maps directly onto the RPF's artifact-driven evaluation spine: each iteration of task prompts, feedback scripts, and governance routines generates data that feeds the next design revision.

This commitment to operationalizing outcomes is perhaps most consequential for humor. Humor serves multiple functions in intercultural communication: it establishes rapport and in-group membership, manages face-threatening situations, signals playful intent, and creates affective bonds that facilitate learning (Martin, 2007). It is also deeply culturally bound. What reads as affiliative in one context may be perceived as aggressive, dismissive, or incomprehensible in another. Attardo's (1994) linguistic theories of humor identify incongruity, superiority, and relief as underlying mechanisms, each carrying different risks across cultural boundaries. An AI-generated icebreaker relying on playful self-deprecation, which may be a low-risk strategy in some North American classrooms, might be perceived as a loss of professional authority in a high-context East Asian business setting. Jegede (2025) further demonstrates how humor operates as a pragmatic tool in multicultural online interactions, where the absence of nonverbal cues makes audience design even more critical. Pan's (2024) research on impoliteness in polylogal intercultural communication among Asian EFL learners adds an important dimension, showing that what one participant intends as teasing may be received as face-threatening by another. These findings underscore why humor cannot be left to chance in AI-mediated settings. To bring the necessary rigor to the classroom, a humor risk spectrum is presented in Table 1.

*Table 1. The humor risk spectrum*

| Category | Description | Risk Level | Pedagogical Use |
|---|---|---|---|
| Affiliative | Inclusive humor that builds rapport without targeting individuals | Low | Model and encourage |
| Self-deprecating | Humor at one's own expense to reduce power distance | Moderate | Discuss cultural variation in appropriateness |
| Ironic / Sarcastic | Humor requiring shared cultural knowledge to decode | High | Analyze with recovery strategies |
| Aggressive / Teasing | Humor that targets others, even when intended playfully | Very High | Identify face-threat potential; practice repair |

Note. Categories are derived from Attardo (1994), Martin (2007), Jegede (2025), and Pan (2024). Risk levels reflect potential face-threat in cross-cultural interaction.

As Table 1 shows, affiliative humor is low-risk and should be modeled and encouraged. Self-deprecating humor carries moderate risk because its appropriateness for reducing power distance varies significantly across cultures, making it an excellent object of discussion. Ironic or sarcastic humor is high-risk: it requires shared cultural knowledge to decode and often leads to misunderstanding. Aggressive or teasing humor, even when intended playfully, carries the highest face-threat potential.

Translating this risk spectrum into assessable practice requires a structured approach. Table 2 presents a rubric for evaluating a learner's competence in intercultural humor use along three criteria. The first, audience analysis, ranges from no consideration of the audience's cultural background at the emerging level to nuanced adaptation with explicit justification at the advanced level. The second, recovery competence, assesses the learner's ability to handle humor misfires, from no recovery strategy at all to graceful recovery that restores rapport. The third, AI interrogation, measures critical engagement with machine-generated humor: progressing from uncritical acceptance through systematic evaluation of cultural fit to creating superior alternatives grounded in community repertoires.

*Table 2. Humor assessment rubric*

| Criterion | Emerging (1) | Developing (2) | Proficient (3) | Advanced (4) |
|---|---|---|---|---|
| Audience Analysis | No consideration of audience cultural background | Basic awareness of audience differences | Explicit rationale for humor choices based on audience analysis | Nuanced adaptation to specific interlocutors with explicit justification |
| Recovery Competence | No recovery strategy; ignores misfires | Generic apology when humor fails | Prepared recovery lines; can explain intent | Graceful recovery that restores rapport and demonstrates learning |
| AI Interrogation | Uncritical acceptance of AI humor suggestions | Identifies obvious cultural problems in AI humor | Systematically evaluates AI humor for cultural fit | Creates superior alternatives drawing on community repertoires |

Note. Levels are cumulative; advanced-level performance presupposes the capacities described at lower levels.

A concrete illustration shows how these principles come together in practice. Consider a first-year writing course for engineers with a multinational cohort, where teams co-author a project update email to community stakeholders. The AI proposes a draft. Students annotate where the draft implicitly positions power, identify stance markers that might misfire for the local audience, and explain how they would repair the message. They then submit a revised version with a brief disclosure of the AI's role and a note on what they verified.

One team, for instance, notices that the AI's draft opens with a joke about tight deadlines, a move that reads as affiliative among their Canadian peers but risks sounding dismissive to the Japanese partner institution, where project timelines carry stronger face implications. The team replaces the joke with a warm acknowledgment of the partner's contribution, flags the original humor as a moderate-risk move in their rationale, and documents how the AI was used and where human judgment intervened. The feedback return models empathic correction: "I read your intent as building rapport with the stakeholders; for this audience, an alternative that preserves your collegial stance while softening the time-pressure framing would be..." The interface displays provenance labels for AI-generated segments. Because deliverables include both the product and the process record, the instructor can recognize intercultural reasoning even when the surface text looks unremarkable. Research shows that people tend to prefer algorithmic judgment by default (Logg et al., 2019); making the process explicit helps students move from passive deference to active, informed engagement.

In terms of the assessment rubric (Table 2), this team's performance illustrates a shift from Emerging to Proficient on Audience Analysis: they moved from uncritical acceptance of the AI's humor to an explicit rationale grounded in audience-specific face concerns. On Recovery Competence, the team demonstrated Developing-level skill by preparing an alternative that preserved rapport, though a fully Advanced response would also reflect on what the misfire revealed about their own assumptions. This process ensures that humor is treated as a designed and repairable resource, not as a stochastic garnish. The RPF is not meant to be implemented wholesale on day one. Programs can phase adoption by starting with governance and interface elements (disclosures, provenance labels, prompt journals), then layering in feedback scripts that model repair, and finally redesigning tasks so that perspective-taking, humor analysis, and bias checks are integral rather than add-ons. Scaling is supported by lightweight staff development: short, cross-cultural workshops that walk through disclosure exemplars, demonstrate bias checks, and rehearse empathic feedback phrasing (Korte et al., 2024; Volcic et al., 2024).

*Table 3. Evaluation rubric for the RPF in AI-mediated ICC*

| Dimension | Operational Definition | Observable Indicators | Evaluation Criteria / Evidence |
|---|---|---|---|
| Empathy | The ability to recognize, understand, and respond to others' perspectives and emotions in intercultural encounters, including face-saving repair. | • Perspective-taking in AI-mediated tasks<br>• Face-saving repair when misunderstandings occur<br>• Intent recognition and reformulation in process records | High: Consistently interprets intentions across cultural contexts; repairs with nuance.<br>Moderate: Shows awareness but repair is inconsistent.<br>Low: Minimal perspective-taking; surface-level responses. |
| Humor | The appropriate, context-sensitive use of humor as a relational resource, with planned recovery strategies. | • Identifies culturally specific humor<br>• Uses affiliative humor to build rapport<br>• Demonstrates recovery competence when humor misfires | High: Uses humor strategically; adapts to audience with explicit rationale.<br>Moderate: Attempts humor with limited audience analysis.<br>Low: Avoids humor or uses it without cultural consideration. |
| Ethical Awareness | Routine transparency about AI use, including disclosure, attribution, and systematic bias monitoring. | • Complete, traceable AI-use disclosure statements<br>• Accurate source attribution<br>• Periodic bias spot-checks on AI outputs | High: Disclosure is complete and traceable; bias audits identify risks.<br>Moderate: Disclosure present but incomplete.<br>Low: Minimal or no disclosure; no bias monitoring. |
| Governance Integration | The institutionalization of transparency, accountability, and human oversight as habitual course practices. | • Disclosure templates and bias-check routines in course shell<br>• Human sign-off for high-stakes communications<br>• Prompt journals and provenance badges maintained | High: Governance routines embedded and consistently followed.<br>Moderate: Some elements present but inconsistently applied.<br>Low: Governance is ad hoc or absent. |

Table 3 maps each design mediator to concrete design moves, observable behaviours, and evidence sources. Instruments can include selected items from intercultural sensitivity measures, counts of successful repair in discourse, prompt journals and provenance badges, and periodic bias-audit snapshots (McCallum, 2024; Jenks, 2025; Sarwari et al., 2024; Chen & Wei, 2025).

Seen as a whole, the RPF attempts three things: preserving the human relational core of learning, leveraging AI as a pedagogical instrument rather than an oracle, and embedding accountability in classroom infrastructure. If the design works, two outcomes should follow. First, learners will be able to explain and evidence why a given formulation is interculturally appropriate for a particular audience, including when that formulation departs from the model's default. Second, programs will have a routine, auditable trail of how AI was used, verified, and corrected. Those are the conditions under which AI can help widen intercultural dialogue without erasing the differences that make dialogue worth having.

## 5. EVALUATION AND MEASUREMENT

If rehumanization is more than rhetoric, it must generate evidence that the RPF's target outcomes develop in AI-mediated ICC. The evaluation task is not to reduce intercultural judgment to a single number but to make growth legible across complementary traces: self-report dispositions, interactional behaviour, and ethical practice. Alignment is the guiding principle. Instruments should track what the RPF explicitly designs, so that assessment reinforces rather than distorts pedagogy.

The first layer concerns self-reported orientations that ICC research has long associated with growth: interaction enjoyment, respect for difference, and confidence in intercultural encounters. Dispositions alone do not constitute competence, but they plausibly mediate gains when combined with interactional practice. In a large study of engineering undergraduates (n = 990), features of AI learning environments positively predicted ICC, with learning adaptability partially mediating that effect (Chen & Wei, 2025). Programs should therefore track a small set of dispositions at baseline and post, particularly those capturing adaptability and willingness to repair.

The second layer is interactional evidence. The object here is not surface polish but the sequences by which meaning is negotiated: how learners signal recognition of intent, soften or strengthen stance, avoid or repair face-threats, and deploy humor to affiliate rather than exclude. In telecollaboration settings where AI is positioned as an object of critique, the strongest gains occur when instructors model repair rather than merely pointing out misalignment (Dai et al., 2025). A practical evaluation routine asks for side-by-side versions, the AI-influenced first pass and the revised, audience-tuned version, accompanied by a short rationale naming likely face-threats and explaining how the team repaired them.

The third layer evaluates ethical practice as ordinary behaviour. If governance covaries with perceived benefit (Sarwari et al., 2024), then embedding disclosure, attribution, and small bias audits into assignments is not mere compliance but a pedagogy that conditions trust. Evaluation should score the completeness and traceability of AI-use statements and the quality of bias spot-checks. Because these are visible artifacts, they can be sampled across sections to monitor whether ethical awareness is becoming habitual.

A fourth concern is fairness and equity. Distance language programs routinely contend with uneven connectivity, device access, and digital literacies; AI layers on additional resource demands (Aderinoye, 2005; Ergin et al., 2022). Evaluation must disaggregate results by access tier so that program leaders have early warning when structural supports are needed. Validity deserves explicit attention because measurement regimes can distort practice. Content validity means scoring what the framework claims to teach. Construct validity calls for triangulation: self-report shifts that travel with interactional evidence and ethical behaviour. Reliability requires internal consistency for self-report scales and inter-rater agreement for artifact scores. Generalizability can be addressed pragmatically by sampling artifacts across sections over time, supported by stable rubrics and short rater-calibration sessions.

A credible programme-level cycle begins with baseline profiling: a brief dispositions survey and a short diagnostic task drafting for a concrete audience. During the module, the artifact routine (paired versions, rationale, disclosure, and micro-bias check) generates consistent evidence. At the end of the module, students repeat the survey and submit a final artifact set, scored with the RPF rubric. Programs can then inspect three simple deltas: shifts in dispositions, prevalence of successful repairs, and improvements in ethical practice. When these move together, the framework is not just a slogan, but a practice that learners have internalized. Calibrated trust must itself be evaluated as agentic AI increases both opportunity and risk. A short reflective prompt such as "Where did you accept the model's suggestion? Where did you override it? What audience or ethical consideration drove that decision?" generates rationales that improve over time, becoming less about grammar and more about audience design, facework, and provenance (O'Regan & Ferri, 2025).

Implementation quality depends on staff readiness. Cross-cultural AI-literacy workshops build shared terminology and provide concrete exemplars, lowering the barrier to routine adoption (Korte et al., 2024). Over successive offerings, programs can curate a local repository of good practice: repair exemplars, audience-safe humor examples, and effective counter-prompts. Two risks require direct attention. First, over-quantification: because perspective-taking and humor are delicate interactional achievements, crude counts mislead. The solution is to keep numbers modest and attach them to interpretable events. Second, privacy drift: as course analytics expand, opaque pipelines and secondary use can corrode trust. Evaluation protocols should follow least-data principles and strip identifying details from stored artifacts (O'Regan & Ferri, 2025).

When assembled, these elements form a coherent measurement story. Dispositions tell us whether students are becoming learners who will attempt intercultural repair. Interactional artifacts show whether repair and audience-safe humor actually occur. Ethical routines demonstrate whether authorship and bias are handled with accountability. Together, they answer the performance question that matters: appropriateness and effectiveness for a particular audience and purpose.

## 6. CONCLUSION AND FUTURE DIRECTIONS

This chapter has argued that the pedagogical promise of AI-supported distance language education becomes durable only when intercultural communication is designed around the human capacities that machines cannot assume. The Rehumanizing Pedagogical Framework treats these capacities as intentional outcomes, realized through task and feedback designs that foreground empathic positioning and repair, interface affordances that make provenance and authorship visible, and governance routines that normalize disclosure and bias audits.

### 6.1 Implications for Practice

Two implications follow for curriculum and classroom practice. First, assessment should shift from a narrow emphasis on textual products to the quality of interactional processes: how learners document their prompting and verification decisions, negotiate stance and face, repair misalignments, and justify tone or humor choices for specific audiences. Second, programme-level policies should institutionalize what individual faculty often improvise: disclosure-by-default for AI use, auditable bias-check routines around culturally sensitive tasks, and interface cues that label AI-generated text and human verification. In practical terms, learning management systems such as Canvas or Moodle can be configured to include disclosure templates, prompt-journal submission points, and peer-review protocols that make process artifacts visible alongside final products.

At the professional learning level, institutions should treat AI literacy as intercultural literacy. Cross-cultural AI-literacy workshops show that shared vocabulary and reflective routines can be built across culturally diverse cohorts and carry over into more consistent classroom practice (Korte et al., 2024). In distance contexts, such capacity building needs to be coupled with design choices that preserve the felt presence of others, understood through the Community of Inquiry lens as the degree to which participants project themselves as real people in mediated communication (Garrison et al., 2000; Sun, 2025).

## 6.2 Prioritized Research Agenda

A forward-looking research agenda follows from the constraints identified in this chapter, organized into three tiers based on urgency and feasibility.

Tier 1: Immediate Priorities (1 to 2 years). (a) Design-based research should iterate on task- and feedback-level mediators to estimate what changes when interfaces add provenance cues or when rubrics credit high-quality AI-use documentation. (b) Fairness-aware analytics are urgently needed: programs should implement bias and differential item functioning checks disaggregated by language background and access strata. (c) Professional-learning pathways should be studied as interventions, comparing sequences of micro-credentials, peer coaching, and cross-cultural workshops.

Tier 2: Medium-Term Priorities (2 to 4 years). (a) Longitudinal, multi-site studies should track how the RPF's target outcomes develop across terms and how these trajectories relate to achievement and participation, particularly for learners who differ in access and language backgrounds. (b) Translanguaging-compatible tooling merits sustained experimentation, for example retrieval-augmented generation grounded in community corpora combined with guided reflection, so that learners see, contest, and improve the cultural scripts embedded in AI suggestions.

Tier 3: Longer-Term Priorities (4+ years). (a) Develop standardized assessment instruments for AI-mediated ICC that can be validated across diverse educational contexts. (b) Investigate the long-term impact of RPF-aligned pedagogy on learners' intercultural citizenship and professional communication beyond the classroom.

## 6.3 Limitations and Closing Remarks

Limitations deserve candor. The current empirical base on AI-mediated humor and affect is thin; brittle pragmatics and culturally misaligned warmth persist, requiring human mediation in high-stakes interactions. The black-box properties of AI systems and unresolved questions about data provenance complicate trust and accountability in education (von Eschenbach, 2021). Uptake costs are nontrivial: instructors need time and coaching to internalize disclosure norms, run bias audits, and design tasks that make reading the interlocutor's stance and repair discussable rather than hidden. None of these constraints invalidate the approach; they make visible the institutional investments needed to move from enthusiasm to sustained practice.

The decisive question for AI in distance language education is not whether models can produce fluent text but whether educators can orchestrate AI-mediated environments that deepen intercultural understanding while keeping human judgment and accountability at the centre. The RPF is a pragmatic answer. By treating taking the other's viewpoint as a practice enacted through repair, humor as culture-safe play that sustains rapport, and ethical awareness as routine transparency and bias monitoring, it offers a way to govern AI with pedagogical purpose rather than be governed by its speed and scale. If programs embed these routines into everyday practice, through clear interfaces, credit for reflective AI use, and scheduled bias reviews, AI can become a trustworthy partner in the long project of intercultural education rather than a detour away from it.

## REFERENCES


Aderinoye, R. A. (2005). Distance Education and Languages: Evolution and change. *International Review of Research in Open and Distance Learning*, *6*(3). Advance online publication. DOI: 10.19173/irrodl.v6i3.269

Atay, D., Kurt, M., Camlıbel Ersin, P., & Kaşlıoğlu, Ö. (2009). The role of intercultural competence in foreign language teaching. *Inonu University Journal of the Faculty of Education*, *10*(3), 123–135.

Attardo, S. (1994). *Linguistic theories of humor*. Mouton de Gruyter.

Byram, M. (1997). *Teaching and assessing intercultural communicative competence*. Multilingual Matters.

Byram, M. (2021). *Teaching and assessing intercultural communicative competence: Revisited*. Multilingual Matters. DOI: 10.21832/9781800410251

Chen, Y., & Wei, L. (2025). Effects of artificial intelligence learning environments on engineers' intercultural communication competence: The mediating role of learning adaptability. *Interactive Learning Environments*, *33*(2), 1404–1421. DOI: 10.1080/10494820.2024.2371937

Dai, D. W., & Hua, Z. (2025). When AI meets intercultural communication: New frontiers, new agendas. *Applied Linguistics Review*, *16*(2), 747–751. DOI: 10.1515/applirev-2024-0185

Dai, D. W., Suzuki, S., & Chen, G. (2025). Generative AI for professional communication training in intercultural contexts: Where are we now and where are we heading? *Applied Linguistics Review*, *16*(2), 763–774. DOI: 10.1515/applirev-2024-0184

Deardorff, D. K. (2006). Identification and assessment of intercultural competence as a student outcome of internationalization. *Journal of Studies in International Education*, *10*(3–4), 241–266. DOI: 10.1177/1028315306287002

Ergin, D. Y., Asutay, H., & Doğan, C. (2022). Distance education problems in foreign language education during the pandemic period. *Open Journal of Educational Research*, *6*(1), 43–56. DOI: 10.32591/coas.ojer.0601.04043e

Fantini, A. E. (2009). Assessing intercultural competence: Issues and tools. In Deardorff, D. K. (Ed.), *The SAGE handbook of intercultural competence* (pp. 456–476). SAGE., DOI: 10.4135/9781071872987.n27

Ferrara, E. (2023). Should ChatGPT be biased? Challenges and risks of bias in large language models. *First Monday*, *28*(11). Advance online publication. DOI: 10.5210/fm.v28i11.13346

Garrison, D. R., Anderson, T., & Archer, W. (2000). Critical inquiry in a text-based environment: Computer conferencing in higher education. *The Internet and Higher Education*, *2*(2–3), 87–105. DOI: 10.1016/S1096-7516(00)00016-6

Goodell, J., & Kolodner, J. (Eds.). (2022). *Learning engineering toolkit: Evidence-based practices from the learning sciences, instructional design, and beyond.* Routledge., DOI: 10.4324/9781003276579

Guzman, A. L., & Lewis, S. C. (2020). Artificial intelligence and communication: A human–machine communication research agenda. *New Media & Society*, *22*(1), 70–86. DOI: 10.1177/1461444819858691

Hall, J. K. (2018). *Essentials of SLA for L2 teachers: A transdisciplinary framework.* Routledge. DOI: 10.4324/9781315181271

Hauck, M., & Hampel, R. (2005). The challenges of implementing online tuition in distance language courses: Task design and tutor role. In Holmberg, B., Shelley, M., & White, C. (Eds.), *Distance education and languages: Evolution and change* (pp. 258–277). Multilingual Matters., DOI: 10.2307/jj.27710941.19

Hornyak, T. (2025). Agentic AI is here—But are we ready? *Research Technology Management*, *68*(5), 59–60. DOI: 10.1080/08956308.2025.2532320

Hua, Z., Dai, D. W., Brandt, A., Chen, G., Ferri, G., Hazel, S., Jenks, C., Jones, R., O'Regan, J., & Suzuki, S. (2025). Exploring AI for intercultural communication: Open conversation. *Applied Linguistics Review*, *16*(2), 809–824. DOI: 10.1515/applirev-2024-0186

Jegede, O. O. (2025). Humour as a pragmatic tool in multicultural online interactions. *Integrative Psychological & Behavioral Science*, *59*(4), 67. Advance online publication. DOI: 10.1007/s12124-025-09930-7

Jenks, C. (2025). Communicating the cultural other: Trust and bias in generative AI and large language models. *Applied Linguistics Review*, *16*(2), 787–795. DOI: 10.1515/applirev-2024-0196

Kelly, R., & Hou, H. (2022). Empowering learners of English as an additional language: Translanguaging with machine translation. *Language and Education*, *36*(6), 544–559. DOI: 10.1080/09500782.2021.1958834

Korte, S. M., Cheung, W. M. Y., Maasilta, M., Kong, S. C., Keskitalo, P., Wang, L., Lau, C. M., Lee, J. C. K., & Gu, M. M. (2024). Enhancing artificial intelligence literacy through cross-cultural online workshops. *Computers and Education Open*, *6*, 100164. Advance online publication. DOI: 10.1016/j.caeo.2024.100164

LeCun, Y. (2022). *A path towards autonomous machine intelligence* (Version 0.9.2) [Preprint]. OpenReview. https://openreview.net/forum?id=BZ5a1r-kVsf

Logg, J. M., Minson, J. A., & Moore, D. A. (2019). Algorithm appreciation: People prefer algorithmic to human judgment. *Organizational Behavior and Human Decision Processes*, *151*, 90–103. DOI: 10.1016/j.obhdp.2018.12.005

Martin, R. A. (2007). *The psychology of humor: An integrative approach.* Elsevier Academic Press. DOI: 10.1016/B978-012372564-6/50024-1

McCallum, L. (2024). New takes on developing intercultural communicative competence: Using artificial intelligence tools in telecollaboration task design and task completion. *Journal for Multicultural Education*, *18*(1/2), 153–172. DOI: 10.1108/JME-06-2023-0043

McConachy, T., Golubeva, I., & Wagner, M. (Eds.). (2022). *Intercultural learning in language education and beyond: Evolving concepts, perspectives and practices.* Multilingual Matters.

Moore, M. G. (1993). Theory of transactional distance. In Keegan, D. (Ed.), *Theoretical principles of distance education* (pp. 22–38). Routledge.

O'Regan, J., & Ferri, G. (2025). Artificial intelligence and depth ontology: Implications for intercultural ethics. *Applied Linguistics Review*, *16*(2), 797–807. DOI: 10.1515/applirev-2024-0189

Pan, Z. (2024). Impoliteness in polylogal intercultural communication among Asian EFL learners. *Intercultural Pragmatics*, *21*(2), 227–254. DOI: 10.1515/ip-2024-2003

Sarwari, A. Q., Javed, M., Adnan, M., & Abdul Wahab, M. N. (2024). Assessment of the impacts of artificial intelligence (AI) on intercultural communication among postgraduate students in a multicultural university environment. *Scientific Reports*, *14*(1), 13849. Advance online publication. DOI: 10.1038/s41598-024-63276-5

Schneider, B. (2022). Multilingualism and AI: The regimentation of language in the age of digital capitalism. *Signs and Society (Chicago, Ill.)*, *10*(3), 362–387. DOI: 10.1086/721757

Seo, K., Tang, X., Roll, A., Fels, S., & Yoon, J. (2021). The impact of artificial intelligence on learner–instructor interaction in online learning. *International Journal of Educational Technology in Higher Education, 18*(1), 54. Advance online publication. DOI: 10.1186/s41239-021-00292-9

Sun, L. (2025). Enhancing intercultural competence of Chinese English majors through AI-enabled Collaborative Online International Learning (COIL) in the digital era. *Education and Information Technologies, 30*(6), 7995–8027. DOI: 10.1007/s10639-024-13143-7

Tuncel, İ., & Paker, T. (2018). Effects of an intercultural communication course in developing intercultural sensitivity. *International Journal of Higher Education, 7*(6), 198–217. DOI: 10.5430/ijhe.v7n6p198

Volcic, Z., Tran, I., Palepu, V., & Baath, R. (2024). Intercultural communication during pandemic: New ways to build intercultural dialogue and relationships. *Intercultural Education, 35*(1), 42–61. DOI: 10.1080/14675986.2023.2279832

von Eschenbach, W. J. (2021). Transparency and the black box problem: Why we do not trust AI. *Philosophy & Technology, 34*(4), 1607–1622. DOI: 10.1007/s13347-021-00477-0

Young, R. F. (2008). *Language and interaction: An advanced resource book.* Routledge.

## KEY TERMS AND DEFINITIONS

**Agentic AI:** Artificial intelligence systems that plan, reason, and act toward high-level goals through tool calls and multi-step orchestration, operating with less human micromanagement than traditional prompt-bound generation.

**Calibrated Trust:** A learner disposition toward AI that is neither credulous nor cynical, involving informed decisions about when to accept, modify, or override AI-generated suggestions based on intercultural and ethical considerations.

**Community of Inquiry (CoI):** A theoretical framework identifying three interdependent elements, namely relational connectedness, cognitive presence, and teaching presence, as necessary conditions for meaningful educational experience in online and distance learning environments.

**Ethical Simulacra:** AI-generated outputs that appear ethically well-formed and norm-consistent on the surface but lack genuine judgmental rationality, thereby obscuring responsibility and potentially reproducing inequality.

**Intercultural Communicative Competence (ICC):** The ability to communicate appropriately and effectively across cultural boundaries, encompassing attitudes of openness, knowledge of sociocultural contexts, skills of interpretation and interaction, and critical cultural awareness.

**Rehumanizing Pedagogical Framework (RPF):** A design architecture for distance foreign language education that treats the RPF's three target outcomes as explicit, assessable learning outcomes, operationalized through four design mediators: task design, feedback design, interface affordances, and governance.

**Social Presence:** The degree to which participants in mediated communication are able to project their personal characteristics into the interaction, thereby presenting themselves as real people and fostering interpersonal relationships.

**Transactional Distance:** The psychological and communicative space between learner and instructor in distance education, which expands when dialogue is limited and structure is rigid, requiring deliberate relational design to bridge.

# Chapter 7
# Coded Stories, Cultural Scripts Intercultural Communication in AI-Driven Children's English Learning Apps

**Alperen Avci**
http://orcid.org/0000-0003-2395-9495
*Mus Alparslan University, Turkey*

**Duygu Yalman Polatlar**
*Fatih Sultan Mehmet Vakif University, Turkey*

## ABSTRACT

*As artificial intelligence (AI) becomes more embedded in children's English language education through story-driven apps, questions arise about the cultural and ecological assumptions encoded in algorithmic narratives. This chapter examines how AI-powered platforms, particularly Lingokids, represent cultural diversity, spatial norms, and nature. Although presented as neutral language-learning tools, these narratives operate as coded stories that subtly reproduce specific cultural scripts. Drawing on intercultural communication theory, ecocriticism, and critical media literacy, the study conducts a qualitative visual content analysis of five alphabet-based Lingokids stories. Findings show recurring Western suburban imagery, anthropomorphized characters, sanitized ecological settings, and simplified story structures indicating algorithmic cultural reductionism. The chapter introduces an*

DOI: 10.4018/979-8-3373-6325-7.ch007

*interdisciplinary framework for evaluating AI-mediated storytelling and recommends culturally inclusive, ecologically responsive narrative practices for educators, designers, and policymakers.*

## INTRODUCTION

### AI, Early Childhood, and the Cultural Politics of Educational Platforms

In the rapidly expanding landscape of educational technology, artificial intelligence (AI) has emerged not only as a pedagogical instrument but as an infrastructural force reorganising how knowledge, interaction, and authority circulate within early childhood learning environments. AI-driven English learning applications designed for young learners—such as Lingokids, Duolingo Kids, and similar conversational learning systems—are frequently framed as playful, adaptive ecosystems that support vocabulary growth, phonological awareness, and early literacy development (Holmes et al., 2019; OECD, 2021). Their design logic emphasises gamification, repetition, and personalisation, promising to optimise engagement while reducing cognitive overload.

Yet a growing body of scholarship in critical educational technology studies cautions against viewing AI as a neutral efficiency-enhancing layer (Selwyn, 2019; Williamson, 2017; Knox, 2020). Educational AI systems are socio-technical assemblages embedded within broader political, economic, and cultural structures. They do not merely transmit content; they curate representational environments. Through algorithmic sequencing, interface aesthetics, and narrative design, such platforms repeatedly stage particular visions of childhood, domestic life, emotional expression, and environmental settings.

This chapter begins from the premise that AI-mediated English-learning story apps function simultaneously as linguistic tools and as cultural infrastructures. While they undoubtedly contribute to lexical and phonological development, they also construct symbolic worlds that children inhabit repeatedly during the process of "learning English." These worlds are not random. They are shaped by platform economies, global media aesthetics, training datasets, and design decisions that privilege recognisability, scalability, and legibility across markets (Williamson, 2017; Srnicek, 2017).

Educational platforms operate within what has been described as "platform capitalism," a model in which data extraction, algorithmic optimisation, and user engagement drive design priorities (Srnicek, 2017). In children's educational apps, optimisation often targets retention metrics, progression rates, and engagement loops. However, optimisation also influences representational choices. When designers seek globally marketable visual templates, they frequently select culturally legible and commercially familiar imagery—suburban houses, temperate forests, pastel animal characters—forms that circulate widely in Western children's media industries. Over time, these selections solidify into aesthetic defaults.

Scholars analysing algorithmic bias have demonstrated that digital systems frequently reproduce dominant cultural norms under the guise of neutrality (Noble, 2018). Similarly, Bender et al. (2021) argue that AI systems inherit the statistical patterns embedded in their training data, thereby amplifying hegemonic linguistic and cultural regularities. In early childhood AI applications, such inheritance may not manifest in overtly discriminatory outputs but in subtle standardisation: a narrowing of representational plurality into a small set of recurring templates.

The cultural stakes of this standardisation are heightened in early childhood. Developmental research emphasises that between the ages of four and eight, children engage intensively in symbolic play, narrative immersion, and socio-emotional categorisation (Bruner, 1986; Vygotsky, 1978). Stories serve not merely as entertainment but as interpretive scaffolds through which children construct expectations about social life. Repeated exposure to stable narrative environments can strengthen vocabulary acquisition, but it can also stabilise cultural assumptions about what homes look like, which animals are familiar, and how problems are resolved.

This dual function of repetition—cognitive reinforcement and representational normalisation—makes AI-driven story apps particularly significant. Unlike traditional printed storybooks, AI platforms are designed for iterative interaction. Characters recur across modules; settings remain consistent; aesthetic palettes are standardised to support brand identity. Through this iterative structure, children repeatedly rehearse the same symbolic landscapes while advancing linguistically.

From a socio-cultural perspective, learning is always mediated through cultural artefacts (Vygotsky, 1978). AI-mediated stories are such artefacts. They embed assumptions about politeness routines, emotional expressivity, and domestic organisation. Even when presented in simplified form, these assumptions reflect broader cultural scripts.

The notion of cultural scripts, developed within cultural linguistics, refers to shared norms and expectations that guide communication and social interaction within communities (Goddard & Wierzbicka, 2004). In early language-learning apps, scripts may be encoded into routine greetings, tidy-up sequences, helping behaviours, and repair-oriented conflict resolutions. Because these scripts are embedded in seemingly universal childhood situations, their cultural specificity can remain invisible.

This invisibility is not accidental. Global educational platforms frequently aim for cross-cultural legibility. To avoid alienating diverse markets, designers may opt for imagery and narrative structures perceived as culturally neutral. However, neutrality is rarely culture-free; it often aligns with dominant Western media conventions that appear universal precisely because they circulate widely (Gray, 2010).

The tension between global accessibility and representational plurality becomes particularly salient in the context of English as a global lingua franca. Contemporary scholarship emphasises that English functions less as a marker of belonging to a specific national culture and more as a flexible communicative resource used across multilingual contexts (Seidlhofer, 2011; Jenkins, 2014). Yet pedagogical materials—including digital ones—often continue to embed English within Anglo-American childhood imaginaries. AI story apps risk perpetuating this pattern by linking English vocabulary to specific domestic architectures, ecological settings, and behavioural scripts that reflect particular socio-cultural norms.

The question, therefore, is not whether AI apps teach English effectively in a narrow linguistic sense. Rather, it is whether the symbolic worlds accompanying that instruction align with the plural realities of global English use. Do AI-mediated narratives expand children's intercultural imagination by presenting varied social and ecological contexts? Or do they stabilise a narrow configuration of childhood as implicitly universal?

This chapter situates these questions within a broader theoretical shift in educational research: the recognition that learning technologies are not culturally transparent. Critical scholars argue that digital systems structure what becomes visible, measurable, and legitimate within educational spaces (Selwyn, 2019; Knox, 2020). When AI systems curate children's story environments, they also curate visibility. They determine which homes appear as default, which habitats count as "nature," and which emotional expressions are modelled as normative.

Importantly, this chapter does not adopt a technologically deterministic stance. Children are not passive recipients of digital narratives. Research in media studies demonstrates that young learners actively interpret and negotiate meaning within family and classroom contexts (Buckingham, 2003; Livingstone, 2020). Parental and teacher mediation significantly shapes children's understanding of digital content (Nikken & Jansz, 2015). However, agency does not negate representational structure. The range of available contrasts within a storyworld influences what can be noticed, compared, and questioned.

When a platform repeatedly depicts a single housing prototype, a limited set of woodland animals, and a consistent pastel aesthetic, it constrains the internal variability of the narrative environment. Educators can introduce external comparisons, but the platform itself provides fewer triggers for intercultural reflection.

Moreover, AI personalisation often operates primarily at the level of performance metrics—adjusting task difficulty, repetition frequency, or progression pathways (Holmes et al., 2019). Cultural and ecological variation rarely form part of personalisation logics. As a result, linguistic scaffolding may adapt while representational context remains static. This asymmetry produces what may be termed contextual rigidity: the child's lexical pathway is individualised, but the symbolic environment is not.

The educational implications of contextual rigidity are subtle but significant. Intercultural Communicative Competence (ICC) theory emphasises that language learning involves not only grammatical mastery but also openness to difference, interpretive flexibility, and critical awareness (Byram, 1997). In early childhood, such dispositions are nurtured through exposure to varied perspectives and guided discussion. When narrative worlds lack representational plurality, opportunities for within-text comparison decrease.

Simultaneously, ecocritical scholarship reminds us that environmental imagination is cultivated through narrative framing (Glotfelty, 1996; Garrard, 2011). When AI story apps depict nature as static, risk-free, and homogenous, they may inadvertently flatten ecological complexity. This does not imply a need for crisis narratives; rather, it suggests the value of subtle ecological variability—seasonal shifts, habitat diversity, interdependence cues—that can be integrated without increasing linguistic difficulty.

Against this backdrop, this chapter approaches AI-mediated English-learning stories as cultural–ecological micro-worlds. It does not seek to evaluate the technical efficacy of vocabulary instruction. Instead, it examines how narrative architecture—housing models, landscape templates, character repertoires, and conflict-resolution logics—structures symbolic meaning.

By analysing Lingokids ABC stories as an illustrative case, the chapter contributes to a growing conversation about the cultural politics of AI in early childhood education. As AI systems become embedded in formative learning environments, representational design becomes a pedagogical concern rather than a peripheral aesthetic choice.

## Narrative Worlds, Multimodality, and the Formation of Symbolic Normalcy

If AI-mediated language learning applications are approached as cultural infrastructures, it becomes necessary to examine not only what linguistic content they present but how they structure narrative experience. Stories are not neutral containers for vocabulary; they are meaning-making systems that organise time, causality, character, and space. Narrative theory has long emphasised that human beings understand social reality through storied forms (Bruner, 1986; Ricoeur, 1984;

Fisher, 1987). For young children in particular, narrative is a primary cognitive scaffold through which categories of self, other, home, and environment are formed.

Jerome Bruner (1986) distinguishes between paradigmatic and narrative modes of thought, arguing that narrative thinking enables individuals to make sense of human action within culturally structured plots. In early childhood, this narrative mode precedes abstract reasoning; children grasp moral logic and social norms through repeated exposure to story patterns. When AI-driven platforms repeatedly stage similar domestic settings, character roles, and resolution logics, they participate in shaping what Bruner describes as "canonical narratives" patterns that define what is expected, ordinary, or desirable.

Paul Ricoeur's (1984) work on narrative temporality further deepens this insight by suggesting that narratives configure experience through emplotment: they arrange events into coherent sequences that generate meaning. In AI story apps, emplotment frequently follows a compressed structure: introduction of a minor problem, brief disruption, and technical resolution. While this structure supports clarity and comprehension, its repetition may also stabilise particular causal logics. If problems are consistently framed as material damage repaired through individual effort, social and ecological complexity remains backgrounded.

Narrative rationality theory (Fisher, 1987) similarly posits that humans evaluate stories based on coherence and fidelity whether narratives appear internally consistent and resonant with lived experience. For young children, fidelity may be shaped by repetition rather than critical comparison. When AI-mediated narratives maintain high internal coherence through aesthetic standardisation and consistent character design, they enhance narrative rationality while potentially limiting exposure to alternative social configurations.

## Multimodality and Visual Semiotics in AI Story Apps

AI-supported language-learning stories are not purely textual; they are multimodal artefacts combining image, sound, animation, and interaction. Kress and van Leeuwen's (2020) theory of multimodality emphasises that visual composition communicates meaning through framing, colour, perspective, and spatial arrangement. In children's story apps, housing prototypes, landscape backdrops, and character positioning are semiotic resources that construct social meaning.

For example, symmetrical suburban houses with fenced lawns may connote order, safety, and middle-class domestic stability. Pastel colour palettes and rounded character shapes evoke emotional warmth and non-threatening environments. These design choices are pedagogically strategic: they reduce anxiety and enhance affective engagement. However, multimodal theory reminds us that such choices are not culturally empty. They reflect aesthetic conventions associated with specific media traditions.

Visual repetition reinforces semiotic normalcy. When the same housing form appears across multiple story units, its semiotic meaning becomes backgrounded, and it is no longer noticeable as a particular type of home but becomes "home" itself. The absence of urban density, rural variation, or alternative architectural forms further naturalises this template. In this sense, multimodal stability can function as cultural stabilisation.

## Repetition, Familiarity, and Symbolic Internalisation

Repetition is foundational in early childhood pedagogy. Cognitive research demonstrates that repeated exposure strengthens memory consolidation and category formation. In language learning, repetition supports phonological mapping and lexical retention. AI systems leverage repetition strategically: characters recur, songs reappear, settings remain stable.

Yet repetition does not operate solely at the lexical level. It also operates symbolically. Sociologist Pierre Bourdieu (1977) conceptualised habitus as a system of durable dispositions formed through repeated exposure to structured environments. While Bourdieu's framework addresses broader social reproduction, its insight is relevant here: repeated symbolic exposure shapes what feels familiar and taken-for-granted.

In AI story apps, repeated exposure to specific domestic and ecological templates may cultivate a micro-habitus of normalcy within the narrative world. This does not determine children's beliefs about reality, but it can influence which images feel culturally unmarked. Representational plurality, by contrast, introduces variability that disrupts automatic normalisation.

## Digital Childhood and Algorithmic Mediation

Research in digital childhood studies emphasises that contemporary children encounter media through interactive, algorithmically curated platforms rather than through static broadcast channels (Marsh, 2004; Livingstone, 2020). Unlike printed books, AI-driven apps can adapt content sequences based on user interaction. This adaptation creates an illusion of responsiveness and intimacy.

However, algorithmic mediation also introduces what has been termed "algorithmic authority" (Gillespie, 2014). When digital systems select and present content without visible authorship, their outputs may appear neutral and inevitable. In AI story apps, the narrative voice is not attributed to a named author; it is embedded within interface design. This invisibility can enhance perceived objectivity.

For young children, whose epistemic frameworks are still developing, such invisibility may strengthen the sense that the story world is simply "how things are." Unlike a printed book, which clearly signals authorship and boundedness, AI-mediated narratives are seamlessly integrated into interactive environments. The frictionless quality of interface design can obscure the constructed nature of representation.

## Affect, Emotional Scripts, and Norm Production

Beyond spatial and narrative structures, AI story apps encode affective norms. Characters frequently display exaggerated smiling expressions, cooperative attitudes, and emotionally legible gestures. Affect theory scholars argue that emotional representations contribute to the formation of social expectations (Ahmed, 2004). In children's media, smiling anthropomorphic characters create emotionally safe environments, but they also normalise particular affective repertoires.

When emotional expression is standardised for example, when characters consistently resolve frustration through calm repair rather than negotiation children are exposed to a limited range of affective scripts. Again, this does not imply harm; emotional clarity supports early learning. However, limited affective variability may reduce exposure to more complex interpersonal dynamics.

## Interface Authority and the Disappearance of Context

AI-driven educational apps are frequently positioned as globally accessible tools. To achieve cross-market legibility, they often minimise culturally specific markers. Yet minimisation of specificity does not equate to universality. Instead, it may reflect dominant design conventions perceived as broadly marketable.

The disappearance of contextual markers geographic cues, linguistic variation, socio-economic diversity produces what could be termed representational decontextualisation. Homes appear without location; forests appear without climate; communities appear without social differentiation. This decontextualisation simplifies narrative comprehension but also reduces opportunities for children to encounter contextual variability within the story world.

## From Narrative Stability to Representational Centring

Taken together, these theoretical perspectives suggest that AI-mediated story apps may cultivate what can be described as representational centring. Through multimodal repetition, narrative coherence, and aesthetic standardisation, a particular configuration of domestic life, environmental setting, and emotional expression becomes centred as default.

This centring is not necessarily intentional or ideological in a narrow sense. It may arise from design priorities focused on clarity, emotional safety, and brand consistency. However, centring has consequences. When a single configuration dominates, alternative configurations remain peripheral or absent.

From an intercultural perspective, exposure to difference is not solely achieved through explicit cultural lessons. It also emerges through narrative contrast. When multiple housing types, habitats, or social arrangements appear within story environments, children encounter variability as normal. When variability is limited, the symbolic repertoire narrows.

### Linking Narrative Formation to Intercultural and Ecological Inquiry

The theoretical discussion in this section underscores why representational analysis matters in AI language-learning contexts. Narrative worlds shape early symbolic categories. Multimodal repetition stabilises semiotic meaning. Algorithmic authority obscures authorship. Affective scripts normalise emotional expectations.

These dynamics collectively raise a central concern: how might AI-mediated story worlds influence the symbolic conditions under which intercultural communicative competence and ecological imagination develop?

The next section deepens this question by explicitly situating AI story apps within ICC theory and English as a Lingua Franca scholarship, examining how symbolic formation intersects with global language use.

## INTERCULTURAL COMMUNICATIVE COMPETENCE, GLOBAL ENGLISH, AND THE LIMITS OF NARRATIVE PLURALITY IN AI LANGUAGE LEARNING

If AI-mediated English-learning environments are approached as symbolic worlds, their relationship to intercultural communicative competence (ICC) becomes central. ICC reframes language learning as an interpretive, relational, and reflexive practice rather than as mere grammatical acquisition. Byram's (1997) influential model conceptualises ICC as comprising five interrelated dimensions: attitudes (curiosity and openness), knowledge (of social groups and their practices), skills of interpreting and relating, skills of discovery and interaction, and critical cultural awareness. Importantly, this model positions language learning as inseparable from engagement with cultural difference.

Subsequent frameworks have expanded ICC beyond European language pedagogy. Deardorff (2006) conceptualises intercultural competence as a process model in which attitudes, knowledge, and skills interact dynamically to produce internal outcomes (adaptability, empathy, flexibility) and external outcomes (effective and appropriate communication). Bennett's (1993) Developmental Model of Intercultural Sensitivity (DMIS) similarly emphasises movement from ethnocentric to ethnorelative orientations. These models converge on a core insight: intercultural competence is cultivated through exposure to difference and guided reflection on that difference.

In early childhood contexts, ICC does not manifest as abstract comparative analysis. Rather, it develops through narrative immersion, dialogic interaction, and adult mediation. Children notice variation in clothing, housing, food, family structure, and communicative routines through story exposure and guided discussion. When narrative worlds provide limited representational variability, opportunities for noticing and comparison are reduced.

## English as a Lingua Franca and Cultural Multiplicity

The relationship between English learning and cultural representation is further complicated by the global status of English. English today operates less as a national language tied to specific Anglo-American contexts and more as a lingua franca used across diverse sociolinguistic settings (Seidlhofer, 2011; Jenkins, 2014). ELF scholarship emphasises variability, accommodation strategies, and pragmatic negotiation across speakers from different linguistic backgrounds.

Canagarajah (2013) argues that global English communication is characterised by translanguaging practices and flexible norm negotiation rather than adherence to fixed native-speaker standards. Pennycook (2007) similarly critiques monolithic representations of English culture, advocating for recognition of English as a site of hybridity and cultural mixing. From this perspective, embedding English learning within narrow suburban and temperate-forest imagery risks misaligning pedagogy with sociolinguistic reality.

If AI-mediated story apps implicitly link English to a particular visual-cultural template, they may reinforce what Gray (2010) describes as the "cultural packaging" of English within Western consumerist imagery. While such packaging enhances global marketability, it may obscure the plural and hybrid contexts in which English is actually used.

## Intercultural Pragmatics and Communicative Variation

Beyond visual representation, ICC also involves pragmatic competence the ability to use language appropriately across contexts. Brown and Levinson's (1987) politeness theory introduced the concept of face management in interaction, highlighting how cultural norms shape indirectness, mitigation, and deference. Spencer-Oatey (2008) later refined relational management theory to account for culturally variable expectations of rapport and obligation.

Kecskes (2014) argues that intercultural pragmatics involves dynamic meaning negotiation shaped by participants' prior experiences and socio-cultural frames. In early childhood AI language apps, pragmatic routines are often simplified: greetings follow formulaic patterns; requests are direct; conflicts are resolved swiftly. While simplification supports comprehension, it may flatten pragmatic variation.

For example, if requests are consistently modelled in direct imperative forms without alternative strategies (e.g., hints, softened requests), children may encounter limited pragmatic repertoires within the storyworld. This does not imply pedagogical failure; early learners require clarity. However, absence of variation may limit exposure to communicative flexibility central to ICC.

## Cultural Hybridity and the "Third Space"

Homi Bhabha's (1994) concept of the "third space" provides another lens for examining intercultural representation. Bhabha argues that cultural interaction produces hybrid spaces in which identities are negotiated rather than fixed. English as a global language operates within such hybrid spaces.

If AI-mediated narratives consistently depict culturally homogeneous environments stable housing prototypes, uniform ecological settings, standardised characters they may underrepresent hybridity. Hybrid representation need not involve overt multicultural markers; it can involve subtle layering: mixed architectural cues, multilingual signage, varied dress styles, or blended celebration practices.

Hybrid narrative worlds could reflect the fluidity of global childhoods, particularly in urban and diasporic contexts. When story environments remain culturally unmarked yet visually aligned with Western templates, hybridity remains peripheral.

## AI, Standardisation, and the Compression of Cultural Variation

Algorithmic systems favour standardisation for scalability. Consistent visual assets reduce production costs and enhance brand coherence. However, this standardisation can compress cultural variation into a limited set of defaults.

From an ICC perspective, the issue is not whether AI systems explicitly exclude cultures, but whether they provide sufficient narrative plurality to support interpretive comparison. Exposure to difference is not achieved solely through token inclusion of diverse characters; it also requires variability in setting, architecture, social routines, and communicative styles.

Moreover, AI personalisation algorithms rarely incorporate cultural diversity metrics. Adaptation focuses on task difficulty, repetition rates, and learner performance data (Holmes et al., 2019). Cultural variation is seldom parameterised. As a result, children may experience highly individualised lexical pathways within representationally uniform worlds.

## Early Childhood, Category Formation, and Cultural Imagination

Developmental research emphasises that young children construct categories through perceptual regularity and contrast. When multiple exemplars of a category are presented, children learn to recognise variability within that category. When exemplars are homogeneous, categories become narrower.

If "home" is repeatedly represented through a single suburban template, children may form a narrower internal representation of domestic possibility within the narrative context. If "nature" consistently appears as a temperate forest, ecological diversity remains underrepresented.

Importantly, this does not equate to children generalising such templates to real life without question. Rather, it concerns the symbolic conditions under which intercultural imagination develops. ICC involves the ability to recognise that one's own perspective is partial and situated. Narrative plurality supports this recognition by normalising variability.

## AI Story Worlds and the Risk of Cultural Neutralisation

Educational technology often aspires to cultural neutrality to ensure global market acceptance. However, neutrality may mask dominance. When specific cultural forms appear unmarked, they are positioned as universal.

This phenomenon aligns with postcolonial critiques of English language pedagogy, which highlight how Western norms are frequently presented as globally standard

(Pennycook, 2007). AI-mediated English apps risk replicating this pattern through aesthetic defaults rather than explicit ideology.

### Linking ICC Theory to Representational Analysis

The preceding discussion suggests that evaluating AI language apps solely on linguistic metrics is insufficient. ICC theory demands attention to representational conditions. Narrative plurality, pragmatic variation, and ecological diversity contribute to intercultural learning by expanding symbolic repertoires.

This chapter therefore investigates not whether Lingokids effectively teaches alphabetic principles, but how its storyworlds structure cultural and ecological meaning. By analysing recurring housing forms, landscape templates, character repertoires, and conflict-resolution logics, the study examines whether narrative environments reflect the plural realities of global English use or centre a narrow template.

## ECOLOGICAL REPRESENTATION, ALGORITHMIC REDUCTIONISM, AND THE ETHICS OF AI STORYTELLING IN EARLY CHILDHOOD

While intercultural representation addresses how cultural plurality becomes visible within AI-mediated story worlds, ecological representation raises parallel questions concerning how nature, environment, and human–nonhuman relations are framed. Ecocritical scholarship has long argued that literary and visual texts do not merely depict landscapes; they encode environmental imaginaries that influence how readers conceptualise the natural world (Glotfelty, 1996; Garrard, 2011). In children's media, nature often appears as aesthetically pleasing background a pastoral, conflict-free setting populated by friendly animals and stable weather conditions. This aestheticisation can cultivate affection toward nature, yet it may also obscure ecological interdependence, environmental vulnerability, and habitat diversity.

Ursula Heise (2008) introduces the concept of "eco-cosmopolitanism," emphasising the need for narratives that situate local environments within global ecological networks. Rob Nixon (2011) similarly draws attention to "slow violence" environmental degradation that unfolds gradually and invisibly, often escaping narrative representation. Although early childhood stories are not expected to depict environmental crisis, ecocritical theory underscores the importance of representational complexity. Even subtle cues seasonal change, species diversity, varied terrains can expand ecological imagination without overwhelming young audiences.

In AI-mediated language-learning apps, ecological representation is frequently simplified to enhance clarity and emotional safety. Forests appear as homogeneous green hills; skies remain perpetually pastel; environmental disturbance is absent. This sanitised aesthetic aligns with pedagogical goals of reassurance and cognitive manageability. However, repeated depiction of static, risk-free environments may flatten ecological variability.

The issue is not that AI story apps should introduce environmental catastrophe into early literacy modules. Rather, it is whether they provide sufficient ecological plurality to reflect the diversity of habitats children inhabit globally. Desert environments, coastal regions, mountainous terrains, tropical climates, and urban ecologies represent lived realities for millions of children learning English. When AI storyworlds repeatedly centre temperate woodland ecologies, they privilege a specific environmental imaginary.

Ecological simplification intersects with cultural standardisation. If domestic architecture and natural landscapes remain consistent across narrative units, the storyworld becomes geographically unmarked yet aesthetically specific. This pattern may reflect what can be described as algorithmic reductionism a structural tendency of AI-mediated systems to compress representational variability into scalable templates.

## Algorithmic Reductionism and Governance

Algorithmic reductionism does not imply deliberate cultural exclusion. Rather, it refers to a systemic compression of diversity driven by optimisation logics. Educational AI platforms operate under constraints of scalability, usability, and cross-market appeal. Consistent asset libraries reduce production costs; stable templates enhance recognisability; simplified environments support user retention metrics.

However, governance scholars argue that algorithmic systems shape social reality by structuring visibility (Beer, 2017; Gillespie, 2014). When particular forms are repeatedly selected by design and optimisation processes, they become infrastructural norms. In educational contexts, such norms influence symbolic exposure during formative years.

International policy discussions increasingly recognise ethical dimensions of AI in education. UNESCO's (2021) Recommendation on the Ethics of Artificial Intelligence emphasises transparency, diversity, and cultural inclusion in AI systems. The European Union's AI Act similarly foregrounds accountability and risk mitigation in AI deployment, including educational contexts. While these frameworks primarily address data governance and bias prevention, they implicitly raise questions about representational equity.

Representation is an ethical issue because it shapes whose experiences are visible. In early childhood education, representational narrowing may not manifest as explicit discrimination but as absence of varied housing, absence of ecological diversity, absence of hybrid cultural cues. Such absences are subtle yet consequential.

## Representational Ethics in Early Childhood AI

Ethics in AI-mediated education is often framed in terms of privacy, data protection, and algorithmic fairness. These concerns are critical. Yet representational ethics how cultural and environmental plurality is depicted remains underexamined. In early childhood contexts, where symbolic formation is rapid and impressionable, representational narrowing may influence which worlds feel familiar within language learning.

Importantly, this chapter does not argue that AI story apps determine children's worldviews. Children inhabit complex ecological systems shaped by family, community, media, and school (Bronfenbrenner, 1979). However, AI-mediated narratives constitute a recurring symbolic resource within those systems. As such, their design merits scrutiny.

Balancing developmental simplicity with representational plurality is not an impossible task. Ecological variation can be introduced through seasonal rotation, diverse habitat modules, or regionally adaptive imagery. Cultural plurality can be reflected through varied architectural forms, mixed social settings, and hybrid celebratory scenes. Such variability need not increase linguistic complexity; it can operate visually while lexical scaffolding remains stable.

## From Reductionism to Plural Design

Moving beyond algorithmic reductionism requires rethinking design priorities. Currently, personalisation in AI language apps often targets performance data adjusting repetition frequency, pacing, or task difficulty. Representational context rarely adapts. Yet technological capacity exists for dynamic variation. AI systems could rotate environmental settings, incorporate culturally diverse housing prototypes, or integrate subtle geographic cues without compromising clarity.

This shift would align AI pedagogy with intercultural and ecological educational goals. Intercultural competence is strengthened when learners encounter difference as normal rather than exceptional. Ecological imagination expands when environments vary rather than remain static.

Such redesign does not imply abandoning emotional safety. Developmentally appropriate storytelling can coexist with representational plurality. Indeed, plurality itself may cultivate cognitive flexibility a trait associated with intercultural adaptability (Deardorff, 2006).

## Positioning the Present Study

Against this theoretical backdrop, this chapter undertakes a qualitative document analysis of selected Lingokids ABC stories as an illustrative case. Lingokids is not treated as uniquely problematic nor as representative of all AI-supported platforms. Rather, it provides a focused site for examining how narrative architecture constructs cultural and ecological meaning within early English-learning contexts.

By analysing housing models, spatial configurations, animal repertoires, affective scripts, and conflict-resolution structures, the study investigates whether representational plurality is embedded within the narrative system or compressed into standardised templates. The aim is interpretive rather than causal. The analysis does not claim developmental outcomes but identifies symbolic patterns that may shape conditions for intercultural and ecological learning.

## Contribution to the Field

This chapter contributes to three intersecting scholarly conversations:

1. **AI in Education**: It extends evaluation beyond efficacy metrics to include representational analysis, responding to calls for critical scrutiny of AI's cultural dimensions (Selwyn, 2019; Knox, 2020).
2. **Intercultural Communication**: It situates AI-mediated storytelling within ICC and ELF frameworks, linking symbolic formation to global language realities (Byram, 1997; Seidlhofer, 2011).
3. **Ecocriticism and Childhood Studies**: It foregrounds environmental representation in digital learning environments, connecting ecological imagination to narrative design (Glotfelty, 1996; Heise, 2008).

In doing so, the chapter reframes AI-driven English-learning apps as cultural–ecological infrastructures rather than purely instructional technologies. As AI becomes embedded in early childhood education, attention to representational ethics becomes integral to responsible design.

## Closing Framing

Language learning in AI-mediated contexts is not only about acquiring phonics or vocabulary. It involves inhabiting curated narrative worlds. Ensuring that these worlds reflect plurality cultural, ecological, and social is a pedagogical challenge and an ethical responsibility.

The sections that follow present the methodological approach and detailed findings of the Lingokids case analysis, examining how spatial norms, ecological imagery, character representation, and narrative logic structure the symbolic environment of AI-mediated English learning.

## 3. METHOD

### 3.1 Epistemological Positioning and Research Design

This study is grounded in an interpretivist epistemological orientation, which assumes that meaning is socially constructed and embedded within cultural artefacts rather than objectively given (Schwartz-Shea & Yanow, 2012). Within this paradigm, AI-mediated children's stories are treated not as neutral instructional tools but as symbolic texts that encode culturally situated assumptions about social life, environment, and normalcy.

Rather than evaluating measurable learning outcomes, this chapter seeks to examine representational structures and symbolic patterns within AI-supported story environments. Accordingly, the study adopts a **theory-informed qualitative document analysis**, a methodological approach appropriate for analysing written, visual, and multimodal artefacts within their socio-cultural contexts (Bowen, 2009; Schreier, 2012).

Document analysis is particularly suited to this inquiry for three reasons:

1. AI-mediated stories function as textual and visual documents that can be systematically examined.
2. The research questions concern representation, meaning-making, and symbolic construction rather than behavioural effects.
3. The method enables integration of theoretical frameworks directly into analytic procedures.

This study does not aim to establish causal claims about children's intercultural development. Instead, it offers an interpretive analysis of how AI-supported storytelling constructs cultural and ecological imaginaries within early English-learning contexts.

The research design is best described as a **theory-driven qualitative case analysis**, in which an illustrative case (Lingokids) is examined in depth to generate analytically transferable insights (Yin, 2018). The case is not treated as statistically representative of all AI platforms but as a theoretically generative site for examining broader structural tendencies in AI-mediated early language learning.

## 3.2 Case Selection and Rationale

Lingokids was selected as the focal case for several theoretically grounded reasons.

First, the platform occupies a prominent position within the global early childhood edtech market, with widespread international distribution and multilingual user bases. Its reach positions it as a meaningful site for examining globally circulating narrative templates.

Second, Lingokids integrates multimodal storytelling combining text, image, animation, and interactivity making it particularly suitable for semiotic and narrative analysis (Kress & van Leeuwen, 2020). Because this chapter investigates symbolic representation across linguistic and visual modalities, multimodality was a crucial selection criterion.

Third, Lingokids relies heavily on recurring characters and settings across learning modules. This structural repetition makes it analytically appropriate for investigating representational stability and narrative patterning.

The case was therefore selected through theoretical sampling logic (Patton, 2015), prioritising analytic relevance rather than representativeness.

## 3.3 Corpus Delimitation and Sampling Strategy

A purposive sampling strategy was employed to select five ABC stories from the Lingokids story library.

The sampling process followed three explicit criteria:

(1) Pedagogical Centrality ABC stories introduce foundational literacy concepts and are typically encountered early in user engagement. Because early exposure may shape first impressions of the platform's narrative environment, these stories were considered particularly significant.

(2) Algorithmic Visibility Stories that appear prominently in introductory or recommended sections were prioritised. Algorithmic visibility was defined as placement within default user pathways during initial platform navigation. This criterion reflects the study's concern with what children are most likely to encounter.

(3) Multimodal Density Selected stories integrated textual narration with full-page illustrations and character-driven visual scenes, enabling analysis of linguistic, spatial, and semiotic elements.

The decision to analyse five stories reflects the study's emphasis on analytic depth rather than breadth (Guest, Namey, & Mitchell, 2013). The goal was not coverage of the entire platform but saturation within a bounded corpus. Repeated coding cycles across five stories allowed identification of recurring structural patterns.

## 3.4 Data Collection Procedures

For each selected story, the following materials were systematically collected:

- Full-page screenshots capturing visual composition
- Complete textual transcriptions of narration and dialogue
- Researcher-generated narrative summaries documenting plot structure
- Field notes documenting contextual observations during platform navigation

Screenshots preserved spatial configuration, colour palettes, character positioning, and environmental framing. Textual transcriptions ensured accurate representation of linguistic content. Narrative summaries enabled macro-level structural comparison across stories.

All materials were organised within a structured analytic archive, facilitating cross-story comparison.

## 3.5 Analytical Framework

The analysis employed **directed content analysis** (Hsieh & Shannon, 2005), a method appropriate when existing theory informs initial coding categories. Unlike purely inductive approaches, directed content analysis allows theoretical constructs to guide interpretive attention while remaining open to emergent patterns.

## 3.6 Coding Process

The coding process unfolded in four stages:

### Stage 1: Immersive Familiarisation

Each story was reviewed multiple times to identify narrative flow, spatial patterns, and representational features (Braun & Clarke, 2019). Memos documented preliminary observations.

### Stage 2: Initial Theoretical Coding

Open codes were generated within each analytic category. For example:

- "Western suburban house prototype"
- "Pastoral forest background"
- "Anthropomorphic facial standardisation"
- "Technical repair resolution"
- "Absence of geographic markers"

Codes were applied systematically across stories to identify repetition and variation.

### Stage 3: Cross-Story Pattern Identification

Codes were compared across the corpus to detect structural regularities. Recurring features were grouped into higher-order themes such as "Representational Standardisation" or "Ecological Simplification."

### Stage 4: Interpretive Synthesis

Themes were interpreted in relation to ICC theory, ecocriticism, and AI representation scholarship. Importantly, interpretations focused on representational structures rather than presumed developmental outcomes.

## 3.7 Reflexivity and Researcher Positionality

Because qualitative interpretation is shaped by researcher perspective, reflexive practice was integrated throughout analysis (Finlay, 2002). Reflexive memos documented:

- The researcher's disciplinary background in intercultural and early childhood studies
- Potential interpretive biases regarding Western media templates
- Decisions made when resolving ambiguous coding cases

This reflexive process aimed to enhance analytic transparency.

## 3.8 Trustworthiness and Rigor

To strengthen credibility and methodological rigour, multiple strategies were employed (Lincoln & Guba, 1985):

### Credibility

- Theoretical grounding in established frameworks
- Thick description of visual and narrative elements
- Iterative coding cycles

### Dependability

- Audit trail documenting analytic decisions
- Systematic category definitions

### Confirmability

- Reflexive memos
- Explicit separation of description and interpretation

### Intercoder Agreement

A second researcher independently coded a subset of the corpus (two stories). Intercoder reliability was calculated using Miles and Huberman's (1994) formula:

*Reliability = Agreements / (Agreements + Disagreements)*

The resulting agreement rate exceeded the commonly accepted threshold of .80, indicating substantial consistency. Discrepancies were resolved through analytic dialogue, leading to refinement of category definitions.

Intercoder agreement was not treated as proof of objectivity but as a procedural tool to enhance clarity and analytic precision.

## 3.9 Scope and Limitations

This study analyses a limited corpus of five stories within a single platform. It does not examine user interaction data, learning outcomes, or longitudinal developmental effects. Nor does it compare multiple AI platforms.

The findings should therefore be understood as analytically transferable rather than statistically generalisable (Yin, 2018). The purpose is to illuminate structural tendencies in AI-mediated narrative design rather than to produce universal claims.

## 3.10 Ethical Considerations

The study relies exclusively on publicly accessible digital materials and does not involve human participants. Accordingly, no institutional ethical approval was required. However, ethical sensitivity was maintained by avoiding evaluative claims about platform intent and by situating findings within structural design considerations rather than individual responsibility.

# 4. FINDINGS: CULTURAL AND ECOLOGICAL REPRESENTATION IN LINGOKIDS ABC STORIES

To address the guiding question—within the Lingokids case—"To what extent do the narratives in AI-supported English learning apps foster intercultural empathy, openness, and global understanding?", visual materials from five ABC stories were analysed through thematic content analysis. Each image was coded across spatial configuration, ecological imagination, species diversity, narrative problem–solution structure, and cultural markers. Open codes were grouped into categories and synthesised into higher-order themes.

*Table 1. Cultural and ecological representation in Lingokids ABC stories*

| Theme | Category | Codes (Open Codes) |
|---|---|---|
| **Theme 1: Housing and Spatial Norms (Monocultural Housing)** | 1A. Housing Typology | – Western suburban house prototype<br>– Red pitched roof, beige walls<br>– Standardized wooden door<br>– Symmetrical window placement<br>– Same house model repeated across scenes |
| | 1B. Interior/Exterior Spatial Elements | – Recurrent fence–lawn–flower box<br>– Standard ramp design<br>– Absence of cultural traces in interiors<br>– Lack of alternative architectural forms |
| **Theme 2: Nature Depiction and Ecological Simplification (Romanticized Nature)** | 2A. Nature Backgrounds | – Single-type green hill landscape<br>– Pastel sky and cloud motifs<br>– Risk-free, sanitized forest floors<br>– Lack of habitat diversity |

continued on following page

*Table 1. Continued*

| Theme | Category | Codes (Open Codes) |
|---|---|---|
| | 2B. Absence of Ecological Issues | – No pollution elements<br>– No seasonal variation<br>– No climate/weather events<br>– Environmental threats rendered invisible |
| **Theme 3: Animal and Character Representation (Symbolic Homogenization)** | 3A. Species Diversity | – Dominance of Western forest fauna<br>– Absence of region-specific species<br>– Animal selection tied to a single ecological zone |
| | 3B. Anthropomorphism | – Human-like facial expressions<br>– Smiling, emotional posing<br>– Human behavioral mimicry<br>– Stylized pastel cartoon aesthetic |
| **Theme 4: Conflict–Resolution Structures (Technical Fix Framing)** | 4A. Problem Presentation | – Structural damage in the house (door, floor, wall)<br>– Presence of spider webs<br>– Dark, unusable interior spaces |
| | 4B. Resolution Structure | – Building a new house<br>– Technical repair/reconstruction<br>– No social context<br>– No ecological context |
| **Theme 5: Diversity Gaps (Cultural and Biological Diversity Absence)** | 5A. Lack of Cultural Markers | – No cultural motifs in clothing<br>– Absence of ethnic markers<br>– No geographical symbols |
| | 5B. Spatial/Biological Diversity Gaps | – Single habitat representation<br>– Single housing style<br>– Limited animal typology<br>– Lack of cultural–ecological integration |

Below, the themes are presented with interpretive detail and evidence anchors. Rather than claiming learner outcomes, the findings describe representational tendencies that shape the symbolic environment of the storyworlds.

## Theme 1: Housing and Spatial Norms (Monocultural Housing)

Across scenes, domestic architecture is anchored to a single suburban prototype. The beige façade, pitched red roof, symmetrical windows, and tidy garden layout recur across the corpus. Interiors and exteriors include few cultural traces; there are no vernacular architectural forms, apartment living, rural dwellings, or region-specific materials.

**Evidence vignette 1 (Story 1):** In Story 1, "home" is depicted through repeated fence–lawn–flower box elements and symmetrical window placement. Even when the narrative introduces "damage" (e.g., broken door, dark interior, spider webs), the repaired version returns to the same suburban template. The house functions as a stable symbol of domestic normalcy rather than as a culturally situated place (Figure I; Table 1, Theme 1).

**Evidence vignette 2 (Story 2):** In Story 2, a near-identical house model reappears with minor changes in object placement or interior emptiness. The recurring ramp-and-door layout and consistent garden symmetry reinforce the impression that "home" is a standardised container. Domestic space is framed as private, orderly, and economically neutral—suggesting a particular spatial ideology aligned with suburban imaginaries (Figure I; Table 1, Theme 1).

These patterns indicate that domestic architecture operates as a repeated representational anchor that stabilises the storyworld. The absence of architectural variety does not prove intentional exclusion; rather, it shows how one template becomes the default visual grammar of "home."

*Figure 1. House tipology*

## Theme 2: Nature Depiction and Ecological Simplification (Romanticised Nature)

Nature is consistently rendered as a simplified and aesthetically safe backdrop: green hills, rounded trees, pastel skies, and uniform clouds. Environmental complexity—soil texture, seasonal change, habitat diversity, ecological interaction, and disturbance—remains largely absent. Animals sometimes appear in non-specific settings that do not correspond to ecological realism.

**Evidence vignette 1 (Story 3):** In Story 3, characters are placed against rolling green hills and a pastel sky with uniform cloud motifs. Nature provides atmosphere but minimal ecological specificity. The landscape signals "outdoors" as a generic space rather than a habitat with material detail (Figure 2; Table 1, Theme 2).

**Evidence vignette 2 (Story 4):** In Story 4, a forest scene includes stylised trees and simplified ground textures, but there is little indication of leaf litter, insects, water sources, or microhabitats. Even when a frog appears, it is not embedded in a wetland or water-adjacent habitat; it is placed within a generalised green space. This reinforces a pastoral imaginary: nature is stable, clean, and conflict-free (Figure 2; Table 1, Theme 2)

A related pattern is the systematic absence of ecological disturbance. Across scenes, there are no indicators of pollution, drought, extreme weather, fire, flooding, or seasonal transition. The climate remains consistently pleasant. Representationally, the environment is framed as timeless and risk-free. Ecologically, nature is present but depoliticised and decontextualised.

*Figure 2. Nature visual*

## Theme 3: Animal and Character Representation (Symbolic Homogenisation)

Animal characters display limited species diversity and strong anthropomorphic standardisation. Species selection is concentrated on familiar woodland animals frequently found in Western children's literature (e.g., bear, fox, rabbit, owl, squirrel). Region-specific or non-forest species do not appear in the selected stories, and the animal world is compressed into a narrow ecological zone.

**Evidence vignette 1 (Story 5):** In Story 5, multiple species share similar facial structures—large round eyes, simplified mouth curvature, and uniform smiling affect. Emotional states are made immediately legible, but species differentiation is reduced. The design foregrounds cuteness and affective readability within a consistent pastel aesthetic (Figure III; Table 1, Theme 3).

**Evidence vignette 2 (cross-story pattern):** Across the corpus, anthropomorphism reconfigures animals through human-like emotional codes, prioritising social legibility over ecological specificity. This semiotic strategy supports quick comprehension for early learners, yet it can blur habitat specificity and reduce opportunities to notice biodiversity as diversity rather than as interchangeable friendly characters (Figure 3; Table 1, Theme 3).

Cultural markers are similarly minimal. Characters do not display culturally specific clothing, accessories, or symbolic motifs. A disability marker (wheelchair) appears once, potentially signalling inclusion; however, the marker is not developed into a narrative context addressing accessibility or environment. Difference is signalled briefly but not structurally expanded.

*Figure 3. Animal visual*

## Theme 4: Conflict–Resolution Structures (Technical Fix Framing)

Narrative conflicts rely on a consistent technical fix schema. Problems are introduced as structural damage (e.g., broken door, hole in the floor, collapsed ceiling, spider webs, unusable rooms) without social, economic, or ecological context. The narratives do not specify why deterioration occurs, who is responsible, or how community relations shape responses. Resolutions follow a mechanical repair logic: rebuilding, replacing, or fixing physical parts of the house.

**Evidence vignette 1 (Story 1):** In Story 1, the conflict is framed as material deterioration. The resolution is repair or reconstruction, often executed quickly. The schema supports clear sequencing (problem → fix → happy ending), facilitating comprehension and basic procedural vocabulary (Figure 4; Table 1, Theme 4).

**Evidence vignette 2 (Story 2):** In Story 2, a similar arc repeats: the problem is object-based and the solution is mechanical. Social negotiation, cooperative planning, or resource constraints do not appear. This narrows the representational repertoire for problem-solving and limits opportunities to model relational pragmatics (asking for help, persuading, coordinating) as part of narrative resolution (Figure 4; Table 1, Theme 4).

*Figure 4. Structural issues*

## Theme 5: Diversity Gaps (Cultural and Biological Diversity Absence)

Across the corpus, cultural, spatial, and ecological diversity is limited. Visuals repeat a single housing model, a single habitat template, a restricted set of animals, and a consistent pastel aesthetic. Cultural markers—traditional clothing motifs, geographical symbols, ethnic identifiers, local artefacts, multilingual signage—do not appear.

As a result, the storyworld appears culturally unmarked yet is structured by a standardised suburban and Western-coded aesthetic regime. Representationally, locality is erased and diversity is minimally signalled. This does not allow claims about children's outcomes; instead, it indicates that the analysed stories offer limited representational resources for depicting cultural plurality, diverse habitats, or alternative worldviews within early language-learning story contexts.

*Table 2. Representation–meaning matrix for symbolic story framing*

| Theme | Category | Codes (Open Codes) | Symbolic Framing / Interpretive Implications |
|---|---|---|---|
| **T1. Spatial Representation as a Symbolic World Builder** | 1A. Normalized Home Imagery | – Single suburban house prototype<br>– Pastel, economically neutral home<br>– Safe and sanitized outdoor space | Frames "home" through a standardized, orderly, suburban template that centers a single domestic model as visually normative. |
| | 1B. Absence of Local/ Urban Forms | – No apartments<br>– No rural structures<br>– No local/ vernacular architecture | Limits representational visibility of diverse housing forms and universalizes one spatial configuration of domestic life. |
| **T2. Aesthetic Standardization as a Semiotic Frame** | 2A. Color Palette and Visual Simplification | – Pastel tones<br>– Constructed optimistic atmosphere<br>– Sanitized environment | Establishes a visually consistent, emotionally safe aesthetic that minimizes environmental or socio-material complexity. |
| | 2B. Flattened Detail | – Absence of extra-textual signs<br>– Lack of cultural objects<br>– Lack of natural detail | Reduces semiotic layering and limits opportunities for culturally or ecologically complex visual interpretation. |
| **T3. Character–Environment Semiotics** | 3A. Zoological Limitation | – Only Western forest animals<br>– Absence of local species | Narrows ecological representation toward a single woodland fauna template while excluding region-specific biodiversity. |
| | 3B. Anthropomorphized Expressions | – Single face–eye structure<br>– Human-like emotional expressions | Reconfigures animals through humanized emotional codes, foregrounding affective familiarity over species differentiation. |
| **T4. Narrative and Ecological Meaning-Making** | 4A. Absence of Socio-Ecological Causality | – Contextless problems<br>– Ecology, climate, and society invisible | Frames problems as decontextualized material disruptions rather than as socially or ecologically embedded processes. |
| | 4B. Technical Fix Narratives | – Every problem solved through repair<br>– No community involvement | Centers mechanical repair as the dominant narrative resolution logic while backgrounding communal or environmental dimensions. |

continued on following page

*Table 2. Continued*

| Theme | Category | Codes (Open Codes) | Symbolic Framing / Interpretive Implications |
|---|---|---|---|
| **T5. Diversity Construction** | 5A. Symbolic Inclusion/Exclusion | – Disability implied only once<br>– No ethnic/cultural diversity | Signals minimal difference while leaving broader cultural plurality visually underrepresented. |
| | 5B. Habitat + Housing Monolith | – Single habitat + single house model<br>– Single ecological setting | Standardizes the storyworld around a singular habitat–housing configuration with limited locality cues. |

Synthesis: Taken together, the patterns indicate high representational consistency across spatial, ecological, aesthetic, narrative, and character-related dimensions. The stories repeatedly mobilise a limited set of templates. The analysis thus identifies the semiotic parameters within which meaning-making is invited to occur in these narratives and establishes the foundation for interpretive discussion.

## 5. TRANSITION: FROM REPRESENTATION TO REFLECTION

The findings reveal a coherent representational logic rather than isolated design choices. Across spatial design, ecological framing, character construction, and narrative resolution, the stories rely on stable templates: a single suburban home model, a simplified pastoral ecology, anthropomorphised woodland fauna, and technical-fix problem-solving. These recurring patterns foreground aesthetic consistency, emotional safety, and narrative simplicity—common goals of early childhood interface design—while backgrounding cultural plurality, ecological variability, and contextual causality.

This chapter does not infer direct developmental outcomes. Instead, it examines how representational range constrains or enables what can be noticed, compared, and discussed within AI-mediated storyworlds. In ICC terms, exposure to difference is not limited to explicit cultural facts; it also involves the presence of contrasting spatial forms, social practices, and symbolic cues. In ecocritical terms, the flattening of ecological complexity reduces opportunities to depict interdependence, variability, and habitat specificity. The discussion therefore focuses on representational scope and the pedagogical implications of AI-mediated narrative architectures.

# 6. DISCUSSION: REIMAGINING AI NARRATIVES FOR INTERCULTURAL AND ECOLOGICAL LEARNING

## 6.1 From Representational Range to ICC and Language Learning (Mechanism Mapping)

ICC, particularly in Byram's (1997) framework, emphasises that intercultural learning includes not only knowledge of cultural practices but also the attitudes and interpretive skills needed to engage with difference. In early childhood, these components do not develop primarily through explicit instruction about "cultures." They develop through repeated encounters with contrast: noticing that homes can be organised differently, that routines vary, that politeness and cooperation can take diverse forms, and that meanings depend on context. Kramsch's (2006) symbolic competence similarly foregrounds ambiguity and interpretive flexibility as core to meaning-making. Within AI-mediated story worlds, representational range functions as the substrate for such flexibility. When multiple spatial forms and social arrangements are depicted, children have more opportunities—especially with adult mediation—to practise noticing, comparing, and imagining alternative perspectives.

The findings suggest that the Lingokids corpus offers a low-ambiguity representational environment. Low ambiguity is not inherently negative. For young learners, narrative stability reduces cognitive load and supports comprehension. The educational value of stable templates is widely recognised: repeated settings and predictable schemas help children anticipate events and allocate attention to language forms. However, from an ICC standpoint, the pedagogical challenge is to preserve stability while avoiding representational narrowing that positions one configuration of domesticity and nature as silently universal. A low-ambiguity world can support vocabulary acquisition, but it may also limit the kinds of cultural questions the story world itself invites.

To make the link between representation and intercultural learning analytically explicit, this chapter proposes a mechanism mapping across three layers:

### Layer 1: Representational inputs (observed patterns).

- Domestic architecture: repeated suburban prototype
- Ecology: pastoral, static, single-habitat aesthetic
- Character design: anthropomorphic uniformity, limited species repertoire
- Narrative resolution: technical fix, decontextualised causality

### Layer 2: ICC-related interpretive opportunities (what children can notice/practise).

- **Attitudes (openness/curiosity):** Curiosity toward difference partly depends on encountering difference as visible and narratively meaningful. When settings rarely vary, curiosity requires external prompts rather than being triggered by the text itself.
- **Knowledge (cultural practices/everyday life):** Early cultural knowledge is often everyday-life knowledge: what homes look like, what routines are typical, what social relations are implied. Limited everyday-life variability narrows the knowledge repertoire presented as normal.
- **Skills of interpreting/relating:** Interpreting meaning across contexts requires contexts to differ. If routines and scripts remain stable, children have fewer within-text opportunities to compare "how else it could be."
- **Critical cultural awareness:** Noticing that representations are partial becomes easier when texts offer contrasts or explicit cues that "stories look different in different places." Without such cues, representational defaults can appear natural.

### Layer 3: Language learning functions (pragmatics and discourse).

Language learning in narrative contexts is not only lexical. It includes pragmatic functions: asking for help, negotiating, persuading, apologising, coordinating, expressing uncertainty, and responding to difference. Technical-fix narratives often foreground procedural vocabulary (fix, build, clean) but underrepresent relational discourse (let's decide, can you help, what if, I'm sorry). Consequently, representational narrowing can correspond to pragmatic narrowing. This is not a claim about children's outcomes; it is a claim about what the storyworld makes readily available for modelling and imitation.

From this perspective, the key question shifts from "Does AI personalise learning?" to "What dimensions of learning does AI personalise?" Many platforms adapt the difficulty of lexical items or repetition schedules, yet the representational context may remain fixed. If linguistic scaffolding advances while representational scaffolding remains static, children may practise language forms within a limited symbolic field, which can constrain the intercultural imagination that ICC frameworks aim to cultivate (Byram, 1997; Kramsch, 2006).

## 6.2 Ecological Imagination and Environmental Semiotics

Ecocriticism emphasises that narratives shape environmental imagination by encoding assumptions about nature, dwelling, and human–nonhuman relations (Glotfelty, 1996; Garrard, 2011). In the Lingokids corpus, nature is present but simplified: landscapes are pastoralised, sanitised, and temporally static. Forests are green and hazard-free; skies remain pastel and unchanging; no environmental disruption, seasonal transition, or ecological tension emerges within the narrative logic.

Such representation aligns with the pastoral trope, in which nature functions as a benign background rather than a dynamic system. This does not necessarily indicate environmental neglect; it often reflects a design preference for emotional safety and aesthetic cohesion. Yet ecological imagination develops not only through safety but through awareness of variability and interdependence. Children's environmental literacy is supported when narratives illustrate cause-and-effect relationships, seasonal cycles, habitat diversity, or interspecies interaction. Even subtle cues—falling leaves, migrating birds, changing light, different soil textures—expand the semiotic field of ecological meaning.

The absence of ecological variation in the Lingokids stories does not imply that children will misunderstand nature. Instead, it signals that the analysed narratives prioritise environmental neutrality over ecological process. The forest is not polluted, but it is also not evolving. It is safe, but not interdependent. It is harmonious, but not contextualised.

This observation highlights a design frontier. AI storytelling platforms possess technological capabilities that traditional print texts lack. They can alter environments across iterations. Seasons could rotate. Habitats could shift geographically. Weather could be represented at developmentally appropriate scales. Such variation need not increase linguistic complexity; it can diversify representational range while preserving narrative clarity. The challenge is not to introduce environmental crisis into early childhood stories but to avoid flattening nature into purely decorative aesthetic.

## 6.3 Algorithmic Cultural Reductionism, Design Implications, and Pedagogical Mediation

The term algorithmic cultural reductionism, as used here, does not suggest deliberate cultural exclusion. Rather, it describes a structural tendency for AI-mediated narrative systems to compress representational diversity into standardised templates. Algorithmic systems privilege forms that are statistically common, visually consistent, and broadly legible. In globally distributed children's platforms, dominant motifs—suburban housing, woodland fauna, pastel aesthetics—may be overrepresented in training data and design precedents (Noble, 2018; Bender et al.,

2021). When platforms aim for cross-cultural usability, they often select culturally ambiguous but Western-coded templates perceived as neutral. Neutrality, however, is rarely culture-free; it often corresponds to dominant norms that appear universal precisely because they are widespread.

The Lingokids case illustrates a design asymmetry: linguistic personalisation is advanced (difficulty adapts; repetition adjusts; feedback is individualised), while representational context remains comparatively static (the house remains the same; the forest remains the same; the aesthetic register remains stable; narrative resolution remains technical-fix oriented). This asymmetry suggests that future AI storytelling systems might move beyond performance-based personalisation toward contextual and representational responsiveness.

## Design implications (from narrative safety to narrative plurality):

1. **Representational diversification without linguistic burden.** Platforms can maintain simple syntax and vocabulary while varying housing forms (urban apartments, rural dwellings, region-specific architecture), habitats (coastal, desert, mountain, wetland), animal species (locally diverse fauna), and family/community arrangements. This enriches context without complicating language.
2. **Contextualised problem-solving.** Instead of exclusively technical repair narratives, stories could incorporate cooperative action, relational negotiation, or environmentally mindful solutions. This expands narrative logic beyond mechanical causality and provides richer pragmatic language functions (asking, offering, persuading, coordinating).
3. **Adaptive cultural framing without tokenism.** AI systems could rotate story-world motifs to normalise plurality for all users rather than stereotyping users by geography. Diversity should be integrated into narrative structure, not added as decorative fragments.

## Pedagogical mediation (critical media literacy as interpretive infrastructure):

AI narratives can obscure authorship and present representations as natural outputs of technology, creating epistemic opacity. Critical media literacy reintroduces transparency by supporting guided noticing (Kellner & Share, 2007). In early childhood, this is operationalised through playful co-interpretation rather than abstract critique. Educators and caregivers can transform representational regularities into discussion prompts:

- Comparative storytelling ("What would this story look like in our town?")

- Environmental recontextualisation (“What happens in winter?”)
- Species substitution (“Which animals live near us?”)
- Alternative resolutions (“Who could help fix this problem?”)

Such practices align with ICC’s dimension of critical cultural awareness (Byram, 1997) and position the child as an active co-constructor of meaning.

## LIMITATIONS AND FUTURE RESEARCH

This study is limited by its focus on a small purposive corpus of five introductory ABC stories from a single platform. The analysis therefore does not aim for statistical generalisation across AI language-learning systems. Instead, it offers an analytically transferable account of representational patterns within a clearly bounded subset. Additionally, the study analyses story materials as texts and images rather than measuring children’s learning outcomes. While the chapter theorises plausible pedagogical implications, it does not claim causal effects on intercultural competence or ecological literacy.

Future research can extend this work in four directions. First, comparative corpus studies across platforms (e.g., Lingokids vs. other children’s AI language apps) could identify whether representational standardisation is platform-specific or industry-wide. Second, mixed-method studies could examine how children interpret such narratives across different cultural contexts, including the role of adult mediation in amplifying or counteracting representational narrowing. Third, design-based research could test the feasibility of representational rotation (housing types, habitats, seasonal variation) while holding linguistic difficulty constant, evaluating whether representational plurality can be increased without sacrificing developmental clarity. Finally, ethical and governance-focused studies could explore transparency in algorithmic curation: how platforms explain representational choices, how cultural stakeholders are involved, and what accountability mechanisms can ensure that “global” design does not default to hegemonic templates (Noble, 2018; Bender et al., 2021; Luckin et al., 2016).

## CONCLUSION: SYMBOLIC WORLDS AND THE FUTURE OF INTERCULTURAL AI PEDAGOGY

This chapter argued that AI-driven children’s language-learning applications function not only as linguistic tools but also as symbolic infrastructures. Through a qualitative document analysis of five Lingokids ABC stories, the chapter identified recurring representational patterns: architectural homogeneity anchored in a suburban home prototype, ecological simplification through pastoral and static nature imagery, anthropomorphic character standardisation within a narrow woodland fauna repertoire, and a dominant technical-fix narrative logic.

These findings do not imply pedagogical failure. Simplification supports clarity, predictability, and emotional safety—important qualities for early learners. However, as AI increasingly mediates early childhood learning experiences, evaluation must extend beyond functional efficacy to symbolic scope. ICC and symbolic competence frameworks suggest that intercultural learning depends not only on explicit cultural lessons but also on representational range: the availability of contrasting homes, habitats, communicative styles, and social practices (Byram, 1997; Kramsch, 2006). Ecocriticism similarly highlights the importance of depicting nature as process and interdependence rather than as decorative backdrop (Glotfelty, 1996; Garrard, 2011).

The chapter therefore proposes a recalibration of AI storytelling priorities. The next frontier is not merely stronger linguistic personalisation but contextual and representational responsiveness: story worlds that maintain developmental simplicity while expanding cultural and ecological plurality. Such a move would strengthen the ethical and pedagogical quality of AI-mediated language learning by ensuring that the worlds children inhabit while learning English reflect multiplicity, locality, and interdependence rather than a singular normalised template.

Language learning in AI-mediated contexts is not only about acquiring words and structures; it is also about inhabiting digitally curated worlds. Ensuring that those worlds make diversity visible—culturally, socially, and ecologically—is both a design challenge and an educational responsibility.

## REFERENCES


Ahmed, S. (2004). *The cultural politics of emotion*. Edinburgh University Press.

Beer, D. (2017). The social power of algorithms. *Information Communication and Society*, *20*(1), 1–13. DOI: 10.1080/1369118X.2016.1216147

Bender, E. M., Gebru, T., McMillan-Major, A., & Shmitchell, S. (2021). On the dangers of stochastic parrots: Can language models be too big? In *Proceedings of the 2021 ACM Conference on Fairness, Accountability, and Transparency*(pp. 610–623). DOI: 10.1145/3442188.3445922

Bennett, M. J. (1993). Towards ethnorelativism: A developmental model of intercultural sensitivity. In Paige, R. M. (Ed.), *Education for the intercultural experience* (pp. 21–71). Intercultural Press.

Bhabha, H. K. (1994). *The location of culture*. Routledge.

Bourdieu, P. (1977). *Outline of a theory of practice*. Cambridge University Press. DOI: 10.1017/CBO9780511812507

Bowen, G. A. (2009). Document analysis as a qualitative research method. *Qualitative Research Journal*, *9*(2), 27–40. DOI: 10.3316/QRJ0902027

Braun, V., & Clarke, V. (2019). Reflecting on reflexive thematic analysis. *Qualitative Research in Sport, Exercise and Health*, *11*(4), 589–597. DOI: 10.1080/2159676X.2019.1628806

Bronfenbrenner, U. (1979). *The ecology of human development*. Harvard University Press. DOI: 10.4159/9780674028845

Brown, P., & Levinson, S. C. (1987). *Politeness: Some universals in language usage*. Cambridge University Press. DOI: 10.1017/CBO9780511813085

Bruner, J. (1986). *Actual minds, possible worlds*. Harvard University Press. DOI: 10.4159/9780674029019

Buckingham, D. (2003). *Media education: Literacy, learning and contemporary culture*. Polity Press.

Byram, M. (1997). *Teaching and assessing intercultural communicative competence*. Multilingual Matters.

Canagarajah, A. S. (2013). *Translingual practice: Global Englishes and cosmopolitan relations*. Routledge. DOI: 10.4324/9780203120293

Deardorff, D. K. (2006). Identification and assessment of intercultural competence. *Journal of Studies in International Education, 10*(3), 241–266. DOI: 10.1177/1028315306287002

Finlay, L. (2002). Negotiating the swamp: The opportunity and challenge of reflexivity. *Qualitative Research, 2*(2), 209–230. DOI: 10.1177/146879410200200205

Fisher, W. R. (1987). *Human communication as narration.* University of South Carolina Press.

Garrard, G. (2011). *Ecocriticism* (2nd ed.). Routledge., DOI: 10.4324/9780203806838

Gillespie, T. (2014). The relevance of algorithms. In Gillespie, T. (Eds.), *Media technologies* (pp. 167–194). MIT Press. DOI: 10.7551/mitpress/9042.003.0013

Glotfelty, C. (1996). Introduction: Literary studies in an age of environmental crisis. In Glotfelty, C., & Fromm, H. (Eds.), *The ecocriticism reader* (pp. xv–xxxvii). University of Georgia Press.

Goddard, C., & Wierzbicka, A. (2004). Cultural scripts: What are they and what are they good for? *Intercultural Pragmatics, 1*(2), 153–166. DOI: 10.1515/iprg.2004.1.2.153

Gray, J. (2010). *The construction of English: Culture, consumerism and promotion in the ELT global coursebook.* Palgrave Macmillan. DOI: 10.1057/9780230283084

Guest, G., Namey, E., & Mitchell, M. (2013). Collecting qualitative data. A Field Manual for Applied Research. *Sage (Atlanta, Ga.).* Advance online publication. DOI: 10.4135/9781506374680

Heise, U. K. (2008). *Sense of place and sense of planet.* Oxford University Press. DOI: 10.1093/acprof:oso/9780195335637.001.0001

Holmes, W., Bialik, M., & Fadel, C. (2019). *Artificial intelligence in education.* Center for Curriculum Redesign.

Hsieh, H.-F., & Shannon, S. E. (2005). Three approaches to qualitative content analysis. *Qualitative Health Research, 15*(9), 1277–1288. DOI: 10.1177/1049732305276687 PMID: 16204405

Jenkins, J. (2014). *Global Englishes* (3rd ed.). Routledge. DOI: 10.4324/9781315761596

Kecskes, I. (2014). *Intercultural pragmatics.* Oxford University Press.

Kellner, D., & Share, J. (2007). Critical media literacy is not an option. *Learning Inquiry, 1*(1), 59–69. DOI: 10.1007/s11519-007-0004-2

Knox, J. (2020). Artificial intelligence and education in China. *Learning, Media and Technology*, *45*(3), 298–311. DOI: 10.1080/17439884.2020.1754236

Kramsch, C. (2006). From communicative competence to symbolic competence. *The Modern Language Journal, 90,* 249–252. https://doi.org/ _3.xDOI: 10.1111/j.1540-4781.2006.00395

Kress, G., & van Leeuwen, T. (2020). *Reading images: The grammar of visual design* (2nd ed.). Routledge. DOI: 10.4324/9781003099857

Lincoln, Y. S., & Guba, E. G. (1985). Naturalistic inquiry. *Sage (Atlanta, Ga.)*.

Livingstone, S. (2020). *Parenting for a digital future*. Oxford University Press. DOI: 10.1093/oso/9780190874698.001.0001

Luckin, R., Holmes, W., Griffiths, M., & Forcier, L. B. (2016). *Intelligence unleashed: An argument for AI in education*. Pearson Education.

Marsh, J. (2004). The techno-literacy practices of young children. *Journal of Early Childhood Research*, *2*(1), 51–66. DOI: 10.1177/1476718X0421003

Miles, M. B., & Huberman, A. M. (1994). *Qualitative data analysis* (2nd ed.). Sage.

Nikken, P., & Jansz, J. (2015). Developing scales to measure parental mediation of young children's internet use. *Learning, Media and Technology*, *40*(2), 250–266. DOI: 10.1080/17439884.2013.782038

Nixon, R. (2011). *Slow violence and the environmentalism of the poor*. Harvard University Press.

Noble, S. U. (2018). *Algorithms of oppression: How search engines reinforce racism*. New York University Press. DOI: 10.18574/nyu/9781479833641.001.0001

OECD. (2021). *AI in education: A roadmap for the future*. OECD Publishing.

Patton, M. Q. (2015). *Qualitative research & evaluation methods* (4th ed.). Sage.

Pennycook, A. (2007). *Global Englishes and transcultural flows*. Routledge.

Ricoeur, P. (1984). *Time and narrative* (Vol. 1). University of Chicago Press.

Schreier, M. (2012). *Qualitative content analysis in practice*. SAGE Publications., DOI: 10.4135/9781529682571

Schwartz-Shea, P., & Yanow, D. (2012). *Interpretive research design*. Routledge.

Seidlhofer, B. (2011). *Understanding English as a lingua franca*. Oxford University Press.

Selwyn, N. (2019). *Should Robots Replace Teachers? AI and the Future of Education*. Polity Press.

Spencer-Oatey, H. (2008). *Culturally speaking* (2nd ed.). Continuum.

Srnicek, N. (2017). *Platform capitalism*. Polity Press.

UNESCO. (2021). *Recommendation on the ethics of artificial intelligence*. UNESCO.

Vygotsky, L. S. (1978). *Mind in society: The development of higher psychological processes*. Harvard University Press.

Williamson, B. (2017). Big data in education. The digital future of learning, policy and practice. *Sage (Atlanta, Ga.)*. Advance online publication. DOI: 10.4135/9781529714920

Yin, R. K. (2018). *Case study research and applications* (6th ed.). Sage.

# Section 3
# Developing Intercultural Communicative Competence

Chapter 8

# Developing Intercultural Communication Competence in an ELT Context through the Integration of AI-Tools

**Turan Paker**
http://orcid.org/0000-0002-3941-3975
*Pamukkale University, Turkey*

## ABSTRACT

*It is crucial to educate prospective language teachers to create awareness towards intercultural competence and arrange activities in their courses so that they can develop their intercultural competence. Thus, they may be interculturally sensitive to better serve their future students' needs. In this chapter, the importance and the role of intercultural communication, how intercultural competence can be enhanced through employing AI-supported activities, and opportunities and challenges in this process have been discussed. For this purpose, to what extent various AI tools such as Chat GPT, Gemini, QuillBot, Canva, Grammarly, and others can be employed has been discussed in line with the syllabus of the intercultural communication course in the English Language teaching Department. All the activities have been based on Byram's (1997) language-pedagogical model, through diaries, focus group discussions, and reflections of the students.*

DOI: 10.4018/979-8-3373-6325-7.ch008

## 1. INTRODUCTION

Our globalized and digitally interconnected world requires effective communication, both linguistically and culturally in education, business or international settings. Consequently, individuals and organizations need to engage meaningfully with people from diverse cultural backgrounds. Considering these types of needs, the United Nations' Sustainable Development Goals (SDG) emphasize quality education SDG 4 (Quality Education) by advocating for AI literacy and intercultural competence in teacher preparation programs, reducing inequalities, SDG 10 (Reduced Inequalities), through equitable access to AI-enhanced learning opportunities. Next, promoting dialogue, empathy, and inclusivity across cultures is in line with peace, justice, and strong institutions, SDG 10 (Reduced Inequalities). However, interactions among people are frequently challenged by language barriers, cultural misunderstandings, bias or other invisible factors.

The integration of artificial intelligence (AI) into language education is a contemporary phenomenon exerting a significant influence on the experiences of both teaching professionals and their students. In the contemporary era, learners' daily routines have become increasingly dependent on AI tools such as ChatGPT, Quillbot and Grammarly, among others. These technologies have paved the way for novel avenues of intercultural communication (ICC), a domain that has been widely recognised as being of paramount importance in fostering the development of global citizens who are adept at navigating a myriad of communicative contexts and who are endowed with empathy and cultural awareness (Byram, 1997; Deardorff, 2006). For this reason, it is crucial to educate prospective language teachers to create awareness towards intercultural competence by arranging various activities in their courses so that they can develop their intercultural competence. Thus, they may be interculturally sensitive to better serve their future students' needs.

## 2. INTERCULTURAL COMMUNICATION COMPETENCE (ICC)

The ability to effectively communicate across cultures has never been more crucial due to the fact that globalization facilitates the movement of people, goods, and ideas across the globe. Consequently, intercultural communication has become an indispensable skill for individuals, organizations, and nations in the 21$^{st}$ century. Thanks to globalization, the world has been transformed into a global village (McLuhan & Powers, 1989), where people from various cultures frequently meet for various reasons. Hence, businesses, governments, international teachers and students and individuals have to communicate with people from diverse backgrounds, making intercultural communication a key to success. Thus, critical thinking, creativity, teamwork, higher-order thinking skills and cultural empathy are among these essential qualities that 21st century citizens should have in order to develop intercultural competence.

Creating intercultural communication awareness and helping students improve their 'intercultural communication competence' (Byram, 1997) are now in the curriculum of schools for a peaceful world. It is the cement to build a multicultural civil society across nations and regions (Byram, 2018). Deardorff (2006, p. 248) defines intercultural competence as "the ability to communicate effectively and appropriately in intercultural situations based on one's intercultural knowledge, skills, and attitudes." Intercultural communication competence includes attitudes, knowledge, and critical cultural awareness in addition to linguistic skills (Byram 1997; Chen & Starosta, 1996; Deardorff; 2006). Besides linguistic abilities, intercultural competency necessitates empathy, social awareness, and the ability to negotiate meaning among diverse worldviews (Chen & Starosta, 1996; Deardorff, 2006). Key components of intercultural competence cover intercultural awareness, intercultural sensitivity, intercultural effectiveness, and cultural intelligence.

Byram's model of intercultural communicative competence (1997) was developed in relation to the Council of Europe's (Council of Europe, 2001) project to construct the Common European Framework of Reference for Languages (CEFR). According to Hoff (2020), the model of ICC provides a basis for the development of the conceptual model which underpins the recent Reference Framework of Competences for Democratic Culture (2018). Its five savoirs (attitudes, knowledge, skills of interpreting/relating, skills of discovery/interaction, and critical cultural awareness) have offered educators a systematic approach for integrating interculturality into language instruction. This model is an additional component of the communicative competence model proposed by Canal and Swain (1980), which encompasses linguistic, discourse, sociolinguistic, and strategic competencies in effective communication. Byram's model of intercultural citizenship education (Byram, 2008, 2012) emphasizes values such as democratic culture, the rule of law, and human rights ideals, and seeks to counter racism, extremism, and intolerance in society (Hoff, 2020). Thanks to this model, we can create a third culture among our students who can be mediators between or among various cultures. This is relevant for curricula integrating human rights education and democratic participation as learning outcomes.

The intercultural competence model proposed by Byram (1997) is one of the most influential frameworks, and his model reframes language teaching beyond functional proficiency in language teaching, incorporating additional ethical, critical, and civic objectives. It has five key components focusing on the skills necessary for effective communication in intercultural contexts.

- Knowledge: Understanding of social groups, products, and practices in one's own and other cultures.
- Attitudes: Curiosity and openness towards other cultures.
- Skills of interpreting and relating: Ability to interpret cultural phenomena and relate them to one's own culture.
- Skills of discovery and interaction: Ability to acquire new cultural knowledge and operate in real-time communication.
- Critical cultural awareness: Ability to critically evaluate cultural practices and products, including one's own.

According to Byram (1997), intercultural competence covers five interconnected components. The savoirs articulate not only the knowledge that learners should possess about "other" cultures, but also the attitudes (curiosity, openness), skills (interpreting, relating, discovery, interaction), and critical cultural awareness needed to engage responsibly in intercultural encounters. Knowledge is related to knowledge of self and others while interacting in a social group, either in their own country or other countries. Attitudes are about relativizing the self and valuing the other. The skills of interpreting and relating are the ability to analyse a document or event from another culture, interpret it, and relate it to one's own. The skill of discovery and interaction is related to the ability to acquire new knowledge of a culture and apply that knowledge in communication and interaction when needed. Finally, critical cultural awareness is the capacity to assess, using defined criteria, the viewpoints, practices, and outputs of both one's own culture and others. ICC involves knowledge of cultural norms, self-awareness, emotional regulation, and language proficiency (Fantini, 2000). It is argued that promoting ICC requires pedagogical approaches that go beyond content delivery, involving experiential learning, critical reflection, and dialogic exchange (Byram, 1997). On the other hand, recent reviews (Xu et al., 2025) emphasize that Byram's framework remains integral across EFL contexts due to its structured focus on attitudes, knowledge, skills, and critical cultural awareness. They posit that recent frameworks, such as Byram's (2020) model, underscore the pivotal role of ICC in language learning, which emphasizes the integration of both linguistic and cultural sensitivity (Byram, 2020). In addition, Wang (2024) explains that Byram's model offers actionable, pedagogically relevant categories, which are of particular value for curriculum design endeavors that aspire to cultivate intercultural attitudes, knowledge, and skills. In addition, the pedagogical efficacy of the model is attributable to its clearly delineated categories, which can be integrated into curriculum goals, classroom tasks, and assessment criteria.

Intercultural communication is the process of exchanging information, ideas, and emotions across different cultural backgrounds. Hence, intercultural communication helps conflict resolution among people from different cultures because misunderstandings and conflicts often arise due to cultural differences, prejudice, ethnocentrism, and so on. Effective intercultural communication can help mitigate conflicts and promote peaceful resolutions. Additionally, enhanced cultural awareness may result in effective communication among people with different cultures. Hence, engaging in intercultural communication fosters greater cultural awareness and sensitivity among students in foreign/second language courses, leading to greater appreciation, tolerance and respect for different cultures.

In this chapter, the importance and the role of intercultural communication, how intercultural competence can be enhanced through employing various AI-supported activities, as well as the opportunities and challenges in this process have been discussed through an intercultural education course syllabus. For this purpose, to what extent various Generative AI tools such as ChatGPT, Gemini, QuillBot, and the others can be employed has been addressed. Depending on the topic studied, these generative tools can help the students find videos, websites, written documents, stories, articles or can create simulations. All the activities are based on Byram's (1997) language-pedagogical model, through cases, scenarios, focus group discussions, sharing students' experiences and reflection sheets because Byram (2020) suggests hybrid or updated models suited to 21st century realities. Throughout the academic semester, each topic in the syllabus can contribute to key components of Byram's (1997) model in terms of introducing knowledge to students and helping them understand social groups, products, and practices in their own and other cultures and co-cultures. Next, watching related video films, discussions, and sharing the learners' experiences could trigger their attitudes, create openness towards other cultures, help them interpret cultural phenomena and relate them to their own culture by comparing and contrasting. Hence, they could have a chance to critically evaluate cultural practices and products, including their own, because we need to integrate digital intercultural literacies as well as the learners' experiences into the competence construct. Finally, all these activities may result in having the ability to acquire new cultural knowledge and operate in real-time communication, which will lead them to have critical cultural awareness. Consequently, there are some research questions posed:

1- Do the topics and activities provide knowledge and understanding for the students to be aware of culture, co-culture, social groups, products, and practices?
2- Do the topics and activities help the students create openness towards other cultures, and help them interpret cultural phenomena and relate them to their own culture in terms of attitude?
3- Do the topics and activities help them critically evaluate cultural practices and products, including their own?
4- Do the topics and activities lead them to have critical cultural awareness?

## 3. METHOD

This is a qualitative study with 40 English Language Teaching (ELT) students at a state university in Denizli, Türkiye. The participants consisted of 24 female and 16 male students, with an age range of 20-24. The elective course on intercultural communication was carried out in the Department of English Language Teaching, Faculty of Education, Pamukkale University. In this two-hour-a-week course, first the syllabus was introduced to the students, and they had some brainstorming related to the topics, and then, the students formed their groups of three in order to prepare and present the topic of the week. Throughout the semester, as a group, they prepared presentations on various topics in the syllabus, then presented the topic in the class, and the class discussed it altogether, and shared their experiences regarding the topic of the week over the 14-week course. In order to find related video films, dialogues, simulations or stories, the students used ChatGPT, Chatbots, Gemini, YouTube, etc., and shared them during their presentations. After each session, each student wrote his/her reflections on what they had learned about the topic, what the implications were, and how they could integrate these ideas into their teaching. The students uploaded their reflections to Moodle on a weekly basis and shared them with the instructor. The following week, they shared their reflections orally within their groups and with the whole class, which created a peer group learning environment and awareness towards the topic. Consequently, the instructor gave feedback about their reflections both orally and in writing. For this study, the data were collected through their written reflections throughout the semester. The data were analysed through content analysis (Miles & Huberman, 1994) in terms of codes and themes by the instructor and a staff member who held a PhD in the field of ELT. The results were compared and contrasted, and an agreement was reached on the codes and themes in order to provide validity and reliability. In order to assess the reliability of the thematic analysis, the researcher employed the interrater reliability formula proposed by Miles and Huberman (1994). In line with this formula, reliability is calculated as the number of agreements divided by the total number of agreements and disagreements, and a minimum of 80% agreement is recommended for acceptable reliability. In this study, the interrater reliability was calculated at 86%. In reporting the participants' reflections, they were labelled as P1, P2, P3 ...... P40 to ensure confidentiality.

## 4. APPLICATION OF INTERCULTURAL COMMUNICATION CLASSES THROUGH VARIOUS TOPICS AND ACTIVITIES WITH AI TOOLS AND MULTIMEDIA

Generative AI tools provide a range of opportunities for situated context-sensitive learning. Zhang and Zhou (2024) report that AI-enhanced learning environments have improved Chinese students' intercultural communicative competence through collaborative, adaptive simulations. In addition, Dai and Hua (2025) posit that generative artificial intelligence (AI) signifies a novel paradigm in the domain of intercultural communication, facilitating the emergence of innovative content creation and interaction methodologies. Yang et al. (2024) emphasize that AI tools, particularly simulation and generative systems, facilitate more profound experiential engagement with different cultures and support identity-building processes in intercultural encounters. This type of learning context helps students engage in culturally diverse scenarios in a controlled but responsive space, which promotes reflection, empathy, and adaptability. Many universities still utilize AI-based tools for cross-cultural learning and tutoring, and the COVID-19 epidemic has increased the adoption of digital platforms for intercultural communication (Godwin-Jones, 2023). AI-supported solutions have the potential to improve inclusion and customization in educational settings, which focus on fostering intercultural communication competence.

AI is used in language learning applications to provide cultural information, real-world conversation scenarios, reflections from learners, and individualized feedback. For instance, ChatGPT or Gemini offer instant feedback on language accuracy and style, which may improve learners' international communicative competence as well as their language competence (Zou et al., 2023). The utilization of these tools has been demonstrated to facilitate the development of cognitive and emotional aspects of intercultural competence, including empathy, perspective-taking, and critical cultural awareness. This facilitation is achieved by enabling students to engage in intercultural behaviours within low-risk virtual settings (Deardorff, 2006; Jenks, 2025).

While teaching the intercultural communication course, several strategies were integrated into our syllabus, such as getting to know oneself, home culture, values, cultural sensitivity training, active listening, avoiding stereotypes, adaptability, empathy, clarifying misunderstandings, and so on. On the other hand, some significant challenges were also dealt with during the courses, such as language barriers, cultural norms, cultural bias, ethnocentrism, ethnophaulism, racism, as well as nonverbal communication. In terms of AI tools, ChatGPT and Gemini were employed for conversational simulations. In addition, Replika was employed as an AI companion application that demonstrates how empathy is simulated in affective computing.

The students used Grammarly or QuillBot to check their accuracy or to paraphrase some statements when they wrote their reflections. While using these applications, the instructor guided the students on how to navigate the affordances and risks of AI-supported tools. Despite some inefficiencies of AI tools, such as bias, missing nuances between cultural discourse, and so on, these tools are very practical and effective as they provide sources for our students in a foreign language context. Finally, the students wrote reflection sheets after each session, and they shared and discussed their reflections in the subsequent session because encouraging students to engage in regular self-assessment and reflection helps them become more aware of their biases, cultural assumptions, and areas for growth (Li, 2021).

In our course, intercultural communication, we dealt with various topics week by week so that the students could be aware of their own culture and other cultures, be aware of cultural differences, and hopefully, be more understanding and tolerant towards them. Our syllabus covered:

- Introduction to the course, basic concepts and principles in cultural and intercultural studies: culture, home culture, dominant culture, co-culture.
- Self, family and society
- Critical thinking in communication
- Communication perspectives: small talk, relating and receiving information, catharsis or tension release, ritual, affective communication, instrumental communication
- Encountering differences in cultural patterns and communication
- Cultural identity, cultural bias, ethnocentrism and prejudice in communication
- Observations on nonverbal communication across cultures
- Social distance and zones in communication in various cultures
- Implementing an intercultural approach in ELF
- Challenges and barriers in intercultural communication in practice

First of all, knowledge about culture, home culture, dominant culture and co-cultures was the starting point. Understanding one's own culture is the first step in developing intercultural competence. Thus, students could develop self-awareness, which helps individuals recognize their own cultural biases and assumptions. They could also become aware of their cultural values, norms and their cultural differences from region to region within the country. They try to understand how they feel and their attitudes towards other cultures, their relationship with the dominant culture as a new generation compared to older generations within the nation. From these perspectives, we introduced other cultures and discussed their attitudes towards them because acquiring knowledge about other cultures, including their values, beliefs, customs, and communication styles, helps individuals understand and appreciate cultural differences (Deardorff, 2006; Hofstede & Bond, 1984). As a follow-up, we analysed various characters through videos or films and sometimes cases shared in the stories, as well as using ChatGPT scenarios. In this way, the students attempted to understand the interactions between people, both verbally and nonverbally. In addition, the students who lived in another country shared their experiences, and foreign students also shared their experiences related to the topic of the week. Furthermore, we prompted ChatGPT to come up with scenarios based on our descriptions and prompts. In the end, all these discussions led us to study the critical thinking procedures because an essential part of intercultural competence is the ability to think critically. Consequently, all these activities could create intercultural sensitivity, which helps them to be respectful and non-judgmental about cultural differences and foster an environment of mutual respect and understanding (Bennett, 1993; Chen & Starosta, 1997). Finally, the students wrote their reflections based on the topic of the week. In their reflections, they summarized the topic, wrote about its implications, and discussed how they could use these ideas in their lesson plan in their teaching activities. Incorporating reflective activities allows students to reflect on their intercultural experiences and learn from them (Dewey, 1933; Schön, 1983). In the following week, they shared their reflections in a group work and got to know each other's ideas. Hence, they attempted to employ knowledge and sensitivity by means of effective communication, conflict resolution, and adaptability in diverse cultural settings, taking into account the real-world interactions (Hammer et al., 2003).

## 5. RESULTS AND DISCUSSION

As a result of content analysis of the data, some themes were identified, and they were arranged to respond to research questions. In this context, the first research question is: Do the topics and activities provide knowledge and understanding for the students to be aware of culture, co-culture, social groups, products, and practices? Our data revealed that the topics and activities, such as presentations, short video films, ChatGPT simulations, discussions, and sharing experiences, created a knowledge base and awareness among the participants towards their own and other cultures, co-cultures, products and practices. The participants reported their ideas and feelings in their reflections, such as:

*First, I learned the difference between culture and a nation. Culture is about the daily life of people, their beliefs, values, language, and customs. A nation is a large group of people with a shared identity, often in one country. Understanding this difference is the key. In my classroom, I will have students from different cultures, even if they are from the same nation. I should not generalize and think everyone is the same and shares the same cultural values and norms (P7).*

*Learning about cultures, co-cultures, nations, and systems helped me understand people in a deeper way. Before this session, I thought culture was only about food, music, clothes, or traditions. But now I see that culture is much more than that. It is the way people live, think, and act every day. It includes how we talk, what we believe, what we respect, and even how we see time and family. Culture shapes our habits and our feelings toward others. When I learn about other cultures, I start to see how beautiful and different people can be, and it makes me want to understand the world more (P35).*

*I think that as a prospective teacher, understanding the terms and their differences is important because they teach us to be respectful of students' cultures and co-cultures. I also pay attention to language because, in my view, it is the most essential component of culture, and without it, we cannot fully explain our culture. Therefore, I will show the importance of language to my future students. Additionally, the differences between a nation and a culture are deeper than I had thought (P12).*

*Culture gives people a sense of identity and belonging. Every nation has its own culture that reflects its history, geography, and lifestyle. For example, Japan values respect and working together, while the United States values freedom and individuality. These differences do not make one culture better than another; they simply show how people learn to live in unique ways. Understanding this helps me become more open-minded and less quick to judge others (P26).*

As can be seen in the quotations of the participants, the activities carried out in the course helped them construct knowledge and understanding of the topic and reflect on their ideas regarding culture and co-culture.

Communication perspective was another topic we dealt with during the course. The students tried to understand various concepts and their functions in intercultural communication, such as small talk, relating and receiving information, catharsis or tension release, ritual, affective communication, and instrumental communication. Following the presentation of definitions and the provision of real-life examples by the past experiences of students, various discourses in films and some scenarios from Gemini were analysed in order to raise awareness of the concepts. The students appeared to understand much better how these concepts are actualized during conversations, depending on the themes in the films. In addition, films reflect real life much better than any other material and bring the native speakers' discourse into the classroom. As a follow-up, they wrote reflections and shared them as group work in the following lesson, which led to peer learning and reflection. Here are some quotes from the reflection sheets of my students regarding communication perspectives:

*Another aspect of my communication perspectives involves cultural awareness. Growing up in Türkiye, I noticed that certain gestures, like a simple nod or a smile, carry different weight depending on the context. When I met international students at university, I realized that the gestures I considered polite could be misunderstood. For instance, maintaining strong eye contact is a sign of confidence in some cultures, while in others it can be seen as aggressive or disturbing for the interlocutor. Experiencing these differences firsthand has helped me adopt a more flexible perspective, understanding that effective communication is highly situational and cultural (P2).*

*Another insight is that communication is not complete when a message is sent; it continues through interpretation and feedback. I remember a situation where a friend from another country said "maybe" when she actually meant "no." This misunderstanding arose from cultural differences in expressing disagreement. This experience made me more aware of how perception, interpretation, and evaluation can differ between individuals depending on cultural background. I learned to focus more on nonverbal cues and tone rather than relying solely on literal meanings (P11).*

*Distinguishing between affective and instrumental communication has made me more conscious of my own communication style. When comforting a friend, I naturally use affective communication by showing empathy and warmth. In contrast, when coordinating tasks in a group project, I adopt an instrumental style that prioritizes clarity and efficiency. Being aware of this shift allows me to adapt my tone and approach according to context and purpose (P33).*

In the study, the second research question is as to what extent the topics and activities help the students create openness towards other cultures, help them interpret cultural phenomena, and relate them to their own culture in terms of attitude. Some topics such as self, family and society that the participants have studied provided both a knowledge base and an awareness of their attitudes. In order to help the prospective teachers understand the relationship between themselves, their family, and society, I asked them to describe themselves using an identity wheel after the presentation. Then, I expected them to see their place in the social network in various roles and characteristics. The students thought about the complex ways in which our identities were created, and the ways in which socialization shaped their perspectives and behaviours. Hence, they were aware that as we got older and took on various roles and personas, many facets of our lives influenced who we were. Consequently, they learned that they lived as members of a social network. As a result of filling out the wheel, they discussed the questions next to the identity wheel (see Figure 1).

*Figure 1. The identity wheel (Kalish et al., 2021)*

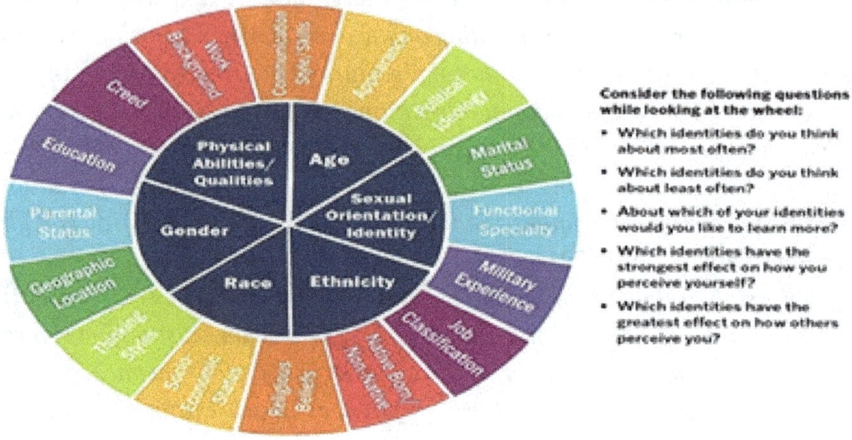


https://www.mgma.com/resources/human-resources/how-medical-practices-can-continue-the-journey-tow

Here are some quotes from the reflection sheets of the participants regarding self, family and society:

*The identity wheel section also made me think a lot. It has demonstrated that we all have a myriad of various aspects: gender, nationality, age, belief, and they all impact how we communicate. It has reminded me that we do not always receive the complete picture of a person's identity when we are communicating with that person. Being aware of this makes me remain open and patient (P30).*

*The identity wheel also helped me see that everyone's identity was made up of different parts, such as gender, ethnicity, religion, experiences, and so on. When I thought about my own identity, I realized how these parts shaped the way I think and interact with others. Being aware of this helps me become more open-minded and respectful when communicating with people who have different backgrounds (P5).*

*In a classroom setting, integrating activities like the Identity Wheel, scenario-based discussions, and role-playing exercises could help students practice these skills in realistic contexts. This is especially valuable in diverse educational environments, such as in Turkey, where students often come from various cultural and socio-economic backgrounds. Encouraging them to explore their own identities and listen actively to others can enhance mutual understanding and reduce communication barriers (P17).*

The topic of encountering differences in cultural patterns and communication led the students to create openness towards other cultures and helped them interpret cultural phenomena and related them to their own culture in terms of attitude. The term 'encountering differences' refers to cultural differences in spoken language, certain gestures, customs, climate, and cuisine, or communication that involves actions, perceptions, choices, interpretations, and expectations. The purpose is how we perceive the differences and what we understand and feel related to them as well as how we cope with them. For this purpose, during the lesson, the students shared their experiences within the country or abroad. Especially, those who had been in a European country for the Erasmus+ mobility for one or two semesters had effective stories to share and strange implications. Next, we analysed various cases in formal and informal contexts. We watched films and discussed what the problem would be, and how it could be resolved. Some quotes reflect their attitude regarding encountering differences in cultural patterns and communication:

*Through studying and observing these cultural differences, I have learned that there is no single correct way to communicate. What one culture considers polite, another might see as distant; what one sees as honest, another may view as too direct. In developing countries, people often rely on cooperation and shared understanding, which makes communication more indirect and emotionally sensitive. For example, Richard's experiences (London & Yousef, 1989), in cross-cultural contexts demonstrate that these differences, while sometimes challenging, also create opportunities for learning and growth (P12).*

*While analysing the case about Richard's experiences (London & Yousef, 1989), I reflected on how easily misunderstandings can happen even with good intentions. For example, his behaviour in Japan, trying to explain himself after a mistake, seemed normal to him but inappropriate to others because Japanese culture values group harmony over self-defence. It reminded me of moments when I unintentionally offended someone just because I did not know their cultural expectations. This made me more aware of the importance of empathy and cultural sensitivity. This topic helped me see that intercultural communication is not just about learning another language; it is about understanding another way of seeing the world. To truly connect with others, we must move beyond stereotypes and approach every culture with respect, curiosity, and openness (P8).*

*The presentation addressed the importance of intercultural competence, the ability to communicate effectively and appropriately with people from other cultures. It requires not only knowledge of cultural patterns but also open-mindedness, flexibility, and emotional intelligence. I found this idea very relevant, especially for teachers, students, and professionals who work in multicultural environments. In today's globalized world, intercultural competence is a necessary skill for building mutual respect and understanding among people (P27).*

*Now I know that cultural awareness is not just about knowing facts or stereotypes about different groups. It is about developing cultural humility, which is the willingness to recognize our own biases and to approach others with openness and respect (P13).*

In the study, the third research question is as to what extent the topics and activities help the students critically evaluate cultural practices and products, including their own. One of the most important topics is critical thinking in intercultural communication. Traditional critical thinking frameworks prioritize competencies, including analysis, assessment, inference, and self-regulation (Ennis, 1985; Facione, 1990). Contemporary approaches broaden critical thinking to encompass attitudes, epistemic humility, and reflective judgment. According to Deardorff (2006), intercultural competence (ICC) is a cyclical process comprising attitudes, knowledge, internal outcomes, and external behaviours. Essentially, critical reflection serves as a conduit between internal and external outcomes. In addition to possessing strong critical-thinking skills, one must be disposed to engage in problems and make decisions using those skills. Critical thinking employs certain universal intellectual values such as clarity, credibility, accuracy, precision, relevance, depth, breadth, significance, and fairness (Glaser, 1941). In order to help students understand the importance of critical thinking, we analysed various scenarios. For example, we discussed a scenario such as: "Imagine that when you visit a foreign country, your bag is stolen in a shopping mall. Would you consider that all people are thieves in that city or country?" Apart from scenarios, they watched films, and we discussed the issues from different perspectives, such as clarity, credibility, accuracy, precision, relevance, depth, breadth, significance, and fairness. I believe that films reflect real life more than anything else, though they are written as scenarios. Here are some quotes from the reflection sheets of my students regarding how they critically evaluated cultural practices and products, including their own critical thinking:

> *Critical thinking techniques tie all these ideas together: asking questions, recognizing bias, evaluating evidence, perspective-taking, and reflective thinking, and they serve as practical tools for developing both communication and problem-solving skills. For instance, the short quiz about "Bob" was a creative way to make the audience think critically about how bias and assumptions influence perception (P22).*

> *The techniques like recognizing bias, evaluating evidence, and reflective thinking are not only academic skills but life skills. They can help us make better decisions and build stronger relationships with people from other cultures. Overall, the presentation and the scenarios reminded me that communication without critical thinking could easily lead to misunderstanding. Developing this skill takes time and practice, but it is a valuable tool for becoming a more thoughtful and culturally aware individual (P28).*

> *At the beginning of the course, I thought critical thinking simply meant finding mistakes or criticizing other people's ideas. Later, I discovered that it actually involves a much deeper process. It requires open-mindedness, curiosity, and the willingness to consider from different perspectives. One of the most valuable*

*lessons I have learned is that there is often more than one correct answer, and to reach a strong conclusion, we need to explore all sides of an argument. Our professor's story related to the lunch with his female student who graduated 10 years ago was a good scenario. This approach has helped me develop a more balanced and reflective way of thinking (P35).*

*I found it particularly enlightening to see how critical thinking is not just about logical reasoning but also about recognizing biases, questioning assumptions, and exploring diverse perspectives. In this session, it has been emphasized that critical thinking is a process rather than an instant reaction, requiring time, reflection, and continuous practice. This perspective resonates strongly with my own experience as a student because I have often realized that initial impressions or cultural assumptions can easily mislead us unless we pause to examine them (P9).*

The fourth research question sought answers as to what extent the topics and activities led the students to have critical cultural awareness. In the syllabus, the topic on observations on nonverbal communication across cultures helped the students to have critical cultural awareness. During the presentation, the focus was on the power of nonverbal communication, and the proverb, i.e., "actions speak louder than words" explained the meaning effectively. The students gave examples concerning nonverbal communication from our culture and other nations' cultures, such as mime, gestures, body language, and tone of voice. We concluded that not all nonverbal actions were universal. The students drew various nonverbal actions and acted them out through various role plays and simulations they created. They preferred using Canva in their drawings and discussed their functions in daily life discourse. Especially, watching how people used nonverbal communication in various films was very effective. Short film analysis helped them to be aware of how nonverbal actions differ from culture to culture. According to Gudykunst (2005), activities can be designed to develop both verbal and nonverbal communication skills, thereby fostering the ability to navigate cultural misunderstandings and conflicts. The students reflected their critical cultural awareness regarding the topic in their reflection sheets as in the following:

*Another impressive concept was Hall's theory of proxemics, which examines how individuals use personal space in communication. The idea that comfort zones differ across societies made me reflect on my own behavior. In Turkey, people tend to communicate closely and touch you on your arm or shoulder as a friendly gesture. However, I sometimes noticed foreign classmates stepping back during conversations. At first, I perceived it as rude, but now I understand it as their way of maintaining comfort within their cultural norms. The presentation also highlighted the contradictions between verbal and nonverbal messages. People may say one thing but express another through their tone, posture, or facial expressions. In real life, I have experienced moments where a person claimed to be "fine," yet their body language—crossed arms, lack of eye contact, or a forced smile—revealed discomfort (P15).*

*I found nonverbal communication interesting. Things like gestures, facial expressions, tone of voice or even small pauses can mean different things depending on the culture. For instance, what might seem like a normal thinking gesture in one culture could be confusing or even rude in another. This makes intercultural communication complex and delicate, requiring not just language skills, but cultural sensitivity and awareness (P40).*

*In some cultures, people say things with body language, not just with words. For example, how close people stand, if they look into your eyes or not, or how they use silence—these can all give meaning. In Japan, for example, not saying something can be more important than saying it. That is very different from my culture (P25).*

*Thanks to the presentation on nonverbal communication, I have learned that body language, eye contact, and personal space are also part of how people communicate. For example, how close we stand to someone or how we look at them can have different meanings in different cultures. I found this part very important because it shows that even when people use the same words, misunderstandings can still happen due to cultural habits (P10).*

Another topic was social distance and zones in communication in various cultures in the syllabus. We discussed the norms in our culture regarding social distance. The students came up with some rigorous examples based on their experiences. They brought some examples through using AI, and we discussed to what extent they were similar or different, and even odd compared to our culture. In this context, online forums, virtual exchange programs, and social media can facilitate intercultural interactions and learning (Guth & Helm, 2010). For example, having close and constant eye contact with someone when you talk is considered disturbing in Turkish culture, but it is expected behaviour in Western culture. The students reflected their critical cultural awareness regarding the topic in their reflection sheets:

*Social distance is another important point that affects the way we communicate with people from different cultures. I am one of those people who do not prefer people around me when they are too close. I like keeping people in my social space rather than my personal or intimate space. Otherwise, I do not feel comfortable during communication, and it creates a negative impact. This impact can lead to misunderstandings. On the other hand, some people like to keep their partners close to themselves during communication. Keeping the appropriate distance changes from culture to culture (P2).*

*Social distance refers to the emotional and physical space individuals maintain between themselves and others in social interactions. Recognizing and respecting social distance is crucial in the classroom. Some students may prefer a more personal and closer teacher-student relationship, while others may feel uncomfortable with excessive familiarity. As a prospective teacher, understanding and respecting varying social distances is essential in building trust and rapport with students while ensuring that no one feels intruded upon or uncomfortable (P18).*

*My friend's first observation was about personal space and greetings. In Turkey, it is common to greet friends and even acquaintances with a handshake or sometimes a kiss on the cheek. However, in the U.S., especially among younger people, she noticed that greetings were often limited to a simple wave, a verbal "hi," or sometimes even just a smile. She realized that attempting to greet her American classmates with a cheek kiss made them visibly uncomfortable. Back home, such behavior would have been considered warm and friendly, but in the American context, it was seen as too intimate. Another example was the communication style. She noted that Americans often express their opinions directly, even in classrooms or casual conversations. In contrast, in Turkey, students sometimes hesitate to contradict a teacher or to speak very frankly in public discussions. In the U.S., her tendency to soften criticism or to hesitate before sharing her thoughts was sometimes misunderstood as uncertainty or lack of confidence. This difference highlighted the cultural value Americans place on individual expression and assertiveness (P26).*

While studying the topic, from values to beliefs: cultural identity, cultural bias, ethnocentrism and prejudice in communication, the students from different regions in Türkiye gave examples from their own experiences. We analysed cases, and they also shared some expressions regarding ethnocentrism or prejudice in various discourses. They compared and contrasted cultures in Western and Eastern countries in the world and Turkish cultures by watching some short films or videos as well as their personal accounts in various countries. AI helps them find cases and films, and share them with their friends in class. All these activities led them to have critical cultural awareness regarding the topic. They seemed to have awareness of their cultural barriers. The students reflected their critical cultural awareness in their reflection sheets as follows:

*Our identity shapes how we interpret everything around us. For example, someone growing up in a collective society might naturally value group harmony more than individual success, without even realizing it. Prejudice heavily affects communication, too. When people form opinions without real knowledge but based on stereotypes rather than facts, they block honest and open communication. If we approach others with prejudice, we are likely to misinterpret their words, intentions, or behaviour, leading to unnecessary conflict. Critical thinking plays a vital role in overcoming prejudice (P28).*

*It reminds me that promoting critical thinking about cultural assumptions will not only broaden students' minds but also foster mutual respect among them. Teaching students to recognize cultural biases, ethnocentrism and prejudice in communication can improve communication and collaboration in diverse settings, which are increasingly common today (P14).*

*Concepts like cultural identity, cultural bias, and ethnocentrism made me think about how easy it is to judge other cultures based on our own perspectives. The idea of cultural relativism showed me that behaviour which seems strange or wrong to me might be completely normal and meaningful in another culture. When we only view the world through our own cultural lens, stereotyping and prejudice become almost automatic. I found the distinction between individual prejudice and institutional prejudice especially eye-opening because it showed me how unfair treatment can be reinforced by systems, not just personal attitudes. These concepts helped me realize that effective communication requires awareness, empathy, and an understanding of hidden cultural assumptions (P17).*

*The discussion of cultural identity, bias, ethnocentrism, and cultural relativism reminded me how easily people judge other cultures using their own norms as the benchmark. The examples given, such as assuming one's own language is superior or preferring job candidates from a similar background, illustrate how unconscious these biases can be. The idea of cultural relativism, which encourages understanding beliefs in their own context, seems essential for reducing prejudice (P29).*

The topic of implementing an intercultural approach in ELF is related to a brief historical perspective in second and foreign language teaching, and how intercultural communication is handled by various approaches and methods. Initially, language teaching focused on accuracy and tried to improve the language competency of learners in this way. Later, it was realized that having communicative competence was not enough to have effective communication and Byram (1997) introduced intercultural communication competence. Thus, we discussed how we could integrate intercultural communication elements into our lesson plans, activities and materials in ELT so that prospective teachers could teach the second or foreign language by considering interlanguage communication. Here are some quotes from the reflection sheets of my students regarding implementing an intercultural approach in ELF:

*This topic has broadened my perspective on what it means to teach a language. It reminded me that language teaching is also culture teaching, and that developing intercultural sensitivity is crucial for both teachers and learners in today's interconnected world. I feel more prepared and motivated to integrate cultural elements into my lessons and to help my students become not only successful language users but also respectful global citizens (P8).*

*This topic made me more curious about languages and cultures. I understand that learning a language is not only about grammar or vocabulary. It is also about learning how people from other cultures live and think and behave when they communicate. I think this will help me a lot when I speak English with people from different countries. I will try to understand not only their words, but also their feelings, habits, and culture (P28).*

*The course also emphasized the role of cultural awareness in creating inclusive and supportive ELT classrooms. As language teachers, it is essential that we recognize and respect the various cultural backgrounds of our students. This involves moving away from a narrow focus on British or American English and integrating a broader range of global voices and English varieties. Doing this not only enriches the learning experience but also allows students to view themselves as valid users of English, regardless of their accent or cultural norms (P32).*

*A powerful concept introduced is the idea of English as a lingua franca (ELF), where the language serves as a shared medium between speakers from different mother tongues. In these interactions, mutual understanding and cultural sensitivity are more important than adhering strictly to native-speaker models. This perspective has changed how I define successful communication—not by perfect grammar or pronunciation, but by the ability to communicate effectively across cultures (P33).*

*As a prospective teacher, I will raise my students' awareness of the different practices related to different cultures. I can bring videos of different cultures. I can encourage them to make friends from different countries and cultures. Above all, I will explain to them that each culture is special and unique just the way it is (P3).*

The final topic we dealt with was the challenges and barriers in intercultural communication in practice. The challenges and barriers may result from the dynamics of surface and deep culture, differences in values and beliefs, stereotyping and prejudice influenced by our own worldview, the environment and media. As a follow-up activity, after the presentation, we watched various films, and while watching the films, we paused whenever there was a cultural barrier in communication, and thus, we had an opportunity to discuss why it was a challenge in this context. In this way, our prospective teachers were aware of the challenges and barriers people had in their communication. Some cases were analysed and discussed, and students' past personal accounts were shared and explained, related to what the challenge was and how it could be resolved. The participants reflected their opinions and attitudes regarding the challenges and barriers in intercultural communication in practice are illustrated below:

*The presentation identifies major intercultural communication challenges such as differences in language, stereotypes, and other assumptions about cultures. There are certain languages that have idioms or statements that cannot be translated directly into other languages, and communication becomes a problem. People may also have unconscious cultural prejudices, assuming universal cultural norms. Differences in nonverbal communication, for instance, eye contact, personal spaces, and body language, may lead to misunderstandings (P10).*

*After the presentation and films, the discussions touched on negative outcomes like stereotyping, prejudice, and discrimination. These issues reminded me of the importance of promoting empathy and open-mindedness in the classroom. One practical strategy discussed was using films or series to teach cultural differences instead of listing customs. This helps students see people as individuals rather than as fixed representations of a culture (P4).*

*Thanks to the presentation and the films we watched, I was aware of some problems in intercultural communication. For example, language problems, stereotypes, and different communication styles can make people confused or uncomfortable. I realized that sometimes, teachers are not ready to talk about cultural topics, or the books only show British or American culture. This can make students feel left out or misunderstood (P26).*

It can be claimed that intercultural communication courses can create awareness and intercultural sensitivity towards the conflicting cultural dynamics categorized into high- and low-context cultures, individualism versus collectivism, varying power distance, and long-term versus short-term orientations. In the Turkish context, Tuncel and Paker (2018) investigated the effectiveness of an intercultural communication course in the department of English language teaching on the level of students' intercultural sensitivity. The results revealed that the intercultural communication course contributed significantly to the development of intercultural sensitivity among students, and the activities in the course contributed a lot to increasing their awareness of intercultural communication components and the development of their intercultural sensitivity.

Reconciling the opposing forces and beliefs poses a significant challenge in establishing a worldwide community; however, acknowledging the advantages of building a third culture (Casmir, 1993) as a collectively negotiated culture is a crucial step in fostering global communities. According to Casmir (1993), the third culture is based on creative and adaptive development and interdependence in a continuous process of dialogic communication that requires people to change their attitudes in order to survive within the third culture community.

## 6. THE CHALLENGES & ETHICAL CONSIDERATIONS

Among these challenges, there are concerns about preserving traditional values amid cultural pluralism and avoiding the marginalization of individuals who may be perceived as 'the other' (Lestinen et al., 2004). Another one is resistance to change, which can stem from both students and educators. The resistance may be because of deeply ingrained cultural biases or a lack of understanding regarding the benefits of intercultural competence (Gay, 2010). If intercultural learning is not approached thoughtfully and sensitively, it may result in the risk of cultural stereotyping, when oversimplified and fixed ideas about other cultures are reinforced rather than dismantled. Next challenge is due to its complex and multifaceted nature, assessing intercultural competence can be difficult. Standardized testing methods may not adequately capture the depth of students' intercultural understanding and skills (Fantini, 2000). In addition, the challenge is the cross-cultural engagement through online platforms. Online platforms can be a friend or foe because the digital realm exposes individuals to risks, including hate speech, stereotypes, and discrimination, particularly on social media (Sandu & Bajja, 2018). In addition, Dai and Hua (2025) claim that the use of generative artificial intelligence (AI) has the potential to misrepresent identity and history, thereby emphasizing authenticity as a pivotal intercultural criterion.

Algorithms are not impartial, instead, they embody the biases and perspectives embedded in their design and training datasets, as evidenced by extensive study in computer science and critical data analysis (Benjamin, 2019; Noble, 2018). Learners' perceptions of culture, identity, and belonging are directly impacted by these biases, which is particularly concerning when it comes to intercultural communication. On the other hand, algorithms are not neutral; rather, they reflect the datasets and design choices that inform them, which was reported in an expanding body of study in AI ethics (Crawford, 2021; Noble, 2018). This knowledge has led to the development of a number of ethical standards for the appropriate use of AI, directly addressing intercultural concerns. The UNESCO Recommendation on the Ethics of Artificial Intelligence (2021) has created a global framework for addressing these challenges, which outlines the principles in terms of:

- Fairness and non-discrimination
- Transparency and explainability
- Human oversight and accountability
- Inclusivity and cultural diversity

Here, these principles are very compatible with ICC theory, especially the emphasis on transparency, respect, and critical cultural awareness. Thus, AI ethics requires caution against adding negative presumptions into algorithms.

Despite these challenges, students could develop the ability to analyse situations from multiple viewpoints, fostering more comprehensive and creative problem-solving abilities by engaging with diverse perspectives (Byram, 1997). Consequently, all the activities carried out during the classes in the intercultural communication course will result in prospective teachers who are sensitive, understanding and tolerant towards other cultures. Hence, they are expected to educate their students in this vein in the future.

## 7. CONCLUSION

Intercultural competence requires an understanding of one's own cultural framework and an appreciation of other cultures. Thus, students recognize and value cultural differences, and also understand how these differences influence communication and behaviour. As an initial component of intercultural competence, intercultural awareness involves both cognitive understanding and recognition of cultural differences and similarities. Next, intercultural sensitivity is predicated on affective understanding of cultural differences, which involves empathy and openness towards other cultures, fostering an environment where intercultural interactions can occur respectfully and effectively. On the other hand, intercultural effectiveness is the practical application of cultural knowledge and sensitivity. It is the ability to resolve conflicts, adapt to new cultural environments, and exhibit culturally appropriate behaviours. Consequently, the concept of "cultural intelligence (CQ)" integrates these components to form a comprehensive ability to function effectively in diverse cultural settings. While trying to construct such key components among our students, we can use various activities supported with AI tools under the supervision of instructors. The structured intercultural development activities are highly effective in fostering a deeper understanding and practical application of intercultural skills (Tuncel & Paker, 2018). In addition, using digital tools and platforms to connect students with their peers worldwide should be integrated into the syllabus. All in all, experiential and reflective learning should be emphasized as they are effective in developing intercultural competence. Sharing students' experiences, role-playing, simulations, case studies, and project-based learning encourages students to engage actively in cultural scenarios, enabling them to apply theoretical knowledge in practical contexts (Ceo-DiFrancesco et al., 2016).

I believe that human judgement is better than computer judgement because it covers cognitive, metacognitive, motivational, affective and behavioural dimensions.

In order to ensure that students are engaged in reflective activities, discussions and feedback sessions, educators should consider integrating AI technology as supplementary tools rather than replacements for human interaction.

The efficacy of these activities underscores the significance of experiential learning, wherein students actively engage in scenarios that challenge their preconceptions and expand their worldview. Intercultural competence should be a fundamental element in education, equipping students with the skills required to thrive in diverse cultural environments. An intercultural communication course should be a key component of the curriculum. In this respect, teachers' professional development should also be prioritized to ensure that language teachers are well-prepared to teach intercultural competence. Thanks to all these efforts, a third culture can be constructed among our students to build a civic society that is understanding, tolerant, and more flexible towards cultures different from their own.

## REFERENCES


Benjamin, R. (2019). *Race after technology: Abolitionist tools for the new Jim code*. Polity Press.

Bennett, M. J. (1993). Towards ethnorelativism: A developmental model of intercultural sensitivity. In Paige, R. M. (Ed.), *Education for the intercultural experience* (pp. 21–71). Intercultural Press.

Byram, M. (1997). *Teaching and assessing intercultural communicative competence*. Multilingual Matters.

Byram, M. (2008). *From foreign language education to education for intercultural citizenship: Essays and reflections*. Multilingual Matters.

Byram, M. (2012). Conceptualizing intercultural (communicative) competence and intercultural citizenship. In J. Jackson (Ed.), *The Routledge handbook of language and intercultural communication* (pp. 85–98). Routledge.

Byram, M. (2020). Teaching and assessing intercultural communicative competence. In *Multilingual Matters eBooks*. DOI: 10.21832/BYRAM0244

Casmir, F. L. (1993). Third-culture building: A paradigm shift for international and intercultural communication. *Annals of the International Communication Association, 16*(1), 407–428. DOI: 10.1080/23808985.1993.11678861

Ceo-DiFrancesco, D., Mora, O., & Collazos, A. S. (2016). Developing intercultural communicative competence across the Americas. In *New directions in telecollaborative research and practice* (pp. 59–67). DOI: 10.14705/rpnet.2016.telecollab2016.490

Chen, G., & Starosta, W. J. (1996). Intercultural communication competence: A synthesis. *Annals of the International Communication Association, 19*(1), 353–383. https://doi.org/DOI: 10.1080/23808985.1996.11678935

Chen, G. M., & Starosta, W. J. (1997). A review of the concept of intercultural sensitivity. *Human Communication, 1*(1), 1–16. https://files.eric.ed.gov/fulltext/ED408634.pdf

Council of Europe. (2001). *Common European framework of reference for languages: learning, teaching, assessment*. Cambridge University Press.

Crawford, K. (2021). *Atlas of AI: Power, politics, and the planetary costs of artificial intelligence*. Yale University Press.

Dai, D. W., & Hua, Z. (2025). When AI meets intercultural communication: New frontiers, new agendas. *Applied Linguistics Review, 16*(2), 747–751. DOI: 10.1515/applirev-2024-0185

Deardorff, D. K. (2006). Identification and assessment of intercultural competence as a student outcome of internationalization. *Journal of Studies in International Education, 10*(3), 241–266. DOI: 10.1177/1028315306287002

Dewey, J. (1933). *How we think: A restatement of the relation of reflective thinking to the educative process*. Heath & Co Publishers.

Ennis, R. H. (1985). A logical basis for measuring critical thinking skills. *Educational Leadership, 43*(2), 44–48.

Facione, P. A. (1990). *Critical thinking: A statement of expert consensus for purposes of educational assessment and instruction*. American Philosophical Association., DOI: 10.1016/0022-4405(92)90029-T

Fantini, A. E. (2000). A central concern: Developing intercultural competence. *SIT Occasional Papers Series, 1*, 1–50. Retrieved from https://culturewise.ie/library/wp-content/uploads/2023/12/A_Central_Concern__Developing_Intercultural_Competence.pdf

Gay, G. (2010). *Culturally responsive teaching: Theory, research, and practice* (2nd ed.). Teachers College Press.

Glaser, E. M. (1941). *An experiment in the development of critical thinking*. Teacher's College, Columbia University.

Godwin-Jones, R. (2023). Emerging technologies: AI-mediated communication and language learning. *Language Learning & Technology, 27*(1), 1–12. DOI: 10.10125/73494

Gudykunst, W. B. (2005): *Theorizing about intercultural communication,* (ed.). Sage Publications.

Guth, S., & Helm, F. (Eds.). (2010). *Telecollaboration 2.0: Language, literacies and intercultural learning in the 21st century*. Peter Lang. DOI: 10.3726/978-3-0351-0013-6

Hammer, M. R., Bennett, M. J., & Wiseman, R. (2003). Measuring intercultural sensitivity: The intercultural development inventory. *International Journal of Intercultural Relations, 27*(4), 421–443. DOI: 10.1016/S0147-1767(03)00032-4

Hoff, H. E. (2020). The evolution of intercultural communicative competence: Conceptualisations, critiques and consequences for 21st century classroom practice. *Intercultural Communication Education, 3*(2), 55–74. DOI: 10.29140/ice.v3n2.264

Hofstede, G., & Bond, M. H. (1984). Hofstede's culture dimensions. *Journal of Cross-Cultural Psychology, 15*(4), 417–433. DOI: 10.1177/0022002184015004003

Jenks, C. J. (2025). Communicating the cultural other: Trust and bias in generative AI and large language models. *Applied Linguistics Review, 16*(2), 1–9. DOI: 10.1515/applirev-2024-0196

Kalish, C., Adams, D., & Medley, T. (2021). How medical practices can continue the journey toward diversity, acceptance and inclusion. https://www.mgma.com/articles/how-medical-practices-can-continue-the-journey-toward-diversity-acceptance-and-inclusion

Lestinen, L., Petrucijová, J., & Spinthourakis, J. A. (2004). *Identity in multicultural and multilingual contexts*. Metropolitan University.

Li, X. (2021). Promoting English learners' intercultural competence through technology-enhanced model. *2021 2nd International Conference on Information Science and Education (ICISE-IE)*, 1592–1595. DOI: 10.1109/ICISE-IE53922.2021.00352

London, J. C., & Yousef, F. S. (1989). *An introduction to intercultural communication*. Collier Macmillan Publishers.

McLuhan, M., & Powers, B. R. (1989). *The global village: Transformations in world life and media in the 21st century*. Oxford University Press.

Miles, M. B., & Huberman, A. M. (1994). *Qualitative data analysis: An expanded Sourcebook* (2nd ed.). Sage.

Noble, S. U. (2018). *Algorithms of oppression: How search engines reinforce racism*. NYU Press. DOI: 10.18574/nyu/9781479833641.001.0001

Sandu, O. N., & Bajja, N. L. (2018). *T-Kit 4 Intercultural Learning*. Council of Europe.

Schön, D. A. (1983). *The reflective practitioner: How professionals think in action*. Basic Books.

Tuncel, İ., & Paker, T. (2018). Effects of an intercultural communication course in developing intercultural sensitivity. *International Journal of Higher Education*, 7(6), 198–211. DOI: 10.5430/ijhe.v7n6p198

UNESCO. (2021). *Artificial intelligence in education: Challenges and opportunities for sustainable development*. UNESCO Publishing.

UNESCO. (2021). *Recommendation on the ethics of artificial intelligence*. United Nations Educational, Scientific, and Cultural Organization.

Wang, J. (2024). Analysis of development of intercultural communicative competence in English education. *The Educational Review USA*, *8*(4), 593–597. DOI: 10.26855/er.2024.04.018

Xu, H., Wang, Y., & Ma, J. (2025). A comprehensive review of intercultural communicative competence in EFL education and global business. *Cogent Education*, *12*(1), 2557608. Advance online publication. DOI: 10.1080/2331186X.2025.2557608

Yang, S., Zhao, H., & Luo, W. (2024). The impact of artificial intelligence on intercultural communication.In *IntechOpen eBooks*. DOI: 10.5772/intechopen.1006172

Zou, D., Huang, Y., & Xie, H. (2023). Generative artificial intelligence for language education: Applications, challenges, and future directions. *Computers and Education: Artificial Intelligence*, *4*, 100119. DOI: 10.1016/j.caeai.2023.100119

Chapter 9

# AI Chatbots as Intercultural Companions in Literature Learning: Between Words and Worlds

**Kadir Lüta**
http://orcid.org/0000-0001-6813-7407
*Kırklareli University, Turkey*

**Oya Tunaboylu**
http://orcid.org/0009-0003-9711-3625
*Kırklareli University, Turkey*

## ABSTRACT

*This chapter examines AI chatbots as intercultural companions in literature education, proposing a framework to develop students' Intercultural Communicative Competence (ICC) and empathy. Based on Byram's ICC model and Davis's empathy framework, it describes a four-week intervention using conversational AI for dialogic exploration of culturally diverse texts. The approach stresses critical AI literacy, treating AI outputs as interpretive texts for analysis, not authoritative sources. A baseline survey of English Literature students at Kırklareli University showed moderate-to-high intercultural sensitivity (M=3.86, SD=0.37) and empathy (M=3.59, SD=0.41), with strengths in interaction enjoyment, respect for differences, and cognitive perspective-taking, but moderate active engagement and affective empathy. The chapter extends ICC and empathy models to digital contexts, offers practical guidance for AI-enhanced pedagogy, and confirms students' readiness for AI-mediated learning while preserving humanistic values in humanities education.*

DOI: 10.4018/979-8-3373-6325-7.ch009

# 1. INTRODUCTION

The integration of artificial intelligence into higher education has created new opportunities for reimagining pedagogical practice, particularly in humanities disciplines where meaning-making, empathy, and cultural understanding constitute core learning objectives. This chapter explores how AI chatbots can serve as intercultural companions in literature education, facilitating students' development of intercultural communicative competence (ICC) and empathy through dialogic engagement with culturally diverse texts.

Literature has long been recognized as a powerful vehicle for cultural learning. Through encounters with narratives from diverse contexts, readers gain access to worldviews and values different from their own, cultivating what Nussbaum (1995) terms "narrative imagination." Recent scholarship demonstrates that literature classrooms can serve as sites of intercultural development when pedagogy intentionally foregrounds cultural dialogue (Byram, 2021; Kramsch, 2009), and that fiction reading measurably enhances prosocial dispositions (Kidd & Castano, 2013). However, traditional approaches often prioritize textual analysis over the emotional and dialogic dimensions that deepen cultural empathy.

AI chatbots present a novel pedagogical opportunity. Recent reviews confirm that when integrated thoughtfully, AI tools can significantly enhance students' intercultural communication competence by bridging linguistic and cultural gaps (Klimova & Chen, 2024). Unlike traditional educational technologies, conversational AI systems engage students in sustained, exploratory dialogue about culturally complex texts. They can articulate multiple cultural perspectives, pose challenging questions, and provide low-stakes conversational spaces where students practice perspective-taking without fear of judgment—crucial for intercultural learning, which requires vulnerability (Bennett, 2004). Educational technology research recognizes that AI's value lies in augmenting human capacities for personalized learning (Holmes et al., 2019) rather than replacing human teaching.

However, AI integration raises critical questions. Can algorithmic systems genuinely support deeply human capacities like empathy and cultural sensitivity? How do we ensure AI serves as reflective tool rather than authoritative source that reinforces biases? This chapter responds by proposing a theoretically grounded framework that integrates Byram's (1997) model of ICC with Davis's (1980) multidimensional empathy model, examining how AI dialogue can develop both intercultural skills and emotional understanding while cultivating critical AI literacy.

The context of the study is significant. Conducted with English Literature students at Kırklareli University in Turkiye, the research involves students who regularly engage with Anglophone texts while situated in a Turkish context. They occupy a complex intercultural position, navigating cultural differences embedded in texts they study, making them particularly relevant participants for exploring AI-supported intercultural learning. As AI systems become ubiquitous in students' lives, literature educators must proactively design pedagogies that harness AI's potential while cultivating critical awareness of its limitations and biases.

## 2. THEORETICAL FRAMEWORK

This pedagogical framework rests on three interconnected theoretical pillars: Byram's model of Intercultural Communicative Competence, Davis's (1980) multidimensional conception of empathy, and emerging scholarship on AI as dialogic partner in humanistic education.

### 2.1 Intercultural Communicative Competence in Literature Education

Byram's (1997) model conceptualizes ICC as complex integration of attitudes, knowledge, skills, and critical cultural awareness—the five *savoirs*. The model emphasizes curiosity and openness (*savoir être*), cultural knowledge (*savoirs*), interpretive skills (*savoir comprendre*), discovery skills (*savoir apprendre/faire*), and critical cultural awareness (*savoir s'engager*). Subsequent scholarship has refined understanding of how ICC develops through iterative cycles of experience and reflection (Deardorff, 2006) and foregrounded the political dimensions of critical cultural awareness as essential for democratic citizenship (Guilherme, 2002).

Traditional literature pedagogy often develops cultural knowledge and interpretive skills while neglecting attitudinal development and critical awareness. AI chatbots present distinctive opportunities: by articulating multiple cultural perspectives, they can prompt curiosity, provide on-demand cultural knowledge, model interpretive processes, and—when paired with critical reflection—support critical cultural awareness by making visible cultural assumptions in both AI outputs and students' interpretations.

### 2.2 Empathy as Multidimensional Construct

Davis (1980, 1983) demonstrated that empathy comprises distinct dimensions: perspective-taking (cognitive component), fantasy (imaginative transposition), empathic concern (affective component), and personal distress (self-oriented anxiety). For literature education, the distinction between cognitive perspective-taking and affective empathic concern proves particularly illuminating. Students may develop sophisticated analytical skills without emotional connection or feel moved without understanding why characters act as they do. Contemporary empathy research has expanded this framework, examining neural mechanisms (Decety & Jackson, 2004) and demonstrating how cultural contexts shape empathy's expression (Chiao & Mathur, 2010).

Research shows fiction reading enhances both cognitive and affective empathy through simulation processes (Keen, 2007; Mar & Oatley, 2008). However, when characters come from culturally unfamiliar contexts, readers may lack cultural knowledge for accurate perspective-taking or respond with distress rather than concern. AI can support this learning by articulating culturally situated interpretations that scaffold perspective-taking, prompting attention to emotional dimensions, and developing meta-cognitive awareness about empathy's cultural situatedness.

## 2.3 AI as Dialogic Partner in Humanistic Learning

From a pedagogical standpoint, dialogue has long been recognized as central to humanities learning. Bakhtin's (1981) dialogism emphasizes that meaning emerges through interaction between multiple voices. AI chatbots introduce a new dialogic partner: not human, yet capable of sophisticated linguistic interaction; not an authority, yet able to articulate perspectives. Luckin et al. (2016) propose AI as learning companion supporting exploratory learning through conversation.

As Laquintano and Vee (2024) argue, these generative tools are likely to integrate with existing literacy practices rather than replace them, provided that educators emphasize the quality of ideas over mere output. However, critical concerns must be addressed. Large language models reflect cultural biases and dominant perspectives in their training data (Bender et al., 2021). Critical scholarship documents how algorithmic systems perpetuate bias across domains (Crawford, 2021; Eubanks, 2018; O'Neil, 2016), revealing that algorithmic bias reflects deeper issues about whose knowledge counts and how power operates through technology. In educational contexts, this requires developing “critical data literacy” (Pangrazio & Selwyn, 2019), capacity to question data sources, recognize algorithmic politics, and understand technology as socially constructed.

Rather than positioning AI as problem to avoid, effective pedagogy treats AI as object of critical inquiry. Students must approach AI-generated interpretations with the same critical lens applied to any source: asking whose perspectives are centered, what assumptions underlie analysis, and what might be missing. This dual focus transforms AI from merely a tool into a site of critical reflection about technology, culture, and interpretation.

Furthermore, the integration of AI companions aligns with Benson's (2011) conceptualization of learner autonomy, as it grants students control over the pace and direction of their cultural inquiry, allowing for self-regulated learning beyond the classroom. From a motivational perspective, interacting with a non-judgmental AI partner can support what Dörnyei (2009) terms the 'Ideal L2 Self.' By practicing intercultural dialogue in a low-stakes environment, students can visualize themselves as competent communicators, thereby reducing anxiety and enhancing their motivation to engage in future real-world interactions.

### 2.4 Synthesis: Toward an Integrated Framework

These theoretical strands articulate how AI-mediated dialogue might facilitate intercultural and empathic learning. First, AI chatbots serve as conversational scaffolds supporting Byram's five savoirs. Second, AI dialogue activates both cognitive and affective empathy dimensions. Third, critical AI literacy becomes integral to intercultural learning, as students evaluate AI outputs using the same critical cultural awareness they apply to texts. Fourth, AI complements rather than replaces human interaction, serving as preparatory space for intercultural dialogue. Finally, the framework maintains humanistic values while embracing technological innovation, with AI creating opportunities for dialogue and critical thinking about culture and technology. While the theoretical pillars establish the 'why,' the practical application of this integration is detailed in the subsequent methodology section (see Section 5.2.1 and Table 2 for the operational framework).

## 3. METHODOLOGY

This study employed a cross-sectional survey design to establish baseline measures of intercultural communicative competence and empathy among undergraduate English Literature students, providing insight into students' current capacities and establishing foundation for evaluating readiness for AI-mediated intervention.

### 3.1 Participants and Context

Participants were undergraduate students enrolled in English Literature programs at Kırklareli University in Turkey. The study group consisted of 84 undergraduate students (52 female, 32 male) ranging in age from 18 to 24. The participants possessed a minimum of B2 English proficiency level according to the CEFR standards. Prior to this study, the majority of participants reported moderate experience with AI tools for academic purposes, though all were familiar with the concept of generative AI.

These students occupy a distinctive intercultural position: they study literature produced primarily in Anglophone contexts while situated in a Turkish cultural and educational environment, routinely navigating cultural differences embedded in texts they read. The geographic position of Turkiye, bridging Europe and Asia, creates educational environments where questions of cultural identity and intercultural encounter carry particular resonance.

### 3.2 Instruments

The Intercultural Sensitivity Scale (ISS; Chen & Starosta, 2000) measures sensitivity to cultural differences across five subscales: Interaction Engagement, Respect for Cultural Differences, Interaction Confidence, Interaction Enjoyment, and Interaction Attentiveness. Participants respond using 5-point Likert scales. The ISS demonstrates strong psychometric properties and aligns well with Byram's conceptualization of ICC.

The Interpersonal Reactivity Index (IRI; Davis, 1980) assesses dispositional empathy across four dimensions: Perspective-Taking (cognitive empathy), Fantasy (imaginative engagement), Empathic Concern (affective empathy), and Personal Distress (self-oriented anxiety). The 28-item instrument uses 5-point scales and is considered a gold standard in empathy research.

Both instruments were administered via online survey, with demographic information collected while maintaining participant anonymity.

### 3.3 Data Analysis and Ethics

Descriptive statistics characterize the sample's baseline intercultural sensitivity and empathy levels. Mean scores and standard deviations were calculated for overall scales and subscales. The study received institutional approval, with voluntary anonymous participation and informed consent procedures.

## 4. FINDINGS

This section presents the baseline assessment results, beginning with overall patterns in intercultural sensitivity and empathy before examining subscale-level findings that provide more nuanced understanding of students' capacities.

## 4.1 Sample Characteristics and Overall Patterns

*Table 1. Descriptive statistics for ICC and IRI scales*

| Scale/Subscale | | Mean (*M*) | *SD* | Min. | Max. |
|---|---|---|---|---|---|
| ISS | Overall ICC | 3.86 | 0.37 | 2.92 | 4.88 |
| | Interaction Enjoyment | 4.05 | - | - | - |
| | Respect for Cultural Differences | 4.00 | - | - | - |
| | Interaction Confidence | 3.77 | - | - | - |
| | Interaction Attentiveness | 3.77 | - | - | - |
| | Interaction Engagement | 3.69 | - | - | - |
| IRI | Overall IRI | 3.59 | 0.41 | 2.46 | 4.46 |
| | Perspective-Taking | 3.81 | - | - | - |
| | Fantasy | 3.78 | - | - | - |
| | Empathic Concern | 3.67 | - | - | - |
| | Personal Distress | 3.11 | - | - | - |

Note. All scores measured on 5-point Likert scales. $N = 80$

The baseline assessment revealed that participants demonstrated moderate-to-high levels of both intercultural sensitivity and empathy. On the Intercultural Sensitivity Scale, the overall mean score was 3.86 ($SD = 0.37$) on the 5-point scale, with individual scores ranging from 2.92 to 4.88. This overall level, substantially above the scale midpoint, indicates that participants generally possess positive attitudes toward intercultural interaction and cultural difference. The relatively low standard deviation suggests considerable consistency across participants, with most students clustering around the moderate-to-high range rather than showing extreme variation.

On the Interpersonal Reactivity Index, the overall mean empathy score was 3.59 ($SD = 0.41$), also above the scale midpoint and indicating moderate empathic capacity. Individual scores ranged from 2.46 to 4.46. The slightly higher standard deviation compared to the ISS suggests somewhat greater variability in empathy levels across participants, though the distribution still centers around the moderate range. These overall patterns establish that the student population begins with foundational capacities in both intercultural sensitivity and empathy that the proposed AI intervention can build upon and develop further.

## 4.2 Intercultural Sensitivity Patterns

Subscale analysis revealed meaningful variation. Highest means appeared in Interaction Enjoyment ($M = 4.05$) and Respect for Cultural Differences ($M = 4.00$), indicating students derive pleasure from intercultural encounters and demonstrate strong appreciation for diversity—aligning with Byram's *savoir être*. Moderate-to-high scores in Interaction Confidence and Attentiveness (both $M = 3.77$) suggest reasonable self-assurance and cultural awareness, while the lowest mean in Interaction Engagement ($M = 3.69$), though still moderate, suggests students are somewhat less proactive in seeking intercultural encounters.

## 4.3 Empathy Patterns

Perspective-Taking showed highest mean ($M = 3.81$), indicating moderate-to-high cognitive empathy capacity—foundational for literary interpretation and intercultural empathy. Fantasy ($M = 3.78$) suggests students readily engage imaginatively with texts. Empathic Concern ($M = 3.67$), while above midpoint, is lower than Perspective-Taking, suggesting stronger cognitive than affective empathy. Personal Distress ($M = 3.11$) indicates emotional regulation allowing engagement with difficult material without becoming overwhelmed—crucial for intercultural learning involving uncomfortable content.

## 4.4 Synthesis of Baseline Findings

The findings reveal students with positive attitudes toward cultural difference, cognitive empathy skills, and imaginative capacities providing solid foundations for intercultural learning. Simultaneously, somewhat lower active engagement and moderate affective empathy identify specific developmental opportunities the proposed intervention addresses.

# 5. DISCUSSION

This section interprets the findings of the study within the theoretical frameworks established earlier and explores their implications for theory, pedagogy, and practice. The discussion is organized around five major themes: interpreting the baseline assessment data in relation to students' readiness for AI-mediated intercultural learning, examining theoretical contributions to scholarship on intercultural communicative competence and empathy, articulating pedagogical implications for literature instruction, addressing ethical and critical dimensions of AI integration in humanities education, and acknowledging the study's limitations while pointing toward future research directions.

## 5.1 Interpreting Baseline Findings and Readiness for AI-Mediated Learning

The baseline data provide crucial insights into students' readiness for AI-mediated intervention. Overall moderate-to-high scores establish that students enter with foundational capacities rather than minimal competence, having important implications for pedagogical design. While these moderate-to-high baseline scores might initially suggest that students are already sufficiently competent, educational scholarship cautions against interpreting such data as a ceiling. Instead, these scores indicate 'readiness' rather than 'mastery.' As Vygotsky's Zone of Proximal Development suggests, students at this level are precisely positioned to benefit from scaffolding to reach higher levels of critical awareness. Without the proposed intervention, there is a risk that students will remain at a plateau of 'passive appreciation' of culture. The framework aims to disrupt this comfort zone, pushing students from merely respecting differences (a moderate skill) to critically analyzing the power dynamics and biases inherent in cultural representations (an advanced skill).

High Interaction Enjoyment and Respect scores indicate students approach intercultural learning with curiosity and openness rather than resistance—creating favorable conditions for intervention to deepen engagement rather than first cultivating basic openness. However, lower Interaction Engagement reveals an important need: while students appreciate cultural difference, they demonstrate less proactive engagement. The AI-mediated activities, requiring students to formulate questions and actively construct understanding rather than passively receive information, directly target this dimension.

Moderate Interaction Confidence and Attentiveness scores suggest room for growth in navigating cultural dynamics. The intervention addresses confidence by providing low-stakes conversational environments where students practice intercultural inquiry without fear of causing offense. As confidence grows through AI interaction, students may become more willing to engage in higher-stakes dialogue with actual people.

High Perspective-Taking scores indicate strong cognitive empathy providing essential foundation. Students can build on existing skills to develop more culturally informed perspective-taking. High Fantasy scores facilitate empathic imagination activities. Moderate Empathic Concern scores reveal an area requiring attention: students demonstrate stronger cognitive than affective empathy. This underscores importance of activities explicitly targeting empathic concern and connecting emotional responses to cultural understanding. The relatively low Personal Distress scores constitute positive findings, indicating emotional regulation enabling sustained intercultural inquiry.

These patterns inform intervention implementation importantly. The intervention can build on enjoyment and respect by providing structured opportunities for active engagement currently showing lower levels. It can leverage cognitive empathy while targeting affective empathy development. It can support confidence-building through low-stakes practice before higher-stakes human dialogue.

## 5.2 Proposed AI-Mediated Pedagogical Framework

Building on baseline insights revealing students' strong attitudinal foundations but moderate active engagement and affective empathy, this section presents a four-week intervention framework tailored to demonstrated readiness and developmental needs.

The framework privileges dialogue as primary learning mode, with students engaging in sustained conversation where meaning emerges through interaction. It follows scaffolded progression from cultural awareness to critical engagement, positions critical AI literacy as explicit learning objective, integrates cognitive and affective learning, balances AI and human interaction, and embodies culturally responsive pedagogy.

### 5.2.1 Four-Week Intervention Model

*Table 2. Four-week AI-mediated intervention framework*

| Week | Focus | Key Activities | Learning Objectives |
|---|---|---|---|
| 1 | Foundations | Introduction to AI as a dialogic partner; cultural context exploration; basic perspective-taking practice | Develop openness toward culturally unfamiliar texts; learn AI engagement strategies; recognize how culture shapes interpretation |
| 2 | Deepening | Multi-perspective analysis; challenging stereotypes; comparative framework building | Strengthen interpretive skills; practice systematic cultural comparison; recognize cultural complexity and avoid essentialism |
| 3 | Empathy | Emotional landscape mapping; empathic imagination exercises; exploring empathic limits | Develop affective empathic concern; recognize how culture shapes emotion; understand empathy's possibilities and limits |
| 4 | Synthesis | Deconstructing AI interpretations; developing personal AI use guidelines; integrative reflection | Integrate ICC and empathy with critical AI literacy; evaluate AI outputs critically; articulate ethical AI use guidelines |

### *Week 1: Foundations - Cultural Awareness and Dialogic Practice*

The first week establishes foundational capacities for AI-mediated intercultural learning. Students develop openness and curiosity toward culturally unfamiliar texts, corresponding to attitudes of openness in Byram's model, while practicing basic skills of cultural observation and description. Equally important, they learn to engage AI chatbots as conversational partners rather than answer-providers and begin recognizing how cultural perspectives shape literary interpretation.

The week opens with an introduction to AI as conversational partner for exploring literary texts. Rather than presenting AI as an expert system, the instructor frames AI as a dialogic tool with particular affordances, including the ability to articulate multiple perspectives and patience with exploratory questioning, alongside significant limitations such as lack of lived cultural experience and potential for bias. Students experiment with different types of prompts, discovering how the framing of questions shapes AI responses. They might compare, for instance, AI responses to asking what a text is about versus how readers from different cultural backgrounds might interpret the same text. This activity introduces the meta-cognitive practice of attending to how questions shape answers, a skill essential both for effective AI interaction and for intercultural inquiry more broadly.

Building on this introduction, students engage AI in dialogue about cultural contexts that inform a selected culturally diverse text, such as a short story from postcolonial literature, contemporary global fiction, or literature in translation. The goal at this stage is not comprehensive cultural knowledge but rather developing curiosity and openness alongside basic cultural understanding. Students follow a structured protocol: they identify cultural practices, values, or references in the text that are unfamiliar, ask AI to provide cultural context for these elements, request explanations of how cultural insiders might understand these elements differently than cultural outsiders, and reflect on how this contextual knowledge affects interpretation. Critically, students are instructed to approach AI-provided information as one perspective to be verified rather than definitive truth, and they are encouraged to compare AI explanations with scholarly sources while noting discrepancies or oversimplifications.

The week's third major activity focuses on perspective-taking practice. Students use AI to practice adopting others' psychological viewpoints by asking the chatbot to articulate how different characters in the text might view a particular event or conflict. This targets Davis's (1980) cognitive empathy dimension while introducing the idea that perspectives are culturally situated. In a text featuring cultural conflict between characters, students might prompt AI to explain how one character would view a situation based on their cultural background, then ask how another character from a different cultural context would understand the same situation. Students then reflect on what cultural values or assumptions inform each perspective, beginning to recognize the cultural construction of viewpoint itself.

Each week concludes with structured reflection where students document their learning process. In the first week, students consider what surprised them about using AI to explore cultural contexts in literature, what questions proved most productive in generating useful AI responses, when they noticed their own cultural assumptions affecting interpretation, and what limitations they observed in AI's cultural explanations. These reflections develop meta-cognitive awareness essential for both intercultural learning and critical AI use.

### *Week 2: Deepening - Cultural Analysis and Comparative Perspectives*

The second week builds on foundational capacities to develop more sophisticated skills in interpreting and relating cultural perspectives. Students strengthen cognitive perspective-taking capacities, practice comparing multiple cultural interpretations systematically, and begin recognizing cultural complexity while avoiding essentialist thinking that reduces cultures to simple generalizations.

Building on the foundation in the previous week, students now engage in multi-perspective analysis of culturally significant moments, symbols, or relationships in texts. They select an element and systematically explore how readers from different cultural positions might interpret it. The protocol guides them to prompt AI to analyze the element from the perspective of the culture represented in the text, request analysis from the perspective of the target language culture such as contemporary American readers, ask AI to identify additional cultural frameworks that might yield different interpretations, and then compare these interpretations to identify where cultural values lead to divergent meanings. A student reading Jhumpa Lahiri's work, for instance, might explore how concepts of family obligation are understood differently in South Asian and American cultural contexts, using AI to articulate both perspectives before analyzing how these different frameworks affect interpretation of character choices.

A crucial activity in this week specifically targets critical cultural awareness by helping students recognize and question stereotypical cultural representations. Students identify moments in texts or in AI-generated responses where cultural groups might be represented in reductive or stereotypical ways. They ask AI to describe how a particular cultural group is represented in the text, prompt AI to identify potential stereotypes or oversimplifications in this representation, request more nuanced or complex perspectives on the culture, and reflect critically on whether AI's own responses contain stereotypical assumptions. This activity makes visible the tendency toward cultural essentialism in both literary texts and AI outputs, developing students' critical capacity to recognize when cultural complexity is being flattened into simple generalizations.

Students also work with AI to develop comparative frameworks for understanding cultural differences in values, communication styles, social structures, or worldviews as they appear in literary texts. Rather than simply noting that cultures differ, students practice articulating the specific dimensions along which difference operates and recognizing diversity within cultures. They might ask AI to compare how concepts of individual autonomy versus collective responsibility are culturally constructed, then apply this framework to analyze character conflicts in texts where these values clash. Importantly, students are guided to recognize that such frameworks are analytical tools rather than rigid classifications of entire cultures, and that any framework inevitably simplifies the complexity of actual cultural practices and beliefs.

Weekly reflection in this phase asks students to consider how their understanding of cultural difference has become more complex or nuanced, when they caught themselves or AI making stereotypical assumptions about a culture, what strategies helped them move beyond surface-level cultural knowledge to deeper understanding, and how they decide when AI-provided cultural analysis is reliable versus oversimplified. These reflections consolidate learning while developing meta-cognitive awareness about the interpretive process itself.

### *Week 3: Empathy and Emotional Engagement*

The third week shifts focus toward affective dimensions of intercultural learning. Students develop empathic concern alongside cognitive perspective-taking, practice emotional engagement with culturally unfamiliar characters and situations, recognize how culture shapes emotional expression and experience, and explore both the possibilities and limits of empathy across cultural difference.

The week begins with activities designed to explore the emotional landscape of literary texts. Students use AI to investigate the emotional dimensions of characters' experiences, particularly attending to how cultural contexts shape emotional life. They identify a moment of emotional intensity in the text, such as grief, joy, shame, or anger, and ask AI to describe what the character might be feeling and why. They then prompt AI to explain how cultural values or norms might influence how this emotion is experienced or expressed, before reflecting on similarities and differences between the character's emotional experience and their own. A student reading a text where a character experiences shame about bringing dishonor to their family, for instance, might explore with AI how concepts of honor, shame, and family obligation are culturally constructed, and how the character's emotional experience is shaped by these cultural frameworks. This activity develops students' capacity to recognize that emotions themselves, while universal in some sense, are also culturally mediated. What triggers shame, how shame is experienced, and how it is expressed all vary across cultural contexts.

Drawing on Davis's (1983) concept of empathic concern, students engage in empathic imagination exercises that invite them to enter characters' experiences while maintaining awareness of cultural differences. Students write brief first-person reflections as if they were a character at a crucial moment in the text, then use AI to generate an alternative first-person reflection from the same character. They compare the two reflections, noting what cultural knowledge or emotional understanding each captures or misses, and reflect on what this comparison reveals about empathy's possibilities and limits. This activity makes visible the interpretive and imaginative work involved in empathy while highlighting how cultural knowledge informs empathic accuracy. When students' own imaginative reconstructions differ significantly from AI-generated alternatives informed by cultural context, they gain insight into how their own cultural frameworks shape even their most intimate attempts at understanding others.

Moving toward critical reflection, the week addresses a key tension in intercultural empathy, which is the risk of assuming we can fully understand others' experiences, particularly across significant cultural differences. Students use AI dialogue to explore when empathy becomes problematic, such as when it erases difference, appropriates others' experiences, or substitutes feeling for understanding. They identify a character or situation in the text where cultural difference is particularly significant, then discuss with AI what readers from outside this culture can understand about this character's experience and what they might inevitably misunderstand or fail to grasp. They ask AI to articulate why some experiences may not be fully accessible to empathic imagination, then reflect on how to balance empathic engagement with recognition of difference and epistemic humility. This activity introduces students to the concept that empathy, while valuable, has ethical limits. Claiming to fully understand another's experience, especially across power differentials or significant cultural difference, can be a form of epistemic violence that denies the other's irreducible alterity.

Reflection prompts for this week ask students to consider how focusing on emotional dimensions changed their engagement with the text, when they experienced genuine empathic connection with culturally unfamiliar characters and what facilitated this connection, when they encountered limits to their empathic understanding and how they responded to these limits, and how empathy can be both valuable for intercultural learning and potentially problematic. These reflections help students develop a nuanced understanding of empathy as neither always possible nor always appropriate, but rather as a practice that requires both emotional openness and critical awareness.

### *Week 4: Critical Synthesis and AI Literacy*

The final week integrates intercultural communicative competence and empathy development with critical AI literacy. Students evaluate AI-generated interpretations using explicit criteria, synthesize their learning across the intervention, and articulate guidelines for ongoing ethical use of AI in literary study.

The culminating activity asks students to apply critical analytical skills to AI outputs themselves, treating them as texts to be interpreted and evaluated. This solidifies critical AI literacy while reinforcing intercultural and empathic competencies. Students select a complex moment of cultural significance in a text and generate multiple AI interpretations by varying their prompts. They then analyze these interpretations by asking what cultural perspectives are centered and which are marginalized or absent, what assumptions about culture the interpretation makes, where it demonstrates cultural knowledge versus stereotype, and how it handles cultural complexity and within-culture diversity. Students compare AI interpretations with scholarly literary criticism on the same text before synthesizing their findings into an evaluation of AI's affordances and limitations for intercultural literary analysis. This activity brings together all the skills developed over the previous weeks, including cultural knowledge, perspective-taking, critical awareness, and empathic engagement, while explicitly focusing them on the technology itself as an object of critical inquiry.

Drawing on their four weeks of experience, students develop personal guidelines for how they will use AI chatbots ethically and effectively in their ongoing literary studies. This activity promotes meta-cognitive awareness and student agency by positioning students as thoughtful practitioners who can make informed decisions about technology use. Students create guidelines addressing when AI dialogue is most useful for intercultural literary learning, what types of prompts generate productive versus problematic responses, how to verify AI-provided cultural information, when to prioritize human sources, such as lived experience narratives or scholarship by cultural insiders over AI, and how to maintain critical awareness while still benefiting from AI's conversational affordances. Rather than prescribing a single correct approach, this activity honors the diversity of students' learning styles and needs while ensuring that all students develop principled frameworks for AI engagement.

The intervention concludes with substantial integrative reflection where students synthesize their learning across all four weeks, connecting their experiences to course concepts and to broader questions about literature, culture, and technology. Students trace their development of intercultural communicative competence through this process, identify which aspects of empathy they have strengthened, and which remain challenging, articulate how working with AI has changed their approach to culturally diverse literature, specify what they will carry forward from this experience into future literary studies, and voice any concerns or questions they still have about using AI for intercultural learning. This final reflection serves multiple purposes: it consolidates learning by requiring students to articulate their development, it provides instructors with rich qualitative data about the intervention's effects, and it positions students as ongoing learners whose intercultural and empathic development extends beyond this particular intervention.

### 5.2.2 Pedagogical Strategies and Best Practices

Regular peer discussions contextualize AI-mediated learning by bringing diverse student perspectives into dialogue. Instructors model effective AI dialogue practices, making visible meta-cognitive processes. Text selection follows progressive complexity principles. Formative assessment emphasizes growth rather than mastery, creating conditions where students feel safe acknowledging uncertainty. Throughout, instructors maintain explicit focus on ethical dimensions of intercultural engagement and AI use.

### 5.2.3 Assessment Framework

The intervention employs multiple methods: pre-post quantitative measures (ISS and IRI) provide standardized data; weekly reflection journals offer qualitative evidence of developing awareness and skills; AI dialogue transcripts demonstrate students' developing competence; integrative essays synthesize intercultural competence, empathic capacity, and critical AI literacy; and participation in discussions recognizes that intercultural learning is inherently social. Assessment emphasizes growth and process, acknowledging that ICC and empathy develop over extended periods.

## 5.3 Theoretical Implications: Extending Models of Intercultural Competence and Empathy

The framework extends Byram's ICC model into AI-mediated contexts, demonstrating how digital tools can scaffold humanistic capacities. It illuminates how AI dialogue can serve as a preparatory space for human intercultural engagement, with lower stakes allowing students to develop foundational competencies before higher-stakes encounters. This extension aligns with calls for attention to digital mediation of intercultural encounters (O'Dowd, 2018; Helm, 2018) and recent scholarship emphasizing the role of virtual exchange in fostering communication for the digital age (Potolia & Derivry-Plard, 2023).

The framework also extends Davis's (1980) empathy model by foregrounding cultural dimensions. Effective empathy across cultural difference requires not only general capacities Davis identified but also cultural knowledge, awareness of how culture shapes emotional experience, and recognition of empathy's limits. This culturally informed extension has implications beyond literature education for intercultural psychology and cross-cultural counseling.

The framework contributes to theory on digital mediation of humanistic learning, challenging technological determinism by demonstrating how technology and humanism can be complementary when thoughtfully integrated. It theorizes a new role for algorithmic systems by positioning AI outputs as interpretive texts worthy of critical analysis, contributing to critical algorithm studies by demonstrating how humanistic interpretation methods can be applied to algorithmic outputs.

## 5.4 Pedagogical Implications: Designing and Implementing AI-Mediated Literature Learning

The framework demonstrates importance of structured scaffolding when introducing AI tools, as effective interaction requires skills students do not automatically possess. The consistent emphasis on reflection prevents passive consumption and cultivates active critical engagement. Integration of peer discussion alongside AI dialogue proves vital, as AI cannot replicate embodied cultural knowledge and relational dynamics. Assessment practices must evolve to evaluate complex, process-oriented learning through multiple methods emphasizing formative feedback.

These implications resonate with conversations in literature education about decentering traditional canons and interpretive authorities (Mignolo, 2011). As Patel (2016) argues, decolonial approaches require transforming interpretive practices to honor multiple epistemologies. AI integration, approached critically, can support transformation by making visible how interpretive authority operates.

The framework also has implications for instructor development, curricular design across multiple courses, and thoughtful text selection prioritizing works presenting cultural complexity and resisting easy generalization.

## 5.5 Ethical and Critical Dimensions: Responsible AI Integration in Humanities Education

Central ethical concerns include algorithmic bias, as large language models reflect biases in training data. The framework addresses this by making critical AI literacy explicit and teaching students to question AI outputs. However, instructors must remain vigilant about how biases manifest in specific contexts.

Related concerns involve whose knowledge AI represents, with training data overrepresenting certain regions and groups. The framework emphasizes AI provides one perspective requiring verification with other sources, particularly scholarship by cultural insiders. Recent work emphasizes need for participatory design involving end users (Costanza-Chock, 2020) and attention to how AI systems reproduce or challenge power structures.

The framework grapples with technological solutionism by explicitly positioning AI as supplement rather than substitute, maintaining substantial human interaction, and cultivating critical awareness. Questions of intellectual property arise when students use AI to generate content, addressed through documentation and citation requirements. Equity and access concerns require institutions to ensure all students can access AI tools. Environmental costs of AI systems warrant consideration in adoption decisions.

## 5.6 Effectiveness, Limitations, and Future Directions

The cross-sectional baseline design cannot establish causality or document developmental change. Future research implementing full intervention with pre-post assessment would provide crucial evidence about whether the framework produces intended outcomes, ideally with delayed post-tests examining persistence of gains.

The study's specific context—Turkish students engaging with Anglophone texts—shapes intercultural dynamics and AI-mediated learning affordances. Comparative research in different contexts would illuminate how context shapes outcomes. Reliance on self-report measures introduces limitations including social desirability bias; future research might complement with behavioral assessments.

The four-week duration may be insufficient for deep changes in ICC and empathy, which develop over extended periods. Future research examining longer interventions would provide insight into necessary duration and intensity. The study does not examine instructor experience or institutional conditions; research attending to teacher perspectives and institutional factors would help identify conditions enabling effective AI integration.

Additionally, this study did not explicitly control students' prior attitudes toward artificial intelligence. As user trust and 'algorithm aversion' can significantly influence interaction quality, future iterations of this research should include specific measures of AI acceptance as a potential moderating variable.

# 6. CONCLUSION AND FUTURE DIRECTIONS

This chapter has explored the intersection of artificial intelligence, intercultural learning, and literary education by proposing a theoretically grounded pedagogical framework for using AI chatbots as intercultural companions in literature classrooms. At a moment when AI technologies are rapidly becoming ubiquitous in students' lives yet remain largely unexamined in humanities pedagogy, this work contributes both conceptual clarity and practical guidance for literature educators seeking to harness AI's potential while maintaining fidelity to humanistic values.

The central argument advanced here is that AI chatbots, when integrated thoughtfully into literature pedagogy, can serve as valuable tools for developing students' intercultural communicative competence and empathy. This argument rests on several key insights that emerge from the theoretical synthesis and pedagogical framework presented in preceding sections. First, the dialogic nature of conversational AI aligns well with the conversational and exploratory processes central to intercultural learning. Unlike educational technologies that primarily deliver content or assess performance, AI chatbots can engage students in the kind of sustained, reflective dialogue that supports perspective-taking, cultural inquiry, and empathic imagination. Second, AI's capacity to articulate multiple cultural perspectives on demand provides scaffolding for students who are developing intercultural competence but lack the cultural knowledge or analytical frameworks to independently generate alternative interpretations. Third, when paired with critical reflection activities, AI dialogue can make visible the cultural assumptions embedded in interpretation itself, whether those interpretations are generated by humans or algorithms, thereby supporting the development of critical cultural awareness.

Crucially, this chapter has positioned AI not as replacement for human interaction or expertise but as supplementary tool that complements and prepares students for intercultural dialogue with actual people. The framework recognizes that intercultural competence and empathy ultimately develop through human relationships characterized by vulnerability, reciprocity, and ethical responsibility. AI chatbots lack lived cultural experience, embodied knowledge, and the relational qualities that make human dialogue transformative. What AI can offer, however, is a low-stakes conversational space where students practice perspective-taking, explore cultural contexts, test interpretations, and develop the meta-cognitive awareness necessary for productive intercultural engagement. By conceptualizing AI as catalyst and scaffold rather than authority or peer, the framework maintains humanistic commitments while embracing technological innovation.

The four-week intervention model detailed in this chapter provides a replicable structure for implementing AI-mediated intercultural learning across diverse institutional contexts. The model's progression from foundational cultural awareness through increasingly sophisticated analytical and empathic engagement reflects developmental principles drawn from both Byram's intercultural communicative competence framework and Davis's multidimensional model of empathy. By scaffolding students' development across cognitive, affective, and critical dimensions, the intervention ensures that AI dialogue serves multiple learning objectives simultaneously. Students develop cultural knowledge and interpretive skills while also cultivating openness, empathic concern, and critical awareness of both cultural and algorithmic dynamics.

Importantly, the framework integrates critical AI literacy as a core learning outcome rather than treating it as peripheral or instrumental concern. In an era when students already use AI tools extensively, often without critical frameworks for evaluation, literature classrooms have a responsibility to develop students' capacities for thoughtful engagement with these technologies. The intervention addresses this responsibility by positioning AI outputs as interpretive texts subject to the same critical analysis students apply to literary works. Students learn to ask whose perspectives AI centers and marginalizes, what cultural assumptions underlie AI-generated interpretations, where algorithmic outputs demonstrate genuine cultural insight versus stereotype, and how to verify and supplement AI-provided information. This dual focus on intercultural competence and critical AI literacy prepares students not only to read literature more thoughtfully but also to navigate a world where algorithmic systems increasingly mediate cultural knowledge and communication.

The baseline assessment component of this study, while modest in scope, provides essential groundwork for implementing the proposed intervention. Understanding students' existing levels of intercultural sensitivity and empathy allows educators to design activities appropriately calibrated to students' developmental needs. It also establishes a foundation for future research examining whether and how the intervention produces measurable changes in these capacities. The assessment data reveal important patterns regarding students' readiness for AI-mediated intercultural learning, including areas of relative strength and aspects requiring particular pedagogical attention. These insights inform not only the current intervention design but also broader questions about how literature education can more effectively cultivate intercultural and empathic capacities.

Looking forward, this work opens multiple directions for future research and pedagogical development. First, longitudinal studies tracking students' intercultural competence and empathy development over extended periods would provide insight into whether gains achieved through focused interventions like the one proposed here persist and transfer to other contexts. Such studies might examine whether students who participate in AI-mediated intercultural learning demonstrate sustained changes in how they approach culturally diverse texts, engage in intercultural dialogue, or navigate cultural difference in their broader lives.

Second, comparative research examining different approaches to AI integration in literature education would help refine understanding of what pedagogical strategies most effectively support intercultural and empathic learning. Questions worth exploring include how different intervention durations affect outcomes, whether certain types of literary texts prove more conducive to AI-mediated intercultural dialogue than others, how instructor facilitation strategies influence learning, and what role student characteristics such as prior intercultural experience or technological fluency play in shaping outcomes. Comparative designs might contrast AI-mediated approaches with traditional pedagogical methods or with alternative technological interventions to establish the specific value added by conversational AI.

Third, cross-cultural research implementing the framework in diverse educational contexts would illuminate how cultural setting shapes both the challenges and opportunities of AI-mediated intercultural learning. The current study takes place in Türkiye with students studying Anglophone literature, positioning students in particular intercultural relationships to the texts they read. How might the framework need adaptation for students in different cultural contexts, studying different literatures, or navigating different intercultural dynamics? Such research would both test the framework's generalizability and generate insights into how cultural context mediates learning processes.

Fourth, technological developments in AI systems themselves warrant ongoing attention. As conversational AI capabilities continue advancing, new affordances may emerge for supporting intercultural learning. Multimodal AI systems that integrate text, image, and voice might offer richer conversational experiences. AI systems with more sophisticated cultural knowledge bases or better capacity to recognize and mitigate bias might address some current limitations. Simultaneously, new concerns may arise requiring pedagogical responses. Continuous dialogue between educational practitioners, educational researchers, and AI developers will be essential for ensuring that technological evolution serves rather than undermines humanistic learning goals.

Fifth, research examining how AI-mediated intercultural learning transfers to actual intercultural interaction would address a critical question: does practicing perspective-taking and empathic engagement through AI dialogue translate to improved intercultural competence in human relationships? While the intervention includes peer discussions designed to bridge AI and human dialogue, empirical research tracking whether participants demonstrate enhanced intercultural skills in subsequent human interactions would strengthen claims about the intervention's ultimate value.

Beyond research directions, this work also points toward practical needs in teacher education and institutional support. Literature instructors require professional development opportunities to develop their own critical AI literacy, to learn effective prompting and facilitation strategies, and to navigate the ethical complexities of integrating AI into humanities teaching. Many instructors have received limited training in intercultural pedagogy generally and none in AI-mediated learning specifically. Workshops, teaching communities, and resources supporting instructors in implementing frameworks like the one proposed here would facilitate wider adoption and more effective practice.

Institutionally, educational leaders must grapple with policy questions about AI use in academic contexts. Rather than blanket prohibitions or uncritical embrace, institutions need nuanced policies that distinguish between AI uses that undermine learning and those that enhance it. The framework presented here offers one example of how AI can be integrated ethically and pedagogically soundly into humanities education. Institutional policies should create space for such innovative pedagogies while establishing guardrails against problematic uses. This requires ongoing dialogue among faculty, students, administrators, and educational technology specialists to develop shared understandings of AI's appropriate roles in higher education.

The broader contribution of this work lies in demonstrating that humanities education can engage thoughtfully and critically with emerging technologies without abandoning humanistic values or goals. There is sometimes tendency in humanities contexts to view technology as inherently opposed to humanistic inquiry or to approach technological developments with skepticism bordering on resistance. While critical skepticism is indeed warranted, particularly given well-documented concerns about algorithmic bias and the commercialization of educational technology, wholesale rejection risks ceding important pedagogical territory. The framework proposed here charts a middle path: embracing AI's affordances for supporting intercultural dialogue while maintaining critical awareness of its limitations and cultivating students' capacities to engage with these technologies thoughtfully.

As literature educators, our fundamental commitments remain unchanged by technological developments. We seek to help students become more thoughtful, empathic, and critically aware readers who can engage meaningfully with diverse texts and perspectives. We aim to cultivate capacities for cultural understanding, ethical reasoning, and humanistic inquiry. We value the distinctly human qualities of imagination, vulnerability, and relational connection that make literature transformative. The question facing us is not whether to use AI but how to shape its use in service of these enduring commitments. This chapter has argued that with appropriate pedagogical frameworks, critical awareness, and humanistic grounding, AI chatbots can become valuable companions in the essential work of intercultural and empathic learning through literature.

The title of this chapter, "Between Words and Worlds," captures the dual nature of the work we undertake in literature classrooms. We dwell between words on the page and the worlds they evoke, between the language we use to articulate understanding and the lived realities that language represents, between our own cultural worlds and those of others. AI chatbots now occupy space in this between as well—neither fully human nor simply tool, neither author nor reader, but conversational partners in the ongoing negotiation of meaning across difference. By learning to engage with these algorithmic companions thoughtfully and critically, students develop capacities that extend far beyond literature classrooms. They learn to navigate a complex cultural and technological landscape with curiosity, empathy, and critical awareness. They develop habits of questioning, reflecting, and revising understanding in light of new perspectives. They practice the difficult but essential work of recognizing both connection and difference across cultural boundaries. These are precisely the capacities our diverse, interconnected, technologically mediated world urgently needs.

Ultimately, this chapter addressed the pedagogical gap between passive reading of multicultural texts and active intercultural engagement. The proposed framework offers a concrete solution to this challenge by transforming the solitary act of reading into a dialogic encounter. By leveraging AI as a scaffold, the intervention effectively bridges the distance between the learner's world and the text's world, ensuring that empathy and cultural competence are not just abstract goals but practiced skills.

In conclusion, this chapter contributes to emerging scholarship on AI in humanities education by offering a theoretically grounded, pedagogically detailed, and ethically informed framework for using AI chatbots to support intercultural communicative competence and empathy development in literature learning. It demonstrates that thoughtful integration of AI can enhance rather than diminish the humanistic goals of literature education. It provides practical guidance for instructors seeking to implement AI-mediated intercultural learning in their own contexts. Furthermore, it points toward a vision of humanities pedagogy that embraces technological change while remaining rooted in enduring commitments to critical thinking, cultural understanding, and human flourishing. As we continue navigating the evolving landscape of AI in education, frameworks like the one proposed here can help ensure that technological innovation serves humanistic ends, that efficiency never substitutes for depth, and that in our engagement with artificial intelligence, we remember and honor what makes us most profoundly human.

## REFERENCES


Bakhtin, M. M. (1981). *The dialogic imagination: Four essays (M. Holquist* (Emerson, C., & Holquist, M. Eds. & Trans.). University of Texas Press.

Bender, E. M., Gebru, T., McMillan-Major, A., & Shmitchell, S. (2021). On the dangers of stochastic parrots: Can language models be too big? In *Proceedings of the 2021 ACM Conference on Fairness, Accountability, and Transparency* (pp. 610-623). Association for Computing Machinery. DOI: 10.1145/3442188.3445922

Bennett, M. J. (2004). Becoming interculturally competent. In Wurzel, J. S. (Ed.), *Toward multiculturalism: A reader in multicultural education* (2nd ed., pp. 62–77). Intercultural Resource Corporation.

Benson, P. (2011). *Teaching and Researching: Autonomy in Language Learning* (2nd ed.). Routledge., DOI: 10.4324/9781315833767

Byram, M. (1997). *Teaching and assessing intercultural communicative competence*. Multilingual Matters.

Byram, M. (2021). *Teaching and assessing intercultural communicative competence: Revisited* (2nd ed.). Multilingual Matters. DOI: 10.21832/9781800410251

Chen, G.-M., & Starosta, W. J. (2000). The development and validation of the Intercultural Sensitivity Scale. *Human Communication, 3*, 1–15.

Chiao, J. Y., & Mathur, V. A. (2010). Intergroup empathy: How does race affect empathic neural responses? *Current Biology, 20*(11), R478–R480. DOI: 10.1016/j.cub.2010.04.001 PMID: 20541493

Costanza-Chock, S. (2020). *Design justice: Community-led practices to build the worlds we need.* MIT Press. DOI: 10.7551/mitpress/12255.001.0001

Crawford, K. (2021). *Atlas of AI: Power, politics, and the planetary costs of artificial intelligence*. Yale University Press.

Davis, M. H. (1980). A multidimensional approach to individual differences in empathy. *Catalog of Selected Documents in Psychology, 10*, 85.

Davis, M. H. (1983). Measuring individual differences in empathy: Evidence for a multidimensional approach. *Journal of Personality and Social Psychology, 44*(1), 113–126. DOI: 10.1037/0022-3514.44.1.113

Deardorff, D. K. (2006). Identification and assessment of intercultural competence as a student outcome of internationalization. *Journal of Studies in International Education, 10*(3), 241–266. DOI: 10.1177/1028315306287002

Decety, J., & Jackson, P. L. (2004). The functional architecture of human empathy. *Behavioral and Cognitive Neuroscience Reviews, 3*(2), 71–100. DOI: 10.1177/1534582304267187 PMID: 15537986

Dornyei, Z. (2009). The L2 Motivational Self System. In Dornyei, Z., & Ushioda, E. (Eds.), *Motivation, Language Identity and the L2 Self.* Multilingual Matters. DOI: 10.21832/9781847691293-003

Eubanks, V. (2018). *Automating inequality: How high-tech tools profile, police, and punish the poor.* St. Martin's Press.

Guilherme, M. (2002). *Critical citizens for an intercultural world: Foreign language education as cultural politics.* Multilingual Matters.

Helm, F. (2018). *Emerging identities in virtual exchange.* Research-publishing.net.

Holmes, W., Bialik, M., & Fadel, C. (2019). *Artificial intelligence in education: Promises and implications for teaching and learning.* Center for Curriculum Redesign.

Keen, S. (2007). *Empathy and the novel.* Oxford University Press. DOI: 10.1093/acprof:oso/9780195175769.001.0001

Kidd, D. C., & Castano, E. (2013). Reading literary fiction improves theory of mind. *Science, 342*(6156), 377–380. DOI: 10.1126/science.1239918 PMID: 24091705

Klimova, B., & Chen, J. H. (2024). The impact of AI on enhancing students' intercultural communication competence at the university level: A review study. *Language Teaching Research Quarterly, 43*, 102–120. DOI: 10.32038/ltrq.2024.43.06

Kramsch, C. (2009). *The multilingual subject.* Oxford University Press.

Laquintano T, Vee A. AI and the Everyday Writer. *PMLA/Publications of the Modern Language Association of America.* 2024;139(3):527-532. DOI: 10.1632/S0030812924000609

Luckin, R., Holmes, W., Griffiths, M., & Forcier, L. B. (2016). *Intelligence unleashed: An argument for AI in education.* Pearson.

Mar, R. A., & Oatley, K. (2008). The function of fiction is the abstraction and simulation of social experience. *Perspectives on Psychological Science, 3*(3), 173–192. DOI: 10.1111/j.1745-6924.2008.00073.x PMID: 26158934

Mignolo, W. (2011). *The darker side of Western modernity: Global futures, decolonial options*. Duke University Press.

Nussbaum, M. C. (1995). *Poetic justice: The literary imagination and public life*. Beacon Press.

O'Dowd, R. (2018). From telecollaboration to virtual exchange: State-of-the-art and the role of UNICollaboration in moving forward. *Journal of Virtual Exchange, 1*, 1–23. DOI: 10.14705/rpnet.2018.jve.1

O'Neil, C. (2016). *Weapons of math destruction: How big data increases inequality and threatens democracy*. Crown.

Pangrazio, L., & Selwyn, N. (2019). 'Personal data literacies': A critical literacies approach to enhancing understandings of personal digital data. *New Media & Society, 21*(2), 419–437. DOI: 10.1177/1461444818799523

Patel, L. (2016). *Decolonizing educational research: From ownership to answerability*. Routledge.

Potolia, A., & Derivry-Plard, M. (Eds.). (2023). *Virtual exchange for intercultural language learning and teaching: Fostering communication for the digital age*. Routledge.

# Chapter 10
# AI-Supported Telecollaboration for Promoting Intercultural Communicative Competence

**Saliha Toscu**
http://orcid.org/0000-0002-8179-5444
*Çankaya University, Turkey*

## ABSTRACT

*Artificial Intelligence offers modern pedagogical innovations by supporting telecollaboration to develop language skills in authentic contexts. This chapter aims to give insights regarding how AI-supported telecollaboration fosters Intercultural Communicative Competence, grounded in a theoretical framework based on recognized ICC models. The chapter addresses the synergy between telecollaboration and AI, discussing how telecollaboration facilitates authentic interaction while AI helps overcome linguistic/cultural barriers, provides personalized feedback, and supports learner autonomy. The chapter also addresses ethical and pedagogical challenges and outlines implications for both learners and teachers, offering specific pedagogical considerations for integrating AI effectively. The chapter emphasizes the importance of an integrated approach to authentic communication experiences, demonstrating how AI-enhanced tools can fundamentally enrich intercultural education.*

DOI: 10.4018/979-8-3373-6325-7.ch010

## INTRODUCTION

In today's interconnected world, English serves as a lingua franca, which is a crucial medium of communication. Speaking English today involves engaging with interlocutors with diverse cultural backgrounds (Alptekin, 2002). Hence, the emphasis on native-like proficiency has already been replaced by a focus on developing intercultural competence in language education (Alptekin, 2002). As technology advances, the boundaries of the classroom are expanding, allowing speakers of English to communicate with one another, which in turn helps them improve their foreign language and intercultural communicative competence (ICC) (Byram, 1997; McComb, 1994; Simpson, 2002).

Telecollaboration, which is a dialogic process that supports geographically distant collaborative work, intercultural exchange, and social interaction through communication tools, has long been recognized as an effective means of promoting intercultural dialogue (Dooly, 2016; Kramsch, 2013; O'Dowd, 2011). Telecollaboration is considered an effective tool for fostering intercultural competence, providing EFL learners with authentic opportunities to communicate with individuals from varied linguistic and cultural backgrounds (O'Dowd, 2011). As Corbett (2003) and Byram (2008) argue, computers constitute an essential component of intercultural learning. Telecollaboration projects are considered essential for fostering intercultural dialogue, as they offer learners the opportunity to connect with peers from diverse cultural backgrounds through guided activities (Anikina et al., 2015). Depending on the objectives and participants, such projects can contribute to teachers' professional growth and support students in developing language skills, technological competence, and intercultural awareness. Because they promote genuine communication with native speakers, telecollaboration initiatives are particularly well-suited for enhancing intercultural competence (Anikina et al., 2015).

The advancements in technology have also led to the development of Artificial Intelligence (AI) tools. As a result of advancements in deep learning and intelligent neural networks, AI has been integrated into various aspects of social life, including speech recognition, financial markets, education, and training (Yang et al., 2024). The use of AI in language education enhances real-time interaction, provides feedback, improves linguistic accuracy, and cultural understanding for effective communication (Xia et al., 2024). AI technologies have the potential to transform traditional pedagogy in language classrooms, offering an authentic and creative language-learning experience. Therefore, it is essential to integrate AI technologies to redefine educational strategies and make learning more engaging and personalized (Yeh, 2024). Generative AI (GenAI) is particularly significant in education due to its potential to enhance the study of teaching and learning (Wang & Chen, 2025; Yu & Guo, 2023). It generates new forms of data, such as images, music, and text, by utilizing machine learning and deep learning (Yu & Guo, 2023). Its advantages, such as content generation, delivery of individualized learning opportunities, evaluation, feedback, and an adaptive educational system, make GenAI effective in yielding efficient learning outcomes (Wang & Chen, 2025). As explained by Wang and Chen (2025), the application of generative AI in education encompasses the automatic generation of content, the provision of individualized learning opportunities, and the provision of evaluation and feedback. Artificial intelligence and virtual technologies have the potential to be effectively utilized in cross-cultural communication, enhancing cultural awareness and experiences, and thereby facilitating a deeper understanding of different cultures (Yang et al., 2024). GenAI can be effective for cross-cultural education through online education environments and virtual reality technology by bringing students from diverse countries together and engaging them in communication, thereby enhancing their cultural skills (Yu & Guo, 2023). Therefore, integrating GenAI into online education or virtual exchange is valuable for educational purposes, as it enables authentic intercultural communication and skill development.

## THE CONTRIBUTION OF THE CHAPTER

This chapter explores the integration of AI-supported telecollaboration into education as a pedagogical innovation that promotes intercultural communicative competence and language skills. Based on ICC frameworks (Byram, 199; Deardorff, 2006), the chapter contributes to the current knowledge of telecollaboration and ICC development by extending the pedagogical potential of telecollaboration practices enhanced by emerging AI technologies. One key contribution of the current chapter is its connection of theoretical perspectives on ICC with concrete pedagogical applications of AI-supported telecollaboration practices. The chapter readdresses telecollaboration as a practice enhanced by AI technologies, enabling deeper cultural understanding (Angelova & Zhao, 2016; Belz, 2007), increasing confidence by reducing speaking anxiety (Chen & Sevilla-Pavón, 2023), and increasing motivation (Csizér & Kormos, 2009; Ueki & Takeuchi, 2013).

In addition, the chapter gives insights into the practical applications that can be benefited from before, during, and after AI-enhanced telecollaboration activities, such as intercultural simulations (Godwin-Jones, 2025), role-play activities (Chen & Sevilla-Pavón, 2023), and facilitating reflections (McCallum, 2024; Tang et al., 2025). As a result, the chapter provides an understanding of how AI can be used as a tool that supports meaningful intercultural communication between people across cultures. By adopting a critical perspective, the chapter also addresses challenges of AI-enhanced telecollaboration, including failure to give cultural and pragmatic discrepancies (Grab, 2025; Klimova & Chen, 2024), lack of training (Dai & Hua, 2024) and ethical considerations regarding the use of AI in telecollaboration, such as insufficient technical skills (Bueno-Alastuey & Kleban, 2016), uneven access to resources (Farrelly & Baker, 2023), and data security (Lamy & Hampel, 2007).

Furthermore, the chapter presents insights regarding the implications of AI-supported telecollaboration for learners and teachers in intercultural exchange, such as increasing learners' awareness of cultural similarities and differences (You et al., 2025), changing the attitudes towards people from different cultures through authentic communication (Klimova & Chen, 2024; Wang & Chen, 2025). Thus, the changing roles of learners and teachers in intercultural exchanges are highlighted in the chapter through the presentation of future research directions and pedagogical implementation of AI technologies into education. Overall, the chapter contributes to the field by providing an understanding of how theory, pedagogy, and technology are combined and by guiding telecollaboration practitioners and researchers in integrating telecollaboration practices enhanced and supported by AI tools into language education to improve ICC.

## THEORETICAL BACKGROUND

This section presents the theoretical background of ICC by reviewing its models and examining its development through telecollaboration. Furthermore, the section details how AI is integrated into telecollaboration practices to facilitate intercultural competence.

### An Overview of Intercultural Communicative Competence

With the influence of the communicative approach, the concept of culture in language learning shifted to emphasizing everyday life and shared experiences (Kramsch, 2013), while native-speaker norms and culture persisted (Byram et al., 2013). Nevertheless, the rise of English as a global language has brought a more international and intercultural perspective on language learning (Alptekin, 2002). In today's increasingly diverse and multicultural societies, engaging with people from different cultures is crucial for navigating personal, social, and professional lives effectively, as communication is a fundamental aspect of human life and intercultural communication is particularly important and indispensable (Sarwari et al., 2024).

Intercultural Communicative Competence is the capacity to engage in effective and appropriate communication with people from different cultural backgrounds, grounded in one's knowledge, skills, and attitudes (Deardorff, 2006). To develop ICC, individuals' attitudes play a crucial role; namely, they need to be open to other cultures, show respect for different perspectives, demonstrate a willingness to learn about others, and have an understanding of diverse worldviews (Byram, 1997). Intercultural competence encompasses diverse models, falling into five categories (Deardorff, 2009):

## Compositional and Co-orientational Models

Compositional models identify the key traits that interculturally competent speakers should possess without explaining their interrelationships (Deardorff, 2009). Deardorff's (2006) Pyramid Model of Intercultural Competence conceptualizes intercultural competence as progressing from essential attitudes, such as respect, openness, and curiosity, to cultural comprehension and cognitive abilities, such as observing, interpreting, and relating (Deardorff, 2006). The intercultural understanding in co-orientational models, in contrast, is based on interaction (Deardorff, 2009). Byram's (1997) Intercultural Competence Model, which explains that the ultimate goal of foreign language education should be the development of intercultural speaking competencies, is a representative model for this category. Byram (1997) explains that ICC is a combination of attitudes, knowledge, skills, and critical cultural awareness. All of these components help individuals develop an intercultural identity and engage in intercultural communication effectively for a mutual interpretation between interlocutors (Byram, 1997; Byram et al., 2002), although it has been criticized for the lack of an explicit focus on the developmental process of intercultural competence (Navaitienė et al., 2015).

## Developmental and Adaptation Models

Developmental models focus on the process-oriented nature of intercultural competence by emphasizing that intercultural understanding develops gradually as individuals engage in communication (Deardorff, 2009). Bennett's (1993) Developmental Model of Intercultural Sensitivity includes a shift from denial and defense to acceptance and integration. According to this model, people initially view their own culture as superior to others, but later they recognize and appreciate other cultures, adapting to cultural differences (Bennett, 1993). Deardorff's (2006) Process Model of Intercultural Competence highlights that intercultural competence (ICC) develops continuously over time. Deardorff (2011) explains that internal changes in an individual's knowledge, attitudes, and skills result in external outcomes reflected in one's behavior and communication in intercultural situations, which leads to greater adaptability to new cultural settings. Adaptation models address the transformation of a person's worldview from an ethnocentric to an ethnorelative perspective (Navaitienė et al., 2015). Berry's (1992) model of acculturation categorizes adaptation strategies (assimilation, separation, integration, and marginalization) into two groups: maintaining one's original cultural identity and adapting to the host culture.

### Causal Models

Causal process models display cause-and-effect relationships by explaining how different components influence one another (Navaitienė et al., 2015). Arasaratnam and Banerjee (2011) examined the causal process model of ICC. Accordingly, intercultural communicative competence is positively associated with sensation seeking, together with other variables, and their study indicated that this relationship is influenced by motivation and a positive attitude toward people from different cultures.

Taken together, intercultural education seeks to help individuals adopt attitudes that are receptive to different ideas and cultures, be aware of their own and others' cultures, question ideas, and make reasonable judgements, thereby helping them recognize diversity and benefit from communication with people from other cultures (Council of Europe, 2016). As a result, developing intercultural skills is a necessity emerging as a response to reach higher education standards, the goal of which is to improve the quality of education and increase learners' academic achievement, and enhance the shared values and goals in the society (Council of Europe, 2016). Upon the advancements in technology, its use in education has encouraged more utility of the Internet, smart phones for collective tasks and software to boost the effectiveness of the class materials (British Council, 2015). As one of the assets of technological developments, telecollaboration stands out to be valuable to receive authentic input, and engage learners in meaningful interaction with people living in distant locations and having distinct cultural backgrounds (O'Dowd, 2011).

## Telecollaboration and ICC development

Telecollaboration, which is described with different terminologies, such as "*online intercultural exchange, virtual exchange, collaborative online international learning*" (O'Dowd, 2015, p.63), refers to an interactive process that enables individuals in different locations to engage in cooperative tasks, intercultural communication, and social interaction through both real-time and delayed digital communication tools, to achieve shared goals and generate collective knowledge (Dooly, 2016). Telecollaboration projects are essential for promoting intercultural dialogue, as they enable students to interact with peers from diverse cultural backgrounds through guided tasks (Anikina et al., 2015). Telecollaboration offers valuable opportunities for teachers and students to engage in new global experiences, fostering effective intercultural communication and making it a powerful tool for bringing people from diverse cultures together (Sladovníková, 2020). With the introduction of personal computers and the Internet, the opportunity to communicate with people who live far away has increased significantly, enabling people to move more freely and with greater flexibility (Akayoğlu et al., 2021). Meanwhile, it enhances teachers' instructional skills and students' language proficiency, digital literacy, and intercultural competence through authentic communication experiences (Anikina et al., 2015).

Telecollaboration projects facilitate easy contact with people speaking different languages. As learners interact with one another, their communication abilities and cultural understanding develop, which positively reflects on their cultural awareness by helping them explore different cultures and enabling them to reflect on their own culture from an outside perspective (Kern, 2006). Kern et al. (2004) emphasize that engaging in online interactions alone does not necessarily lead to intercultural competence. Accordingly, innovative pedagogical designs that use literature, email exchanges, and digital platforms such as CULTURA have the potential to promote ICC and mutual understanding (Kern et al., 2004). Hence, traditional teacher-centered instruction can be replaced with a learner-centered, reflective approach to language and culture learning (Kern et al., 2004). Different classroom strategies and materials, such as collaborative role-plays (Woragwong et al., 2017), intercultural tasks, songs (Shayakhmetova et al., 2017), and literary texts (Gomez, 2012), can be integrated in foreign language education to improve intercultural competence through telecollaboration.

Virtual exchange methods have been a part of foreign language education since the advent of the Internet, evolving from the early e-tandem model, which focused on learner autonomy and language practice, to the more recent intercultural collaboration model, which emphasizes intercultural communication, online interaction, and teacher-guided projects (Sladovníková, 2020). While e-tandem models primarily focus on developing linguistic competence, CULTURA models, based on the CULTURA project by Furstenberg et al. (2001), aim to promote intercultural understanding among learners from different cultures by providing opportunities to share and discuss cultural materials online. Hence, it is an interactive and constructivist model that enables learners to explore others' attitudes and beliefs (Furstenberg et al., 2001). Generally speaking, virtual exchange models have evolved to shift from language-focused interaction to global interaction, encompassing intercultural awareness and mutual understanding.

Kern et al. (2004) explain that the primary benefit of telecollaboration projects is the development of intercultural competence, emphasizing that research shifted from classroom-based language learning to studies focusing on intercultural interaction, cultural learning, and cultural literacy. You et al. (2025) posit that the interactive processes in telecollaboration help arouse students' curiosity about the target culture and foster recognition and respect for cultural differences. Interacting with English speakers from diverse parts of the world encourages learners' open-mindedness toward other cultures and increases their curiosity about them (Liu et al., 2025).

Additionally, Liu et al. (2025) assert that virtual environments established through telecollaboration can reduce learners' anxiety and foster positive attitudes and perceptions toward online intercultural communication. They attribute this outcome to the user-friendly design of the online platform, which has enabled learners to easily find suitable partners for their telecollaborative tasks. Likewise, Jin and Erben (2007) explain that foreign language learners' intercultural awareness is enhanced through telecollaboration and fosters more respectful attitudes towards different cultures. In addition, Turula et al. (2025) emphasize the potential of telecollaboration projects to foster social interaction and critical thinking in online intercultural exchanges, underscoring the importance of integrating both asynchronous and synchronous communication tools.

## Artificial Intelligence in Telecollaboration for Developing ICC

AI significantly enhances telecollaboration by improving communication, reducing misunderstandings, and providing personalized feedback, thereby enhancing learners' overall linguistic and cultural experience (Sarwari et al., 2024). In particular, AI helps learners overcome language and cultural barriers, by this means preventing miscommunication and facilitating smoother intercultural dialogue. AI technologies also provide authentic exposure to different cultural norms and practices by assisting learners in engaging in real-time intercultural communication, revising and modifying their language, and benefiting from AI-generated feedback (Ma & Yang, 2025).

AI tools are also considered non-judgmental conversation partners. This is particularly important when exploring sensitive cultural topics, such as religion and gender. Students may not always feel comfortable discussing these issues with their peers, but AI tools in intercultural contexts provide a safe space for learners (Hastomo et al., 2025; Ma & Yang, 2025). In line with this, research has noted the positive effects of AI bots on demonstrating respect for cultural diversity and increased attentiveness during interactions (Chang, 2023).

Moreover, AI-supported simulations and virtual exchanges encourage learners to reconsider stereotypes and biases, fostering self-reflection and developing intercultural competencies (Klimova & Chen, 2024). AI can facilitate progress in intercultural sensitivity, as described in Bennett's (1993) model, through simulations, telecollaboration tasks, and personalized learning experiences that help students adopt a mindset that is based on accepting and understanding cultural differences without bias rather than evaluating other cultures according to the assumptions in one's own culture (Klimova & Chen, 2024, p. 105).

The integration of AI into education has brought benefits ranging from personalized learning opportunities to increased intercultural awareness. This section presents how those benefits could be relevant to ICC development in telecollaboration practices. Figure 1 indicates the contribution of AI tools to the users who are engaged in telecollaboration practices.

*Figure 1. The contribution of AI-enhanced telecollaboration to ICC development*

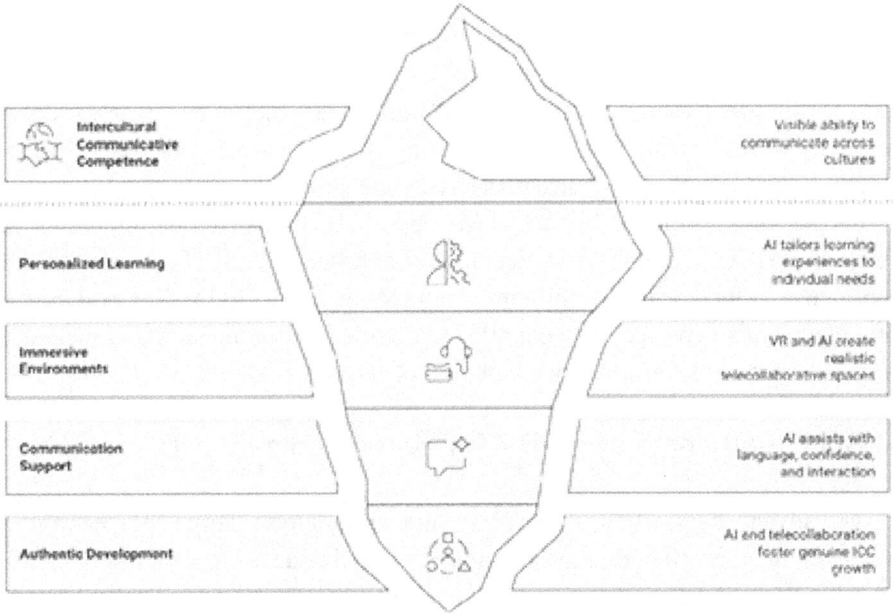


As Figure 1 shows, the values of AI integration into telecollaboration practices are categorized under the subheadings: AI-enhanced personalized and adaptive learning, AI-supported immersive VR/AR environments for ICC, AI for communication support, and incorporation of AI into telecollaboration for authentic ICC development, each of which is detailed in the following section.

## AI-Enhanced Personalized and Adaptive Learning in Telecollaboration

Artificial Intelligence (AI), which has recently become an integral part of every facet of life, including education, is also playing a significant role in telecollaboration by enhancing intercultural communication through adaptive AI tools. The integration of AI technologies in education has become a transformative trend, making educational platforms more effective and efficient by modifying them according to students' learning needs (Kuleto et al., 2021).

In this regard, AI can enhance education by providing personalized learning, language support, and feedback on students' work, thereby assisting students improve their language skills and performance (Wang et al., 2023). It offers students a tailored learning experience, enabling teachers to understand diverse learning styles and adapt their teaching methods to better support students (Kuleto et al., 2021). Likewise, adaptive learning technologies personalize education by adjusting content, pace, and difficulty based on learners' needs and performance in language learning (Xia et al., 2024). These technologies utilize AI to tailor culturally embedded language tasks, helping learners understand cultural norms and practice real-world scenarios, gradually increasing difficulty and enhancing cross-cultural interactions (Xia et al., 2024). As a result, they help learners to become active receivers of information.

Furthermore, studies highlight that AI-supported personalized learning contributes positively to ICC. Through AI, students can be exposed to cultural scenarios and build confidence in intercultural communication (Ma & Yang, 2025). Telecollaboration strengthens this experience by enabling authentic communication and meaningful language practice supported by adaptive tools (Mont et al., 2025).

## AI-Supported Immersive VR/AR Environments for ICC

The advances in virtual reality (VR) and augmented reality (AR) technologies are changing game, health, tourism industries, and education (Abbasi et al., 2024). They facilitate immersive experiences by uniting digital content with virtual settings (Abbasi et al., 2024). AI-enhanced VR and AR environments further support ICC development in telecollaboration. AI-supported immersive VR presents opportunities for multimodal social and cultural communication through VR simulations and role-playing (Godwin-Jones, 2025). Thus, learners can engage in authentic interactions in simulated environments, which is highly relevant for getting ready and rehearsing for real-life telecollaboration practices.

Virtual reality and augmented reality technologies also provide immersive learning opportunities by enabling learners to hear authentic pronunciations and experience the target culture through applications such as ImmerseMe and Virtual Reality Language Learning (Cheng, 2025). Such experiences enable students to use the target language in actual cultural settings, thereby enhancing their confidence in communication (Cheng, 2025).

The combination of immersive 3D environments and multimodal AI is crucial because it offers learners adaptive, personalized, and collaborative learning prospects (Godwin-Jones, 2025). However, Godwin-Jones (2025) highlights that privacy and ethical issues should be considered in AI-driven virtual reality environments.

These issues are important because their absence can negatively affect the quality and authenticity of intercultural communication.

## AI as Support for Communication in Telecollaboration

AI can support telecollaborative communication by enhancing interaction quality and enabling meaningful exchanges between practitioners. Technology-enhanced project-based learning through telecollaboration helps incorporate digital tools into collaborative activities, which makes it possible for students to engage in authentic communication (Mont et al., 2025). By interacting with AI-enhanced platforms, students can develop authentic communication skills and experience natural, contextually meaningful language learning (Mont et al., 2025).

AI chatbots also help learners overcome limitations such as limited class time, studying in a crowded classroom, or a lack of a speaking partner or a teacher (Romadhon & Yulianti, 2025). Chatbots offer various benefits for learners, such as enhancing vocabulary and improving grammatical accuracy, and allow learners to practice pronunciation and fluency independently (Grab, 2025; Khasawneh, 2023). In addition, thanks to the personalized, immediate, and non-judgmental feedback which AI chatbots provide, learners' motivation and confidence increase, and thus, learners prepare for real-life telecollaboration practices more effectively (Dooly, 2022; Grab, 2025).

AI tools can be also used in asynchronous telecollaboration practices and yield effective results for the users by increasing their interest and commitment (Lee et al., 2024). When integrated into online discussions, AI tools such as ChatGPT promote learners' involvement and provide more active participation (Lin et al., 2024). This is because learners critically examine the texts which AI generates, evaluate their credibility, and explore the uncertainties or partialities they may contain. Such activities stimulate critical thinking while also expanding intercultural understanding (Lin et al., 2024; You et al., 2025).

In addition, telecollaborative activities that AI tools enhance can foster meaning negotiation, a central aspect of language learning (Yamo & Sutin, 2024). Such activities positively impact learners' autonomy by providing prompt responses and assistance (Yeşil, 2025). Through ongoing, autonomous intercultural exchanges, learners' intercultural sensitivity improves, particularly in terms of interaction, enjoyment, and confidence (You et al., 2025).

## Combining AI and Telecollaboration for Authentic ICC Development

Telecollaboration fosters cultural awareness (Katsumata & Guo, 2020), teamwork, digital literacy (Hauck et al., 2025), problem-solving, and critical thinking skills

(Saricaoglu, 2021). Extending the discussion of AI in education to telecollaborative ICC development, research indicates that combining AI with human interaction has a positive effect on language learning and enhances its effectiveness (Mont et al., 2025). Through collaborative negotiation and discussion, students gain a deeper understanding of global perspectives (Mont et al., 2025).

When AI tools and telecollaboration are combined, learners benefit from real-time conversations with native speakers, AI-generated guidance, and adaptive learning experiences. These interactions promote authentic communication and support language acquisition in meaningful, context-rich situations (Mont et al., 2025). AI-supported learning and telecollaboration both aim for authentic learning—developing relevant, engaging, and real-world communication skills that are central to ICC development (Dooly, 2022; Grab, 2025; Mont et al., 2025).

## IMPLICATIONS FOR LEARNERS AND TEACHERS

The incorporation of AI technologies and telecollaboration into language education is renovating teaching and learning practices. On the one hand, these technologies are beneficial for learners because they enable learners to communicate authentically, reflect critically, and engage in intercultural dialogue. On the other hand, such technologies contribute to teachers' instructional processes by challenging them to integrate technology responsibly, facilitate cultural understanding, and constantly adapt their educational strategies. This section outlines the key implications for learners and teachers by presenting how AI-enhanced telecollaboration can foster ICC and pedagogical transformation.

### Implications for Learners

AI-supported telecollaboration presents various implications for learners. To begin with, it enhances intercultural awareness and sensitivity (You et al., 2025). Thanks to AI-supported environments and telecollaboration activities, learners have the opportunity to interact authentically with peers from diverse cultures and countries, which helps to develop open-mindedness, empathy, and intercultural sensitivity (Byram, 1997; Bennett, 1993; Klimova & Chen, 2024). Hence, AI-enhanced telecollaboration activities enable learners to move from a monocultural to a multicultural perspective (Navaitienė et al., 2015).

Learners benefit from exposure to real-world contexts through intercultural dialogues (Xia et al., 2024), which leads students to improve their communicative competence, motivation, and confidence in interacting in intercultural settings. Moreover, integrating telecollaboration activities with AI technologies helps to develop autonomous learning. To illustrate, Wang and Chen (2025) and Xia et al. (2024) note that AI tools provide individualized feedback, enabling real-time interaction, which fosters learner autonomy and reflection on both linguistic and cultural aspects of communication. In addition, AI-supported telecollaboration improves students' language proficiency and technological adaptability (Anikina et al., 2015; Mont et al., 2025). Thus, AI technologies such as translation tools and virtual platforms enable students to gain experience in developing their language and technology skills.

## Implications for Teachers

The integration and adaptation of diverse teaching models, along with the use of AI and other emerging technologies, are crucial for educators to enhance students' communication, collaboration, and practice in multicultural environments (Cheng, 2025). In addition, Godwin-Jones (2025) explains that AI and VR have the potential to enhance education; however, they do not undervalue teachers' roles, as they should provide active guidance and mentoring in the use of technology. Godwin-Jones (2025) defines language teachers as "informed consumers of AI" who guide students in using AI properly (p. 238). Building on these ideas, Dooly (2022) underscores that with the advancements in AI technology and its integration into education, teachers are required to prepare their students to adapt to this new system by helping them to develop new communication competencies for interacting effectively with non-human agents, specifically bots, avatars, and AI-supported assistants, besides their human partners. Undoubtedly, AI-supported education redefines teachers' roles (Meylani, 2024). Teachers' traditional roles in the classroom have been replaced with roles that facilitate understanding, communication, and collaboration among learners (Almegren et al., 2025). Teachers also support and guide students in their learning process regarding the use of AI technologies (Chang, 2023).

The redefined role of teachers requires them to develop AI literacy, which involves understanding how to design prompts, evaluate outputs, and consider ethical issues while effectively integrating AI into telecollaboration projects (McCallum, 2024). This can be effectively developed through teacher training programs that include practical guidance on using AI tools, such as ChatGPT, translation tools, and adaptive learning systems. When teachers are equipped with the skills to critically evaluate AI-produced content and to design AI-supported tasks, they can enhance their teaching practices and learner engagement. Anikina et al. (2015) emphasize that engagement with AI and telecollaboration practices provides teachers with opportunities for continuous professional development. Thus, teachers become a part of a global professional network.

Another implication derived from the research regarding AI tools and telecollaboration relates to ethical and equity issues. Teachers are supposed to ensure fair access to AI technologies and be aware of socio-economic disparities in AI tool availability (Farrelly & Baker, 2023). They are expected to adopt practices that utilize alternative resources or engage in collaborative activities to promote equity in AI-assisted learning environments. Additionally, teachers should take responsibility for fostering students' ethical awareness regarding the potential issues that data bias and privacy concerns may cause. Therefore, they should help their learners become more reflective and responsible in their use of technology.

In summary, AI-supported telecollaboration presents opportunities for both learners and teachers. While learners experience authentic, culturally relevant, and personalized learning, teachers redefine their roles to create ethical and intercultural classrooms. These technologies, overall, enhance ICC and promote adaptive and more reflective teaching and learning experiences.

## Ideas for Practical Applications

This section offers some implementations of AI that could be employed in telecollaboration in practice. AI tools can be used before, during, and after telecollaboration activities. Namely, AI tools can be beneficial before telecollaboration practices for translation (Klimova & Chen, 2024; Tahara, 2024), role-playing (Godwin-Jones, 2023), and simulation of real-life cultural encounters, and for enhancing cultural understanding (Chen & Sevilla-Pavón, 2023). While collaborating in an online intercultural exchange, AI functions as a live resource and visual or immersive mediator. Finally, AI enables increasing cultural awareness by fostering reflection through the analysis of transcripts and feedback (McCallum, 2024). Some ideas on how to use AI tools at each step, pre, during, and post, are detailed in the following section.

### Pre-Telecollaboration

One of the contributions of AI advancements is to translation and cross-cultural dialogue (Tahara, 2024). AI translation is opening a new space for intercultural interaction by eliminating language barriers in language exchanges (Busch, 2025). Accordingly, when GenAI is involved in translation, the tool is not merely for word substitution; it actively supports dialogue and creates new meaning (Tahara, 2024). To illustrate, when learners from different countries worked on a literary text via ChatGPT-4, ChatGPT could enhance a diffractive process, yielding interpretations with diverse perspectives and cultural understandings (Tahara, 2024). Thus, partners in an intercultural exchange can negotiate meaning with each other and adopt an understanding accepting the other cultures, which is directly related to the attitude and knowledge dimensions of ICC.

The practical applications of AI-supported translation tools, such as Google Translate, DeepL, and AI-based language models, can allow learners speaking different languages to communicate smoothly (Klimova & Chen, 2024); however, the use of such tools requires a critical pedagogical approach, which enables learners to edit a text and reflect on it critically. Namely, a learner should be able to review AI-generated translations for cultural appropriateness and assess whether they convey the intended tone and meaning, thereby developing critical cultural awareness (Byram, 1997).

In addition to translation, AI serves as a safe space for pragmatic practice before learners are engaged in real intercultural encounters (Godwin-Jones, 2023). By means of programs such as SimCon or role-playing with AI bots, users experience pragmatic norms and appropriateness in simulations (Godwin-Jones, 2023). Thus, students can practice making pragmatic choices about what is appropriate to say in specific situations before they enter a real virtual exchange. Such a practice might enable learners to prepare for intercultural collaboration through videoconferencing, thereby compensating for the drawbacks of role-playing with AI agents that lack semiotic resources (Godwin-Jones, 2023). Even though AI cannot communicate using semiotic resources like humans, it still opens new directions for research, education, and the teaching of language and intercultural communication.

The primary use of AI, such as ChatGPT and Gemini, in telecollaboration could involve using it as a cultural resource to quickly obtain information on culture, norms, and appropriate manners (Hastomo et al., 2025). As learners become accustomed to AI tools, they employ them more effectively through "iterative prompting", which can help deepen their cultural understanding by progressing from surface-level information to deeper understanding (Hastomo et al., 2025, p. 12). By making the context more specific with iterative questioning, learners can adopt cultural understandings (Hastomo et al., 2025). In a virtual exchange, AI can mediate for learners to practice culturally acceptable norms and manners before they genuinely engage in intercultural contact.

## During Telecollaboration

During a telecollaboration activity, AI-supported tools can also foster cultural exploration. Godwin-Jones (2023), for example, highlights the use of digital maps for learning about a particular local area and its culture in a virtual exchange. Digital maps are dynamic images with interfaces that can design and explain themselves thanks to the effects of GenAI (Kang & Wang, 2025). Such maps can be used in telecollaboration activities in which learners collaborating with a partner from a different culture can use them to create narratives together and share media and history specific to their local cultures (Godwin-Jones, 2023). Thus, such an activity can serve as a basis for exploring each other's cultures and histories.

Furthermore, immersive technologies such as VR have a value in teaching culture as they make real-life experiences possible for increasing cultural awareness and turn learning environments into interactive settings (Tafazoli, 2024). Immersive VR technologies can be integrated into virtual exchanges by moving communication beyond chat between people from different cultures (Chen & Sevilla-Pavón, 2023). Platforms such as Spatial, for example, are based on GenAI and enable 3D environments where learners from different cultures exchange information and role-play the given scenarios via avatars (Chen & Sevilla-Pavón, 2023). For example, Chen and Sevilla-Pavón (2023) explain that participants can meet in a virtual room with their 3D avatars, reflect on their behaviors, mimic, and introduce themselves by acting out a scenario, such as being an international student. Such scenarios, based on exploring cultural differences, can enhance online interactions through immersive technologies, enabling learners to engage with greater empathy and reduced anxiety and preparing them for life outside the school (Chen & Sevilla-Pavón, 2023). However, Tafazoli (2024) notes that to make the most of such technologies, training is essential so that teachers can move beyond safe zones and better understand that VR immersive environments are more than games; they have the potential to enhance learning.

## Post-Telecollaboration

AI-enhanced tools can also serve after telecollaboration practices by facilitating reflection. For instance, people engaged in a telecollaboration activity can generate the transcript of their intercultural exchange and analyze it by using GenAI tools (McCallum, 2024). As demonstrated by Tang et al. (2025), GenAI could be employed for an automatic coding of students' reflections with "a few-shot prompting strategy", which helps to identify specific difficulties or solutions during a virtual exchange (p. 251). Accordingly, learners can benefit most from GenAI by defining the purpose and task, providing the rules or theoretical definitions, and, most importantly, giving examples (Tang et al., 2025). Consequently, GenAI can effectively analyze the given texts.

Similarly, Otten et al. (2025) indicated GenAI tools such as ChatGPT can be used to automatically analyze how learners can build on one another's ideas with "a multi-layered validation process" to avoid deviation and vagueness of the outputs generated by AI (p. 321). Essentially, by using GenAI tools to identify the key parts of a meaning negotiation in a virtual exchange, learners can control their interaction data set and ask the AI to analyze it. Thus, based on evidence, they can develop an understanding of how they have constructed meaning together with their intercultural partners.

## PEDAGOGICAL CONSIDERATIONS IN AI-SUPPORTED TELECOLLABORATION

AI will become an essential component of future information technology education, incorporated into educational settings in various forms via smart, modern tools such as software and websites (Long & Lin, 2022). Given its nature, AI aligns closely with the education sector, making its integration highly compatible and a growing focus in AI applications (Long & Lin, 2022). Hence, it generates motivation to reshape course plans and instructional strategies for teachers (McCallum, 2024) and presents an opportunity for collaborative learning in virtual classrooms and discussion forums (Mont et al., 2025).

Dooly (2022) explains that as the world becomes more digital, educators need to reconsider and improve their pedagogies for language learning, which requires them to prepare their students to communicate with non-human agents in virtual exchange projects that involve AI-enhanced communication tasks. As a result, pedagogical approaches based on task-based learning and communicative approaches can be adjusted for AI-supported tasks by reconsidering traditional classroom teaching methods and replacing them with technology-enhanced tools (Çelik, 2025). This may pose challenges for teachers, including a lack of technological knowledge, limited access to AI tools, and resistance to adopting new technologies (Karimov et al., 2024).

AI-supported tools have become a part of language education, so teachers involved in telecollaboration projects need to develop AI literacy as a required competence (McCallum, 2024). For instance, McCallum (2024) suggests that teachers can maximize the benefits of AI tools for telecollaboration by crafting clear prompts with specific criteria, enabling them to generate output tailored to their teaching needs. As a result, AI tools can produce scripts for students to practice speaking (Lu et al., 2026), cultural case studies for comparing cultures (Jayasinghe et al., 2025), and comprehension exercises to check factual information (Wetzel & Kani, 2024) about a particular culture.

By providing opportunities to practice and improve pronunciation and fluency, AI chatbots enable learners to overcome the limitations of traditional classroom-based instruction, which are often due to class time, size, and students' diverse proficiency levels (Grab, 2025). These tools allow learners to practice language anywhere, eliminating time and location constraints (Wiboolyasarin et al., 2025), and when trained with relevant cultural content, they can also facilitate learners' intercultural competence (Weng & Fu, 2025). Grab (2025) emphasizes that different chatbots offer various pedagogical benefits, ranging from supporting vocabulary acquisition to enhancing grammatical accuracy. Therefore, teachers need to decide which tool to use depending on their educational purposes, aligning chatbots with specific instructional objectives—for example, using one chatbot for conversation practice and another for grammar exercises.

Using an AI tool does not mean learners are passive in the learning process. Instead, while using AI, learners need to be active evaluators of information that evaluate the accuracy, relevance (Fan et al., 2025), and potential bias of AI-generated information (Hastomo et al., 2025). Hastomo et al. (2025) emphasize that learners must critically evaluate information generated by AI technologies, particularly for outputs that may be biased or stereotypical. In this regard, teachers can integrate tasks that involve evaluating and comparing AI-generated texts with trusted sources, thereby helping learners recognize bias. As a result, teachers can reduce potential barriers and increase learning opportunities for critical thinking, interpretation, and relating skills. This critical process, which enables learners to evaluate biases in both human texts and in the AI tools they use, is also vital for adopting critical cultural awareness (Byram, 1997). Consequently, students should ponder AI responses as starting points for their learning and confirm the information using various sources, such as peer-reviewed journals and reliable websites (Lin et al., 2024). In this context, teachers take on the role of guides, helping learners identify bias through tasks that require evaluating AI outputs and comparing them with dependable sources.

According to Dooly (2022), with the advancements in AI technology and its integration into education, teachers are required to prepare their students to adapt to this new system by helping them develop new communication competencies for interacting effectively with non-human agents, specifically bots, avatars, and AI-supported assistants, in addition to their human partners. Unlike traditional multimedia learning materials, AI bots function not only as conversational partners but also as learning facilitators (Ling & Jan, 2025), suggesting that teachers' roles as knowledge transmitters and guides may need to be redefined. Chang (2023) emphasizes that integrating AI into English instruction requires developing an AI-assisted language-learning model, demonstrating its effectiveness, and carefully implementing it in practice.

Taken together, regarding the responsible integration of AI into language learning, one may suggest that teachers should develop AI knowledge, guide students in evaluating AI outputs in a critical way, and strategically implement AI tools to improve both language and intercultural competence.

## CHALLENGES AND ETHICAL CONSIDERATIONS OF AI IN TELECOLLABORATION AND ICC

AI has the potential to enhance language learning and intercultural communication; however, several limitations must be acknowledged. First, AI systems can struggle to recognize diverse accents and dialects, hindering effective communication and learning (Wang et al., 2023). Additionally, these systems often have a narrow cultural viewpoint, which can negatively impact both communication and the overall learning experience (Wang et al., 2023). Similarly, AI translation tools may not convey cultural nuances, such as tone, context, and body language, which are fundamental to cultural meaning (Klimova & Chen, 2024). Likewise, AI chatbots, while producing accurate and contextually relevant language, may not capture cultural or pragmatic differences in intercultural interaction, which attracts attention to the need for culturally informed, contextually rich content created by educators (Grab, 2025).

Second, issues of equity and accessibility present challenges. Farrelly and Baker (2023) note that the use of GenAI in education raises concerns about fair assessment and equitable access, as some emerging models may be costly, and this may give students whose economic status is better than others an advantage. Despite these challenges, GenAI offers significant opportunities for international students to enhance their writing and speaking skills (Farrelly & Baker, 2023), so Farrelly and Baker (2023) emphasize the importance of equipping students with AI literacy and competencies to succeed in the twenty-first century and suggest that higher education staff revise programs to effectively integrate AI. Furthermore, governments, educational institutions, and technology companies might collaborate to provide solutions related to such problems, depending on the learning goals, and should provide services for various learners (Rasheed et al., 2025). Furthermore, teachers might prioritize cost-effective open-source AI tools (Bobboi et al., 2026), or, for digital equity, design tasks that ensure collaboration between students with access to advanced AI technologies and those without.

Third, limitations related to AI-generated content should also be considered. Dai and Hua (2024) explain that the outputs generated by AI are based on training datasets, which can reproduce stereotypes existing in human language. The fact that AI can produce stereotypes should be turned into a learning goal that includes giving learners tasks through which they can critically and collaboratively evaluate AI-generated cultural texts. Zhai et al. (2024) stress that when learners are engaged in critically evaluating the content that AI has produced, learners not only make the most of AI technologies but also develop important skills, such as "critical analysis, problem-solving, and decision making" (p. 27). Besides, an authentic interaction will be enhanced, and students' interpreting and relating skills will be improved.

Finally, Klimova and Chen (2024) highlight ethical concerns, emphasizing that AI may reinforce cultural biases and social prejudices if not carefully monitored. They also stress that unequal access to AI technologies can worsen educational inequalities and limit opportunities for developing ICC. Given AI's limitations and potential biases, teachers must carefully evaluate AI tools and their outputs to avoid prejudice, inequality, and overgeneralization (McCallum, 2024). Different chatbots offer distinct pedagogical benefits, ranging from vocabulary support to grammatical accuracy, which necessitates that educators select tools based on their educational goals (Grab, 2025). Lim et al. (2023) emphasize that awareness and guided use of GenAI can foster a balanced approach, whereas Lin et al. (2024) argue that banning AI entirely may limit its educational potential, suggesting that institutions should adopt proactive roles in guiding the integration of AI. Thoughtful evaluation of AI's strengths and weaknesses can help universities maximize its educational benefits while mitigating risks (Kuleto et al., 2021; Wang et al., 2023).

## CONCLUSION AND FUTURE DIRECTIONS

This chapter sought to explore how to integrate AI tools into telecollaboration activities as pedagogical renovation to foster ICC in English language education. With an understanding of the limitations of traditional language exchange models, this chapter presents existing theoretical foundations of ICC, specifically defined by Byram (1987) and Deardorff (2006), and highlights their transformative capabilities when telecollaboration practices supported by generative and adaptive AI technologies are integrated in intercultural communication.

The integration of AI into telecollaboration has been analyzed to reveal its effects on fostering ICC in English language learning. Accordingly, the chapter suggests that AI-enhanced telecollaboration offers pedagogical opportunities for learners and teachers, including the potential for realistic intercultural communication, individualized feedback, and increased learners' autonomy. Language learners can enhance their language skills and intercultural awareness by adopting an intercultural perspective that exceeds the limitations of traditional classroom-based learning. Essentially, telecollaboration provides genuine human-to-human interaction and the analytical application of learned skills, but the findings suggest that AI offers personalized scaffolding and instant cultural cues.

The chapter also highlights the renewed and responsible role of language teachers in integrating AI into their instruction. Specifically, it suggests that teachers need to develop AI literacy, guide learners in critically analyzing AI-generated texts, and design tasks that intentionally engage learners in meaningful, culturally relevant interactions. Learners can benefit from AI tools to practice cross-cultural understanding. As a result, telecollaboration activities can facilitate authentic interaction, critical thinking, and cultural understanding, and this supports learners' effective engagement.

Ethical concerns, inequalities in access to technology and AI tools, and the limitations of AI tools, such as their vulnerability to prejudice and stereotypes, should be carefully considered in future studies and in the practice of telecollaboration. There is a need for future research to deepen the understanding of how to design adaptive AI systems that serve to different types of learners and enhance effective intercultural experiences. Precisely, future studies need to go beyond linguistic indicators to sophisticated AI-enhanced technologies that can measure intangible and abstract facets of ICC, such as adaptability, empathy-driven interaction, and intercultural attitudes (Byram, 1997). Additionally, there is a need for studies examining the long-term effectiveness of human-AI collaborative exchanges to investigate the impact of interaction with AI agents on pragmatic competence and anxiety levels during human telecollaboration. Furthermore, educational institutions must develop ethical frameworks based on research for AI-driven virtual exchange. For example, protocols for data transparency and security must be established to mitigate education inequalities.

All in all, AI-supported telecollaboration activities hold promise for ICC development due to their innovative potential, which transforms language education, enhances intercultural and digital skills, and redefines the role of language teachers in the classroom. Ultimately, the integration of AI to support telecollaboration is crucial for educating learners who are proficient in linguistics, critical thinkers, reflective, technologically skilled, and ethically responsible, thereby meeting the demands of modern language education.

## REFERENCES

Abbasi, M., Váz, P., Silva, J., & Martins, P. (2024). Enhancing visual perception in immersive VR and AR environments: AI-driven color and clarity adjustments under dynamic lighting conditions. *Technologies*, *12*(11), 216. DOI: 10.3390/technologies12110216

Akayoğlu, S., Yazan, B., & Üzüm, B. (2021). Designing telecollaboration projects for developing intercultural communicative competence. *Çankaya University Journal of Humanities and Social Sciences (CUJHSS)*, *15*(2), 348-362. DOI: 10.47777/cankujhss.1047511

Almegren, A., Almegren, R. M., Hazaea, A. N., Mahdi, H. S., & Ali, J. K. M. (2025). AI powered ELT: Instructors' transformative roles and opportunities. *PLoS One*, *20*(5), 1–10. DOI: 10.1371/journal.pone.0324910 PMID: 40440266

Alptekin, C. (2002). Towards intercultural communicative competence in ELT. *ELT Journal*, *56*(1), 57–62. DOI: 10.1093/elt/56.1.57

Angelova, M., & Zhao, Y. (2016). Using an online collaborative project between American and Chinese students to develop ESL teaching skills, cross-cultural awareness, and language skills. *Computer Assisted Language Learning*, *29*(1), 167–185. DOI: 10.1080/09588221.2014.907320

Anikina, Z., Sobinova, L., & Petrova, G. (2015). Integrating telecollaboration into EFL classroom: Theoretical and practical implications. *Procedia: Social and Behavioral Sciences*, *206*, 156–161. DOI: 10.1016/j.sbspro.2015.10.045

Arasaratnam, L. A., & Banerjee, S. C. (2011). Sensation seeking and intercultural communication competence: A model test. *International Journal of Intercultural Relations*, *35*(2), 226–233. DOI: 10.1016/j.ijintrel.2010.07.003

Belz, J. A. (2007). The role of computer mediation in the instruction and development of L2 pragmatic competence. *Annual Review of Applied Linguistics*, *27*, 45–75. DOI: 10.1017/S0267190508070037

Bennett, M. J. (1993). Towards a developmental model of intercultural sensitivity. In Paige, R. M. (Ed.), *Education for the intercultural experience* (pp. 21–72). Intercultural Press.

Berry, J. W. (1992). Acculturation and adaptation in a new society. *International Migration (Geneva, Switzerland)*, *30*(s1), 69–85. DOI: 10.1111/j.1468-2435.1992.tb00776.x

Bobboi, S. M., Abdullahi, B. M., Abdulrazak, A. Y., Saleh, Y. S., Ibrahim, L., & Ahmad, S. (2026). Bridging the digital gap: Ensuring equity and access to AI in education. [IJCSMT]. *International Journal of Computer Science and Mathematical Theory, 12*(2), 40–49. DOI: 10.56201/ijcsmt.vol.12.no2.2026.pg40.49

British Council. (2015). *The state of English in higher education in Turkey*. TEPAV.

Bueno-Alastuey, M. C., & Kleban, M. (2016). Matching linguistic and pedagogical objectives in a telecollaboration project: A case study. *Computer Assisted Language Learning, 29*(1), 148–166. DOI: 10.1080/09588221.2014.904360

Busch, D. (2025). AI translation and intercultural communication: New questions for a new field of research. *SocArXiv*. DOI: 10.1007/978-3-658-48522-1_12

Byram, M. (1997). *Teaching and assessing intercultural communicative competence*. Multilingual Matters.

Byram, M. (2008). *From foreign language education to education for intercultural citizenship*. Multilingual Matters.

Byram, M., Gribkova, B., & Starkey, H. (2002). *Developing the intercultural dimension in language teaching: A practical introduction for teachers*. Council of Europe.

Byram, M., Holmes, P., & Savvides, N. (2013). Intercultural communicative competence in foreign language education: Questions of theory, practice and research. *Language Learning Journal, 41*(3), 251–253. DOI: 10.1080/09571736.2013.836343

Çelik, Ö. (2025). Evolution of foreign language education in the age of AI. *ELT Research Journal, 14*(1), 61–77. DOI: 10.71362/eltrj.1703861

Chang, H. J. (2023). The effect of AI chatbot-based tourism English instruction on intercultural communicative competence. *Journal of English Teaching through Movies and Media, 24*(2), 15-30. DOI: 10.16875/stem.2023.24.2.15

Chen, H. I., & Sevilla-Pavón, A. (2023). Negotiation of meaning via virtual exchange in immersive virtual reality environments. *Language Learning & Technology, 27*(2), 118–154. https://hdl.handle.net/10125/73506. DOI: 10.64152/10125/73506

Cheng, H. (2025). Research on strategies for cultivating intercultural communication competence in AI-assisted English teaching. *Advances in Educational Technology and Psychology, 9*(1), 101–107. DOI: 10.23977/aetp.2025.090113

Corbett, J. (2003). *An intercultural approach to English language teaching*. Multilingual Matters. DOI: 10.21832/9781853596858

Council of Europe. (2016). *Guide for the development and implementation of curricula for plurilingual and intercultural education*. Council of Europe Publishing.

Csizér, K., & Kormos, J. (2009). Learning experiences, selves and motivated learning behavior: A comparative analysis of structural models for Hungarian secondary and university learners of English. In Dörnyei, Z., & Ushioda, E. (Eds.), *Motivation, language identity and the L2 self* (pp. 98–119). Multilingual Matters.

Dai, D. W., & Hua, Z. (2024). When AI meets intercultural communication: New frontiers, new agendas. *Applied Linguistics Review*. Advance online publication. DOI: 10.1515/applirev-2024-0185

Deardorff, D. K. (2006). Identification and assessment of intercultural competence as a student outcome of internationalization. *Journal of Studies in International Education*, *10*(3), 241–266. DOI: 10.1177/1028315306287002

Deardorff, D. K. (2009). *The SAGE handbook of intercultural competence*. SAGE Publications, Inc. DOI: 10.4135/9781071872987

Deardorff, D. K. (2011). Assessing intercultural competence. *New Directions for Institutional Research*, *149*(149), 65–79. DOI: 10.1002/ir.381

Dooly, M. (2016). 'Please remove your avatar from my personal space': Competences of the telecollaboratively efficient person. In T. Lewis & R. O'Dowd (Eds.), *Online intercultural exchange: Policy, pedagogy, practice* (pp. 192-208). Routledge.

Dooly, M. (2022). Language teaching, language learning, and virtual exchange in an age of complexity. *International Journal of Computer-Assisted Language Learning and Teaching*, *12*(3), 1–18. DOI: 10.4018/IJCALLT.316459

Fan, L., Deng, K., & Liu, F. (2025). Educational impacts of generative artificial intelligence on learning and performance of engineering students in China. *Scientific Reports*, *15*(1), 1–15. DOI: 10.1038/s41598-025-06930-w PMID: 40691450

Farrelly, T., & Baker, N. (2023). Generative artificial intelligence: Implications and considerations for higher education practice. *Education Sciences*, *13*(1109), 1109. Advance online publication. DOI: 10.3390/educsci13111109

Furstenberg, G., Levet, S., English, K., & Maillet, K. (2001). Giving a virtual voice to the silent language of culture: The CULTURA project. *Language Learning & Technology*, *5*(1), 55–102. DOI: 10.64152/10125/25113

Godwin-Jones, R. (2023). Emerging spaces for language learning: AI bots, ambient intelligence, and the metaverse. *Language Learning & Technology*, *27*(2), 6–27. DOI: 10.64152/10125/73501

Godwin-Jones, R. (2025). AI and VR converge: The future of language learning in an emerging metaverse. In Chun. D., Lan, Y.-J., & Qi, G. (Eds.), *AI-mediated Language Education in the Metaverse Era* (pp. 221–246). Springer.

Gomez, L. F. R. (2012). Fostering intercultural communicative competence through reading authentic literary texts in an advanced Colombian EFL classroom: A constructivist perspective. *Profile, 14*(1), 49–66. DOI: 10.15446/profile.v14n1.29177

Grab, M. Ö. (2025). Integrated AI chatbot practice. A pathway to improved ESL speaking skills. *Social Sciences & Humanities Open, 12*, 1–9. DOI: 10.1016/j.ssaho.2025.101933

Hastomo, T., Widiate, U., Ivone, F. M., Zen, E. L., Hasbi, M., & Khulel, B. (2025). AI-powered conversational agents and intercultural learning: Insights from Indonesian EFL students. *Intercultural Communication Education, 8*(1), 1–20. DOI: 10.29140/ice.v8n1.103127

Hauck, M., Salomão, A. C. B., Satar, M., & Primo, G. (2025). Internationalization at home through critical virtual exchange. *AILA Review, 38*(2), 262–293. DOI: 10.1075/aila.24044.hau

Jayasinghe, S., Arm, K., & Gamage, K. A. A. (2025). Designing culturally inclusive case studies with generative AI: Strategies and considerations. *Education Sciences, 15*(6), 1–17. DOI: 10.3390/educsci15060645

Jin, L., & Erben, T. (2007). Intercultural learning via instant messenger interaction. *CALICO Journal, 24*(2), 291–311. DOI: 10.1558/cj.v24i2.291-312

Kang, Y., & Wang, C. (2025). Envisioning generative artificial intelligence in cartography and mapmaking. *International Cartographic Association*. 1-9. /arXiv.2508.09028DOI: 10.48550

Karimov, A., Saarela, M., & Kärkkäinen, T. (2024). Teachers' adoption of AI tools: Motivations, challenges, and skills required. In Bonk, C. J., & Marks, G. H. (Eds.), *Proceedings of E-Learn 2024: World Conference on E-Learning in Corporate, Government, Healthcare, and Higher Education* (pp. 610–615). Association for the Advancement of Computing in Education., https://www.learntechlib.org/primary/p/225103/

Katsumata, E., & Guo, S. (2020). Intercultural learning through a telecollaboration project: Video conferences and presentations between Taiwanese and Japanese university students. *The Aoyama journal of International Politics and Communication, 105*, 1-24.

Kern, R. (2006). Perspectives on technology in learning and teaching languages. *TESOL Quarterly, 40*(1), 183–210. DOI: 10.2307/40264516

Kern, R., Ware, P., & Warchauer, M. (2004). Crossing frontiers: New directions in online pedagogy and research. *Annual Review of Applied Linguistics, 24*, 245–260. DOI: 10.1017/S0267190504000091

Khasawneh, M. A. S. (2023). Integrating AI-based virtual conversation partners in enhancing speaking skills in foreign languages: Insights from university students. *Journal of Southwest Jiaotong University, 58*(5), 575–587. DOI: 10.35741/issn.0258-2724.58.5.43

Klimova, B., & Chen, J. H. (2024). The impact of AI on enhancing students' intercultural communication competence at the university level: A review study. *Language Teaching Research Quarterly, 43*, 102–120. DOI: 10.32038/ltrq.2024.43.06

Kramsch, C. (2013). Culture in foreign language teaching. *Iranian Journal of Language Teaching, 1*(1), 57–78.

Kuleto, V., Ilić, M., Dumangiu, M., Ranković, M., Martins, O. M. D., Păun, D., & Mihoreanu, L. (2021). Exploring opportunities and challenges of artificial intelligence and machine learning in higher education institutions. *Sustainability (Basel), 13*(18), 1–16. DOI: 10.3390/su131810424

Lamy, M., & Hampel, R. (2007). *Online communication in language learning and Teaching*. Palgrave Macmillan. DOI: 10.1057/9780230592681

Lee, H., Lee, E., & Kwon, H. (2024). Online support for international students' engagement in learning: A case study on Padlet usage at a university in Korea. *Social Sciences (Basel, Switzerland), 13*(5), 1–18. DOI: 10.3390/socsci13050232

Lim, W. M., Gunasekara, A. N., Pallant, J. L., Pallant, J. I., & Pechenkina, E. (2023). Generative AI and the future of education: Ragnarök or reformation? A paradoxical perspective from management educators. *International Journal of Management Education, 21*(2), 1–13. DOI: 10.1016/j.ijme.2023.100790

Lin, X., Luterbach, K., Gregory, K. H., & Sconyers, S. E. (2024). A case study investigating the utilization of ChatGPT in online discussions. *Online Learning : the Official Journal of the Online Learning Consortium, 28*(2), 1–23. DOI: 10.24059/olj.v28i2.4407

Ling, Y., & Jan, J. M. (2025). Voices from the flip: Teacher perspectives on integrating AI chatbots in flipped English classrooms. *Education Sciences, 15*(9), 1–17. DOI: 10.3390/educsci15091219

Liu, G.-Z., Fathi, J., & Rahimi, M. (2025). Enhancing EFL learners' intercultural communicative effectiveness through telecollaboration with native and nonnative speakers of English. *Computer Assisted Language Learning, 38*(1-2), 97–127. DOI: 10.1080/09588221.2022.216477

Long, J., & Lin, J. (2022). An empirical study on cultivating college students' cross-cultural communicative competence based on the artificial-intelligence English-teaching mode. *Frontiers in Psychology, 13*, 976310. DOI: 10.3389/fpsyg.2022.976310 PMID: 36562067

Lu, C. T., Chen, Y. J., Wu, T. Y., & Lu, Y. Y. (2026). An intelligent English-speaking training system using generative AI and speech recognition. *Applied Sciences (Basel, Switzerland), 16*(1), 1–31. DOI: 10.3390/app16010189

Ma, G., & Yang, X. (2025). Fostering intercultural competence through AI-driven tools: A case study of linguistic and cultural adaptability in Chinese EFL education. *Digital Technologies Research and Applications, 4*(1), 158–169. DOI: 10.54963/dtra.v4i1.1131

McCallum, L. (2024). New takes on developing intercultural communicative competence: Using AI tools in telecollaboration task design and task completion. *Journal for Multicultural Education, 18*(1/2), 153–172. DOI: 10.1108/JME-06-2023-0043

McComb, M. (1994). Benefits of computer-mediated communication in college courses. *Communication Education, 43*(2), 159–170. DOI: 10.1080/03634529409378973

Meylani, R. (2024). Artificial intelligence in the education of teachers: A qualitative synthesis of the cutting-edge research literature. *Journal of Computer and Education Research, 12*(24), 600–637. DOI: 10.18009/jcer.1477709

Mont, M., Dooly, M., & Masats, D. (2025). Enhancing foreign language learning through AI-driven telecollaboration. *Journal of Responsible Technology, 25*, 1–9. DOI: 10.2139/ssrn.5201351

Navaitienė, J., Račelytė, D., & Rimkevičienė, V. (2015). Adaptation of Handbook for Development of Intercultural Competence: The Experiences. *Pedagogika, 119*(3), 33–44. DOI: 10.15823/p.2015.021

O'Dowd, R. (2011). Intercultural communicative competence through telecollaboration. In Jackson, J. (Ed.), *The Routledge handbook of language and intercultural communication* (pp. 342–358). Routledge.

O'Dowd, R. (2015). Supporting in-service language educators in learning to telecollaborate. *Language Learning & Technology, 19*(1), 63–82. DOI: 10.64152/10125/44402

Otten, D. M., Papadopoulos, P. M., Haeri, M. A., & Endedijk, M. D. (2025). Automatic analysis of transactivity in collaborative problem-solving dialogues: The relationship of novelty and reference. In A. I. Cristea, E. Walker, Y. Lu, O. C. Santos, & S. Isotani (Eds.), *Artificial Intelligence in Education: 26th International Conference, AIED 2025, proceedings* (pp. 156-163). Springer. DOI: 10.1007/978-3-031-98462-4_20

Rasheed, T., Bashir, A., Hanif, S., & Gul, H. (2025). Leveraging AI to mitigate educational inequality: Personalized learning resources, accessibility, and student outcomes. *The Critical Review of Social Sciences Studies*, *3*(19), 2399–2412. DOI: 10.59075/j4959m50

Romadhon, R., & Yulianti, N. (2025). Emerging technologies in English writing: AI chatbots' benefits, challenges, and implications. *MULTIPLE: Journal of Global and Multidisciplinary*, *3*(1), 4553–4562.

Saricaoglu, A. (2021). A telecollaborative approach to foster students' critical thinking skills. *Focus on ELT Journal*, *3*(1), 18–32. DOI: 10.14744/felt.2021.00043

Sarwari, A. Q., Adnan, H. M., Rahamad, M. S., & Wahab, M. N. A. (2024). The requirements and importance of intercultural communication in the 21st century. *SAGE Open*, *14*(2), 1–10. DOI: 10.1177/21582440241243119

Shayakhmetova, L., Shayakhmetova, L., Ashrapova, A., & Zhuravleva, Y. (2017). Using songs in developing intercultural competence. *Tarih Kültür ve Sanat Arastirmalari Dergisi*, *6*(4), 639–646. DOI: 10.7596/taksad.v6i4.1157

Simpson, J. (2002). Computer-mediated communication. *ELT Journal*, *56*(4), 414–415. DOI: 10.1093/elt/56.4.414

Sladovníková, Š. (2020). Telecollaborative language learning. *4th international scientific conference communication trends in the post-literacy era: Multilingualism, multimodality, multiculturalism. KnE Social Sciences, 2020*, 1-13. DOI: 10.18502/kss.v4i2.6300

Tafazoli, D. (2024). From virtual reality to cultural reality: Integration of virtual reality into teaching culture in foreign language education. *Journal for Multicultural Education*, *18*(1/2), 6–24. DOI: 10.1108/JME-12-2023-0135

Tahara, M. (2024). How does generative AI function as an active cross-cultural communication agent? A case study of Japanese literature translation using ChatGPT-4. *INContext*, *4*(2), 63–83. DOI: 10.54754/incontext.v4i2.103

Tang, S., Yip, K., Chan, C. K. K., & Hu, X. (2025). Using generative AI for analyzing student reflections on collaborative virtual reality creation. In Oshima, J., Chen, B., Vogel, F., & Järvelä, J. (Eds.), *Proceedings of the 18th International Conference on Computer-Supported Collaborative Learning - CSCL 2025* (pp. 250-258). International Society of the Learning Sciences. DOI: 10.22318/cscl2025.136951

Turula, A., Grau, M. K., Chun, D., & Cano, J. (2025). Social and Cognitive Affordances of Chat Technologies in Telecollaboration: A Critical Look at the COI Model. *Teaching English with Technology*, *25*(1), 4–25. DOI: 10.56297/vaca6841/OZFH1876/MNJU1091

Ueki, M., & Takeuchi, O. (2013). Forming a clearer image of the ideal L2 motivational self-system and learner autonomy in a Japanese EFL context. *Innovation in Language Learning and Teaching*, *7*(3), 238–252. DOI: 10.1080/17501229.2013.836205

Wang, T., Lund, B. D., Marengo, A., Pagano, A., Mannuru, N. R., Teel, Z. A., & Pange, J. (2023). Exploring the potential impact of artificial intelligence (AI) on international students in higher education: Generative AI, chatbots, analytics, and international student success. *Applied Sciences (Basel, Switzerland)*, *13*(11), 1–15. DOI: 10.3390/app13116716

Wang, Z., & Chen, K. (2025). The application of generative artificial intelligence in education: An analysis of the 25th international conference on artificial intelligence in education (AIED 2024). *2025 International Conference on Artificial Intelligence and Education*, 491-497. DOI: 10.1109/ICAIE64856.2025.11158359

Weng, Z., & Fu, Y. (2025). Generative AI in language education: Bridging divide and fostering inclusivity. [IJTE]. *International Journal of Technology in Education*, *8*(2), 395–420. DOI: 10.46328/ijte.1056

Wetzel, D. A., & Kani, J. (2024). Enhancing information literacy through generative AI in the library classroom. *Pennsylvania Libraries: Research & Practice*, *12*(2). Advance online publication. DOI: 10.5195/palrap.2024.302

Wiboolyasarin, W., Wiboolyasarin, K., Tiranant, P., Jinowat, N., & Boonyakitanont, P. (2025). AI-driven chatbots in second language education: A systematic review of their eficacy and pedagogical implicatons. *Ampersand (Oxford, UK)*, *14*, 100224. Advance online publication. DOI: 10.1016/j.amper.2025.100224

Woragwong, K., Charttrakul, K., & Damnet, A. (2017). Promoting intercultural competence of Thai university students through role-play. *Advances in Language and Literary Studies*, *8*(6), 37–47. DOI: 10.7575/aiac.alls.v.8n.6p.37

Xia, Y., Shin, S. Y., & Kim, J. C. (2024). Cross-cultural intelligent language learning system (CILS): Leveraging AI to facilitate language learning strategies in cross-cultural communication. *Applied Sciences (Basel, Switzerland)*, *14*(13), 5651. DOI: 10.3390/app14135651

Yamo, P., & Sutin, W. (2024). Negotiation of Meaning Strategies to Improve English Conversations between EFL University Students and a Native Speaker. *Interdisciplinary Academic and Research Journal*, *4*(3), 505–528. DOI: 10.60027/iarj.2024.275696

Yang, S., Zhao, H., & Luo, W. (2024). The impact of artificial intelligence on intercultural communication. In Muenstermann, I. (Ed.), *Belonging in culturally diverse societies-official structures and personal customs* (pp. 57–64). IntechOpe., DOI: 10.5772/intechopen.1006172

Yeh, H. (2024). Revolutionizing language learning: Integrating generative AI for enhanced language proficiency. *Journal of Educational Technology & Society*, *27*(3), 335–353. DOI: 10.30191/ETS.202407_27(3).TP01

Yeşil, Ş. (2025). Fostering learner autonomy in AI-mediated language learning environments: A review of literature. *ELT Research Journal*, *14*(2), 243–259. DOI: 10.71362/eltrj.1817405

You, H.-J., Yeh, H.-C., & Qi, G. Y. (2025). Fostering intercultural sensitivity in language learning: Quality Talk in telecollaboration. *Language Learning & Technology*, *29*(1), 1–26. DOI: 10.64152/10125/73624

Yu, H., & Guo, Y. (2023). Generative artificial intelligence empowers educational reform: Current status, issues, and prospects. *Frontiers in Education*, *8*, 1–10. DOI: 10.3389/feduc.2023.1183162

Zhai, C., Wibowo, S., & Li, L. D. (2024). The effects of over-reliance on AI dialogue systems on students' cognitive abilities: A systematic review. *Smart Learning Environments*, *11*(28), 1–37. DOI: 10.1186/s40561-024-00316-7

## KEY TERMS AND DEFINITIONS

**Adaptive Learning:** This refers to educational systems that are adapted according to students' performance.

**AI Literacy:** It includes the knowledge and skills necessary for the effective and ethical use of AI technologies.

**Generative Artificial Intelligence:** Machine learning and deep learning models of Artificial Intelligence, which can create new and original content.

**Intercultural Competence:** It is a skill to communicate effectively and appropriately across cultures.

**Personalized learning:** This is a pedagogical approach that takes an individual student's needs and preferences as a basis.

**Virtual Exchange:** A planned technology-mediated collaboration process between geographically distant participants through online platforms.

**Virtual Reality:** This refers to computer-generated and immersive three-dimensional environments.

# Chapter 11
# AI-Supported Collaborative Online Programs for Promoting Intercultural Communication

**Indranil Mutsuddi**
http://orcid.org/0000-0002-4202-8744
*JIS University, India*

## ABSTRACT

*In today's interconnected world, clear communication across diverse cultures and languages is vital for success in business, education, and diplomacy. However, language gaps and cultural differences often cause misunderstandings and hinder teamwork. AI-powered collaborative platforms now offer real-time translation, cultural adaptation, and personalized messaging using advanced machine learning and natural language processing. These tools interpret tone and idioms, going beyond literal translation to improve clarity and foster respect among participants. In educational and professional settings, AI customizes interactions based on users' language skills and cultural backgrounds, enhancing engagement through interactive features. This chapter delves into the transformative impact of AI on intercultural communication, exploring practical uses, ethical dilemmas & future opportunities. It advocates for a balanced approach where technological advancements are carefully guided by human values - ensuring that AI supports inclusive, respectful, and effective global communication.*

DOI: 10.4018/979-8-3373-6325-7.ch011

## INTRODUCTION

In the context of the increasingly globalized and interconnected digital landscape we find ourselves in today, the importance of effective intercultural communication has perhaps never been more vital. Whether it is in the context of business, education, or global politics, it is often the ability of people or organizations to communicate effectively with those from diverse cultural backgrounds that can make or break success. Unfortunately, this has often been hindered by factors such as language, cultural, and communication differences.

With the increase in the scale and depth of inter-cultural communication, there is an increasing need for new and creative tools that can ensure inclusive and sensitive communication. Among the most impactful advancements in the field of inter-cultural communication is the integration of artificial intelligence (AI) in inter-cultural communication platforms. These AI-based communication platforms are revolutionizing inter-cultural communication by offering real-time translation and tailoring the communication process according to cultural and individual user needs.

Today's AI tools have come a long way from simple text translation. Thanks to advances in machine learning and natural language processing, these systems can now pick up on tone, understand idioms, and consider cultural context. This makes communication not only accurate but also respectful, reducing misunderstandings between people from different backgrounds. In schools and workplaces, AI-powered platforms are transforming how we learn and work together. They offer personalized experiences that adapt to each person's language skills, learning speed, and cultural background. Features like video calls, live chats, shared online workspaces, and virtual role-playing help users develop real-world skills for navigating cultural differences. However, relying too much on AI also brings challenges. Issues like bias in algorithms, privacy concerns, and the risk of losing human empathy need careful attention. If not managed properly, AI could unintentionally reinforce stereotypes or silence minority voices. That is why it is important to use AI thoughtfully with ethical guidelines and human judgment so that it supports genuine human connection rather than replacing it.

This chapter looks at how AI-powered collaboration tools are changing the way people from different cultures communicate and work together. It offers practical advice on using AI to close cultural gaps and boost teamwork across countries. The chapter further highlights who can benefit most, including global managers trying to unite diverse teams, HR professionals using AI to improve cultural understanding, policymakers working to ensure AI is used ethically in areas like education and diplomacy, and researchers studying the intersection of AI, learning, and cross-cultural communication.

By exploring current uses, challenges, and future possibilities, this chapter gives a clear picture of how AI tools can support better global communication. Above all, it stresses the need for balancing technological progress with respect for human values to create a more inclusive and connected world.

## LITERATURE REVIEW

The digital space has been recognized as an effective platform that facilitates intercultural collaborative learning through the creation of an immersive environment where people of different cultural, linguistic, and social backgrounds can interact with each other in real time. The digital ecosystem thus facilitates interaction, communication, and cooperation among the learners.

Developing intercultural skills—those abilities that help people successfully interact in diverse social and work settings—has been highlighted as crucial by scholars like Pinna Pintor and Premazzi (2024). They emphasize that these skills are not only useful but necessary for young individuals who want to succeed in today's global job market. Traditionally, such skills were gained through programs involving travel or direct multicultural experiences. However, virtual spaces now provide a more accessible and scalable way to gain these experiences, making intercultural learning available to a wider audience.

Supporting this idea, Hasler (2011) pointed out the importance of embedding cultural sensitivity into the design of virtual learning environments. Her research showed that taking cultural differences into account when creating educational platforms can foster mutual respect, reduce misunderstandings, and improve communication among users from different backgrounds. When learners feel acknowledged and respected in a culturally inclusive setting, they tend to engage more deeply and achieve better learning results. This approach aligns with the broader aim of building intercultural literacy, which is essential for effective participation and collaboration in our increasingly multicultural world.

Recent progress in artificial intelligence (AI) has opened up new opportunities for intercultural learning and communication. AI technologies are becoming more interactive and better at responding to social cues. Researchers like Cheng and Jiang (2022), as well as Cheng et al. (2024) have shown that using conversational language and creating a stronger sense of social presence in AI systems greatly increases user engagement. This improved interaction helps build trust and strengthens connections between people and institutions, whether in education or the workplace.

AI is also proving to be a powerful tool in education, particularly for language learning and communication skills. Systems powered by AI can offer real-time feedback on writing, tailor assessments to individual needs, and create personalized learning paths. Salas-Pilco et al. (2022) explored how AI and emerging technologies affect learning in diverse sociocultural contexts, with a focus on students from minority groups. Their research suggests that these tools can help close educational gaps by supporting language learning and improving digital skills. Additionally, Alhusaiyan (2025) emphasized that while AI plays an important role in language development, its success in encouraging lively, interactive communication depends largely on educators' careful involvement in designing instruction.

One significant recent development is the emergence of Artificial Intelligence-Generated Content (AIGC), which is changing the way knowledge is shared and managed within organizations. AIGC plays a key role in digitizing organizational knowledge and supporting collaboration across multiple languages—both of which are essential in today's international and multicultural workplaces (Cheng et al., 2025). These technologies do more than only facilitating communication; they are reshaping how people perceive and engage with cultural diversity.

A common example of AI integration in daily life is seen in Conversational User Interfaces (CUIs), such as voice assistants like Apple's Siri and Amazon's Alexa, along with text-based chatbots and virtual agents. Brandt and Hazel (2025) point out that these systems are designed based on developers' interpretations of how humans converse. This means CUIs carry important consequences for intercultural communication because the cultural assumptions embedded in their design can reflect or even amplify certain norms and biases. This, in turn, affects how users from different cultural backgrounds interact not only with technology but also with each other.

In today's interconnected world, people from diverse cultural backgrounds rely on each other more than ever. This growing interdependence has brought greater attention to the ideas and language surrounding Intercultural Communicative Competence (ICC) (Gibson & Zhong, 2005). As global interactions become more frequent and complex, being able to communicate effectively across cultures has become an essential skill (Zhang & Zhou, 2019). The increase in international cooperation across fields like education, healthcare, business, religion, and the military has made culturally competent communication a necessity. Professionals in these areas often work with colleagues from different cultural and linguistic backgrounds. For this reason, ICC is no longer a side topic but a core part of successful global engagement.

Intercultural communication is a broad field that explores how people from various cultures and identities—including differences in language, religion, age, gender, sexuality, and profession—interact. One important focus is understanding how stereotypes form and how they can be challenged or broken down through open dialogue and empathy. With AI technologies becoming more common in everyday communication, it is increasingly important to study how they affect intercultural relationships (Dai & Hua, 2025).

In our globalized society, ICC is fundamental for success in education, international teamwork, and business. The ability to cross cultural boundaries is no longer optional but vital for personal, academic, and professional growth (Sarwari et al., 2024). Research consistently shows that a lack of ICC is a major cause of misunderstandings and failures in multicultural and international professional settings. Those who struggle with intercultural interactions often face obstacles that limit collaboration, trust, and productivity. This makes developing intercultural skills a pressing priority in both schools and workplaces.

One significant issue in this area is the hidden cultural biases present in AI systems, especially in large language models (LLMs). These models learn from massive amounts of data that often contain existing social inequalities, including biases related to race and gender. Researchers like Hancock et al. (2020) have highlighted that AI brings new challenges to human communication, prompting a need to rethink many basic ideas in the study of Computer-Mediated Communication (CMC). Similarly, Swiatek et al. (2022) stressed the importance of updating and broadening CMC theories to better understand how AI-generated conversations impact communication.

A recent study by Huertas-Abril and Palacios-Hidalgo (2024) examined the benefits of Collaborative International Online Learning (COIL), a program that connects students from different countries through virtual exchanges. The research showed that participants generally felt COIL helped increase their awareness of other cultures and broaden their global perspective. It also supported the development of important skills needed for future careers. Interestingly, the study noted that females tended to have a more positive view of COIL than males. Additionally, those who had not traveled internationally before saw COIL as a valuable way to experience different cultures, highlighting its role as an inclusive educational method.

Despite the progress made in AI technology, concerns about built-in biases persist. Studies have repeatedly found that machine learning algorithms and large language models can reinforce harmful stereotypes (Bender et al., 2021; Mehrabi et al., 2022). These problems are not only limited to text but also affect generative AI tools that produce content in many forms, including images and videos (Fischer, 2023). To better grasp the societal effects of these technologies, Spolsky's (2004) framework on language policy offers valuable insight. Language policy deals with how language use is regulated and standardized within communities, shaping how people communicate and understand each other. Applying this framework to conversational AI sheds light on the social and political consequences of algorithmic choices around language, tone, and expression.

In today's diverse global workforce, strong Interactional Competence—the skill to navigate and adjust communication across cultures—is more crucial than ever. Yet, the complex relationship between the key aspects of Professional Communication in Intercultural Contexts (PCIC)—which includes culture, workplace dynamics, and human interaction—has not been fully explored in academic research (Dai, 2024). There is an urgent call for scholars to examine how AI is influencing these interactions, especially in professional and educational environments. In this context, Jenks (2025) urges intercultural communication experts to engage more deeply with generative AI technologies. He points out that although large language models may seem neutral or unbiased, they often mirror dominant cultural viewpoints, subtly shaping public conversations. This has significant consequences for how society understands and talks about issues such as racism, discrimination, and cultural representation.

## ANALYTICAL REVIEW OF PRIOR STUDIES AND GAP ASSESSMENT

The literature reviewed shows that despite notable advances in using virtual environments and AI to improve intercultural communication and collaborative learning, important research gaps still exist. While many studies highlight the value of culturally aware design in virtual spaces and the promise of AI to aid language learning and engagement, there is still little concrete research on how hidden cultural biases within AI—especially large language models—impact intercultural communication outcomes. Additionally, the complex relationship between culture, workplace communication, and AI-driven interactions remains largely unexplored, particularly in terms of how AI tools affect professional communication across different cultural settings. Although theoretical frameworks like language policy help us understand the social and political effects of AI, there is a shortage of applied research investigating these impacts in real-world educational and organizational contexts.

Moreover, the varied experiences of different learner groups—for example, how gender influences perceptions of virtual intercultural programs—and the crucial role educators play in addressing AI's limitations deserve more attention. Overall, there is a pressing need for interdisciplinary studies that critically explore how new AI technologies are reshaping intercultural communicative skills and interaction abilities, ensuring these tools foster inclusivity and fair participation in a connected global community.

## OVERVIEW OF INTERCULTURAL COMMUNICATION IN THE GLOBAL DIGITAL AGE

In today's connected and technology-driven world, intercultural communication is essential for building meaningful relationships across borders. The fast growth of globalization, aided by the widespread use of digital communication tools and social media, has created new opportunities for people to connect with others from different cultural backgrounds. Intercultural communication means exchanging ideas, perspectives, and information between individuals from various cultural contexts. It involves much more than language; nonverbal expressions, social behaviors, and cultural values all play a role in how messages are shared and understood.

As the world becomes increasingly interconnected, the need for understanding and respecting cultural differences has never been more important. Being able to communicate with sensitivity and genuine awareness is crucial for building effective partnerships and fostering mutual understanding across borders. Historically, many methods for studying intercultural communication have come from Western perspectives, like Geert Hofstede's cultural dimensions theory. This framework attempts to explain cultural differences through broad categories such as individualism versus collectivism or high versus low power distance. While these models provide a useful starting point, they can sometimes reduce the nuanced and diverse nature of real cultural experiences to overly simple opposites.

In the increasingly diverse world, it is more important than ever to have intercultural training programs that focus on self-awareness, thoughtful reflection, and real-world skills instead of simply labeling cultures. The best training encourages people to explore how cultural expectations develop, question assumptions, and build the social skills needed to connect meaningfully with others, no matter where they come from. By learning to recognize and adapt to different ways of communicating, thinking, and behaving, we can create an environment of mutual respect and greatly minimize misunderstandings.

Both verbal and nonverbal communication are central to how people interact across cultures. Spoken language may carry the intended message, but tone of voice, facial expressions, gestures, and body language significantly influence how that message is perceived. Awareness of these subtle cues and an openness to learning how they vary across cultures is crucial. Just as important is developing cultural sensitivity—being aware of one's own biases and assumptions and understanding how they might impact interactions with others. Genuine intercultural competence involves a willingness to adapt without expecting others to fully conform to one's own cultural norms. This mutual process of learning and adjusting supports effective dialogue and relationship-building.

The relevance of intercultural communication extends across multiple domains, including business, education, international diplomacy, and local community life. In the business world, the ability to communicate effectively with partners, clients, and colleagues from different cultural backgrounds is vital for success in global markets. In educational settings, teachers and students benefit from intercultural skills that promote inclusive learning environments and enrich classroom interactions. Similarly, international relations and diplomacy rely on respectful communication to build alliances, resolve conflicts, and promote global cooperation. Even within countries, diverse societies require intercultural awareness to navigate the complexities of multicultural interactions in workplaces, institutions, and public life.

## Digital Technology as a Catalyst for Bridging Cultural Barriers

The rise of digital technologies has significantly transformed the landscape of intercultural communication, offering innovative ways to bridge cultural divides. Tools such as social media, video conferencing platforms, and online education systems now enable real-time interaction among individuals from diverse cultural backgrounds, regardless of geographical location. These digital spaces not only support the exchange of information but also provide platforms where cultural identities can be expressed, shared, and co-constructed. Research from countries such as Cambodia, China, and Japan illustrate how digital media is reshaping intercultural dynamics, making cultural understanding more accessible and participatory. Through these platforms, individuals can engage in global conversations, share traditions, and participate in collaborative learning—thereby reducing cultural isolation. Virtual environments offer opportunities to explore different worldviews, appreciate cultural diversity, and develop intercultural competence.

Despite the above-mentioned opportunities, the digital age also brings new complexities. While technology can foster cross-cultural connections, it may also perpetuate cultural stereotypes, spread biased or inaccurate information, and limit exposure to diverse viewpoints due to algorithmic filtering. Social networks now influence how people consume information, form opinions, and engage with cultural others. As digital technologies—particularly those driven by artificial intelligence—play a growing role in shaping user experiences, concerns over privacy, cultural misrepresentation, and content bias have become areas of concern for policy makers and academic researchers.

*Figure 1. Digital communication & its impact on intercultural communication*

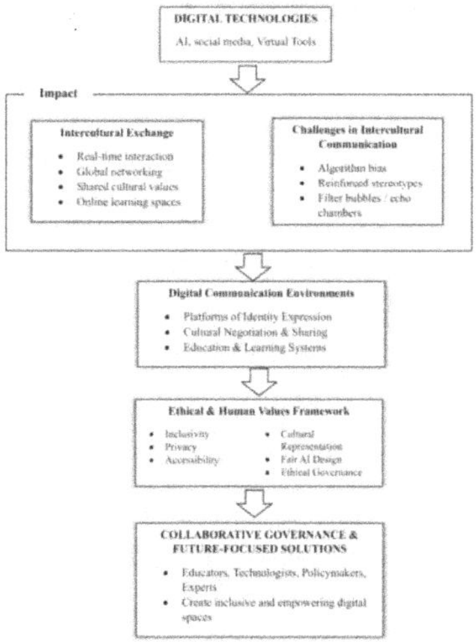

As depicted above (Figure 1), digital communication holds the capability to break down cultural barriers, build global networks, and foster mutual understanding. Yet, this potential comes with ethical responsibilities. Ensuring that digital platforms are inclusive, equitable, and culturally sensitive requires intentional design, ethical oversight, and collaboration among educators, technologists, policymakers, and communication professionals. Technological solutions alone cannot eliminate cultural barriers. They must be supported by ethical frameworks and human-centered approaches to truly promote intercultural harmony. Creating respectful and accessible digital environments is essential for empowering individuals from all cultures to participate fully in the global digital conversation.

## THEORETICAL FRAMEWORKS UNDERPINNING INTERCULTURAL COMMUNICATIVE COMPETENCE

### Intercultural Communicative Competence (ICC)

ICC refers to the ability to engage successfully and respectfully with individuals from diverse cultural backgrounds. It encompasses awareness of cultural variations, the flexibility to adjust one's communication approach, and the capacity to foster meaningful connections across cultural boundaries. As global interactions become more frequent and essential, ICC plays a crucial role in shaping effective communication, influencing both personal relationships and professional achievements in multicultural settings.

## Hofstede's Framework for Inter-Cultural Communicative Competence (ICC)

Hofstede's framework, centered on key cultural dimensions such as power distance, individualism vs. collectivism, masculinity vs. femininity, uncertainty avoidance, long-term orientation, and indulgence vs. restraint, provides valuable insight into how cultures differ in values and behavior. In the context of intercultural communicative competence, this model helps individuals recognize and adapt to these cultural variations, allowing for more effective, respectful, and context-sensitive communication across cultural boundaries. By understanding how cultural norms shape communication styles and social expectations, individuals can develop the skills needed to engage appropriately and effectively in diverse cultural settings, reducing misunderstandings and enhancing mutual understanding. It equips individuals with the tools to interpret and navigate behaviors, values, and communication styles across cultural boundaries—an essential skill in today's globalized world (see Table 1)

*Table 1. Hofstede's framework for explaining inter-cultural competence*

| Items | Details |
|---|---|
| Enhancing Cultural Awareness | This involves the ability to recognize that people from different cultures often approach life, work, and communication in diverse ways. Hofstede's model outlines key dimensions—such as power distance, individualism versus collectivism, and uncertainty avoidance—that highlight these differences. Understanding where a culture falls within these dimensions helps individuals anticipate how others might think or behave. |
| Promoting Effective Communication | Cultural values significantly impact communication styles. For instance, individuals from low-context, individualistic cultures may prefer direct communication, while those from high-context, collectivist cultures might rely on indirect or nuanced expressions. By applying Hofstede's insights, people can adjust their communication strategies to bridge these differences, reducing the chances of misunderstanding |
| Building Stronger Relationships | Respecting and adapting to another culture's norms helps foster mutual trust and respect. Whether in personal interactions or professional partnerships, demonstrating cultural sensitivity strengthens connections. Hofstede's framework encourages people to step outside their cultural lens and approach others with empathy and understanding. |
| Facilitating Collaboration Across Cultures | In diverse teams—whether in international business, education, or community projects—awareness of cultural dynamics is crucial. Hofstede's dimensions help identify potential sources of tension or misunderstanding, enabling team members to find common ground and work together more effectively. |
| Minimizing Cross Cultural Misunderstandings | Misinterpretations often arise when behaviors are judged through the lens of one's own culture. Hofstede's model helps people recognize that different responses or practices may be culturally driven rather than personal. This reduces the risk of offense or misjudgment and encourages more thoughtful, inclusive interactions. |

## Professional Communication and Interactional Competence in Multicultural Settings

Professional Communication in Intercultural Contexts (PCIC) refers to the exchange of information, ideas, and messages within workplace environments where individuals from diverse cultural backgrounds interact. Unlike casual or everyday interactions, PCIC is inherently high-stakes due to its dual complexity—first, the professional or organizational setting, and second, the cross-cultural nature of the participants involved. Communication in such contexts is often governed by formal expectations, institutional norms, and performance outcomes, all of which may vary significantly across cultures. These differences can influence not only the content and form of messages but also how meaning is interpreted, relationships are built, and decisions are made. As a result, effective PCIC demands a nuanced understanding of both professional communication protocols and intercultural competence, making it a particularly critical area of study and practice in today's globalized work environment. Developing interactional competence and professional communication in diverse contexts thus requires a combination of cultural awareness, adaptability, and strong interpersonal skills.

Corporate leaders and practicing managers must recognize that communication norms vary across cultures—what is considered polite, clear, or assertive in one culture may be misinterpreted in another. Building competence involves active listening, adjusting communication styles based on context, and using clear, respectful language. Practical strategies such as intercultural training, seeking feedback, and engaging with diverse teams help professionals become more effective and empathetic communicators. Ultimately, mastering interactional competence enhances collaboration, reduces misunderstandings, and fosters inclusive and productive workplaces in a globalized world.

# TRANSFORMATIVE ROLE OF ARTIFICIAL INTELLIGENCE IN INTERCULTURAL COMMUNICATION

Artificial Intelligence (AI) is reshaping the way people interact across different cultures by offering innovative tools that overcome language barriers, enhance cultural awareness, and support seamless global communication. These technologies are not only making international dialogue more accessible but also promoting inclusivity and mutual understanding (see Table 2).

*Table 2. How AI technologies are transforming intercultural communication*

| Role of AI for transforming Intercultural Communication | Details |
|---|---|
| Breaking Language Barriers with AI Translation | AI translation tools, including real-time speech translators and advanced machine translation software, are revolutionizing multilingual communication. These tools allow individuals from different language backgrounds to converse more naturally and accurately, reducing misunderstandings and fostering smoother interactions. |
| Facilitating Deeper Cultural Awareness | AI can analyze vast amounts of communication data to uncover cultural norms, preferences, and values. By recognizing these subtle cultural cues, AI can help users understand different perspectives, reducing the risk of cultural missteps and enhancing cross-cultural sensitivity. |
| Supporting Global Communication and Collaboration | When people from different countries team up, AI-powered tools are making it much easier for everyone to communicate and work together. Instant translation, intelligent email assistants, and chatbots that understand cultural differences help break down barriers between diverse groups. Thanks to these smart technologies, international teams can collaborate more smoothly, avoid misunderstandings, and get things done more efficiently, making global partnerships truly productive. |
| Customizing Learning for Intercultural Competence | AI-driven learning applications personalize language and cultural education by adapting to a learner's background, skill level, and learning style. These platforms provide tailored feedback, simulate real-world interactions, and integrate cultural context to build both language proficiency and intercultural skills. |
| Enhancing Accessibility and Inclusion | AI also plays a crucial role in making communication accessible to people with disabilities or those lacking traditional educational resources. Features like speech-to-text, audio translations, and AI tutors ensure that everyone, regardless of their circumstances, has the opportunity to engage in intercultural dialogue. |

## Artificial Intelligence in Online Collaborative Systems

The corporate hold a significant position in driving progress by utilizing their financial strength, advanced technologies, and research and development expertise to tackle complex global challenges. Through strategic investments and innovation, they can contribute to solving issues related to cross-cultural communication challenges. AI is becoming an essential driving force behind the development of collaborative online platforms. These platforms, which enable people to work together remotely, are evolving rapidly as AI technologies are integrated into their foundational features. AI brings capabilities such as automating repetitive tasks, delivering personalized content recommendations, and providing instant feedback, all of which contribute to higher productivity and deeper user engagement. By streamlining communication processes and improving coordination among team members, AI helps create work and learning environments that are more customized and efficient.

Collaborative learning is a teaching strategy that emphasizes active participation and cooperation among learners to reach common educational goals. It encourages students to engage with their peers, share perspectives, and construct knowledge collectively. When AI is incorporated into this approach, the quality and impact of collaborative learning improve considerably. AI helps manage group interactions by fostering clearer communication and smoother teamwork. It also delivers timely, personalized feedback to learners, enabling them to address errors and deepen their understanding immediately. Furthermore, AI adjusts learning content and support based on each student's unique abilities and preferences, creating a more individualized learning experience within the group context. These advancements make collaborative learning more engaging and effective, promoting both personal growth and collective achievement. In addition, AI's ability to analyze detailed data on students' performance and learning habits allows for the customization of educational content and activities to meet diverse learner needs. By interpreting this information, AI systems can predict future performance levels and identify students who may be at risk of falling behind.

## Natural Language Processing (NLP), Machine Learning (ML), and Adaptive Algorithms for effective Inter-Cultural Communication

In today's digitally connected world, Artificial Intelligence (AI) technologies like Natural Language Processing (NLP), Machine Learning (ML), and adaptive algorithms are reshaping how people from different cultures and languages interact. These tools (see Table 3) are playing a pivotal role in bridging linguistic gaps, fostering mutual understanding, and enhancing global cooperation.

*Table 3. Natural language processing, machine learning, and adaptive algorithms for effective inter-cultural communication*

<table>
<tr><th>Items</th><th>Functions/Applications</th><th>Impact on Inter-Cultural Communication</th><th>Practical Applications</th></tr>
<tr><td rowspan="2">Role of NLP</td><td>Real-Time Translation and Interpretation</td><td>NLP algorithms make it possible to translate spoken and written language in real time, helping individuals communicate across language barriers. Capabilities such as speech recognition, machine translation, and emotion-aware language processing ensure messages are accurately delivered while accounting for cultural subtleties.</td><td rowspan="5">Global Business Negotiations:<br><br>AI tools assist in international meetings by translating both language and cultural etiquette, helping parties avoid misunderstandings<br><br>Intercultural Learning & Development:<br><br>Learning platforms powered by AI adapt course materials to suit students' linguistic and cultural backgrounds, making education more accessible and effective.<br><br>Multilingual Customer Support:<br><br>AI systems offer round-the-clock support in multiple languages while adapting tone and style to align with customers' cultural expectations.</td></tr>
<tr><td>Understanding Context and Culture</td><td>Modern NLP systems go beyond literal translation. They increasingly grasp idiomatic expressions, cultural metaphors, and context-specific language use, making conversations more nuanced and respectful of cultural differences.</td></tr>
<tr><td rowspan="2">Role of ML</td><td>Learning from Cultural Data</td><td>ML models analyze large-scale datasets that include global texts, speech, and online communications. This helps them understand and interpret diverse dialects, accents, and regional expressions, resulting in more precise and inclusive language tools.</td></tr>
<tr><td>Culturally Aware Personalization</td><td>ML allows digital systems to adapt their content and recommendations based on individual users' cultural norms and communication preferences. This reduces misunderstandings and creates a more personalized user experience.</td></tr>
<tr><td rowspan="2">Role of Adaptive Algorithms</td><td>Real-Time Adaptation</td><td>Smart adaptive algorithms are always learning from how people interact with them, tweaking their responses to better fit each user</td></tr>
<tr><td>Promoting Cultural Respect</td><td>These smart algorithms can spot when something you have written might accidentally cross cultural boundaries. By recommending different words or suggesting a better way to phrase things, they help keep conversations respectful and make sure everyone communicates in a way that is sensitive to different cultures</td><td></td></tr>
</table>

Technologies like NLP, ML, and adaptive algorithms are game changers when it comes to breaking down language and cultural barriers in our interconnected world. These tools make it possible for people to communicate in real time, no matter what language they speak, by understanding not only the words but also the cultural context behind them. NLP helps people have smooth conversations across languages without losing any of the subtle meaning or intent. Machine learning takes things a step further by picking up on different dialects, customs, and ways people express themselves, making communication feel more natural and authentic. Adaptive algorithms personalize every interaction—they can shift their tone, clarify what you mean, and respond to cultural signals on the fly. The result is that these technologies are not only making workplaces more inclusive—they are transforming how we connect in classrooms, hospitals, social media, and everyday life. Together, they are paving the way for a world where everyone feels understood and included, no matter where they come from.

## AI-Powered Real-Time Translation and Contextual Understanding for Inter-Cultural Communication

AI has dramatically changed the way people connect and communicate across different languages and cultures. Thanks to advanced, AI-powered translation tools, it is now possible for individuals who do not share a common language to have seamless conversations. This breakthrough is reshaping how we work together worldwide, opening doors in education, healthcare, travel, and international business.

Modern AI translation systems rely on several cutting-edge technologies working together:

- Automatic Speech Recognition (ASR): This technology listens to spoken words and instantly turns them into written text in the original language.
- Neural Machine Translation (NMT): It then takes that text and translates it into the listener's language, paying close attention to grammar, context, and even subtle shades of meaning.
- Text-to-Speech (TTS): The translated text is brought to life as spoken words, often sounding natural and carrying the right emotional tone.
- Low Latency Processing: With super-fast neural networks, these systems can deliver accurate translations in just a few hundred milliseconds, making truly real-time conversations possible.

Altogether, these innovations are breaking down barriers like never before, making global teamwork and understanding part of everyday life.

***Emphasis on Contextual and Cultural Accuracy:*** Modern AI translation goes far beyond swapping words from one language to another—it is designed to capture the real meaning behind what is being said. Rather than relying on word-for-word translations, today's AI tools pick up on idioms, subtle cultural references, and even the emotional mood of the speaker. Advanced models like transformers (think GPT or BERT) and other generative AI systems can grasp the bigger picture of a conversation, ensuring that what is translated makes sense in context and respects cultural differences. Some platforms take things even further by using knowledge graphs and conversation memory. This means the AI can keep track of who said what, remember important details, and hold the thread in longer or multi-language conversations. These features are especially important during virtual meetings, international conferences, and any situation where people from around the world need to work together smoothly. The end result is communication that is not only accurate, but also meaningful and culturally aware—making global collaboration feel more natural than ever.

## Conversational User Interfaces and Socially Responsive AI Systems for Inter-Cultural Communication

Conversational User Interfaces (CUIs) are digital tools, such as chatbots, voice assistants, or apps that respond to gestures, that make interacting with technology feel natural and intuitive. Instead of forcing users to navigate menus or learn special commands, CUIs let people communicate in everyday language—whether they are speaking, typing, or even using gestures. This makes technology more approachable and accessible for everyone. When it comes to bridging cultures, CUIs are built with features that focus on empathy, cultural awareness, and reading the room. Below is outlined how they stand out in cross-cultural situations:

- Natural Language Processing (NLP): CUIs use NLP to go beyond just understanding words. They pick up on the intent behind what is said, recognize emotions, and catch subtle language differences that can vary from one culture or language to another.
- Cultural Adaptability: These interfaces adjust their language, tone, and the way they interact to match the cultural norms of each user, helping to build trust and prevent misunderstandings.
- Dialogue Management: CUIs remember previous conversations, so they can keep chats on track and avoid confusion, even as context or topics shift.
- Transparency & Feedback: With features like "typing" indicators or prompts for clarification, these systems help users feel heard and understood—especially when conversations touch on sensitive cultural topics.

- Personalization: By taking into account things like where a user is from or their preferences, CUIs can tailor their responses, making the interaction feel more genuine and comfortable

## Socially Responsive AI and Intercultural Engagement

Socially responsive AI does much more than only understanding words—it is built to pick up on the social and cultural signals that shape how we communicate. These advanced systems can read between the lines, paying attention not only to what is being said, but also to tone of voice, body language, facial expressions, and even cultural etiquette that might be unique to a particular community. By tuning in to these subtle cues, socially aware AI can reply in ways that feel more thoughtful, respectful, and sensitive to each person's background and situation. This leads to smoother conversations, fewer misunderstandings, and stronger feelings of trust—especially when people from different cultures interact. Ultimately, these systems have the power to close communication gaps and make technology feel more fair, welcoming, and truly centered around human needs.

## Case Illustration: Cultural Training Robots for enhancing Intercultural Competence through Realistic Simulation

In our increasingly connected world, being able to understand and adapt to different cultures is more important than ever. That is where cultural training robots like Furhat come in—they are changing the way people build intercultural communication skills by making the learning process hands-on and engaging. Instead of sitting through lectures or reading from a textbook, learners interact with these robots in realistic social situations. What sets these robots apart is their lifelike features: they can express themselves with facial movements, speak naturally, and use body language just like a real person. This means users get to practice everything from greetings and gestures to etiquette that is unique to certain cultures—like bowing in Japan or making eye contact in Western countries—all in a safe, low-pressure setting. As users chat with these robots, they get instant feedback on how they are doing, so they can fine-tune their skills as they go. This kind of immersive practice is especially valuable for anyone working in fields like international business, healthcare, education, or diplomacy where truly connecting with people from other cultures can make all the difference.

### Artificial Intelligence-Generated Content (AIGC) in Multicultural Settings

Artificial Intelligence-Generated Content (AIGC) refers to articles, images, or videos created mostly by AI, with little help from people. This technology is opening up exciting new possibilities—especially in multicultural environments—but it also brings some real challenges. On the bright side, AIGC makes it easier for people from all backgrounds to share their stories and ideas. With user-friendly tools, anyone can create and share content, helping more voices be heard. AI can also break down language barriers, making cross-cultural communication smoother and adapting content to suit different cultures and learning styles.

## VIRTUAL WORLDS AND IMMERSIVE ENVIRONMENTS FOR INTERCULTURAL LEARNING

Breakthroughs in digital technology—especially virtual reality (VR) and interactive 3D platforms—are completely changing the way people connect with other cultures. Instead of just reading about cultural differences or watching videos, these immersive tools let people step right into new environments. They offer lively, interactive spaces where exploring different cultures becomes something you actually experience, not just learn about in theory. These virtual worlds are transforming education by giving students the chance to "live" other perspectives. Learners can interact with realistic settings, observe traditions, hear new languages, and even participate in cultural events—all from their own classrooms or homes. This hands-on approach helps students build stronger communication skills and truly understand what life is like in another part of the world.

These cutting-edge platforms also make it possible for students from all over the globe to connect and work together. In shared virtual spaces, learners develop important intercultural skills like tolerance, flexibility, and an appreciation for different perspectives. Group projects and discussions in these environments closely mimic the way people collaborate in international workplaces, giving students a head start on working in multicultural teams. Immersive technology also breathes new life into language learning and cultural exchange. Students can practice speaking with avatars that sound and act like native speakers, or wander through virtual markets, homes, and neighborhoods. This kind of hands-on practice makes learning a new language much more practical and engaging, since it is paired with real-life cultural context.

## AI-enabled Virtual Collaborative Learning Spaces for Inter-Cultural Communication

Artificial intelligence is changing the game when it comes to virtual collaborative learning spaces (VCLSs), making them smarter, more engaging, and welcoming to everyone. With the help of technologies like machine learning, natural language processing (NLP), virtual reality (VR), and augmented reality (AR), these digital classrooms are becoming more interactive and better able to adapt to each student's needs. AI-powered VCLSs go far beyond traditional online learning. They personalize lessons, communication, and feedback for each student—taking into account language skills, cultural backgrounds, and individual learning styles. Real-time translation tools and chatbots powered by NLP make it easy for students from around the world to talk and work together, while also helping spot and clear up any cultural misunderstandings that might pop up.

## Designing Culturally Sensitive Virtual Environments for Inter-Cultural Communication

Creating virtual environments that truly respect and reflect diverse cultures is the key to building meaningful connections online. As more of our learning, teamwork, and social lives move into digital spaces, it is vital that these environments go beyond surface-level representations and avoid falling into stereotypes. To get this right, it is important for designers to partner with people who really know the culture—ensuring every detail, from language to customs, is authentic. Accessibility needs to be front and center, too, with features like language options, easy-to-use interfaces, and inclusive design that welcomes people with different physical and communication abilities.

A well-designed virtual space should let users express both their group identity and their individuality so that everyone feels seen and respected. By weaving in meaningful cultural touches—like familiar places, stories, or artifacts—and using immersive tools such as VR and AR, these environments can help people genuinely experience and understand another culture. AI can play a big role as well, guiding users through new cultural settings with stories, interactive scenarios, and adaptable communication styles. When done thoughtfully, these digital spaces become more than just platforms—they become bridges that connect people, encourage empathy, and make intercultural learning a truly transformative experience

### Role of Immersion and Simulation in Developing Intercultural Competencies

Immersion and simulation are two powerful approaches that work hand in hand to help people develop intercultural competence. Immersion, especially when enhanced with AI-driven technology, means diving headfirst into new cultural experiences—living, working, or studying in environments that are different from what you are used to. Being surrounded by unfamiliar customs, traditions, and ways of thinking, people naturally build a deeper understanding and appreciation for diversity. This kind of "real-life" exposure not only sharpens communication skills (both spoken and unspoken), but also helps individuals become more adaptable and empathetic, often leading to personal growth and a more open-minded worldview. Classic examples include studying abroad, staying with host families, or joining community-based programs—experiences that leave a lasting impact.

Simulation technologies can help to build critical thinking, teamwork, and communication skills, as participants experiment with new behaviors and attitudes. Tools like BaFa BaFa or Barnga are great examples—they simulate cultural adaptation, push people to question their own assumptions, and make learning engaging and memorable. The supportive, reflective environment of simulations encourages participants to think more deeply, feel more empathy, and strengthen their intercultural awareness, all while having the freedom to make mistakes and learn from them.

## AI-SUPPORTED COLLABORATIVE ONLINE PROGRAMS: MODELS AND APPLICATIONS

AI is changing the landscape of online collaboration, bringing a whole new level of engagement and teamwork to both schools and workplaces. With AI woven into digital platforms, organizations and institutions are making remote work and learning not only more efficient, but also more interactive and productive. As highlighted in Table 4, these advancements are redefining how people connect, share ideas, and get things done together—no matter where they are in the world.

*Table 4. Models of AI-enabled collaborative online applications*

| Model Name | Hallmarks | Illustrations | AI Capabilities |
|---|---|---|---|
| AI-enabled Collaborative Learning Platforms | AI tools offer instant feedback, help organize tasks, create personalized learning paths, and track progress in detail. They make it easier for users to work together, join discussions, and share resources—all automatically—so collaboration feels smooth and seamless. | 360Learning, Howspace | Generative AI is making it easier than ever to design new courses, empower subject matter experts, and streamline assessments with automated tools. Features like task assistants, process helpers, and tools that visualize interactions all work together to simplify complex tasks and support both educators and learners throughout the learning journey. |
| Collaborative ML Platforms | Collaborative work environments with version tracking and simultaneous input from several team members—ideal for coding, data analysis, and data science initiatives. | Google Colab, Kaggle | Collaborative coding and analytics, version control, shared datasets |
| AI-enabled Project Management | These platforms simplify everything from scheduling meetings and assigning tasks to generating meeting summaries—all automatically. Plus, they offer smooth integration for chatting and editing documents together, making teamwork more efficient and connected | Taskade, ClickUp | With AI-powered platforms, you get real-time document editing, project management tools, chat, and video—all in one place. This integration makes it easy for teams to collaborate, communicate, and stay organized without switching between different apps |
| Virtual Labs | Experience virtual hands-on experiments where AI provides instant feedback and in-depth analysis as you work. This real-time support helps you learn, adjust, and understand results more effectively, making experiments both interactive and insightful. | Labster, PhET simulations | Automatically transcribe meetings, generate concise summaries, and identify who said what. This makes it easy to review discussions, track action items, and keep everyone on the same page—without any manual effort |
| Content Creation & Online Peer Assessment Tools | AI-driven collaborative writing platforms offer automated review and feedback, while also tracking each person's contributions. This ensures the writing process is fair, transparent, and everyone's input is recognized and accountable | Bit.ai, Peergrade | Work together on documents and share content seamlessly, all while AI helps organize and manage knowledge. These tools make it easy to collaborate, find information, and keep everyone up to date with the latest insights. |

AI-powered platforms are transforming the way people work and learn together—both in schools and across industries. In education, collaborative learning systems like 360Learning and Howspace use AI to give real-time feedback, manage tasks intelligently, personalize learning paths, and provide analytics on progress, all while making it easy for groups to work, discuss, and share resources. For coding and data science, environments such as Google Colab, Kaggle, and Azure ML let multiple users work side by side in shared spaces, complete with version control and live editing—making team projects smoother and more efficient. Project management tools like Taskade and ClickUp automate the nitty-gritty, from scheduling and assigning tasks to generating meeting summaries, and they integrate with chat and document editing to keep everyone connected.

Virtual labs and simulation platforms bring hands-on experiments online, delivering instant AI feedback and detailed analytics—perfect for science and engineering students working from anywhere. Content creation and peer review tools—think Google Docs, Bit.ai, and Peergrade—make it simple to co-author documents, give and receive AI-supported feedback, and track who did what, ensuring fairness and transparency. In higher education, AI takes things further by automatically grouping students, grading assignments, and giving adaptive feedback. These platforms can even summarize and visualize class discussions, helping everyone make sense of complex group conversations. Real-time peer interactions are boosted by AI that monitors participation and analyzes feedback to keep students engaged.

## Collaborative Online International Learning (COIL) for Inter-Cultural Communication

Collaborative Online International Learning (COIL) is a forward-thinking educational model that brings together students and teachers from different countries through online platforms. Instead of relying on travel, COIL creates opportunities for people from all over the world to work together on shared projects and discussions, breaking down cultural and geographical barriers in the process. Through joint curriculum planning and teaching, everyone gets a chance to participate equally, and the classroom becomes a place where all perspectives are welcomed and respected.

COIL is especially valuable for building intercultural communication skills. By connecting students from various backgrounds, it gives them a chance to interact directly with peers who see the world differently. This helps learners develop key skills like empathy, openness to new ideas, and attentive listening—all of which are vital for navigating cultural differences with confidence. As students work together on real-life challenges and reflect on what they have learned, they often end up questioning stereotypes, shedding biases, and gaining a much deeper understanding of other cultures. This kind of experience could be seen as great preparation for life in an increasingly connected and diverse world.

## AI-driven Personalized Learning and Adaptive Intercultural Training

AI-powered personalized learning transforms education by tailoring the experience to fit each student's unique needs, goals, and cultural background. Using data analysis, AI figures out how each learner prefers to absorb information—whether that is through videos, reading, or interactive activities—and delivers content in ways that work best for them. Students get real-time feedback that pinpoints their weak spots and helps them grow, while the material adapts in difficulty and pace based on how well they are doing and what interests them most. AI also uses predictive tools to spot when someone might be struggling, so teachers can step in early to offer extra help. Importantly, modern AI systems do not only focus on academics—they can pick up on students' emotional and social cues, supporting their overall well-being as part of the learning journey.

When it comes to adaptive intercultural training, the goal is to help people thrive in diverse cultural environments. This approach mixes hands-on experiences, empathy-building, and resilience training so learners can feel confident navigating cultural differences. Traditional methods focus on practical exercises and self-reflection, but AI takes things further. It personalizes lessons to each learner's cultural context, creates realistic virtual reality simulations of global scenarios, and tracks progress with adaptive assessments. Real-time feedback and sentiment analysis keep learners engaged, while AI-powered platforms connect people from all over the world for genuine intercultural exchanges. This makes the training richer, more authentic, and better prepares learners for success in our increasingly connected world.

## CASE STUDY OF SUCCESSFUL AI-SUPPORTED INTERCULTURAL PROGRAMS

Hyperspace is a cutting-edge training platform that uses advanced AI to create engaging, hands-on learning experiences for global teams. With self-paced modules and lifelike simulation exercises, Hyperspace helps employees build the soft skills they need to communicate and collaborate effectively across cultures in today's diverse workplaces. What sets Hyperspace apart is its ability to use AI to simulate real-world intercultural situations, capturing the subtle challenges of working with colleagues from different backgrounds. Through interactive role-plays, team members can practice skills like navigating virtual meetings, negotiating with international partners, and resolving conflicts across cultural lines—all in a safe, supportive environment that mirrors actual workplace dynamics.

Hyperspace's AI engine offers instant, personalized feedback on how participants communicate—including their style, tone, and cultural awareness—in this way users can quickly see where they shine and where there is room to grow. This real-time advice encourages ongoing learning and flexibility, helping everyone sharpen their people skills. The platform also puts learners into team-based scenarios that require group problem-solving, decision making, and overcoming the natural challenges that come with cross-cultural teamwork. These realistic, hands-on exercises help team members develop empathy, adaptability, and respect for one another's differences.

When global organizations add Hyperspace's AI-powered simulations to their training mix, they can dramatically boost employees' cultural intelligence and soft skills. The immersive, practice-focused design lets learners gain confidence in handling intercultural situations and develop more effective ways to communicate. With immediate feedback, people pick up new skills faster and are more likely to change their behavior for the better—leading to international teams that are more united, productive, and positive. In the end, Hyperspace helps organizations turn cultural diversity into a source of strength, creating workplaces where everyone feels included and valued.

## DYNAMIC INTERPLAY BETWEEN CULTURE, WORKPLACE COMMUNICATION AND AI

The relationship between organizational culture, workplace communication, and AI is rapidly changing how companies function and connect with their people. This is not just about machines taking over tasks—it is about blending AI with a company's core values and communication habits to build workplaces that are more dynamic, inclusive, and efficient. AI is having a growing influence on company culture, not only by automating repetitive work but also by shaping how feedback is given, how employees feel connected to their organization's mission, and even how a sense of belonging is created—especially for teams spread out across different locations. While technology adds a new layer, the heart of culture—values like openness, purpose, and inclusivity—remains essential. AI can help reinforce these values by recognizing and celebrating employee achievements that reflect company culture or by analyzing internal communications to keep the workplace respectful and welcoming.

AI also encourages a culture of ongoing learning by personalizing development opportunities and mentorship to match each person's goals, sparking innovation and flexibility within the workforce. When it comes to workplace communication, especially in multicultural teams, AI makes interactions more personal and inclusive. AI-powered platforms can adapt messages to fit different roles and preferences, making conversations more meaningful across global and hybrid teams. With features that read the emotional tone and context of messages, these systems help make communication clearer, more empathetic, and less prone to misunderstandings—an especially big deal for remote teams. AI also removes barriers by translating jargon, suggesting meeting times that work across time zones, and supporting asynchronous collaboration, connecting colleagues around the world.

The best results come when humans and AI work together as partners, with AI acting as a helpful catalyst rather than a replacement. By taking care of repetitive tasks, AI frees employees to focus on creative problem-solving, strategic planning, and building relationships. It is up to leadership to make sure AI supports a strong, unified culture by setting clear guidelines and encouraging open conversations about how technology is used. When AI is introduced without input or transparency, it can cause confusion and division. On the other hand, involving a diverse range of voices in AI development and keeping communication open builds trust and a sense of inclusion. Employee forums and regular feedback loops make sure this partnership stays healthy and responsive, so AI can support everyone's well-being. AI is also making a difference throughout the employee journey. In hiring and onboarding, it helps reduce unconscious bias by using objective criteria, while also personalizing the experience for new team members and setting expectations for an inclusive culture. During learning and development, AI curates training paths that fit both personal and company-wide goals, encouraging continuous growth. For performance management, AI-driven analytics provide real-time insight into communication trends, team morale, and workflow challenges, helping leaders step in early to support both individuals and teams.

## ETHICAL, SOCIAL, AND PRACTICAL CHALLENGES OF AI IN INTERCULTURAL COMMUNICATION

Using AI in intercultural communication brings a range of ethical, social, and practical challenges that need careful attention to ensure technology supports respectful and inclusive interactions. Some of these challenges are explained as follows.

**Ethical Challenges:** One major concern is algorithmic bias. Because AI systems learn from the data they are trained on, they can pick up and even strengthen stereotypes or biases present in that data. If not monitored closely, this can lead to unfair or misleading portrayals of certain groups, making existing inequalities worse rather than better.

Data privacy is another big issue. AI-powered communication tools often process huge amounts of information, sometimes including sensitive or private cultural details. Without strong security and clear data practices, there is a real risk of privacy violations—especially for vulnerable or marginalized communities who may be most at risk.

**Social Challenges:** There is also the risk that AI, if relied on too much, could reduce genuine human connection. Machines can struggle to pick up on subtle emotional cues or deep cultural meanings, which can make conversations feel less empathetic and personal. Translation errors and unequal access to technology present further hurdles. Mistakes in translation can cause misunderstandings, while not everyone has the same access to cutting-edge AI tools. This digital divide can leave some groups behind, deepening existing social gaps.

**Practical Challenges:** AI often prioritizes major languages and cultures tied to economic or political power, meaning minority languages and communities can get overlooked. This influences which voices are heard and can reinforce global imbalances.

Finally, many AI systems do not fully account for the range of gender identities, cultural backgrounds, and social experiences. When these differences are missed, certain groups can be excluded or misrepresented, making it harder to achieve true inclusivity.

## SCOPE OF FURTHER STUDIES

Looking ahead, research in intercultural communication should dive into how AI and digital tools are shaping the way people from different cultures connect in our ever-more linked world. Important questions include how well AI-powered solutions—like instant translation, culturally aware interfaces, and personalized learning programs—actually help people communicate and understand each other better. It is also worth exploring how digital identities are formed and expressed across cultures, and how immersive technologies like virtual reality can foster intercultural skills and awareness. At the same time, researchers need to keep a close eye on the ethical side of things, including issues like bias, privacy, and fair representation of all cultures in digital spaces.

Finally, evaluating new approaches, such as Collaborative Online International Learning (COIL), and making sure that less commonly spoken languages are included, will be key to building communication systems that are truly inclusive and culturally sensitive. This research will help ensure that as technology evolves, it brings people together rather than driving them apart.

## IMPLICATIONS OF THE STUDY

**Theoretical Implications:** This study points to a major shift in how we think about intercultural communication in the digital era. Instead of relying solely on traditional, language-focused models, we now see the rise of flexible, technology-driven frameworks. The addition of AI and digital tools is expanding Intercultural Communicative Competence (ICC), making it possible for people to interact in real time and adapt to different cultures instantly, no matter where they are. These changes push existing theories to evolve, recognizing that communication today is shaped by both human intentions and the influence of intelligent technology. As digital platforms take center stage in global interactions, our theories must keep pace—reflecting the ever-changing, collaborative, and blended nature of modern communication.

**Practical Implications:** On a practical level, the findings underline how important intercultural communication has become in our digital, interconnected world. Thanks to AI and digital platforms, crossing language and geographical boundaries is easier than ever, which boosts collaboration, learning, and professional exchange. These technologies let people and organizations connect more smoothly and work together across cultures. But there are real-world hurdles, too—including algorithmic bias, data privacy issues, and the risk of misrepresenting cultures. To make the most of these opportunities while minimizing harm, it is essential to focus on culturally sensitive design, ongoing intercultural training, and responsible, ethical implementation of AI.

**Social Implications:** Tools like real-time translators and virtual classrooms are helping to bridge gaps, allowing people from different backgrounds to connect, learn, and work together more easily. These advances are breaking down barriers and making spaces more welcoming and inclusive. Still, the study highlights ongoing concerns about cultural bias, privacy, and the potential to overlook minority voices. If we want to fully realize the benefits of these technologies, we need to build systems that are respectful of all cultures and stick to ethical, inclusive best practices—so that genuine understanding and cross-cultural respect can thrive.

## CONCLUSIONS

In today's interconnected world, technology—especially AI—is transforming how we communicate across cultures. Tools like real-time translation, adaptive messaging, and immersive virtual environments make it easier than ever for people from diverse backgrounds to connect, collaborate, and learn from one another. However, while these tools create new opportunities, they also introduce real challenges.

Issues such as bias, privacy, and accurate cultural representation require careful attention to ensure technology unites people rather than divides them. Ultimately, successful intercultural communication is not only about the latest technology—it is also about using these innovations wisely, with respect for cultural differences and a firm commitment to fairness and ethical principles.

## REFERENCES


Alhusaiyan, E. (2025). A systematic review of current trends in artificial intelligence in foreign language learning. *Saudi Journal of Language Studies, 5*(1), 1–16. DOI: 10.1108/SJLS-07-2024-0039

Bender, E. M., Gebru, T., McMillan-Major, A., & Shmitchell, S. (2021). On the dangers of stochastic parrots. *Proceedings of the 2021 ACM Conference on Fairness, Accountability, and Transparency*, 610–623. DOI: 10.1145/3442188.3445922

Brandt, A., & Hazel, S. (2025). Towards interculturally adaptive conversational AI. *Applied Linguistics Review, 16*(2), 775–786. DOI: 10.1515/applirev-2024-0187

Cheng, Q., Zhang, S., Wang, L., & Lu, Y. (2025). Inter-organizational knowledge sharing in the age of artificial intelligence: The mediating role of knowledge digitization and cross-language collaboration. *Journal of Knowledge Management, 29*(8), 2724–2744. Advance online publication. DOI: 10.1108/JKM-12-2024-1423

Cheng, Y., & Jiang, H. (2022). Customer–brand relationship in the era of artificial intelligence: Understanding the role of chatbot marketing efforts. *Journal of Product and Brand Management, 31*(2), 252–264. DOI: 10.1108/JPBM-05-2020-2907

Cheng, Y., Wang, Y., & Lee, J. (2024). Using a chatbot to combat misinformation: Exploring gratifications, chatbot satisfaction and engagement, and relationship quality. *International Journal of Human-Computer Interaction*, •••, 1–13. DOI: 10.1080/10447318.2024.2344149

Dai, D. W. (2024). Interactional competence for professional communication in intercultural contexts: Epistemology, analytic framework and pedagogy. *Language, Culture and Curriculum, 37*(4), 435–455. DOI: 10.1080/07908318.2024.2349781

Dai, D. W., & Hua, Z. (2025). When AI meets intercultural communication: New frontiers, new agendas. *Applied Linguistics Review, 16*(2), 747–751. DOI: 10.1515/applirev-2024-0185

Fischer, J. E. (2023). Generative AI considered harmful. *Proceedings of the 5th International Conference on Conversational User Interfaces*, 1–5. DOI: 10.1145/3571884.3603756

Gibson, D., & Zhong, M. (2005). Intercultural communication competence in the healthcare context. *International Journal of Intercultural Relations, 29*(5), 621–634. DOI: 10.1016/j.ijintrel.2005.07.008

Hancock, J. T., Naaman, M., & Levy, K. (2020). AI-mediated communication: Definition, research agenda, and ethical considerations. *Journal of Computer-Mediated Communication, 25*(1), 89–100. DOI: 10.1093/jcmc/zmz022

Hasler, B. S. (2011). *Intercultural collaborative learning in virtual worlds.*, DOI: 10.1108/S2044-9968(2011)0000004015

Huertas-Abril, C. A., & Palacios-Hidalgo, F. J. (2024). Collaborative international online learning for the development of intercultural awareness: An experience with pre-service language teachers. *Journal for Multicultural Education, 18*(1/2), 67–80. DOI: 10.1108/JME-09-2023-0093

Jenks, C. J. (2025). Communicating the cultural other: Trust and bias in generative AI and large language models. *Applied Linguistics Review, 16*(2), 787–795. DOI: 10.1515/applirev-2024-0196

Mehrabi, N., Morstatter, F., Saxena, N., Lerman, K., & Galstyan, A. (2022). A survey on bias and fairness in machine learning. *ACM Computing Surveys, 54*(6), 1–35. DOI: 10.1145/3457607

Pinna Pintor, S., & Premazzi, V. (2024). The key role of intercultural competencies for effective integration: From theory to practice. *Quality Education for All, 1*(2), 94–111. DOI: 10.1108/QEA-03-2024-0027

Salas-Pilco, S. Z., Xiao, K., & Oshima, J. (2022). Artificial intelligence and new technologies in inclusive education for minority students: A systematic review. *Sustainability (Basel), 14*(20), 13572. DOI: 10.3390/su142013572

Sarwari, A. Q., Adnan, H. M., Rahamad, M. S., & Abdul Wahab, M. N. (2024). The requirements and importance of intercultural communication competence in the 21st century. *SAGE Open, 14*(2), 21582440241243119. Advance online publication. DOI: 10.1177/21582440241243119

Spolsky, B. (2004). *Language policy* (1st ed., Vol. 1). Cambridge University Press.

Swiatek, L., Galloway, C., Vujnovic, M., & Kruckeberg, D. (2022). Artificial intelligence and changing ethical landscapes in social media and computer-mediated communication: considering the role of communication professionals. In *The Emerald handbook of computer-mediated communication and social media* (pp. 653–670). Emerald Publishing Limited., DOI: 10.1108/978-1-80071-597-420221038

Zhang, X., & Zhou, M. (2019). Interventions to promote learners' intercultural competence: A meta-analysis. *International Journal of Intercultural Relations, 71*, 31–47. DOI: 10.1016/j.ijintrel.2019.04.006

# Chapter 12
# Fostering ICC Through AI-Integrated Visual Arts in COIL-Based Vietnamese Higher Education

**Hanh Cao Minh Hong**
http://orcid.org/0009-0002-8828-736X
*Saigon University, Vietnam*

## ABSTRACT

*This chapter examines how intercultural communicative competence (ICC) can be fostered through AI-integrated visual arts within Collaborative Online International Learning (COIL) in Vietnamese higher education. Despite the growing use of COIL worldwide, empirical research on its application in visual arts education, particularly in Vietnam, remains limited. Drawing on a qualitative, constructivist grounded theory approach, the study analyzes AI-supported collaborative visual art projects as spaces of intercultural meaning-making and dialogue. The findings indicate that AI-generated visual practices can mediate intercultural interaction, support reflective engagement with cultural identities, and enable new forms of collaborative creativity. The chapter contributes a contextualized pedagogical model for integrating AI and COIL into visual arts education to enhance ICC development in transnational learning environments.*

DOI: 10.4018/979-8-3373-6325-7.ch012

## 1. INTRODUCTION

In recent years, with globalisation and rapid technological advancement, the development of Intercultural Communicative Competence (ICC) for university students has become a critical priority in higher education. Recognising one's own culture while engaging with others is essential to build intercultural understanding appropriate for a globalised world, without diminishing the importance of national identity. Within this context, visual arts education serves as a powerful medium through which learners can perceive, interpret, and express cultural meanings. Art functions as a bridge for intercultural dialogue, enabling students to translate values, identities, and experiences across linguistic and social boundaries.

Although the Collaborative Online International Learning (COIL) model has been successfully implemented in numerous countries to foster intercultural competence through virtual exchange, its application within the field of visual arts education, especially in Vietnamese higher education, remains underexplored. Meanwhile, the increasing integration of Artificial Intelligence (AI) in arts education is reshaping how people create, interpret, and communicate cultural and aesthetic knowledge. AI tools such as generative design, image synthesis, and intelligent translation are not only expanding access to artistic expression but also transforming aesthetic learning into intercultural encounters where creativity and empathy intersect. However, despite this potential, there exists a research gap regarding how AI-supported COIL projects can systematically enhance ICC in visual arts education within Vietnam. Most COIL research in the Vietnamese context has focused on language learning and internationalisation strategies, with limited attention to aesthetic, cultural, and creative dimensions. This gap reveals a theoretical tension: while COIL provides a framework for intercultural collaboration, and AI enables new modes of visual dialogue, their intersection in art education remains conceptually and pedagogically underdeveloped. Addressing this tension is essential to understand how technology-mediated creativity can foster deeper intercultural understanding.

To respond to these challenges, this chapter proposes a pedagogical model of AI-integrated COIL designed to develop ICC among visual arts students in Vietnamese universities. The model situates AI not merely as a technical aid but as a mediator of intercultural meaning-making, supporting learners in expressing identity, empathy, and reflection through collaborative art-making. Through this approach, the study contributes to ongoing discussions on intercultural education in the arts, expands theoretical perspectives on COIL, and offers practical insights into internationalising Vietnam's creative education sector. Accordingly, this chapter pursues the following objectives:

(1) To assess the potential of AI in supporting visual arts education and creativity as a means to promote ICC development among learners.
(2) To analyse the significance of ICC through COIL in designing programs, teaching activities, and developing institutional policies for visual arts education in Vietnamese higher education.

Following this introduction, Section 2 presents the theoretical framework, outlining key models of ICC, the role of visual arts in intercultural education within the COIL framework, and the potential of AI to enhance creative and intercultural learning. Section 3 reviews relevant literature on ICC development through the arts, COIL-based intercultural collaboration, and AI integration in visual arts education, highlighting current debates and research gaps. Section 4 focuses on integrating AI into COIL visual arts programs in Vietnam, analysing current practices, pedagogical potential, and emerging challenges and opportunities. Section 5 concludes with recommendations and future directions for implementing AI-supported COIL initiatives that strengthen intercultural competence and creativity in Vietnamese higher education.

## 2. THEORETICAL FRAMEWORK

### 2.1. Intercultural Communicative Competence and Intercultural Communicative Competence Education Through the Arts

ICC has long been recognised as a central educational goal in the context of globalisation and internationalisation. Since the late 20th century, various theoretical approaches have sought to define what constitutes intercultural competence and how it can be developed within education. Among these, Byram's (2021) and Deardorff's (Deardorff & Jones, 2022) frameworks remain the most widely cited, providing complementary yet distinct perspectives on intercultural learning and communication.

Byram's (2021) model conceptualises ICC as a set of interrelated components, including attitudes, knowledge, skills, and critical cultural awareness, all of which together enable effective and appropriate interaction across cultures. His framework, grounded in foreign language education, positions learners as mediators between cultures. The model's clarity and structure make it particularly valuable for curriculum design and assessment; however, it has been critiqued for its relative rigidity and for privileging cognitive understanding over experiential or affective dimensions of learning. In the context of arts education, where meaning is often embodied and affective, Byram's focus on structured competence may overlook the imaginative and sensory processes that shape intercultural understanding.

Building on Byram's foundation, Deardorff introduces a developmental and process-oriented model of ICC (Deardorff & Jones, 2022). She emphasises that intercultural competence evolves dynamically through internal shifts, such as openness, curiosity, flexibility, and empathy, which lead to external behaviours like adaptability and effective communication. Unlike Byram's structural approach, Deardorff situates ICC within an ongoing cycle of reflection and transformation. This flexibility allows her model to align more closely with creative and experiential pedagogies. Yet, it can also pose challenges for measurement and curriculum integration because of its open-ended and context-dependent nature.

From the perspective of arts education, the works of Eisner (2002) and Greene (2000) extend these intercultural frameworks into the aesthetic domain. Eisner views the arts as a form of interpretive knowledge, emphasising that artistic creation and appreciation cultivate sensitivity to multiple meanings and perspectives. Through aesthetic inquiry, learners develop interpretive and reflective skills that transcend linguistic barriers which are key aspects of intercultural competence. However, Eisner's approach has been critiqued for focusing predominantly on cognition and perception, with less explicit attention to empathy or dialogue as intercultural dimensions.

Maxine Greene's (2000) philosophy complements Eisner by placing imagination and aesthetic experience at the centre of intercultural education. For Greene, imagination enables individuals to perceive the world through others' eyes, breaking through habitual perceptions and fostering empathy. Her notion of "releasing the imagination" links directly to the affective and ethical dimensions of intercultural learning. Yet, Greene's work, while profound in its humanistic vision, provides less guidance for empirical or structured pedagogical application, a gap in which integrating COIL and AI technologies might help address by operationalising her ideas in interactive and collaborative contexts.

When synthesised, these four frameworks - Byram, Deardorff, Eisner, and Greene - offer a multilayered theoretical foundation for ICC development through the arts (see Figure 1). Byram and Deardorff contribute conceptual and developmental clarity to understanding intercultural interaction, while Eisner and Greene provide an aesthetic and humanistic lens that situates learning within interpretation, emotion, and imagination. The intersection of these perspectives suggests that ICC is not only about knowledge, skills, and attitudes, but also about perceptual awareness, imaginative empathy, and aesthetic engagement.

In the context of AI-supported COIL art education, this synthesis is particularly relevant. Byram's cognitive structure, Deardorff's developmental process, Eisner's interpretive arts framework, and Greene's imaginative humanism together form the conceptual basis for AI-mediated intercultural learning—where students use digital art tools to express, analyse, and empathise across cultural boundaries. These theories collectively underpin the chapter's pedagogical model, which positions visual arts as a transformative site for intercultural dialogue and creativity within global, technology-enhanced learning environments.

*Figure 1. Logical integration of four theoretical frameworks in Intercultural Communicative Competence (ICC) education through the arts*

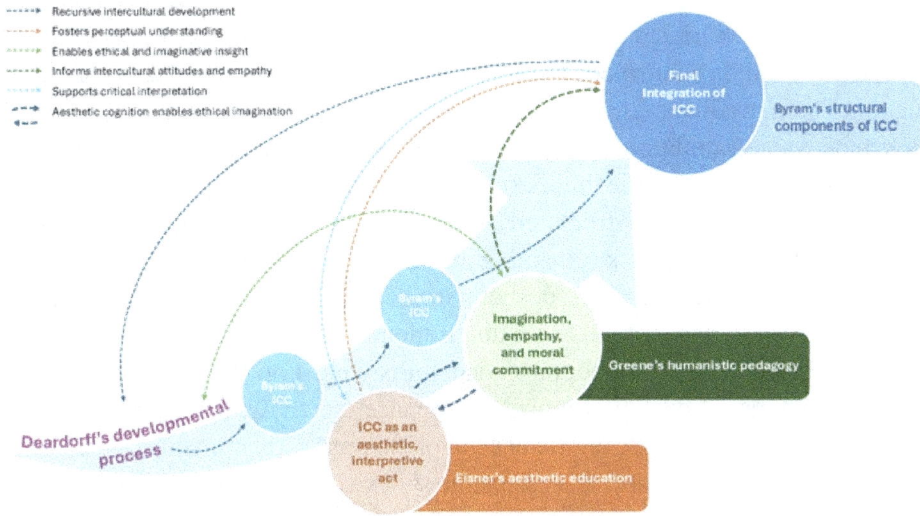


## 2.2. The Role of Visual Arts in Intercultural Education Within the Collaborative Online International Learning Framework

The COIL framework has emerged as a transformative pedagogical model that bridges geographical and cultural divides through structured virtual collaboration. Originally conceptualised under the broader umbrella of Virtual Exchange (VE) (Helm, 2024), COIL emphasises student-to-student engagement, co-created learning content, and shared intercultural reflection. Within this framework, learners from different cultural and linguistic backgrounds engage in joint projects that promote mutual understanding, critical thinking, and intercultural communication. As studies by Hackett et al. (2023) and Asojo et al. (2019) highlight, COIL's educational value lies in integrating disciplinary knowledge with ICC, facilitated by both digital tools and project-based learning. In this intercultural learning landscape, visual arts occupy a distinctive and powerful position. Unlike linguistic exchanges that rely on verbal communication, visual arts enable learners to express and interpret cultural meanings through symbolic, non-verbal, and aesthetic forms. As Asojo et al. (2019) argue, artistic practice provides experiential spaces in which students can engage with diversity through creative problem-solving and aesthetic representation. When situated within COIL, the arts function as a mediating language that transcends words, allowing participants to co-construct meaning through shared images, design, and creative narratives.

From a pedagogical perspective, the visual arts can serve as a medium for what Asojo et al. (2019) call content representation (CoRe), the integration of subject-specific learning with intercultural reflection. This closely aligns with Byram's (2021) emphasis on cultural knowledge and Eisner's (2002) notion of art as interpretive inquiry. Through collaborative artmaking, students encounter cultural systems, such as beliefs, values, traditions, and visual codes, which expand their understanding of self and others. Yet, while these experiences foster intercultural awareness, their effectiveness depends on structured facilitation. Without intentional reflection, intercultural art projects risk remaining at the level of exchange rather than transformation. Thus, effective COIL design must deliberately embed opportunities for dialogue, critique, and cultural contextualisation.

From a technological standpoint, visual arts education within COIL benefits from the integration of digital tools that enhance creativity, communication, and collaboration. Platforms for digital design, photography, or animation, when combined with online discussion spaces, enable students to explore and share aesthetic experiences in multimodal forms. As Greene (2000) emphasises, imagination is essential for intercultural understanding; technology amplifies this imaginative space by extending learners' ability to visualise, simulate, and reinterpret cultural realities. However, technology alone cannot guarantee intercultural depth. As Hackett et al. (2023) caution, the pedagogical and ethical dimensions of online collaboration must be prioritised to ensure that digital art practices promote dialogue and empathy rather than superficial representation.

In terms of intercultural practice, the visual arts cultivate key competencies at the heart of ICC, interpretation, relation, and critical awareness. Through cross-cultural creative projects, students are invited to question their assumptions, analyse visual symbols, and reflect on artistic conventions that carry cultural meanings. These experiences align with Deardorff's (2006) emphasis on empathy, adaptability, and reflexivity as developmental outcomes of intercultural competence. Moreover, the process of co-creation in COIL art projects fosters collective meaning-making, encouraging students to view art not as an isolated act of expression but as a form of intercultural negotiation. This aligns with Greene's (2000) vision of the arts as spaces for social imagination and human connection.

Nevertheless, the integration of visual arts within COIL also presents conceptual challenges. Artistic meaning is inherently subjective, and interpretations of visual symbols may vary widely across cultural contexts. Without critical facilitation, students may misinterpret or exoticise cultural artefacts, reinforcing stereotypes rather than promoting understanding. Thus, educators must frame visual arts COIL projects through reflective dialogue, guiding learners to move beyond representation toward intercultural empathy and co-constructed knowledge. This pedagogical mediation transforms the visual arts from a product of cultural expression into a process of intercultural inquiry.

In summary, within the COIL framework, the visual arts play a multifaceted role:

(1) Pedagogically, they connect disciplinary learning with intercultural awareness through creative practice.
(2) Technologically, they leverage digital platforms to enable multimodal communication and collaborative imagination.
(3) Interculturally, they cultivate empathy, reflection, and interpretive sensitivity essential to ICC.

Through these interconnected dimensions, visual arts-based COIL initiatives embody the principles of aesthetic inquiry and intercultural dialogue, creating transformative learning experiences that prepare students to participate in an increasingly interconnected and culturally diverse world.

## 2.3. The Potential of AI in Visual Arts Education as a Tool for Fostering Intercultural Communicative Competence Through Collaborative Online International Learning-Based Collaborations

Over the past decade, Artificial Intelligence (AI) has revolutionised the educational landscape by transforming how knowledge is created, accessed, and interpreted. Within the field of visual arts education, AI has emerged as both a creative instrument and a cultural interlocutor, influencing how aesthetic knowledge and intercultural understanding are constructed. As Huang (2023) and Ezhilmurugan and Yashavini (2024) observe, AI systems through generative algorithms, virtual simulations, and intelligent design platforms, have expanded opportunities for artistic expression and redefined what it means to learn, create, and collaborate in digital environments. When integrated into COIL programs, AI becomes not only a technological aid but also a pedagogical mediator that can enhance ICC by facilitating creativity, empathy, and dialogue across cultures.

Recent research underscores AI's multifaceted role in transforming aesthetic and intercultural education. Studies such as Then et al. (2023) and Davoodi (2024) suggest that AI fosters "creative co-production" by enabling learners to visualise and reinterpret cultural ideas collaboratively, thereby challenging conventional notions of authorship and ownership in the arts. Similarly, Erişti and Freedman (2024) highlight AI's potential to support originality and divergent thinking, though they also caution against its possible constraints on creativity when used uncritically. Zlateva (2025) further notes that AI democratizes access to artistic production, offering new forms of participation and inclusion, yet this expanded accessibility also introduces ethical questions about cultural representation, bias, and epistemic equity.

In the context of COIL, AI strengthens the triadic relationship between pedagogy, technology, and intercultural practice (Hackett et al., 2023). Pedagogically, AI enables educators to design interactive, student-centred learning experiences that integrate visual creation with intercultural reflection. Through platforms such as Midjourney, Leonardo AI, and Wombo Dream, learners can experiment with cultural symbols, reinterpret traditions, and collaboratively construct visual narratives that embody multiple worldviews. These processes align with Eisner's (2002) notion of art as interpretive knowledge and Greene's (2000) idea of imagination as a vehicle for empathy. Technologically, AI facilitates multimodal communication by combining language, imagery, and design, allowing students to transcend linguistic barriers and engage through shared visual vocabularies. This multimodality resonates with Deardorff's (2006) model of ICC, where internal attitudes of openness and curiosity are externalised through creative, context-sensitive expression (see Figure 2).

*Figure 2. AI, COIL, and visual arts integration in developing intercultural communicative competence*

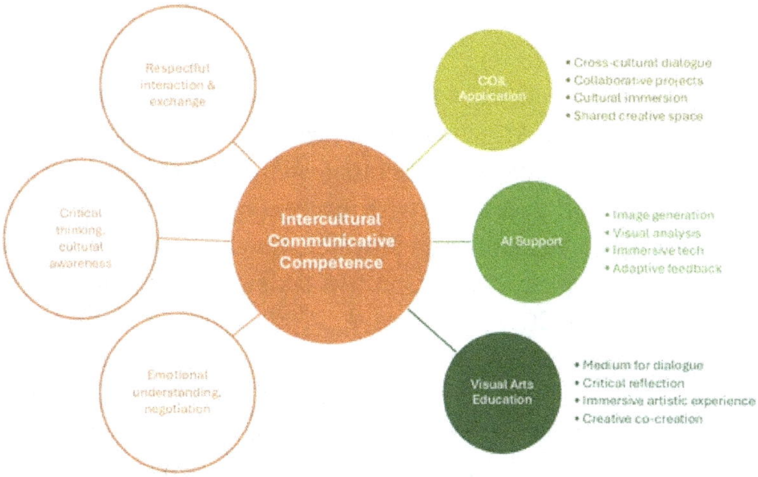


However, despite these pedagogical advantages, the integration of AI in visual arts COIL projects requires careful critical framing to avoid reinforcing cultural bias or superficial understanding. As your empirical synthesis notes, AI systems rely on large datasets that often privilege dominant, especially Western cultural aesthetics. This can result in cultural homogenisation or misrepresentation, where culturally specific visual forms are reduced to stylised abstractions lacking contextual depth. Williamson and Piattoeva (2022) refer to this issue as a form of algorithmic epistemic injustice, in which AI reproduces existing power asymmetries by encoding certain cultural knowledges as universal while marginalising others. To counter this, educators must cultivate critical AI literacy by teaching students to question, interpret, and deconstruct algorithmic outputs as part of the learning process. This approach not only protects cultural integrity but also aligns with the reflective and ethical dimensions of ICC.

From a constructivist perspective, AI also promotes a shift from passive learning toward co-construction of intercultural meaning. In COIL settings, students collaborate to generate, critique, and reimagine artistic representations using AI tools which act as intermediaries in intercultural dialogue. This dynamic corresponds to Charmaz's constructivist view of knowledge as emergent and co-created through interaction (Charmaz & Thornberg, 2021), aligning with Deardorff's (2006) cyclical model of intercultural development. When facilitated through AI-enabled platforms, learners engage in reflective interpretation: examining how machine-generated images represent or distort cultural narratives and collaboratively negotiating meaning through feedback and dialogue. Such processes foster empathy and analytical depth, transforming AI from a mechanical tool into an epistemic partner in intercultural learning.

Moreover, AI's affordances in personalisation and immersion enhance students' capacity for aesthetic and emotional engagement. As Huang (2023) and Jingxiu (2025) highlight, immersive AI technologies, such as Virtual Reality (VR) and Augmented Reality (AR), simulate diverse cultural environments that allow learners to "enter" artistic and social spaces otherwise inaccessible to them. When embedded in COIL projects, these technologies cultivate embodied experiences of cultural difference, nurturing empathy and perspective-taking that are core dimensions of ICC identified by Byram (2021) and Greene (2000). However, these benefits also raise ethical challenges concerning authenticity and emotional manipulation, underscoring the need for reflective debriefing and educator guidance to ensure that affective experiences lead to understanding rather than spectacle.

Integrating AI within COIL visual arts education thus demands a balance between innovation and critical awareness. AI can amplify creativity, connect learners globally, and democratize access to cultural exchange; yet, without critical pedagogy, it risks reinforcing cultural stereotypes, dependence on algorithmic authority, or unreflective consumption of visual culture. As Erişti and Freedman (2024), and Ezhilmurugan and Yashavini (2024) suggest, the pedagogical challenge lies in using AI as a supporting tool rather than a replacing force, a medium for exploring, not substituting, human imagination and intercultural dialogue.

In summary, the potential of AI in visual arts education within COIL environments lies in its ability to create "complex creative spaces" where human creativity, technological mediation, and cultural diversity coexist in dialogue. When grounded in critical reflection and intercultural pedagogy, AI-supported COIL art projects can nurture the attitudes, knowledge, and skills central to ICC: curiosity, empathy, interpretive awareness, and ethical engagement. For Vietnamese higher education, these approaches offer a pathway to reimagine visual arts curricula that not only embrace technological innovation but also sustain cultural authenticity, intercultural understanding, and creative global citizenship.

## 3. LITERATURE REVIEW

This section situates the study within current international and Vietnamese scholarship on ICC, COIL, and the integration of AI in visual arts education. It builds on the theoretical foundations established in Section 2, linking intercultural theory, aesthetic pedagogy, and digital innovation, while identifying existing research gaps and opportunities for development. The review is organised into three interrelated areas: (1) ICC development through the arts, (2) COIL as a framework for intercultural collaboration, and (3) AI integration in visual arts education for intercultural learning.

## 3.1. Intercultural Communicative Competence Development Through the Arts

The arts have increasingly been recognised as a dynamic medium for intercultural communication, offering learners experiential and affective pathways to understand cultural difference. Building on the foundations of Eisner (2002) and Greene (2000), arts education enables students to perceive, interpret, and negotiate meaning through visual and symbolic languages that transcend verbal barriers. In this context, art serves not only as a product of culture but also as a process of meaning-making, encouraging reflection, empathy, and reinterpretation.

Contemporary research supports this view. Studies such as Asojo et al. (2019) and Hackett et al. (2023) have demonstrated how visual arts, when linked to international collaboration, promote deeper intercultural awareness and creativity. These projects highlight the pedagogical value of "learning through making," where art becomes a reflective dialogue between the self and the other. Through creative production, students develop interpretive and relational skills central to Byram's and Deardorff's ICC frameworks, such as openness, curiosity, and the ability to relate and interpret across cultures.

However, much of the existing research remains Eurocentric or discipline-specific, often focusing on Western institutional contexts. As Ezhilmurugan and Yashavini (2024) observe, there is limited empirical attention to how artistic pedagogy fosters ICC in non-Western higher education systems, particularly within Southeast Asia. This gap underscores the importance of exploring how cultural expression and creative practice can support ICC development in contexts like Vietnam, where the intersection of traditional aesthetics and contemporary technology presents unique opportunities for reimagining intercultural learning.

In sum, visual arts education offers fertile ground for cultivating intercultural understanding through imaginative engagement. Yet its integration into structured frameworks such as COIL, and its potential enhancement through AI, remains an emerging field that demands further scholarly inquiry.

## 3.2. Collaborative Online International Learning as a Framework for Intercultural Collaboration

The COIL model represents a pedagogical innovation that merges online learning, intercultural exchange, and project-based collaboration. Initially conceptualised within the broader scope of VE (Helm, 2024), COIL provides structured opportunities for students from different cultural and national contexts to engage in co-designed learning experiences. As Hackett et al. (2023) and Asojo et al. (2019) note, effective COIL programs rely on the interplay of three essential elements: pedagogy, technology, and intercultural practice. This triadic design not only fosters communication and teamwork skills but also builds students' reflective awareness of cultural perspectives.

In the field of arts education, COIL offers distinctive advantages. Artistic collaboration naturally supports experiential learning and symbolic communication, allowing participants to share cultural values through creative forms rather than linguistic exchanges alone. Studies such as Borger (2022) and Asojo et al. (2019) highlight the role of visual storytelling, digital exhibitions, and design-based projects in promoting dialogue and intercultural understanding. Within these projects, the arts serve as both a learning object (through content representation) and a learning medium (through creative practice), aligning with Eisner's (2002) and Greene's (2000) aesthetic-pedagogical theories.

Empirical evidence further demonstrates COIL's capacity to enhance ICC. For instance, Petrova and Kuhnen (2025) examined an AI-supported design project between universities in Mexico and the United States, finding that collaborative digital artmaking strengthened students' self-confidence, intercultural awareness, and creativity. Similarly, Qumbisa et al. (2025) reported that visual exchanges using platforms like Padlet and Zoom encouraged students to reflect on their identities and develop empathy across cultural boundaries. Together, these studies affirm that COIL can serve as a transformative framework for fostering ICC through multimodal, student-centred learning.

Nonetheless, COIL's integration remains limited in Vietnamese higher education, where most virtual collaborations focus on English language learning or entrepreneurship rather than the arts (Lu et al., 2024; Tran & Hoang, 2025; Trang et al., 2021). Existing projects demonstrate positive outcomes, such as improved intercultural sensitivity (Tung, 2022) and communication adaptability, but reveal institutional barriers are listed including inconsistent policy support, technological inequity, and a lack of faculty training (Giang, 2023; Thanh & Anh, 2025). As shown in Figure 3, these challenges reflect Rubin and Guth's (2023) early developmental stage of COIL adoption in Vietnam, where pilot programs have yet to reach full institutionalisation. Addressing these gaps requires systemic approaches to embed

COIL in curricula, supported by policies that recognise intercultural learning as a core educational goal.

### 3.3. Artificial Intelligence in Visual Arts Education for Intercultural Learning

Recent advancements in AI have opened new possibilities for transforming visual arts education into a dynamic and intercultural learning environment. AI application, from generative art tools like DALL·E and Midjourney to immersive AR/VR technologies, offer novel modes of creativity, interaction, and reflection. As summarised in Table 1, current research demonstrates AI's dual potential as both a creative and cognitive tool (Davoodi, 2024; Erişti & Freedman, 2024; Huang, 2023) and as a driver of intercultural and pedagogical innovation (Jingxiu, 2025; Then et al., 2023; Zlateva, 2025).

*Table 1. Summary of key findings on AI in visual arts education related to intercultural and pedagogical transformation*

| Authors | Year | Key findings | Category |
|---|---|---|---|
| Huang | 2023 | AI automates tasks, enhances creativity with tools like GANs/AR, and supports cognitive/artistic growth. Emphasizes AI as complementary. | AI as a creative & cognitive tool |
| Then et al. | 2023 | AI tools deepen learner engagement with cross-modal art forms and enhance intercultural understanding in digital visual environments. | AI in educational innovation & ICC |
| Davoodi | 2024 | AI fosters creative co-production, challenges traditional authorship, and promotes multimodal cultural expression. | AI as a creative & cognitive tool |
| Erişti & Freedman | 2024 | AI enhances learning and originality but also poses risks to creativity. Suggests using AI as a supporting, not replacing tool. | AI as a creative & cognitive tool |
| Ezhilmurugan & Yashavini | 2024 | AI transforms pedagogy and promotes intercultural collaboration but raises concerns over ethics and curricular alignment. | AI in educational innovation & ICC |
| Jingxiu | 2025 | AI encourages collaborative aesthetic learning and supports COIL-based art education by providing cross-cultural visual generation capabilities. | AI in educational innovation & ICC |
| Zlateva | 2025 | Highlights AI's strong application in digital arts and learning. Notes positive perceptions of AI's role in broadening access to education. | AI in educational innovation & ICC |

AI's capacity to automate technical tasks, personalise learning, and generate visual representations enables students to engage with complex cultural themes in unprecedented ways. For example, Jingxiu (2025) found that AI-supported art projects enhanced learners' ability to collaborate across cultures, while Ezhilmurugan and

Yashavini (2024) observed that AI tools fostered inclusivity and reflective dialogue in digital creative environments. These outcomes resonate with Deardorff's process model of ICC where empathy and adaptability evolve through intercultural interaction.

At the same time, the literature warns of ethical and epistemic challenges. AI systems trained on culturally biased datasets can inadvertently reproduce stereotypes or homogenise artistic diversity (Williamson & Piattoeva, 2022). As Davoodi (2024), and Erişti and Freedman (2024) argue, educators must position AI as a supportive rather than substitutive technology: one that augments, rather than replaces, human imagination and cultural dialogue. This critical awareness is essential to prevent the misuse of AI in ways that undermine authenticity or perpetuate cultural inequities.

Integrating AI within COIL frameworks offers promising solutions to these tensions. As illustrated in Figure 2, AI operates as a mediating layer connecting pedagogy, technology, and intercultural practice. Within this triadic model, AI enables multilingual communication, collaborative creation, and reflective feedback, as well as key processes for building intercultural empathy and global citizenship. When strategically applied in Vietnamese visual arts education, AI-supported COIL projects can help overcome linguistic barriers, stimulate creativity, and cultivate cultural sensitivity. Yet to achieve these outcomes sustainably, educators must combine critical AI literacy with constructivist, arts-based pedagogies that emphasise interpretation, dialogue, and ethical engagement.

Collectively, current scholarship underscores that ICC development in visual arts education requires an integrative approach that unites aesthetic inquiry, intercultural collaboration, and technological mediation. While COIL and AI each offer transformative potential, their combined application in the Vietnamese higher education context remains in its infancy. Addressing this research gap, through AI-supported, art-based COIL models, provides both a theoretical contribution to intercultural pedagogy and a practical strategy for advancing educational internationalisation in Vietnam.

## 4. INTEGRATING AI INTO VISUAL ARTS EDUCATION COLLABORATIVE ONLINE INTERNATIONAL LEARNING PROGRAMS IN VIETNAM

### 4.1. The Current State of Collaborative Online International Learning Adoption in Vietnamese Higher Education Level

Most COIL programs in Vietnamese universities currently focus on language education, especially English. Although research on collaborative learning in Vietnam does not always use the term COIL, in general these programs are based on online collaboration among students from different cultural backgrounds or on international cooperation in innovative teaching. From 2021 to 2025, many studies have examined COIL applications in Vietnam across diverse teaching contexts. Based on Rubin and Guth's (2023) stages of COIL development, the structured process of building a COIL project includes five basic steps (Figure 3). These steps help universities organize and implement COIL effectively, including finding international partners, designing shared modules, supporting students and lecturers, and assessing intercultural collaboration outcomes.

*Figure 3. Steps of implementing the COIL project in the university settings by Rubin and Guth (2023)*

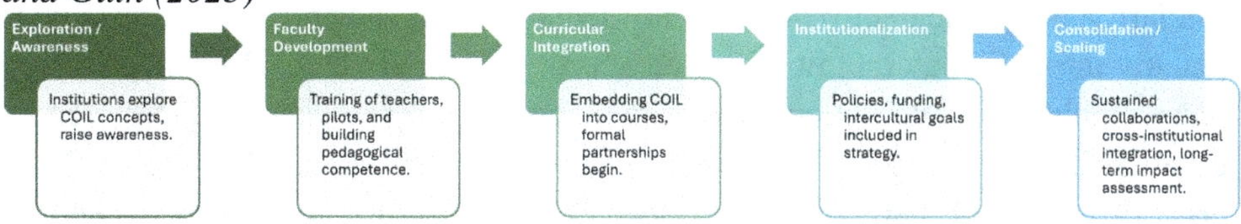


In practice, most studies on COIL in Vietnam indicate that the adoption level in higher education is still at the initial stage, with limited institutional and policy support. According to Rubin and Guth's model, the initial stage includes piloting, experimenting, and building faculty capacity. For example, research at Van Lang University examined EFL students' participation in online collaborative environments but reported challenges with technology and a lack of intercultural integration (Trang et al., 2021). Similarly, research in 2025 showed that online collaboration had mostly individual impacts, with Vietnamese students engaging better when tasks emphasised direct interaction (Thanh & Anh, 2025). Other studies found that while COIL promotes innovation, faculty in Vietnam face institutional barriers, lacking strong support mechanisms (Giang, 2023). In the next stage, COIL is integrated into training courses, and some projects have shown concrete progress. For example, the VIBE program between Vietnam and Ireland allowed faculty training in entrepreneurship, experiential learning, and design methods, applied to real-world teaching contexts (Lu et al., 2024). This represents a more systematic COIL model applied across subjects. Another example is a Vietnam–Taiwan project where lecturers co-designed online classes, creating intercultural group learning environments (Tran & Hoang, 2025). These cases show that COIL in Vietnam is reaching a structured level, though still limited. Some studies also note that projects at this stage focus on sustainability and long-term collaboration, such as offshore programs allowing students to participate in international modules. In short, research and COIL projects in Vietnam are still in the early stages, with many at the pilot or partial implementation level. Only a few have moved toward institutionalisation. The final stage of Rubin and Guth's model, which involves large-scale implementation supported by national networks and long-term policies, has not yet been observed in Vietnam.

In terms of subject areas, the most common COIL-related practices in Vietnam are found in English as a Foreign Language (EFL), entrepreneurship, and interdisciplinary research. EFL education appears to be the field most often linked to online collaboration, frequently using group-based tasks to engage students with diverse perspectives. For example, a study at Van Lang University showed how EFL students interacted via online platforms to develop communication and teamwork skills in intercultural contexts (Trang et al., 2021). While not officially a COIL program, this research reflected core values of COIL and highlighted ICC development potential. Similarly, entrepreneurship education in Vietnam has shown promising growth, particularly through bilateral initiatives such as the VIBE Vietnam - Ireland program, which emphasized international exchange, creative project work, and experiential learning (Lu et al., 2024). These activities were structured similarly to COIL in terms of goals and methods, aiming to build 21st-century skills, entrepreneurial thinking, and connected learning communities. The impact of these programs on students' intercultural communicative competence (ICC) is clear. For instance, a study involving Vietnamese and Taiwanese students found reduced anxiety in intercultural communication and significant improvement in ICC when students engaged in structured online collaboration (Tran & Hoang, 2025). Likewise, other studies showed that Vietnamese students who joined overseas learning programs developed stronger intercultural sensitivity and adaptability, both are key components of ICC (Tung, 2022).

However, challenges remain. Research by Thanh and Anh (2025) indicated that student characteristics, such as introversion, affected participation in collaborative online learning. Many students still preferred traditional face-to-face methods despite the benefits of digital platforms. Additionally, institutional and administrative barriers, such as rigid regulations and insufficient policy support, were major obstacles to scaling COIL systematically in higher education.

In conclusion, although COIL has not yet been widely and formally adopted in Vietnamese higher education, its foundation elements, international collaboration, online platforms, and the growing demand for ICC, are already present across many fields. To align with global modernisation and integration, Vietnamese universities need to embed COIL systematically into curricula. This would involve designing cross-border learning programs and creating institutional and policy frameworks that treat COIL-based international online learning as a core component of modern pedagogy.

## 4.2. The Potential of Integrating AI Tools With the Visual Arts Education Collaborative Online International Learning Programs for Intercultural Communicative Competence Development in Vietnam

From reviewing COIL-related studies in Vietnam, one notable direction is the potential of applying COIL in visual arts and aesthetic education, especially as universities move toward modern curricula supported by digital technologies and international collaboration. Although a specific COIL framework for this field has not yet been established, initiatives such as 3D exhibitions modeled after programs in Japan, Korea, and other countries, show growing interest from Vietnamese universities in combining art exchange with global collaboration (Giang, 2023; Thanh & Anh, 2025). Another relevant area is youth-focused research. For instance, projects involving Vietnamese and UK students on visual storytelling about climate change showed effective ICC development and highlighted COIL's potential for community-based and creative art projects (Jones et al., 2025).

Visual arts COIL projects are connected with design thinking, creativity, and innovation, offering several advantages in Vietnam's higher education context. First, visual arts education in Vietnam currently emphasises practical and professional skills. By applying COIL, students not only gain access to real-world knowledge but also expand their perspectives globally. International collaboration helps them practice critical reflection, creativity, and practical design skills in both local and global contexts. Second, while Vietnamese culture is often included in domestic curricula, it remains less familiar to international audiences. COIL offers opportunities for Vietnamese students to exchange and interpret their cultural heritage with peers abroad. This reflective interaction helps them recognise and evaluate national cultural values in comparison with others. Drawing on frameworks like Eisner and Greene, this process fosters deeper intercultural understanding and appreciation. Third, Vietnam's integration of arts and social engagement creates opportunities for linking COIL with real-life contexts. Through projects, students can explore not only artistic and technical content but also social and community issues. This strengthens their ability to connect creative practice with civic responsibility, building a culture of social engagement in education. Finally, the creative disciplines naturally encourage exploration and risk-taking. COIL thus provides a multidimensional environment where students express individuality while learning intercultural collaboration. This connection not only improves ICC but also broadens career opportunities, equipping Vietnamese students with confidence in a globalised creative labour market.

In conclusion, COIL in Vietnamese visual arts education is not only an academic framework but also carries strong practical significance for developing future creative human resources. These advantages can be further expanded when AI is integrated into the organisation of COIL visual arts projects aimed at developing ICC, as illustrated in Figure 4:

**AI as an intermediary communication tool.** In Vietnam's higher arts education, language barriers and limited opportunities for international exchange remain challenging for students. By integrating AI-based translation and communication tools into COIL projects, students can overcome these barriers, creating conditions to exchange ideas, debate, and reflect on artworks with global peers. At the same time, digitalisation and multilingual outputs foster ICC by helping students express ideas across languages, enhancing global collaboration skills and preparing them for intercultural professional contexts.

**AI as a source of intercultural creative inspiration.** With its ability to simulate, recreate, and generate images from multiple cultures, AI opens new creative directions for Vietnamese art students. Instead of focusing only on basic visual skills, students can use AI to explore cultural diversity, compare and reinterpret Vietnamese art from a global perspective. This integration expands creativity while building students' capacity for critical reflection, dialogue, and empathy with different cultures. Thus, AI supports ICC development by addressing current gaps in technical training and intercultural dialogue in Vietnamese visual arts education.

**AI as a platform for practice and community connection.** Studios and online exhibitions supported by AI allow Vietnamese students to access global art environments throughout their learning process. By displaying, commenting, and reflecting on artworks in international spaces, students can build intercultural awareness, responsibility, and civic engagement. This is especially relevant in Vietnam, where arts education increasingly emphasises community-oriented practice. COIL, combined with AI, creates opportunities for students to experience cultural diversity in virtual spaces, enhancing awareness of art's cultural and social roles.

**AI as a tool for assessment and learning feedback.** In higher arts education, studio teaching often prioritises practice and experimentation, with less focus on evaluating communication and reflection skills. With AI support, teachers can assess participation, communication, and collaboration in COIL projects more effectively. AI tools can generate real-time feedback, highlight intercultural aspects of student outputs, and suggest directions for further creative development. In this way, AI not only strengthens technical training but also contributes to shaping students' ICC and reflective habits in their creative learning process.

*Figure 4. AI-integrated visual arts COIL framework in Vietnamese higher education, showing how AI supports creation, data, display, communication, feedback, and adjustment to foster ICC*

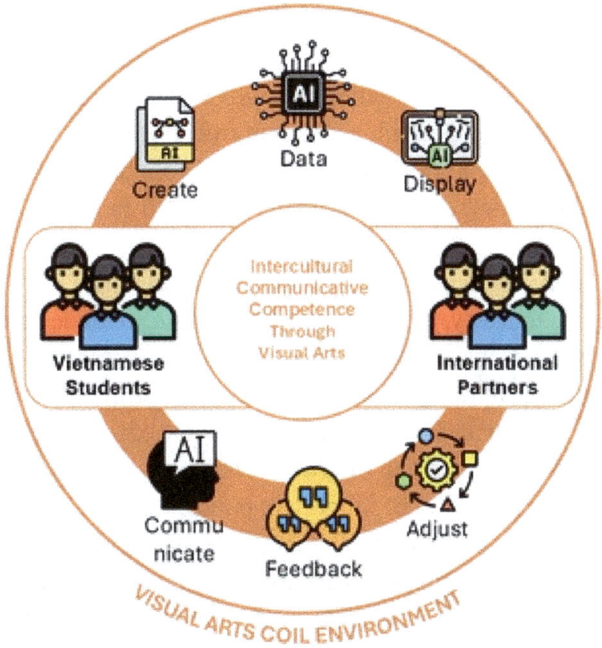


Thus, the integration of AI tools into COIL programs in higher education visual arts in Vietnam offers great potential for developing students' ICC. While current visual arts training mainly focuses on basic technical skills, applying COIL combined with AI has expanded opportunities for creativity, cultural dialogue, and global connection. AI not only acts as a communication bridge, a source of intercultural creative inspiration, and an online exhibition platform, but also serves as a tool for analysis and feedback, helping to reduce language barriers, limitations in international access, and gaps in community engagement. As a result, Vietnamese art students can participate more deeply in intercultural collaborations, strengthen their reflective abilities, enhance cultural awareness, and gradually affirm their position in the global art environment.

### 4.3. Key Challenges and Opportunities in Promoting Intercultural Communicative Competence Through Visual Arts Using the Collaborative Online International Learning Model in the Vietnamese Context

Promoting ICC through visual arts education using the COIL model in Vietnam presents both opportunities and challenges. As Vietnam's higher education system becomes more globally integrated, COIL has emerged as a framework to support intercultural dialogue, creativity, and international collaboration. However, policy, pedagogical methods, and cultural characteristics still present barriers that limit effectiveness.

One of the main challenges is language and communication. Although visual arts rely heavily on imagery, the process of discussion, critique, and interpretation of artworks requires strong language skills. Vietnamese students often struggle to express complex ideas in foreign languages other than English, leading to shallow exchanges. While AI translation tools can reduce some of these barriers, they cannot fully convey the nuance and depth of artistic and cultural expression.

Another challenge is the lack of supportive policies and institutional frameworks. At present, many COIL projects in Vietnam depend mainly on individual faculty efforts or short-term international collaborations, often limited by university strategies. Insufficient funding, management, and policies hinder the sustainability and scalability of COIL models. This restricts ICC development within higher education curricula.

Technological and resource limitations are also notable obstacles. Even large universities in Hanoi and Ho Chi Minh City have invested in infrastructure, but disparities remain, especially for students in smaller institutions or rural areas. The lack of access to advanced design software, 3D platforms, or stable internet connections creates inequality in participation and collaboration in COIL activities.

Traditional teaching approaches in Vietnam also affect ICC development through COIL. Arts education in Vietnam often emphasises technical skills and craftsmanship, with limited attention to dialogue, reflection, or intercultural exchange. This results in students excelling in creative production but lacking the skills to situate their work globally or engage deeply in intercultural discussions. Thus, COIL requires shifting teaching practices from teacher-centred to student-centred approaches.

Cultural limitations and limited international exposure are additional challenges. Many Vietnamese students lack confidence in sharing their cultural values or presenting critical perspectives in global discussions. This hesitation reduces the depth of intercultural exchanges and often leads to passive participation in COIL projects.

On the other hand, COIL offers important opportunities for ICC development in visual arts education. Integrating AI can support multimodal communication. AI translation, image generation, and analysis tools help students overcome language barriers while opening new forms of exchange through visual outputs, online exhibitions, and collaborative creative projects. This makes intercultural communication more diverse, comprehensive, and innovative.

Another key opportunity lies in expanding the global vision of Vietnamese visual arts. Through COIL, students and institutions can introduce their cultural identity, traditional arts, and contemporary creativity to the world. This presence not only promotes Vietnamese culture but also breaks stereotypes, giving students greater confidence in expressing themselves as active cultural creators.

COIL in visual arts also creates opportunities for interdisciplinary learning and community engagement. Many art projects are linked to social issues such as the environment, identity, heritage, or social equity. Incorporating these themes into COIL projects allows students to collaborate with international peers to co-create meaningful cross-cultural narratives. In doing so, students not only learn art but also practice addressing diverse global challenges.

Furthermore, COIL provides an opportunity to innovate teaching methods in Vietnamese universities. By encouraging collaboration, reflection, and intercultural exchange, COIL fosters a shift away from traditional teacher-centred approaches. This transformation not only strengthens ICC but also aligns Vietnamese higher education with international teaching standards.

Finally, COIL in visual arts contributes significantly to training a creative workforce with global potential. Participation in international projects helps students develop critical thinking, creativity, and global collaboration skills, qualities essential for success in today's globalised creative industries. As a result, Vietnamese students are better equipped for integration and can confidently establish themselves in the international creative sector.

In summary, promoting ICC through visual arts education with the COIL model in Vietnam involves both challenges and opportunities. Barriers such as language difficulties, limited policies, technological gaps, traditional pedagogy, and student psychology exist. However, with AI support, cultural promotion, interdisciplinary learning, and creative workforce training, COIL can become an effective framework for Vietnamese higher education to develop ICC and enhance the global impact of Vietnam's visual arts.

## 5. RECOMMENDATIONS AND FUTURE DIRECTIONS

Based on the research analysis, this chapter affirms that developing ICC through COIL programs in visual arts education in Vietnam should be guided by a strategic and sustainable approach. First, universities need to institutionalise COIL in their curricula, treating it as an essential component of the internationalisation process in education, rather than limiting it to pilot projects. This requires clear policies, stable funding, and specific assessment criteria for ICC outcomes among students. At the same time, training and professional development for lecturers are crucial to equip them with knowledge in intercultural pedagogy, skills in designing international collaborative modules, and the ability to apply AI in visual arts teaching.

Another important factor is investment in digital infrastructure, from online exhibition platforms and translation tools to design software and AI-powered creative applications, ensuring equal participation opportunities for students across different regions and institutions. Additionally, supportive policies such as credits, scholarships, or certification of ICC competencies should be introduced to motivate student participation, reduce psychological barriers, and encourage engagement in international collaboration. Particularly, linking COIL visual arts projects with pressing global social issues—such as climate change, gender equality, and cultural heritage preservation—can help students simultaneously build creative skills and develop global citizenship awareness.

For the future, several directions should be prioritized. First, building domestic COIL networks that connect with international partners will ensure greater diversity and sustainability than individual projects. Second, further research is needed to assess AI's role in enhancing ICC in arts education, including empathy, critical thinking, and creativity in intercultural contexts. Third, global digital exhibition models should be piloted to create spaces for exchange where Vietnamese students can present their work and engage in international dialogue, supported by AI tools for creation and analysis. Fourth, COIL should be integrated with national strategies for educational internationalisation, complementing traditional exchange formats to expand access to more students. Finally, long-term studies should evaluate the impact of COIL and AI not only on learning outcomes but also on career development, creativity, and global competencies after graduation.

In conclusion, COIL in visual arts education with AI support is not only an academic approach but also a strategic tool for enhancing Vietnamese students' global cultural competence. If implemented with systematic coordination, supportive policies, and sustainable integration, COIL has the potential to become a driving force for Vietnam's higher education internationalisation while fostering a creative workforce equipped for global challenges.

## REFERENCES


Asojo, A. O., Kartoshkina, Y., Jaiyeoba, B., & Amole, D. (2019). Multicultural learning and experiences in design through collaborative online international learning (COIL) framework. *Journal of Teaching and Learning with Technology*, *8*(1), 5–16. DOI: 10.14434/jotlt.v8i1.26748

Borger, J. G. (2022). Getting to the CoRe of collaborative online international learning (COIL). *Frontiers in Education*, *7*, 987289. Advance online publication. DOI: 10.3389/feduc.2022.987289

Byram, M. (2021). *Teaching and Assessing intercultural communicative competence: Revisited* (2nd ed.). Multilingual Matters & Channel View Publications., DOI: 10.21832/9781800410251

Charmaz, K., & Thornberg, R. (2021). The pursuit of quality in grounded theory. *Qualitative Research in Psychology*, *18*(3), 305–327. DOI: 10.1080/14780887.2020.1780357

Davoodi, A. (2024). EQUAL AI: A framework for enhancing equity, quality, understanding and accessibility in liberal arts through AI for multilingual learners. *Language, Technology, and Social Media*, *2*(2), 178–203. DOI: 10.70211/ltsm.v2i2.139

Deardorff, D. K., & Jones, E. (2022). Intercultural competence as a core focus in international higher education. In *The Handbook of International Higher Education* (2nd ed.). Routledge.

Eisner, E. W. (2002). *The Arts and the creation of mind.* Yale University Press. https://www.jstor.org/stable/j.ctt1np7vz

Erişti, S. D. B., & Freedman, K. (2024). *Integrating digital technologies and AI in art education: Pedagogical competencies and the evolution of digital visual culture. Participatory Educational Research, 11(H. Ferhan Odabaşı Gift Issue), Article H.* Ferhan Odabaşı Gift Issue., DOI: 10.17275/per.24.94.11.6

Ezhilmurugan, P., & Yashavini, E. (2024). Exploring the impact of Artificial Intelligence in the visual arts: A comprehensive study. *ShodhKosh: Journal of Visual and Performing Arts, 5*(2ICITAICT), 74–84. DOI: 10.29121/shodhkosh.v5.iICITAICT.2024.1331

Giang, N. T. (2023). Innovating education in the digital era for the traditional fine arts education professions, the applied fine arts training field in hanoi, vietnam. *Проблемы современной науки и образования*, (8 (186)), 66-73.

Greene, M. (2000). *Releasing the imagination: Essays on education, the arts, and social change*. Jossey-Bass Publishers. (Original work published 1995)

Hackett, S., Janssen, J., Beach, P., Perreault, M., Beelen, J., & van Tartwijk, J. (2023). The effectiveness of collaborative online international learning (COIL) on intercultural competence development in higher education. *International Journal of Educational Technology in Higher Education, 20*(1), 5. DOI: 10.1186/s41239-022-00373-3 PMID: 36713634

Helm, F. (2024). *Intercultural communication in virtual exchange*. Cambridge University Press. DOI: 10.1017/9781009385589

Huang, D. (2023). Exploring the impact of artificial intelligence on arts education: Enhancing students' creative. *Lecture Notes in Education Psychology and Public Media, 32*(1), 152–157. DOI: 10.54254/2753-7048/32/20230842

Jingxiu, H. (2025). Breaking boundaries and reshaping: An exploration of aesthetic competence development in university students in the era of artificial intelligence. *International Journal of Social Science, Management and Economics Research.* DOI: 10.22004/ag.econ.355400

Jones, L., Hu , L., Parsons, K. J., Thu, V. T., & Halstead, F. (2025). From science to storytelling: Advancing a climate knowledge–action framework through reflections on youth-focused, participatory action research in Vietnam. *British Educational Research Journal, n/a*(n/a). DOI: 10.1002/berj.70004

Lu, T. T. L., Linh, D. T. D., Anh, N. T. T., Anh, N.-Q., & Jarvis, S. (2024). Reimagining Vietnamese higher education: Entrepreneurial pedagogy and the Vietnam–Ireland bilateral educational exchange (VIBE) program at Vietnam national university, Hanoi. In Earl, C. (Ed.), *Vietnam's creativity agenda: Reforming and transforming higher education practice* (pp. 149–162). Springer Nature., DOI: 10.1007/978-981-97-7703-7_10

Petrova, M., & Kuhnen, C. (2025). Artificial intelligence as a tool for individual and collaborative creativity in design education. *Design and Technology Education: An International Journal, 30*(1), 86–101.

Qumbisa, N., Khoza, N., & Tshabadira, T. (2025). Employing innovative learning management systems in higher education virtual exchanges projects. *Journal of Inquiry Based Activities, 15*(Special Issue), 83–94.

Rubin, J., & Guth, S. (2023). *The guide to COIL virtual exchange: Implementing, growing, and sustaining collaborative online international learning*. Taylor & Francis.

Thanh, N. H., & Anh, N. N. (2025). Impacts of personality on the use of online collaborative platforms in higher education in Vietnam. *Asian Education and Development Studies*, *14*(4), 742–768. DOI: 10.1108/AEDS-05-2024-0103

Then, C., Soewandi, E. J., Danial, M. F., Achmad, S., & Sutoyo, R. (2023). The impact of artificial intelligence on art—a systematic literature review. *2023 IEEE 9th Information Technology International Seminar (ITIS)*, 1–7. DOI: 10.1109/ITIS59651.2023.10420208

Tran, L., & Hoang, H. (2025). Enhance university students' intercultural competence with collaborative online international learning (coil): A case study of Vietnamese and Taiwanese students. In *Intercultural competence in higher education english language instruction* (pp. 191–226). IGI Global Scientific Publishing., DOI: 10.4018/979-8-3693-3506-2.ch006

Trang, B. T. X., Ha, H. Y., Uyen, N. T. B., Thanh, N. V. U., & Thuy, N. T. C. (2021). A study on collaborative online learning among EFL students in Van Lang University (VLU). *AsiaCALL Online Journal*, *12*(3), 9–21.

Tung, V. N. (2022). Vietnamese international students in offshore programs: Engagement in intercultural communicative competence and intercultural sensitivity. *Journal of Intercultural Communication Research*, *51*(3), 229–253. DOI: 10.1080/17475759.2021.1970612

Williamson, B., & Piattoeva, N. (2022). Education governance and datafication. *Education and Information Technologies*, *27*, 3515–3531.

Zlateva, A. (2025). Artificial intelligence in art education: Transforming visual arts training. *International Journal of Cognitive Research in Science. Engineering and Education*, *13*(2), 481–489.

# Section 4
# Teacher Education and Professional Development

Chapter 13

# Bringing Intercultural Communicative Competence and Artificial Intelligence Into Teacher Education:

## Integrating Training and Lifelong Professional Development

**Ayten Çokçalışkan**
http://orcid.org/0000-0002-5616-1351
*Ministry of National Education, Turkey*

**Sabriye Şener**
https://orcid.org/0000-0003-4926-8940
*Independent Researcher, Turkey*

## ABSTRACT

*Teacher education plays an important role in shaping cultural and technological transformation. As classrooms become more diverse and digital tools influence instruction, teachers need competences that go beyond traditional expectations. Intercultural Communicative Competence (ICC) and Artificial Intelligence (AI) have therefore become key areas of teacher preparation, yet both remain only partly integrated into pre-service and in-service programs. This chapter examines how teacher education can more effectively embed ICC and AI across the continuum of teacher learning. It outlines the historical development of teacher training, highlights cultural and technological priorities, and discusses how globalization, digitalization,*

DOI: 10.4018/979-8-3373-6325-7.ch013

*and evolving pedagogies require a reframing of teacher competences. It further explores how ICC and AI can support each other and presents practical models for implementation. The chapter ultimately proposes a coherent, future-oriented framework for integrating ICC and AI in ethical, sustainable, and meaningful ways.*

## 1. THE HISTORICAL PERSPECTIVES ON TEACHER TRAINING AND PROFESSIONAL DEVELOPMENT

Teacher education has undergone a significant transformation over the past several decades, shifting from traditional models toward more dynamic, interactive, reflective, and technology-enhanced approaches (Mena-Guacas et al., 2025). Understanding the historical evolution of teacher training and professional development (PD) is essential for situating contemporary debates on intercultural competence, digital literacy, and artificial intelligence in education. This section offers an overview of how pre-service training and in-service professional development have changed over time, drawing attention to the pedagogical, technological, and sociocultural factors that continue to shape teacher education today.

Early teacher preparation programmes were shaped by behaviourist and positivist assumptions that positioned teaching as a standardized and linear process centred on content delivery rather than professional judgement (Darling-Hammond, 2006). Cohen et al. (2013) note that these historical orientations reflected broader paradigms in education research, which favoured technical competence over reflective or inquiry-based practice. As a result, teachers were often viewed as implementers of predetermined curricula, and teacher training programmes prioritized subject knowledge and procedural classroom management over the kind of adaptive, context-sensitive expertise that teaching in diverse and rapidly changing classrooms actually demands.

Over time, the limitations of traditional models became increasingly visible. Influenced by constructivist, sociocultural, and humanistic theories, and particularly by Vygotsky's (1978) emphasis on learning as a socially mediated process, teacher education gradually shifted toward acknowledging teaching as a complex, relational, and context-dependent profession that requires reflective practice, pedagogical reasoning, and responsiveness to diverse learners (Schön, 1983). This led to the expansion of practicum experiences, mentorship structures, and school–university partnerships, as well as growing attention to diversity and inclusion in teacher preparation (Darling-Hammond, 2006; Zeichner, 2010). Alongside these shifts, intercultural competences also began to receive greater emphasis in language teacher education, particularly with the influence of Byram's (1997) framework, which moved the field away from purely linguistic goals toward a broader conception of communicative and cultural mediation. Professional development, too, moved beyond short, isolated workshops and began to adopt more continuous, collaborative, and practice-based approaches, such as professional learning communities (Hord, 2009), reflecting a growing recognition that teacher learning is ongoing and deeply embedded in social, cultural, and institutional contexts.

Technological and societal changes in the 21st century further accelerated this evolution. The integration of ICT tools required teachers to develop digital literacy, multimodal pedagogical skills, and fluency in technology-enhanced learning environments (Koehler & Mishra, 2009). More recently, the rise of artificial intelligence has brought new and arguably more urgent expectations, asking teachers not only to use these tools but to critically evaluate how they work, what assumptions they encode, and what ethical implications they carry for data-driven decision-making in education (Holmes et al., 2019). These developments make a compelling case for why ICC, digital literacy, and AI literacy can no longer be treated as peripheral concerns in teacher education; they are, increasingly, central to what it means to teach responsibly and effectively in the 21st century.

## 1.1 Evolution of Pre-Service Teacher Training

Pre-service teacher training refers to the formal preparation prospective teachers undergo before entering the profession, encompassing coursework, supervised practicum experiences, and the development of foundational pedagogical and subject-specific knowledge. The quality of this preparation is widely recognised as one of the most significant determinants of teaching effectiveness and learner outcomes (Darling-Hammond, 2017; Turan, 2023). How this preparation is structured, and what competences it prioritises, has changed considerably over the past several decades, shaped by shifting theoretical frameworks, evolving societal demands, and rapid technological development.

Historically, pre-service programmes operated within a transmission-oriented paradigm in which teaching was understood as the efficient delivery of content (Darling-Hammond, 2017). Prospective teachers were trained to follow prescriptive lesson plans, manage classrooms procedurally, and demonstrate mastery of subject knowledge. Reflective practice, intercultural awareness, and learner-centred pedagogy were largely absent from these curricula, or at best treated as peripheral concerns. Studies highlight that teachers' efforts to integrate culture into lessons often remain at a surface level, largely dependent on textbook content, resulting in inadequate preparation for intercultural teaching (Şallı-Çopur, 2021). This gap is particularly significant given that intercultural competence requires deliberate, structured development rather than incidental exposure (Byram, 1997; Deardorff, 2006).

From the 1980s onwards, these assumptions were increasingly challenged. Reflective teaching (Schön, 1983), practicum experiences, and collaboration with experienced mentors (Hobson et al., 2009) have become more prominent. The turn towards communicative approaches (Canale & Swain, 1980) repositioned language learning around meaningful use, learner autonomy (Little, 1991), and critical thinking rather than memorisation and form-focused instruction. These approaches encouraged teacher candidates to move beyond rote learning and develop the skills needed to facilitate meaningful communication in diverse classrooms. Authentic materials such as videos, podcasts, and real-life interactions became integral to helping learners develop cultural awareness and communicative competence (Reid, 2014). This shift mattered beyond methodology: it signalled a change in how the teaching profession itself was understood, from technical executor to reflective, culturally responsive practitioner.

Computer-Assisted Language Learning (CALL) platforms introduced adaptive tasks, personalised learning, and multimodal resources that earlier textbook-based models could not offer. As Crystal (1987) observed, even early digital tools such as micro-computers meaningfully expanded the possibilities of language instruction by supporting interactive work across all four skills. These developments gradually shifted expectations: prospective teachers were no longer required only to teach effectively but to design digitally mediated learning environments responsive to varied learning styles, abilities, and contexts (Koehler & Mishra, 2009).

The transition from CALL-based tools to AI-driven systems marks a significant shift in the expectations placed on teacher candidates, one that goes beyond technical proficiency and raises fundamental questions about pedagogy, ethics, and professional identity. Tools such as adaptive learning systems, automated feedback applications, natural language processing tools, and intelligent tutoring systems have begun to influence how teachers prepare for the classroom (Holmes et al., 2019; Luckin, 2018). AI-enhanced simulations provide spaces where teacher candidates can practise without risk, while data-informed reflection tools help them evaluate their own performance more accurately. Yet despite these developments, systematic AI training within pre-service programmes remains limited, contributing to uncertainty and hesitation among novice teachers (Taqa, 2025). This gap is not incidental, it reflects a broader pattern in which teacher education struggles to keep pace with technological change. Addressing it requires not only technical familiarity with AI tools but also ethical digital literacy, including awareness of algorithmic bias and data privacy, and the intercultural dimensions of AI-mediated communication (Zawacki-Richter et al., 2019).

This overview illustrates how pre-service teacher education has gradually expanded beyond traditional pedagogical preparation to encompass the digital, ethical, and intercultural dimensions that increasingly define what it means to teach in complex, technology-mediated classrooms. At the same time, these developments also highlight that teacher learning does not end with initial preparation but continues throughout the professional career, making ongoing professional development an essential component of teacher education.

## 1.2 Historical Foundations of Professional Development

While pre-service training provides the foundation for entering the profession, professional development encompasses the ongoing, in-service learning experiences through which teachers refine and expand their competences. Richards and Farrell (2005) emphasise that teachers need continuous professional development to respond effectively to their students' needs in an educational landscape that is constantly evolving and increasingly shaped by technology. Professional development encompasses a wide range of activities, from workshops, seminars, and online courses to more embedded forms of collaborative learning such as mentoring, peer observation, and professional learning communities, and increasingly, AI-mediated development pathways. Research also distinguishes between more traditional activities, such as workshops and short courses, and school-embedded, collaborative forms of learning. Lewis et al. (2009) demonstrate that lesson study, a structured cycle in which teachers collaboratively plan, observe, and revise classroom lessons, fosters deeper pedagogical reflection and more sustained instructional improvement than one-off training events. Similarly, participation in professional learning communities has been shown to strengthen instructional practices and contribute positively to student learning outcomes (Vescio et al., 2008); more recent research further indicates that PLC participation also enhances teacher self-efficacy and professional commitment (Cheng & Zhao, 2023). While traditional activities often take place outside classroom hours and tend to have limited impact because teachers have little opportunity to apply what they learn immediately, school-based models such as mentoring, coaching, study groups, and peer observation are viewed as more effective because they are sustained, collaborative, and closely connected to teachers' daily practice (Garet et al., 2001).

For many years, professional development mostly consisted of brief workshops that provided information but rarely led to meaningful changes in how teachers taught. During this period, PD also focused heavily on curriculum implementation, subject-area updates, and administrative requirements. Research shows that such episodic training has limited long-term impact (Desimone & Garet, 2015). However, as educational contexts have become more complex, the expectations placed upon teachers have expanded significantly. Teachers today are expected to design meaningful learning experiences, foster critical thinking, motivate learners, support autonomy, create inclusive environments, and adapt instruction to diverse learner needs. Recent research highlights that these expectations have expanded alongside the growing importance of 21st-century teaching and learning skills, particularly in relation to technology integration. Nuhoğlu and Güvercin-Seçkin (2021) emphasise that teachers' 21st-century instructional skills are closely linked to their level of information technology use, underscoring the central role of digital competence in contemporary educational practice. Therefore, teacher educators should model pedagogical agility, critical thinking, socio-emotional competence, and openness to innovation to prepare teachers for the complex demands of today's classrooms. In response, PD has increasingly shifted toward sustained, collaborative, and practice-oriented models, including Professional Learning Communities (PLCs). PLCs encourage teachers to reflect collectively, share expertise, analyse student data, and engage in continuous instructional improvement (DuFour & Fullan, 2013; Hord, 2009).

Technological advancements have markedly expanded PD opportunities. Digital platforms enable teachers to access global knowledge networks, participate in virtual learning, and collaborate beyond geographical constraints (Selwyn, 2017; Voogt et al., 2013), while MOOCs provide affordable and flexible access to specialised training (Yuan & Powell, 2013) and social media platforms support informal but meaningful forms of professional exchange (Carpenter & Krutka, 2014). More recently, artificial intelligence has further extended these possibilities by enabling personalised professional learning recommendations, real-time analytics on instructional performance, adaptive feedback, and simulation-based practice. However, these advancements also present challenges, including ethical concerns, data privacy risks, unequal access to digital resources, and the need for teachers to develop new forms of technological and intercultural literacy (UNESCO, 2021). All of this suggests that teachers need support in developing a balanced set of skills, those that help them work confidently with AI tools and those that allow them to respond sensitively to cultural diversity.

## 2. REFRAMING TEACHER EDUCATION IN A CHANGING WORLD

As education systems confront rapid cultural and technological change (Aramayo & Shackleton, 2025), it has become increasingly important for curriculum design and teacher preparation to equip educators with competences that extend beyond traditional pedagogical knowledge. Despite these developments, research indicates that both pre-service training and professional development still lack a consistent focus on intercultural competence and AI literacy. Studies show that intercultural preparation in teacher education often remains insufficient (Şallı-Çopur, 2021), while systematic AI training remains limited (Taqa, 2025). Guan et al. (2025) further report that pre-service teachers tend to use AI only when strictly necessary, reflecting gaps in both foundational knowledge and pedagogical integration. This gap can be seen as a significant limitation in today's teacher education systems. This becomes especially clear when the purposes of ICC and AI literacy in contemporary classrooms are taken into account. Intercultural communicative competence is essential for fostering inclusion, addressing diversity, and supporting learners as global citizens (Byram, 1997; Deardorff, 2006). At the same time, AI literacy has become fundamental for navigating the digitalization of education and making informed decisions about technology integration (Meylani, 2024; Taqa, 2025). Teachers who lack ICC may unintentionally reinforce stereotypes or struggle to respond to learners' diverse needs, while those without AI literacy may resist innovation, misuse emerging tools, or overlook critical ethical issues.

In light of these developments, integrating ICC and AI into training and professional development has become increasingly important for supporting teachers in their work. AI, for example, can enrich ICC-focused learning by providing immersive simulations, adaptive feedback, and multilingual collaboration tools (Godwin-Jones, 2021). Meanwhile, ICC frameworks offer the ethical, reflective, and human-centred perspective teachers need to critically assess AI outputs, identify algorithmic bias, and ensure that technology is used to promote, not compromise, equity (Taqa, 2025). ICC and AI should be viewed as complementary aspects of teacher competence, as these reciprocal contributions show.

## 2.1 Continuous Professional Development in a Changing Landscape

Professional growth does not end at certification; it is a lifelong journey. In this context, continuing professional development (CPD) involves ongoing processes and structured activities that help teachers expand their knowledge, build new skills, and develop their professional attitudes so they can better support student learning (Guskey, 2000). It enables teachers to keep pace with evolving technologies, pedagogical approaches, and global trends (Avalos, 2011). CPD is required in many countries; however, its effectiveness varies greatly depending on the quality, relevance, and design of the programmes (Organisation for Economic Co-operation and Development [OECD], 2019). Research consistently shows that high-quality CPD should be teacher-driven, context-sensitive, and connected to real instructional challenges (Darling-Hammond et al., 2017). Effective professional development must incorporate strong technological skills in addition to pedagogical competence and subject knowledge as classrooms continue to evolve in the digital age. CPD related to technology must be in line with teachers' actual needs (Alivi, 2022), and meaningful changes in teachers' attitudes toward teaching require sustained, long-term support rather than quick interventions.

Teachers now have access to a wide range of CPD options, including peer learning networks, online courses, workshops, and mentorship. However, single training sessions usually do not create long-term change. Sustainable improvement occurs when professional learning is embedded into teachers' daily practice through coaching, collaborative planning, ongoing reflection, and consistent feedback (Desimone & Garet, 2015). Professional learning communities can be given as an example, as they bring teachers together to analyse student data, share strategies, and reflect on teaching (DuFour & Fullan, 2013; Hord, 2009). By working together in these ways, teachers are better able to share responsibility, learn from one another, and maintain steady progress in their professional learning. Continuous professional development thus serves not only to improve instructional quality but also to help teachers adapt to emerging innovations and sustain meaningful professional growth.

## 2.2 Digital Transformation of Teacher Professional Development

In contemporary education, teachers' efforts to make learning more effective increasingly lead them to engage with digital tools and innovative instructional technologies (Kirschner & Selinger, 2003). As technological advancements continue to influence educational practices (Prensky, 2001), both teachers and learners benefit from enriched learning environments and more dynamic learning experiences. To inspire students in areas such as creative thinking, problem solving, inquiry, and lifelong learning, today's teachers must actively explore, implement, and meaningfully adapt emerging educational technologies within their own professional learning processes (Johnson & Adams, 2011; Prensky, 2001).

However, the availability of digital tools does not automatically translate into effective pedagogical use. Research suggests that many teachers still lack the confidence or training to integrate technology in ways that go beyond surface-level application (Koehler & Mishra, 2009). This challenge is particularly relevant in culturally diverse settings, where digital tools need to be adapted not only to different learning styles but also to varied linguistic and cultural expectations. In such contexts, digital transformation requires more than technical training; teachers also need professional learning that combines digital competence with intercultural awareness, enabling them to use technology in ways that are both pedagogically sound and culturally responsive.

Furthermore, digital tools personalize professional learning by enabling self-paced study and offering micro-credentialing opportunities (Pellegrino & Hilton, 2012). Teachers can earn badges and certificates in targeted areas, allowing them to respond flexibly to evolving classroom demands. At the same time, this digital transformation also draws attention to persistent inequities. Without equitable access to devices, connectivity, and digital literacy training, educators in under-resourced contexts risk being excluded from emerging opportunities (UNESCO, 2021). In parallel with these digital developments, AI-supported applications such as adaptive learning platforms and intelligent tutoring systems are increasingly viewed as contributing to meaningful changes in education, with the potential to strengthen teaching and learning processes (Zhang et al., 2023).

These developments suggest that professional learning can no longer rely on isolated technical training. As digital tools and AI applications become part of everyday educational practice, teachers increasingly need support that strengthens both their technological competence and their ability to work effectively in culturally diverse classrooms. Addressing this need requires sustained, well-designed professional development that connects digital skills with intercultural awareness.

## 3. INTERCULTURAL COMMUNICATIVE COMPETENCE IN TEACHER PROFESSIONAL DEVELOPMENT

In recent years, foreign language education has increasingly focused on intercultural communicative competence, as global interconnectedness has made it a central goal rather than an optional skill. One of the most influential frameworks for conceptualizing intercultural competence is Byram's Intercultural Communicative Competence model (Byram, 1997), which outlines the key components teachers and learners need in order to interact meaningfully across cultural boundaries. The model includes attitudes such as curiosity, openness, and a readiness to suspend preconceived assumptions when encountering cultural others; knowledge of social groups, cultural practices, and how these shape communication; and skills that involve interpreting cultural meanings and connecting one's own perspective with those of others. At the centre of this framework lies critical cultural awareness, which encourages individuals to reflect on their own cultural positioning, question biases, and engage responsibly with cultural differences. This conceptualization makes it clear that ICC includes the attitudes, information, and abilities required to successfully negotiate cultural diversity in addition to language proficiency.

In the context of English language teaching and teacher professional development, this model provides an essential foundation because it clarifies not only what intercultural competence entails but also why it matters for contemporary teaching. It helps teachers understand how cultural perspectives influence communication, while also supporting the development of the reflective, ethical, and interpretive abilities needed to guide learners in culturally diverse classrooms. Consequently,

Byram's framework plays a crucial role in preparing teachers to act as intercultural mediators who foster inclusion, global citizenship, and culturally responsive pedagogy.

As educational environments become more multicultural and interconnected, teachers are expected to navigate diverse communicative contexts with greater sensitivity and professionalism. In the 21st century, interaction, communication, and collaboration across cultures have become essential professional competences rather than supplementary skills. Given that English functions as a primary medium of global exchange, foreign language education bears the responsibility of fostering these competences from the earliest stages of schooling (Şallı-Çopur, 2021). Foreign language teachers should therefore develop the ability to act as intercultural mediators if they are to model these skills for their students. When teachers possess a strong foundation in their own ICC, they are better equipped to guide learners toward intercultural understanding and help them cultivate these competences themselves. Byram (1997) argues that teachers who have developed critical cultural awareness are more likely to foster the same capacity in their learners, acting as intercultural mediators rather than simply transmitting cultural information. Lee et al. (2023), in a quasi-experimental study, demonstrate that when teachers actively integrate ICC into their instruction, students show measurable gains in both intercultural competence and language proficiency. Conversely, Şallı-Çopur (2021) shows that where such preparation is absent, teachers' efforts to address culture tend to remain superficial and textbook-dependent.

The teaching–learning process is shaped by culturally embedded assumptions about the nature of the educational relationship, who participates in it, what their roles are, and the purposes underlying their shared activities (Venuleo et al., 2007). Recognising this culturally embedded nature of education, recent policy developments increasingly emphasize the importance of intercultural awareness, inclusive practices, and global citizenship competences. International frameworks such as the CEFR Companion Volume, Byram's (1997) model of Intercultural Communicative Competence, and Deardorff's (2006) process-oriented framework collectively position teachers not merely as knowledge transmitters but as cultural mediators capable of navigating diversity in contemporary classrooms. Both models have continued to inform current research at the intersection of ICC and technology-enhanced education. Byram's five-dimensional model — encompassing attitudes, knowledge, skills of interpreting and relating, skills of discovery and interaction, and critical cultural awareness — remains a widely adopted analytical framework in studies investigating how digital tools and AI-supported environments facilitate intercultural learning (Klimova & Chen, 2024). Deardorff's (2006) process model, which conceptualises intercultural competence as an ongoing developmental process rather than a fixed set of traits, has similarly provided a basis for designing training programmes that incorporate reflective and experiential components. Against this theoretical background, empirical research has begun to demonstrate the practical effects of AI-mediated interaction: Sarwari et al. (2024) show that AI technologies can positively influence intercultural communication among university students in multicultural settings, while Klimova and Chen (2024), in their synthesis of 11 studies, highlight how AI-driven tools such as an AI-powered language tools and virtual reality simulations can contribute to the development of ICC. At the practical level, McCallum (2024) demonstrates how generative AI tools can be used to design telecollaboration tasks that specifically target intercultural communicative competence, offering a concrete model for integrating AI into culture-focused language pedagogy. Despite the growing policy emphasis on intercultural awareness, research consistently indicates that many teachers address cultural dimensions in unplanned and superficial ways, reflecting insufficient preparation for intercultural teaching within teacher education programmes (Byram, 1997; Şallı-Çopur, 2021). These persistent gaps reveal that existing professional development structures, while essential for lifelong learning, remain limited in their integration of sustained, structured intercultural preparation. In the present study, these models serve as the conceptual basis for examining the integration of ICC and AI in teacher education, guiding both the analysis of existing literature and the suggested directions for pre-service and in-service teacher development.

Developing ICC within teacher PD requires moving beyond technical skill acquisition and embracing forms of professional growth that are critical, reflective, and ethically informed. In this sense, critical pedagogy offers a valuable foundation. Giroux (2020) argues that teachers should be empowered as transformative intellectuals who critically examine educational structures rather than functioning solely as curriculum deliverers. Freire's (2018) perspective similarly emphasizes education as a dialogic, liberatory practice, where teachers and learners collaboratively interrogate their world.

When PD programmes draw on critical pedagogy, they encourage teachers to engage with cultural and sociopolitical contexts, recognize their own biases, and develop reflective habits that support intercultural understanding (Ladson-Billings, 2014). Culturally responsive pedagogy exemplifies this approach: it highlights the importance of understanding learners' cultural backgrounds and integrating that knowledge into instructional design in ways that affirm identity and belonging (Gay, 2018). Such practices help teachers foster inclusive environments where all learners can participate meaningfully.

Empowered through ICC-oriented and critically informed PD, teachers can better support students who are not receiving adequate assistance, adjust the curriculum to respond to diverse needs, and work to reduce structural inequalities in schools. In this sense, ICC becomes not only a communicative skill set but a professional stance, one that positions education as a means of empowerment rather than a mechanism of exclusion (Giroux, 2020). Strengthening ICC in teacher professional development is not just about making it easier for people from different cultures to talk to each other; it is also about getting teachers ready to deal with the social issues that affect today's classrooms in a thoughtful and responsible way.

## 4. ARTIFICIAL INTELLIGENCE IN TEACHER PROFESSIONAL DEVELOPMENT

As global education continues to evolve in response to technological and pedagogical change, artificial intelligence is emerging as one of the most influential forces shaping language teaching and teacher learning. The rapid integration of AI into instructional settings is accelerating shifts in educational processes and professional practices (Adelana et al., 2024). In teacher professional development specifically, AI is transforming how teachers access learning opportunities, receive feedback, and refine their instructional decisions.

As AI becomes more embedded in educational contexts, teachers encounter both new opportunities and shifting expectations regarding their professional roles. While AI can reduce teacher workload by automating time-consuming administrative tasks (Shoaib et al., 2024), freeing teachers to focus on relational and instructional work, it also prompts a deeper reflection on the nature of teaching itself. Kim et al. (2022) note that when routine tasks are eased, teachers can devote more attention to activities requiring human judgment, empathy, and pedagogical insight. Ou et al. (2024) further highlight that recent advancements in educational AI increasingly assume tasks once carried out exclusively by teachers, making it essential for educators to reconsider their roles in AI-mediated environments. Consequently, stronger and more forward-looking teacher education programmes are needed to prepare teachers for these evolving expectations.

Building on these broader developments, Guan et al. (2025), drawing on thematic analysis of qualitative interviews with 24 pre-service teachers in Hong Kong and grounded in social cognitive theory, show that teacher candidates still tend to use AI only when they consider it strictly necessary, reflecting limited pedagogical integration. Their findings also reveal gaps in foundational AI knowledge and ethics, as well as a tendency to view AI as a mechanical tool rather than a collaborative partner. These insights underscore the importance of strengthening AI literacy and preparing teacher candidates for changing roles in AI-supported classrooms.

Studies on conversational agents (Xiao et al., 2024), adaptive and personalized learning materials (Essa et al., 2023; Alkhatnai, 2025), and multimodal representations in AI-supported learning (Cheung et al., 2025) demonstrate that AI's influence extends beyond personalization. These tools contribute to immersive learning experiences, support interactive engagement, and reshape how learners experience classroom communication. However, research shows that AI's instructional potential is still emerging in practice. Hwang and Chen (2023) observe that while deeper, pedagogically focused uses of AI are emerging more slowly, teachers frequently use it for familiar tasks like assessment support.

While these studies highlight AI's growing impact on learners, its influence on teachers' professional growth is becoming equally significant. Simulation environments and automated feedback systems offer safe spaces for experimenting with instructional strategies and receiving immediate insights that inform professional growth (Holmes et al., 2019). Such environments hold particular promise for intercultural teacher education, where practising culturally sensitive communication in simulated settings can support the development of both confidence and awareness. These developments suggest that AI is shaping not only what teachers teach, but also how they learn, reflect, and grow as professionals (Meylani, 2024).

At the policy level, national and international initiatives increasingly emphasise the importance of AI literacy and ethical awareness for educators. The Schoolnet Thematic Seminar Report (Çukurova et al., 2024) identifies key areas of AI-focused PD: supporting teaching and learning with AI tools, developing foundational AI concepts and ethical understanding, and rethinking curricula and teacher roles in response to AI-driven change. Frameworks such as DigCompEdu and UNESCO's ICT Competency Framework for Teachers (ICT-CFT) offer structured guidance for embedding digital skills and broader dimensions of inclusive, culturally responsive practice into teacher education, supported by evidence that assistive technologies can expand participation (Seale, 2013) and that inclusive pedagogical approaches help ensure all learners benefit from these opportunities (Florian & Beaton, 2018). At the national level, the Turkish Ministry of National Education's Artificial Intelligence in Education Policy Document (2025–2029) emphasizes the need to strengthen AI literacy, promote human-centred and ethically grounded AI practices, and ensure data protection and inclusivity (Ministry of National Education [MoNE], 2025).

Empirical research further demonstrates why AI must become an integral component of teacher professional development. Shezad et al. (2025) show that AI-supported professional development can enhance teacher performance, though they caution that technology alone is insufficient without reflective and context-aware learning processes. Meylani (2024) similarly argues that intelligent tutoring systems, data-driven dashboards, and VR-based simulations are most effective when integrated into sustained and well-designed PD programmes rather than provided as isolated tools. In such programmes, AI can also analyse learner data to identify strengths and needs, offering tailored pathways that enhance both efficiency and depth of understanding (Aldosari, 2020). Despite growing interest, substantial access gaps remain; Taqa (2025) reports that fewer than one-third of teachers have received formal AI training, highlighting persistent inequities in professional learning. As Prothero (2023) similarly notes, teachers need to understand how AI works and how to use it responsibly in instruction, yet opportunities for such training remain scarce.

Research on digital pedagogy also highlights why AI-related competences matter for teacher well-being in addition to instructional quality. In their studies, Shi et al. (2025) found that digital pedagogy competence predicts increased work engagement and reduced emotional exhaustion, largely due to enhanced digital self-efficacy. Their TPACK-based PD programme strengthened teachers' confidence and improved overall learning experiences. These findings suggest that technology-focused PD should intentionally integrate technological, pedagogical, and content knowledge while building self-efficacy in digital environments.

The evidence reviewed in this section indicates that AI is reshaping how teachers learn, receive feedback, and develop professionally. However, realising this potential requires more than access to advanced tools; it demands sustained, ethically grounded professional development that prepares teachers to work confidently with AI while addressing the intercultural dimensions of contemporary classrooms. It is within this context that the present study reviews and synthesises the existing literature on ICC and AI in teacher education, identifying key themes, gaps, and directions for future research and practice.

## 5. INTEGRATING INTERCULTURAL COMMUNICATIVE COMPETENCE AND ARTIFICIAL INTELLIGENCE INTO TEACHER PROFESSIONAL DEVELOPMENT

The incorporation of artificial intelligence into educational settings offers meaningful opportunities to strengthen not only students' language development but also their intercultural understanding (Ma & Yang, 2025). As the world becomes more interconnected, people engage in cross-cultural communication far more often, making proficient language use increasingly important (Xia et al., 2024). Strong intercultural communication skills are becoming even more important as a result of the rapid technological change, particularly the emergence of artificial intelligence, which is changing how people interact. People now encounter diverse cultural perspectives more frequently, whether online, through globalized workplaces, or within multilingual classrooms (Rahiman & Kodikal, 2023). This shift has made it essential for individuals to understand, adapt to, and effectively engage with cultural differences. In educational settings, these dynamics are already visible: learners come from varied linguistic and cultural backgrounds, and communication requires more than speaking a shared language. It demands sensitivity to cultural norms, values, and interaction styles. For teachers, developing such intercultural awareness has become increasingly important, especially as AI-driven tools intensify global connectivity and reshape how communication and learning take place.

In light of these facts, ICC and AI are best understood not as separate additions to teacher education but as interconnected competences that strengthen each other when developed together. ICC frameworks offer the ethical and reflective tools necessary for critical engagement with AI, particularly in identifying cultural bias and ensuring equitable practices. AI, in turn, provides new opportunities for strengthening ICC learning through simulations, adaptive environments, multilingual interaction tools, and data-informed reflective tasks. In this sense, the integration of ICC and AI is best viewed not as an optional enhancement but as a mutually reinforcing approach that reflects the needs of modern classrooms. For example, learners can improve their ability to navigate cultural diversity by using intelligent language-learning systems that incorporate real-world cultural contexts (Liu, 2025). When AI is used without intercultural sensitivity, there may be a risk that culturally biased data or ethnocentric assumptions embedded in algorithms may go unnoticed, potentially reinforcing stereotypes or marginalising learners from underrepresented backgrounds. For example, an AI-powered language assessment tool trained predominantly on native-speaker norms may penalise pragmatically appropriate but culturally distinct communication styles. Conversely, when ICC is developed without the support of technology, opportunities for authentic cross-cultural interaction may remain limited to what the immediate classroom context can offer. AI can extend these opportunities by connecting learners and teachers across cultural and linguistic boundaries through simulations, telecollaboration platforms, and adaptive feedback systems. In this sense, each domain addresses a limitation of the other.

Bringing intercultural communicative competence together with AI-supported tools helps bridge the gap between linguistic accuracy and cultural appropriateness. While AI can offer real-time correction, feedback, and examples of target-language structures, ICC ensures these structures are used in ways that are socially, pragmatically, and culturally meaningful. When combined, AI provides linguistic scaffolding and ICC contributes the cultural lens needed to use language sensitively and responsibly across contexts. Virtual simulation environments, for instance, allow learners to explore culturally varied scenarios and engage in interactive tasks that promote deeper intercultural understanding (Liu et al., 2023). To illustrate, consider a teacher using an AI-powered language tool to support learners' spoken interaction in English. Without ICC awareness, the teacher may accept the AI-powered language tool's responses as culturally neutral, overlooking the fact that the AI-powered language tool may default to dominant communication norms such as directness or informality. A teacher with ICC training, however, would recognise these defaults, discuss them with learners, and use the interaction as an opportunity to explore how communication styles vary across cultures. In this way, ICC transforms a routine AI-assisted language task into a meaningful intercultural learning experience.

Beyond these conceptual links, practical applications of AI also demonstrate how technology can actively support the development of intercultural competence. AI-supported tools, such as an AI-powered language tools, virtual tutors, and immersive simulation environments, can expose learners to diverse cultural viewpoints through real-time, interactive experiences (Chen et al., 2024). These technologies help move beyond the constraints of traditional classroom settings by enabling learners to practice language and communication skills in culturally authentic, dynamically generated contexts. This convergence suggests a holistic model in which ICC contributes the values, ethics, and intercultural sensitivity, while AI provides the tools, environments, and analytical feedback that make professional development more personalized and scalable.

Our review suggests that ICC and AI are more effectively developed when approached together rather than in isolation. When teachers bring intercultural sensitivity to their use of AI tools, they are more likely to notice cultural biases and respond to learners' diverse needs. At the same time, AI-supported environments can offer more varied and sustained opportunities for developing intercultural competence than traditional classroom settings alone. For teacher education programmes, this suggests that treating ICC and AI as separate modules may be less effective than creating learning experiences where both competences develop in connection with each other.

## 6. PRACTICAL APPLICATIONS AND TRAINING PROPOSALS

There are multiple practical steps that can be taken to move this integration forward. These pathways may vary across programmes, yet many begin with the early stages of teacher preparation. Pre-service settings offer a space where candidates can encounter ICC- and AI-related practices with guidance and feedback. Starting this work early helps teachers build habits that will support them throughout their careers. The studies reviewed in this chapter suggest that AI-based activities, such as VR cultural simulations and an AI-powered language tool can be more effectively integrated into existing curricula when they are aligned with learning objectives and assessment procedures (Ma & Yang, 2025). Such alignment is likely to increase both the pedagogical value and the practical relevance of these tools.

The strongest promise of AI in education lies in its ability to enhance adaptivity and interactivity through learner-centred, personalized instructional pathways (Chiu et al., 2024). However, these advantages can only be realized when pre-service teachers are properly equipped to integrate AI into their future classroom practices. In pre-service programmes, ICC-focused coursework can be paired with AI-supported case studies and interactive simulations, enabling teacher candidates to examine culturally complex scenarios with adaptive, data-informed feedback. A growing body of research demonstrates that AI-enhanced learning environments can personalise tasks and adjust the level of cultural and linguistic support according to learners' needs, creating more responsive opportunities for intercultural learning. Huang et al. (2023), in a bibliometric analysis of over 500 studies, identify personalisation and adaptive feedback as two of the most consistently reported affordances of AI in language education — affordances that are particularly relevant for intercultural learning contexts. Shadiev & Yu (2024), in a comprehensive review of CALL-based approaches, highlight the specific potential of these tools for developing intercultural competence. Empirical studies further support these claims: Sarwari et al. (2024) show that AI-mediated interaction can positively influence intercultural communication among students in multicultural university settings, while Klimova & Chen (2024), synthesising 11 studies conducted globally, demonstrate that AI-driven tools, including AI-powered language tools and virtual reality simulations, can meaningfully enhance intercultural communicative competence, though challenges related to cultural sensitivity and unequal access remain.

Yet, both educators and learners often require targeted training and ongoing support to use these tools effectively; professional development and student-friendly tutorials can help reduce technical barriers and improve learning experiences. In addition, mentor teachers and teacher candidates can collaboratively explore AI tools in culturally diverse classroom settings. This collaborative exploration allows candidates to observe how experienced teachers navigate cultural dynamics while using AI, bridging the gap between theoretical ICC knowledge and practical AI application. Including AI literacy in various parts of teacher preparation, with particular attention to ethics, understanding data, and thoughtful decision-making, supports candidates in learning how to use AI tools responsibly in culturally diverse classrooms.

In professional development, recent research shows that AI-supported workshops can merge intercultural case studies with real-time analytics (Huang et al., 2023), enabling teachers to reflect more closely on their communication strategies. Online modules may integrate ICC frameworks with adaptive AI tasks, and studies on adaptive systems indicate that such tasks can adjust to teachers' developing needs and levels of expertise (Yu et al., 2022), offering personalized pathways for ongoing learning. To reduce resistance to new technologies, research suggests that involving learners in choosing and using AI tools and designing AI-based tasks that resonate with students' interests and learning preferences can increase acceptance and sustained engagement (Ma & Yang, 2025). Reflective AI journals, in which teachers document their experiences with AI tools in culturally diverse contexts, can also serve as a formative assessment tool within professional development. Such journals encourage teachers to critically examine how AI-generated feedback interacts with cultural assumptions and communication norms.

As suggested by Shezad et al. (2025), blended programmes can further strengthen this process by connecting face-to-face seminars with AI-mediated reflective assignments, ensuring continuity and depth. They also note that micro-credentialing systems can be used to monitor teachers' progress across both ICC and AI literacy dimensions, aligning with emerging work on AI-enhanced professional learning. Based on our review, these structures offer a more coherent and transparent pathway for teacher development. Creating clear markers of progress can also promote sustained engagement with both ICC and AI-related competences over time. We would argue that without such structured pathways, efforts to integrate ICC and AI into teacher education risk remaining fragmented and short-lived. A more systematic approach, one that connects micro-credentials, reflective tasks, and collaborative learning within a sustained framework, is more likely to support meaningful and lasting professional growth.

Professional Learning Communities provide another avenue for sustained development. Embedding ICC–AI integration into PLC structures supports ongoing collaboration, mentoring, and peer reflection, which aligns with Wenger's (1998) framework for situated professional learning. Recent studies on AI-enabled platforms also highlight their potential to enhance multilingual and cross-regional collaboration by recommending relevant resources and facilitating communication across linguistic boundaries (Shadiev et al., 2021). Building on McCallum's (2024) work, AI-supported telecollaboration tasks can also connect teachers across different cultural and linguistic contexts, enabling them to practise intercultural communication while simultaneously developing AI literacy through the tools that facilitate these exchanges. Integrating these components within collaborative structures may make professional growth more continuous and better supported. When teachers work together within shared communities of practice, the development of both ICC and AI literacy can become more sustainable and more closely connected to real classroom challenges.

In line with other studies examining the role of artificial intelligence in teacher learning, Meylani (2024) outlines several domains through which AI may influence teachers' professional growth. The researcher highlights AI's support for continuous learning, the development of digital and AI literacy, and the use of reflective and adaptive tools that inform instructional decisions. Attention is also drawn to ethical considerations, accessibility, and the institutional conditions that shape meaningful AI use. These ideas are consistent with broader discussions in the field and help explain why educators are now expected to engage with data, ethics, and human–AI collaboration, especially in classrooms that are digitally mediated and culturally diverse.

These developments also bring a number of ethical considerations into view. As AI systems collect and analyse educational data, teachers inevitably face questions around privacy, data ownership, and surveillance, concerns widely discussed in the literature (Meylani, 2024). These debates underline how ethical decision-making is becoming a routine part of teachers' work rather than an occasional concern. Algorithmic bias further raises questions about fairness, while the digital divide limits access to AI-supported professional development in under-resourced contexts. Addressing these issues requires explicit ethics modules that are grounded in intercultural sensitivity and reflective engagement, an approach echoed in recent discussions of responsible AI use in diverse classrooms (Chiu et al., 2022). Embedding such components in teacher preparation may encourage more thoughtful and context-aware uses of AI, helping educators navigate complex situations with greater clarity and confidence. In this respect, ethics-focused ICC perspectives offer a valuable lens for understanding how technological decisions intersect with cultural dynamics, linguistic diversity, and everyday patterns of classroom interaction.

What emerges from our review is that effective integration of ICC and AI in teacher education is not simply a matter of adding new tools or topics to existing programmes. Rather, it requires a rethinking of how these competences are developed together — through sustained, reflective, and ethically grounded learning experiences that connect cultural sensitivity with technological confidence. The recommendations outlined above are not intended as a prescriptive model but as evidence-based directions that teacher educators and programme designers can adapt to their own institutional and cultural contexts.

Equipping teachers for an AI-enhanced educational landscape requires long-term curriculum planning that embeds AI literacy and is supported by sustained professional development (Chiu & Chai, 2020; Van Brummelen, Heng & Tabunshchyk, 2021). Preparing educators for such environments involves a comprehensive approach that strengthens their technical understanding of AI, develops their ethical awareness, and supports innovation in curriculum design, ensuring that teachers are ready to use AI meaningfully and responsibly in their instructional practice. Ultimately, these combined efforts can help create an educational ecosystem in which AI supports inclusion, intercultural understanding, and more responsive forms of teaching and learning.

## 7. EXPECTED CONTRIBUTIONS AND IMPLICATIONS FOR TEACHERS, TEACHER EDUCATORS, AND POLICYMAKERS

The discussion of how ICC and AI can be integrated into teacher education offers conceptual clarity, identifies existing gaps in current preparation models, and outlines practical pathways for strengthening both competences across pre-service and in-service contexts. A key contribution lies in showing how cultural and technological competences, often developed separately, can be strengthened when approached through a unified, mutually reinforcing framework.

For teachers, the integration of ICC and AI highlights the importance of developing the interpretive, ethical, and intercultural capacities needed to navigate today's diverse and technologically mediated classrooms. Consistent with longstanding understandings of intercultural competence (Byram, 1997), teachers benefit from cultivating the ability to interpret learners' linguistic and cultural perspectives and respond in ways that support inclusive participation. Beyond technical familiarity with AI tools, educators also need reflective habits that help them critically interpret AI-generated feedback and recognize the assumptions encoded in algorithmic outputs, a concern widely addressed in the ethics of AI (Floridi et al., 2018). Strengthening these competences enhances teachers' professional autonomy and better equips them to respond to rapidly evolving instructional demands.

For teacher educators, the implications centre on rethinking programme design and the everyday practices that support it. Preparing future teachers for culturally diverse and AI-rich learning environments requires more than simply adding new elective courses; it calls for integrated pedagogical models that blend experiential learning, case-based inquiry, simulation, and sustained reflection. Insights from experiential learning theory (Kolb, 1984) and culturally responsive pedagogy (Gay, 2018) remind us that these approaches help teacher candidates connect theoretical ideas to the realities they will face in their classrooms. By engaging with these models, candidates can develop the ethical, intercultural, and reflective habits that will help them navigate classroom complexities with greater confidence and sensitivity.

For policymakers, the implications emphasise the need to align national reforms with international competence frameworks and to create long-term, sustainable structures that support both ICC and AI literacy. This includes investing in technological infrastructure, providing equitable access to digital tools, and establishing clear guidelines to ensure ethical, transparent, and bias-aware AI use in education. Addressing the digital divide and supporting resource-constrained schools are also essential to ensuring that AI-enhanced professional development benefits all teachers, not only those in well-resourced environments.

In addition to these priorities, policymakers must also contend with the regulatory and policy questions that arise as AI becomes more embedded in education.

The rapid pace of technological change makes it difficult for schools and education systems to keep up, often leaving them without clear guidelines for using these tools in ethical and effective ways (Caerio Rodríguez et al., 2020). To address this, it is essential for educational authorities to work closely with technology specialists to develop standards that ensure responsible use, safeguard student data, and promote equitable access (Mena-Guacas et al., 2025).

These implications point toward a more culturally responsive, technologically informed, and ethically grounded vision of teacher development, one that supports educators in meeting the complex demands of contemporary classrooms. All three stakeholder groups, teachers, teacher educators, and policymakers, should work together to advance this vision. Teachers strengthen their intercultural, ethical, and reflective skills; teacher educators create cohesive, practice-based preparation models; and policymakers create fair and encouraging environments for the use of AI. Each group makes a unique but related contribution. The integration of ICC and AI becomes more practical and sustainable when these three factors cooperate, offering a stronger basis for meeting the changing needs of modern classrooms.

## 8. CONCLUSION

In this chapter, we examined how ICC and AI have been addressed in teacher education by synthesising historical developments, contemporary needs, and practice-based recommendations. Drawing on research, policy documents, and trends in teacher preparation, we traced how pre-service training and professional development have evolved in response to globalization, digitalization, and changing pedagogical expectations. We also highlighted several ongoing gaps that continue to shape teachers' preparedness for culturally diverse and technologically mediated classrooms and suggested that ICC and AI literacy should be understood as complementary elements of contemporary teacher professionalism. Across the subsequent sections, we explored the foundations of ICC and AI in teacher learning, discussed how each area contributes to teachers' interpretive, ethical, and pedagogical capacities, and offered practical recommendations for integrating them into both initial preparation and ongoing professional development. We aimed to provide a coherent, forward-looking synthesis that supports teachers, teacher educators, and policymakers in developing more inclusive, informed, and future-ready approaches to teacher education. By bringing ICC and AI together within a single analytical frame, we sought to address a gap in the existing literature, where these two areas tend to be examined separately. Our synthesis suggests that ICC and AI function as complementary rather than separate competences: ICC provides the reflective and culturally sensitive lens, while AI offers tools and adaptive feedback that can support more responsive professional development.

Teacher education has changed considerably as cultural diversity, new technologies, and evolving pedagogical ideas reshape what teachers are expected to know and do. Looking at how pre-service training and professional development have developed over time makes it clear that many long-established structures, although useful in their own moment, no longer fully prepare teachers for the realities of today's classrooms. The review of earlier sections also brought forward a recurring concern: intercultural communicative competence and artificial intelligence literacy are still too often treated as side topics rather than as essential, interconnected elements of professional preparation.

Examining ICC revealed how essential it has become for teachers to understand the cultural backgrounds and communication styles that shape students' experiences. The discussion of AI showed how digital tools now influence lesson design, assessment, feedback, and daily interaction in classrooms. What becomes clear when these strands are considered together is that neither cultural nor technological competence can stand alone. Teachers need both: the sensitivity to navigate human diversity and the confidence to work with tools that increasingly shape communication, access to information, and learning opportunities.

Several practical possibilities emerged from this synthesis. In pre-service settings, candidates can learn to connect cultural knowledge with digital tools through simulations, case studies, and guided reflection. In professional development, blended learning, AI-supported feedback, multilingual communities of practice, and flexible micro-credentials can help teachers build these skills over time. These approaches work best when they encourage ethical thinking, critical data use, and awareness of equity, especially in contexts where technological resources are unevenly distributed.

The broader implications reach beyond individual classrooms. Teachers benefit from stronger preparation that acknowledges both the human and digital dimensions of their work. Teacher educators can redesign programmes in ways that bring theory and practice closer together. Policymakers can support this direction by offering coherent frameworks, sustainable investment, and guidance that balances innovation with responsibility.

These insights point toward a vision of teacher preparation that is more responsive to the realities of today's classrooms. Strengthening teachers' intercultural awareness alongside their ability to engage thoughtfully with AI does not replace the core of what teachers do; rather, it reinforces the judgment, sensitivity, and professional agency required in diverse and technologically mediated learning environments. When teacher-education programmes and policy frameworks support this combined development in a sustained and coherent way, they lay the groundwork for classrooms

## REFERENCES


Adelana, O. P., Ayanwale, M. A., & Sanusi, I. T. (2024). Exploring pre-service biology teachers' intention to teach genetics using an AI intelligent tutoring-based system. *Cogent Education, 11*(1), 2310976. DOI: 10.1080/2331186X.2024.2310976

Aldosari, S. A. M. (2020). The future of higher education in the light of artificial intelligence transformations. *International Journal of Higher Education, 9*(3), 145–151. DOI: 10.5430/ijhe.v9n3p145

Alivi, J. S. (2022). *Explaining why teachers use ICT for teaching and learning: A case study of English as a foreign language teachers in a university in Indonesia.* [Unpublished doctoral dissertation]. University of Warwick.

Alkhatnai, M. (2025). The role of artificial intelligence tools in mediating Sino-Arab cultural exchanges through intercultural translation. *Babel, 71*(6), 740–769. DOI: 10.1075/babel.25101.alk

Aramayo, M., & Shackleton, J. (2025). Foreword. In Motteram, G., & Dawson, S. (Eds.), *What's changed in English Language Teaching? A review of change in the teaching and learning of English and in teacher education and development from 2014-2024 British Council.*, DOI: 10.57884/FPE8-5130

Avalos, B. (2011). Teacher professional development in *Teaching and Teacher Education* over ten years. *Teaching and Teacher Education, 27*(1), 10–20. DOI: 10.1016/j.tate.2010.08.007

Byram, M. (1997). *Teaching and assessing intercultural communicative competence.* Multilingual Matters.

Caerio Rodríguez, M., Ordoñez Fernández, F. F., Callejón Chinchilla, M. D., & Castro León, E. (2020). Diseño de un instrumento de evaluación de aplicaciones digitales (Apps) que permiten desarrollar la competencia artística. *Pixel-Bit. Revista de Medios y Educación, 58,* 7–25. DOI: 10.12795/pixelbit.74071

Canale, M., & Swain, M. (1980). Theoretical bases of communicative approaches to second language teaching and testing. *Applied Linguistics, 1*(1), 1–47. DOI: 10.1093/applin/1.1.1

Carpenter, J. P., & Krutka, D. G. (2014). How and why educators use Twitter: A survey of the field. *Journal of Research on Technology in Education, 46*(4), 414–434. DOI: 10.1080/15391523.2014.925701

Chen, X., Ma, L., Su, D., Zhang, Y., Liu, X., Xing, J., Li, L., & Ryoo, J. (2024). AI-enhanced cross-cultural competence in STEM education. *Proceedings of the International Conference on New Findings in Humanities and Social Sciences, 1*(1), 29–43. DOI: 10.33422/hsconf.v1i1.267

Cheng, C., & Zhao, J. (2023). The impact of professional learning communities on pre-service teachers' professional commitment. *Frontiers in Psychology*, *14*, 1153016. DOI: 10.3389/fpsyg.2023.1153016 PMID: 37448713

Cheung, K. K. C., Pun, J., Kenneth-Li, W., & Mai, J. (2025). Exploring students' multimodal representations of ideas about epistemic reading of scientific texts in generative AI tools. *Journal of Science Education and Technology*, *34*(2), 284–297. DOI: 10.1007/s10956-024-10182-0

Chiu, T. K., Ahmad, Z., Ismailov, M., & Sanusi, I. T. (2024). What are artificial intelligence literacy and competency? A comprehensive framework to support them. *Computers and Education Open*, *6*(6), 100171. DOI: 10.1016/j.caeo.2024.100171

Chiu, T. K. F., & Chai, C. S. (2020). Sustainable curriculum planning for artificial intelligence education: A self-determination theory perspective. *Sustainability (Basel)*, *12*(14), 5568. DOI: 10.3390/su12145568

Chiu, T. K. F., Meng, H., Chai, C.-S., King, I., Wong, S., & Yam, Y. (2022). Creation and evaluation of a pretertiary artificial intelligence (AI) curriculum. *IEEE Transactions on Education*, *65*(1), 30–39. DOI: 10.1109/TE.2021.3085878

Cohen, L., Manion, L., & Morrison, K. (2013). *Research methods in education* (7th ed.). Routledge. DOI: 10.4324/9780203720967

Crystal, D. (1987). *The Cambridge encyclopedia of language*. Cambridge University Press.

Çukurova, M., Kralj, L., Hertz, B., & Saltidou, E. (2024). *Professional development for teachers in the age of AI: European Schoolnet Academy thematic seminar report.* European Schoolnet Academy. http://www.eun.org/documents/411753/11183389/EUNA-Thematic-Seminar-Report-V5.pdf/b16bf795-b147-43ac-9f58-4dd1249b5e48

Darling-Hammond, L. (2006). *Powerful teacher education: Lessons from exemplary programs*. Jossey-Bass.

Darling-Hammond, L. (2017). Teacher education around the world: What can we learn from international practice? *European Journal of Teacher Education*, *40*(3), 291–309. DOI: 10.1080/02619768.2017.1315399

Darling-Hammond, L., Hyler, M. E., & Gardner, M. (2017). *Effective teacher professional development.* Learning Policy Institute. DOI: 10.54300/122.311

Deardorff, D. K. (2006). Identification and assessment of intercultural competence as a student outcome of internationalization. *Journal of Studies in International Education, 10*(3), 241–266. DOI: 10.1177/1028315306287002

Desimone, L. M., & Garet, M. S. (2015). Best practices in teachers' professional development in the United States. *Psychology, Society, &. Education, 7*(3), 252–263. https://ojs.ual.es/ojs/index.php/psye/article/view/515

DuFour, R., & Fullan, M. (2013). *Cultures built to last: Systemic PLCs at work.* Solution Tree Press.

Essa, S. G., Celik, T., & Human-Hendricks, N. E. (2023). Personalized adaptive learning technologies based on machine learning techniques to identify learning styles: A systematic literature review. *IEEE Access : Practical Innovations, Open Solutions, 11*, 48392–48409. DOI: 10.1109/ACCESS.2023.3276439

Florian, L., & Beaton, M. C. (2018). Inclusive pedagogy in action: Getting it right for every child. *International Journal of Inclusive Education, 22*(8), 870–884. DOI: 10.1080/13603116.2017.1412513

Floridi, L., Cowls, J., Beltrametti, M., Chatila, R., Chazerand, P., Dignum, V., Luetge, C., Madelin, R., Pagallo, U., Rossi, F., Schafer, B., Valcke, P., & Vayena, E. (2018). AI4People—An ethical framework for a good AI society: Opportunities, risks, principles, and recommendations. *Minds and Machines, 28*(4), 689–707. DOI: 10.1007/s11023-018-9482-5 PMID: 30930541

Freire, P. (2018). *Pedagogy of the oppressed* (50th anniversary ed.). Bloomsbury.

Garet, M. S., Porter, A. C., Desimone, L., Birman, B. F., & Yoon, K. S. (2001). What makes professional development effective? Results from a national sample of teachers. *American Educational Research Journal, 38*(4), 915–945. DOI: 10.3102/00028312038004915

Gay, G. (2018). *Culturally responsive teaching: Theory, research, and practice* (3rd ed.). Teachers College Press.

Giroux, H. A. (2020). *On critical pedagogy* (2nd ed.). Bloomsbury. DOI: 10.5040/9781350145016

Godwin-Jones, R. (2021). Evolving technologies for language learning. *Language Learning & Technology, 25*(3), 6–26. http://hdl.handle.net/10125/73443. DOI: 10.64152/10125/73443

Guan, L., Zhang, Y., & Gu, M. M. (2025). Pre-service teachers' preparedness for AI-integrated education: An investigation from perceptions, capabilities, and teachers' identity changes. *Computers and Education: Artificial Intelligence*, *8*, 100341. DOI: 10.1016/j.caeai.2024.100341

Guskey, T. R. (2000). *Evaluating professional development*. Corwin press.

Hobson, A. J., Ashby, P., Malderez, A., & Tomlinson, P. D. (2009). Mentoring beginning teachers: What we know and what we don't. *Teaching and Teacher Education*, *25*(1), 207–216. DOI: 10.1016/j.tate.2008.09.001

Holmes, W., Bialik, M., & Fadel, C. (2019). Artificial intelligence in education: Promises and implications for teaching and learning. *Center for Curriculum Redesign*. https://www.researchgate.net/publication/332180327_Artificial_Intelligence_in_Education_Promise_and_Implications_for_Teaching_and_Learning

Hord, S. M. (2009). Professional learning communities: Educators work together towards a shared purpose. *Journal of Staff Development*, *30*, 40–43. https://learningforward.org/wp-content/uploads/2018/03/hord301.pdf

Huang, X., Zou, D., Cheng, G., Chen, X., & Xie, H. (2023). Trends, research issues and applications of artificial intelligence in language education. *Journal of Educational Technology & Society*, *26*(1), 112–131. DOI: 10.30191/ETS.202301_26(1).0009

Hwang, G.-J., & Chen, N.-S. (2023). Editorial position paper: Exploring the potential of generative artificial intelligence in education: Applications, challenges, and future research directions. *Journal of Educational Technology & Society*, *26*(2), I–XVIII. DOI: 10.30191/ETS.202304_26(2).0014

Johnson, L., & Adams, S. (2011). *Technology outlook for UK tertiary education 2011-2016: An NMC Horizon Report Regional Analysis*. The New Media Consortium., https://www.learntechlib.org/p/182074/

Kim, J., Lee, H., & Cho, Y. H. (2022). Learning design to support student–AI collaboration: Perspectives of leading teachers for AI in education. *Education and Information Technologies*, *27*(5), 6069–6104. DOI: 10.1007/s10639-021-10831-6

Kirschner, P., & Selinger, M. (2003). The state of affairs of teacher education with respect to information and communications technology. *Technology, Pedagogy and Education*, *12*(1), 5–17. DOI: 10.1080/14759390300200143

Klimova, B., & Chen, J. H. (2024). The impact of AI on enhancing students' intercultural communication competence at the university level: A review study. *Language Teaching Research Quarterly*, *43*, 102–120. DOI: 10.32038/ltrq.2024.43.06

Koehler, M. J., & Mishra, P. (2009). What is technological pedagogical content knowledge? *Contemporary Issues in Technology & Teacher Education, 9*(1), 60–70. https://citejournal.org/volume-9/issue-1-09/general/what-is-technological -pedagogicalcontent-knowledge/

Kolb, D. A. (1984). *Experiential learning: Experience as the source of learning and development.* Prentice Hall.

Ladson-Billings, G. (2014). Culturally relevant pedagogy 2.0: Aka the remix. *Harvard Educational Review, 84*(1), 74–84. DOI: 10.17763/haer.84.1.p2rj131485484751

Lee, T. Y., Ho, Y. C., & Chen, C. H. (2023). Integrating intercultural communicative competence into an online EFL classroom: An empirical study of a secondary school in Thailand. *Asian-Pacific Journal of Second and Foreign Language Education, 8*(1), 4. DOI: 10.1186/s40862-022-00174-1

Lewis, C. C., Perry, R. R., & Hurd, J. (2009). Improving mathematics instruction through lesson study: A theoretical model and North American case. *Journal of Mathematics Teacher Education, 12*(4), 285–304. DOI: 10.1007/s10857-009-9102-7

Little, D. (1991). *Learner Autonomy: Definitions, Issues and Problems.* Authentik.

Liu, J. (2025). Exploring the impact of artificial intelligence-enhanced language learning on youths' intercultural communication competence. *Humanities & Social Sciences Communications, 12*(1), 1757. DOI: 10.1057/s41599-025-06033-x

Liu, S., Gao, S., & Ji, X. (2023). Beyond borders: Exploring the impact of augmented reality on intercultural competence and L2 learning motivation in EFL learners. *Frontiers in Psychology, 14*, 1234905. DOI: 10.3389/fpsyg.2023.1234905 PMID: 37860297

Luckin, R. (2018). *Machine learning and human intelligence: The future of education for the 21st century.* UCL IOE Press.

Ma, G., & Yang, X. (2025). Fostering intercultural competence through AI-driven tools: A case study of linguistic and cultural adaptability in Chinese EFL education. *Digital Technologies Research and Applications, 4*(1), 158–169. DOI: 10.54963/dtra.v4i1.1131

McCallum, L. (2024). New takes on developing intercultural communicative competence: Using AI tools in telecollaboration task design and task completion. *Journal for Multicultural Education, 18*(1/2), 153–172. DOI: 10.1108/JME-06-2023-0043

Mena-Guacas, A. F., López-Catalán, L., Bernal-Bravo, C., & Ballesteros-Regaña, C. (2025). Educational Transformation Through Emerging Technologies: Critical Review of Scientific Impact on Learning. *Education Sciences, 15*(3), 368. DOI: 10.3390/educsci15030368

Meylani, R. (2024). Artificial intelligence in the education of teachers: A qualitative synthesis of the cutting-edge research literature. *Journal of Computer and Education Research, 12*(24), 600–637. DOI: 10.18009/jcer.1477709

Ministry of National Education. (2025). *Artificial Intelligence in Education Policy Document (2025–2029)*. Türkiye.

Nuhoğlu, H., & Güvercin Seçkin, G. (2021). The analysis of relationship between teachers' 21st-century teaching-learning skills and information technology usage levels. *Kırşehir Ahi Evran University Faculty of Education Journal, 22*(3), 1358–1388. https://izlik.org/JA65JK95KB

Organisation for Economic Co-operation and Development (OECD). (2019). TALIS 2018 results (Volume I): Teachers and school leaders as lifelong learners. OECD Publishing. DOI: 10.1787/1d0bc92a-en

Ou, A. W., Stöhr, C., & Malmström, H. (2024). Academic communication with AI-powered language tools in higher education: From a post-humanist perspective. *System, 121*, 103225. DOI: 10.1016/j.system.2024.103225

Pellegrino, J. W., & Hilton, M. (Eds.). (2012). *Education for life and work: Developing transferable knowledge and skills in the 21st century*. National Academies Press.

Prensky, M. (2001). Digital natives, digital immigrants part 1. *On the Horizon, 9*(5), 1–6. DOI: 10.1108/10748120110424816

Prothero, A. (2023). *3 simple ideas for introducing AI into your teaching*. Education Week. https://www.edweek.org/technology/3-simple-ideas-for-introducing-ai-into-your-teaching/2023/06

Rahiman, H. U., & Kodikal, R. (2023). Revolutionizing education: Artificial intelligence empowered learning in higher education. *Cogent Education, 11*(1), 2293431. DOI: 10.1080/2331186X.2023.2293431

Reid, E. (2014). Authentic materials in developing intercultural communicative competences. *In LLCE2014: Conference proceedings (pp. 160–167).* Constantine the Philosopher University in Nitra.

Richards, J. C., & Farrell, T. S. C. (2005). *Professional development for language teachers*. Cambridge University Press. DOI: 10.1017/CBO9780511667237

Şallı-Çopur, D. (2021). Integrating intercultural communicative competence into teacher education for young learners. *Cankaya University Journal of Humanities and Social Sciences, 15*(2), 330–347. DOI: 10.47777/cankujhss.1047509

Sarwari, A. Q., Javed, M. N., Adnan, H. M., & Wahab, M. N. A. (2024). Assessment of the impacts of artificial intelligence (AI) on intercultural communication among postgraduate students in a multicultural university environment. *Scientific Reports, 14*(1), 13849. DOI: 10.1038/s41598-024-63276-5 PMID: 38879546

Schön, D. A. (1983). *The reflective practitioner: How professionals think in action*. Basic Books.

Seale, J. (2013). *E-learning and disability in higher education: Accessibility research and practice* (2nd ed.). Routledge. DOI: 10.4324/9780203095942

Selwyn, N. (2017). *Education and Technology: Key Issues and Debates* (2nd ed.). Bloomsbury Academic., DOI: 10.5040/9781474235952

Shadiev, R., Wang, X., & Huang, Y. M. (2021). Cross-cultural learning in virtual reality environment: Facilitating cross-cultural understanding, trait emotional intelligence, and sense of presence. *Educational Technology Research and Development, 69*(5), 2917–2936. DOI: 10.1007/s11423-021-10044-1

Shadiev, R., & Yu, J. (2024). Review of research on computer-assisted language learning with a focus on intercultural education. *Computer Assisted Language Learning, 37*(4), 841–871. DOI: 10.1080/09588221.2022.2056616

Shezad, F., Goswami, R., Shaheen, A., & Khan, I. (2025). AI in Teacher Training and Professional Development: A Tool for Continuous Learning and Skill Enhancement. *Review of Education, Administration & Law, 8*(1), 179-191. https://real.spcrd.org/index.php/real/article/view/416

Shi, Y. R., Sin, K. F. K., & Wang, Y. Q. (2025). Teacher professional development of digital pedagogy for inclusive education in post-pandemic era: Effects on teacher competence, self-efficacy, and work well-being. *Teaching and Teacher Education, 168*, 105230. DOI: 10.1016/j.tate.2025.105230

Shoaib, M., Sayed, N., Singh, J., Shafi, J., Khan, S., & Ali, F. (2024). AI student success predictor: Enhancing personalized learning in campus management systems. *Computers in Human Behavior, 158*, 108301. DOI: 10.1016/j.chb.2024.108301

Taqa, A. R. (2025). Teacher training and professional development in the age of AI. *Enhanced Research Publications*. https://www.researchgate.net/publication/388910863

Turan, R. (2023). An overview of the history teacher training programs of education faculties in Turkey from the perspective of pedagogical content knowledge. *Journal of Innovative Research in Teacher Education*, *4*(2), 311–335. DOI: 10.29329/jirte.2023.572.9

United Nations Educational, Scientific and Cultural Organization. (2021). *AI and education: Guidance for policy-makers*. https://www.unesco.org/en/articles/ai-and-education-guidance-policy-makers

Van Brummelen, J., Heng, T., & Tabunshchyk, V. (2021). Teaching tech to talk: K-12 conversational artificial intelligence literacy curriculum and development tools. *Proceedings of the AAAI Conference on Artificial Intelligence*, *35*(17), 15655–15663. DOI: 10.1609/aaai.v35i17.17844

Venuleo, C., Salvatore, S., Mossi, P., Grassi, R., & Ruggeri, R. (2007). The teaching relationship in the changing world: Outlines for a theory of the reframing setting. *European Journal of Social Psychology*, *5*(2), 151–180.

Vescio, V., Ross, D., & Adams, A. (2008). A review of research on the impact of professional learning communities on teaching practice and student learning. *Teaching and Teacher Education*, *24*(1), 80–91. DOI: 10.1016/j.tate.2007.01.004

Voogt, J., Knezek, G., Cox, M., Knezek, D., & ten Brummelhuis, A. (2013). Under which conditions does ICT have a positive effect on teaching and learning? A call to action. *Journal of Computer Assisted Learning*, *29*(1), 4–14. DOI: 10.1111/j.1365-2729.2011.00453.x

Vygotsky, L. S. (1978). *Mind in society: The development of higher psychological processes*. Harvard University Press.

Wenger, E. (1998). *Communities of practice: Learning, meaning, and identity*. Cambridge University Press. DOI: 10.1017/CBO9780511803932

Xia, Y., Shin, S. Y., & Kim, J. C. (2024). Cross-cultural intelligent language learning system (CILS): Leveraging AI to facilitate language learning strategies in cross-cultural communication. *Applied Sciences (Basel, Switzerland)*, *14*(13), 5651. DOI: 10.3390/app14135651

Xiao, F., Zhao, P., Sha, H., Yang, D., & Warschauer, M. (2024). Conversational agents in language learning. *Journal of China Computer-Assisted Language Learning*, *4*(2), 300–325. DOI: 10.1515/jccall-2022-0032

Yu, H., Wang, J., Murugesan, M., & Rahman, A. S. (2022). Artificial intelligence-based quality management and detection system for personalized learning. *Journal of Interconnection Networks*, *22*(Supp02), 2143004. DOI: 10.1142/S0219265921430040

Yuan, L., & Powell, S. J. (2013). *MOOCs and open education: Implications for higher education*. JISC CETIS.

Zawacki-Richter, O., Marín, V. I., Bond, M., & Gouverneur, F. (2019). Systematic review of research on artificial intelligence applications in higher education. *International Journal of Educational Technology in Higher Education*, *16*(1), 39. DOI: 10.1186/s41239-019-0171-0

Zeichner, K. (2010). University-based teacher education: Rethinking the connections between campus courses and field experiences in college- and university-based teacher education. *Journal of Teacher Education*, *61*(1-2), 89–99. DOI: 10.1177/0022487109347671

Zhang, C., Schießl, J., Plößl, L., Hofmann, F., & Glaser-Zikuda, M. (2023). Acceptance of artificial intelligence among pre-service teachers: A multigroup analysis. *International Journal of Educational Technology in Higher Education*, *20*(1), 49. DOI: 10.1186/s41239-023-00420-7 PMID: 36743849

Chapter 14
# Teacher Training and Professional Development in AI-Supported ICC

**Binnur Ilter**
*Akdeniz University, Turkey*

**Burak Asma**
http://orcid.org/0000-0002-3602-3867
*Akdeniz University, Turkey*

## ABSTRACT

*This chapter examines how teacher education and professional development can foster intercultural communicative competence (ICC) in AI-mediated, digitally rich classrooms. Drawing on established ICC models, it introduces intercultural digital literacy, which links digital, media, and critical literacies with intercultural competence and highlights teachers as cultural mediators and critical evaluators of online and AI-generated content. The chapter reviews telecollaboration, virtual exchange, and AI-supported tools such as large language models, authoring and presentation platforms, gamified quizzes, automated writing feedback, and translation systems, outlining opportunities for scenario-based learning, reflection, and differentiation, as well as challenges including bias, limited pedagogical guidance, workload, and unequal access. It argues that sustainable professional development must embed intercultural digital literacy in curricula and build supportive, cross-national frameworks so AI promotes inclusive, dialogic, and socially just education.*

DOI: 10.4018/979-8-3373-6325-7.ch014

## 1. INTRODUCTION

In contemporary education systems, teachers are no longer regarded only as transmitters of subject knowledge. They are increasingly positioned as cultural mediators who guide learners in navigating complex, pluralistic societies. Intercultural communication competence (ICC) is therefore not confined to language education; it is a central professional requirement across subject areas and educational levels. In mathematics, science, history, arts, vocational education, and other fields, teachers work with culturally diverse groups of learners, respond to transnational mobility, and engage with curricula framed by global references and comparisons.

Processes of globalization and intensified mobility have multiplied everyday intercultural encounters, both offline and online. As Deardorff (2006) notes, higher education and schooling more broadly are expected to develop learners' intercultural competence as part of preparing them for participation in a global society. Classrooms have become spaces where individuals bring different cultural backgrounds, linguistic repertoires, beliefs, and communicative norms. Teachers are expected to support learners in engaging constructively with such differences, entering into dialogue, and reflecting critically on their own assumptions and positioning. In Byram's (1997) influential model, ICC encompasses attitudes of curiosity and openness, knowledge of one's own and others' social identities and practices, skills of interpreting and relating, skills of discovery and interaction, and critical cultural awareness. Though these elements originated in the field of foreign language education, they are growing more applicable to education across disciplines because any teacher, regardless of subject, can use these elements to create an inclusive, dialogic and critically engaged classroom, promoting participation, reasoning and equitable learning.

Digital technologies add an additional layer to this intercultural landscape. The widespread availability of online resources, learning platforms, automated feedback systems, and translation services means that learners routinely access information, texts, and media that present other cultures and societies. Warschauer and Kern (2000) already showed how networked communication environments were reshaping language use and intercultural contact. Today, these environments are embedded across the curriculum. A history teacher searching for sources on colonial encounters, a science teacher looking for examples of climate change impacts in different regions, or a civics teacher exploring debates on migration can quickly draw on large collections of digitized texts, images, and videos. Learners themselves use online tools to translate, summarize, and rework material, often outside teachers' direct supervision.

These developments create significant opportunities. Teachers can more readily introduce multiple perspectives, compare representations from different contexts, and design tasks that draw on authentic materials, as advocated by Kramsch (1993) and later by Gilmore (2007). Learners may also investigate the ways in which ideas, events and social issues are framed and represented in other linguistic and cultural contexts and share digital resources from their own linguistic and cultural backgrounds online too. Digital resources lack cultural neutrality. Particular historical contexts, specific discourses, and power relations produce them. These contexts, discourses, and relations privilege some voices. These contexts, discourses, and relations marginalise other voices in how material is organised on a digital platform. Critical media literacy scholars have also examined how online texts reinforce stereotypes, mute minority voices, and universalize dominant norms (e.g., Kellner & Share, 2007).

For teachers in all subjects, this brings up questions that go beyond just using digital tools. When a history teacher relies on automatically generated summaries of an event, they need to think about which narratives are highlighted and which are missing. When a science teacher uses complex word problems or case studies found online, cultural references might resonate more with some students than others, which could reinforce feelings of exclusion or inadequacy. When a teacher of literature invites students to engage with different readings of a novel on-line, s/he must also remain attentive to the culturally situated perspectives that frame those readings, including those that are not acknowledged or are invisible, because effective teaching in such contexts requires that we not only evaluate the truth of claims, but also the representation of identities, values, and cultural communities and the power relations that constitute those representations.

The need for professional development in ICC in digitally rich environments comes from these observations. Learners already use many tools, platforms, and resources when they search for information, translate texts, or prepare assignments. If teachers are not ready to address and thoughtfully frame this reality, a gap appears between formal education and students' actual communication practices. Helm (2015) points out that in virtual exchange, simply offering technology for contact is not enough; intercultural learning needs careful teaching and reflection. Likewise, in school and university classrooms, having digital access alone does not ensure intercultural understanding. Teachers require structured chances to develop the knowledge, skills, and attitudes they need to help learners use and assess digital resources with cultural content critically.

Studies of online translation and multilingual communication have demonstrated, for instance, that machine translation systems frequently handle culturally laden expressions poorly and may tacitly sanction particular language varieties (Pym, Malmkjær & Gutiérrez-Colón Plana, 2013), and therefore, without deliberate preparation, teachers may mistakenly reproduce such distortions through the examples they select, the tasks they assign, or the materials they recommend. Moreover, teachers need concrete ways to identify bias, cross-check information across multiple sources, and promote learners' critical reading and viewing practices in digital environments, because this will enable them to effectively support their students in navigating complex digital landscapes.

The professional role of teachers is becoming more inclusive with an integrated competence profile, and in addition to subject matter and pedagogical competence, teachers must also possess cultural-linguistic awareness, as well as a sensitivity to how digital tools impact communication practices and the construction of knowledge. In other words, short-term tool training is no longer sufficient, because Sleeter (2012) argues that long-term engagement is required for teachers to develop deep, reflective competencies that pertain to diversity and social justice in the context of multicultural teacher education. Moreover, in the context of digitally saturated learning environments, long-term engagement must also include awareness about how cultures are represented online, whose narratives and experiences are being amplified or marginalized, and how to help learners articulate and value their own perspectives.

In practical terms, this means changing how we think about teacher learning. Instead of viewing digital tools and intercultural goals as separate subjects, professional development should combine them under the larger idea of intercultural digital literacy. This includes the ability to navigate and create digital content, to understand and respect cultural differences, and to act ethically and reflectively when using and recommending resources. For example, teachers might learn to design classroom activities where students compare how a global issue such as climate change, migration, or public health is represented in different national media outlets, to discuss how frames differ, and to consider whose interests are served by specific narratives. Such activities align with calls by UNESCO (2013) for media and information literacy that is explicitly connected to intercultural dialogue and democratic participation.

This chapter responds to these developments by focusing on teacher training and professional development in relation to intercultural communication in digitally mediated educational contexts. It begins by outlining conceptual foundations that connect established theories of ICC (e.g., Byram, 1997; Deardorff, 2006; Bennett, 1993) with current understandings of technology use in education. It then reviews existing practices in initial teacher education and in-service professional development that engage with digital tools in support of intercultural learning, highlighting both promising examples and persisting inequities in access and support. Subsequent sections examine the challenges teachers report when they attempt to integrate intercultural aims with digital practices, discuss the potential of simulations, role plays, and reflective tasks supported by technology for teacher learning, and propose recommendations for designing sustainable, long-term professional development models. The chapter argues that equipping teachers in all subjects with the skills, knowledge, and ethical orientation required to foster ICC in digitally rich environments is essential for building inclusive and culturally responsive education in the twenty-first century.

## 2. CONCEPTUAL FOUNDATIONS

Conceptual foundations and frameworks serve as the operating system for preparing teachers for the future. The frameworks of theory provide a means of articulating the purpose and process of educational practice by defining the key concepts, the relationships between them and their broader significance, and they provide a basis for needs diagnosis, for anticipating new developments, and for making informed decisions in a rapidly changing environment. The frameworks of theory also provide the basis for translating theory into practice in terms of curriculum design, pedagogy, assessment and the use of technology. They outline what to prioritize, how to stage learning, and what criteria to use when selecting tools. Together, they offer stable anchors like ethics, equity, intercultural dialogue, and learning impact. This approach allows for the thoughtful integration of new AI capabilities instead of just reacting to them. It also helps stakeholders find a common language and turn uncertainty into opportunities for design.

### 2.1 Defining intercultural communicative competence

Intercultural communicative competence (ICC) has been conceptualized in several complementary ways that are particularly relevant for teacher education. One of the most important frameworks is Byram's (1997) model. It was created for foreign language education, but it is now often cited in wider conversations about intercultural learning. Byram proposes five components, often referred to as *savoirs*:

- **Attitudes (savoir-être):** curiosity, openness, and a readiness to suspend disbelief about other cultures and beliefs about one's own.
- **Knowledge (savoirs):** understanding of social groups, products, practices, and interaction processes in one's own and in other cultures.
- **Skills of interpreting and relating (savoir-comprendre):** the ability to interpret documents and events from another culture and relate them to one's own.
- **Skills of discovery and interaction (savoir-apprendre / savoir-faire):** the ability to acquire new cultural knowledge and operate attitudes and skills in real-time interaction.

- **Critical cultural awareness (savoir-s'engager):** the ability to critically evaluate, on the basis of explicit criteria, perspectives, practices, and products in one's own and other cultures.

This model shifts the focus from imitating a normative "native speaker" towards developing an "intercultural speaker" who can mediate between perspectives and negotiate meanings across cultural boundaries. For teachers in all subjects, this implies a need to help learners compare viewpoints, question taken-for-granted assumptions, and understand that knowledge is often culturally situated rather than neutral.

Deardorff's (2006) process model of intercultural competence, based on a Delphi study with experts, provides a complementary perspective that is widely used in higher education and internationalization discourses. Her model distinguishes:

- **Attitudes:** respect, openness, curiosity, and discovery.
- **Knowledge and comprehension:** cultural self-awareness, deep understanding of other worldviews, sociolinguistic awareness.
- **Skills:** listening, observing, evaluating, analysing, interpreting, and relating.

When internalized in an integrated and sustained manner, these internal dimensions are then externally demonstrated through effective and appropriate communication and behaviour in intercultural contexts. Deardorff emphasizes that intercultural competence is a process that develops over time as a cycle, rather than as a state of being, and, as such, ICC can never be covered in one course; therefore, it must be revisited, scaffolded and deepened progressively in pre-service preparation and in-service professional development.

From a developmental psychology perspective, Bennett (1993) offers the Developmental Model of Intercultural Sensitivity (DMIS), which is a framework that conceptualizes the individual experience of cultural difference through a progression of stages from ethnocentrism to ethnorelativism. The model proposes a progression through six stages of increasing sensitivity to cultural difference, each representing a more complex perception and experience of cultural difference, and these six stages are:

1. **Denial** of difference
2. **Defence** against difference
3. **Minimization** of difference
4. **Acceptance** of difference
5. **Adaptation** to difference
6. **Integration** of difference

The early stages are marked by limited recognition of difference or by defensiveness and a need to protect one's worldview. The later stages involve recognizing cultural complexity, shifting perspective, and incorporating multiple cultural frames into one's identity. Teacher education programs can use this model diagnostically and pedagogically, designing learning experiences (e.g., case studies, simulations, critical incidents) that gently challenge ethnocentric assumptions and support movement toward more ethnorelative orientations.

Taken together, these frameworks conceptualize ICC as a composite of attitudes, knowledge, skills, and critical awareness. For teachers, they highlight the importance of being able to recognize cultural dimensions in curricula and classroom interaction, to mediate between different perspectives, and to foster learners' own intercultural development in a reflective and ethically grounded manner.

## 2.2 Frameworks for technology integration in education

Discussions of technology in education have generated several conceptual frameworks that, while not always explicitly focused on intercultural aims, are highly relevant for understanding how digital tools intersect with teaching for ICC.

One of the most widely cited is the Technological Pedagogical Content Knowledge (TPACK) framework (Mishra & Koehler, 2006). TPACK identifies three primary forms of teacher knowledge:

- **Content knowledge (CK):** understanding of the subject matter.
- **Pedagogical knowledge (PK):** understanding of teaching and learning processes.
- **Technological knowledge (TK):** understanding of how to use digital tools and resources.

The TPACK framework also suggests how pedagogical content knowledge (PCK), technological content knowledge (TCK) and technological pedagogical knowledge (TPK) come together to form a new, integrated knowledge base that enables teachers to integrate technology, pedagogy and content in principled ways. When intercultural learning goals are introduced, intercultural communicative competence becomes an intrinsic part of both content and pedagogy, therefore teachers should intentionally intertwine these goals with their understanding of technology. While the ability to operate tools is not sufficient, educators should be able to select, sequence and orchestrate technologies to encourage critical, dialogic and explicitly intercultural forms of learning, because research on online language education and telecollaboration also underscores the social and intercultural affordances of technology. Hampel and Stickler's (2005) skills pyramid for online language tutors describes a developmental progression from basic technical proficiency to more advanced pedagogical and interpersonal skills. Building on this framework, empirical studies on telecollaboration and virtual exchange (e.g., O'Dowd, 2013; Helm, 2015) have shown that technology-mediated interaction across contexts can foster intercultural competence, but only if tasks are carefully designed, reflective activities are embedded, and issues of power, language dominance and inequitable participation are explicitly addressed.

Puentedura's (2006) SAMR model also provides a useful complement to this thinking about the levels of technology integration. At the lower tiers (substitution and augmentation), digital tools supplant or mildly augment existing practices, but at the upper tiers (modification and redefinition), technology allows for considerable task redesign and new forms of learning that were difficult or impossible, thus enabling sustained virtual exchanges between geographically distant classrooms, collaborative inquiry into global problems, and co-authorship of multilingual, multimodal artifacts. Moreover, the broader implication is that effective technology use for intercultural competence requires support that extends beyond technical training to include the design of learning experiences that exceed substitution, because the goal should be transformative integration in which intercultural dialogue and collaborative knowledge building are central to the pedagogy.

Together, these frameworks suggest that technology integration should be understood as pedagogically and culturally situated. They provide a basis for designing teacher education that treats digital tools as part of a broader ecology of communication, knowledge, and culture, rather than as isolated technical add-ons.

## 2.3 Teachers as cultural mediators and critical evaluators in digital environments

In the context of digitalized education, teachers' roles as cultural mediators acquire new significance. Kramsch (1993) describes language teachers as "cultural brokers" who help learners interpret symbolic systems of meaning and understand the relationships between language, culture, and identity. This mediating role now extends to the ways in which teachers choose, frame, and critique digital resources used in class.

Teachers select which texts, videos, tasks, and platforms are brought into the learning environment. They decide how to contextualize these materials historically, politically, and socially, and how to relate them to learners' own experiences. In doing so, they inevitably foreground certain narratives and voices while leaving others in the background. Critical media literacy researchers, like Kellner and Share (2007), argue that education should help students understand how media messages are created, whose interests they serve, and how they shape views of social reality.

Teachers need to deliberately scaffold students to ask the following questions in relation to the classroom text: Who is speaking in this text, who is included/excluded, what assumptions about normality are being communicated, and how might this look from another perspective, because these questions are even more critical in digital environments.

Digital texts are widely distributed, algorithmically curated and multimodal, consisting of text, image, video, and sound, and can convey strong tacit messages about cultures and social groups. Teachers need to evaluate digital texts critically before, during and after classroom use to consider when materials perpetuate stereotypes, rely on deficit narratives about particular communities, or oversimplify complex phenomena, and this requires them to be attentive to the relational and affective dimensions of intercultural engagement.

When students read texts that challenge their assumptions, they may feel uncomfortable, tense, resistant, and therefore teacher educators can help teachers anticipate and respond productively to these reactions by normalizing discomfort as a part of intercultural learning, facilitating dialogue rather than debate, and inviting multiple interpretations rather than policing a single correct reading. This can be achieved using frameworks such as Bennett's (1993) Developmental Model of Intercultural Sensitivity, which highlights that evaluative practice is far more than checking factual accuracy or technical quality, but requires ethical judgement, intercultural attunement, and reflexivity about one's own interpretive stance. Consequently, teachers need structured professional spaces to interrogate digital materials together, to explore alternative readings, and to deliberate about pedagogically responsible ways to engage with learners in relation to such materials.

## 2.4 Beyond technical skills: towards intercultural digital literacy

The ideas mentioned earlier suggest we need a wider understanding of competence beyond just “digital skills”. A helpful way to view this is through the concept of intercultural digital literacy, which combines digital literacy, media literacy, and intercultural competence.

Digital literacy, Lankshear and Knobel (2008) argue, is more than operational competence in using devices or software, but it is about participating in socially situated practices of reading, writing, and communicating through digital media. Media literacy involves understanding how media texts are constructed, how they construct meanings, how audiences interpret them, and how they are located in broader social and political contexts (Buckingham, 2003), and critical media literacy extends this to the analysis of power, ideology, and representation in and through media (Kellner & Share, 2007).

When we bring these elements together with ICC frameworks, intercultural digital literacy becomes a competence that includes:

- The ability to navigate and use digital tools and platforms for communication and learning.
- The capacity to analyse and evaluate digital texts and practices in terms of how they represent cultures, identities, and social issues.
- Sensitivity to cultural and linguistic diversity in online interactions, including awareness of unequal access and hierarchy.
- Skills for engaging in respectful, dialogic communication across difference in digital spaces.
- Ethical awareness regarding privacy, consent, authorship, and the potential impact of sharing certain representations.

UNESCO's *Global Media and Information Literacy Assessment Framework* (2013) explicitly associates media and information literacy with intercultural dialogue and democratic participation, and it suggests that learners require a comprehensive set of critical thinking and communication skills in order to effectively participate in knowledge societies today. For teachers, this means that their professional development should treat technology as not only a content delivery mechanism, but as a set of sociocultural environments in which meanings, identities and power relations are constantly being negotiated.

Embedding intercultural digital literacy in teacher education can take various forms. For example, teacher candidates might be asked to:

- Compare coverage of the same international event in news sites from different countries, analysing framing, language choices, and source selection.
- Analyse social media posts or advertising campaigns for implicit messages about gender, ethnicity, language, or nation.
- Collaborate with peers in another country to co-design digital materials that incorporate multiple perspectives on a shared theme.
- Reflect on their own online practices, including which voices they tend to follow, which languages they see represented, and how this shapes their understanding of the world.

In fact, these practices explicitly bring together core dimensions of intercultural communicative competence and media literacy while directly involving teachers and learners in digital media environments. They also highlight that teachers are part of digital cultures, not just outside observers. Their habits, preferences, and ways of understanding affect the choices they make about what to include in the classroom.

Taken together, the principles of ICC, models of technology integration, changing teacher roles, and intercultural digital literacy offer a cohesive framework for reconceptualizing teacher education in digitally mediated environments, which implies professional development that goes beyond tool proficiency to produce reflective, ethically aware, and culturally responsive educators who design learning where students critically engage with and contribute to the complex cultural systems of contemporary education.

## 3. CURRENT PRACTICES IN TEACHER TRAINING AND PROFESSIONAL DEVELOPMENT

Current practice in teacher training and development is an uneven and rapidly changing field in which AI-supported and digital tools are integrated into day-to-day work, telecollaboration, and virtual exchange form the basis for intercultural learning, and professional learning ranges from short workshops to longer, embedded programs. Teachers use language models, educational generators, multimodal authoring platforms, gamified quizzing, writing feedback systems, and translation systems to create materials and as objects of critique; however, such tools can have a meaningful impact only when used with facilitation, reflection, and alignment with intercultural goals rather than convenience. Telecollaboration and virtual exchange remain the most compelling examples of practice when tasks are carefully designed and ethically moderated; however, similar gains can be made locally by engaging learners with digital traces of diverse cultures and by systematically debriefing how media represent identities and power. Professional development is most effective when sustained, collaborative, discipline-relevant, and cycling through design, enactment, and reflection; isolated tool trainings raise awareness but rarely shift pedagogy. Across regions and institutions, access and support are uneven, and language, workload, and policy gaps affect who can participate and sustain innovation. Overall, current practice demonstrates potential and growing expertise, but also highlights the need for integrated, equity-focused strategies that connect technology use with intercultural objectives and provide consistent institutional support.

### 3.1 Digital tools in practice: language models, learning platforms, and translation systems

A range of AI-supported tools is now a regular part of teachers' daily work. These tools vary in function and complexity, but they share two important characteristics for teacher education and intercultural communication: they create or change content dynamically, and they organize interactions in specific ways. It is essential for current teacher training and professional development to understand how to use them creatively and with critical awareness.

One prominent category includes large language models like ChatGPT, Gemini, DeepSeek, and Grok. These systems can create, summarize, translate, and adjust texts in various languages and formats. Teachers across different subjects are already using them to:

- draft lesson plans, unit outlines, and thematic sequences that can be further refined for specific groups
- create parallel versions of reading texts or instructions at different proficiency levels
- rewrite explanations in a more accessible language while preserving disciplinary content
- generate short case studies, classroom incidents, or intercultural dilemmas as prompts for discussion in teacher education courses
- simulate dialogues that can be analysed for pragmatic choices, turn-taking, and politeness strategies.

Recent reviews of such models have pointed out that, although they can foster idea generation and differentiation, their products always need to be human-checked for accuracy, bias, and cultural sensitivity (Kasneci et al., 2023; Zawacki-Richter et al., 2019), and in professional development contexts, this evaluative work can be reframed as a learning opportunity. For instance, teacher candidates may examine a machine-generated scenario to determine whose perspectives are represented and whose are not, and then collaboratively revise the text according to intercultural communication principles.

A second AI-assisted tool category relevant to this project consists of tools designed for explicit educational use, such as MagicSchool AI, which offers structured templates with which teachers can generate quizzes, rubrics, feedback statements, and reading passages by inputting topic, age group, and learning objectives. These tools formalize common instructional routines and can save teachers substantial time, and in teacher education, they can also serve as a foundation for critical design tasks: participants assess auto-generated materials for fairness, inclusivity, and intercultural relevance, and iteratively revise them to meet these standards.

Authoring and presentation platforms like Genially and Prezi combine templates, interactive features, and more AI-assisted design suggestions. Teachers can use these to create:

- interactive timelines that juxtapose events or developments from multiple regions or traditions

- exploratory "click-through" case studies where learners follow different branches of an intercultural scenario and then compare outcomes
- multimodal infographics representing comparative data (for instance, on education, environment, or health indicators across countries) as a basis for critical discussion.

Because these tools support multimodal design, they are particularly suited to tasks where learners express and negotiate meaning through combinations of text, image, layout, and hyperlinking, all of which can carry cultural significance.

Game- and quiz-based platforms such as Quizizz and Kahoot deserve special attention because they foreground gamification. They allow teachers to transform review or assessment activities into competitive or collaborative games, often with immediate feedback, leaderboards, and visual rewards. Research on game-based learning indicates that such features can enhance engagement and motivation when used thoughtfully (Deterding et al., 2011). For ICC-oriented work, these platforms can be used not only for checking factual knowledge, but also for:

- surfacing prior assumptions and stereotypes about cultures in a low-threat way, followed by debriefing and discussion
- comparing how different groups of students respond to the same culturally themed items
- designing "myth vs. fact" quizzes about widely held beliefs concerning particular communities, which then serve as entry points for more nuanced exploration.

In teacher education, asking participants to design and then analyse their own Genially presentations or Quizizz/Kahoot activities encourages them to consider how question wording, images, and examples may reflect or challenge particular cultural narratives.

A third cluster of tools focuses more narrowly on language form and mediation. Automated writing feedback systems such as Grammarly, Write & Improve, or ProWritingAid provide suggestions on grammar, vocabulary, cohesion, and aspects of style. Empirical work suggests that such tools can help learners notice recurring problems and improve accuracy, provided they engage actively with feedback rather than accepting all changes mechanically (Ranalli, 2018). For teachers, these tools serve several purposes. They help with their own writing. They can also be used for classroom analysis, such as when a suggestion is grammatically correct but doesn't fit the situation. Additionally, they show how certain ideas about "standard" language are built into the design of the software.

Online translation systems, most prominently Google Translate and DeepL, are also firmly embedded in everyday practice. Studies of their role in language learning emphasize both their potential and their risks (Pym, Malmkjær, & Gutiérrez-Colón Plana, 2013). Used uncritically, they can encourage dependence and obscure gaps in understanding. Used as objects of inquiry, they can:

- prompt reflection on equivalence, formality, and cultural references by comparing machine and human translations
- reveal how idioms, humour, or culturally specific terms are simplified, altered, or omitted
- support classroom activities where learners hypothesize why certain translations fail and propose contextually appropriate alternatives.

Across all these tools, a common pattern emerges. On the one hand, they can greatly expand what is practically feasible for teachers: generating multiple variants of tasks, visualising complex information, creating gamified practice, and giving rapid language feedback. On the other hand, they introduce pre-structured ways of representing knowledge, language, and culture. For teacher training and professional development, the central challenge is, therefore, to move from tool use as convenience to tool use as a site of pedagogy and critique.

Working with tools such as ChatGPT, Gemini, DeepSeek, Grok, MagicSchool, Genially, Prezi, Quizizz, Kahoot, Grammarly, and translation systems can help future and practicing teachers:

- experiment with creative tasks and material design
- practice identifying bias, stereotyping, and omission in automatically generated or template-based content
- rehearse how to adapt digital outputs to diverse groups of learners and intercultural aims
- reflect on how gamification, multimodality, and automation shape participation and classroom dynamics.

In this way, digital tools become both resources for innovation and objects of critical inquiry, supporting the development of teachers as reflective, interculturally aware professionals in digitally saturated educational environments.

## 3.2 Applications in language courses, telecollaboration, and virtual exchanges

The most documented uses of digital tools for intercultural purposes remain in language education, particularly in relation to telecollaboration and virtual exchange. Over the past two decades, numerous projects have linked classes across borders for collaborative tasks, often in higher education and teacher education programs. These initiatives have used a variety of platforms (e.g., learning management systems, videoconferencing, shared document editors, forums) to enable learners to work together on projects that require them to explore cultural topics, compare perspectives, and negotiate meaning.

Research on such projects shows that, when carefully designed and facilitated, telecollaboration can foster the development of ICC, critical cultural awareness, and digital literacies (O'Dowd, 2013; Helm, 2015). Tasks commonly include comparative analysis of media representations, joint creation of digital artifacts (blogs, videos, wikis), and collaborative inquiry into global issues such as sustainability, migration, or social justice. In many cases, student teachers participate as part of their practicum or methodology coursework, reflecting on their experiences and considering how they might later implement similar designs in their own classrooms.

In more recent projects, teachers have begun to combine these established formats with newer tools. For instance, learners may use online translation to support early stages of communication, then critically examine differences between machine-produced and human-produced texts. Automated writing feedback may be used as a resource during joint text production, followed by class discussion on which suggestions are accepted or rejected and why. Conversational tools may be used to generate alternative viewpoints or sample dialogues that learners then critique from an intercultural and pragmatic perspective.

Language courses that do not involve cross-border exchanges still draw on digital tools to simulate intercultural encounters. Teachers may ask learners to analyze comment threads on international news sites, to explore multilingual websites of global organizations, or to compare school websites from different countries. In teacher education, such activities are often accompanied by reflective tasks in which student teachers examine how they selected materials, how they framed them for learners, and how they might respond to sensitive or controversial issues arising from the content.

These practices illustrate that technology-supported intercultural work is not limited to direct communication with distant partners. Teachers can design local activities in which learners engage with digital traces of other cultures and perspectives, provided that tasks and reflection prompts are informed by ICC frameworks and by critical media literacy principles.

## 3.3 Professional development formats: workshops, MOOCs, and institutional training

Teacher training and professional development related to digital tools and intercultural communication currently take multiple forms, each with particular strengths and limitations.

Short, tool-focused workshops remain the most widespread format. These sessions typically introduce teachers to specific platforms (for example, Quizizz, Genially, or videoconferencing tools), demonstrate possible classroom activities, and allow limited time for hands-on practice. Research on professional development in educational technology shows that such workshops can raise awareness and build basic confidence but often have limited impact on long-term pedagogical change, especially when they are isolated events that are not embedded in ongoing support or school-wide strategies (Dede et al., 2009; Lawless & Pellegrino, 2007). In the context of ICC, purely technical workshops risk overlooking deeper questions about representation, ethics, and diversity.

In addition, universities and professional organizations have also been using online courses and MOOCs to spread practices and examples across national contexts in areas such as online teaching, virtual exchange, global competence and media and information literacy. For example, the European Commission has supported online training for educators involved in virtual exchange through modules on telecollaborative task design, assessment of intercultural learning and facilitating online interaction (Helm, 2015; Dooly & O'Dowd, 2018), and MOOCs on global citizenship education and intercultural learning typically involve video lectures, curated readings, discussion forums and peer-assessed assignments (Stacey, 2018). While this format can be effective for spreading practices and examples across national contexts, it is often limited by the same persistent problems as previous iterations of online training, such as low completion rates, lack of opportunities for meaningful interaction and difficulties in relating generic course content to the specific local contexts and needs of participants (Veletsianos & Shepherdson, 2016).

More promising for lasting change are professional development programs that focus on technology and intercultural goals within wider frameworks of teacher learning. Some universities have included virtual exchange components in initial teacher education programs. They have made these components required parts of methodology or practicum courses instead of optional additions (Hauck & MacKinnon, 2016; O'Dowd, 2018). Others have created "global competence" or "internationalization at home" modules. These modules blend seminars on ICC theory, analysis of digital resources, and small design projects where teachers try out digitally supported intercultural tasks in their own classrooms (Deardorff, 2015; Beelen & Jones, 2015).

Research on effective professional development in technology-enhanced and intercultural education shows several common elements: duration and intensity over time, chances for collaborative work, relevance to teachers' own subjects, and cycles of design, implementation, and reflection (Desimone, 2009; Dooly & Sadler, 2016). When professional development includes these features, teachers are more likely to develop a cohesive understanding of technology, pedagogy, and intercultural knowledge instead of seeing technology as something extra.

There are also emerging examples of communities of practice and professional networks focused on virtual exchange, global education, and intercultural digital learning. These include networks associated with EU-funded projects such as UNI-Collaboration, EVALUATE, and EVOLVE, which provide repositories of tasks, case studies, and research insights, as well as online events where teachers share experiences (O'Dowd, 2018; O'Dowd & Beelen, 2021). Such communities can serve as important "bridging spaces" between research and practice, and between institutions with different levels of resources.

Despite these developments, several reviews point out that professional development often treats "technology integration" and "intercultural competence" as separate topics, even though they are closely connected in practice (Zawacki Richter et al., 2019; Dooly & O'Dowd, 2018). Programs that specifically help teachers investigate how digital tools interact with culture, identity, and power in classrooms are still quite rare. These often rely on the efforts of individual academics or small project teams.

## 3.4 Uneven access: disparities between regions, institutions, and teacher communities

Current practices in teacher training and professional development for digitally mediated ICC are marked by significant disparities in access, participation, and support. These inequalities appear at multiple levels: between countries and regions, between institutions, and between different groups of teachers.

On a macro level, differences in infrastructure and education funding determine what is possible, and UNESCO and OECD reports document persistent connectivity, access to devices and high-quality digital learning resources gaps regularly (UNESCO, 2021; OECD, 2020). In practice, some teachers have stable broadband, institutional subscriptions, and dedicated technical support; others work with unstable connections, shared devices and limited access to licensed tools, which influence classroom practices directly, curtailing opportunities for online professional development, telecollaboration and international networks.

Institutional settings further amplify these differences, because ICT integration research has demonstrated that some schools and universities pursue coherent strategies, such as allocating time for training, providing incentives and recognizing digitally innovative teaching, while others depend on the voluntary and unsupported efforts of individual educators (Lawless & Pellegrino, 2007; Tondeur et al., 2012). Similar patterns are evident in virtual exchange, as O'Dowd (2018) and Helm (2015) highlight, many projects rely on a small group of highly motivated practitioners who receive little institutional recognition and struggle to sustain activity once external funding ends; consequently, inequities within teacher communities are also related to employment conditions, teaching environments and language proficiencies.

Teachers in temporary positions, working in rural or under-resourced settings or carrying heavy teaching loads are less likely to have the time and flexibility to participate in sustained professional learning opportunities or international partnerships (Dede et al., 2009; Tondeur et al., 2012), because language is another barrier, in that the majority of MOOCs, webinars and virtual exchange resources are produced in English, which effectively excludes educators whose own language skills or preferences do not lie in English (Helm, 2015; O'Dowd & Beelen, 2021). Inequalities can also exist within telecollaborative partnerships themselves, since when the two partner institutions have differing levels of access to technology, institutional support or students' language resources, this can impact participation patterns and power dynamics within the partnership; therefore, groups that are more familiar with the tools or confident in the lingua franca may assume more leadership or dominant roles, while their partners become more passive or compliant (O'Dowd, 2013; Helm, 2016). If left unchecked, such dynamics may serve to reinforce existing hierarchies; moreover, there is also a risk that the most innovative practices in digitally mediated intercultural communication will continue to remain confined to the more privileged sectors of education, such as well-funded universities, teacher education programs with strong international connections or schools participating in externally financed initiatives, while educators outside of such networks have limited opportunities to experiment with the tools themselves or to see tangible examples of how digital technologies and intercultural aims can be meaningfully integrated across subjects and age groups.

Collectively, these differences indicate that "current practice" is a profoundly unequal terrain whose topography is determined by structural conditions, policy choices and professional cultures rather than a level playing field; thus, tackling these inequalities will demand action across levels, including:

- policy initiatives that prioritize investments in infrastructure and teacher development as fundamental aspects of digital and intercultural education policy (UNESCO, 2021; OECD, 2020),
- institutional arrangements that acknowledge and support educators' engagement with digitally mediated intercultural projects as legitimate professional activity,

- professional development opportunities that are multilingual, multimodal and flexible, and explicit consideration of inequalities in telecollaboration and virtual exchange, including task designs and reflection components that make asymmetries visible and problematic (Helm, 2015; Dooly & O'Dowd, 2018).

Without such actions, the benefits of AI-supported and digitally mediated ICC are likely to accrue to the most privileged contexts, further entrenching existing differences in educational opportunity and professional learning.

## 4. CHALLENGES IN AI-SUPPORTED ICC FOR TEACHERS

Intercultural learning through AI tools presents significant challenges for educators, and these challenges relate to conceptual, ethical, pedagogical and institutional issues that transcend mere technical implementation. They concern the ways in which teachers perceive their role in technology-mediated, intercultural learning environments, and the manner in which they facilitate learning, assessment and communication in the classroom, because the moral principles that guide them in assisting learners with the use of technology and the acquisition of intercultural knowledge are also a crucial aspect.

### 4.1 Absence of transparent pedagogical models for AI integration

One central difficulty is the lack of clear, research-informed pedagogical models that show teachers how to integrate AI tools in ways that support ICC. While there is a growing body of work on technology integration in general (e.g., Mishra & Koehler, 2006; Tondeur et al., 2012) and on telecollaboration and virtual exchange for ICC (O'Dowd, 2013; Helm, 2015), systematic guidance on using AI-supported tools specifically for intercultural aims is still in its early stages.

Studies on AI in education often focus on technical affordances or on outcomes such as performance gains and efficiency (Zawacki-Richter et al., 2019; Holmes, Bialik, & Fadel, 2019), with less attention to how such tools shape cultural representations or classroom discourse. As a result, teachers frequently experiment with large language models, automated feedback systems, or AI-driven platforms in an ad-hoc fashion, without a clear framework for aligning tool use with ICC models such as Byram's (1997) or Deardorff's (2006).

This absence of transparent models can lead to several problems:

- AI tools may be used primarily for language correction, content delivery, or quiz generation, without exploiting their potential for perspective-taking, intercultural comparison, or critical media literacy.
- Activities may remain at the level of substitution or augmentation in terms of the SAMR framework (Puentedura, 2006), rather than moving towards redesigned tasks that genuinely foster intercultural dialogue.
- Teachers may unintentionally reinforce traditional, teacher-centered patterns by using AI to produce more materials and explanations, rather than creating space for student-led inquiry into how AI itself constructs knowledge and culture.

Research on teacher beliefs and technology use suggests that in the absence of explicit pedagogical models, teachers tend to appropriate new tools in ways that fit existing practices (Ertmer & Ottenbreit-Leftwich, 2010; Tondeur et al., 2012). For AI-supported ICC, this means that without targeted professional development, AI is likely to be used to "do the same things faster" rather than to open up new intercultural learning opportunities.

## 4.2 Risks of stereotypes, biases, and cultural misrepresentations in AI content

A second major challenge concerns the cultural quality of AI-generated content. AI systems, including large language models and recommendation algorithms, are trained on large datasets that reflect existing social biases, hegemonic discourses, and patterns of under-representation (Buolamwini & Gebru, 2018; Bender et al., 2021). As a result, their outputs can reproduce or amplify stereotypes, marginalize certain voices, and normalize particular worldviews as "neutral."

In teaching language and subjects, this can show up in several ways:

- Automatically generated examples, stories, or scenarios often default to Western, English-speaking, or majority group settings, with little representation from other contexts.
- Descriptions of countries, cultures, or social groups may depend on old clichés, exotic views, or negative perspectives.
- Translations can simplify culturally specific expressions or adopt standards linked to a certain variety, unintentionally implying that others are less valid or incorrect (Pym, Malmkjær, & Gutiérrez Colón Plana, 2013).

Critical research on language technologies indicates that machine translation and text generation systems tend to reproduce gendered, ethnic, and religious stereotypes (Caliskan et al., 2017; Prates et al., 2020), and in educational contexts, Kasneci et al. (2023) point out that large language models may generate fluent and authoritative-sounding text that conceals biased or incomplete information, making these issues difficult for learners to spot. For teachers interested in developing intercultural communicative competence, these risks are of particular concern because AI-generated texts can be treated as productive artefacts for critical inquiry and allow students to diagnose stereotyping, omissions, and framing effects, yet, without sufficient time, training, or confidence to systematically check the outputs of tools, educators may inadvertently adopt problematic content, thereby reinforcing rather than challenging biased representations. This concern is especially acute in subjects like history, civic education, literature, and the social sciences, where questions of power, identity, and representation are constitutive of the curriculum (Gay, 2010; Ladson-Billings, 2014), and meeting this challenge requires more than procedural familiarity with tools. This includes robust critical media literacy and intercultural digital literacy, involving the ability to interrogate sources and identify bias, as well as to support students in ethical and culturally responsive interpretation and production (Buckingham, 2003; Kellner & Share, 2007; Lankshear & Knobel, 2008), however, many current professional development initiatives focus primarily on the technical operation of tools, at the expense of these more complex conceptual, ethical, and intercultural dimensions, consequently leaving a critical gap in teacher preparation.

## 4.3 Workload, sustainability, and the challenge of continuous upskilling

AI-supported tools are often marketed as time-saving solutions, but teachers often find that they increase an already heavy workload. For effective and responsible use of AI in ICC-oriented teaching, time is needed for:

- experimenting with different tools and understanding their affordances and limitations
- critically evaluating AI-generated outputs for accuracy, bias, and cultural appropriateness
- redesigning or adapting auto-generated materials to fit specific learner groups and intercultural objectives
- monitoring how students use AI tools themselves, and responding to issues such as overreliance, plagiarism, or uncritical acceptance of suggestions.

The research on technology-related professional development suggests that teachers face a "double workload" when integrating new technologies, because they have to maintain their current teaching practices while they learn about, try out and refine their use of innovations (Dede et al., 2009; Lawless & Pellegrino, 2007). The fast development of AI and its technologies worsens this burden, since many teachers feel they have to "keep up" but are not provided with sufficient time, institutional recognition or structured support for the learning involved, which results in fatigue, anxiety and resistance (König et al., 2020; Selwyn, 2011). Furthermore, the challenge is compounded in the context of intercultural communicative competence, because teachers are expected not only to learn new technologies but also to engage with complex intercultural theories and concepts, interrogate their own positionalities and participate in discussions about sensitive topics such as racism, colonialism, and discrimination (Sleeter, 2012; Deardorff, 2006), and adding AI to this already heavy agenda is likely to be seen as overwhelming, especially in the context of limited or fragmented support structures.

Sustainability is a critical issue, therefore, because without longer-term planning for AI-related professional learning, schools are likely to be trapped in patterns of short-term enthusiasm, superficial adoption and little lasting change in practice. However, research on effective professional development tells a different story, suggesting that sustained, content-focused, coherent with other initiatives and embedded in teachers' day-to-day work approaches are more effective (Desimone, 2009; Tondeur et al., 2012), and in the case of AI-supported ICC, this means developing systems that enable educators to build competence incrementally through iterative practice, collaborative inquiry and reflective feedback, rather than one-off workshops or quick fixes.

## 4.4 Institutional gaps: lack of policy frameworks and systemic support

While the problems teachers face in using AI to support intercultural communicative competence are located at the policy and institutional level, schools, universities and education systems are generally lacking in guidelines for the educational, ethical and intercultural implications of AI, and educators are therefore without coherent principles to inform practice.

Several issues are particularly notable:

- **Lack of explicit guidelines:** Many institutions have started drafting policies on academic honesty and AI. However, these often concentrate on plagiarism and assessment rather than how AI can or should be used in teaching and intercultural contexts (Selwyn, 2022; Floridi & Chiriatti, 2020). As a result, teachers may be uncertain about what is allowed, what is encouraged, and how to communicate these expectations to students.

- **Limited institutional recognition:** Getting involved with AI-supported ICC projects, telecollaboration, or virtual exchange often relies on individual teachers' efforts. This involvement does not always receive recognition in workload models, promotion criteria, or quality assurance processes (Helm, 2015; O'Dowd, 2018). This lack of recognition can discourage ongoing participation, especially for teachers in insecure or heavily burdened roles.
- **Inconsistent access and support:** As mentioned in the previous chapter, differences in infrastructure and support staff mean that some teachers can easily access AI-enhanced platforms, training, and technical help, while others cannot (OECD, 2020; UNESCO, 2021). Where institutional support is weak, teachers have to deal with technical, legal, and ethical questions mostly on their own.
- **Fragmented approaches to internationalization and digitalization:** Policy frameworks on internationalization, digital change, and inclusion are often created separately, even though they clearly overlap (Beelen & Jones, 2015; O'Dowd & Beelen, 2021). Consequently, AI initiatives may focus on efficiency or innovation without connecting to ICC and equity goals, and intercultural initiatives may ignore AI's role in shaping modern communication.

UNESCO's 2021 report calls for a new social contract for education that specifically addresses how digitalization affects equity, democratic participation and cultural diversity. Similarly, recent policy debates on AI in education have emphasized the need for human-centered, rights-based approaches that protect learner and teacher agency, privacy and cultural diversity, as highlighted by UNESCO and OECD in 2023 and 2021, respectively. However, the translation of these general commitments into concrete institutional policies and everyday school practices has been inconsistent and incomplete, suggesting a significant implementation gap between high-level principles and local realities.

For teachers, the lack of strong institutional and policy frameworks means they often bear the individual responsibility of addressing complex ethical and intercultural questions without enough support. This situation supports the view that AI-supported ICC cannot be tackled only at the classroom level. It also needs systemic focus on infrastructure, governance, teacher training, and curriculum design so that teachers do not have to resolve competing demands alone.

## 5. POTENTIAL OF AI IN TEACHER EDUCATION FOR ICC

Artificial intelligence (AI) is spreading the educational experience, shaping the ways in which learners access knowledge, the organization of communication and the assessment of learning, and for teacher education, this represents a double challenge and opportunity. While AI can be used to enhance efficiency, it can also be harnessed to create new spaces for examining culture, communication and power in digital contexts, and from an intercultural communicative competence perspective, the issue is not whether teachers should use AI, but how they can appropriate AI to cultivate curiosity, critical cultural awareness and dialogue across differences.

## 5.1 Interactive simulations and role-playing with AI-driven cultural scenarios

Interactive, AI-supported simulations can place teachers in rich, ambiguous situations where cultural expectations, values, and communication styles collide. Such environments resonate strongly with Byram's (1997) view of intercultural communicative competence (ICC) as involving attitudes, skills of interpreting and relating, and critical cultural awareness, and with Deardorff's (2006) emphasis on intercultural competence as a lifelong, reflective process.

In teacher education, simulations can be set up so participants take on the role of classroom teachers, mentors, or school leaders facing intercultural tensions. These tensions could include disagreements between parents and the school about religious holidays, conflicts among students sparked by media coverage of international events, or complaints about perceived "unfair" content in history or literature classes. AI can create branching narratives where different teacher responses lead to different directions in the interaction. This allows participants to try out various options, including those that might seem risky in real life but provide valuable lessons in training.

The value of these simulations does not depend on producing the "right" answer on the first try but is predicated instead on the iterative cycle of action, observation, and reflection. At the end of a scenario, participants can rewind to critical points, reformulate their responses, and compare the consequences of different responses, because this process allows them to reflect on their decisions and their impact. Teacher educators can ground these experiences in established frameworks such as Bennett's (1993) Developmental Model of Intercultural Sensitivity, and ask participants to identify whether their responses fall in the denial, defence, minimization, acceptance, adaptation, or integration stage. Research on scenario-based and reflective teacher education indicates that structured engagement with such "critical incidents" can uncover tacit beliefs, make them discussable, and thereby support professional development, as supported by the work of Korthagen (2010) and Loughran (2006).

Interactive role-play using AI can also support discipline-specific ICC. In mathematics or science education, situations might centre on students contesting the relevance of content because it appears disconnected from their lived realities, or on debates about how examples and case studies represent particular regions or communities. In social studies or language arts, simulated parent-teacher meetings or staff-room discussions can foreground contested narratives of history, identity, and citizenship. Across subjects, the key design principle is that simulations must be embedded in structured debriefing that links practical choices to broader questions of power, representation, and voice, rather than being treated as decontextualized "practice in communication".

## 5.2 AI-based intercultural chatbots for exploring diverse communication styles

Conversational agents offer another avenue for developing ICC-related insights in teacher education. While their technical sophistication varies, they can be configured to enact specific communicative profiles across dimensions such as directness, turn-taking, face-saving strategies, and degrees of emotional expressiveness. When framed appropriately, these agents become tools for exploring how norms of "appropriate" communication differ across contexts, rather than prototypes of any culture.

In practice, teacher educators can create sequences where participants interact with chatbots representing different interlocutors: a concerned caregiver who uses highly indirect hints rather than explicit criticism; a colleague from another department who communicates in brief, very direct messages; or a school principal whose style is formal and heavily hedged. Afterwards, participants analyse how they interpreted these moves, which aspects they found challenging, and how they might adapt their own responses. Connections can then be drawn to constructs such as high- and low-context communication, uncertainty avoidance, and power distance (Gudykunst, 2004; Hofstede et al., 2010), and to Byram's (1997) "skills of discovery and interaction".

Studies on pedagogical chatbots indicate that they can provide low-stakes environments for exploratory dialogue and promote learner engagement when their limitations are made transparent and interaction is followed by guided reflection (Kerly, Hall, & Bull, 2007; Winkler & Söllner, 2018). In an ICC-oriented teacher education context, their primary function is to help participants:

- notice how much they rely on tacit norms when interpreting utterances
- articulate expectations about roles (teacher–student, teacher–parent, colleague–colleague)
- experiment with alternative formulations and observe shifts in the simulated interlocutor's reactions.

Language teachers can use such agents to examine pragmatic choices across varieties of a language; subject-area teachers can focus on professional genres such as staff emails, feedback to students, or communication with external partners. In both cases, the aim is to heighten awareness of how different ways of "doing" professionalism and politeness may be perceived by interlocutors with differing cultural frames of reference.

## 5.3 Adaptive learning systems and analytics for teacher self-reflection

Adaptive learning systems and learning analytics, originally developed to monitor and support student learning, can also be turned toward teachers' own intercultural development. When employed with clear ethical safeguards and critical intent, analytics can make visible patterns in interaction and task design that might otherwise remain unnoticed (Ifenthaler & Yau, 2020).

In blended or online teacher education, learning analytics dashboards can display participation data from forums, collaborative documents, and synchronous sessions. Rather than being used purely for performance management, such data can anchor reflective inquiry. When a cohort of pre-service teachers works in international virtual exchange projects, for instance, patterns may show that contributions from some national or linguistic groups receive fewer responses, or that particular topics consistently elicit high engagement while others are avoided. Drawing on research into telecollaboration and virtual exchange (Helm, 2015; O'Dowd, 2018), teacher educators can encourage participants to interrogate these patterns: Who is being heard. Who tends to remain silent. Which perspectives are treated as central or peripheral.

Adaptive systems can also offer individualized prompts based on teachers' interaction histories. Participants who rarely pose open-ended questions in discussion forums may receive targeted resources on dialogic teaching. Those who participate actively but seldom reference learners' cultural backgrounds might be encouraged to design tasks that explicitly invite such connections. Used in this way, adaptation is not about prescribing a single "ideal" teaching style, but about supporting movement toward more ethnorelative, reflective orientations in line with Bennett's (1993) model.

However, the use of analytics in ICC teacher education centred on the ICC raises important ethical questions because participation, language use, or collaboration metrics are easily misinterpreted and can quickly shift from formative support to surveillance (Slade & Prinsloo, 2013). Thus, PD efforts must clarify the purposes for which analytics are being used, obtain informed consent, and involve participants in interpreting results, and if these conditions are met, analytics can serve as a reflective mirror, enabling teachers to make sense of their own and others' roles in online intercultural exchanges and to identify specific areas for intentional development.

## 5.4 Reimagining teacher education: from tool adoption to pedagogical transformation

The examples above show that AI tools can support ICC-focused teacher education in various ways. They can generate complex scenarios, sustain exploratory dialogue, and highlight patterns in interaction. However, their biggest potential is not in automating current practices, but in encouraging a broader rethink of how we prepare teachers for culturally diverse, digitally rich classrooms.

Transformative approaches to teacher education emphasize the interpenetration of theory and reflective inquiry into one's own practice, participation in professional learning communities, and sustained critical engagement, as discussed by Korthagen (2010) and Loughran (2006). From this perspective, AI constitutes one element in a broader resource ecology that enables educators to interrogate issues of representation, power, and participation, while simulations can show how institutional routines and expectations can marginalize certain students or families. Moreover, conversational agents can show how easily assumptions of “clear communication” can break down, and learning analytics can reveal whose voices are amplified in digital spaces and whose remain peripheral.

A reimagined teacher education curriculum can integrate these elements into iterative cycles of design, implementation, and reflection. Pre-service teachers might co-create an AI-mediated intercultural task, pilot it with peers or school students, collect interactional data, analyse outcomes with reference to ICC frameworks (Byram, 1997; Deardorff, 2006; Bennett, 1993), and then redesign the activity. In-service programs can support school-based teams in using similar cycles to examine their own communication with parents, colleagues, and local communities in multilingual and multicultural settings.

At the institutional and policy levels, moving from tool adoption to pedagogical transformation requires sustained support. Short, tool-focused workshops are insufficient to address the intertwined challenges of interculturality and digital mediation (Dede et al., 2009). Instead, programs need:

- time and recognition for collaborative inquiry into practice
- explicit links between ICC, media and information literacy, and subject-specific pedagogy (UNESCO, 2013)
- attention to inequities in access to technology, professional development, and international partnerships (Helm, 2015; Dooly & O’Dowd, 2018).

Only under such conditions can AI be appropriated in ways that strengthen teachers' roles as cultural mediators and ethical professionals, rather than reinforcing existing hierarchies or standardizing cultural perspectives. Used critically and creatively within robust theoretical and ethical frameworks, AI can support a shift in teacher education from viewing technology as an add-on to conceiving it as part of the communicative fabric in which ICC is learned, enacted, and continually renegotiated.

## 6. RECOMMENDATIONS FOR SUSTAINABLE PROFESSIONAL DEVELOPMENT

Recommendations for sustainable professional development in AI-supported ICC need to begin with the curriculum of teacher education itself. Intercultural digital literacy cannot be treated as an optional add-on but must be embedded as a core competence across initial teacher education and in-service programs. Drawing on work that positions intercultural competence as central to contemporary teaching (Byram, 1997; Deardorff, 2006) and on research into digital and media literacies (Buckingham, 2003; Lankshear & Knobel, 2008; UNESCO, 2013), teacher education curricula should explicitly connect intercultural theory, critical media analysis, and hands-on engagement with AI-mediated tools. This involves designing modules where student teachers examine how digital environments show cultures, languages, and identities. They learn to choose, adjust, and create tasks that encourage curiosity, empathy, and critical awareness. Instead of offering separate "technology" and "intercultural" courses, programs can integrate ICC and digital elements into subject methods, practicum seminars, and research projects. This approach encourages candidates to see intercultural digital literacy as part of being a competent teacher in mathematics, science, language, or arts.

To achieve this integration, professional development models must go beyond one-time workshops. They should combine theory, practice, peer collaboration, and ongoing reflection. Research on effective teacher learning highlights that meaningful change happens when teachers connect conceptual frameworks to their practice, experiment over time, and discuss experiences with colleagues (Dede et al., 2009; Korthagen, 2010; Loughran, 2006). Blended models that mix online and face-to-face components are especially suitable for AI-mediated ICC. For example, teacher candidates could study key ICC frameworks (Byram, 1997; Bennett, 1993; Deardorff, 2006) in seminars. They could design AI-assisted intercultural tasks in small groups, implement them in practicum or micro-teaching settings, and then use digital recordings, discussion logs, or simple analytics for joint reflection. Online spaces can host reflective journals, peer feedback, and discussions across institutions. Meanwhile, on-site sessions can focus on reviewing emotionally charged or ethically complex moments and connecting experiences to larger discussions about diversity, equity, and representation.

These blended approaches rely on institutional frameworks that support this kind of work. At the program level, curriculum committees and leadership teams need to set clear goals for AI-supported ICC and link them with current quality assurance and teacher standards. This includes intercultural digital literacy outcomes in program specifications, recognizing the time needed for design-based experimentation in workload models, and providing access to appropriate technical and teaching support. At the system level, policy documents on teacher competence, digital strategies, and internationalization should explicitly mention the need for teachers who can act as critical, interculturally aware users and mediators of AI-related technologies. This approach should not frame technology use solely in terms of efficiency or innovation. Studies of teacher professional development show that ongoing institutional commitment, clear policy signals, and chances for local adaptation are essential in moving past disconnected, tool-focused initiatives (Dede et al., 2009; Sleeter, 2012).

Lastly, sustainable development in this area requires cooperation between countries and strong networks for sharing knowledge. Telecollaboration and virtual exchange projects in higher education have shown both the potential and challenges of connecting classrooms across borders for intercultural learning (Helm, 2015; O'Dowd, 2018; Dooly & O'Dowd, 2018). Similar principles can guide professional communities of teachers and teacher educators who want to share practices related to AI-supported ICC. Online communities of practice, joint research projects, and international professional development programs can help lessen the isolation of educators in under-resourced settings and share examples of context-sensitive, ethically grounded AI uses in intercultural teaching. Social and professional networks, webinars, and open educational resources support this cooperation. However, they must also address the differences in access, language, and institutional support that often determine participation and influence in these models (Helm, 2015).

Together, integrating intercultural digital literacy into curricula, using blended and reflective professional development models, establishing supportive institutional frameworks, and creating cross-national networks provide a clear pathway for sustainable growth in AI-supported ICC. These recommendations view teachers not as passive recipients of technological change but as active, critically informed professionals who collaboratively shape how AI supports intercultural understanding and equitable education.

## 7. CONCLUSION

This chapter argues that preparing teachers for intercultural communication in AI-mediated environments demands a fundamental shift away from tool-focused training towards a more comprehensive, critical, and sustainable model of professional development, building on established frameworks of intercultural communicative competence (Byram, 1997; Deardorff, 2006; Bennett, 1993) and research in digital, media, and information literacy (Buckingham, 2003; Lankshear & Knobel, 2008; UNESCO, 2013). We claim that AI-based simulations, conversational agents, and learning analytics can only support teacher education when embedded in coherent pedagogical designs that foreground inquiry into practice, structured reflection, and collaborative sense-making over the limited goal of "mastering" specific tools, because this approach emphasizes the need to integrate intercultural digital literacy into teacher education curricula, adopt blended models linking theory, practice, peer collaboration, and reflection, establish supportive institutional and policy conditions, and create cross-national networks to sustain development over time.

A central argument is that AI-supported intercultural communication is not only a technical or methodological issue but also an ethical one, since AI systems contribute to content creation, interaction facilitation, and visibility curation in digital spaces, shaping the circulation of cultural representations, narratives, and power relations. For teacher education, this yields at least three interrelated ethical imperatives: first, preservice and in-service teachers must have structured opportunities to interrogate the cultural assumptions, biases, and exclusions inscribed in training datasets, interface designs, and default outputs, including whose languages and varieties are normalized or marginalized, whose histories and experiences are amplified or obscured, and how stereotypes may be reproduced under claims of neutrality or intelligence; second, programs must address privacy, consent, and data governance in the use of learning analytics and AI-facilitated communication, ensuring that tools do not become instruments of surveillance or control and that participants have meaningful roles in interpreting and acting on data (Slade & Prinsloo, 2013; Ifenthaler & Yau, 2020); third, teacher education must address the global inequities of access to technology, infrastructure, and professional learning that shape the AI-mediated teaching and learning contexts of teachers and their students.

Preparing teachers for intercultural dialogue in the AI era requires building attitudes and skills that go beyond just technical skills. Teachers will encounter classrooms and communities where students move between offline and online spaces. They will interact with information shaped by algorithms and connect in networks influenced by complex histories of migration, inequality, and resistance. AI-driven environments can both create new opportunities for communication and increase the risks of division, misunderstanding, and exclusion. Therefore, teacher education must foster a long-term commitment in teachers to be curious, humble, and critically hopeful. This means being willing to listen across differences, question commonly accepted ideas, and collaborate with students to imagine fairer ways to coexist.

This means training teachers to create and lead learning experiences where AI tools support intercultural inquiry without taking centre stage. Simulations can provide spaces to explore differing viewpoints. Chatbots can encourage reflection on communication norms and assumptions. Analytics can reflect on whose voices are heard or ignored. However, these advantages only contribute to intercultural learning when guided by strong theoretical perspectives. They should be embedded in dialogic teaching methods and paired with critical reflection on power and responsibility. Teacher educators also need institutional and policy environments that recognize the complexity of this work and permit experimentation, teamwork, and long-term commitment.

The main challenge isn't just keeping pace with technological progress. We must consider what types of intercultural relationships AI-based education should foster. We need to examine whose interests are served by specific mixes of technology, teaching methods, and policies. By emphasizing intercultural communication skills, ethical awareness, and social justice in teacher education, and by viewing AI as one part of a broader communication and cultural network, we can prepare teachers to handle uncertainty, find meaning, and promote dialogue. This way, teacher education can help develop professionals who view AI not just as a tool but also as a source of ongoing ethical and intercultural responsibility. These teachers, along with their students, will critically and creatively shape the nature of dialogue in the AI era.

## REFERENCES


Beelen, J., & Jones, E. (2015). Redefining internationalization at home. In Curaj, A., Matei, L., Pricopie, R., Salmi, J., & Scott, P. (Eds.), *The European higher education area: Between critical reflections and future policies* (pp. 59–72). Springer. DOI: 10.1007/978-3-319-20877-0_5

Bender, E. M., Gebru, T., McMillan-Major, A., & Shmitchell, S. (2021). On the dangers of stochastic parrots: Can language models be too big? In *Proceedings of the 2021 ACM Conference on Fairness, Accountability, and Transparency* (pp. 610–623). New York: ACM. DOI: 10.1145/3442188.3445922

Bennett, M. J. (1993). Towards ethnorelativism: A developmental model of intercultural sensitivity. In Paige, R. M. (Ed.), *Education for the intercultural experience* (pp. 21–71). Intercultural Press.

Buckingham, D. (2003). *Media education: Literacy, learning and contemporary culture*. Polity Press.

Buolamwini, J., & Gebru, T. (2018). Gender shades: Intersectional accuracy disparities in commercial gender classification. In *Proceedings of the 1st Conference on Fairness, Accountability and Transparency* (pp. 77–91). New York: PMLR.

Byram, M. (1997). *Teaching and assessing intercultural communicative competence*. Multilingual Matters.

Caliskan, A., Bryson, J. J., & Narayanan, A. (2017). Semantics derived automatically from language corpora contain human-like biases. *Science*, *356*(6334), 183–186. DOI: 10.1126/science.aal4230

Deardorff, D. K. (2006). Identification and assessment of intercultural competence as a student outcome of internationalization. *Journal of Studies in International Education*, *10*(3), 241–266. DOI: 10.1177/1028315306287002

Deardorff, D. K. (2015). Demystifying outcomes assessment for international educators: A practical approach. *International Educator*, *24*(1), 54–57.

Dede, C., Jass Ketelhut, D., Whitehouse, P., Breit, L., & McCloskey, E. M. (2009). A research agenda for online teacher professional development. *Journal of Teacher Education*, *60*(1), 8–19. DOI: 10.1177/0022487108327554

Desimone, L. M. (2009). Improving impact studies of teachers' professional development: Toward better conceptualizations and measures. *Educational Researcher*, *38*(3), 181–199. DOI: 10.3102/0013189X08331140

Deterding, S., Dixon, D., Khaled, R., & Nacke, L. (2011). From game design elements to gamefulness: Defining "gamification". In *Proceedings of the 15th International Academic MindTrek Conference* (pp. 9–15). New York: ACM. DOI: 10.1145/2181037.2181040

Dooly, M., & O'Dowd, R. (Eds.). (2018). *In this together: Teachers' experiences with transnational, telecollaborative language learning projects*. Peter Lang. DOI: 10.3726/b14311

Dooly, M., & Sadler, R. (2016). Becoming little scientists: Technologically-enhanced project-based language learning. *Language Learning & Technology, 20*(1), 54–78. DOI: 10.64152/10125/44446

Ertmer, P. A., & Ottenbreit-Leftwich, A. T. (2010). Teacher technology change: How knowledge, confidence, beliefs, and culture intersect. *Journal of Research on Technology in Education, 42*(3), 255–284. DOI: 10.1080/15391523.2010.10782551

Floridi, L., & Chiriatti, M. (2020). GPT-3: Its nature, scope, limits, and consequences. *Minds and Machines, 30*(4), 681–694. DOI: 10.1007/s11023-020-09548-1

Gay, G. (2010). *Culturally responsive teaching: Theory, research, and practice* (2nd ed.). Teachers College Press.

Gilmore, A. (2007). Authentic materials and authenticity in foreign language learning. *Language Teaching, 40*(2), 97–118. DOI: 10.1017/S0261444807004144

Gudykunst, W. B. (2004). *Bridging differences: Effective intergroup communication* (4th ed.). Sage. DOI: 10.4135/9781452229706

Hampel, R., & Stickler, U. (2005). New skills for new classrooms: Training tutors to teach languages online. *Computer Assisted Language Learning, 18*(4), 311–326. DOI: 10.1080/09588220500335455

Hauck, M., & MacKinnon, T. (2016). Exploring the link between telecollaboration and intercultural communicative competence. In S. Jager, M. Kurek, & B. O'Rourke (Eds.), *New directions in telecollaborative research and practice* (pp. 214–238). Dublin: Research-publishing.net.

Helm, F. (2015). The practices and challenges of telecollaboration in higher education in Europe. *Language Learning & Technology, 19*(2), 197–217. DOI: 10.64152/10125/44424

Helm, F. (2016). Facilitated dialogue in online intercultural encounters. In S. Jager, M. Kurek, & B. O'Rourke (Eds.), *New directions in telecollaborative research and practice* (pp. 150–174). Dublin: Research-publishing.net.

Hofstede, G., Hofstede, G. J., & Minkov, M. (2010). *Cultures and organizations: Software of the mind* (3rd ed.). McGraw-Hill.

Holmes, W., Bialik, M., & Fadel, C. (2019). *Artificial intelligence in education: Promises and implications for teaching and learning*. Center for Curriculum Redesign.

Ifenthaler, D., & Yau, J. Y.-K. (2020). Utilising learning analytics to support study success in higher education: A systematic review. *Educational Technology Research and Development, 68*(4), 1961–1990. DOI: 10.1007/s11423-020-09788-z

Kasneci, E., Sessler, K., Küchemann, S., Bannert, M., Dementieva, D., Fischer, F., Gasser, U., Groh, G., Günnemann, S., Hüllermeier, E., Krusche, S., Kutyniok, G., Michaeli, T., Nerdel, C., Pfeffer, J., Poquet, O., Sailer, M., Schmidt, A., Seidel, T., & Kasneci, G. (2023). ChatGPT for good? On opportunities and challenges of large language models for education. *Learning and Individual Differences, 103*, 102274. DOI: 10.1016/j.lindif.2023.102274

Kellner, D., & Share, J. (2007). Critical media literacy, democracy, and the reconstruction of education. In Macedo, D., & Steinberg, S. R. (Eds.), *Media literacy: A reader* (pp. 3–23). Peter Lang.

König, J., Jäger-Biela, D. J., & Glutsch, N. (2020). Adapting to online teaching during COVID-19 school closure: Teacher education and teacher competence effects among early career teachers in Germany. *European Journal of Teacher Education, 43*(4), 608–622. DOI: 10.1080/02619768.2020.1809650

Kramsch, C. (1993). *Context and culture in language teaching*. Oxford University Press.

Ladson-Billings, G. (2014). Culturally relevant pedagogy 2.0: A.k.a. the remix. *Harvard Educational Review, 84*(1), 74–84. https://psycnet.apa.org/doi/10.17763/haer.84.1.p2rj131485484751. DOI: 10.17763/haer.84.1.p2rj131485484751

Lankshear, C., & Knobel, M. (2008). *Digital literacies: Concepts, policies and practices*. Peter Lang.

Lawless, K. A., & Pellegrino, J. W. (2007). Professional development in integrating technology into teaching and learning: Knowns, unknowns, and ways to pursue better questions and answers. *Review of Educational Research, 77*(4), 575–614. DOI: 10.3102/0034654307309921

Loughran, J. (2006). *Developing a pedagogy of teacher education: Understanding teaching and learning about teaching*. Routledge.

Mishra, P., & Koehler, M. J. (2006). Technological pedagogical content knowledge: A framework for teacher knowledge. *Teachers College Record*, *108*(6), 1017–1054. DOI: 10.1111/j.1467-9620.2006.00684.x

O'Dowd, R. (2013). Telecollaborative networks in university higher education: Overcoming barriers to integration. *The Internet and Higher Education*, *18*, 47–53. DOI: 10.1016/j.iheduc.2013.02.001

O'Dowd, R. (2018). From telecollaboration to virtual exchange: State-of-the-art and the role of UNICollaboration in moving forward. *Journal of Virtual Exchange*, *1*, 1–23. DOI: 10.14705/rpnet.2018.jve.1

O'Dowd, R., & Beelen, J. (2021). The role of virtual exchange in fostering internationalisation at home in European higher education. In A. Turula, M. Kurek, & T. Lewis (Eds.), *Telecollaboration and virtual exchange across disciplines: In service of social inclusion and global citizenship* (pp. 21–38). Dublin: Research-publishing.net.

OECD. (2020). *Teaching in the time of COVID-19 (TALIS Spotlight 1)*. OECD.

OECD. (2021). *OECD Digital Education Outlook 2021: Pushing the frontiers with AI, blockchain and robots*. OECD.

Prates, M. O. R., Avelar, P. H. C., & Lamb, L. C. (2020). Assessing gender bias in machine translation: A case study with Google Translate. *Neural Computing & Applications*, *32*(10), 6363–6381. DOI: 10.1007/s00521-019-04144-6

Puentedura, R. R. (2006). Transformation, technology, and education. Unpublished manuscript.

Pym, A., Malmkjær, K., & Gutiérrez-Colón Plana, M. (Eds.). (2013). *Translation and language learning: The role of translation in the teaching of languages in the European Union*. Publications Office of the European Union.

Ranalli, J. (2018). Automated written corrective feedback: How well can students make use of it? *Computer Assisted Language Learning*, *31*(7), 653–674. DOI: 10.1080/09588221.2018.1428994

Selwyn, N. (2011). *Education and technology: Key issues and debates*. Continuum.

Selwyn, N. (2022). *Is technology good for education?* (2nd ed.). Polity Press.

Slade, S., & Prinsloo, P. (2013). Learning analytics: Ethical issues and dilemmas. *The American Behavioral Scientist*, *57*(10), 1510–1529. DOI: 10.1177/0002764213479366

Sleeter, C. E. (2012). Confronting the marginalization of culturally responsive pedagogy. *Urban Education*, *47*(3), 562–584. DOI: 10.1177/0042085911431472

Stacey, E. (2018). Massive open online courses and teachers' professional learning. *Professional Development in Education, 44*(2), 232–244.

Tondeur, J., van Braak, J., Ertmer, P. A., & Ottenbreit-Leftwich, A. (2012). Understanding the relationship between teachers' pedagogical beliefs and technology use in education: A systematic review of qualitative evidence. *Educational Technology Research and Development, 60*(1), 135–149.

UNESCO. (2013). *Global media and information literacy assessment framework: Country readiness and competencies*. UNESCO.

UNESCO. (2021). *Reimagining our futures together: A new social contract for education*. UNESCO.

UNESCO. (2023). *Guidance for generative AI in education and research*. UNESCO.

Veletsianos, G., & Shepherdson, P. (2016). A systematic analysis and synthesis of the empirical MOOCs literature published in 2013–2015. *International Review of Research in Open and Distance Learning, 17*(2), 198–221. DOI: 10.19173/irrodl.v17i2.2448

Warschauer, M., & Kern, R. (Eds.). (2000). *Network-based language teaching: Concepts and practice*. Cambridge University Press. DOI: 10.1017/CBO9781139524735

Winkler, R., & Söllner, M. (2018). Unleashing the potential of chatbots in education: A state-of-the-art analysis. In *Academy of Management Annual Meeting Proceedings*. DOI: 10.5465/AMBPP.2018.15903abstract

Zawacki-Richter, O., Marín, V. I., Bond, M., & Gouverneur, F. (2019). Systematic review of research on artificial intelligence applications in higher education – Where are the educators? *International Journal of Educational Technology in Higher Education, 16*(1), 39. DOI: 10.1186/s41239-019-0171-0

# Chapter 15
# Smart Starts:
## Using AI Tools to Plan and Create Engaging English Lessons for Young Learners

**Gökçe Nur Türkmen**
http://orcid.org/0000-0002-8755-1803
*Çanakkale Onsekiz Mart University, Turkey*

**Kürşat Cesur**
http://orcid.org/0000-0001-5091-9793
*Çanakkale Onsekiz Mart University, Turkey*

**Tatyana Mikhailova**
http://orcid.org/0000-0001-6032-3846
*Sh.Ualikhanov Kokshetau University, Kazakhstan*

## ABSTRACT

*This chapter investigates the pedagogical implications of artificial intelligence (AI) within teaching English to young learners (EYL). The authors draw on contemporary research in the field AI-mediated education, addressing the potential of tools for lesson planning, language input and learner engagement with materials. The implications of reducing teacher workload, personalization of materials, and support for motivation building through gamified and interactive learning experiences, as potential of AI tools are discussed. In addition, important considerations related to ethics, cultural representations and data safety concerning child centered AI related resource and considered pedagogies are highlighted. The chapter concludes that AI works best as a co-creative partner enhancing teacher knowledge rather than*

DOI: 10.4018/979-8-3373-6325-7.ch015

*replacing the teacher. Finally, the chapter finishes with ideas for future research, suggestions for teacher education, and recommendations for policy that supports equitable, reflective, and human-centered AI integration into early language education.*

## 1. INTRODUCTION

Over the last couple of years, artificial intelligence (AI) has become indispensable for education, transforming how teachers design lessons, tasks, and assessments, and how students engage with language learning. Since being introduced into the educational field, AI has very quickly gained traction in lesson design, task design, gamification, translation, and personalized support for learning (Powell & Courchesne, 2024; Lo et al., 2024). In respect of language learning specifically, AI tools are transforming not only how students practice their language learning, but how teachers design and deliver content, thus developing more interactive, adaptive and student-centered learning experiences.

Foreign language teaching and teacher education in Türkiye do prioritize grammatical and lexical competence over communicative and intercultural dimensions (Akpınar, 2020). The disjunct between idealized curriculum and reality restricts children of opportunities for intercultural understanding and communicative confidence. Furthermore, teachers still lack suitable, age-appropriate, culturally relevant resources that would allow them to be creative and inclusive (Akpınar, 2020).

AI tools can act as logistical support for teachers by highlighting the tedious aspects of their work that lead them to eventually burnout, such as lesson planning, task design, and differentiation. Generative AI tools such as ChatGPT, Eduaide.ai, and Canva's Magic Write and many more can assist teachers in developing rich lesson content, creating visual materials, and producing scaffolded tasks to support different levels of proficiency (Prilop et al., 2024). Research has indicated that using AI to support lesson design lessens workload while generating comparable quality of instruction and pedagogy (Khan et al., 2024; Memarian & Doleck, 2023). Furthermore, with a call to engage more intentionally with AI literacy in K-12, educators and students need to be ready to encounter and interact critically with AI technologies (Laupichler et al., 2022; Memarian & Doleck, 2023).

This chapter serves as a bridge between early language teaching and AI-loaded teaching by considering how teachers can create "smart starts" with AI, using it as a creative and culturally responsive co-designer instead of a substitute for pedagogical knowledge. It shows teachers how to use AI technology for lesson design through interactive personalized content which matches student developmental levels and maintains human empathy and intercultural awareness that supports early language education. The chapter also discusses teaching approaches and particular classroom instances which prove that AI technology transforms early language learning into a worldwide creative environment that enables teachers and students to participate actively.

## 1.1. Using AI Tools for Young Learners

AI has emerged in recent years as a disruptive friend for educators in the way they plan lessons, design materials, and assess learning. AI tools enable educational systems to improve learning through customized approaches that boost student achievement and enable innovative teaching methods (Lo et al., 2024; Prilop et al., 2024). Corroborating evidence from higher-education EFL in Türkiye shows that General English Language MOOC (GELMOOC) produced substantial pre- to post-test gains and high learner satisfaction, underscoring how well AI-structured online designs can support language outcomes. (Uygun & Cesur, 2025). Research also shows that chatbots and adaptive platforms and AI storytelling systems enhance student engagement and literacy development and motivation when used in language learning classrooms for young students (Sun et al., 2025; Verma et al., 2025). Students achieve better vocabulary growth and narrative development and comprehension learning through multimodal tutoring systems which provide visual and audio learning materials (Chen, 2024; Liu et al., 2025). The research conducted on early learning environments demonstrates that adaptive feedback systems and gamified learning approaches and tutoring agents with emotional intelligence led to improved cognitive and socio-emotional growth (Bayrak, 2025; Sun et al., 2025).

Research in early education shows that new AI-supported tools for children have become more diverse. The selection includes chatbots and intelligent tutoring systems and interactive robots and storytelling applications and adaptive learning systems. These educational technologies draw from children's instinctive interest in new things to create learning environments that combine multiple learning modes with game elements and individualized content which results in active student participation and sustained motivation (Kanero et al., 2021; Kwon et al., 2023; Verma et al., 2025). The educational development of children depends on conversational AI tools which use age-appropriate teaching methods and instant feedback and emotional responses that range from compliance prompts to imaginative play support to help students stay focused and enhance their social and emotional skills. The educational approach which focuses on play-based learning demonstrates that young children achieve superior results when teachers combine play activities with interactive meaningful learning experiences and supportive learning environments (Haznedar & Uysal, 2020).

Early AI education for children enables them to operate AI tools and understand how AI systems process information and generate responses. Research shows that early AI exposure to students results in enhanced awareness of social and ethical AI issues while helping them grasp AI as both a technological system and cultural force that shapes human behavior and relationships (Casal-Otero et al., 2023; Memarian & Doleck, 2023). The research shows that students who learn about AI from an early stage develop better understanding of AI's social effects and ethical issues while recognizing AI as a technological system and cultural force which shapes how people behave and connect with each other (Casal-Otero et al., 2023; Memarian & Doleck, 2023). Future citizens must learn to operate ethically with technology because digital systems control their learning and work and social interactions. AI literacy functions as a digital global citizenship extension because it demands users to think critically about their digital actions while promoting equal participation and moral responsibility in digital spaces.

The main elements which enhance the language-learning process include authentic materials and learner independence and teamwork and learning through relevant real-world situations. Hypermedia learning environments enhanced by AI features like adaptive feedback and automated scaffolding enable students to control their learning speed and direction while receiving authentic language input through meaningful learning environments. Students acquire digital competencies and basic intercultural knowledge through their independent language practice in multiple learning environments.

Research conducted by Sun et al. (2025) and Chen (2024) demonstrates that AI-based learning environments produce substantial improvements in early literacy and oral language skills through interactive storytelling and pronunciation modeling and vocabulary enhancement activities. AI storytelling systems would monitor how children react to the story and modify the narrative based on their responses to boost their engagement and empathy and imagination. The study results show that AI reaches its highest teaching potential when technology functions as a tool to support educators rather than replace them because it enables teachers to deliver customized learning experiences that keep the human elements of play and personal interaction in early childhood education.

## 1.2. Young Learners' Needs: Attention, Multimodality and Interaction

To teach English to young learners, teachers must be deeply pedagogically sensitive to children's unique developmental, cognitive and emotional traits. An effective English lesson should encourage young learners' curiosity, creativity, and communication whilst managing large amounts of attention and interactions from young learners. Haznedar and Uysal (2020) point out that much of the literature regarding teacher-education continues to prioritize teacher-centered grammar-based instruction which is not an effective reflection of how children learn languages, which is through exploration, play, and engagement with society.

Research frequently demonstrates that children have distinct advantages regarding second-language acquisition. A faster progression for adults may occur at the outset because of the greater maturity of their cognition; nonetheless, children have advantages in achieving greater native-like proficiency over time when second-language learning begins early (Haznedar & Uysal, 2020). It is for this reason that early instruction should be meaning-oriented, playful, and experiential. In fact, Haznedar and Uysal (2020) state that effective classrooms for English for young learners integrate all four skills through stories, songs, rhymes, drama, and hands-on activities, all in a relaxed, low-anxiety atmosphere, often enhanced with visuals and gestures. Akcan (2020) similarly contends that children learn best when instruction focuses on relevant, meaningful content, as opposed to abstract linguistic form, and when children engage with frequent opportunities to communicate. Ellis (1996) argues that child-centered learning should be experiential and interactive in nature, allowing reflection to emerge spontaneously from authentic communication. Akpınar (2020) further reminds that children's intrinsic qualities of curiosity, openness, and lack of prejudice make them outstanding participants in intercultural and multilingual learning, as these qualities are considered essential for an education that promotes global citizenship.

## 2. PEDAGOGICAL IMPLEMENTATIONS FOR EARLY EDUCATION

### 2.1. Foundations of Language Learning in Childhood

Early childhood is a period of significant opportunity for language learning, as cognitive, emotional, and social capacities work together to create favorable conditions for linguistic and communicative development. In contrast to adults who tend to rely upon analytical and metalinguistic reasoning, children learn language implicitly through social interaction, imitation, and multimodal exploration. Consequently, early years language pedagogy should foreground experiences and play through a communication process and contextual meaning as opposed to abstracting linguistic form (Khan et al, 2024; Sampanis, 2025).

Research in early childhood pedagogy indicates the need to ensure that AI and AI applications are congruent with a children's realities of development. Su and Yang (2022) undertook a scoping review which examined how, in the field of AI literacy, young children must not only use AI tools but understand them as cognitive cultural artifacts. Because of this, Su and Yang (2022) argue that AI should be introduced through play and guided engagement to foster both conceptual conceptualizations of understanding and form good and effective digital habits. Casal-Otero et al. (2023) argued in their systematic review that when AI tools were integrated into teacher mediated contexts where children are engaged collaboratively, they contributed to creativity, emotional regulation, and literacy outcomes.

One notably creative example of an innovative system is Tinker Tales, a tangible-digital storytelling system that pairs physical tokens with an AI driven narrative engine (Choi et al., 2025). Each object represents a character, setting, or emotion that prompts the AI to continue the story. By interacting with these tangible elements, children furthermore anchor their abstract conceptions of AI with a physical and embodied experience. The system also served as an example of a design for children that follows the principle of appropriate developmental practice: that young children learn and build knowledge through hands-on experiences and social interaction. The examples within this literature illustrate that successful AI integration in early childhood space must be developmentally responsive, scaffolded, multi-modal, interactive, and play driven (Choi et al., 2025; Khan et al., 2024).

## 2.2. Embedding Play, Storytelling and Gamification

Play, storytelling, as well as gamified learning, are integral to language development in the early years, where children create meaning, negotiate social roles, and internalize language patterns in contexts that are intrinsically motivating. AI-mediated environments show a strengthening of these characteristics through the use of personalized content and interactive features and multiple forms of content delivery. The research done by Chen in 2024 shows that AI storytelling tools help young children learn new words and understand stories better and stay interested in their early learning activities. The tools proved to be effective because their design enables them to adjust to individual needs through their ability to understand user input and their language skills. The research by Sun et al. (2025) demonstrated that AI storytelling combined with game-based systems enabled users to maintain their focus while learning new language elements through integrated text and visual and auditory content within structured stories. At the same time, AI-supported storytelling can introduce cultural bias or stereotypical representations (e.g., family structures, lifestyles, gender roles) if prompts and generated content are not carefully curated and localized. Because young learners are still forming social categories, teachers should treat AI-generated characters, images, and plotlines as drafts that require cultural checking, inclusive redesign, and classroom discussion, rather than "ready-made truth" (Grassini, 2023). Teacher mediation therefore becomes the safeguard that preserves both developmental appropriacy and cultural representation.

The research reveals multiple educational advantages which stem from human-AI collaboration during the creation process. Ye et al. (2025) describe a setting where children and teachers engaged with an AI storytelling system, with the AI scaffolding the narrative structure, while the children and teachers contributed the characters and dialogue. These results indicated a measurable increase in children's expressive language and coherence in story development, suggesting that AI can extend beyond being a didactic tutor to being a responsive narrative partner. For instance, Azzopardi (2025) documents instances of a kindergarten teacher negotiating story reading between a traditional story, AI-supported narrative reading, and traditional storytelling. This example depicts the value of AI during storytelling to maintain emotional connection and social interaction, while utilizing the adaptive visual and audio features of the AI system to afford additional support of stories.

Gamified AI systems, such as tangible interactive games for AI literacy, as described by Sampanis (2025), engage play and technology to maintain motivation and knowledge of procedural knowledge. Gamified AI literacy systems embed basic concepts of AI such as decision-making and pattern recognition within tasks linked to narrative or language being developed. Although children are engaged within narrative and language tasks linked to familiar stories, they are developing understanding of the mechanics of AI and pragmatics of communication. AI-mediated play creates contexts for enhancing linguistic, cognitive, and socio-emotional growth at the same time, reinforcing one aspect of holistic language learning.

There is an increasing amount of empirical evidence that describes how AI tools are being used in early childhood classrooms to support language and literacy learning. Here are two examples that vary in their approach but share similar pedagogical foundations. The Colin multimodal storytelling system (Ye et al., 2024) allows children to collaboratively co-construct stories with AI support. By adding visual prompts and the ability to recognize children's speech and implement narrative sequencing, Colin helps scaffold children's understanding of narrative and coherence while also supporting imaginative expression. Tinker Tales (Choi et al., 2025) also combines physical (tangible) manipulatives with AI narration that transforms storytelling from a solitary into a collaborative sensory experience while developing children's narrative competence and foundational AI literacies. AI-enhanced storybooks created at MIT Media Lab present AI concepts to children through interactive robot characters which include Doodlebot to help children learn basic decision-making processes (MIT Media Lab, 2023). Storybooks serve two functions by helping young readers understand artificial intelligence and building their vocabulary and reading skills through repeated language patterns and conversational exchanges.

## 2.3. Design Principles for Implementing AI in Early Childhood Language Education

AI-mediated learning during early childhood requires a combination of learner independence and structured assistance to create *scaffolded agency* which serves as its fundamental characteristic. AI tools enable children to actively control storytelling and dialogue and problem-solving tasks through their interactive features which also include language and visual support to enhance understanding and maintain involvement. The design method protects children's creative abilities and learning independence while giving them age-appropriate guidance during their developmental stages. The research by Ye et al. (2025) demonstrates that children achieved better narrative coherence and expressive language development through their collaborative storytelling activities with the Colin multimodal storytelling system. Likewise, Azzopardi (2025) studied teacher-mediated AI storytelling to foster learner emotional engagement and agency during shared reading sessions, and children perceived the AI as a partner rather than a prescriptive teacher. Ultimately, these studies reflect that the most meaningful and productive AI environments uphold and preserve the child's voice in guided, meaningful interaction.

Young learners acquire and retain new information most efficiently through instruction that includes *multimodal integration* - multiple sensory and cognitive channels. AI-enabled learning experiences can integrate text, image, voice, gesture, and the experience of the physical world to reflect children's affinities for concrete and embodied learning. For example, Chen (2024) and Sun et al. (2025) reported that when presented in synchronized visual and auditory modes, a multimodal AI storytelling tool resulted in significantly greater vocabulary growth and comprehension than traditional didactic literacy instruction. Taking this a step further, Choi et al. (2025) investigated tangible-digital hybrid systems, such as Tinker Tales, that supported embodied learning and retention of concepts over time, and their findings showed that when children physically manipulated the storytelling elements to impact AI-generated outcomes, not only did they support embodied learning, but also attention and engagement with literacy practice. This body of work moves multimodal interfaces beyond enhancing comprehension and provides the basic premise of bridging abstract linguistic forms with sensory experience through AI modality, consequently, the abilities of AI-supported lessons.

A key design principle is *adaptive complexity*, the ability of AI systems to adaptively modify the difficulty of tasks, the speed of tasks, and feedback based on each learner's proficiency level, attention span, and some prior knowledge. Adaptivity contributes to the sustained motivation of learners by maintaining a "challenge zone" that is neither too easy to risk boredom or too difficult to lead to frustration. Chen (2024) showed how adaptive narrative branching and graded vocabulary exposure facilitated continuous learner engagement because children were encountering stories that changed as their language ability changed. Sun et al. (2025) also affirmed that the adaptivity of intelligence was a key contributor to maintaining attention and deeper cognitive engagement when stories were enhanced by AI. Practical adaptive AI allows educators to develop unique experiences for diverse learners while maintaining a shared sense of progression and discovery.

Even though AI is complex in its technology, mediating the AI experience in early years classrooms is integral to the role of educators. Teachers continue to play the role of interpreters, curators, and emotional support while maintaining ethics, cultural relevance, and aligned development. This principle of *teacher mediation and reflection* acknowledges that effectiveness with AI tools depends not only on the algorithms used but also on how educators mediate and provide context to those tools. Sun et al. (2025) stated that guided mediations provide a guided as well as personalized, child-centered, supportive backdrop to build children's understanding of AI and stop misconceptions about what AI is, and how AI works. Azzopardi (2025) and Casal-Otero et al. (2023) also found that AI-based interventions are most effective in teacher-led, socially rich environments where children are supported to discuss, empathetic and critically reflect. So rather than reducing the teacher's role, the use of AI enhances the teacher role to design meaningful moments of reflection between children and technology.

Young learners' use of AI tools must operate in *playful and culturally responsive contexts* that are representations of children's lived experiences and diversity. Play and culturally relevant representation amplify motivation, support learners' identity, and promote intercultural awareness. For instance, Sampanis (2025) showed that interactive games with physical manipulatives contextualized AI concepts through culturally relevant storytelling, enabling children to engage with language and culture playfully and participatorily. In a similar study, researchers at the MIT Media Lab (2023) reported that robot-based storybooks developed on local and ethical knowledge led to curiosity and moral reflection in preschoolers. These examples make clear that playful learning environments grounded in culture situate AI as a tool for inclusion and not uniformity, increasing AI's capacity to develop global citizenship and empathy from a young age.

Overall, these design principles indicate agreement that AI should serve as a pedagogical partner and not a replacement educator. Scaffolded agency and adaptivity allow children to co-construct meaning with AI; multimodality and play create engagement and holistic learning opportunities; and teacher mediation protects the ethical and emotional aspects of education. When viewed through these principles, AI integration bolsters, rather than replaces, the creative, relational, and intercultural underpinnings of early language learning (Chen, 2024; Sun, 2025; Ye et al., 2025).

## 3. BENEFITS OF AI-SUPPORTED LEARNING AND TEACHING

Learning environments that use AI *help improve learners' intrinsic motivation and engagement* by providing new and interactive, responsive learning environments. In an important research study, Fryer and Carpenter (2006) revealed six pedagogical advantages of online language learning chatbots. These included discovering that learners felt more fearlessness about interacting with chatbots than with human partners; could review and repeat materials at their own pace; were able to practice listening and reading skills; were motivated because of the novelty; were introduced to rich language input; and were able to attain immediate feedback on their mechanical errors (Fryer et al., 2020). Each of these affordances encourages learning all the more for young learners, who learn best in low-anxiety environments that integrate repetition along with play and discovery. Using conversational AI, young learners are able to experiment with language without fear of disapproving evaluation, which follows principles of affective engagement and reflects foundational principles of early language teaching pedagogy. Recent studies confirm that children do enjoy engaging more because of AI-supported interactions. For example, Sun et al. (2025) examined these engagements, noting that children's handling of today's high level of digital learning has been significantly improved by AI-driven story time applications. This study revealed that children attended to their learning for longer periods of time when the read-to-me digital book included AI features and functions where the AI storytelling systems adjusted to children's comprehension, modulating voice to sustain curiosity for greater length in digital story mid learning engagement than traditional read-a-loud sessions. Likewise, Bayrak (2025) noted how gamified AI systems enhance socio-emotional engagement by providing meaningful rewards and agency, crucial sources of motivation for continued language learning. These types of multimodal learning environments adapt to the learner and can turn routine practice into an interactive, emotional experience for the learner.

In addition to engagement, AI has considerable promise for the *enhancement of young children's early literacy and vocabulary growth.* Wei (2023) suggests that reading systems enhanced with AI can support vocabulary acquisition and reading fluency through adaptive contextualized input. Likewise, Chen (2024) reports that AI storytelling platforms in which on-the-fly the stories changed based on children's responses to recognize words, comprehension of meaning and narrative competence. These platforms use adaptive algorithms to scaffold new vocabulary in meaningful contexts while expanding the child's semantic networks, in which all learned new vocabulary becomes informed by three modalities - text, voice, image, and animation. Moreover, Liu et al. (2025) shared that children would have significant gains in both expressive and receptive language when engaging with an AI tutoring system that provided continuous feedback and individualized prompts for students to consider.

Unlike conventional digital materials, AI-based tools maintain a "zone of proximal development" design through immediate differentiated feedback as a mechanism to motivate children to embellish their language production in a safe environment. With teacher mediation, technologies can develop active, reflective learning opportunities that promote cognitive, linguistic, and socio-emotional growth.

AI technology is a *functional collaborator for teachers*, helping to ease the time burden related to intensive workloads like lesson planning, assessment design, or differentiation. Prilop et al. (2024) demonstrate how generative AI can create lesson frameworks, intended learning outcomes, and formative assessments aligned to curricular goals, which allow teachers to direct more content focus towards higher order thinking and creative instruction. Memarian & Doleck (2023) and Khan et al. (2024) also found that AI contributed to their ability to design lessons that tied in personalization of materials, digital resources, and responding to diversity within the learner's needs all in an efficient manner. Educators receive support through cognitive workload offloading which allows them to create learning experiences that welcome all students while respecting their cultural backgrounds and social needs. AI systems generate quick task variations for students who have different learning needs through the creation of multiple task versions and the use of first language translation and the presentation of content in culturally relevant visual and textual formats. AI systems provide educational content to students through their ability to modify learning resources according to individual requirements and specific learning situations (Grassini, 2023). The system gives equal access to all users and supports educational progress through its design. AI functions as a co-designer for teachers who use its capabilities to support their empathetic understanding of human learning environments which enables them to create new learning experiences.

AI-supported teaching methods provide an additional benefit by *supporting multimodal learning and cultural inclusivity* which serve as core elements for successful early language education. The multimodal AI systems combine text and speech with images and gesture recognition and emotional detection to support various learning methods of young children. The research studies by Bayrak (2025) and Sun et al. (2025) demonstrate that AI story environments which use multiple modes of presentation help users understand and remember content better through their use of various sensory inputs at the same time. The recommendation supports early childhood education principles because it builds upon the concepts of embodied learning and play-based activities and sensory exploration. Multi-modal AI systems, therefore, can also support many of the principles of early language pedagogy.

AI applications function as intercultural awareness tools when they undergo design processes which prioritize cultural representation and diversity inclusion. The educational tools which use local content together with multiple languages and cultural topics create better learning encounters for students when they connect worldwide concepts with their nearby environment. According to Selwyn (2019), AI systems perform automated tasks in education but they lack the ability to make ethical decisions and provide human interaction which remains vital for educational settings. The educational content created by AI systems needs teachers to select and organize and interpret it so that technology can help students maintain their cultural and social learning experiences.

## 4. AI TOOLS FOR LESSON PLANNING

Artificial intelligence systems perform educational functions which support teachers because they automate routine tasks to help educators build student-focused lesson plans. Teachers who use AI planning tools generate teaching materials which combine educational theories with visual design elements and flexible content structures and maintain their control over creative decisions and content localization (Prilop et al., 2024; Liu et al., 2025). The tools provide teachers with suggestions for learning goals and lesson organization and evaluation methods which align with student needs and educational standards, so teachers need to think less about these tasks (Memarian & Doleck, 2023).

During the ideation stage, tools like ChatGPT, Gemini, and MagicSchool.ai allow teachers to brainstorm on lesson themes, communicative tasks, warm-ups, and games in the classroom. Generative AI can extend teachers' flexibility to create activities that are age-appropriate, interactive, and include important elements of play, conversation, and inquiry-based approaches in young learner pedagogy (Liu et al., 2025; Sun et al., 2025). In an example, an AI could provide a teacher with a story text prompt asking for a story where the setting is "a magic garden!" or could brainstorm scaffolding ideas for dialogues on everyday topics such as at "the supermarket", which would permit the teacher to linguistically or culturally adapt the outcome. Such applications support the idea of co-creativity in which AI serves as a partner that stimulates teacher imagination rather than serves as a replacement for pedagogical judgement (Grassini, 2023).

In the instance of lesson structure, AI tools such as Eduaide.ai and LessonPlans.ai generate entire lesson outlines, including objectives, timing, and assessment suggestions, according to learners' proficiency (Prilop et al., 2024). These structures use natural language processing to categorize the activities of the lesson into semi-coherent stages such as presentation, practice, and production or inquiry-based sequences (i.e. "engage-explore-explain-extend"). The overall benefit is fewer hours of preparation - clearly aiding novice teachers visualize the course of a well-balanced lesson. According to Khan et al. (2024), teachers can use generative AI to shift from routine lesson planning to thoughtful educational choices about content selection and instructional methods.

AI functions as a visual design tool which operates as a vital motivational force for young students during their initial learning process. Teachers have access to three main tools which include Canva Magic Write and Curipod and DALL·E to develop vibrant visual materials that transform complex vocabulary and grammar content into understandable child-friendly illustrations. Research on multimodal learning environments confirms that visualized and interactive input enhances attention and retention in children, particularly when combined with narration or gestures (Bayrak, 2025; Chen et al., 2025; Choi et al., 2025). The AI image generator enables teachers to request visual content about "farm animals in winter" which generates instant images for educational purposes such as storytelling and vocabulary development.

Lastly, AI facilitates collaboration and co-creation among educators as well as shared functions that support educators. AI platforms allow teachers to co-design materials, share strategies for improvement, and collaborate in marking student work while remaining true to the principles of distributed expertise (Selwyn, 2019). Most importantly, while AI will take care of the mechanical aspects of design, the educator's expertise, empathy, and situational sensitivity will remain relevant. As Selwyn (2019) and Grassini (2023) stipulate, for AI to be successful in educational contexts (such as lesson planning and assessments), educators must examine and contextualize the products of AI, and maintain the human aspects of encouragement, humor, and empathy, which AI can never substitute.

Creating lesson plans may be one of the most rigorous demands of the teacher's workload, but this is particularly true in early language classrooms where lessons need to be engaging, multimodal, and developmentally appropriate. AI tools can assist the teacher by allowing them time to generate ideas, sequence lessons and differentiate, thus allowing the teacher to be creative and have time for personal interaction.

Recent research suggests that by using AI-assisted planning, teachers will be efficient and pedagogically innovate, as it allows teachers to spend more time designing lessons that are interactive and communicative with children instead of excluding them because of a desire for enhanced child-centeredness (Grassini, 2023; Prilop et al., 2024). The following tools will help to inspire the teacher while brainstorming related themes, designing objectives and creating the entire lesson structure around the needs of the young learner.

*Table 1. Key uses of AI in lesson planning*

| Function | AI Contribution | Pedagogical Benefit for YLs | Supporting Studies |
|---|---|---|---|
| **Idea Generation** | Suggests themes, dialogues, warm-ups, games | Boosts teacher creativity; ensures varied, playful input | Agherai et al. (2025); Cui, & Alias (2024); Liu et al. (2025); Lo et al. (2024); Sun et al. (2025); Toscu (2025) |
| **Lesson Structuring** | Builds objectives, stages, and assessments | Supports balanced, CEFR-aligned planning | Azzopardi (2025); Chen (2024); Choi et al. (2025); Kanero et al. (2021); Khan et al. (2024); Prilop et al. (2024); Trust et al. (2023); Ye et al. (2025) |
| **Visual Design** | Generates slides, posters, story scenes | Increases attention and comprehension through visuals | Bayrak (2025); Chen (2024); Chen et al. (2025) |
| **Collaboration** | Enables co-editing, shared grading, peer feedback | Promotes professional growth and reflective teaching | Memarian & Doleck (2023); Sampanis (2025); Selwyn (2019); Song & Glazewski (2023); Verma et al. (2025) |

## 4.1. Smart Starts: AI Tools for Teachers

Generating new ideas is one of the most time-consuming parts of lesson planning. AI platforms such as ChatGPT, Gemini, and MagicSchool.ai can quickly generate suggested thematic topics, communicative situations, and play-based activities, thus allowing teachers to think and focus their time on adapting and ensuring cultural relevance (Liu et al., 2025; Lo et al., 2024). This is especially useful in early-age classrooms, where the storytelling and imagination drive motivation and engagement. Teachers can prompt AI to create sample dialogues, rhymes, or role plays, then adapt the language or visuals for their learners. Embedding intercultural aims and global-awareness themes in these prompts may enhance ICC development (Mikhailova & Cesur, 2025).

Effective lesson planning is one of the most time-consuming and challenging elements of a teacher's workload, particularly in early language teaching where activities must be engaging, multimodal, and developmentally appropriate. AI tools can support plan the segment on creating ideas, Sequencing, and differentiation so that teachers have more time available for ideation and creativity, as well as human interaction. Recent studies indicate that AI-supported planning will improve teacher efficiencies and pedagogical innovation that allow teachers the opportunity to create more interactive and communicative lessons (Grassini, 2023; Prilop et al., 2024). However, AI-generated lesson plans may also be generic, culturally mismatched, or over-standardized, and they can unintentionally reduce teacher agency if adopted without critical adaptation. To avoid "automation," teachers should verify alignment with local curriculum aims, developmental needs, and classroom realities, using AI for augmentation rather than replacement of professional judgment (Selwyn, 2019; Prilop et al., 2024). The following tools are addressed for teachers to assist and as a springboard to brainstorm themes, create objectives, and plan and write a complete lesson based on the developmental needs of your young learners.

*Table 2. AI tools for lesson planning*

| Tool | Function | Example Classroom Use | Teacher's Role | Student's Role |
|---|---|---|---|---|
| **ChatGPT** | Generates lesson ideas, dialogues, warm-ups | Creates a "My Favorite Toy" speaking task | Prompt, edit, adapt for level | Participate in created task |
| **Gemini (Google)** | Brainstorms themes, objectives, and CEFR-aligned ideas | Designs "Weather Around the World" lesson plan | Guide idea refinement | Engage with sample visuals |
| **MagicSchool.ai** | Builds structured lesson frameworks | Generates full "Colors and Clothes" lesson | Adjust timing and scaffolding | Follow lesson flow |
| **LessonPlans.ai** | Suggests objectives, procedures, and assessments | Prepares a reading + craft lesson on "Animals" | Select relevant stages | Complete guided activity |
| **Eduaide.ai** | Produces rubrics, objectives, and reflection tasks | Generates "My Daily Routine" formative rubric | Review and modify | Self-assess learning |
| **Twee** | Generates CEFR-based communicative tasks | Produces listening questions for a short story | Select & localize tasks | Listen and answer |
| **Brisk Teaching** | Automates lesson summaries and tasks | Creates worksheet summaries of past units | Evaluate and print | Review summaries |
| **Debate AI** | Creates age-appropriate debate topics | "Which pet is better?" structured mini debate | Model debate language | Express opinions |
| **Mizou** | Develops critical thinking and short exchanges | "Should kids recycle?" role-play debate | Scaffold vocabulary | Respond to prompts |

Given the rapid spread of classroom AI, early childhood educators need a concise, age-appropriate guide to tools that scaffold reading and writing while ensuring teacher mediation and data minimization. Following table summarizes each tool's function, example classroom use, and the complementary roles of teachers and students.

*Table 3. AI tools for reading and writing support*

| Tool | Function | Example Classroom Use | Teacher's Role | Student's Role |
|---|---|---|---|---|
| **Diffit** | Simplifies or rewrites texts | Adjusts "Goldilocks" story for CEFR A1 | Choose difficulty | Read simplified version |
| **Rewordify** | Converts complex words into simple terms | Makes graded readers accessible | Verify accuracy | Build vocabulary list |
| **Quillbot** | Paraphrases or rephrases writing | Rewrites student journal sentences | Check meaning | Compare AI vs. original |
| **ProWritingAid** | Corrects grammar and improves style | Revises story drafts | Review feedback | Edit own writing |
| **Scholarcy** | Summarizes long texts | Condenses "The Three Little Pigs" into short summary | Guide summarization | Identify main ideas |
| **AI Essay Grader** | Provides rubric-based writing feedback | Grades simple paragraph writing task | Review AI comments | Reflect and improve |

Children learn best when they can see, hear, and do. AI-driven design and media tools create engaging visual and auditory materials for teachers that anchor vocabulary and structures in meaningful contexts. Multimodal engagement increases attention and retention (Bayrak, 2025), creating memorable, concrete experiences with abstract language. The following tools help teachers create illustrations, videos, polls, and slides that make engaging language experiences in their lessons.

*Table 4. AI tools for visual and multimodal input*

| Tool | Function | Example Classroom Use | Teacher's Role | Student's Role |
|---|---|---|---|---|
| **Canva Magic Write / Magic Design** | Designs posters, flashcards, story visuals | Create "My Family" poster | Curate safe templates | Add images or text |
| **DALL·E / Bing Image Creator** | Generates illustrations from text | "At the Zoo" vocabulary visuals | Guide prompt writing | Describe pictures |
| **Curipod** | Interactive lesson builder | Slide-based poll on favorite foods | Present and monitor | Respond interactively |
| **ClassPoint** | Converts slides into live quizzes | Use drag-and-drop word sorting | Facilitate feedback | Participate in polls |
| **Veed.io** | Video editing and subtitling | Record and subtitle short story | Support video narration | Watch and retell |
| **Suno AI** | Creates AI-generated music and sound effects | Add soundscape to stories | Adjust rhythm and tone | Sing or move along |

continued on following page

*Table 4. Continued*

| Tool | Function | Example Classroom Use | Teacher's Role | Student's Role |
|---|---|---|---|---|
| **DeepAI** | Generates quick illustrations | Create "Seasons" picture set | Filter content | Identify seasons visually |
| **Zapper / Deep Nostalgia** | Animates characters or historical figures | Animate fairy tale scenes | Select age-safe content | Observe and narrate |

Communication skills such as speaking and listening are core to communicative competence, though they are often constrained by time in the classroom, or the stress of students having to perform (Trust et al., 2023). AI-driven speech technology offers learners safe, repeatable, and individualized oral practice, with reduced anxiety and the benefit of instantaneous feedback (Fryer & Carpenter, 2006). For teachers, these represent a digital co-tutor that can increase pronunciation, fluency, and listening exercises previously only done in class. The table below lists AI tools that can facilitate conversational practice, pronunciation modeling, and real-time correcting.

*Table 5. AI tools for listening and speaking*

| Tool | Function | Example Classroom Use | Teacher's Role | Student's Role |
|---|---|---|---|---|
| **Murf AI** | Text-to-speech generator | Narrate bedtime stories in English | Choose natural voice | Listen and repeat |
| **Speechify** | Converts written texts into audio | Read aloud students' own stories | Control playback speed | Listen and follow text |
| **ELSA Speak** | Pronunciation and accent feedback | Practice "th" sound words | Assign pronunciation drills | Record and repeat words |
| **Speechling** | Gives pronunciation corrections | Shadow short dialogues | Monitor improvement | Compare and repeat |
| **Praktika** | Simulated speaking partner | Role-play "At the Supermarket" | Supervise safe use | Converse naturally |
| **Debate AI / Mizou** | Develops structured argumentation | Conduct "Agree or Disagree" mini sessions | Scaffold sentence frames | Present arguments |
| **Build-a-Bot** | Custom chatbots for interaction | "Ask the Robot about Animals" | Design questions | Engage in dialogue |

Gamification converts repetitive drills into play-based activities, appealing to children's drive for competition and creativity. Quiz and game platforms enhanced by AI automatically create many tasks that support the learning outcome of the lesson, keeping students motivated while reinforcing core skills (Kanero et al., 2021). These platforms assist teachers in sustaining engagement, differentiating levels of difficulty, and collecting data on students' progression. The tools below illustrate how AI can create dynamic routines of drills with active participation and self-correction.

*Table 6. AI tools for gamification and practice*

| Tool | Function | Example Classroom Use | Teacher's Role | Student's Role |
|---|---|---|---|---|
| **Kahoot!** | Creates AI-generated quizzes | Vocabulary revision on "Colors" | Host quiz and review | Compete and answer |
| **Quizzillion** | Generates adaptive grammar games | Verb tense practice game | Moderate and assess | Play and self-check |
| **Redmenta** | Online tests with auto-grading | Multiple-choice test on "Animals" | Analyze results | Review feedback |
| **ClassPoint** | Turns slides into quizzes | Spelling quiz integrated in lesson | Facilitate pacing | Respond actively |
| **Build-a-Bot** | Custom chatbot quiz | "Guess the Food" interactive quiz | Supervise responses | Ask and answer |
| **Zapper / Deep Nostalgia** | Adds visual animation | Animate winning characters | Ensure appropriateness | Watch animations |

Assessment in early learning should be formative, nurturing, growth-focused, and not punitive. AI systems can help teachers efficiently develop rubrics, mark student work, and produce helpful comments to make feedback timely and personal (Prilop et al., 2024). When used ethically, tools like the ones listed below can optimize the mechanical grading process so that teachers can spend more of their time being empathic and connected. The following table lists different products or tools that can promote fair, transparent, and feedback-rich assessments in EYL classrooms.

*Table 7. AI tools for assessment and feedback*

| Tool | Function | Example Classroom Use | Teacher's Role | Student's Role |
|---|---|---|---|---|
| **ExamSoft** | Creates secure online tests | End-of-unit vocabulary exam | Review analytics | Take online test |
| **MagicSchool AI** | Generates rubrics and feedback templates | "Story Writing" rubric | Adjust rubric criteria | Self-evaluate work |
| **Co-Grader AI** | Co-grades and comments on writing | "My Pet" essay feedback | Review suggestions | Reflect and edit |
| **Ed Café AI** | Peer reflection and assessment | Share favorite activity ideas | Moderate discussion | Post feedback |
| **Scholarcy / ProWritingAid** | Checks writing clarity and coherence | Grade short descriptive texts | Interpret AI insights | Apply corrections |

Collaborative work is essential to professional growth and to innovation in the classroom. Artificial Intelligence-enabled platforms allow teachers and students to co-create, co-edit and co-reflect as a collective group, making their once individual work a shared inquiry (Memarian & Doleck, 2023). Collaborative learning promotes metacognition, peer support and community, and promotes engagement in more participatory learning. For example, the tools below illustrate ways that AI engaged teachers collaboratively, fostered student reflection, and provided safe spaces for conversation.

*Table 8. AI tools for collaboration and reflection*

| Tool | Function | Example Classroom Use | Teacher's Role | Student's Role |
|---|---|---|---|---|
| **Ed Café AI** | Collaborative teacher workspace | Share "Seasons" unit plans | Guide reflection | Observe planning |
| **Google Workspace AI** | Shared AI-assisted writing | Co-write group story in Docs | Facilitate revision | Write together |
| **Co-Grader AI** | Joint grading & feedback | Collaborative story grading | Moderate comments | Peer-assess |
| **Replika** | Reflective journaling chatbot | "My Day" reflection dialogue | Supervise responses | Reflect on daily learning |
| **MagicSchool.ai** | Team planning assistant | Co-design multi-teacher project | Review AI output | Collaborate in projects |

Cross-curricular projects blend language learning with art, science, and design and promote more holistic learning, including 21st-century skills such as creativity, problem solving, and global awareness (Chen et al. 2025). The AI-enhanced tools deepen learning in cross-curricular projects to experiment and invent while communicating meaningfully across subject boundaries that meet a blend of language and disciplinary goals. The following tools help students experiment, invent, and communicate in an authentic, multimodal way that transcends disciplinary boundaries and captures the very essence of what Smart Starts embodies.

*Table 9. AI tools for cross-cultural and creative projects*

| Tool | Function | Example Classroom Use | Teacher's Role | Student's Role |
|---|---|---|---|---|
| **Wordela** | Personalized vocabulary trainer | Review words from "Nature" unit | Assign review sets | Practice independently |
| **BookCreator** | Interactive story and comic maker | Create "My Dream School" e-book | Guide story sequence | Write and illustrate |
| **CranioCatch** | Visual analysis tool | Science–English "Teeth and Smile" unit | Introduce visual vocab | Label visuals |
| **AlphaFold** | Biology structure predictor | English for Science "Parts of the Body" | Integrate STEM, CLIL lessons | Describe scientific visuals |
| **Suno AI** | Creates background music or narration | Compose song for "My Family" | Choose tempo | Sing and perform |
| **Veed.io** | Edits and subtitles video projects | "My Hometown" presentation | Support technical side | Record and narrate |

## 4.2. And Many More: There's an AI for That

In the rapidly evolving and crowded realm of educational technology, teachers often find it difficult to navigate the potential of all the AI tools available. There's an AI for That (https://theresanaiforthat.com) offers a needed solution, in the form of a comprehensive, updated, list of AI tools, across many sectors and industries, including education, creativity, assessment, and productivity. For language teachers this site is essentially a discovery tool for teachers to find AI tools to support their lesson planning, storytelling, pronunciation, gamification, or translation needs. The site is organized by categories and searchable by keywords which takes the guessing out of finding those excellent tools that align with their classroom goals or learners' profiles. If thoughtful and judicious, websites like this can help teachers maintain relevancy, and utilize new tools mindfully, while developing a collection of tools that are consistent with their educational beliefs, and that of their learners. Nevertheless, teachers will still need to practice caution in using them, such as verifying credibility, privacy or student compliance, and developmental appropriateness for young learners (Laupichler et al., 2022; Memarian & Doleck, 2023).

Taken together, the tools and use-cases above illustrate the breadth of AI support for early language teaching; however, effective use depends less on how many tools are available and more on the conditions under which they are selected, mediated, and governed. For that reason, the next section synthesizes the highest-stakes risks and practical safeguards—particularly around teacher agency, cultural bias, and child data protection—so that innovation remains educationally and ethically responsible.

## 5. RISKS, ETHICS, AND BEST PRACTICES

### 5.1. Contextual constraints in Public-schools

While AI tools can enrich early language teaching, their classroom use is often shaped by structural constraints that differ sharply across school contexts. In many public-school settings, limited infrastructure (e.g., a single computer or projector), unequal access to devices, unreliable internet, and overcrowded classes can make "one-device-per-child" assumptions unrealistic. These constraints influence not only whether AI can be used, but how: in low-resource contexts, AI may function primarily as a teacher-facing planning and materials tool (e.g., generating differentiated worksheets, visuals, and story scripts for printing) rather than a student-facing, always-online tutor. Practical mitigation includes "one-device" or "station rotation" models, offline-first routines (pre-downloaded audio, screenshots, printed prompts), and whole-class, teacher-mediated demonstrations that minimize student data entry and keep pedagogy play-based and interactive (Selwyn, 2019; Prilop et al., 2024).

### 5.2. Risks of Over-Reliance

Though AI tools can provide extraordinary assistance with lesson planning and management, teachers' overreliance on automated systems may present danger of deskilling, thereby slowly undermining teachers' creative and pedagogical agency. Research on AI supported design prescribes that educators, when relying too heavily on machine generated plans or materials, could miss potentiality for developing novel strategies and reflective judgment (Selwyn, 2019). In contexts like Türkiye, where communicative language teaching and intercultural competence have been highlighted as policy objectives, classroom realities frequently still consist mostly of grammar-centric instruction (Akpınar, 2020). These classroom realities are echoed in a recent netnographic analysis of 154 teacher comments: the most frequent failure causes were educational (e.g., grammar-focused lessons, little real practice, overcrowding), alongside personal, linguistic, and social factors (Acar et al., 2024)

Generative AI tools, like ChatGPT, Eduaide.ai, and Canva Magic Write, have the potential to help bridge that gap in lesson design as they begin with teachers to design visually rich, communicative tasks, but they also risk homogenizing instruction if not critically adopted into teaching practices. Furthermore, Prilop et al. (2024) emphasize that the goal of AI implementations should be for "augmentation rather than automation" where teachers continue to be the "curriculum designers," providing guidance on the AI outputs to "inform instruction by being cognizant of context, nuance, and pedagogical sensitivity." Moreover, pre-generated lesson materials may limit experimentation and professional development, while also risking reflective artistry that embodies effective early language instruction.

## 5.3. Bias, Stereotypes, and Cultural Representation in AI Outputs

Additionally, another important matter to consider in AI-enriched learning spaces is the potential for bias, stereotypes, and cultural underrepresentation to persist in, or be exploited by, AI-generated materials. As large language models and generative systems draw upon massive datasets collected from various sources, these datasets may open the possibility for the generated content to reflect cultural hierarchies, gender stereotypes, or a Western point-of-view (Grassini, 2023). For example, image or text prompts developed in the production of classroom material could reproduce limited representations of families, ethnicity, or lifestyles that conflict with the local culture or inclusive purposes. For early learners, this could be particularly damaging as early education is a significant opportunity to construct equity foundations surrounding diversity and belonging.

Therefore, as an act of ethical pedagogy, educators must serve as critical mediators of AI outputs and engage with that AI data, modify, and/or recontextualize that output before using it in their classroom. To serve in this capacity, educators are required to engage in a practice referred to as critical AI literacy, which Laupichler et al. (2022) defined as the ability to understand and critique how AI systems produce information. Educators who engage in critical AI literacy can interrogate biased patterns in generated outputs and ensure equitable representation. They can also modify the output to include pluriversality and intercultural perspectives. When thoughtfully curated, AI can even support educators to interrogation of stereotypes by generating alternative inclusive narratives and images, shifting the data of technology from one of culture reproduction to cultural reflections for consideration.

## 5.4. Safeguarding Child Data and Digital Safety

Since very young children are vulnerable given their age, data privacy and digital safety are critical ethical challenges when considering the use of AI in education. Many applications in AI rely on the collection of important data (e.g. voice recordings, keystrokes, or analytics of use), and without oversight, data may put children at risk of security issues and potentially violate informed consent. UNESCO (2023) identifies children's digital rights as fundamental to educational institutions' ethical

AI policies which also emphasize the importance of transparency, anonymity and the risk of data fatigue.

The educational environment requires educators and schools and policy makers to follow local legal requirements including General Data Protection Regulation (GDPR) and Children's Online Privacy Protection Act (COPPA) and child protection laws while keeping track of AI tools they use and their timing. Teachers should use institution-approved passwords and follow data-minimization practices, collecting only what is necessary for learning. Educators can teach digital citizenship by explaining to students how AI stories process and reuse information. Digital citizens need to realize that AI-generated responses are not automatically logical, neutral with integrity within discourse, or do not reveal any information. These constructs could be part of ethical literacy at the level of early childhood education.

Finally, with young learners, AI use frequently extends beyond the classroom through homework, family devices, and children's independent media habits. This makes parental communication and consent central to responsible implementation, especially regarding screen time, data privacy, and the quality of language exposure at home. Schools can reduce anxiety and build trust by offering brief parent orientations (or one-page guides) clarifying what tools are used, what data is (and is not) collected, and what "safe use" looks like in practice - e.g., encouraging co-use with an adult, limiting logins/accounts, prioritizing offline or teacher-curated materials, and recommending short, purposeful use aligned with classroom goals rather than open-ended chatting. Such home-school alignment supports children's digital rights and helps ensure that AI supplements - rather than displaces - human interaction and developmentally appropriate language play (Chauncey & McKenna, 2023; UNESCO, 2023).

## 5.5. Encouraging Teacher Adaptation and Creativity

The most effective form of sustainable AI use is predicated on teacher creativity and flexible pedagogy, as opposed to reliance on technology. Generative systems function as tools to help educators plan and supply various educational materials although teachers serve as the essential decision-makers who transform AI results into suitable developmental learning content that also keeps students emotionally connected. The research conducted by Memarian and Doleck (2023) shows that K-12 education will continue to use AI because teachers need to adjust their teaching methods through personal reflection and individual adaptation to this technology. The research conducted by Khan et al. (2024) demonstrated that teachers who used AI tools gained additional time to develop advanced teaching methods which included personalized learning approaches and intercultural communication strategies and socio-emotional learning techniques.

The educational method of teacher experimentation leads AI to function as an active creative partner instead of its typical role as a passive educational tool. The process of teaching AI literacy to educators enables them to develop educational materials which combine human empathy with technological accuracy through workshop-based professional development programs. AI integration in early language education needs to protect the fundamental human aspects of teaching because algorithms lack the ability to duplicate creative responses and warm emotional connections and individualized feedback.

# 6. FUTURE DIRECTION

## 6.1. Adaptive Learning Platforms for Young Learners

Emerging adaptive platforms such as KidSense, Lingokids, and Sora, are at the forefront of innovating how we can personalize language learning. The adaptive systems use speech recognition technology and data analytics to change their operation speed and task complexity and deliver personalized feedback based on each student's learning process. Personalized learning methods help students stay within their zone of proximal development by providing suitable challenges and necessary support according to Ellis (1996). AI systems that adapt through learning will achieve success when they handle localization and produce content that respects various cultural and linguistic backgrounds instead of using a single learning model for all users. The assessment of early education requires future studies to evaluate context-sensitive AI systems which support both multilingual capabilities and equitable learning experiences.

AI enabled oral feedback systems such as ELSA Speak, Speechling, and Praktika, are increasingly in a position to analyze in real time for pronunciation accuracy, intonation and fluency. The systems provide instant individual feedback and endless practice sessions which enable students to repeat activities for building their endurance. The evaluation process in future instances will integrate phonetics with affective computing to identify both vocal tone and communicative goals which will generate a more complete assessment. Research should continue to examine how these systems influence confidence, motivation and speech development when combined with modeling from teachers and interaction with peers.

The intersection of artificial intelligence with augmented and virtual reality provides new opportunities for experiential language learning. A full immersion storytelling app can take students into an interactive cultural space, festival, marketplace, or narrative world, where students have the opportunity to practice the language in a meaningful context. These environmental experiences are designed to develop intercultural empathy and contextual understanding by engaging their senses. Future directions for research on AR/VR will address student access to immersive language experiences, the diversity of content across the context's culture, and the lasting effects of immersive language experiences on cognitive and social development.

## 6.2. Research Priorities in AI for Early Language Learning

Notwithstanding the increasing enthusiasm, empirical evidence about the durability of AI in early education is still limited. Existing evidence suggests that short-term vocabulary gains, motivation, and engagement could be enhanced through the use of AI (Bayrak, 2025; Song & Glazewski, 2023; Wei, 2023). Longitudinal studies are important, so future studies can identify and assess reading, creativity, and socio-emotional development-critical to a holistic early childhood education, but often missing or hard to assess in current AI use (Casal-Otero et al., 2023; Chauncey & McKenna, 2023).

Furthermore, as early language classrooms are becoming increasingly diverse, the role of AI in promoting intercultural competence and inclusive pedagogy should be explored systematically. Recent work in Türkiye underscores why these matters: migrant and multilingual learners face language and adaptation challenges that demand culturally responsive classrooms and well-prepared teachers (Kırcalı & Cesur, 2024). Their CLD Self-Efficacy Beliefs Scale provides evidence that teachers' beliefs toward cultural and linguistic diversity are consequential for equitable practice. AI storytelling, virtual exchange platforms, and other multilingual tutoring systems, such as SingaKids, show intercultural promise but present questions about bias, cultural representation, and context (Azzopardi, 2025; Liu et al., 2025; MIT Media Lab, 2023). Finally, there is a need to create teacher education within AI literacy and the ethics of using AI. Teachers must know not only how to efficiently use AI but also to be able to assess the pedagogical implications, cultural implications, and data used (Laupichler et al., 2022; Memarian & Doleck, 2023).

Future teacher preparation models would benefit from an emphasis on the idea of co-design practices where educators collaboratively impose change on AI-based learning environments but with reflective change instead of passive implementation (Prilop et al., 2024; Trust et al., 2023). Lastly, policy and governance frameworks must accompany technological changes to ensure transparency, security of data, and fairness for potential child-centered AI systems. The research studies emphasize an immediate requirement for creating ethical guidelines and accountability systems which safeguard young students' privacy while supporting their educational growth (Casal-Otero et al., 2023; Cui & Alias, 2024; Grassini, 2023).

Prioritizing these changes requires collaboration across disciplines of educators, linguists, engineers, and developmental psychologists to develop shared frameworks that prioritize the new possibilities AI brings to early language learning while continuing to demonstrate humane and ethical accounts of responsibility. AI functions as an educational resource which also serves as an ethical tool to support early language learning through creating educational spaces that focus on inclusion and human-centered adaptive learning.

## 7. ANTICIPATED CONTRIBUTIONS AND SIGNIFICANCE

The current chapter adds to the emerging field of AI-assisted early language instruction by providing examples of how technology can foster creativity, differentiation, and engagement in pedagogically meaningful ways. AI serves teachers as flexible, adaptable resources for lesson design, gamification, and formative assessment, while providing learners with individualized, interactive practice. As Grassini (2023) notes, AI offers scalable pedagogy that can be customized to different scenarios, lightening workload and facilitating inclusive learning. Toscu (2025) similarly points to AI-supported technologies as possibilities for personalized tutors that can scaffold instruction in relation to students' needs and preferences. At the same time, the chapter also addresses ethical considerations and challenges to the profession shaped by this innovation. The heavy dependence on AI-generated lesson plans results in reduced teacher creativity while AI content errors and cultural prejudices present challenges to educational trustworthiness and fairness (Chen et al., 2025). Nevertheless, as Cui and Alias (2024) note, both technology and teachers' critical awareness will evolve together. Teachers who perform reflective practice to develop critical AI literacy will learn to create AI outputs which follow humanistic and developmental standards.

In conclusion, the chapter highlights AI's double-edged promise in early language education: to support teachers as innovative designers and reimagine learning experiences by providing personalized, culturally relevant, and multimodal learning experiences. The framework establishes a safe environment for students to explore new teaching methods through its combination of ethical principles with innovative approaches and its fusion of automated systems and artistic methods and presents AI as a humanizing educational partner which from the beginning of language acquisition promotes creative learning and cultural exchange and inclusive education.

## 8. CONCLUSION

Artificial Intelligence is beginning to reshape what is possible in early language education by closing the gap between traditional teaching methods and the rapidly changing digital world. Through lesson design, task creation, gamification, and feedback, AI tools offer teachers increasingly flexible ways to promote creativity, engagement, and differentiation. These tools, when used purposefully, can produce lesson outlines, scaffolded materials, and multimodal experiences in accordance with how young learners acquire language in a playful, interactive, and meaning-making context. Research indicates that adaptive and generative systems mediated by a teacher can decrease teacher workload while also increasing opportunities for imaginative and culturally responsive instruction (Grassini, 2023; Prilop et al., 2024). Surprisingly, AI supports the teacher as a collaborator, not as a replacement but as an opportunity to magnify the imagination of the pedagogical professional in planning exciting learning experiences for developmentally appropriate interactive and engaging learning environments.

The primary issue for educators is not whether to use AI, but how to use it effectively. AI functions at its best when teachers keep their ability to assess generated content and make changes to outputs which then become human-centered results. The educational content produced by AI systems needs human teachers to analyze and process and present it to students. Selwyn (2019) explains that automation adoption threatens to eliminate vital teaching elements which include reflection and relational engagement and creative educational practices. The educational partnership between AI and teachers allows AI to generate ideas and different learning paths while teachers preserve the complete emotional, ethical and intercultural learning experience. The approach enables technology to enhance teaching methods rather than replace them so teachers can dedicate their time to building curiosity and teamwork skills and communication abilities which define early childhood learning behaviors.

In the future, the real challenge of AI's educational potential will be its cultural and ethical responsiveness. AI-generated educational content should show the diverse backgrounds of children while eliminating any unfair or misleading information. The design of intercultural digital spaces needs educators and developers to work with community members to develop digital environments that support diversity and respect and empathy. The teacher education program needs to include AI literacy education which teaches both technical and critical skills for teachers to help students learn AI usage and develop AI-related questioning abilities. AI systems that receive inclusive design principles will function as tools to study cultural diversity, but they will not perpetuate existing cultural differences.

The integration of AI technology in early childhood language education requires teachers to shift back to their roles as experience designers and meaning facilitators instead of information transmitters. However, with a critical awareness and intercultural awareness attuned into the teacher's own lived experiences, AI can broaden and expand the possibilities of human creativity, empathy, and curiosity. The teacher can create lessons that are efficient, interactive, personal, and globally connected. AI operates as an educational resource in this context which helps students and teachers collaborate to build joyful and inclusive learning experiences for language and cultural understanding.

## REFERENCES

Acar, S. C., Cesur, K., Mikhailova, T., & Akshulakova, B. (2024). A netnographic study on the reasons why people fail to learn English. *Participatory Educational Research, 11*(6), 134–151. DOI: 10.17275/per.24.83.11.6

Agherai, O., Aoula, E. S., & Ahriz, S. (2025). AI applications in education: A review. *International Journal of Education and Information Technologies, 19*, 33–38. DOI: 10.46300/9109.2025.19.4

Akcan, S. (2020). Teaching English to young learners in Turkey. In Haznedar, B., & Uysal, H. H. (Eds.), *Teaching English to young learners: New insights and practices* (pp. 65–85). Ankara University Press.

Akpınar, K. D. (2020). Intercultural communication and foreign language teaching in Turkey. In Haznedar, B., & Uysal, H. H. (Eds.), *Teaching English to young learners: New insights and practices* (pp. 275–292). Ankara University Press.

Azzopardi, S. (2025). Whimsical wonders or digital dangers: Exploring the influence of artificial intelligence during story reading in an early years classroom. *Minds and Machines Unite, 6*(1), 44–60. DOI: 10.62695/WSRI5131

Bayrak, T. (2025). Artificial intelligence in digital games: Technological development and applications. *İletişim Çalışmaları Dergisi, 11*(1), 89-97. DOI: 10.17932/IAU.ICD.2015.006/icd_v011i1005

Casal-Otero, L., Catala, A., Fernández-Morante, C., & Suárez-Vázquez, A. (2023). AI literacy in K–12: A systematic literature review. *International Journal of STEM Education, 10*(29), 29. Advance online publication. DOI: 10.1186/s40594-023-00418-7

Chauncey, S. A., & McKenna, H. P. (2023). A framework and exemplars for ethical and responsible use of AI chatbot technology to support teaching and learning. *Computers and Education: Artificial Intelligence, 5*, 100182. Advance online publication. DOI: 10.1016/j.caeai.2023.100182

Chen, D., Aaltonen, K., Lampela, H., & Kujala, J. (2025). The design and implementation of an educational chatbot with personalized adaptive learning features for project management training. *Technology. Knowledge and Learning, 30*(6), 1047–1072. DOI: 10.1007/s10758-024-09807-5

Chen, G. Z. (2024). The impacts of AI-driven storytelling applications on language acquisition and literacy development in early childhood education: A systematic review. *Asian Journal of Advanced Research and Reports, 18*(11), 1–12. DOI: 10.9734/ajarr/2024/v18i11770

Choi, N., Cyebukayire, P., & Choi, J. D. (2025, April 22). *Tinker tales: Interactive storytelling framework for early childhood narrative development and AI literacy* (Version 2). arXiv.

Cui, P., & Alias, B. S. (2024). Opportunities and challenges in higher education arising from AI: A systematic literature review (2020–2024). *Journal of Infrastructure. Policy and Development, 8*(11), 8390. DOI: 10.24294/jipd.v8i11.8390

Ellis, R. (1996). *The study of second language acquisition.* Oxford University Press.

Fryer, L. K., & Carpenter, R. (2006). Bots as language learning tools. *Language Learning & Technology, 10*(3), 8–14. DOI: 10.64152/10125/44068

Fryer, L. K., Coniam, D., Carpenter, R., & Lăpu neanu, D. (2020). Bots for language learning now: Current and future directions. *Language Learning & Technology, 24*(2), 8–22. DOI: 10.64152/10125/44719

Grassini, S. (2023). Shaping the future of education: Exploring the potential and consequences of AI and ChatGPT in educational settings. *Education Sciences, 13*(7), 692. DOI: 10.3390/educsci13070692

Haznedar, B., & Uysal, H. H. (Eds.). (2020). *Teaching English to young learners: New insights and practices.* Ankara University Press.

Kanero, J., Tunalı, E. T., Oranç, C., Göksun, T., & Küntay, A. C. (2021). When even a robot tutor zooms: A study of embodiment, attitudes, and impressions. *Frontiers in Robotics and AI, 8*, 679893. DOI: 10.3389/frobt.2021.679893 PMID: 34368237

Khan, M. A., Kurbonova, O., Abdullaev, D., Radie, A. H., & Basim, N. (2024). Is AI-assisted assessment liable to evaluate young learners? Parents support, teacher support, immunity, and resilience are in focus in testing vocabulary learning. *Language Testing in Asia, 14*(1), 48. Advance online publication. DOI: 10.1186/s40468-024-00324-x

Kırcalı, M., & Cesur, K. (2024). Development and validation of a cultural and linguistic diversity scale to measure pre-service EFL teachers' self-efficacy beliefs. *SAGE Open, 14*(1), 1–19. DOI: 10.1177/21582440241236589

Kwon, S. K., Shin, D., & Lee, Y. (2023). The application of chatbot as an L2 writing practice tool. *Language Learning & Technology, 27*(1), 1–19. DOI: 10.64152/10125/73541

Laupichler, M. C., Aster, A., Schirch, J., & Raupach, T. (2022). Artificial intelligence literacy in higher and adult education: A scoping literature review. *Computers & Education: Artificial Intelligence, 3*, 100101. DOI: 10.1016/j.caeai.2022.100101

Liu, Z., Lin, G., Tan, H. L., Zhang, H., Lu, Y., Gao, X., Yin, S. X., Sun, H., Goh, H. H., Wong, L. H., & Chen, N. F. (2025). *SingaKids: A multilingual multimodal dialogic tutor for language learning*. arXiv. https://arxiv.org/abs/2506.02412 DOI: 10.18653/v1/2025.acl-industry.86

Lo, C. K., Yu, P. L. H., Xu, S., Ng, D. T. K., & Jong, M. S.-Y. (2024). Exploring the application of ChatGPT in ESL/EFL education and related research issues: A systematic review of empirical studies. *Smart Learning Environments, 11*(50), 50. Advance online publication. DOI: 10.1186/s40561-024-00342-5

Memarian, B., & Doleck, T. (2023). Fairness, accountability, transparency, and ethics (FATE) in artificial intelligence (AI) and higher education: A systematic review. *Computers and Education: Artificial Intelligence, 5*, 100152. Advance online publication. DOI: 10.1016/j.caeai.2023.100152

Mikhailova, T., & Cesur, K. (2025). Enhancing global awareness and intercultural competence in English language teacher education. In Bafralı, G. (Ed.), *Challenges in teacher education: pedagogy, management, and materials* (pp. 235–266). IGI Global Scientific Publishing., DOI: 10.4018/979-8-3693-7342-2.ch008

MIT Media Lab. (2023). *AI storybook project: Teaching children to understand AI through storytelling*. https://www.media.mit.edu/projects/ai-storybook/overview

Powell, W., & Courchesne, S. (2024). Opportunities and risks involved in using ChatGPT to create first grade science lesson plans. *PLoS One, 19*(6), e0305337. DOI: 10.1371/journal.pone.0305337 PMID: 38885244

Prilop, C. N., Mah, D.-K., Jacobsen, L. J., & Hansen, R. R. (2024, December). *Generative AI in teacher education: Using AI-enhanced methods to explore teacher educators' perceptions. OSF Preprints*. DOI: 10.31219/osf.io/szcwb

Sampanis, N. I. (2025). *Innovative tangible interactive games for enhancing AI knowledge and literacy in elementary education: A pedagogical framework*. arXiv. https://arxiv.org/abs/2506.00651

Selwyn, N. (2019). *Should robots replace teachers? AI and the future of education*. Polity Press.

Song, D., & Glazewski, K. (2023). Scaffolding self-regulated learning in student-generated questioning using mobile phones. *Education and Information Technologies*, *28*(8), 10781–10802. DOI: 10.1007/s10639-023-11627-6

Su, J., & Yang, W. (2022). Artificial intelligence in early childhood education: A scoping review. *Computers and Education: Artificial Intelligence*, *3*, 100049. Advance online publication. DOI: 10.1016/j.caeai.2022.100049

Sun, H., Tan, J., & Lim, M. C. (2025). AI and early language learning: A scoping review. *AI and Education*, *2*(1), 1–23. DOI: 10.1007/s44436-025-00005-3

Toscu, S. (2025). A systematic review on AI technologies in English as a foreign language education. *Sakarya University Journal of Education*, *15*(2), 156–172. DOI: 10.19126/suje.1623401

Trust, T., Whalen, J., & Mouza, C. (2023). Editorial: ChatGPT, challenges, opportunities, and implications for teacher education. *Contemporary Issues in Technology & Teacher Education*, *23*(1). https://citejournal.org/volume-23/issue-1-23/editorial/editorial-chatgpt-challenges-opportunities-and-implications-for-teacher-education

UNESCO. (2023). *Guidance for generative AI in education and research*. UNESCO. https://unesdoc.unesco.org/ark:/48223/pf0000386693

Uygun, E., & Cesur, K. (2025). Teaching English for general purposes through a MOOC in higher education: A quasi-experimental study to explore its effects on learner achievement and satisfaction. *Education and Information Technologies*, *30*(3), 3389–3409. DOI: 10.1007/s10639-024-12948-w

Verma, R., Weber, I., & Cannanure, V. K. (2025). Exploring AI in education: Child-computer interaction in the Global South. *ACM Journal on Computing and Sustainable Societies*, *3*(3), 20. Advance online publication. DOI: 10.1145/3736645

Wei, L. (2023). Artificial intelligence in language instruction: Impact on English learning achievement, L2 motivation, and self-regulated learning. *Frontiers in Psychology*, *14*, 1261955. Advance online publication. DOI: 10.3389/fpsyg.2023.1261955 PMID: 38023040

Ye, L., Jiang, J., Liu, Y., Ran, Y., & Chang, D. (2025, April). Colin: A multimodal human-AI co-creation storytelling system to support children's multi-level narrative skills. In *Extended Abstracts of the CHI Conference on Human Factors in Computing Systems* (pp. 1–11). Association for Computing Machinery. DOI: 10.1145/3706599.3719837

## ADDITIONAL READING


Aliakbari, M., & Maadikhah, M. M. (2024, September). *Enhancing intercultural competence in AI-enabled classrooms: Investigating effectiveness of AI-assisted instruction in EFL cultural syllabi* [Conference presentation]. Digital Transformation in Education International Conference (DITEC24), Ege University, İzmir, Türkiye. DOI: 10.13140/RG.2.2.27259.94242

Conesa, I. M. G. (2024). Gamification in an EFL classroom and the use of games for learning English: Spanish technical engineering degree. In *Enhancing education with intelligent systems and data-driven instruction* (pp. 163–191). IGI Global., DOI: 10.4018/979-8-3693-2169-0.ch008

Cviko, A., McKenney, S., & Voogt, J. (2014). Teachers as co-designers of technology-rich learning activities for early literacy. *Technology, Pedagogy and Education, 23*(3). Advance online publication. DOI: 10.1080/1475939X.2014.953197

Marengo, A., Pagano, A., Lund, B., & Santamato, V. (2025). Research AI: Integrating AI and gamification in higher education for e-learning optimization and soft skills assessment through a cross-study synthesis. *Frontiers of Computer Science, 7*, 1587040. Advance online publication. DOI: 10.3389/fcomp.2025.1587040

Singha, S., Singha, R., & Jasmine, E. (2024). Enhancing language teaching materials through artificial intelligence: Opportunities and challenges. In Pan, F. (Ed.), *AI in language teaching, learning, and assessment* (pp. 22–42). IGI Global., DOI: 10.4018/979-8-3693-0872-1.ch002

Suh, S. (2025, May). *Investigating the impact of personalized AI tutors on language learning performance*. arXiv. https://doi.org//arXiv.2505.02443DOI: 10.48550

Wambsganss, T., Benke, I., Maedche, A., Koedinger, K., & Käser, T. (2024). Evaluating the impact of learner control and interactivity in conversational tutoring systems for persuasive writing. *International Journal of Artificial Intelligence in Education*, •••, 1–32. DOI: 10.1007/s40593-024-00409-x

Wei-Xun, L., & Jia-Ying, Z. (2024). Impact of AI-driven language learning apps on vocabulary acquisition among English learners. *Research Studies in English Language Teaching and Learning, 2*(1), 1–11. DOI: 10.62583/rseltl.v2i1.32

Wu, R., & Yu, Z. (2024). Do AI chatbots improve students learning outcomes? Evidence from a meta-analysis. *British Journal of Educational Technology, 55*(1), 10–33. DOI: 10.1111/bjet.13334

## KEY TERMS AND DEFINITIONS

**Artificial Intelligence (AI):** A discipline within computer science that aims to create machines which can perform tasks that usually require human memory, perception, and reasoning to solve problems and learn. AI in education is instrumental for personalized learning, lesson planning, translation, and assessment using intelligent tutoring systems, chatbots, and generative content tools (Prilop et al., 2024).

**Critical AI Literacy:** An advanced version of AI literacy that focuses on the ability to critique, analyze, and question biases, ethics, and cultural portrayals with AI systems. It empowers learners and educators to engage with AI tools respectfully and reflectively, promoting equity, transparency, and informed participation while learning with AI (Laupichler et al., 2022).

**Differentiated Instruction (AI-Supported):** A teaching approach that adapts the learning experience according to student needs. AI tools support some of the aspects of differentiation by simplifying texts for different language proficiency levels or presenting a variety of versions of tasks, while providing adaptive and personalized feedback to match learning preferences (Choi et al, 2025).

**Early Language Learning (ELL):** The development of a foreign or second language as children, typically from ages 5 to about grade 6 or 12 years old. ELL focuses on meaning-focused, play-based, and experiential forms of learning that adapt listening (comprehension) and speaking (production) while integrating reading and writing using storytelling, songs, and multimodal experience to create low-anxiety, supportive learning environments (Haznedar & Uysal, 2020).

**Gamification:** The integration of gaming-based technologies—reward systems, badges, challenges, feedback loops, etc.—in non-game educational contexts to improve engagement and motivation levels. AI-enabled gamified platforms (e.g., Kahoot!, Redmenta) modify challenges based on the learner's performance, as a means of maintaining interest and providing opportunities for autonomous, enjoyable language practice (Bayrak, 2025).

**Generative AI:** A type of artificial intelligence that is capable of generating new content, such as text, images, or sounds, based on recognizing patterns improved from very large datasets. In English language teaching contexts, generative AI tools (e.g., ChatGPT, Canva Magic Write) enhance educators' ability to design ideas for lessons, materials, and creative output with efficiency, and while maintaining pedagogical authenticity (Lo et al., 2024).

**Intercultural Communication Competence (ICC):** The ability to communicate effectively and appropriately in various cultural contexts. In early language classrooms, AI resources can cultivate intercultural awareness by providing culturally diverse settings and creating opportunities for empathy through storytelling (Ye et al., 2025).

**Multimodal Learning:** A style of learning that includes different sensory and cognitive modes—visual, auditory, textual, and kinesthetic—to enhance solidifying understanding and memory. AI systems such as Murf AI, Canva, and DALL·E facilitate multimodal instruction by producing visuals, sounds, and animations that enrich the language experience of young learners (Kanero et al., 2021).

**Teacher–AI Co-Design:** Teachers and AI work together to create educational materials and assessments, continually evaluating and refining them. AI platforms function as collaborative partners that deliver automated solutions to help educators dedicate more time to self-reflection and development of culturally sensitive teaching methods (Selwyn, 2019; Sun et al., 2025).

# About the Contributors

**Turan Paker** works as a Prof. Dr. in the ELT Department, Faculty of Education, Pamukkale University. He had his BA degree from Selçuk University, his MA degree from Bilkent İhsan Doğramacı University, and his Ph.D. degree from Çukurova University in the field of English Language Teaching (ELT). Prof. Paker has been in the field of ELT as a teacher in MoNE schools, an instructor in Preparatory Schools, a teacher educator, a researcher in ELT Departments, a Head of ELT Department, a Director of School of Foreign Languages, a member of the Institute of Educational Sciences, and a Member of University Senate of Pamukkale University. He teaches Approaches and Methods, ELT Methodology, Teaching Language Skills, Assessment and Evaluation in ELT, Intercultural Communication, World Englishes and Culture, Material Adaptation and Evaluation, and Curriculum Development in undergraduate, MA and Ph.D. programs. He has published book chapters and articles and presented papers in International and National Symposiums as well as local, national and international seminars and webinars on TEFL, pre-and in-service teacher education, teaching practicum, and assessment and evaluation in ELT.

**Gonca Ekşi** is a Professor in English Language Teaching (ELT) in the Department of Foreign Language Education, Gazi University where she teaches several undergraduate and graduate courses and supervises MA and PhD dissertations. She received her MA in ELT in Hacettepe University, Department of ELT and she holds her PhD in ELT in Gazi University. She has worked in a number of projects including the national project for the development of the national English curriculum for Primary and Secondary schools. She managed an Erasmus KA2 Project with distinguished universities in Turkey and abroad. She has published various research articles nationally and internationally focusing on with teaching and learning English as a foreign language. Her research interests include computer-assisted language learning, pre- and in-service teacher education, curriculum and materials development, teaching skills and language components, young learners, use of corpus in language teaching. She is the editor of ELT Research Journal.

**Çağla Atmaca** is an Assoc. Prof. Dr. at Pamukkale University (PAU), Faculty of Education, English Language Teaching (ELT) Department. She graduated from Pamukkale University in 2011 with the highest degree at the Faculty of Education. She worked as a research assistant and got her MA and PhD degrees at Gazi University ELT Department between 2012-2016. She has delivered various BA, MA, PhD courses at PAU ELT Department since 2017. She got national scholarships for MA and PhD degrees and was involved various national and international projects. Her teaching interests are teaching language skills, discourse analysis and ELT, methodology, approaches and methods in ELT, grammar, listening and pronunciation, school experience and teaching practicum courses. Her fields of interest are teacher education, educational technology, discourse analysis, media literacy, second language acquisition, and intercultural communication.

***

**Karlygash Ashirkhanova** is an Asst. Prof. Dr. at Kh. Dosmukhamedov Atyrau University in Kazakhstan, where she also serves as Head of the Department for International Partnerships and Internationalization. Her research focuses on Modern Turkic Languages and Literatures, with particular emphasis on Kazakh folk medicine, animistic belief-based healing practices, and the theoretical foundations of sentence structure in modern linguistics.

**Burak Asma** holds a PhD in Turkish language teaching by Akdeniz University and is a researcher who has approximately 10 years of teaching and academic experience. He is currently working in the Department of Turkish Language Teaching at Akdeniz University, Antalya, Turkey. His primary areas of interest and research include testing and evaluation in language teaching, scale/test development, teacher training, and language teaching.

**Dila Bozkurt** is a PhD candidate in English Language Teaching at Çanakkale Onsekiz Mart University, Türkiye. Her research focuses on critical pedagogy, multicultural education in ELT, and the professional experiences of English language teachers, including issues such as occupational stress, resilience, and burnout. She has published on critical pedagogy in English language teaching and on the stressors faced by novice EFL teachers in the Turkish context in journals such as Innovational Research in ELT and the Turkish Journal of Education.

**Hanh Cao Minh Hong** has focused on teaching and studying Fine Arts practice and education. She has been a lecturer in the Faculty of Arts since 2015, working to incorporate modern methods and technologies into Fine Arts education while maintaining a connection to local socio-cultural traditions. From 2020 to 2024, she has been involved in projects exploring contemporary approaches to Fine Arts education, aiming to balance traditional values with modern developments in the field. Looking ahead, Hanh plans to expand her research on innovative teaching methodologies, particularly focusing on the integration of digital tools and interactive platforms to enhance creativity and engagement in Fine Arts education, while continuing to uphold the importance of cultural heritage in artistic practice.

**Kürşat Cesur** got his BA degree from the ELT Department of Hacettepe University in 2004 and his MA degree from the ELT department of Çanakkale Onsekiz Mart University in 2008. In 2012, he got his PhD degree in the field of ELT at Gazi University. He became Associate Professor Doctor in 2020 in the ELT department of COMU, where he started working as an instructor of English in 2004. Now, he has been working and giving the course named "Teaching English to Young Learners" both at BA and MA levels and "Instructional Technologies" both at MA and PhD levels at the ELT Department of Faculty of Education, COMU since 2013.

**Bora Demir** holds a PhD in English Language Teacher Education and was promoted to Associate Professor in 2023. He is currently a faculty member at the School of Foreign Languages, Çanakkale Onsekiz Mart University. He has published extensively in national and international journals and edited volumes on various aspects of language teaching and language teacher education. Since 2019, he has been the founder and Editor-in-Chief of the academic journal Innovational Research in ELT. His main research interests include technology-assisted language teaching, cognitive dimensions of language learning, and the psychological aspects of language learning and teaching, with a particular focus on teacher education contexts.

**Binnur Ilter** holds a PhD in English by the University of Ankara and is a professor who has approximately 25 years of teaching and academic experience. She is currently working in the Department of Foreign Language Education at Akdeniz University, Antalya, Turkey. Her areas of interest and research include teaching foreign languages to children, methods and techniques in foreign language teaching, bilingual children, developing language skills in foreign language teaching, developing materials and programs in foreign language teaching.

**Mehmet Gökce** is a researcher working in the fields of open and distance learning (ODL), online learning, and artificial intelligence–supported instructional materials. His academic interests focus on AI-generated and AI-assisted video-based learning, learner performance, pedagogical interaction, and the evolving roles of instructors and learners in digital learning environments. His work adopts an interdisciplinary perspective, examining the pedagogical implications of artificial intelligence within ODL contexts, with particular attention to instructional effectiveness, learning outcomes, and digital transformation in higher education.

**Kadir Lüta** is a PhD student at Çanakkale Onsekiz Mart University, in the ELT department, focusing on adult EFL education. He is currently working as a research assistant at English language and literature department at a state university in Turkey.

**Tatyana Mikhailova** is an Assistant Professor at Sh. Ualikhanov Kokshetau University, Kazakhstan. She holds a BA in Translation Studies (English, 2003), an MA in English Philology (2005), and a PhD in Foreign Language: Two Foreign Languages from Ablai Khan University of International Relations and World Languages. Her research interests include ELT, intercultural communication, critical thinking, MOOC design, and the use of creative and digital technologies in language education.

**Indranil Mutsuddi** holds a Ph.D. in Management from Amity University, Uttar Pradesh, India, and currently serves as Associate Professor and Head of the Department at JIS University, Kolkata. With over 22 years of academic experience, he has established himself as a distinguished educator and researcher specializing in Human Resources (HR) and Organizational Behavior. Dr. Mutsuddi is the author of three textbooks on Human Resource Management and has published more than 65 research papers in reputed national and international journals, including 21 indexed in Scopus. He has also contributed 28 book chapters to various edited volumes and presented 57 papers at national and international conferences and seminars. A frequent chair of technical sessions at prestigious management forums, Dr. Mutsuddi is a Double Gold Medalist from AIMA-CME and a recipient of the Prof. Narendra Mohan Basu Award from Presidency College, Kolkata, for academic excellence. He is a life member of several professional bodies, including the National HRD Network (NHRDN), the Indian Commerce Association, and the Presidency College Alumni Association. His primary research interests focus on employee retention and job skills, reflecting his commitment to advancing contemporary HR practices. Most recently, he served as the editor of a management research volume published by Bentham Books. Dr. Mutsuddi's enduring contributions to teaching and research continue to earn him widespread recognition and respect within academic and professional circles.

**Mustafa Kemal Şen** is a foreign language instructor at Kütahya Dumlupınar University, Türkiye. Currently, he is doing his Ph.D study on English Language Teaching at Çanakkale Onsekiz Mart University, Türkiye. His research areas include second language acquisition, materials development, and foreign language teaching policies. Besides teaching, he has written textbooks and supplementary materials.

**Saliha Toscu** is a lecturer in foreign languages department at Çankaya University, Turkey. She received her Master's and doctorate degrees in English Language Teaching from Bilkent University and Hacettepe University respectively. Her primary research interests include research into language teaching and learning, educational research, language learning and technology and intercultural competence.

**Gökçe Nur Türkmen** is a PhD student in the English Language Education program at the School of Graduate Studies, Çanakkale Onsekiz Mart University, Türkiye. Her research focuses on English as a second/foreign language, particularly multiculturalism, race representation in EFL coursebooks, and inclusive language education. She has published in Participatory Educational Research and co-authored work on internationalizing children's songs for teaching English to young learners.

**Sude Uyğun** currently holds an MSc in Information Technology and is an MA student at Çanakkale Onsekiz Mart University, in the ELT department, focusing on Computational Linguistics, Computational Social Sciences, and the integration of AI into language education.

**Pankaj Vaishnav** is a seasoned academic and researcher with extensive experience in English Language Teaching (ELT). Having taught at both undergraduate and postgraduate levels, Dr. Pankaj has worked with a diverse international student body, spanning 17 countries. A published author, Dr. Pankaj's work, 'Current Trends and Future Prospects in English Language Teaching', has garnered international recognition. HIs research spans a wide array of topics, including innovations in ELT, task-based learning, and cultural identity in language learning, particularly in Oman. Dr. Pankaj continues to explore cutting-edge research at the intersection of linguistics, technology, and cultural studies, with ongoing projects in ESP and STEM education.

# Index

## A



## B



## C



## D

## E



## F



## G



## H



## I

## L

## M



## P



## T



## V

www.ingramcontent.com/pod-product-compliance
Lightning Source LLC
LaVergne TN
LVHW061529290926
849162LV00004B/721